HISTORICAL DICTIONARY

The historical dictionaries present essential information on a broad range of subjects, including American and world history, art, business, cities, countries, cultures, customs, film, global conflicts, international relations, literature, music, philosophy, religion, sports, and theater. Written by experts, all contain highly informative introductory essays of the topic and detailed chronologies that, in some cases, cover vast historical time periods but still manage to heavily feature more recent events.

Brief A–Z entries describe the main people, events, politics, social issues, institutions, and policies that make the topic unique, and entries are cross-referenced for ease of browsing. Extensive bibliographies are divided into several general subject areas, providing excellent access points for students, researchers, and anyone wanting to know more. Additionally, maps, photographs, and appendixes of supplemental information aid high school and college students doing term papers or introductory research projects. In short, the historical dictionaries are the perfect starting point for anyone looking to research in these fields.

HISTORICAL DICTIONARIES OF LITERATURE AND THE ARTS

Jon Woronoff, Series Editor

Science Fiction Literature, by Brian Stableford, 2004.
Hong Kong Cinema, by Lisa Odham Stokes, 2007.
American Radio Soap Operas, by Jim Cox, 2005.
Japanese Traditional Theatre, by Samuel L. Leiter, 2006.
Fantasy Literature, by Brian Stableford, 2005.
Australian and New Zealand Cinema, by Albert Moran and Errol Vieth, 2006.
African-American Television, by Kathleen Fearn-Banks, 2006.
Lesbian Literature, by Meredith Miller, 2006.
Scandinavian Literature and Theater, by Jan Sjåvik, 2006.
British Radio, by Seán Street, 2006.
German Theater, by William Grange, 2006.
African American Cinema, by S. Torriano Berry and Venise Berry, 2006.
Sacred Music, by Joseph P. Swain, 2006.
Russian Theater, by Laurence Senelick, 2007.
French Cinema, by Dayna Oscherwitz and MaryEllen Higgins, 2007.
Postmodernist Literature and Theater, by Fran Mason, 2007.
Irish Cinema, by Roderick Flynn and Pat Brereton, 2007.
Australian Radio and Television, by Albert Moran and Chris Keating, 2007.
Polish Cinema, by Marek Haltof, 2007.
Old Time Radio, by Robert C. Reinehr and Jon D. Swartz, 2008.
Renaissance Art, by Lilian H. Zirpolo, 2008.
Broadway Musical, by William A. Everett and Paul R. Laird, 2008.
American Theater: Modernism, by James Fisher and Felicia Hardison Londré, 2008.
German Cinema, by Robert C. Reimer and Carol J. Reimer, 2008.
Horror Cinema, by Peter Hutchings, 2008.
Westerns in Cinema, by Paul Varner, 2008.
Chinese Theater, by Tan Ye, 2008.
Italian Cinema, by Gino Moliterno, 2008.
Architecture, by Allison Lee Palmer, 2008.
Russian and Soviet Cinema, by Peter Rollberg, 2008.
African American Theater, by Anthony D. Hill, 2009.
Postwar German Literature, by William Grange, 2009.
Modern Japanese Literature and Theater, by J. Scott Miller, 2009.
Animation and Cartoons, by Nichola Dobson, 2009.
Modern Chinese Literature, by Li-hua Ying, 2010.
Middle Eastern Cinema, by Terri Ginsberg and Chris Lippard, 2010.

Historical Dictionary of Jazz

John S. Davis

The Scarecrow Press, Inc.
Lanham • Toronto • Plymouth, UK
2012

Published by Scarecrow Press, Inc.
A wholly owned subsidiary of The Rowman & Littlefield Publishing Group, Inc.
4501 Forbes Boulevard, Suite 200, Lanham, Maryland 20706
www.rowman.com

10 Thornbury Road, Plymouth PL6 7PP, United Kingdom

British Library Cataloguing in Publication Information Available

Library of Congress Cataloging-in-Publication Data

Davis, John S., 1960–
  Historical dictionary of jazz / John S. Davis.
      p. cm. — (Historical dictionaries of literature and the arts)
  Includes bibliographical references.
  ISBN 978-0-8108-6757-4 (cloth : alk. paper) — ISBN 978-0-8108-7898-3 (ebook)
  1. Jazz—Dictionaries. I. Title.
  ML102.J3D38 2012
  781.6503—dc23
                                                                     2012016422

∞™ The paper used in this publication meets the minimum requirements of American National Standard for Information Sciences—Permanence of Paper for Printed Library Materials, ANSI/NISO Z39.48-1992.

Printed in the United States of America

Contents

Editor's Foreword

We all know where jazz comes from, namely African-American musicians who, in the early 20th century, began mixing or fusing various genres such as Blues and Ragtime, with its first major site being New Orleans. But, at that time, no one could have known where jazz would go—and we still don't know today. It moved from New Orleans, where it is admittedly still big, to Chicago and New York in the north, and also to the West Coast, and on to Europe as well as Latin America, to say nothing of Japan. During this trajectory, it mixed with other trends, like Swing and Bebop, and assumed many forms, such as Traditional Jazz, Mainstream Jazz, Straight-Ahead, and Modal Jazz, among others. It proved attractive to an amazingly varied group of musicians, including and just to name a few, Jelly Roll Morton, Charlie Parker, Dizzy Gillespie, Miles Davis, and of course Louis Armstrong, but also George Gershwin. It was often popular in the broader sense, but took on tinges of Classical music as well, and it enthused one generation after another of listeners, men, women, and children, of every age, class, and color, around the world. So, in some sense this is a moving target, and one that is hard to define simply and accurately. But that does not matter; jazz doesn't really care.

Still, it is always handy to have a useful compendium on any musical genre, even one as elusive as jazz, and it is high time that it was added to our list in this *Historical Dictionary of Jazz*. Among other things, it specifies more accurately where jazz came from and where it has gone to, this in the chronology. The introduction provides a broad overview showing the various phases it has gone through since its origin, some of the many forms it has adopted, and who contributed to its often surprising and always intriguing evolution. Naturally, the core of the book is the dictionary section, with entries on literally hundreds of musicians, scores of bands and locales, dozens of variations on the basic form, and a smattering of record labels known for jazz, to say nothing of the growing array of musical instruments it is played on. For those really keen on learning more, the last part can be one of the most important, namely a comprehensive bibliography.

This volume was written by John S. Davis, who, like some of those listed in this book, is both a musician and an educator. He plays the trumpet and presents workshops at numerous festivals in the United States and Canada.

He is also a conductor, and under his direction the University of Colorado Jazz Ensemble I performed at the International Association of Jazz Education conference in 2004 and was recognized as one of the country's outstanding big bands by *DownBeat* magazine in 2003 and 2005. He also teaches trumpet and holds performance seminars while at the same time becoming well recognized as a clinician. More on the academic side, John Davis is associate professor and director of jazz studies at the University of Colorado at Boulder, a position he has held since 1999. Prior to this he was assistant director of jazz studies at the University of Northern Colorado, where he was also festival coordinator of the UNC/Greeley Jazz Festival, one of the largest noncompetitive jazz festivals in the world. He spends many of his summers on the faculties of jazz camps, including the Birch Creek Music Academy, the Texas All-Star Jazz Camp, and the Mile High Jazz Camp. Like all academics, he has written on jazz, but he has admittedly never taken on anything as ambitious as this book. Still, given his background and interests, it is not surprising that he has produced an encyclopedic work that is not only informative but also an interesting and lively read.

Jon Woronoff
Series Editor

Reader's Note

In this dictionary, occasional shorthand references are made to instruments like the acoustic bass (commonly referred to simply as *bass*), baritone saxophone (*bari*), and drum set (*drums*). Certain definitions in this text use the shorthand references as they are very commonly used among jazz musicians and scholars.

Record labels in this work are abbreviated to just their name and usually do not include their full working business title. For instance, Blue Note Records is referred to simply as Blue Note. Some entries might include jazz-specific shorthand terms, such as *standard* or *rhythm changes*. In these instances, the shorthand reference is cross-referenced to their fully expanded title.

Musician biographies are listed alphabetically with the last name first, for example, *Ayler, Albert*. Furthermore, a musician's full name is listed followed by any nickname in quotations. The use of nicknames is very common to jazz, and many musicians developed nicknames that were frequently used instead of their given name. Examples of this include *Gillespie, John Birks "Dizzy,"* or *Rollins, Theodore "Sonny."* The use of royal or monarch nicknames were frequently used during the early eras of jazz with musicians like "King" Joe Oliver, "Count" Basie, and "Duke" Ellington. Musicians such as these are also listed as last name, first name, and finally their nickname in quotations. These entries will read *Oliver, Joseph "King"*; *Basie, William "Count"*; and *Ellington, Edward K. "Duke."*

References to recordings are listed with the recording's name in italics followed by parentheses that contain the recording's release date and record label.

Cross-referencing is frequently used in many definitions and will either be presented in bold within the text or added as *See also*. These references will usually be in regard to musicians or styles associated with the entry. This is done to assist the reader in linking specific entries to specific styles, musicians, instruments, records labels, and the like.

Acronyms and Abbreviations

AFM	American Federation of Musicians
AACM	Association for the Advancement of Creative Musicians
ARC	American Radio Company
ASCAP	American Society of Composers, Authors and Publishers
bass	acoustic bass
BMI	Broadcast Music, Inc.
Bop	Bebop
changes	chord changes, the harmonic progression of chords
comp, comping	rhythmic or harmonic accompaniment
drums	drum set
ECM	Edition of Contemporary Music (independent European label)
EWIG	European Improvising Women's Group
HRS	Hot Record Society
IAJE	International Association for Jazz Education
IASJ	International Association of Schools of Jazz
jam	jam session
JATP	Jazz at the Philharmonic
JEN	Jazz Educators Network
JIC	Jazz Institute of Chicago
LJCO	London Jazz Composers Orchestra
M-base	macro-basic array of structured extemporization
MJQ	Modern Jazz Quartet
MPS	Musik Produktion Schwarzwald
LCJO	Lincoln Center Jazz Orchestra
NAJE	National Association of Jazz Educators
NEA	National Endowment for the Arts
NJSO	National Jazz Service Organization
NORK	New Orleans Rhythm Kings
ODJB	Original Dixieland Jazz Band
R&B	Rhythm and Blues
RCA	Radio Corporation of American
sax	saxophone
WSQ	World Saxophone Quartet

Chronology

1881   24 October: Tony Pastor debuts a clean, family-friendly version of Vaudeville at the 14th Street Theater in New York City.

1885   6 July: Benjamin Franklin Keith and Edward Franklin Albee II, having purchased the Boston Bijou Theatre, begin hosting continuous Vaudeville variety shows.

1895   Buddy Bolden, an African-American cornetist involved in Ragtime music in New Orleans, forms his first band.

1897   December: Tom Turpin publishes the piano rag "Harlem Rag." It is the first rag ever published by an African-American.

1899   The "Maple Leaf Rag" by Scott Joplin is published. While sales of the piece are initially slow, it would become a landmark as the first instrumental piece to sell over a million copies of sheet music.

1904   Jelly Roll Morton leaves New Orleans and moves about in the Northwestern United States, spreading the sound of New Orleans music.

1911   The Original Creole Jazz Band, led by Freddie Keppard, relocates from New Orleans to Los Angeles and is subsequently influential in spreading the music of New Orleans.

1913   Charles "Luckey" Roberts, having worked in Vaudeville as a child, becomes the first pianist from Harlem to be published, with his "Junk Man Rag."

1915   Jelly Roll Morton's "Jelly Roll Blues" becomes the first published jazz work.

1916   October: Charles "Luckey" Roberts becomes the first Harlem pianist to be recorded, although the recordings were never released.

1917   26 February: The Original Dixieland Jazz Band makes the first jazz recording, "Livery Stable Blues." It would prove successful, selling a million copies.

1918 Record label OKeh releases its first record, performed by the New Orleans Jazz Band. The label would later become well known for its "race" recordings, featuring African-American jazz and Blues artists.

1920 **28 October:** After the override of a presidential veto, Prohibition begins in the United States. "Speakeasies" arise and serve alcohol on the black market and became synonymous with jazz music.

1922 Pianist, bandleader, and composer Fletcher Henderson begins leading his successful band in New York City with a residence at the Roseland Ballroom. **July:** Edward "Kid" Ory records the first record by an African American, "Ory's Creole Trombone." **October:** Recording for OKeh label, Fats Waller makes his debut with "Muscle Shoals Blues" and "Binningham Blues."

1923 **March:** The New Orleans Rhythm Kings, from Chicago, record "Tin Roof Blues." **August:** Sidney Bechet makes one of his first notable recordings on Clarence Williams' "Kansas City Man Blues." **September:** The Cotton Club opens in Harlem and becomes an important venue for jazz, later featuring Duke Ellington and his Cotton Club Orchestra. **23 September:** Pianist Bennie Moten and his orchestra make their first recordings of early Kansas City Jazz and Blues. This is the first time a Kansas City band records its material on phonograph. **October:** James Johnson's Broadway show "Runnin' Wild" debuts, featuring his hit "Charleston."

1924 Greek-born bandleader Jean Goldkette founds the Victor Recording Orchestra, which would feature musicians such as Tommy Dorsey, Bix Beiderbecke, and Hoagy Carmichael. **12 February:** George Gershwin's "Rhapsody in Blue" is performed for the first time by Paul Whiteman's Orchestra at New York City's Aeolian Hall.

1925 **12 November:** Trumpeter Louis Armstrong makes his first recording under his own name, using the band that would become known as his Hot Five.

1926 **12 March:** The Savoy Ballroom opens on Lenox Avenue in Harlem.

1927 **4 February:** Saxophonist Frankie Trumbauer records "Singin' the Blues," which will later be inducted into the Grammy Hall of Fame in 1977. On the recording he played the C-melody saxophone, a now uncommon instrument pitched between an alto and a tenor. The recording, which along with "I'm Coming, Virginia" would prove influential in the development of the jazz ballad, also features Bix Beiderbecke on one of his most lauded solos. **7 May:** Louis Armstrong records his highly regarded Hot Seven recordings in five sessions, lasting through **14 May**. **6 October:** The first feature film with talking sequences, *The Jazz Singer*, is released by Warner Bros. **26 October:** "Creole Love Call" becomes the first recording credited to Duke Ellington's orchestra.

1928 5 December: Trumpeter Louis Armstrong and pianist Earl Hines record "Weatherbird," a trumpet and piano duet. **11 July:** Drummer William McKinney and his band, McKinney's Cotton Pickers, make their first recordings with Victor. The group would disband in 1934 due to financial stress from the Great Depression.

1929 Cladys "Jabbo" Smith makes many of his most famous recordings, including "Jazz Battle" (**January**), "Sweet and Low Blues" (**February**), and "Aces of Rhythm" (**March**). **2 August:** Fats Waller's "Ain't Misbehavin'" is released. **November:** The Blue Devils, a band formed by bassist Walter Page in Oklahoma City, records "Blue Devil Blues." Vocalist Jimmy Rushing makes his debut on this recording.

1930 October: Lionel Hampton plays the first recorded vibraphone solo in Louis Armstrong's version of Eubie Blake's "Memories of You." **17 October:** Duke Ellington records what would become his first big hit, "Mood Indigo."

1931 March: Cab Calloway's orchestra, replacing the Duke Ellington Orchestra, becomes the house band for the Cotton Club and records "Minnie the Moocher," featuring Calloway's singular scat singing.

1932 5 August: Pianist Art Tatum, known for his superb technique and Stride Piano playing, records his famous version of "Tea for Two."

1933 21 March: Art Tatum records "Tiger Rag." This would become the piece perhaps most associated with Tatum. Following his virtuosic recording, "Tiger Rag" would become an important piece of the jazz piano repertoire.

1934 Stéphane Grappelli and Django Reinhardt form the Quintette du Hot Club de France, producing a European jazz style not directly linked with American jazz. **26 January:** In Harlem, the Apollo nightclub is opened. **May:** Chick Webb's orchestra records "Stompin' at the Savoy." **July:** The jazz magazine *DownBeat* is founded.

1935 23 September: Eddie Durham is the first person to record an electric guitar solo in "Hittin' the Bottle," played by Jimmie Lunceford and His Orchestra. **30 September:** George Gershwin's opera *Porgy and Bess* premieres at Boston's Colonial Theater. **October:** Tommy Dorsey records "I'm Getting Sentimental Over You," featuring what would become his trademark smooth style.

1936   May: Artie "Shaw" Arshawsky and his octet perform his innovative "Interlude in B-flat." **August:** Jimmie Lunceford's band debuts Sy Oliver's arrangement of "Organ Grinder's Swing." **November:** Lester Young, having rejoined Count Basie's band, records highly regarded solos on "Lady Be Good" and "Shoe Shine Boy."

1937   January: Trumpeter Roy Eldridge records one of his most celebrated solos on "Heckler's Hop." **20 February:** Pianist and composer Raymond Scott first records his "Powerhouse," which would later become famous from its use in Warner Bros. cartoons. **2 May:** Ella Fitzgerald records "A Tisket, a Tasket" with Chick Webb and His Orchestra, which brought her wide public acclaim. **30 May:** Gene Sedric, saxophonist with Fats Waller, records the first solo saxophone piece in jazz: "Saxophone Doodles." **July:** Count Basie and his big band record the 12-bar Blues, "One O'Clock Jump," which would become their first hit.

1938   16 January: Benny Goodman and his racially integrated quartet, including Teddy Wilson, Charlie Christian, Lionel Hampton, and Gene Krupa, perform at Carnegie Hall. **3 March:** Gene Krupa leaves Benny Goodman and soon thereafter starts his own orchestra. **Spring:** Milt Gabler, owner of the Commodore Music Shop in Manhattan, New York City, starts the record label Commodore, one of the first labels devoted to jazz, as well as one of the first to list the full personnel on records.

1939   January: Willie "the Lion" Smith records "Finger Buster" and "Rippling Waters." **20 April:** Billie Holiday records the political protest song "Strange Fruit," based on a poem by Abel Meeropol about lynching. This song would provide a surge in her popularity. **May:** Glenn Miller records his "Moonlight Serenade." **8 June:** Saxophonist Sidney Bechet records "Summertime," the first hit for upstart label Blue Note. **16 June:** Upon Chick Webb's death, Ella Fitzgerald takes over his band. **July:** Saxophonist Charlie Barnet's big band successfully bridges Swing and Bebop in its rendition of Ray Noble's "Cherokee." **August:** Electric guitarist Charlie Christian joins Benny Goodman's band. **5 September:** Lester Young and his small group record "Lester Leaps In," which would influence the style of younger saxophonists of the era. **11 October:** Coleman Hawkins records the popular standard "Body and Soul," which would be considered a landmark recording in Early Jazz.

1940   March: The American Society of Composers, Artists, and Producers (ASCAP) proposes an increase of 100 percent for royalties. This would result in a considerable boost for the Pop music industry, as broadcasters shunned ASCAP in favor of Broadcast Music Inc. (BMI) artists.

1941 **4 March:** Guitarist Charlie Christian, an innovator who helped to establish the electric guitar as a solo instrument in jazz, records his "Solo Flight" with Benny Goodman. **May:** Roy Eldridge is featured with Gene Krupa's orchestra on the hit "Let Me Off Uptown."

1942 **31 July:** After an announcement by the president of the American Federation of Musicians (AFM), James Petrillo, a widespread recording ban begins. During the course of the ban, declared due to royalty disagreements, no union musician was allowed to record for any record company. The two largest record companies, Victor and Columbia, would hold out on a settlement until 11 November 1944. **November:** Saxophonist and bandleader Boyd Raeburn and his big band debut at the Arcadia Ballroom and become very successful in Chicago.

1943 **23 January:** Duke Ellington's first Carnegie Hall performance. The only full-length version of "Black, Brown, and Beige," his piece on the history of African-Americans, is recorded. **November:** Stan Kenton's first orchestra records *Artistry in Motion*, as well as their first hit, "Eager Beaver." **30 November:** Popular jazz vocalist Nat "King" Cole records his first big hit, "Straighten Up and Fly Right." The song was co-written by Cole and Irving Mills.

1944 **22 May:** Coleman Hawkins finishes the recording of his album *Rainbow Mist*. Included in the project were several prominent young players, including trumpeter Dizzy Gillespie, bassist Oscar Pettiford, and drummer Max Roach. **15 December:** The plane carrying bandleader and composer Glenn Miller disappears while flying over the English Channel.

1945 Italian composer Pete Rugolo becomes the chief arranger for Stan Kenton and would play an important role in the development of Kenton's modern sound. **9 January:** Trumpeter John "Dizzy" Gillespie makes his first major Bebop recordings, including "Salt Peanuts," "Be Bop," and Tadd Dameron's "Good Bait." **28 February:** Dizzy Gillespie's quintet, the All Stars, which included Charlie Parker on tenor saxophone and Al Haig on piano, record "Groovin' High" and "Dizzy Atmosphere." **28 March:** Miles Davis records with Charlie Parker for the first time. **May:** Stan Kenton records his intriguing hit composition, "Opus in Pastels." **11 May:** Dizzy Gillespie's All Stars record "Shaw 'Nuff" and Tadd Dameron's "Hot House," based on Cole Porter's "What Is This Thing Called Love?" **4 October:** Ella Fitzgerald makes inventive and influential use of "scat" singing on a version of "Flying Home." It would be remembered as one of the most influential vocal jazz records of the decade. **26 November:** Using his newly developed harmonic language, Charlie Parker records "Now's the Time," "Billie's Bounce," "Anthropology," and "Ko Ko," based on Ray Noble's "Cherokee."

1946   28 March: Charlie Parker records "Yardbird Suite" and "Ornithology" with his septet, which includes trumpeter Miles Davis. **September:** Woody Herman's group, the Second Herd, records "Summer Sequence," by pianist Ralph Burns. The group was characterized by its approach of featuring the reeds section over those of the brass and rhythm.

1947   Jazz enters academia when North Texas State University is the first to offer a degree in jazz. At the time, it was referred to as a major in Dance Band. **April:** Third Stream composer Bob Graettinger records his four-movement suite, "City of Glass." **May:** The Claude Thornhill Orchestra records their hit "A Sunday Kind of Love." **September:** The Claude Thornhill Orchestra records "Love for Love." **December:** Dizzy Gillespie records George Russell's "Cubano Be, Cubano Bop." The recording yields some of the first experimentation with modal improvisation. **27 December:** Woody Herman records Jimmy Giuffre's "Four Brothers" with his Second Herd.

1948   28 January: Edmund Martinez Tostado, or "Don Tosti" as he was known, records his hit "Pachuco Boogie." It would become the first million-selling Latin song.

1949   21 January: Miles Davis begins the first of three recording sessions that will result in the seminal album *Birth of the Cool*. **16 March:** The blind pianist Lennie Tristano records two pieces with his sextet that would come to be credited as the first Free Jazz: "Intuition" and "Digression." **8 August:** Earl "Bud" Powell records "Dance of the Infidels" and "Bouncing with Bud" with trumpeter Theodore "Fats" Navarro and tenor saxophonist Sonny Rollins. **30 November:** Charlie Parker records his first project with strings, released as *Charlie Parker with Strings*. The success of the album would lead to several similar sessions.

1950   January: Stan Kenton records *Innovations in Modern Music Orchestra* with his 40-piece orchestra, which includes a 16-piece string section.

1951   27 August: Baritone saxophonist Gerry Mulligan records his arrangements for nonet on *Mulligan plays Mulligan*. **November:** Vibraphonist Teddy Charles Cohen makes his debut with the album *The Teddy Cohen Trio*. **November:** Vibraphonist and drummer Cal Tjader records his pioneering album *The Cal Tjader Trio*, important for its novel fusion of Mambo and jazz. The album also features pianist Vince Guaraldi in his first recording.

1952   Vibraphonist Milt Jackson forms the Modern Jazz Quartet, the first attempt at presenting jazz in a chamber ensemble setting.

1953   George Russell publishes the first edition of his influential book *The Lydian Chromatic Concept of Tonal Improvisation*. **31 January:** Trumpeter

Milton "Shorty" Rogers Rajonsky, a past band member with the bands of Woody Herman and Stan Kenton, completes the album *Modern Sounds*, along with Gerry Mulligan. The album, two years in the making, features the compositional efforts of the pair. **2 March:** Dave Brubeck performs his famous concert at Oberlin College. **28 May:** Stan Kenton records composer Bob Graettinger's six-movement piece "This Modern World." **June:** Lennie Tristano records *Descent into the Maelstrom*, featuring overdubbed piano and harsh atonality that would later influence the work of Cecil Taylor and Borah Bergman. **23 November:** Hard Bop pianist Horace Silver records his first important album, *Trio*. **30 November:** Canadian-born pianist Paul Bley records his debut, *Introducing Paul Bley*, with Charles Mingus and Art Blakey. **8 December:** Tenor saxophonist Ben Webster achieves mainstream success with his album *King of the Tenors*, which also features alto saxophonist Benny Carter and pianist Oscar Peterson. It is originally released as *The Consummate Artistry of Ben Webster*.

1954 The Clifford Brown/Max Roach Quintet is formed. Clifford Brown receives *DownBeat*'s Critics Award for Best New Star on Trumpet. **February:** The group that would become the Jazz Messengers releases a successful album of a live performance, *A Night in Birdland*. The album is credited to "The Art Blakey Quintet." **June:** Miles Davis records his album *Bag's Groove*, featuring several pieces by the group's saxophonist, Sonny Rollins, whose compositions "Doxy," "Airegin," and "Oleo" would all become important pieces of jazz repertoire. **July:** George Wein holds the first Newport Jazz Festival, becoming the first outdoor jazz festival. **27 July:** Pianist Erroll Garner records his composition "Misty," which would become a popular hit. **August:** The notable album *Clifford Brown and Max Roach* is recorded by the prolific duo. The album contains pieces that would remain very important in the jazz repertoire, including "Daahoud" and "Joy Spring." **September:** Trumpeter Chet Baker records *Chet Baker Sextet* with Bud Shank on saxophone and Bob Brookmeyer on trombone. **December:** The Jazz Messengers, at this early period under the direction of pianist Horace Silver, begin recording as a group.

1955 **9 January:** The Modern Jazz Quartet finishes recording for their hit album, *Django*. It is released the following year. **May:** Pianist Herbie Nichols records his album *The Third World*, his first of original music. **August:** Los Angeles drummer Chico Hamilton and his quintet make their debut with the album *Spectacular*. **19 September:** Pianist Erroll Garner records his live album *Concert by the Sea*, featuring Eddie Calhoun on bass and Denzil Best on drums, which becomes a best seller. **October:** Composer and theorist George Russell records his first album as a leader, *Jazz Workshop*, which features his developed system of mode-based jazz.

1956 The U.S. State Department begins sending jazz ambassadors through-out the world. **January:** Bassist Charles Mingus establishes himself as a creative force with his *Pithecanthropus Erectus*. The title piece is a four-movement tone poem that includes elements of Free Jazz that would be influential in the birth of that movement. **May:** Saxophonist Sonny Rollins records the album *Tenor Madness* using the rhythm section from Miles Davis' band: Red Garland on piano, Paul Chambers on bass, and Philly Joe Jones on drums. The album features a tenor duel between Rollins and John Coltrane. **30 May:** Guitarist Kenny Burrell begins his career as a leader with *Introducing Kenny Burrell*. **June:** Sonny Rollins records his potentially most influential album, *Saxophone Colossus*, which includes the Calypso "St. Thomas." **October:** Japanese guitarist Masayuki Takayanagi begins his recording career with his album *Swing Journal All-Star Orchestra*. **15 October:** Thelonious Monk records his inventive masterwork, *Brilliant Corners*. **5 November:** The Nat King Cole Show debuts on NBC Television. Because Cole is black, the program stirs controversy during a volatile time for race/ethnicity relations in the United States. **9 November:** Blind tenor saxophonist Roland Kirk makes his debut with *Triple Threat*. Kirk would become known for his bluesy style and use of unusual techniques, such as circular breathing and playing multiple instruments simultaneously. **December:** Clarinetist, flutist, and saxophonist Jimmy Giuffre records his album *Jimmy Giuffre 3* with guitarist Jim Hall and bassist Ralph Peña. It is on this album that he debuts his signature "The Train and the River."

1957 Henry "Red" Allen records what is widely considered to be one of his finest works, "Ride, Red, Ride in Hi-Fi." Charles Mingus records "Fables for Faubus," a statement against the refusal by the government of Arkansas to desegregate Little Rock Central High School. **February:** The Compilation *Birth of the Cool* is released, featuring Miles Davis's nonet. It was important for its novel setting for Bebop and influenced the Cool Jazz style that followed. **March:** Charlie Mingus' quintet records *The Clown*, which features what is perhaps his most well known piece, "Haitian Fight Song." The album also includes his lyrical tribute to Charlie Parker, "Reincarnation of a Lovebird." **April:** Trumpeter Clark Terry's album *Serenade to a Bus Seat* is released and features the trumpet player's compositional skills. **9 April:** Tenor saxophonist and multi-instrumentalist Yusef Lateef records the album *Jazz Mood*, which is notable for featuring his sophisticated compositional style. By this point, Lateef's writing is beginning to incorporate exotic sounds and melodies. **3 May:** Trombonist J. J. Johnson with his quartet records his highly regarded album *Blue Trombone*. **July:** Thelonious Monk and John Coltrane historically collaborate on the album *Thelonious Monk with John Coltrane*. **August:** The first European jazz festival is held in Sopot, Poland, called the

Sopot Jazz Festival. **September:** Composer and arranger Gil Evans records his album *Gil Evans and Ten*, comprised of jazz standards arranged for large ensemble. The work features saxophonists Lee Konitz and Steve Lacy. **October:** Tenor saxophonist Benny Golsen records *New York Scene*, in which his jazz classic, "Whisper Not," is found. **8 October:** Frank Sinatra records the album *Come Fly with Me*, his first collaborative work with conductor and arranger Billy May. The album is released the following year to much acclaim. **December:** Dizzy Gillespie records and releases *Sonny Side Up*, featuring saxophonists Sonny Rollins and Sonny Stitt.

1958   1 January: Latin Jazz and Mambo musician Tito Puente releases his popular album, *Dance Mania*. **7 January:** Vocalist Sarah Vaughan records "Broken Hearted Melody," which would represent the peak of her commercial success. **February:** Organist Jimmy Smith fuses jazz with Soul music in "The Sermon." **Spring:** Dave Brubeck embarks on a tour across the Iron Curtain as an ambassador of the U.S. State Department. **August:** Fifty-seven jazz greats gather for *Esquire*'s famous picture, "A Great Day in Harlem." **3 October:** Jimmy Lyons presents the first annual Monterey Jazz Festival.

1959   3 February: Saxophonist John Coltrane teams up with Cannonball Adderley for their album *Cannonball and Coltrane*. **22 April:** Miles Davis records *Kind of Blue*, widely considered one of his finest works. This album would be frequently cited as the best-selling jazz album ever. **May:** Marking his departure from Bebop, John Coltrane records "Giant Steps." His use of unusual major-third chord movements would make this landmark piece enormously influential and significant. **22 May:** Saxophonist Ornette Coleman records his groundbreaking Avant-Garde album, *The Shape of Jazz to Come*. This important album, which is received with shock and surprise, would be a harbinger of the Free Jazz movement. **25 June:** Flutist Herbie Mann, known for his efforts in fusing jazz with various types of world music, records his album *Flautista! Herbie Mann Plays Afro-Cuban Jazz*. **18 August:** Pianist Dave Brubeck's *Time Out* is recorded. The album, representing an influential foray into odd meters, would become extraordinarily popular, quickly going platinum. **28 December:** Bill Evans' album *Portrait in Jazz* reflects an important milestone in the development of piano trios by featuring a more interactive, democratic conception between the musicians.

1960   Baritone saxophonist Gerry Mulligan and valve trombonist Bob Brookmeyer establish the Concert Jazz Band, which would produce critically acclaimed work for the few years of its existence. **January:** Guitarist Wes Montgomery records *The Incredible Jazz Guitar of Wes Montgomery*, which features two of his most famous compositions, "Four on Six" and "West Coast Blues." **February:** Tenor saxophonist Hank Mobley records his masterpiece album *Soul Station*. **March:** Miles Davis and Gil Evans' collaborative work peaks with the album *Sketches of Spain*. **April:** Organist Jimmy Smith records his *Back at the Chicken Shack*, which features tenor saxophonist Stanley Turrentine and guitarist Kenny Burrell. **1 April:** Eric Dolphy records his first album as a leader, *Outward Bound*. It also serves to boost the career of pianist Jaki Byard, who was recruited for the album. **July:** Free Jazz trumpeter Don Cherry records his first major album, *The Avant-Garde*, which also features saxophonist John Coltrane. **September:** Drummer Max Roach records his politically charged *We Insist! Freedom Now Suite*, featuring his nonet and vocals by Abbey Lincoln. **November:** Clark Terry records what is arguably his most sophisticated album, *Color Changes*, featuring an octet that includes saxophonist and multi-instrumentalist Yusef Lateef and pianist Tommy Flanagan. **18 November:** Pianist Randy Weston records his four-movement suite, *Uhuru Africa*. The performers include musicians such as Yusef Lateef, trumpeters Clark Terry and Freddie Hubbard, guitarist Kenny Burrell, bassist Ron Carter, and drummer Max Roach, in addition to African percussionist Babatunde Olatunji and two conga players. **December:** Gunther Schuller, noted for his work to integrate jazz and Classical music, or "Third Stream," records *Jazz Abstractions*.

1961   January: Alto saxophonist Phil Woods records his five-movement suite *Rights of Swing*. **February:** Vocalist Abbey Lincoln records her album *Straight Ahead*, featuring an impressive cast including Coleman Hawkins, Eric Dolphy, Mal Waldron, and her husband, Max Roach. **23 February:** Saxophonist Oliver Nelson records his most acclaimed album, *The Blues and the Abstract Truth*. The piece "Stolen Moments" would become his most well known from the album. **25 June:** Bill Evans records *Sunday at the Village Vanguard (Live)*. **27 June:** Pianist Mal Waldron records his album of seven original sonatas, entitled *The Quest*. The work includes saxophonist and multi-instrumentalist Eric Dolphy, tenor saxophonist Booker Ervin, and Ron Carter on cello. **October:** Los Angeles trumpeter Art Farmer records his album *Perception*, which proved to be a notable departure from Hard Bop. **November:** Jamaican-born alto saxophonist Joe Harriet, having developed Free Jazz independently of Ornette Coleman, releases *Free Form* and *Abstract*. **7 December:** Pianist Ran Blake and vocalist Jeanne Lee complete their duo album *The Newest Sound Around*. Their effort was met with success in Europe, although largely ignored in the United States.

1962   14 May: Bill Evans and guitarist Jim Hall record their first collaborative album, *Undercurrent*. It is released the following year. **September:** Art Farmer records a collection of arrangements by Oliver Nelson for big band, called *Listen to Art Farmer and the Orchestra*. Farmer was notably featured prominently on flugelhorn instead of trumpet. **19 November:** After a successful tour of Latin America for the U.S. State Department, saxophonist Paul Winter and his sextet are the first jazz group to perform at the White House. Coinciding with the trip, Winter also records his first album for Columbia, *Jazz Meets the Bossa Nova*, which would become a minor hit. **23 November:** Pianist Cecil Taylor records his live album *Nefertiti the Beautiful One Has Come* with alto saxophonist Jimmy Lyons and drummer Sunny Murray. This recording represents more freedom in Taylor's approach to improvisation, as compared with his earlier recordings.

1963   January: Hard Bop trumpeter Donald Byrd records his innovative *A New Perspective*, featuring Hank Mobley, Herbie Hancock, and guitarist Kenny Burrell, as well as a Gospel choir. **February:** Pianist Bill Evans records *Conversations with Myself*, in which he overdubs three corresponding piano tracks for each song. He would earn his first Grammy Award for this album. **12 October:** The New York Contemporary Five, a quintet featuring Don Cherry on trumpet and John Tchicai and Archie Shepp on saxophones, complete their debut album, *Consequences*. Their work on the album is closely related to Ornette Coleman's *Free Jazz* from 1960. **18 November:** John Coltrane records "Alabama," in memory of the bombing of an African-American church in Birmingham, Alabama, in which four girls were killed. **December:** Trumpeter Lee Morgan's title track on *Sidewinder* becomes a hit.

1964   Saxophonist and multi-instrumentalist Günter Hampel forms a quintet and is credited with launching Free Jazz in continental Europe. **February:** Clarinetist Tony Scott, after leaving the United States for Asia, collaborates with koto player Shinichi Yuize and shakuhachi flute player Hozan Yamamoto for the album *Music for Zen Meditations*. This is his first project involving the fusing of jazz with music from other cultures, a practice for which he would become best known. **25 February:** Saxophonist, flutist, and bass clarinetist Eric Dolphy records perhaps his most important Free Jazz album, *Out to Lunch*. He is joined by trumpeter Freddie Hubbard, vibraphonist Bobby Hutchinson, bassist Richard Davis, and a young Tony Williams on drums. **March:** Saxophonist Stan Getz teams up with Brazilian João Gilberto to release *Getz/Gilberto*, one of the best-selling jazz albums of all time. **31 March:** Pianist and composer Andrew Hill, having studied notably with Classical composer Paul Hindemith, records *Point of Departure*, featuring Eric Dolphy. Hill's style would come to represent a border between total Free Jazz and more traditional paradigms. **29 April:** Saxophonist Wayne Shorter records his first solo album for Blue Note, *Night Dreamer*. Shorter's work with Blue Note would be pivotal to his success, with such notable albums as *Speak No Evil* and *Ju Ju* appearing during this era. It is also at this time that Shorter joins Miles Davis to form Davis' "second great quintet"—the first included John Coltrane. **10 July:** Cleveland-born saxophonist Albert Ayler records the album that would become one of the most important in Free Jazz, *Spiritual Unity*. Accompanied by bassist Gary Peacock and percussionist Sunny Murray, Ayler's performance is unconventional in its emphasis on soundscapes. **October:** Bill Dixon is responsible for organizing the October Revolution in Jazz, the first Free Jazz festival. Though himself a skilled trumpeter, he would become best known for the festival. **26 October:** Horace Silver completes his album *Song for My Father*. Commercially a successful album, it was recorded over the span of two years and features two completely different quintets: one notably features tenor saxophonist Joe Henderson, and the other, trumpeter Blue Mitchell. **30 November:** Tenor saxophonist Joe Henderson records the album *Inner Urge*. **9 December:** John Coltrane's important four-movement suite *A Love Supreme* is recorded. A work with spiritual significance for Coltrane, the piece served to bridge his earlier Hard Bop efforts with his later Free Jazz period. **11 December:** Saxophonist and composer Sam Rivers makes his debut album as a leader with *Fuchsia Swing Song*.

1965 January: Post-Bop pianist Adolph "Dollar" Brand (who later changed his name to Abdullah Ibrahim) records a five-part suite, *Anatomy of a South African Village*. The piece is important in its novel fusion of jazz with African rhythms. Brand would continue for decades to incorporate African themes into his music. **April:** Vibraphonist Bobby Hutcherson records his successful debut album, *Dialogue*. Hutcherson would become known for his experiments with Free Jazz while still incorporating traditional forms and structures. **13 April:** *Getz/Gilberto*, featuring Stan Getz and João Gilberto playing the music of Antônio Carlos Jobim, wins several Grammy Awards. **May:** The Association for the Advancement of Creative Musicians (AACM) is formed. The group would begin changing the nature of performance venues by organizing concerts in theaters and lofts, as opposed to playing in local clubs. **September:** John Coltrane invites fellow saxophonist Pharoah Sanders to join his band. Their relationship would result in several collaborative efforts over the next few years. **8 September:** Trumpeter Lee Morgan records his album *Cornbread*, featuring Herbie Hancock, alto saxophonist Jackie McClean, and tenor saxophonist Hank Mobley. His beloved Latin composition, "Ceora," is found on this album. **October:** Alto saxophonist Joe Harriott and violinist John Mayer, after experimenting with Indian-Jazz fusions, record the album *Indo-Jazz Suite* with their group Indo-Jazz Fusions. **23 November:** Tenor saxophonists John Coltrane and Pharoah Sanders collaborate to record *Meditations*, much of which was Avant-Garde, featuring free rhythm sections and unusual saxophone techniques, such as multiphonics and squealing.

1966 Drummer Mel Lewis teams up with trumpeter Thad Jones to start the Thad Jones–Mel Lewis big band. **February:** The Spontaneous Music Ensemble, created by British drummer/trumpeter John Stevens and saxophonist Trevor Watts, records its first album, *Challenge*. **March:** Avant-Garde keyboardist Sun Ra with his group, "The Arkestra," rises to an early peak in recognition and popularity. **7 June:** Saxophonist Eddie Harris records his well-known piece, "Freedom Jazz Dance." **July:** Pianist Joe Zawinul's bluesy hit, "Mercy, Mercy, Mercy," is recorded. **3 September:** The Free Jazz ensemble, the Globe Unity Orchestra, formed by German pianist Alexander von Schlippenbach, makes its debut at the Berliner Philharmonie. **8 September:** Saxophonist Charles Lloyd records his live album, *Forest Flower*, which would garner wide acclaim.

1967 Dutch pianist and composer Misha Mengelberg and drummer Han Bennink co-found the Instant Composers Pool, an organization promoting Avant-Garde Dutch jazz. **April:** Tenor saxophonist Archie Shepp records his album, *The Magic of Ju-Ju*, which marks the beginning of his long focus on the music and culture of the African continent. **21 April:** Pianist McCoy Tyner, after his departure from John Coltrane's quartet, records his important *The Real McCoy*. The album, which would become a key work in Tyner's discography, features Joe Henderson on tenor saxophone, Ron Carter on bass, and Elvin Jones on drums. **October:** Swiss pianist Irène Schweizer combines jazz with Indian music in her album *Jazz Meets India*. **December:** Drummer Han Bennink and saxophonist Willem Breuker record *New Acoustic Swing Duo*, a seminal recording for Dutch improvised music.

1968 Gunther Schuller's *A History of Jazz* is published. The National Association of Jazz Educators (later to be renamed the International Associate of Jazz Educators, then the International Association for Jazz Education) is formed. **February:** Dave Brubeck's orchestral oratorio "A Light in the Wilderness," based on biblical teachings of Jesus, is premiered by the Cincinnati Symphony Orchestra. **9 March:** Alto saxophonist Julian "Cannonball" Adderley records his seminal album, *Somethin' Else*, featuring Miles Davis, pianist Hank Jones, bassist Sam Jones, and drummer Art Blakey. **April:** Saxophonist, clarinetist, and flutist Paul Horn records the first of his series of influential albums, *Inside the Taj Mahal*. This series of records, featuring solo instrumentals, also would come to include recordings made at the Great Pyramid and the Kazamieras Cathedral. **June:** Alto saxophonist Phil Woods debuts *The Birth of the ERM* with his experimental quartet, European Rhythm Machine. **July:** The Avant-Garde Jazz Composer's Orchestra, led by trumpeter Michael Mantler, records the double album *The Jazz Composer's Orchestra*, also known as *Communications*. Featuring Avant-Garde Jazz musicians such as Pharoah Sanders, Don Cherry, Steve Swallow, and Charlie Haden, the album would prove to be an important work in the history of Avant-Garde Jazz.

1969 Miles Davis begins experimenting with the electric sounds of Rock music, which would lead to his work on *Bitches Brew*. **February:** Anthony Braxton records the first album featuring entirely solo saxophone, *For Alto*. The pieces are dedicated to various artists, including pianist Cecil Taylor and composer John Cage. **May:** Beginning with his album *Blues in Orbit*, which was named after the composition of the same name by George Russell, Gil Evans becomes a notable pioneer in combining electric and acoustic instruments. **June:** German trumpeter Manfred Schoof releases *European Echoes* with the Manfred Schoof Orchestra. **November:** Munich-based record label ECM is founded by producer Manfred Eicher. The label would focus exclusively on jazz for the first several years of its existence.

1970 The National Endowment for the Arts (NEA) awards the first grant for jazz. **29 January:** Freddie Hubbard's venture into Jazz-Rock matures with his album *Red Clay*, featuring a quintet with Joe Henderson, Herbie Hancock, bassist Ron Carter, and drummer Lenny White. **31 January:** Canadian trumpeter Maynard Ferguson, known for his accurate and impressive upper register, releases the first of his successful *M. F. Horn* albums. **April:** Miles Davis releases his most famous Fusion offering, *Bitches Brew*. **25 May:** The Thad Jones–Mel Lewis big band records one of their most important albums, *Consummation*. The best-received piece from the album was "A Child Is Born." **13 July:** British saxophonist Evan Parker records his magnum opus, *Topography of the Lungs*, exemplifying his violent, dissonant style. **October:** Chris McGregor, a pianist from South Africa, records *Chris McGregor's Brotherhood of Breath*, featuring aspects of Swing, Rock, and Free Jazz. **9 December:** After previously working with Horace Silver and Max Roach, trumpeter Woody Shaw makes his debut as a leader on his *Blackstone Legacy*.

1971 The Mahavishnu Orchestra with John McLaughlin integrates elements of Indian music into jazz. **17 March:** The band Weather Report, let by saxophonist Wayne Shorter and pianist Joe Zawinul, records its first album, *Weather Report*. The album would become influential for its place in early Jazz Fusion. **1 May:** Dave Brubeck's cantata *Truth Is Fallen*, a protest of the Vietnam War, is premiered in Midland, Michigan. **June:** Carla Bley's music from *Escalator over the Hill*, commonly referred to as a jazz opera, is released in a triple-LP set.

1972 **26 January:** Saxophonist Archie Shepp, known for his civil rights involvement, records his *Attica Blues* in response to the Attica Prison riots from early September 1971. **March:** Violinist Leroy Jenkins and his Revolutionary Ensemble, a trio including bassist Norris "Sirone" Jones and percussionist Jerome Cooper, record their first album together. The Avant-Garde *Vietnam*, which contains elements of Jazz, Folk, and Classical music, is meant to depict the atrocities of the Vietnam War. **May:** Frank Zappa records his album *The Grand Wazoo*, an experiment with big band Jazz-Rock fusion. **15 October:** Keyboardist Chick Corea and his Fusion group, Return to Forever, records the album *Light as a Feather*. The album features one of Corea's most famous compositions, "Spain." **November:** Polish-born vocalist Urszula Dudziak records her debut album, *Newborn Light*. Dudziak would become known for her use of electronics to alter the sound of her voice. **24 November:** Trumpeter Donald Byrd finishes his wildly successful *Black Byrd*, which would become Blue Note's biggest seller of all time. **December:** German trombonist Albert Mangelsdorff releases *Trombirds*, the first of several solo albums on which he would feature his newly developed method of performing multiphonics.

1973 The Charlie Parker tribute band, called Supersax, records its first album, *Supersax Plays Bird*. This group would release several more such albums. **May:** Pianist Oscar Peterson records the album *The Trio*, featuring Joe Pass on guitar and Niels-Henning Ørsted Pedersen on bass; this work earns a Grammy the following year. **September:** The Headhunters, a Jazz Fusion group formed by Herbie Hancock, records their first album. The album, *Head Hunters*, would become one of the best-selling Fusion records of all time. **30 November:** Guitarist Joe Pass records his highly regarded solo album, *Virtuoso*.

1974 British composer and double bassist Barry John Guy forms the group London Jazz Composers' Orchestra to play his piece "Ode." The group, however, would stay together for many years; the group's active years would end in the mid-1990s. **4 April:** The Toshiko Akiyoshi–Lew Tabackin Big Band records its first album, the successful *Kogun*. Featuring the compositions of pianist Akiyoshi, the album would be awarded a Grammy for Best Jazz Instrumental Performance by a Big Band.

1975 The Heath Brothers are formed, featuring Jimmy, Percy, and Albert "Tootie" Heath. **January:** Saxophonist Michael Brecker and his brother, trumpeter Randy Brecker, collaborate to release *Brecker Bros*. The album would mark the beginning of a long and successful working relationship. **24 January:** Pianist Keith Jarrett performs a concert of solo improvisation in Cologne (Köln), Germany. The recorded concert eventually would result in the album *The Köln Concert*, which as of 2011 remains the best-selling piano album, as well as the best-selling solo jazz album, in history.

1976 After 15 years in Europe, Dexter Gordon returns to the United States. **August:** Jaco Pastorius' debut album, *Jaco Pastorius*, is released, and would be regarded as a breakthrough album for the electric bass. **November:** British bassist Graham Collier's Avant-Garde four-movement "Symphony of Scorpions" is released.

1977 The Feminist Improvising Group is formed in London by vocalist Maggie Nichols and bassoonist/composer Lindsay Cooper. **22 February:** Alto saxophonist Roscoe Mitchell records his creative double album *Nonaah*. Featuring solo, duo, trio, and quartet performances, the album would win him the Album of the Year Award from *DownBeat* magazine.

1978 Saxophonist Chico Freeman records his Free Jazz *The Outside Within*, although it would not be released until 1981. The magazine *Stereo Review* would award Freeman the Album of the Year Award for this effort. **April:** The Pan Afrikan Peoples Arkestra, founded by pianist Horace Tapscott in 1959, makes its first recordings: *Flight 17* and *The Call*. The large ensemble is comprised of six reeds, two trombones, tuba, cello, two pianos, two basses, as well as two percussionists. **July:** Vocalist Jeanne Lee and German saxophonist Günter Hampel notably collaborate on the double LP *Oasis*. **November:** Italian percussionist Andrea Centazzo records *Environment for Sextet* in New York City during a live broadcast on radio station WKCR.

1979 **March:** Spyro Gyra, a Fusion group from Buffalo, New York, gains its first wide recognition with the album *Morning Dance*. Due especially to the title track, the album would go platinum, helping to establish the group's commercial success. **31 October:** The vocal group The Manhattan Transfer records Weather Report's "Birdland." The recording would become very popular and earn the group its first Grammy in 1980. **December:** Vocalist Betty Carter releases her double LP *The Audience*, which features a notable 25-minute version of "Sounds."

1980 **13 October:** The Russia-based Ganelin Trio, featuring pianist Vyacheslav Ganelin, saxophonist Vladimir Chekasin, and drummer Vladimir Tarasov, records *Ancora da Capo*.

1981 **1 January:** Guitarist Emily Remler releases her acclaimed debut album, *Firefly*. **1 October:** Saxophonist and flutist Henry Threadgill, a founding member of the Association for the Advancement of Creative Musicians, records his first of three critically acclaimed LPs with the Henry Threadgill Sextet, entitled *When Was That?* **13 December:** Guitarist John Scofield records his notable live album *Shinola* in Munich, accompanied by bassist Steve Swallow and drummer Adam Nussbaum.

1983   The Feminist Improvising Group becomes the European Women's Improvising Group (EWIG). **29 November:** Saxophonist Branford Marsalis, after working with such jazz personalities as Art Blakey and Herbie Hancock, records his first album as a leader, *Scenes in the City.*

1984   December: Austrian trumpeter and composer Franz Koglmann forms the Chamber Jazz Ensemble Pipetet and releases *Schlaf Schlemmer Schlaf Magritte.*

1985   November: Saxophonist Joe Henderson achieves commercial success with his live trio album, *The State of the Tenor.* **20 December:** Wynton Marsalis begins his significant long-term collaboration with pianist Marcus Roberts with the recording of *J Mood,* referring to "J Master" Roberts.

1986   The Thelonious Monk Institute for Jazz is founded. **9 May:** Saxophonist John Zorn finishes his double LP *Cobra.*

1987   Michael Dorf and Bob Appel open "The Knitting Factory" in New York City, a club that features jazz and experimental music. **February:** After recovering from a 1980 brain aneurysm, guitarist Pat Martino records his impressive comeback album, *The Return.* **3 October:** The Lincoln Center begins hosting jazz. Jazz at Lincoln Center's first concert is "Ladies First—A Tribute to the Great Women in Jazz."

1988   30 August: Wynton Marsalis' notable *Standard Time: Volume I* is released, winning him a Grammy for Best Jazz Instrumental Album.

1989   26 May: The vocal jazz group the New York Voices, after forming in 1987, record their debut album, *New York Voices.*

1990   Meyer Kupferman's *Atonal Jazz* is published. **25 October:** Clarinetist Eddie Daniels, accomplished in both jazz and Classical music, releases his album *Breakthrough,* combining the two.

1991   April: Soprano saxophonist Steve "Lacy" Lackritz records his "Time of Tao—Cycle" on the album *Remains.* On the album, Lackritz, known for his interpretation of Thelonious Monk's work, also includes Monk's "Epistrophy." **July:** British Acid Jazz group Incognito release *Inside Life,* featuring the hit that brought the group wide commercial success, "Always There." **November:** Tenor saxophonist Joshua Redman wins the Thelonious Monk International Jazz Competition. After winning, despite having been accepted to Yale University's law program, Redman would focus on his music career.

1992   30 July: In a father-son effort, established tenor saxophonist Dewey Redman features his son, Joshua, on the album *Choices.* This is Joshua's first recorded appearance.

1993 Composer Maria Schneider forms what is now called the Maria Schneider Orchestra. **6 February:** Avant-Garde trombonist George Lewis records his album *Voyager*, which utilizes software that interacts with the instrumentalists in response to their playing. Lewis is best known for this and similar interactive works with computers.

1994 **29 March:** Panamanian pianist Danilo Perez releases his album *The Journey*. The album, which would serve to thrust Perez into wider recognition, depicts the capture and enslavement of Africans brought to the United States.

1995 John Zorn founds Tzadik, a record label featuring Avant-Garde and creative music. **22 January:** Tenor saxophonist Joe Lovano records *Quartets: Live at the Village Vanguard*, for which he would earn the Album of the Year Award from *DownBeat* magazine. **14 April:** The McCoy Tyner Trio, along with guest saxophonist Michael Brecker, records the Grammy-winning album *Infinity*. In addition to winning a Grammy for the album, Brecker would win the Best Jazz Instrumental Solo Award in 1996 for his solo on "Impressions."

1996 The first Vision Festival is held in Manhattan, New York, featuring Avant-Garde Jazz. **7 February:** Clarinetist Paquito D'Rivera, a successful artist in both Latin Jazz and Classical music, records his notable album *Portraits of Cuba*. **24 September:** The Count Basie big band, led by trombonist Grover Mitchell, releases *Live at the Manchester Craftmen's Guild*; the album would win the ensemble its first Grammy Award in 1997.

1997 Ted Gioia's *The History of Jazz* is published. The text would win the Bay Area Book Reviewer's Association award for Best Nonfiction Book of the Year, in addition to other accolades. **11 February:** Kenny Wheeler releases his drummerless album *Angel Song* to critical acclaim. **7 April:** Wynton Marsalis is awarded a Pulitzer Prize for his slavery-inspired "Blood on the Fields." **September:** The American Jazz Museum Opens in Kansas City.

1998 **19 May:** Cuban trumpeter Arturo Sandoval releases his acclaimed album, *Hot House*, featuring Latin big band music. The album would earn Sandoval a Grammy Award for Best Latin Jazz Performance. **1 October:** The Esbjörn Svensson Trio garners international attention with its album *From Gagarin's Point of View*.

1999 **8 June:** Canadian vocalist Diana Krall's *When I Look in Your Eyes* is released, which would earn her the first Grammy of her career for Best Jazz Vocal Album. **27 October:** Pianist Andrew Hill, who had already played an important role in the development of Free and Avant-Garde Jazz, records his album *Dusk*. The album would win awards for Best Album from both *Down-Beat* and *Jazz Times* magazines.

2000   **25 July:** Béla Fleck and the Flecktones release the album *Outbound*. The band, which features Fleck on the banjo, draws on many genres, including Bluegrass, Fusion, and jazz. The album would earn the group its first Grammy Award in a jazz category the following year: Best Contemporary Jazz Album. **17 October:** Saxophonist Bob Mintzer and his big band release *An Homage to Count Basie*. Featuring many favorites from the Basie repertory, the album would be awarded a Grammy Award in 2002 for Best Large Jazz Ensemble Album. **28 December:** Shortly upon its founding, the trio The Bad Plus records its debut album. Consisting of Berklee graduates Ethan Iverson on piano, Reid Anderson on bass, and David King on drums, this album would mark the beginning of the group's trademark reworking of Rock, Pop, and jazz repertoire.

2001   *The New History of Jazz*, by London Times jazz critic Alyn Shipton, is published. The text would become one of the most important on the subject. **8 January:** *Jazz*, the 19-hour documentary by Ken Burns, first airs on PBS. **22 August:** The Classical Jazz Quartet, known for its arrangements of Classical repertoire, records its first album, *Classical Jazz Quartet Plays Tchaikovsky*. The group features Stefon Harris on vibraphone and marimba, Kenny Barron on piano, Ron Carter on bass, Lewis Nash on drums, and Bob Beldon as arranger.

2002   The Smithsonian Institution declares April to be Jazz Appreciation Month. **26 February:** Vocalist Norah Jones achieves huge commercial success with the release of her debut album, *Come Away with Me*. **April:** Branford Marsalis announces the formation of Marsalis Music, a new record company that is to feature the work of creative musicians. **August:** Brad Mehldau releases *Largo*, a well-received album blending Jazz and Rock.

2003   The website and nascent business model ArtistShare is founded. The site, which features many successful modern jazz musicians, provides a way for fans to fund the creative projects of their favorite artists. **12 August:** After two years of production, guitarist Kurt Rosenwinkel releases his first collaborative work with Hip-hop musician Q-Tip, called *Heartcore*. The album blends jazz with other genres, including Hip-hop, Rock, and Electronica. **28 August:** The John Hollenbeck Large Ensemble records its successful and influential album, *A Blessing*. The album, featuring expansive compositions by the drummer Hollenbeck, makes use of unusual instrumentation, including bowed vibraphone and English horns.

2004   March: Maria Schneider records her album *Concert in the Garden*, which would the following year become the first Grammy Award–winning album sold exclusively on the Internet. **24 August:** Guitarist Bill Frisell releases his Fusion album *Unspeakable*, which would earn him a Grammy in 2005 for Best Contemporary Jazz Album. **September:** Alto saxophonist Travis Sullivan debuts his 18-piece jazz orchestra, the Björkestra, at New York City's Knitting Factory. The orchestra performs arranged music of Icelandic Pop artist Björk. **22 October:** Guitarist Ben Monder records his epic CD *Oceana*. Featuring the wordless vocals of Theo Bleckmann, the dense album is unusual for a jazz work in that it is almost entirely through-composed.

2005   The National Endowment for the Arts launches "NEA Jazz in the Schools." **1 February:** The British jazz group Led Bib records its debut CD, *Arboretum*, earning the group the Peter Wittingham Jazz Award. **March:** The British experimental jazz group Polar Bear achieves wide recognition with their jazz-electronica album, *Held on the Tips of Fingers*.

2006   January: Tenor saxophonist Chris Potter, upon forming his groove-based band, Underground, releases the first of several successful albums with the group, the first simply entitled *Underground*. **August:** Tenor saxophonist Michael Brecker records his final album, *Pilgrimage*. The well-received album would earn Brecker, who died the next year from complications of leukemia, two posthumous Grammy Awards. **September:** Dave Brubeck's jazz opera, *Cannery Row Suite*, based on characters of author John Steinbeck, debuts at the 29th Monterey Jazz Festival.

2007   14 August: Trumpeter Terence Blanchard releases his album *A Tale of God's Will (A Requiem for Katrina)*. The album features Blanchard's quintet playing with the Northern Sinfonia, a 40-member string orchestra. The work would earn Blanchard a Grammy in 2008 for Best Large Jazz Ensemble Album. **25 September:** Herbie Hancock releases his album *River: The Joni Letters*, a homage to his friend, songwriter and performer Joni Mitchell.

2008   10 February: Herbie Hancock's *River: The Joni Letters* becomes the second jazz album in history to receive the Album of the Year Award at the Grammy Awards. **April:** Saxophonist Miguel Zenón receives a John Simon Guggenheim Foundation grant, which would result in his well-received 2009 release, *Esta Plena*. **18 April:** The International Association for Jazz Education (IAJE) declares bankruptcy, putting an end to 40 years of service. **September:** New York alto saxophonist Rudresh Mahanthappa releases his album *Kinsmen*, featuring a blending of Western and Indian approaches to improvisation. The recording was a collaborative effort with Indian saxophonist Kadri Gopalnath. **November:** Guitarist Jim Hall teams up with his former student, Bill Frisell, to release the double-CD set *Hemispheres* through ArtistShare.

2009   The JVC Jazz Festival (formerly the Newport Jazz Festival) is canceled. George Wein comes out of retirement to form a new New York City jazz festival to be held in 2010, sponsored by CareFusion but retaining the iconic Newport Jazz Festival name. **6 November:** Wynton Marsalis receives the French insignia of Chevalier of the Legion of Honor, the highest award given by the French government.

2010   June: The Jazz Education Network (JEN) hosts its first annual conference for performers and educators. The conference, held in St. Louis, includes nearly 1,000 educators, students, and musicians. **October:** Under the direction of Wynton Marsalis, Jazz at Lincoln Center Orchestra holds a six-day residency in Havana, Cuba, involving concerts and clinics for young Cuban musicians.

2011   Pianist Marian McPartland steps down as host of NPR's *Piano Jazz*, having hosted the program since 1979. **13 February:** Bassist and vocalist Esperanza Spalding becomes the first jazz artist to win the Grammy for Best New Artist. **19 July:** Drummer, composer, and bandleader Terri Lynne Carrington releases *The Mosaic Project*, which features an all-female collection of performers including Esperanza Spalding, Dee Dee Bridgewater, Dianne Reeves, Ingrid Jensen, and others.

Introduction

The genre of jazz has always been challenging to describe. By its very nature, jazz is a music formed from a combination of influences. In its infancy, jazz was a melting pot of military brass bands, work songs and field hollers of U.S. slaves during the 19th century, European harmonies and forms, and the rhythms of Africa and the Caribbean. Later, the Blues and the influence of Spanish and French Creoles who possessed European Classical training nudged jazz further in its development. Jazz has always been a world music in the sense that music from around the globe has been embraced and incorporated. This is still true today. At the present time, there seem to be as many stylistic variations within jazz as there are performers. At best, we can approximate the characteristics of the music and find a category in which to place it, but this is more for the convenience of the aficionado than a realistic representation of any actual delineation of the music or musicians. Jazz musicians do not wake up one morning and declare to be a Bebop player or a Cool Jazz player from that day forward. Rather, each musician seeks to make the music his own, combining whatever influences feel most personal, and allows the critic or fan to assign his music to a particular category.

The origin of the word *jazz* is obscure, at best. The word itself was in use at least as early as 1913 in San Francisco by sports editor William "Spike" Slattery, used as a part of baseball slang referring to pep and enthusiasm. Later, the word was used in reference to a type of music, reaching Chicago by 1915, but was not heard of in New York until a year later. Early jazz musicians stated that the word did not appear in New Orleans until 1917. Other sources offer different possibilities for the word's origin, including the Creole patois *jass*, referring to strenuous activity, especially sexual intercourse, but also used of Congo dances; from *jasm* (energy, drive) of African origin; a word connected to the Jasmine perfume worn by prostitutes in the New Orleans red-light district; and in reference to individuals, for example Chicago musician Jasbo Brown. Duke Ellington never approved of the word, preferring instead to refer to the music as Negro music or American music.

At the turn of the 20th century, the influences of European syncopation were brought into the piano stylings of Black musicians performing in bars, clubs, and brothels, while minstrel shows and vaudeville were providing

1

opportunities for other Black musicians as well. It was syncopation that defined the music called Ragtime and which would lead to the off-beat accented nature found in much of jazz music ever since. Ragtime pianists included Joseph Lamb, Ferdinand "Jelly Roll" Morton, Luckey Roberts, and the composer of the popular "Maple Leaf Rag," Scott Joplin. In addition to performances by pianists, Ragtime selections could be heard performed by brass bands and dance bands. A precursor to the exciting Stride Piano, Ragtime was at its height between 1890 and 1920.

Following World War I, the style of piano known as Stride was developed and dominated by James P. Johnson (considered the "father" of Stride Piano), Willie "the Lion" Smith, and Fats Waller, among others. These mostly East Coast musicians performed pieces at blazing speeds outlining both the bass notes and harmony in the left hand while playing the syncopated melody in the right. It was from within Stride Piano that the swing feel, one of a loping nature rather than a strict rigid one, began to surface. In clubs and other venues, pianists would participate in "cutting contests" to determine who could outplay the other. Improvisation, one of the core elements associated with jazz music, began to surface during this time.

Being the major port city that it was, New Orleans served as the perfect location for the development of jazz. If there was a birthplace of jazz, most would point to New Orleans. Brothels and bars, dances and parties all required music, and jazz was the music of choice. Among the earliest of those cited as one of the first to perform the new music that would become known as jazz was cornet player Buddy Bolden. Though no recordings of him exist, stories of his amazing sound and volume have been told throughout the intervening years. Pianist and composer Jelly Roll Morton adapted the earlier music of Ragtime to the lighter interpretation of the new music. Jelly Roll, who claimed to have invented jazz and was known to have spent time as a pool hustler, loan shark, pimp, and gambler, became a significant figure in furthering the music. Among the better-known performers and bandleaders of the Early Jazz New Orleans style are included cornetist Joe "King" Oliver, trombonist Kid Ory, and clarinetist/saxophonist Sidney Bechet. The music, along with much of the population, migrated north to Chicago, where a young Louis Armstrong was to change the music forever.

The first recording of jazz was in 1917 in New York City, recorded not by one of the outstanding bands of Black musicians who had developed the music, but by an all-White band named the Original Dixieland Jazz (or "Jass") Band. The two sides ("Livery Stable Blues" and "Dixie Jazz Band One Step") were released by the Victor Talking Machine Company as a novelty, but they soon became a huge hit. The band broke up in the mid-1920s.

Responding to an invitation to join the band of Joe Oliver, Louis Armstrong moved to Chicago in 1922 and began playing second trumpet (to

Joe's first) in Oliver's very popular Creole Jazz Band. After moving on to play with different bandleaders and singers, Armstrong recorded the *Hot Fives* recordings in 1925 under his own name. These recordings, along with the subsequent *Hot Sevens*, proved to alter the direction of jazz. The music that had been one of collective improvisation, in which each member of the band improvised their parts based on traditional roles, now became one that highlighted the soloist and utilized a more formalized approach to the arrangements. These recordings by Armstrong are considered among the most influential in the history of jazz.

Jazz of the 1920s included such artists as Blues singer Bessie Smith and cornetist Bix Beiderbecke, and the bands of Fletcher Henderson, Duke Ellington, Paul Whiteman, and Jean Goldkette. The success of these larger bands led the way into the development of the Swing or Big Band era, in which Swing music as the preeminent style of dance music was established. Jazz was to become the popular music of the people during the Swing era and would not hold that distinction again.

With the success of the Duke Ellington Orchestra, assisted in no small part by his band's tenure as the house band at New York's Cotton Club from 1927 to 1930, big bands began to flourish. Among these were the bands born from Kansas City, Chicago, and New York City, including those of William "Count" Basie, Chick Webb, Benny Goodman, Artie Shaw, Jimmie Lunceford, Harry James, the Dorsey brothers, and more. It was in ballrooms such as the Savoy in New York where a "battle of the bands" would take place squaring two bands off against each other, with the enthusiastic audience of dancers determining the winner. Jazz had finally become commercialized, and it spread nationwide. Many point to the 1935 Benny Goodman Band performance at the Palomar Ballroom in Los Angeles as marking the start of the Swing era. Dances such as the Lindy Hop, Shag, and others became the rage.

Restrictions on transportation and resources brought about by World War II and a recording strike by the musicians' union from August 1942 to mid-1944 made it hard for the public to hear music on the radio or on recordings that was new. During this time, the recording companies featured vocalists singing with vocal groups, rather than with big bands. Singers such as Frank Sinatra, Bing Crosby, Perry Como, and others began to catch the interest of the public while interest in the bands themselves began to wane. At the same time, a new style of jazz that featured instrumentalists emphasizing improvisation in a small group setting was developing largely without public awareness.

Bebop became the latest stage of jazz development during the 1940s and was led by innovators including Charlie Parker, Dizzy Gillespie, Thelonious Monk, Bud Powell, and others. Sessions at the New York establishments Minton's Playhouse and Monroe's Uptown House functioned as the laboratory for the development of Bebop. The changes to the music included more rap-idly occurring chord progressions, an emphasis on technical virtuosity, less emphasis on arrangements, and a vastly increased emphasis on improvisation. This development, though fulfilling to the jazz musician, served to change the music from being a popular music to that of an art music, less appreciated by the general public. As popularity in vocalists rose, interest in the newest style of instrumental jazz decreased. Performers were no longer playing jazz to entertain the public. Instead, they were working on pushing the music to a more sophisticated level, and appealing to fewer listeners outside of the die-hard aficionados. Though big bands were continuing to perform, the decreas-ing public interest forced many to disband, cut personnel, or resort to heavy traveling between performances.

As if in reaction to the elite demands of the Bebop style, two branches that departed from Bebop began to form. One, which would be known as Cool Jazz, returned to an emphasis on arrangement and linear lines, decreased the emphasis on improvisation, and looked to combine instruments typically not associated with jazz to form new timbres. Instruments such as French horn, tuba, muted brass, and a preference for a lighter, warmer sound to the en-semble were embraced. Though not the first music to be recorded in the Cool Jazz style, the Miles Davis–led sessions of 1949 and 1950, which later were released as *Birth of the Cool*, served as a marker for the new style. For years to come, musicians would be classified as more "cool" or "bop," depending on their sound and arrangements. Notable musicians associated with Cool Jazz include Dave Brubeck, Chet Baker, Gerry Mulligan, pianist Bill Evans, Miles Davis, and saxophonist Lee Konitz.

As Cool Jazz was becoming established, another version of jazz was arising as well, that of Hard Bop. With Hard Bop, a return to a more Blues-focused, "earthy" path was preferred. Musicians were not as focused on the technical wizardry that had been so important to the Bebop style, and groups began to incorporate a Rhythm and Blues component, further allowing the listener to embrace the style. Hard Bop is also sometimes referred to as Funky Jazz or as Soul Jazz. Significant artists associated with the Hard Bop style include Horace Silver, Art Blakey's Jazz Messengers, the Max Roach/Clifford Brown Quintet, Cannonball Adderley, Sonny Stitt, and Lee Morgan. Popular in the 1950s and 1960s, Hard Bop remains an important component to a typical jazz performer's development to this day. With its repetitive, "groove"-like approach, audience members feel musically and intellectually challenged but still connected to the performers onstage.

As with much of society, jazz began to seek a deeper, more meaningful exploration of the personal experience. The late 1950s saw the development of Modal Jazz, which was based on less harmonic variety while emphasizing a more personalized improvisational approach that was based on only one or two scales or only a few notes. The challenge for the performer became communicating more with less and on the development of motivic ideas. Modal Jazz shifted the focus from harmony to melody. In 1959, Miles Davis released *Kind of Blue*, a quintessential Modal Jazz recording. The recording featured pianist Bill Evans, alto saxophonist Cannonball Adderley, and tenor saxophonist John Coltrane, who was to become a significant figure in the world of Free Jazz.

Reflecting the societal unrest of the 1960s, Free Jazz, akin to Avant-Garde Jazz, looked to relieve the music from previous restraints in the areas of tonality, form, melodicism, and instrumentation. Though not truly free from all structure, Free Jazz allows the performer to explore ideas that are contrived almost spontaneously, resulting in a performance that is never the same twice. Different instrumentation of ensembles such as the use of two basses, two drum sets, or the use of multiphonics (the production of more than one tone at a time on one's instrument through multiple vibrations achieved by singing while playing or playing two instruments simultaneously) are welcome in Free Jazz. A goal of Free Jazz is that of expressing the music to the highest possible personal degree without regard for traditional performance practice. Leaders of the Free Jazz movement include Albert Ayler, Cecil Taylor, John Coltrane (*A Love Supreme*), the AACM, and Ornette Coleman (*Free Jazz*). Interestingly, Free Jazz found stronger acceptance in Europe than in the United States, with many accomplished Free Jazz artists choosing to spend extended periods of time there.

The music of Latin America has been influential since the early days of jazz. Jelly Roll Morton referred to it as the Spanish tinge, without which "you will never be able to get the right seasoning for jazz" (*The Complete Library of Congress Recordings*, 2005). Latin Jazz is a term used to refer more generally to music that adopts characteristics of the music of Cuba, Africa, Brazil, and/or Puerto Rico. Afro-Cuban Jazz was featured in the bands of Dizzy Gillespie and Billy Taylor during the 1950s, and more contemporary artists such as Arturo Sandoval, Paquito D'Rivera, and Tito Puente are considered influential performers of Latin Jazz. The Samba and Bossa Nova were brought to the attention of the public by Brazilians João Gilberto and Antônio Carlos Jobim. American performers including Stan Getz and Charlie Byrd performed jazz Sambas and Bossa Novas to wide public acclaim.

During the 1960s and 1970s, a merging of Rock or Funk music and electronics with jazz produced the Jazz Fusion and Jazz-Rock style. Artists such as Miles Davis (*Bitches Brew*, 1970), Herbie Hancock (*Head Hunters*, 1973), the Mahavishnu Orchestra, and Weather Report incorporated electric keyboards, electric bass, synthesized sounds, and various electronic sound effects into the music. During the 1980s and 1990s, Great Britain developed an approach that was termed Acid Jazz, a style that combines elements of jazz, Funk, and Hip-hop. Led in large part by saxophonist Steve Coleman, a collective of African-American jazz musicians from New York began utilizing an approach to performance they termed M-base (short for "macro-basic array of structured extemporization"). Though developed as an approach to creating music, critics and the public adopted the term as referring to the music that resulted from the process. M-base strives to express the experiences, culture, and philosophy of the players, and therefore the performer's approach to the music can and will change, depending on the artist's own personal development.

Jazz in the present day offers a rich mixture of all the styles described above and has regularly begun to incorporate world musics. Jazz has an audience, but the audience is divided into many sections. Traditionalists point to the Early Jazz styles of New Orleans and Chicago. Those who grew into adulthood in the 1930s see the great bands of the Swing era as the pinnacle of jazz, remembering the band battles, Lindy Hop, and vocal stylings of Frank Sinatra and Ella Fitzgerald as jazz at its best. Lovers of Bebop still want to hear music reminiscent of the groups of Dizzy Gillespie, Charlie Parker, and Bud Powell, music that was intended to challenge the listener and the performer. The Cool Jazz sounds of Dave Brubeck, the Modern Jazz Quartet, and Chet Baker brought jazz to an audience that required the familiarity and structure of form, melody, and arrangements in order to appreciate the music. Hard Bop and Free Jazz provided the reconnection African-Americans desired to a music that originally felt like their own but that had begun to lose its way. Those seeking a higher plane of aesthetic experience related to the music of John Coltrane and Miles Davis, and the recordings they made years ago are still being explored for their depth of introspection and reflection. Many who grew up with Rock and Roll find the Jazz Fusion stylists to be most accessible and engaging.

Regardless of personal preference, each of the jazz traditions mentioned above remains well represented by jazz musicians of today. For every group or performer who seeks to carry on the legacy of past jazz masters by recreating and paying homage to specific performers or styles, there is another group or performer who is looking toward the next new fusion of jazz with other styles. Jazz is, at its core, music of the people that reflects a personal expression of the human experience. Always changing, always growing, and always celebrating expression of the individual, jazz will continue to exist as long as mankind continues to search for meaning.

A

A&M RECORDS. A record company founded by Herb Alpert and Jerry Moss in 1962. Founded primarily as an outlet for Herb Alpert to record and distribute **albums** for his group the Tijuana Brass, the label had great success in the late 1960s and opened offices overseas. A&M signed several Pop groups that would go on to great success. These artists included the Carpenters, the Police, and Cat Stevens. Alpert and Moss decided to sell the label to Polygram Records in 1989, shortly after the success the label generated with Bryan Adams' smash single "(Everything I Do) I Do It for You." The label had very little success with jazz outside of Herb Alpert and some albums of **arrangements** by Creed Taylor and **Don Sebesky**, which featured strings and several mainstream jazz artists, including **George Benson.**

ABENE, MICHAEL (1942–). Abene began his professional career at an early age playing piano with Marshall Brown's Youth Jazz Band in 1958 before studying at the Manhattan School of Music. During the 1960s, he played in small-group and **big band** settings with many notable musicians including **Clark Terry, Maynard Ferguson,** Al Cohn, **Zoot Sims,** and **Don Ellis.** Abene's **arrangements** were prominently featured in many groups including the bands of **Buddy Rich,** Ferguson, **Harry Edison,** and **Mel Lewis.** Abene's first **album** came later in his career and was entitled *You Must Have Been a Beautiful Baby* (1984, Stash). Held in high regard as both a performer and arranger, he expanded into the production of several projects for the **GRP** record label including the *GRP Big Band, GRP Big Band Live,* and *The GRP Christmas Collection* (Volumes 1, 2, and 3). In addition to providing workshops and clinics worldwide, Abene joined the collegiate ranks in 1998 as a professor at his alma mater, the Manhattan School of Music.

ABERCROMBIE, JOHN (1944–). Originally from Connecticut, Abercrombie's music studies brought him to Boston's Berklee College of Music in 1962 and later to North Texas State University where he refined his guitar-playing skills. After his time at North Texas, Abercrombie relocated to New York and quickly found his way into the jazz scene. From 1969 to 1984, he performed and worked with many established jazz leaders including **Chico**

Hamilton, **Gil Evans**, and Gato Barbieri, and also developed connections with many leaders of the next wave of jazz innovation. These musicians included **Billy Cobham**, the **Brecker** Brothers, Richie Bierach, **Dave Holland**, George Mraz, and **Jack DeJohnette**. From the mid-1970s onward, Abercrombie was recorded regularly on the **ECM** label as both a leader and **sideman**. The first of these recordings was with his group Gateway, featuring Dave Holland and Jack DeJohnette on the albums *Timeless* (1974, ECM) and *Gateway* (1975, ECM).

From the 1980s to today, Abercrombie has led or co-led many groups with different focuses. Experimenting with different guitar synthesizer possibilities and the use of electric mandolin, Abercrombie has explored many innovative uses of the guitar. Abercrombie recorded in duo format in separate sessions with **John Scofield**, Andy LaVerne, Marc Copland, and Richie Beirach, and in trio settings with Peter Erskine and Marc Johnson, and organists Dan Wall and Jeff Palmer. Abercrombie experimented with Free Jazz in a quartet he formed with Marc Johnson, Joey Baron, and violinist Mark Feldman. Abercrombie had a brief reunion with his Gateway trio and recorded another **album** in 1994 entitled *Gateway: Homecoming* (1994, ECM).

ABRAMS, MUHAL RICHARD (1930–). A native of Chicago, Abrams is a multifaceted musician playing the piano, clarinet, and cello in addition to being a prominent composer, arranger, and educator. Abrams first worked on the Chicago Hard Bop scene with musicians such as **Dexter Gordon** and **Eddie Harris** starting in the mid-1950s. From his rehearsal-based Experimental Band, formed in 1962, Abrams would soon form his creative and forward-thinking Free Jazz cooperative, the **Association for the Advancement of Creative Musicians (AACM)** in 1965. In 1975, Abrams relocated to New York City, where he continued to compose along with playing and pursuing Avant-Garde Jazz. In addition to appearing as a **sideman** with the likes of Anthony Braxton, Eddie Harris, **Kenny Dorham**, and **Woody Shaw**, Abrams has recorded and toured extensively throughout out the United States and abroad as a bandleader. Notable recording: *The Hearing Suite* (1989, **Black Saint**). In 2009 the National Endowment for the Arts (NEA) announced that Abrams would be one of the recipients for the NEA's Jazz Masters Award.

ACCORDION. A portable mechanical keyboard-like instrument that generates sound through air pushed by both arms through the center bellows of the instrument. Each side of the instrument has either a small keyboard or bass buttons. The bass buttons are usually located on the left side. There are several different styles of accordion including the melodeon and concertina, which have different cultural importance. While not directly involved in much of jazz's history, many world music styles heavily use instruments from the accordion family such as the use of the bandoneón in Argentinian music.

ACE OF HEARTS. A record label, associated with partner label Ace of Clubs, primarily dedicated to reissuing **albums** made prior to 1932 that were initially released on **Decca, Brunswick,** and **Vocalion**. The majority of these released albums were cheaper **recordings** of early **Swing** and popular music.

ACID JAZZ (I). A term first used to describe the fusion of jazz-influenced improvisation, harmony, and rhythm, with elements of **Funk** and **Soul** styles and other **groove**-based music. Created in the late 1980s and early 1990s, Acid Jazz began to incorporate electronics as it developed and also incorporated the use of digital sequencing and sampling. The Acid Jazz style was created in Great Britain, primarily influenced by Eddie Piller and Gilles Peterson and their **record label** with the same name. Groups that play in the Acid Jazz style include Freak Power, Goldbug, and Galliano.

ACID JAZZ (II). An independent **record label** founded in England that was partially responsible for the development of the Acid Jazz style. Created by two disc jockeys, Acid Jazz sought out obscure, electronic-influenced **Funk** performers from previous decades. Groups signed to the Acid Jazz label include Jamiroquai and the Brand New Heavies. *See also* ACID JAZZ (I).

ACTUELLE. An American-based record label that produced the first lateral-cut records. Founded in 1920, Actuelle expanded to produce international records shortly after its initial U.S.-only based **recordings**.

ACUNA, ALEX (1944–). A self-taught drummer and percussionist, Acuna made a name for himself in Puerto Rico as a performer and **studio musician**. In 1975, Acuna moved to Las Vegas to pursue new musical opportunities and was invited to perform with the group Weather Report. Acuna's tenure as a member of Weather Report lasted two years and two **albums** (*Heavy Weather* and *Black Market*). After leaving Weather Report, Acuna was an in-demand performer who recorded with **Clare Fischer, Ella Fitzgerald, Tania Maria, Chick Corea,** and Joni Mitchell during the early 1980s. Since then, Acuna has performed primarily as a studio musician while branching out into education. He joined the faculty of the University of California, Los Angeles, and has taught at the Berklee College of Music in addition to releasing several instructional videos.

ADDERLEY, JULIAN "CANNONBALL" (1928–1975). A major **bandleader** and **sideman** of the **Hard Bop** era, Cannonball Adderley was a highly influential alto saxophonist with a style of playing accessible to many. Originally from Tampa, Florida, he moved to New York City in 1955, gaining acclaim and launching his career from that point. Shortly after moving to the city, he tried to create a quintet with brother and cornetist **Nat Adderley** but did not find much success early on. However, with his exuberant tone and Blues-rooted improvisations, he was soon noticed by **trumpet** player **Miles Davis** and joined the Miles Davis Sextet in October of 1957.

His work with the Miles Davis group included participation in the two definitive **albums**: *Kind of Blue* and *Milestones*. Adderley worked as a bandleader with his quintet/sextet during 1959–1966 which featured his brother, Nat Adderley, along with a handful of renowned musicians, including **Bobby Timmons**, **Joe Zawinul**, Victor Feldman, Sam Jones, Louis Hayes, and **Charles Lloyd**, among others. The late 1960s began to reflect an influence of electric jazz and **Avant-Garde** Jazz in Adderley's playing. Adderley died from a stroke in 1975 and was soon thereafter inducted in the *DownBeat* Jazz Hall of Fame. He still remains one of the greatest influences on alto saxophonists today. Notable recordings: *Somethin' Else* (1958, **Blue Note**); *Phenix* (1975, Fantasy); and *Mercy, Mercy, Mercy* (1996, **Capitol** rerelease). *See also* SOUL JAZZ.

ADDERLEY, NATHANIEL "NAT" (1931–2000). Nat Adderley was a Hard Bop cornetist and **trumpet** player who played in a style influenced by **Miles Davis**. Adderley played in his brother **Cannonball**'s original group and then went on to work as a sideman with vibraphonist **Lionel Hampton**, trombonist **J. J. Johnson**, and clarinetist **Woody Herman**. He joined the Cannonball Adderley quintet in 1959 and remained with the group until 1975. Many great compositions, including "Work Song" and "The Old Country," were written by Adderley during this time. After his brother's death in 1975, he continued to play with his own groups and recorded extensively with such artists as **Ron Carter**, **Johnny Griffin**, and **Sonny Fortune**, including an exciting group he led with trombonist J. J. Johnson. Adderley joined the faculty of the Florida Southern College in 1997 as an artist-in-residence, just three years before dying from complications with diabetes.

ADLER, LARRY (1914–2001). Adler took up the harmonica at age 10 and began performing professionally as a teenager in New York. Sir Charles Cochran, a theater manager from Sussex England, heard Adler perform at the age of 20 and recruited him to move to London to perform in one of Cochran's revues. Adler further refined his harmonica skills as a Classical performer and quickly gained recognition as being an elite performer. Malcolm Arnold, Darius Milhaud, Vaughn Williams, and Gordon Jacob all wrote pieces for Adler as a featured soloist with orchestra. Toward the later part of Adler's career he began teaching in addition to composing more. Some of his work is captured on the scores to the films *Genevieve* and *King and Country*.

AFFINITY. A post-Bop quartet made up of Bobby Lurie (drums), Rob Sudduth (tenor saxophone), a rotating bass chair of Michael Silverman and Richard Sanders, and led by soprano saxophonist Joe Rosenburg. Inspired by the work of **Ornette Coleman** and other **Free Jazz** leaders, much of the material played is targeted toward collective intellectual improvisation. Repertoire of the group ranges from Free Jazz artists **Eric Dolphy** and **Anthony Braxton** to **Straight-Ahead** artists including **Art Blakey** and **Cedar Walton**.

AFRO-CUBAN JAZZ. A style arising out of New York City, Afro-Cuban Jazz consists of a blending of Cuban and African polyrhythms with jazz improvisation. At the center of the rhythmic identity of Afro-Cuban Jazz is the **clave**, an off-beat, repeated rhythmic pattern. Although Cuban music remained separate from **Swing** music prior to the 1940s, the rise of **Bebop** in 1945 included an increased influence and incorporation of Afro-Cuban styles. The collaboration between Bebop **trumpet** player **Dizzy Gillespie** and Cuban percussionist **Chano Pozo** in Gillespie's orchestra proved significant in the rise of the genre, producing such tunes as "A Night in Tunisia," the original version of "Manteca," and "Tin Tin Deo." Gillespie remained at the forefront of the genre throughout his career, later working with other artists in Afro-Cuban Jazz including **Paquito D'Rivera** and **Arturo Sandoval**. *See also* LATIN JAZZ.

AIRTO. *See* MOREIRA, AIRTO.

AJAX RECORDS. A record company founded by H. S. Berliner in 1921. Berliner had **recording** studios in Montreal, Canada, and New York City. Poor distribution to the southern and central areas of the United States led to a short business life of the company. Prior to their closing in 1926, Ajax cut records for artists Rosa Henderson, Edna Hicks, and Mamie Smith.

AKIYOSHI, TOSHIKO (1929–). Originally from Japan, Akiyoshi made a name for herself in the world of jazz through her work as pianist, arranger, and composer. Discovered in 1952 by pianist **Oscar Peterson** while he was on a tour of Japan, Akiyoshi recorded with Peterson's own **rhythm section** of Herb Ellis, Ray Brown, and J. C. Heard on her first release titled *Toshiko's*

Piano. Upon moving to the United States in 1956 to study at the Berklee College of Music in Boston, Akiyoshi began learning the art of arranging and composition. Along with her husband **Lew Tabackin**, Akiyoshi formed a **big band** in the Los Angeles area in 1973. Using Akiyoshi's compositions and **arrangements** for the group, the Toshiko Akiyoshi–Lew Tabackin Big Band would hold a strong presence in the jazz world by 1980. After moving to New York City in 1982, the band was started up once again and continued touring, **recording**, and performing regularly, all the while driven by the energetic writing and conducting of Akiyoshi. She has been the recipient of countless Grammy nominations, *DownBeat* Critics Poll contests, and in 2007 was honored with the title of NEA Jazz Master by the National Endowment for the Arts (NEA). Today, while her big band is no longer performing or recording, she continues to appear as a pianist and guest **bandleader**. Notable recordings: *Toshiko Akiyoshi–Lew Tabackin Big Band* (1974–1976, Novus) and *Carnegie Hall Concert* (1991, **Columbia**). *See also* JAPAN.

ALBAM, MANNY (1922–2001). Albam started in the music world as a baritone saxophonist but quickly gained a reputation as a standout arranger in New York. His work was performed by jazz **big bands** led by Don Joseph, Bob Chester, **Georgie Auld**, Sam Donahue, **Charlie Barnet**, and Jerry Wald. In the 1950s, he elected to stop performing and focused his efforts on composition and leading ensembles for the next two decades. Many prominent musicians were attracted to Albam's works, which were featured by groups led by **Dizzy Gillespie**, **Gerry Mulligan**, **Stan Getz**, **Count Basie**, **Woody Herman**, **Stan Kenton**, and **Buddy Rich**. Albam released one title under his name during this time, *The Jazz Greats of Our Time* (1957, MCA), which featured top-flight soloists. Albam is not heard on the **album** but is instead featured as a conductor/arranger for most of the material. He also explored Classical music and composed several works including his "Concerto for Trombone and Strings."

Albam became a more active educator in 1964, teaching at Glassboro State College where he served as a faculty member for the next three decades. He further expanded his compositional skills into developing long, large-scale jazz pieces in addition to working on scores for several movies and television shows. He succumbed to cancer in 2001.

ALBUM. A reference to a collection of recorded songs based around a common theme or idea. Originally used in reference to several 78 rpm **recordings** that made up a long Classical work, such as a symphony, the word was later used to define recordings that lasted over 30 minutes. In the 1960s, the idea of "album artists" was founded by Rock groups like the Moody Blues, the Beatles, Pink Floyd, and Led Zeppelin, who created recordings around a central theme that featured no singular material. Jazz recordings like **Miles Davis'** *Sketches of Spain* (1960, **Columbia**) and *Porgy & Bess* (1958, Columbia) were constructed with the album idea. *See also* RECORD LABEL.

ALEXANDER, MONTGOMERY BERNARD "MONTY" (1944–). Inspired by **Nat "King" Cole, Louis Armstrong**, and Calypso music from his native Jamaica, Alexander began studying jazz piano at the age of 14. After moving to the United States in 1961, Alexander struggled at first to find steady work in Miami and then Las Vegas, until heard by Jilly Rizzo, a club owner and friend of **Frank Sinatra**. After being hired to perform in Rizzo's club (sometimes accompanying Sinatra), he soon met vibraphonist **Milt Jackson**. This encounter was important as Jackson referred Alexander to bassist Ray Brown who invited him to join his trio. Alexander soon relocated to New York and saw his career quickly take shape. He was a regular performer at **Minton's Playhouse** with both Jackson and Brown and was featured on several **recordings** made by both.

Alexander led his own groups from 1974 onward, with the first group featuring John Clayton and **Jeff Hamilton**. This group recorded Alexander's first **album**, *Live! Montreux Alexander* (1976, **Verve**). Alexander enjoyed trying to capture the feel of his native Jamaica by using steel drums and other Caribbean percussion on several albums he would record over the next few decades. Alexander maintained a steady touring and recording career throughout the 1980s and 1990s while also performing with jazz legends including **Barney Kessel, Johnny Griffin, Shelly Manne**, and Marshal Royal. In 2000, he was given the title of Commander in the Order of Distinction for outstanding services to Jamaica as a worldwide music ambassador. He served as director of two major works featured at Jazz at Lincoln Center (*Lords of the West Indies* and *Harlem Kingston Express*).

ALI, RASHIED (1935–2009). Ali's musical training started at early age as he was surrounded by music since birth. His mother had sung with **Jimmie Lunceford**, and his brother, Muhammed, was a drummer with **Albert Ayler**. Ali was born Robert Patterson Jr. but elected to change his name to Rashied Ali when his father, Robert Patterson Sr., converted to Islam and also took the name Rashied Ali.

After moving to New York, Ali quickly found work playing drums with Bill Dixon, Paul Bley, **Pharoah Sanders**, and Alice Coltrane before replacing **Elvin Jones** as drummer in **John Coltrane**'s group in 1965. A pioneer of **Free Jazz** drumming, Ali can be heard on Coltrane's **album** *Meditations* (1965, Impulse!) and *Interstellar Space* (1967, Impulse!) recorded before

Coltrane's death. Although a very prominent performer, Ali did not record very much until later in his life. He formed the group Phalanx in the 1980s that featured James "Blood" Ulmer on guitar, Sirone on bass, and George Adams on tenor saxophone. Ali experimented with much new music and incorporated the use of multimedia in two groups, the Gift of the Eagle and Cosmic Legends, and recorded several albums with groups that included Henry Grimes and Marilyn Crispell. In 2009, Ali died in a New York hospital due to a sudden heart attack.

ALLEN, HENRY "RED" (1908–1967). Son of New Orleans **brass band** leader Henry Allen Sr., Henry "Red" Allen was one of the foremost **trumpet** players in the early **Swing** style. Influenced by and in many ways seen as following in the footsteps of fellow trumpeter **Louis Armstrong**, Allen played in an energetic and convincing manner and was known for his innovative rhythmic freedom and idiomatic trumpet devices (trills, half-valve effects, **growls**, falls, etc.) that he used to create interesting and memorable solos. Red Allen moved to New York City in 1927 to play with **King Oliver**'s band and would soon become a featured soloist in **Fletcher Henderson**'s orchestra as well, demonstrating his expertise at playing the **Blues** through the many wonderful **recordings** he produced with the band. Additionally, Allen recorded and played with the likes of **Fats Waller**, **Jelly Roll Morton**, **Billie Holiday**, and **Benny Goodman**. Allen continued to play and tour with his own group throughout the United States and Europe until his death in the spring of 1967. Notable recording: *Swing Out* (1929–1932, Topaz).

ALLEN, STEVE (1921–2000). Pianist, composer, jazz aficionado, and comedian, Steve Allen was instrumental in bringing a greater audience to jazz music via television. *The Steve Allen Show*, which aired on NBC from 1956 to 1958, featured several broadcasts of jazz performances, including one unforgettable one with the **Count Basie** Orchestra from the **Birdland** jazz club. Allen was strongly influenced by jazz, and his love of it prompted him to feature jazz musicians as guests as often as possible. In fact, Allen was one of the first television hosts to showcase many African-American jazz artists on live television. Always an avid musician and composer, Allen won a Grammy in 1963 for Best Jazz Composition for his tune "Gravy Waltz."

ALLISON, JOHN "MOSE," JR. (1927–). Allison's study of piano began at the age of five while he was in grammar school and remained a focal part of his academic life until he chose to pursue a full-time career in music. Studying first at the University of Mississippi followed by a stint at Louisiana State University (where he received a B.A. in English), Allison led a successful piano trio while completing his studies. After graduating, Allison pursued a career in music and moved to New York where he worked with many of the **Cool Jazz** or **West Coast Jazz** leaders including **Stan Getz, Gerry Mulligan**, and Al Cohn while also **recording** several **albums** for the **Prestige** record label. Allison toured Europe on and off in the 1960s and 1970s with his trio or would use local musicians to cover the bass and drum chairs.

Allison's legacy is tied into the musicians whom he would influence as much as his own ability to perform. He is held in high regard by **Blues** and Rock musicians, including Pete Townshend (The Who), Tom Waits, and the Yardbirds. Many of his compositions such as "A Young Man's Blues," "Tell Me Something," and "I'm Not Talking" have been recorded multiple times by artists from other genres. In the late 1990s, Allison saw a resurgence of his popularity, and his music has been used in motion pictures, and several collaborative efforts with musicians including Van Morrison and Ben Sidran have added to his legacy. While being an active performer, Allison has not recorded much since the 1990s.

ALTO SAXOPHONE. Pitched in E♭, the alto saxophone is one of the dominant members of the saxophone family along with the tenor. The alto's range is from the D♭ below middle C to A♭5 (and sometimes A depending on the model of the saxophone). Alto saxophone has been a popular instrument in jazz that was especially heightened during **Charlie Parker**'s prominence in the late 1940s and early 1950s. *See also* ADDERLEY, JULIAN; SAXOPHONE; STITT, SONNY; WOODS, PHIL.

ALTSCHUL, BARRY (1943–). Altschul grew up in New York and was exposed to jazz early on through Charles Tolliver and Junior Cook—musicians who lived in his neighborhood. He took up the drums and studied with **Hard Bop** drummer **Charlie Persip** during his teenage years. His career continually switched between **Straight-Ahead** groups and newer modern free styles. During the mid-1960s, Altschul worked with Paul Bley as well as the group **Circle** that featured **Anthony Braxton, Dave Holland**, and **Chick Corea**, both groups that were considered highly experimental. Altschul would work with each of the members of Circle in their own groups as well. He recorded on Holland's **album** *Conference of the Birds* (1972, **ECM**) that also featured Braxton, and toured with Braxton's quartet, which ironically also featured Holland on bass.

From the late 1970s, Altschul freelanced with many performers including Sam Rivers, **Paul Bley, Dave Liebman**, Roswell Rudd, Pepper Adams, Ray Anderson, and **Kenny Drew**. Altschul would continue to play with Paul Bley's groups throughout the 1980s as well as playing in reunion groups of all the influential groups that he had played for previously. Altschul has done limited **recording** under his own name but did have several notable recordings in the 1970s that included *You Can't Name Your Own Tune* (1977, Muse) and *Another Time, Another Place* (1978, Muse).

ALVAREZ, CHICO (1920–1992). After learning **piano** and **violin**, Alvarez decided to take up the **trumpet** while growing up in Inglewood, California. Performing as a soloist in **Stan Kenton**'s band, Alvarez got his first break before serving in the army from 1943 to 1946. Following his stint in the army, he played with Kenton again before moving first to Hermosa Beach and then to Las Vegas. Alvarez worked for several hotels, backing up artists such as **Ella Fitzgerald** and **Sarah Vaughan** from 1958 to 1982. In 1985 he was a featured performer at the **Sacramento Dixieland Jubilee** and started his own group, the Las Vegas Jazz Band.

AMERICAN FEDERATION OF JAZZ SOCIETIES (AFJS). An international nonprofit organization whose focus is to manage international communication between jazz groups by sharing information, resources, and techniques. The organization was founded in 1985.

AMERICAN JAZZ ORCHESTRA. Founded by Roberta Swann and Gary Giddins, the American Jazz Orchestra focused on performing music from the **big band** repertoire. Starting with its first concert in 1986, the group performed several concerts a year with fluid personnel based on availability and often featured themed concerts or guest artists. The music of **Duke Ellington**, **Count Basie**, **Jimmie Lunceford**, and **Dizzy Gillespie** were all covered during the group's first few years, and from 1987 to 1992 the group featured the music of living composers such as **Benny Carter**, **Gerald Wilson**, **Muhal Richard Abrams**, **Jimmy Heath**, and David Murray. The orchestra eventually was forced to shut down operations in 1993 when funding problems arose.

AMERICAN RECORD COMPANY (ARC). Formed in 1929, ARC was produced as a result of the combination of several smaller companies. The Cameo Record Corporation, Pathe Phonograph and Radio Corporation, Plaza Music Company, and Scranton Button Company all merged to form the American Record Company. From 1929 until 1938, ARC was seen as a label that produced cheap records (often capitalizing on fallout from the Great Depression) until the label was purchased by the **Columbia Broadcasting System (CBS)** in 1938. As a result of this transaction, CBS moved many of the records that had been successful on ARC to their more popular labels, **Columbia** and **OKeh**.

AMMONS, ALBERT (1907–1949). Considered one of the masters of the **Blues**-based **Boogie-Woogie** style, Ammons was a successful and influential pianist from the late 1920s until his death in 1949. After moving from Chicago to New York City in the late 1930s, Ammons worked with fellow Boogie-Woogie pianists Pete Johnson and **Meade Lux Lewis**, whom Ammons had known well in Chicago. Together, they formed the Boogie Woogie Trio, performing at Carnegie Hall and regularly at the famous **Café Society** in New York. He was known for his powerful and enigmatic piano style that can be heard through his classic **recordings** of "Boogie-Woogie Stomp" and "Pinetop's Boogie-Woogie." Ammons continued to perform regularly and tour as an artist throughout the 1940s, despite the declining public interest in the Boogie-Woogie style. He performed at the inauguration of President Harry S. Truman in 1949. Regardless of his death in 1949 at the age of 32, Ammons would prove to have a great influence on an emerging generation of pianists, including the likes of Ray Bryant and **Erroll Garner**. Ammons is considered by most to be the king of the idiomatic Boogie-Woogie genre. *See also* AMMONS, EUGENE "JUG."

AMMONS, (EU)GENE "JUG" (1925–1974). Eugene "Jug" Ammons, the son of notable **Boogie-Woogie** pianist **Albert Ammons**, was a tenor saxophonist and native of Chicago who was greatly influenced by saxophonists **Lester Young** and **Coleman Hawkins**. He got his start in 1943 at the ripe age of 18 when he went on the road with the King Kolax band. Soon thereafter, in 1944, he would join the noteworthy **big band** of vocalist **Billy Eckstine** and remain with the band until 1947 as a featured soloist. Ammons formed his own quintet and in 1949 replaced **Stan Getz** in the **Woody Herman** Orchestra. Additionally, Ammons joined fellow saxophonist **Sonny Stitt** in 1950 and worked closely playing and "battling" him for a few years. His career unfortunately did not go without hardships; Ammons was imprisoned twice on possession of narcotics charges—once from 1958 to 1960 and again from 1962 to 1969.

Ammons soon returned, however, in 1969 and came back onto the Chicago scene as vibrant as ever. Considered part of the Chicago school of tenor saxophone along with Von Freeman, Ammons was known for his recognizable full and soulful tone. Capable of burning Bebop lines like the rest of the great jazz musicians on the scene, Ammons was also well known for his thoughtful and poignant **ballad** playing. Throughout the rest of his life, he recorded with all-star musicians including **John Coltrane** and **Art Farmer**, and performed often with fellow saxophonists **Dexter Gordon** and Sonny Stitt. Ammons, a great influence on the next generation of saxophonists that would follow (including Joshua Redman), died of bone cancer in 1974.

ANDERSON, IVIE MARIE (1905–1949). Anderson began her professional career at the age of 16, performing in Los Angeles and touring the United States and Cuba in 1922–1923. Performing regularly in the mid-1920s, Anderson developed a strong connection with **bandleader** Sonny Clay who took her with his band on his infamous trip to Australia. Anderson's big break occurred when she was invited to perform with **Duke Ellington** in 1931. The two worked together extensively during the 1930s, including tours of England and collaborating on film and **recording** projects together. The two can be seen together in a soundie made of Ellington's composition "I Got It Bad (and That Ain't Good)." Anderson was also the first vocalist to record Ellington's composition "It Don't Mean a Thing (If It Ain't Got That Swing)." Some of these songs are captured on a compilation made of their collaborations, *With Duke Ellington* (1942, EPM Musique). In the early 1940s, Anderson retired due to complications with asthma and became a restaurateur. She made one final record in 1946 with future jazz icon **Charles Mingus** before health complications resulted in her death in 1949.

ANDERSON, RAY (1952–). Born in Hyde Park, Chicago, Anderson took up the trombone in the fourth grade inspired by sounds he had heard from jazz records his father played that included trombonists such as **Vic Dickenson** and **Trummy Young**. Anderson grew up with fellow trombonist George Lewis, and the two have worked together ever since. Anderson bounced around cities in the early 1970s, playing in a variety of bands in Minnesota, Los Angeles, and San Francisco before relocating in New York in 1972. In New York, Anderson's career took off, and he worked with Bennie Wallace, **Barry Altschul**, and took over his friend George Lewis's chair in **Anthony Braxton**'s quartet.

Anderson became an important **bandleader** in the early 1980s with his group BassDrumBone made up of fellow cutting-edge musicians Mark Helias and Gerry Hemingway. The group made several records over the next two decades and helped usher in new ways of approaching trombone. *Right Down Your Alley* (1984, Soul Alley) and *You Be* (1985, Minor Music) were two of the first BassDrumBone **albums** that ushered in this style.

Anderson was diagnosed with Bell's palsy in the early 1980s and responded by taking up **singing** while allowing his **chops** ample time to recover from stress from the disease. After recovering, he continued to sing in several groups including another group he led called the Slickaphonics. Throughout the remainder of the 1980s through today, Anderson remains an in-demand **sideman** and soloist and has performed with **Charlie Haden**, Tim Berne, **John Scofield**, Bobby Previte, **Henry Threadgill**, New York Jazz Composers Orchestra, **Lew Soloff**, **David Murray**, Craig Harris, and

Gary Valente. In 2003, Anderson was hired as director of jazz studies for the Music Department at the State University of New York–Stony Brook. *See also* TROMBONE.

ANDERSON, WILLIAM ALONZO "CAT" (1916–1981). Born William Alonzo Anderson, "Cat" got his nickname while living at Jenkins Orphanage in South Carolina. At the age of 13, Anderson got his first professional experience playing the **trumpet** in a band created at the orphanage, called "The Carolina Cotton Pickers." After leaving the group in 1935, Anderson quickly caught on with several groups over the next eight years in part due to his incredible upper-register playing. Groups Anderson performed with include the **big bands** and orchestras of Claude Hopkins, Lucky Millinder, Erskine Hawkins, **Lionel Hampton**, and Sabby Lewis.

In 1944, Anderson was recruited to join **Duke Ellington**'s orchestra, a band he would continue to play with for the next three decades. From 1951 to 1959, Anderson was featured on many of Ellington's classic **Columbia** dates and played regularly with the band until taking a two-year hiatus from 1959 to 1961. Some of his playing is captured on Ellington's **album** *Ellington at Newport* (1956, Columbia). In addition to playing with Ellington, Anderson freelanced with many big bands over the next two decades including groups led by Lionel Hampton, **Charles Mingus**, **Louie Bellson**, and Bill Berry. Anderson moved to Los Angeles in 1971 and lived there until his passing in 1981. Anderson is remembered for his high-note playing but among musicians was well respected for his general musicality.

ANDERSON'S ANNEX. A nightclub in New Orleans owned by Tom Anderson and managed by Billie Struve on 201 North Basin Street. The **club** was open from 1901 to 1925, and performers included Bill Johnson, Tom Brown, and allegedly **Louis Armstrong**, although later it was determined that he performed at a different club also owned by Anderson.

ANDRE, WAYNE (1931–2003). Andre began his professional career as a **trombonist** performing and **recording** with Charlie Spivak, the Sauter-Finegan Orchestra, and **Woody Herman**'s orchestra starting when he was 19. In 1956, **Kai Winding** recruited Andre to be part of a four-trombone septet of which Andre was a member until he moved to New York in 1958 to pursue work as a **studio musician**. In between **big band** recording **sessions** with artists like **Art Farmer, Sarah Vaughan,** and **Wes Montgomery**, Andre completed a B.A. degree at the Manhattan School of Music. He further developed his reputation as a top-flight performer working with bands led by **Chick Corea, Gerry Mulligan, Jaco Pastorius, Thad Jones,** and **Clark Terry**. In the 1980s, he worked more frequently in smaller groups playing in a quintet with **trumpet** player **Marvin Stamm** and starting another four-trombone septet that was similar to the group he performed in with Winding several decades prior. Andre continued to be a frequent session player through the 1990s until his death in 2003.

ANTHONY, RAYMOND "RAY" (1922–). Anthony began his professional career as a **trumpet** player in the bands of his childhood home in Cleveland before being recruited to join the **Glenn Miller** band in 1940. In 1942, Anthony joined the U.S. Navy and led a service orchestra until 1946 when he was honorably discharged. In the late 1940s, he formed the Ray Anthony Orchestra and would see great success over the next decade. Among his hits were the "Bunny Hop," the "Hokey Pokey," and theme music for the television shows *Dragnet* and *Peter Gunn*. Anthony briefly explored acting in film during the 1950s and starred as trombonist **Tommy Dorsey** in the movie *Five Pennies*. After briefly reducing his orchestra down to a sextet in 1960, he revived his orchestra in the mid-1960s and continued to lead **big bands** throughout the 1990s in the Los Angeles area.

ANTIBES-JUAN-LES-PINS JAZZ FESTIVAL. A jazz festival founded in the New Orleans sister city of Juan-les-Pins located in southeastern France. The festival, which is usually held in July, began in 1960 and often brings in many top jazz talents like **Keith Jarrett** and **Wynton Marsalis** in addition to crossover and Pop artists. *See also* FRANCE.

ANTILLEAN JAZZ. A **Swing** era term that describes a style of jazz that incorporates musical elements from Caribbean countries included Martinique, Guadeloupe, and Haiti. Between 1920 and 1950, many **recordings** were made that featured musicians from the Caribbean area performing with North American jazz musicians as well as having jazz musicians featured on recordings of their own.

ANTOLINI, CHARLY (1937–). Antolini began his musical career as a marching band **drummer** and **Dixieland** drummer in his homeland of Switzerland before the age of 18. At 18, Antolini pursued a professional career as a jazz drummer by moving to Paris and was immediately recruited to perform with many of the top musicians who resided there including **Sidney Bechet** and **Bill Coleman**. Antolini was an original member of the Dixieland group the Tremble Kids with whom he would perform and record through several stints over the next two decades. Antolini was hired to perform with several **big bands** in Germany, and he relocated there in 1962. These big bands were led by Erwin Lehn and Kurt Edelhagen and were some of the initial versions of Europe's popular jazz ensembles the SWR big band and NDR big band. In the 1970s, Antolini was often used by touring American jazz artists, and he further boosted his career accompanying **Thad Jones**, **Roy Eldridge**, Buddy DeFranco, **Benny Goodman**, and Booker Ervin.

Antolini also began to lead his own groups, the first of which was called Jazz Power and featured **trumpet** player **Lew Soloff**, tenor saxophonist **Sal Nistico**, and alto saxophonist **Herb Geller**. Jazz Power toured and performed from 1976 through the 1980s. Throughout the 1980s and 1990s, Antolini performed in a variety of contexts including big bands and piano trios. He was a featured member in Barbara Dennerlein's trio and in the group The Super Trio.

APEX CLUB. A name used by several jazz clubs, predominantly mentioned in reference to the Apex Club formally located on 330 East 35th street in Chicago's South Side. The club was made famous by the Apex Club Orchestra that performed there regularly under the direction of **Jimmie Noone**. The club was shut down in 1930 during a federal raid for breaking prohibition laws.

APOLLO THEATER. An influential theater founded in Harlem, New York, originally owned and operated as a burlesque theater from 1914 to 1933. The Apollo received its name in 1934 when the theater was converted into a performance space for revues and variety shows. In addition to being a very influential and important venue for social reasons, the Apollo featured many leading jazz artists. Jazz musicians **Miles Davis**, **John Coltrane**, **Lionel Hampton**, **Sarah Vaughan**, and **Thelonious Monk** were among the jazz elite that performed there. *See also* BASIE, COUNT; FITZGERALD, ELLA; HOLIDAY, BILLIE.

ARCADIAN SERENADERS. A group of predominantly white musicians originally known as the Original **Crescent City Jazzers** who performed regularly at the Arcadia Ballroom in St. Louis during the 1920s.

ARC-BRC. An abbreviation for the shared operations of the record labels American Record Company and **Brunswick** Record Company during the 1930s.

ARGO RECORDS. Record label founded in Chicago by brothers Phil and Leonard Chess. Founded in 1955, Argo was primarily interested in **recording Blues sessions** but quickly expanded to include jazz musicians like **James Moody**, **Ahmad Jamal**, and **Ramsey Lewis**. The label was very important to Chicago's jazz scene and was viewed as its most important independent record label. **Barry Harris, Ira Sullivan, Illinois Jacquet, Gene Ammons, Max Roach**, and **Red Rodney** were all musicians recorded on the label. After complications with the British Classical record label also named Argo, the brothers renamed the label as Cadet. The label was eventually sold several times, first to GRT (1969), then to Sugar Hill (1979), and finally to MCA (1985). *See also* RECORD LABEL.

ARKANSAS TRAVELERS. An early **Swing** group that recorded on the **OKeh** and **Harmony** labels during the 1920s. Members included **Jimmy Dorsey, Red Nichols, Miff Mole**, and **Pee Wee Russell**.

ARMED FORCES RADIO SERVICE (AFRS). A government and military sponsored organization and record label dedicated to the broadcasting of shows and concerts to American military bases overseas. Jazz artists were very popular on the label, and artists like **Duke Ellington, Benny Carter, Louis Armstrong**, and **Count Basie** all made **recordings** for the AFRS. Seventy-nine transcriptions of concerts were made by the AFRS of the concert series "A Date with Duke" that featured the music of Ellington. In 1948 the AFRS sponsored a short-lived jazz series entitled *Just Jazz* that consisted of recordings made in the Los Angeles area. Much of the material transcribed and recorded as part of the AFRS series was destroyed by the military in the early 1950s.

ARMSTRONG, LILLIAN HARDIN "LIL" (1898–1971). Armstrong began her professional career as a jazz pianist after moving to Chicago in 1917. She was quickly hired by top Chicago musicians **Freddie Keppard**, Lawrence Duke, and **King Oliver**. Being hired by Oliver was a big professional milestone for Armstrong as she was introduced to her future husband, the great **trumpet** player **Louis Armstrong**, who was also a member of the band. Lil and Louis were married in 1924, and divorced in 1938. Lil was a huge contributor to Louis Armstrong's famous *Hot Five* (1926, **Columbia**) **recordings** both as a performer and composer. Her most famous composition from those **sessions** is "Struttin' with Some Barbeque." In the late 1920s, Armstrong left both groups and was rehired by Freddie Keppard and also toured with **Baby Dodds** in addition to leading her own groups.

   In 1937, she was the house pianist for a series of recordings on **Decca**. Many of these recordings featured her fronting bands that included many other top musicians. These records are compiled in an **album** called *1936–1940* (1940, Classics). After ending her relationship with **Decca** in 1940, Armstrong did not record much for the remainder of her career. She had several brief tours in **Europe** in the early 1950s until eventually settling in Chicago. She died due to a heart attack during a concert in 1971.

ARMSTRONG, LOUIS (1901–1971). Armstrong was a performer at a young age, first developing his vocal skills as a street performer in New Orleans at the age of seven. In 1912, Armstrong celebrated New Years by firing a pistol into the air, an event that would end up with him being placed in a waif's home. During his two years at the home, he decided to learn the **cornet**. After his release he was hired by various **brass bands** throughout New Orleans. He progressed so quickly that in 1917 he was befriended by **Joe "King" Oliver**, one of the top **bandleaders** in New Orleans and in the early jazz scene. Oliver started his own band, and Armstrong was hired to take over Oliver's chair in **Kid Ory**'s band.

In 1919, Oliver toured Chicago and decided to relocate there. His popularity increased every year, and by 1922 he was considered to be one of the top jazz artists. At this time, he decided to include Armstrong in his band and sent to New Orleans for him. Also at this time, pianist and Armstrong's future wife "Lil" Hardin was in Oliver's band, and two years later the two would be married. Armstrong's tenure with King Oliver only lasted two years, but the band was considered to be the top working jazz unit of the time. After being talked into leaving Oliver's band by his wife, Armstrong moved to New York and joined **Fletcher Henderson**'s band for one year until being summoned back to Chicago to lead a group with his wife. From 1925 to 1928 he recorded *Hot Fives Vol. 1* (1926, Columbia) and *Hot Fives and Sevens, Vols. 2–3* (1927, Columbia) with groups that included his wife on piano, Kid Ory on **trombone**, and **Johnny Dodds** on **clarinet**. These **recordings** would serve as highly influential jazz landmarks and would be imitated for decades to come.

By 1930, Armstrong was immensely popular and began actively touring the United States. Rarely did Armstrong ever bring a band with him and instead performed as a featured soloist with different house bands. Armstrong toured Europe for the first time in 1932. He continued this trend of touring alone into the 1940s. In 1938 Armstrong and Hardin divorced, and Armstrong quickly remarried. As **Bebop** came into prominence in the 1940s, Armstrong's popularity took a hit after having been one of the most dominant artists for the previous decade. Armstrong responded by forming the All Stars **big band**, which was quickly watered down to a smaller group in 1947. Members of this group changed over the next decade but included trombonists **Jack Teagarden** and **Trummy Young**, clarinetists Barney Bigard and Edmond Hall, and pianist **Earl Hines**.

Armstrong remained a very popular artist and celebrity well into the 1960s but saw his popularity diminish among jazz musicians and was criticized for never changing or adapting his style. In addition to playing his **trumpet**, he was a very popular vocalist (recording "Hello Dolly" in 1964, a number-one Pop hit) and was a major contributor to the development of vocal improvisation. He died in 1971 and is considered to be one of the greatest jazz figures ever. *See also* ARMSTRONG, LILLIAN H.; EARLY JAZZ; SHAW, ARVELL.

ARRANGEMENT. An arrangement is an interpretation of a previously written composition, be it a standard, a jazz tune, or other melody. While the melody is typically worked into the arrangement, there is much artistic freedom in terms of how the arranger chooses to deal with **tempo, form,** orchestration, rhythm, and **harmony (I).** Although arrangements for large groups, namely **big bands,** are mostly written out, some small groups may come up with an improvisational arrangement of a tune on the spot. Jazz arranging first emerged in the late 1920s with **Swing** bands such as the one of **bandleader Fletcher Henderson** who employed arrangements regularly in his band's performances. A prominent arranger of the Swing era was **Duke Ellington**, who, using the Henderson band as a model, took his arrangements and compositions to a new level by experimenting with new combinations of tones, colors, and instrument pairings. Arrangers were oftentimes hired by famous bandleaders in the Swing era to create unique orchestrations for their groups, as **Billy Strayhorn** and **Sammy Nestico** did for the Duke Ellington Orchestra and the **Count Basie** Orchestra, respectively. See also **AKIYO-SHI, TOSHIKO; BROOKMEYER, BOB; DAMERON, TADD; EVANS, GIL; JONES, THAD; NELSON, OLIVER; SCHNEIDER, MARIA.**

ART ENSEMBLE OF CHICAGO. Formed in 1968 in the city of Chicago from the **Association for the Advancement of Creative Musicians (AACM),** the Art Ensemble of Chicago originally involved **saxophonists** Roscoe Mitchell and Joseph Jarman, **trumpet** player **Lester Bowie, bassist** Malachi Favors Maghostut, and later, **drummer** Famodou Don Moye. Despite being at the forefront of **Free Jazz** and blending all sorts of influences from Bop to Rock to **Blues** to **Traditional Jazz** and ethnic music, the ensemble always surrounded their playing with composition, along with an exploration of new sound structures and timbre combinations. With a firm but not necessarily explicitly detailed structure of composition, the ensemble explored new sounds and frequently improvised collectively, evolving their **improvisations** throughout the performance. Theatrical elements such as recitation of poetry and multimedia formats were an element to the ensemble's identity, but what is very noteworthy about the group was their refined ensemble playing in which each individual added a great deal to the group as a whole.

In 1969, the ensemble moved to Paris and from there became one of the preeminent **Avant-Garde** ensembles, experiencing a considerable amount of success. During that time, they made such **recordings** as *Reese and the Smooth Ones* and *People in Sorrow*. In 1972, the ensemble moved back to Chicago and from there continued to grow. Despite the passing on of several musicians throughout the 1980s and 1990s, the group has more or less remained together, adding trumpeter Corey Wilkes and bassist Jaribu Shahid to the ensemble in 2004.

ARTISTS HOUSE. A record label founded in 1977 by John Snyder with the intention of delivering top-notch **recordings** and detailed liner notes. The record label was only in existence a short time (from 1977 to 1979) and put out about 10 **albums** including James "Blood" Ulmer's first album *Tales of Captain Black* (1978, Artists House). Other artists affiliated with the label included **Ornette Coleman**, Paul Desmond, **Charlie Haden**, and **Thad Jones**. After the record label dissolved in 1979, many of the **sessions** that had been recorded were rereleased in the 1980s under different labels.

ASSOCIATION FOR THE ADVANCEMENT OF CREATIVE MUSICIANS INC. (AACM). Regarded as one of the most successful musicians' cooperatives, the Association for the Advancement of Creative Musicians was formed in 1965 by composer and multi-instrumentalist **Muhal Richard Abrams** and the musicians associated with him. The group was based on a commitment to support forward-thinking and innovative musicians and provide performance and composition opportunities for the musician members. Featuring advocates for new music and talented musicians alike including **saxophonist Anthony Braxton, trumpet** player Leo Smith, and violinist Leroy Jenkins among others, the organization emphasized the sharing of creative exploration and expression.

The **Art Ensemble of Chicago**, a similar forward-thinking group of jazz musicians, was formed in 1968 by musicians who were associated with the AACM. Other organizations, including the cooperative **Black Artists' Group (BAG)** based out of St. Louis and formed in the 1970s, were inspired by the model created by the rather successful AACM. The group presented public concerts in churches, local taverns, art galleries, high schools, and colleges in both **big band** and small-group settings featuring original and creative music by its members. In 1969, an educational program was added to the AACM for inner-city youth, and today, the organization still remains very dedicated to jazz education. Supported by grants from the MacArthur Foundation and the National Endowment for the Arts, a charter by the State of Illinois, as well as an association with Columbia College, the AACM continues to thrive today in its commitment and celebration of creative and, coined by the organization itself, "great black music."

ASSUNTO. A family of **Dixieland** musicians made famous by the band they formed named the "**Dukes of Dixieland**." Jacob "Papa Jac" Assunto (b. Lake Charles, Louisiana, 1 November 1905; d. New Orleans, 5 January 1985) was a Jennings, Louisiana-based trombonist and banjo player who relocated to New Orleans in the 1920s to pursue more performance opportunities and education. In 1929 he gave birth to his first son, Freddie Assunto (b. Jennings, Louisiana, 3 December 1929; d. Las Vegas, Nevada, 21 April 1966), who also took up trombone and received instruction from Papa Jac. Frank Assunto (b. New Orleans, Louisiana, 29 January 1932; d. New Orleans, 25 February 1974), Papa Jac's second son, signaled a change in Papa Jac's life as he decided to no longer pursue an active performance career. Frank decided to learn **trumpet** and at the age of 13 started a Dixieland band with Freddie. This band was officially named the Dukes of Dixieland in 1949, and the brothers toured with the band across the United States and Europe. In 1955 the group extended an invitation to their father to join, and after 22 years of inactivity Papa Jac joined the band. After 11 years of touring, Freddie suffered from illness and succumbed to a heart attack in 1966. Almost 10 years later, Frank also died, and Papa Jac left the group to resume his teaching career that he had started almost 40 years prior.

ASTORIA HOT EIGHT. An early **Swing/Dixieland** band founded by tenor saxophonist David Jones and cornetist Lee Collins in 1928. The band worked primarily at the Astoria Garden in New Orleans and had regular members Theodore Purnell, Joseph Robichaux, Emanuel Sayles, Al Morgan, and Joe Strode. The band also used the name Jones and Collins Astoria Hot Eight and recorded four sides: *Astoria Strut* and *Duet Stomp* (1929, **Victor**) and *Damp Weather* and *Tip Easy Blues* (1929, **Bluebird**).

ATCO RECORDS. Through the work of Herb Abramson, Atco was created as a subsidiary of Atlantic records and was committed to popular music. Atlantic Records had primarily focused on **Rhythm and Blues** and jazz styles, and the smaller label was created out of a desire to sign more mainstream artists. The label was made famous through **recordings** and signings of several Pop stars including King Curtis, Otis Redding, the Allman Brothers, and Bobby Darin. The label signed several jazz musicians during the 1960s. These artists included **Herb Geller**, **Betty Carter**, and **Sir Roland Hanna**. The label eventually folded into Atlantic until the 1990s when it had a brief resurgence. The label name Atco was used for reissues by Warner Group music in 2006. *See also* ATLANTIC RECORDS.

ATLANTIC RECORDS. Founded by Herb Abramson and Ahmet Ertegun in 1947 with the intention of **recording** and distributing African-American influenced music, the label became immensely popular in the 1950s and 1960s. The label was divided in 1955 with the creation of the Atco label that featured primarily Pop artists, leaving Atlantic to remain primarily focused on **Rhythm and Blues** music. Atlantic produced many popular jazz **albums** in the late 1950s. **John Coltrane**'s album *Giant Steps* (1959, Atlantic) and **Ornette Coleman**'s *The Shape of Jazz to Come* (1959, Atlantic) were two highly influential albums that were produced on the label. Jazz artists **Lennie Tristano, Lee Konitz, Charles Mingus, Charles Lloyd, Gary Burton, Eddie Harris,** and **Keith Jarrett** also were recorded during a 10-year period in which Atlantic emphasized recording jazz. Warner Bros. bought Atlantic in 1967, although Ahmet Ertegun retained control of the label. This purchase triggered events that led to fewer and fewer jazz recordings as the label pursued interests in recording Soul music and artists like Aretha Franklin and Wilson Pickett. Atlantic eventually expanded to many other different forms of music and has a strong presence in the Rock and Country music recording industries in addition to R&B. *See also* ATCO RECORDS.

AULD, GEORGIE (1919–1990). Auld began his professional career in the 1930s modeling his idol, **Coleman Hawkins**, while performing with several New York–based bands in addition to leading his own groups. In 1939, Auld joined **Artie Shaw**'s band (even leading the band briefly during an extended absence by Shaw) until he left the group to become a member of **Benny Goodman**'s groups. Throughout the 1930s and 1940s, Auld constantly changed his tenor sound to imitate other saxophonists and was noted for sounding like **Charlie Barnet** and **Lester Young** at different points in his affiliation with various groups. Prior to joining the army in 1943, Auld performed and recorded with **Benny Carter, Billie Holiday**, and briefly rejoined Shaw. From 1943 to 1946, Auld formed a **big band** with many top jazz musicians including **Dizzy Gillespie** and **Erroll Garner**, and recorded *Big Band Jazz* (1945, **Musicraft**).

In 1950, Auld was a member of **Count Basie**'s octet before moving to the Los Angeles area and freelancing with several groups in addition to starting some of his own. Auld opened up his own jazz club called the Melody Room and started a quintet that featured Frank Rosolino and Stan Levey. During this time, Auld recorded one of his most popular **albums,** *In the Land of Hi-Fi*

(1955, **EmArcy**), which also featured Rosolino. Throughout the remainder of the 1950s and 1960s, Auld would primarily freelance and tour with bands in Las Vegas, Los Angeles, and Japan. Auld also pursued a short-lived career in acting, performing in a stage play in 1949 entitled *The Rat Race* and also ghosted for actor Robert De Niro in the 1977 film *New York, New York.*

AURORA. A Canadian record label that featured **recordings** of **Duke Ellington** and **King Oliver** during the early 1930s. While the record label was based out of Canada, many of the **albums** were recorded in the United States. Partner companies included **Brunswick** and **Melotone**.

AUSTIN HIGH SCHOOL GANG. The nickname of a group of musicians from the Chicago West Side who had attended Austin High School and formed a group in 1922. The group was influenced by the **New Orleans Rhythm Kings**. In its early years, the band played for high school fraternity dances and at the homes of fellow students. Members included cornetist **Jimmy McPartland** and tenor saxophonist Bud Freeman. *See also* MEZZROW, MEZZ; TOUGH, DAVE.

AUSTRALIAN JAZZ QUARTET/QUINTET. An Australian jazz group featuring pianist Bryce Rohde and Jack Brokensha. There is debate as to whether the group was named after a tour of Australia in 1958 or whether the members of the group had always made the title official when the group began in 1954. The group disbanded in 1959, and Rohde moved to Australia. The group recorded several **albums** on the Bethlehem label included **recordings** of the music of Rodgers and Hammerstein and jazz renditions of the music from "Three Penny Opera." Other members of the group before they disbanded included drummers Frank Capp and Osie Johnson.

AVAKIAN, GEORGE (1919–). After graduating from Yale in 1941 with an English literature degree, Avakian began freelancing and writing for jazz magazines, writing liner notes for **albums**, and serving as a jazz editor for nonmusic magazines like *Mademoiselle*. In 1940, Avakian was hired by **Columbia** to assist with reissuing jazz **recordings**. This proved to be very important, and he and Columbia would continue to work together after Avakian's military service and for the better part of the next two decades. Avakian produced albums for Columbia in addition to several other labels including Warner Bros. and **RCA** Records. As a producer he signed **Benny Goodman**, **Louis Armstrong**, and **Duke Ellington** to deals in addition to his prized Columbia signing of **Miles Davis**. In the 1960s, Avakian left Columbia and freelanced as a producer. He remained an important figure in the careers of several jazz musicians including Paul Desmond, **Sonny Rollins**, and **Keith Jarrett**. Avakian remained connected to Columbia even throughout the 1990s and contributed liner notes for reissued albums and box sets. Most notably, he was awarded a Grammy in 1996 for his liner notes in a boxed set of the works of Miles Davis and **Gil Evans**. In 2011, he was included on the ASCAP Jazz Wall of Fame as a living jazz legend.

AVANT-GARDE. An alternative to the name **Free Jazz** that was made popular during the 1960s and 1970s. The name Free Jazz was often frowned upon because the musicians felt their music was very structured and not as open as the term "free" implied. There is a slight disconnect from the music labeled as Free Jazz such as was performed by **Ornette Coleman** and **Albert Ayler** to those musicians who played under the Avant-Garde style such as **Archie Shepp**. *See also* DOLPHY, ERIC; JOHNSON, REGINALD "REGGIE"; LEADERS.

AX(E). A term used as a reference to one's instrument. Initially used as slang for a **saxophone**.

AYLER, ALBERT (1936–1970). Ayler began his professional career as an alto saxophonist playing with **Rhythm and Blues** bands led by both others and himself. Ayler enlisted in the army and switched to **tenor saxophone** while performing in the army's concert bands. Ayler sat in on jazz **jam sessions** in **France** and decided to remain in **Europe** after he completed his service with the army. Ayler felt that Europeans were more sympathetic toward his style, and he recorded several live **albums** in Denmark and Sweden. After moving to New York in 1963, Ayler found musicians in Henry Grimes, Gary Peacock, and Sunny Murray who were sympathetic to his musical style and recorded several albums from 1964 to 1968 that included *In Greenwich Village* and *Love Cry*, both on the Impulse label. Ayler showcased his spiritual and Rhythm and Blues roots on several albums including *Spirits Rejoice* on ESP. Reasons for Ayler's premature passing are still unclear. His body was discovered by local authorities after being been washed up along the shore of New York City's East River. *See also* AYLER, DONALD; FREE JAZZ.

AYLER, DONALD (1942–2007). Ayler started his musical career as an alto saxophonist but switched to **trumpet** after a short stint in Europe. Donald was asked to spend time focusing on developing his playing with musician and family friend Charles Tyler and was reunited with his brother Albert in 1965. Albert's newly formed band, which also included Tyler, recorded several times including the ESP **album** *Spirits Rejoice*, and *In Greenwich Village* on Impulse. Ayler suffered from a nervous breakdown and alcoholism, causing him to be fired from his brother's band in 1968. Donald continued to play sporadically throughout the remainder of his life including forming a septet that performed in Italy and recorded the album *In Florence. See also* AYLER, ALBERT.

AZIMUTH. A jazz trio formed by British pianist John Taylor, flugelhorn-ist **Kenny Wheeler**, and singer Norma Winstone. The group was founded in 1977 and quickly recorded three **albums:** *Azimuth* (1977, **ECM**); *The Touchstone* (1977, ECM); and *Depart* (1979, ECM). The group remained active through the early 2000s although it did not perform regularly and often played together as part of other larger ensembles.

B

BACKBEAT. A term used in jazz and other popular music referring to accenting the second and fourth beat of each bar.

BAILEY, COLIN (1934–). Growing up in Swindon, England, Bailey taught himself drums until he was able to study formally at the age of seven. Bailey's professional career took off when he moved to Australia and joined Bryce Rohde's Australian Jazz Quartet. During a tour of the United States with the Australian Jazz Quartet, Bailey was heard in San Francisco by pianist **Vince Guaraldi**, who hired him regularly throughout the 1960s. Bailey was on several of Guaraldi's most popular **albums**, including *Jazz Impressions of Black Orpheus* (1962, Original Jazz Classics) and *A Boy Named Charlie Brown* (1964, **Fantasy**). Bailey moved to Los Angeles, although he was still not an official U.S. citizen, and performed with many of the leading Los Angeles musicians in addition to becoming a prominent **studio musician**. During the period from 1962 to 1970, Bailey performed with **Benny Goodman, George Shearing**, Victor Feldman, and also substituted for **Tony Williams** briefly in **Miles Davis'** famous late quintet.

Bailey became an American citizen in 1970. He developed a television presence serving as replacement for Ed Shaughnessy on the NBC *Tonight Show* in addition to playing a crazed drummer on the television show *Fernwood Tonight*. In 1979, Bailey moved to Texas and took a teaching position at North Texas State University. He left his faculty position in 1984 and moved back to California, this time to the San Francisco area. Bailey freelanced with artists such as **Richie Cole, Joe Pass**, Jimmy Rowles, Red Mitchell, and Ron Affif throughout the 1980s and 1990s.

BAILEY, WILLIAM C. "BUSTER" (1902–1967). Bailey began his professional career as a clarinetist with **W. C. Handy**'s orchestra at the age of 15. He moved from Memphis to Chicago in 1919 to pursue opportunities with other prominent jazz leaders like Erskine Tate, Mamie Smith, and **King Oliver**. Bailey studied with clarinetist Franz Schoepp, who also taught **Benny Goodman**. At the recommendation of **Louis Armstrong, Fletcher Henderson** hired Bailey to join his orchestra in New York, and the two would work together throughout the 1920s and for several occasional periods during the 1930s. In 1929, Bailey left Henderson for the first time to pursue touring and **recording** opportunities with Noble Sissle, Edgar Hayes, and the **Mills Blue Rhythm Section**.

Bailey joined bassist **John Kirby**'s sextet, a group that included **trumpet** player **Charlie Shavers**. The sextet developed a great reputation, and Bailey's talents as a clarinetist truly shined. The group stayed together until 1946 and recorded several **albums**, including *Boss of the Bass* (1941, Columbia); *Biggest Little Band in the Land* (1944, Classic Jazz); and *John Kirby and His Sextet* (1946, Alamac). After the band disbanded in 1946, Bailey played with the **Traditional Jazz** influenced bands of Wilbur De Paris and Henry "Red" Allen, in addition to freelancing with many other artists throughout the 1950s and early 1960s. Bailey joined Louis Armstrong's All Stars in 1965 and remained with that group until his passing in 1967. While Bailey was known mostly as being an outstanding **sideman**, he did record a few albums as a leader, most notably *All about Memphis* (1958, Felsted).

BAKER, CHESNEY "CHET" (1929–1988). Baker took up the **trumpet** while attending Glendale Junior High School in California but did not develop as a performer until he completed two stints with two army bands, the 298th Army band in Berlin, Germany, and the Presidio Army band in San Francisco. Upon being discharged in 1952, Baker was hired by jazz icon **Charlie Parker** for two brief periods in 1952 and 1953, while also touring and **recording** with **Gerry Mulligan**. The collaboration with Gerry Mulligan was considered a jazz milestone and was highly influential in the creation of the **West Coast Jazz** style. Baker's melodic approach resembled that of **Miles Davis**, as often Baker played very soft and with a limited range. In 1953, Baker was given *DownBeat*'s Rising Star Award and topped many of the critic's polls for the next two years. Baker left Mulligan to start a solo career and began touring both the United States and Europe during the late 1950s. He was unable to escape his drug problems and was jailed for a drug-related offense.

Baker moved to Italy after his personal life got seemingly out of hand in the United States. However, Baker was involved with several drug-smuggling schemes in Germany, Italy, England, and France and was forced to return to the United States in 1964. Baker attempted to get his professional career back on track by recording several albums that included saxophonist **George Coleman** and pianist Kirk Lightsey. These records included *Lonely Star* (1965, **Prestige**) and *On a Misty Night* (1965, Prestige). Neither critics nor fans really embraced these records, and Baker's life remained in turmoil. In the early 1970s, Baker lost all of his teeth during a bad drug deal and toward the end of the decade, he moved back to Europe. Baker's career witnessed a brief resurgence in the 1980s when he recorded with Rock artist Elvis Costello and acquired a record deal on **SteepleChase**. Drugs continued to take their toll on Baker, although it is unclear as to whether or not they were involved with his death. *See also* COOL JAZZ.

BAKER, DAVID (1931–). After completing both a bachelor's and a master's degree in music education, Baker began his professional career as a trombonist, touring with **Stan Kenton, Maynard Ferguson, George Russell**, and **Quincy Jones** in the late 1950s and early 1960s. Baker stayed close to his native Indiana home and led his own **big bands** in Indianapolis. Baker suffered from muscular problems that forced him to stop playing trombone for almost a decade. During this hiatus, he took up playing the cello in addition to beginning a very influential teaching career at Indiana University in 1966. Baker also developed a reputation as a first-class arranger and composer and was a Pulitzer Prize nominee in addition to being nominated for a Grammy during the 1970s.

While serving in his faculty position, Baker quickly became one of jazz's most famous instructors. Baker is credited with writing 60 books and over 400 articles. In addition to teaching, Baker served on numerous jazz-related committees including the Jazz Advisory Panel to the Kennedy Center, the Jazz/Folk/Ethnic Panel of the National Endowment of the Arts, and was named president of the National Jazz Service Organization.

BAKER, HAROLD "SHORTY" (1914–1966). Baker began his career as a **trumpet** player while still a teenager in the late 1920s, performing in his brother Winfield's band. In the 1930s he toured with many bands, including small groups led by Erskine Tate and Eddie Johnson, and **big bands** led by **Don Redman** and **Teddy Wilson**. After an invitation to perform and record with **Mary Lou Williams**, Baker soon found himself romantically involved with her, and they were married in 1942. Despite a brief interruption due to army service, Baker was hired to take over Arthur Whetsol's chair in the **Duke Ellington** Orchestra until 1952. For the remainder of his career, Baker would work on and off with Ellington's band and would also be featured in other groups led by **Johnny Hodges** and Teddy Wilson. He made only one **recording**, *Shorty & Doc* (1961, Original Jazz Classics), an **album** he co-led with fellow trumpeter Doc Cheatham.

BAKTON RECORDS. A **record label** founded in 1966 by **Randy Weston**. The label only released one **album** of Weston's music, which was eventually sold to **Atlantic Records**.

BALLAD. A phrase used to describe slower songs in the jazz idiom. The ballad is considered a vital part of the jazz repertoire and is often used as a descriptor for pieces that are slower, softer, or more personal than other pieces.

'BAMA STATE COLLEGIANS. A jazz band formed at Alabama State University in the early 1930s. Led by Erskine Hawkins, who was also a student, the band toured in New York and took the name the Erskine Hawkins Orchestra.

BANDLEADER. A term used to describe the person who leads a band. This person can be an instrumentalist (such as **Dizzy Gillespie** who led a **big band** continually from the 1940s until his death), a vocalist (such as **Frank Sinatra**), or someone who just conducts the ensemble, like Gerald Wilson. *See also* BASIE, WILLIAM; ELLINGTON, DUKE; HENDERSON, FLETCHER; HERMAN, WOODY; MILLER, GLENN.

BANJO. A stringed instrument similar to a guitar that can have between four to six strings and is plucked either by fingers or a pick. The body of a banjo is different from that of a guitar, as it is circular and has a head made of a stretched material the bridge presses upon. The banjo was used frequently in early styles of jazz and often was the only chordal instrument in early **Traditional** and **Dixieland Jazz** bands. *See also* EARLY JAZZ; SNOWDEN, ELMER.

BARBER, JOHN WILLIAM "BILL" (1920–2007). Barber fell in love with tuba while in high school and continued to study it while completing undergraduate work at Juilliard and graduate work at the Manhattan School of Music. After moving to Kansas City to play with the Kansas City Philharmonic and serving in the army from 1942 to 1945, Barber moved back to New York and began looking for opportunities to play jazz. Barber was hired by **Claude Thornhill** in 1947 and was considered to be one of the first and most influential jazz tuba players. **Gil Evans** and **Miles Davis** hired Barber to be a part of their highly influential *Birth of the Cool* (1950, **Columbia**) **recording session** and also used him in their other 1950s collaborations. Throughout the 1950s and 1960s, Barber maintained careers in both jazz and Classical music, often playing Broadway shows in between jazz dates. In the 1960s, Barber pursued a teaching career at an elementary school in Long Island. Barber was still considered a first-call session player and was frequently used by Evans and **Gerry Mulligan** for touring and recording over the next few decades. Barber was recorded on Mulligan's *Re-Birth of the Cool* (1992, **GRP**) after he had retired from teaching. Barber died in 2007 due to heart failure.

BARBIERI, GATO (1934–). Born in Argentina, Barbieri first played tenor saxophone in Argentinian house bands before first moving to Europe and eventually the United States. During the 1960s, Barbieri worked with many popular artists including **Don Cherry, Charlie Haden,** and **Carla Bley.** Barbieri led his own groups during the 1970s and began to receive acclaim for his work, which was a fusion of the styles he had absorbed throughout the 1960s. Barbieri frequently toured and recorded during the 1980s and 1990s, in addition to working often in his native Argentina.

BARI. A commonly used, short term referring to **baritone saxophone.** *See also* SAXOPHONE.

BARITONE SAXOPHONE. The lowest-sounding saxophone commonly used in jazz. Like the alto saxophone, the baritone saxophone (or bari sax) is in the key of E♭. Famous jazz baritone saxophone players include Nick Brignola, **Gerry Mulligan,** Pepper Adams, **Serge Chaloff,** Gary Smulyan, and Joe Temperly. *See also* CARRUTHERS, JOCK; CUBER, RONNIE; DE VILLERS, MICHEL; FOWLKES, CHARLIE; GOYENS, AL(PHONSE); GRAHAM, BILL; KONOPASEK, JAN; MAIDEN, WILLIE; PARAPHER-NALIA; PARKER, LEO; PERKINS, BILL.

BARNET, CHARLIE (1913–1991). Barnet learned to play several instruments as a youth and was a proficient alto saxophonist. He primarily led bands during the 1930s and developed into one of the decade's most successful **bandleaders.** Barnet discontinued leading a band in the 1950s. Barnet's bands featured many top musicians, including **Clark Terry, Charlie Shavers, Dizzy Gillespie,** and **Bill Holman.**

BARNYARD EFFECTS. A musical device used specially by **Early Jazz** performers; musicians would imitate animal sounds using their instruments.

BARRELHOUSE. A precursor to the **Boogie-Woogie** piano style, the Barrelhouse was one of the first **Blues** piano styles. The Barrelhouse style received its name from being developed and performed in bars or driving establishments in which drinks were served straight from the barrel. These establishments were generally considered low class, and often this music was considered to be of the same level. Famous Barrelhouse pianists include Will Ezell, Washboard Sam, Joshua Altheimer, Peetie Wheatstraw, and Charlie Spand. *See also* BARRELHOUSE JAZZ.

BARRELHOUSE JAZZ. Barrelhouse Jazz was hybrid of the **barrelhouse** piano style and the New Orleans **Early Jazz** style that had migrated to Chicago in the 1920s. Barrelhouse Jazz served as a precursor to the Chicago Blues style that was formed in the 1930s, and was characterized by the use of nontraditional jazz instruments like the washboard. Groups that performed in the Barrelhouse Jazz style were recorded much more frequently than its piano-style counterpart, and in many cases, groups that recorded the style did not perform it in public. This style was also considered to be an important element to the creation of **Rhythm and Blues**. *See also* BARRELHOUSE.

BARRELHOUSE JAZZ BAND. Founded by Horst Dubuque, the Barrelhouse Jazz Band was created in Germany in the mid-1950s as an **Early Jazz**– and **Traditional Jazz**–influenced group. In addition to utilizing guest artists such as **Al Grey**, **Jimmy McPartland**, and Buddy Tate, the Barrelhouse Jazz Band also made use of themed concerts to attract concertgoers. These concerts included performances dedicated to **Duke Ellington**, **King Oliver**, and **Jelly Roll Morton**. The name, Barrelhouse Jazz Band, has been used by several other groups in **Europe** as well as in the United States.

BARRETTO, RAY(MOND) (1929–2006). Barretto, originally from New York, played in informal settings with many jazz musicians during the 1950s. Primarily a percussionist, Barretto's professional career took off in the late 1950s and 1960s when he performed and recorded with **Lou Donaldson**, **Dizzy Gillespie**, **Oliver Nelson**, and **Wes Montgomery**. A proponent of **Afro-Cuban** and Latin American Jazz, Barretto became increasingly active as a leader during the 1960s and led groups in the 1970s and 1980s. Barretto's groups consistently featured top musicians, and in the 1990s he founded his most popular group, the New World Spirit. *See also* LATIN JAZZ.

BARRON, KENNY (1943–). Hailing from Philadelphia, pianist Barron found work in the 1960s after he moved to New York, working with performers including **Dizzy Gillespie**, **Stanley Turrentine**, **Freddie Hubbard**, and **James Moody**. He did not become a leader until the mid-1970s and was an important original member of the group **Sphere**. In addition to working with Sphere, he freelanced through the 1980s, including time spent working with **Chet Baker**, David Schnitter, **J. J. Johnson**, **Woody Shaw**, and most significantly, **Stan Getz**. The pairing of Barron and Getz resulted in some important **albums** during the mid-1980s that garnered much acclaim for both musicians. Barron continued to remain active as a performer into the 2000s, in addition to becoming a more active educator.

BASIE, WILLIAM "COUNT" (1904–1984). Along with **Duke Ellington,** Basie would prove to be one of the most important **bandleaders** in jazz. While not a standout pianist, Basie was a performer with roots in the **Stride Piano** style, and the bands Basie fronted were frequently considered to be among the finest working. After an incident in which he was stranded in Kansas City, Basie found work in the late 1920s with **Walter Page**, the bassist who ended up playing a vital role in Basie's 1930 bands. Basie was hired along with Page to play with **Bennie Moten**'s group, which Basie was with until the band disbanded in the mid-1930s. From then on, Basie would work primarily as a bandleader of both small and large groups.

Basie's groups in the 1930s included tenor saxophonist **Lester Young** and **rhythm section** mates Walter Page and drummer Jo Jones. The first incarnation of the Basie **big band** lasted approximately 14 years before Basie had to break up the group in favor of smaller, more financially manageable ensembles. After a two-year hiatus from running a big band, Basie began a new band in 1952, which would develop into one of the top-working units of its time. The Basie bands were regarding as the hardest-swinging ensembles in jazz. Other members of the ensemble included **Freddie Green, Thad Jones, Marshall Royal**, and Frank Foster. Basie would continue to lead the group despite health issues during the 1970s and 1980s. After Basie's passing, the band continued to play under Jones' and eventually Foster's leadership. *See also* JONES-SMITH INC.; KANSAS CITY SEVEN; KANSAS CITY SIX; COUNTSMEN.

BASIN STREET. Located in the French Quarter of New Orleans, Basin Street was one of the main streets within the **Storyville** Red Light District. During its development in the early 1900s, jazz was prominently featured in many venues on Basin Street.

BASS. Also referred to as the double bass, it is the largest and consequently lowest-pitched string instrument. The bass is a fixture in **dance bands** and jazz groups, where it is normally played pizzicato. Its use in the **rhythm section** of these groups was established in the late 1920s. From the 1960s and onward it is occasionally replaced in these groups by the **electric bass guitar**. Notable jazz bassists include **Jimmy Blanton**, Ray Brown, **Ron Carter, Dave Holland, Charles Mingus**, and **Scott LaFaro**. *See also* GOMEZ, EDDIE; HINTON, MILT; PASTORIUS, JACO; PEACOCK, GARY; REID, RUFUS; RIDLEY, LARRY; RUSSELL, DILLON "CURLY"; SLAP BASS; STEWART, SLAM; SWALLOW, STEVE; WALKING BASS.

BASS CLARINET. Uncommon to jazz, the bass **clarinet** is a lower-sounding member of the clarinet family. It is usually pitched one octave below the more traditional soprano clarinet. **Eric Dolphy** was one of the first jazz musicians to use the bass clarinet in improvisational settings and recorded a famous solo bass clarinet version of "God Bless the Child" on *The Illinois Concert* (1963, **Blue Note**).

BASS CLEF. A clef sign used to write lower-register notes. The bass clef is commonly used for instruments like **trombone**, baritone, double **bass**, tuba, and the left hand of the **piano**. The bass clef is also known as the F clef, because it is centrally located on the F line of the staff.

BASS DRUM. A lower-pitched drum that began as a large marching drum but was soon modified to be used in orchestral and concert band works. The bass drum remained an important part of marching band instrumentation and was used in New Orleans **brass bands**. When **Early Jazz** bands began performing in clubs and more stable venues, the bass drum was converted into a more stationary instrument and became a building block for the modern **drum set**. The bass drum is played by the right foot through the use of a beater that is attached to a foot pedal. The drum was eventually modified so that tom-toms could be mounted on it and it could also be used as part of the drum set.

BASS GUITAR. Another name for the **electric bass**. It is frequently used in the **Fusion** and **Jazz-Rock** styles in addition to other popular music. *See also* BASS.

BATISTE, ALVIN (1932–2007). Born in New Orleans, Batiste studied the **clarinet** as a youth and performed with a young **Ornette Coleman**. After a brief period of active playing in the late 1950s and early 1960s, Batiste became an educator for almost 20 years, although he considered his academic work to take away from his performing career and elected to retire from education in the 1980s. Batiste worked steadily in the 1990s as both a performer and composer. Batiste played with both **Ed Blackwell** and the New Orleans Philharmonic Orchestra in the 1990s.

BATTLE OF BANDS. Still done today, though no longer as frequently as in the past, a battle of bands is an event in which several groups compete by attempting to outplay one another for a specific prize. Originating in New Orleans, many touring bands of the 1930s would gather in specific New York ballrooms to compete with one another. *See also* SAVOY BALLROOM.

BEAT. A musical term used to describe the steady pulse of time. In some popular music, the beat is always emphasized by the **bass drum** or **cymbals**

and is heard on every beat of a given measure. In Classical music and some freer forms of jazz, the beat is internalized or conducted rather than being dictated by specific instruments. A lot of popular music is based on music that has four beats per measure, although it is common to see some dance music that only has three, such as a waltz. *See also* GROOVE.

BEBOP. A term used to describe a specific style that was developed in the 1940s, it would frequently feature complex melodies based on expanded harmonic structures and technical, fast improvisation. While Bebop adhered to harmonic rules and remained tonal despite the frequent use of passing harmonies, much of the music created during the Bebop era sounded quite frantic at the time in contrast to the polite nature of the music of the 1930s. Important Bebop musicians include **Charlie Parker, Dizzy Gillespie**, and **Bud Powell**. Bebop was a significant shift in jazz improvisation and became the most imitated and copied style of the 1950s. *See also* CLARKE, KENNY; MINTON'S PLAYHOUSE; MONK, THELONIOUS; MONROE'S UP-TOWN HOUSE; PETTIFORD, OSCAR; POTTER, CHARLES "TOMMY."

BECHET, SIDNEY (1897–1959). Born in New Orleans and first developing his musical skills on clarinet, Bechet was mostly self-taught before he began working in New Orleans bands as a teenager. After Bechet discovered the soprano **saxophone** while on a trip to Chicago, he decided to permanently switch to the instrument and became one of the first and most influential voices on it. Bechet toured **Europe** in the 1920s, in addition to working with **Duke Ellington** and leading his own groups. Considered to be a master improviser, Bechet soon became an icon not only to saxophonists but to all jazz musicians.

Bechet toured frequently with his own groups in the 1930s and after a failed attempt to bring back the New Orleans style that had fallen out of favor for **Swing** and eventually **Bebop**. Bechet's popularity overseas grew, and he decided to relocate to **France** in the 1950s. Bechet remained in France for the rest of his career and was considered to be a jazz hero there. Bechet succumbed to cancer in 1959. *See also* SOPRANO SAXOPHONE.

BECHET LEGACY. Founded by **Sidney Bechet** protégé Bob Wilber, the Bechet Legacy was a tribute group in the early 1980s. The group did little touring and **recording** but did reunite several times in the 1990s for various concerts.

BEE HIVE. An important jazz club in Chicago during the 1950s, it featured top touring acts and was featured in a **recording** of the **Clifford Brown–Max**

Roach Quintet. The Bee Hive was so popular that it inspired a record label in the 1970s to adopt the same name.

BEHIND THE BEAT. A term used by jazz musicians to describe the phrasing style of purposefully delaying a note as to not sound in time. Musicians often play behind the beat to achieve a sense of rhythmic tension. Tenor saxophonist **Dexter Gordon** is one of the most notable musicians to frequently use this technique.

BEIDERBECKE, LEON "BIX" (1903–1931). Born in Davenport, Iowa, the self-taught **cornet** player Beiderbecke was first exposed to jazz through records and his visits to **clubs** in Chicago. Beiderbecke's unfortunately short, yet influential career was defined by the groups and musical relationships he forged in the 1920s. The two most notable collaborations Beiderbecke had then were those he had with saxophonist **Frankie Trumbauer** and with the orchestra of **Paul Whiteman,** as a featured soloist.

Beiderbecke was considered to be a significant figure because of his unique cornet style and ability to solo successfully in a style that differed from **Louis Armstrong.** Beiderbecke played the cornet, which has a warmer, darker tone than the **trumpet.** Despite suffering from alcoholism, Beiderbecke had a successful run and freelanced with several important artists in the late 1920s and early 1930s, including **Tommy Dorsey** and **Benny Goodman,** before dying at the age of 28. *See also* WOLVERINES.

BEIRACH, RICHARD (1947–). Pianist Beirach studied at two of the more prestigious jazz schools, the Berklee College of Music and the Manhattan School of Music, before catching on with several important jazz groups in the 1970s. Beirach spent time with **Stan Getz** and also established a musical relationship with **David Liebman** that would span several decades, including work in the Liebman-created group, Quest. For most of the 1980s and 1990s, Beirach would work as a **sideman** or lead his own small groups.

BELLSON, LOUIE (1924–2009). Bellson's career began with a series of youth appearances both as a drummer and a tap dancer before being hired at the age of 18 to play **drum set** with **Benny Goodman.** Between the years of 1946 and 1967, Bellson spent time with many of the top-working **big bands,** including tours with Goodman, **Tommy Dorsey, Duke Ellington,** and briefly with **Count Basie.** Bellson began leading his own groups in the late 1960s and became more interested in education throughout the 1970s. Bellson mostly fronted his own ensembles for the remainder of his career, including several big bands, most notably an all-star band that featured many members of the Count Basie bands, including **Al Grey** and **Harry "Sweets" Edison.**

BEND. A term that describes when an instrumentalist uses the embouchure to alter a pitch either sharp or flat and then return it to its original pitch.

BENNETT, TONY (1926–). Born with the name Joe Bari, showman Bob Hope discovered him and suggested he change his name to the more marketable Tony Bennett. Bennett rose to prominence during the 1950s and had several popular records. Popular with jazz musicians, Bennett would perform with several famous bands during the 1960s, including **Duke Ellington** and **Count Basie**, and was later featured with the **Bill Evans** Trio in the 1970s. In the 1980s, Bennett recorded with **George Benson, Dexter Gordon,** and **Dizzy Gillespie**, and would use pianist Bill Charlap in his later groups.

BENSON, GEORGE (1943–). Despite his excellent **guitar** playing, Benson's career was always split between **singing** and playing, beginning at the age of eight. Benson worked with many popular **Fusion** and **Soul Jazz** artists of the 1960s, including **Miles Davis** and **Freddie Hubbard**, before branching out in his own career. Benson's guitar playing was consistently overshadowed by the commercial nature of his work, including Pop vocal hits during the 1970s. Benson continued to record popular and contemporary **albums** in the 1980s and 1990s but never fully returned to playing jazz full time.

BERIMBAU. A Brazilian stringed instrument frequently used in capoeira. It is not common to jazz.

BERKLEE COLLEGE (SCHOOL) OF MUSIC. A college located in Boston, Massachusetts, that has been active in jazz, Pop, and Rock education since the 1950s. Founded by Lawrence Berk in 1945 as the Schillinger House of Music, the school officially changed its name first in 1954 to the Berklee School of Music, although no degrees were offered until 1962. Berk's son, Lee, was responsible for oversight of the institution from 1979 to 2004 and changed the name one final time to the Berklee College of Music. The college offers degrees in many areas including music production, music business, and jazz performance. Throughout the last few decades, Berklee has created numerous educational programs outside of Boston, including a variety of summer camps across the globe. The Berklee College of Music has a long pedigree of alumni including **Gary Burton, John Scofield, Branford Marsalis,** and **Sadao Watanabe,** and consistently features a faculty of high-caliber teachers and performers. Berklee alumni have garnered more than 200 Grammy Awards.

BERLINER JAZZTAGE. Original name for the **Jazzfest Berlin** founded in 1964. The Jazzfest was referred to as the Berliner Jazztage until 1982.

BETHLEHEM. A record company founded in 1953 that released many significant jazz **albums**. Bethlehem was a diverse label with offices in Hollywood and New York, catering to many different jazz audiences by distributing albums of artists including **Art Blakey, Charles Mingus, Zoot Sims**, and Herbie Nichols. The discs distributed by Bethlehem remained popular throughout the decades and were often rereleased. *See also* RECORD LABEL.

BEY, ANDY (1939–). Born in Newark, New Jersey, Bey's vocal career began as a youth playing in clubs in his hometown. In the 1960s, Bey performed with numerous jazz musicians including **Howard McGhee, Max Roach**, and **Horace Silver**, before spending part of the 1970s working with the **Thad Jones–Mel Lewis** Orchestra. After his tenure with the Jones/Lewis orchestra, Bey semi-retired from performing to focus instead on teaching. Bey's performing career began to pick up again at the end of the late 1980s, and he was actively **singing** again in the 1990s. Bey recorded several times during the 1990s, in addition to frequently being featured in concerts in a variety of contexts.

BIG BAND. A term used to describe a large jazz ensemble, usually between 12 and 18 people. A typical jazz big band is made up of five **saxophones** (two altos, two tenors, and one baritone), four **trumpets**, four **trombones**, **piano, bass**, and **drum set**. There are many variations of a big band, and frequently a trombone or trumpet can be omitted or a guitarist, percussionist, or vocalist may be added. Instruments used rarely in big bands include the oboe, bassoon, and **French horn**, although some **Third Stream** and modern music contains parts for such instruments. Famous big band leaders include **Duke Ellington, Count Basie, Stan Kenton**, and **Benny Goodman**. *See also* CALLOWAY, CAB; DORSEY, TOMMY; GILLESPIE, DIZZY; HENDERSON, FLETCHER; HERMAN, WOODY; MILLER, GLENN; MINGUS, CHARLES; LUNCEFORD, JIMMIE; SHAW, ARTIE; WEBB, CHICK; WHITEMAN, PAUL.

BIG BANDS INTERNATIONAL. An English organization, founded by Roy Belcher in the late 1970s with the intention of providing members the opportunity to discuss various topics regarding rehearsing, performing, and directing **big bands**.

BIG CHIEF JAZZBAND. A Norwegian-based **Early Jazz** septet that remained active for almost 40 years, from 1952 into the 1990s. It frequently recorded and toured.

BIG FOUR. A name frequently used for all-star quartets that recorded. Groups led by **Sidney Bechet, Buddy Rich**, and **Oscar Peterson** all recorded under the name Big Four.

BIRD. Frequently used nickname for **Bebop** saxophonist **Charlie Parker**.

BIRDLAND. The name of a very significant nightclub in New York that was opened in 1949. Birdland, along with the **Village Vanguard**, is considered to be one of the top jazz **clubs** and frequently features big-name performers. The club's name is in reference to the nickname of **Charlie Parker**, "Bird." Pianist **Joe Zawinul** dedicated a famous **Fusion** work, "Birdland," in honor of the club. The club remains active today.

BISTROUILLE AMATEURS DANCE ORCHESTRA. A Belgium-based dance band created in the 1920s that prominently featured many of the country's finest working musicians.

BLACK AND BLUE. A French **record label** that primarily distributed and rereleased **albums** recorded by smaller companies. Significant jazz players to have albums released on Black and Blue include Jay McShann and Jo Jones.

BLACK & WHITE. Only in existence from 1943 to 1949, the Black & White label released many jazz **albums** of artists including **Lil Armstrong** and **Erroll Garner**.

BLACK ARTISTS GROUP (BAG). An artist collective created by Charles "Bobo" Shaw in 1968 and housed in a performance space in St. Louis, Missouri. The Black Artists Group was created with similar principles as the **Association for the Advancement of Creative Musicians** in Chicago, focusing on the creation of free and creative music. Concerts presented by the BAG ranged from solo to large group performances. Included in this group of musicians were **Avant-Garde** Jazz pioneers **Oliver Lake**, Joseph Bowie, Hamiet Bluiett, **Julius Hemphill**, and Marty Ehrlich. The collective only lasted four years and was forced to fold due to a lack of funding and an absence of younger musicians to replace members that had left to pursue individual careers.

BLACK BOTTOM. A style of dance in the 1920s that involved a set number of specific steps and moves. *See also* BLACK BOTTOM STOMPERS.

BLACK BOTTOM STOMPERS. A group founded in the 1920s to record popular music to which people could perform the **Black Bottom** style dance. The group made several **recordings** but did not tour or perform in public.

BLACK LION. Founded in London in the late 1960s, Black Lion primarily reissued older American **albums** in addition to distributing the music of British jazz musicians. Artists to have albums issued or reissued on Black Lion include **Paul Gonsalves, Sun Ra, Dexter Gordon**, and Chris Barber. Black Lion acquired another significant jazz label, Candid, in the 1980s. *See also* FREEDOM, RECORD LABEL.

BLACK SAINT. An Italian record label created in the 1970s that specializes in **Free** or **Avant-Garde** Jazz. Artists to have **albums** released on Black Saint include **David Murray, Steve Lacy**, the **World Saxophone Quartet**, and **Anthony Braxton**. *See also* RECORD LABEL.

BLACKWELL, ED(WARD) JOSEPH (1929–1992). Born in New Orleans, Blackwell grew up inspired by the variety of rhythms he heard in local bands and among tap dancers. Blackwell's most famous musical association, playing with **Ornette Coleman**, began in the late 1940s in Los Angeles. After a short hiatus in the 1950s, Blackwell resumed playing at the end of the decade. Blackwell's associations with Coleman and **Eric Dolphy** helped define a new style of playing **drum set** in **Free Jazz** music. Blackwell would be affiliated with many of the top Free Jazz musicians during the 1960s, including **Archie Shepp** and **Don Cherry**.

After suffering some minor health setbacks in the 1970s, Blackwell continued to be a highly regarded **sideman** for most of the next few years. Blackwell began leading his own groups in the 1980s, although he spent most of the decade working with Cherry on and off again and performing with tenor saxophonist **David Murray**.

BLAKE, EUBIE (1887–1983). One of the most influential pianists of the early part of the 20th century, Blake, along with **James P. Johnson** and **Fats Waller**, played an important role in the development of jazz piano. During the 1920s, Blake performed in a variety of settings, including solo, duo, and with bands fronted by himself. Blake was also a composer of significant substance (including the "Charleston Rag"), while also writing for Broadway shows.

After the 1930s, Blake composed for various shows and acts and was not as prominent a performer as he had been during the previous decades. Blake primarily produced and published music for the remainder of his career, always being held in high regard as a stellar **Ragtime** and **Stride** pianist. A Broadway show written about Blake, entitled *Eubie*, toured for several years in the late 1970s and 1980s.

BLAKEY, ART (1919–1990). Originally a pianist, Blakey's career took off after he started playing **drum set**. Working with several groups in the 1940s, including groups led by **Fletcher Henderson** and **Billy Eckstine**, Blakey developed into a popular drummer who would go on to work with **Miles Davis** and **Dexter Gordon**. In addition to steadily working as a **sideman**, Blakey also began leading his own groups toward the end of the decade, including the first incarnation of the famous group, the **Jazz Messengers**.

Throughout the 1950s, Blakey would work predominately as a leader, oftentimes featuring a band that had many of the top-working musicians of the day. Blakey paired with **Horace Silver** in the first part of the 1950s, and the two made a formidable pairing, putting together several jazz groups that featured musicians including **Clifford Brown, Lou Donaldson, Kenny Dorham**, and **Hank Mobley**. Silver and Blakey split due to creative differences, and Blakey kept the working title of Jazz Messengers for the groups he led over the next several decades.

Wayne Shorter, Lee Morgan, Benny Golson, Bobby Timmons, Curtis Fuller, and **Freddie Hubbard** were all members of the Jazz Messengers during the late 1950s and early 1960s. Throughout the next several decades, many other famous musicians joined the Jazz Messengers, including **Keith Jarrett, Bobby Watson, Chuck Mangione, Woody Shaw, Wynton Marsalis**, and Terence Blanchard. Blakey was considered to be an important figure, giving younger players the opportunity to perform and develop. *See also* HARD BOP.

BLANTON, JIMMY (1918–1942). After working in a variety of show bands and riverboat bands, Blanton's bass playing was heard by **bandleader Duke Ellington** in the late 1930s. Immediately, Blanton became an important bass player because of his tremendous ability to play **walking bass** lines. Before his death at the age of 23, Blanton worked with Ellington and pianist **Billy Taylor**. *See also* BASS.

BLEY, CARLA (1938–). Growing up in a musical family, Bley's composing career began as a teenager writing for popular jazz leaders in the 1950s, including **George Russell** and **Jimmy Giuffre**. Bley played an important role in the development of the **Jazz Composers Guild** Orchestra and continued to be an active composer, primarily of **Free Jazz**, throughout the 1960s. Bley led her own groups throughout the 1970s and 1980s, in addition to frequently working with **Charlie Haden, Steve Swallow**, and Roswell Rudd, while also developing a strong following in Europe. Adept at working in small groups, Bley performed in groups that included musicians **Pharoah Sanders**, Billy Drummond, Peter Brötzmann, and **Steve Lacy**.

BLEY, PAUL (1932–). Born in Canada, Bley's professional career began in Montreal before moving to the United States to study at the Juilliard School in the 1940s. During the 1950s, Bley worked predominantly as a **sideman**, featured with groups led by **Charles Mingus, Jackie McLean**, and **Chet Baker**. Bley's career took off in the 1960s, when he not only began to lead his own groups, but also worked as a sideman with **Jimmy Giuffre, Don Ellis, Sonny Rollins**, and **Steve Swallow**.

Actively involved in several genres of jazz, Bley was an adept soloist who could play within **Straight-Ahead, Free Jazz, Third Stream**, and **Fusion** settings. During the 1970s and 1980s, he worked with a diverse set of musicians that included **Gary Peacock, Steve Lacy, Lester Bowie, Dave Holland**, and Sam Rivers. Bley remains active working as both a sideman and a leader, frequently fronting trios.

BLOOD, SWEAT AND TEARS. A New York–based American **Jazz-Rock** group formed in 1967. It was known for fusing musical styles including Rock, Pop, **Blues**, and jazz. The hybrid of these styles came to be known as Jazz-Rock. They were also known for their **horn arrangements**, which contained elements from the **big band** tradition. *See also* BRECKER, RANDY; SOLOFF, LEW; STERN, MIKE.

BLOW. A term used to describe the act of improvising over a song form.

BLUEBIRD. A record company created in 1932, Bluebird Records was a sublabel of **RCA Victor** Records. Beginning in the 1930s, Bluebird became a popular label for jazz artists such as **Glenn Miller** and **Artie Shaw**, who recorded with Bluebird in 1938. *See also* RECORD LABEL.

BLUE DEVILS. An important **Early Jazz** group that preceded the **Swing** era. Led by **Walter Page** in the 1920s, the Blue Devils featured alumni that included **Lester Young** and **Count Basie**.

BLUE NOTE. A New York–based jazz **record label** created by Alfred Lion and Max Margulis in the late 1930s. Blue Note quickly developed a reputation for creating many of jazz's finest **albums**. Among the musicians who have recorded under the Blue Note label are **John Coltrane, Herbie Hancock, Kenny Dorham**, Sonny Clark, and **Horace Silver**. From 1953 to the late 1960s, sound engineer Rudy Van Gelder recorded most Blue Note releases. His engineering was thought to be equally important and monumental as the music being played.

BLUES. A musical form consisting of 12 measures that is based in African-American Folk music. The Blues was developed during the same time period that **Ragtime** and **Traditional Jazz** were being formed. Highly significant to the development of jazz, the Blues became one of the most common forms used by jazz composers and soloists. Great Blues singers included **Bessie Smith**, **Joe Williams**, Robert Johnson, Blind Lemon Jefferson, and countless others. *See also* ALLEN, HENRY "RED."

BLUES ALLEY. An important night **club** in the Washington, D.C., area that brings in top jazz musicians. Blues Alley was the home for a live **recording** of **Wynton Marsalis'** quartet in the 1980s.

BLUES PROGRESSION. The harmonic sequence of the **Blues**. Frequently, a Blues progression consists of 12 measures, in which the first four bars are in the tonic key, followed by two bars of a dominant chord based off the fourth of the tonic, a return to the tonic for two bars and a cadence for two bars, arriving on the tonic for the final two bars. Jazz composers and instrumentalists have developed several different sets of alterations that replace the Blues progression.

BLYTHE, ARTHUR (1940–). Blythe's professional alto saxophone career began in his native Los Angeles playing with musicians like Horace Tapscott in the 1960s. After moving to New York in the 1970s, Blythe worked with **Chico Hamilton**, **Gil Evans**, **Julius Hemphill**, and **Jack DeJohnette**, and was prominently featured with **Free Jazz** groups. During the 1980s, Blythe became a more active frontman, forming such groups as the Leaders and various other groups, featuring musicians including **Chico Freeman** and John Hicks. Blythe was temporarily a member of the **World Saxophone Quartet** during the end of the 1980s. Blythe would work as both a **sideman** and leader during the 1990s and 2000s, most notably working with drummer Joey Baron.

BOLDEN, BUDDY (1877–1931). Considered one of the first and most significant musicians to play jazz, Bolden's career began and ended in New Orleans. Extremely popular, Bolden's career is defined by his ability to transform the military **brass band** tradition into a new more loosely styled music that became known as the New Orleans brass band style. Unfortunately, Bolden's career was cut short due to problems with addiction, and no **recordings** of him were ever made. He is also considered to be the first **trumpet** "King" in the lineage that includes **Joe Oliver**, **Freddie Keppard**, and **Louis Armstrong**. *See also* EARLY JAZZ.

BOMB. A drumming technique that involves the drummer playing a single, low-note figure, especially loud while accompanying a soloist or a band. *See also* DRUM SET.

BONE. Shorthand term for **trombone**.

BONGOS. A hand percussion instrument that has origins in Cuba, consisting of a pair of drums that are two different sizes. They are most often played by hand and produce a high-pitched sound. They are commonly used in **Latin Jazz** by bands such as Tito Puente and **Ray Barretto**.

BOOGIE-WOOGIE. A style of piano that is highly influenced by the **Blues**. Boogie-Woogie became popular in the late 1930s but began to develop in the early 1920s. One of the most prominent Boogie-Woogie pianists was **Albert Ammons**, whose **recording** of "Boogie Woogie Stomp" in 1936 was pivotal not only for Boogie Woogie, but also for other styles of music such as Rock and Roll. *See also* SMITH, PINE TOP.

BOOK. A reference to the collection of music that a jazz ensemble plays.

BOP. *See* BEBOP.

BOSSA NOVA. A style of Brazilian music that became popular during the 1950s. Tenor saxophonist **Stan Getz** famously recorded several Bossa Novas written by Antônio Carlos Jobim, a Brazilian composer credited for spearheading the increased awareness of the Brazilian style. *See also* CASTRO-NEVES, (CARLOS) OSCAR (DE); GILBERTO, ASTRUD; GILBERTO, JOÃO; POWELL, BADEN.

BOSTIC, EARL (1913–1965). Bostic's career was defined as being an above-average alto saxophonist and arranger. Bostic spent most of the 1930s touring with various bands, attending college for a brief time (although he did not graduate), and leading bands. In the 1940s, Bostic led bands that featured up-and-coming players including **John Coltrane**, **Blue Mitchell**, and **Benny Golson**. Bostic did not shy away from playing more commercial types of music and made several successful **albums** during the 1950s before a heart condition led to early retirement and eventually his death in 1965.

BOWIE, LESTER (1941–1999). A significant **Avant-Garde trumpet** player of the 1970s, Bowie's career was first forged while touring with **Rhythm and Blues** groups in the 1960s, before settling in Chicago. While living there, Bowie was an important part of the creative music scene, frequently **recording** and playing with members of the **Association for the Advancement of Creative Musicians**. After a brief period living abroad, Bowie returned to Chicago with a new group, the **Art Ensemble of Chicago**. This ensemble would become one of Bowie's most acclaimed units.

In the 1980s, Bowie became very active as a leader and started many groups including the New York Hot Trumpet Repertory Company, Brass Fantasy, and From the Root to the Source. Bowie frequently found himself paired with musicians including **Arthur Blythe**, **Archie Shepp**, Roscoe Mitchell, and **Jack DeJohnette**. Bowie died due to complications with liver cancer.

BRAFF, RUBY (1927–2003). Born in Boston, Ruby Braff began studying the **cornet** at a young age against his own wishes, as he wanted to be a tenor **saxophone** player. His music, which was primarily **Dixieland**, was considered to be outdated, and therefore he had difficulty finding work throughout much of his career. He moved to New York in 1953 and recorded live for **Savoy** with clarinetist **Pee Wee Russell**. As a leader, Braff recorded for Vanguard with artists such as **Urbie Green**, **Vic Dickenson**, and **Buck Clayton**. After working with **Benny Goodman** in the mid-1950s, Braff went on to form a quartet with guitarist George Barnes in 1973, which opened the way for him to become more active in the small-group setting.

BRASS BAND. An ensemble, consisting primarily of brass instruments, that is often accompanied by a percussion section. The brass band tradition dates back to the 1800s during the U.S. Civil War and evolved with the development of **Ragtime** and **Early Jazz** in New Orleans. Brass bands were very common to the area. In the early 1900s, influential players including **Buddy Bolden** and **Freddie Keppard** are attributed with fronting many of these bands. During the **Swing** and **Bebop** eras, the brass band tradition was not as popular but experienced resurgence during the 1950s. *See also* DIRTY DOZEN BRASS BAND; EUREKA BRASS BAND; EXCELSIOR BRASS BAND; GREEN, CHARLIE; HANDY, W(ILLIAM) C(HRISTOPHER); ONWARD BRASS BAND; ORIGINAL TUXEDO ORCHESTRA; PRESERVATION HALL JAZZ BAND; YOUNG TUXEDO BRASS BAND.

BRASS (SECTION). A general term used to describe the **trombones, trumpets, French horns, tuba**, and euphonium instruments in a given ensemble. The brass section in jazz ensembles frequently feature four trumpets and four trombones, although some groups, like those led by **Stan Kenton**, have been expanded to feature additional brass.

BRAXTON, ANTHONY (1945–). One of jazz's most creative and forward-thinking artists, Braxton's early saxophone career was forged in Chicago working with members of the **Association for the Advancement of Creative Musicianship (AACM)**. Developing a very unique style and unorthodox playing method, Braxton spent the end of the 1960s leading groups and touring. In the 1970s, Braxton became an important member of the **Chick Corea**–led unit **Circle**, before continuing work on his own career. Braxton would perform in a variety of situations and ensembles, most notably performing many solo concerts. Throughout the 1980s, Braxton would become increasingly active as an educator while performing across the globe in many different contexts. Braxton has remained equally influential as a composer and as a saxophonist, and has had compositions premiered by several groups in the United States and **Europe** during the 1990s and 2000s.

BREAK. A term used to describe a section of a song in which the **rhythm section** stops playing for a period of time. A break can be any length, from one measure to an entire **chorus** of a given tune. A break is done to give the soloist a completely different texture to work with and to help generate excitement.

BRECKER, MICHAEL (1949–2007). Widely considered to be one of the most influential saxophonists to come after **John Coltrane**, Brecker studied **tenor saxophone** at Indiana University during the 1960s before moving to New York. Throughout the 1970s, Brecker was heard in a variety of settings, included **Straight-Ahead sessions** with **Horace Silver**, and with many **Fusion** groups. Along with his brother, **trumpet** player **Randy Brecker**, Brecker formed the Brecker Brothers in 1974, a highly influential Fusion group. After the group disbanded in 1979, the two would continue to record together for the next several decades.

In the 1980s, Brecker began to lead his own groups in addition to performing with notable musicians including **Herbie Hancock** and **Jaco Pastorius**, and playing on a number of Pop and studio sessions. During this time, Brecker's popularity soared, and he became one of the top touring musicians during the 1990s, bringing along sidemen like **Pat Metheny** and Jeff "Tain" Watts. Brecker would continue to be one of the most recorded saxophonists well into the 2000s until his death due to complications with leukemia.

BRECKER, RANDY (1945–). Part of an incredibly musical family, Randy Brecker is older brother of tenor saxophonist **Michael Brecker**. Brecker's career began while a prodigious youth, winning several competitions in both Classical and jazz music. In the 1960s, Brecker played with Pop and jazz groups, most notably **Blood, Sweat and Tears** and **Horace Silver**. Very active in the **Fusion** movement, Brecker worked with several groups in this style during the 1970s, including ones led by **Billy Cobham** and **Larry Coryell**, along with a group founded with his brother, the Brecker Brothers. The Brecker Brothers remained active until the end of 1970s, when each sibling elected to pursue other work.

Throughout the 1980s and 1990s, Brecker remained active as a **sideman** and leader performing with **Eliane Elias, Jaco Pastorius**, Bob Berg, **Stanley Turrentine, Joe Henderson**, and Conrad Herwig. Brecker was one of the top recorded **trumpet** players during this time and was frequently used in **big bands** including the Carnegie Hall Jazz Band and the Mingus Big Band. While not actively involved in education, several books and transcriptions of Brecker's solos have been made available.

BRICKTOP'S. A term for the nightclubs in Paris, Mexico City, and Rome that were owned by singer Ada "Bricktop" Smith.

BRIDGE. A term for a section of a song containing melodic material that is in contrast to the other section. A common **form** in jazz is AABA, in which the A sections are all similar to each other and the B section may contain a modulation in key. "I Got Rhythm" and "Confirmation" are examples of jazz standards with an AABA form. *See also* RELEASE.

BRITISH RHYTHM SOCIETY. A New York–based record label established in 1948, it was created as part of Dante Bolletino's Globe Industries. It was one of the first record labels to release reissues of **Early Jazz** that had previously been released without authorization during the 1920s. *See also* RECORD LABEL.

BROOKMEYER, ROBERT "BOB" (1929–2011). One of the most significant players to perform on valve trombone, Brookmeyer's career is a combination of working as a leader, **sideman**, and arranger for many groups. After freelancing for several years in New York during the 1950s with musicians like **Claude Thornhill, Woody Herman**, and Tex Beneke, Brookmeyer was hired by **Gerry Mulligan**. The two created a formidable pairing and toured frequently throughout the end of the decade.

During the 1960s, while still working and **recording** with Mulligan, Brookmeyer began to develop as a composer and wrote compositions for Mulligan, **Clark Terry**, and the **Thad Jones–Mel Lewis** Orchestra. Brookmeyer's affiliation with the Jones/Lewis band was significant and led eventually to his being given the role of musical director of the group. During the

1970s, he split time leading his own small groups and doing studio work. Brookmeyer's presence overseas increased, and he found much work there during this time as well. Among Brookmeyer's best-known **arrangements** is his interpretation of the **ballad** "Skylark." Throughout the 1990s and 2000s, Brookmeyer became increasingly more involved in education and joined the faculty of the New England Conservatory.

BRÖTZMANN, PETER (1941–). A highly influential **Free Jazz** saxophonist, Brötzmann was born in Germany. He learned several instruments as a youth until settling on the saxophone. **Recording** as a **sideman** and under his own name in the 1960s, Brötzmann would work with many of Europe's finest Free Jazz musicians including Evan Parker and William Parker. Brötzmann continued to experiment with a variety of jazz styles throughout the 1980s and 1990s, including the expanded use of electronic instruments.

BROWN, CLIFFORD (1930–1956). Despite passing away much too young, **trumpet** player Brown was one of the most influential jazz figures of the 1950s, and remains highly influential today. Developing his style and improvisation skills in Philadelphia, Brown worked with **Tadd Dameron** and **Lionel Hampton** in the early 1950s. After a famous but short stint with **Art Blakey**, Brown forged a relationship with **Max Roach**, creating the now famous Clifford Brown–Max Roach Quintet. Sidemen for the group included **Harold Land, Sonny Rollins**, and **Richie Powell**, and the group released several classic **albums** on the **EmArcy** label. On the way home from a performance with the group, Brown was involved in a fatal car accident along with Powell. Brown's legacy is carried on through the **recordings** that he made, in addition to the influence he had on trumpeters including **Freddie Hubbard** and **Lee Morgan**. *See also* HARD BOP.

BRUBECK, DAVE (1920–). One of the most popular jazz musicians of all time, Brubeck's career began in California while attending the University of the Pacific. Brubeck's early career included work with several different-sized groups, including a 12-piece band, and eventually his own trio. Much of Brubeck's fame came from his compositions, most notably "Take Five" and "Blue Rondo a la Turk," both composed in the 1950s when he was in his prime and working with what would be considered his most famous group, a quartet featuring alto saxophonist Paul Desmond. Brubeck spent much time in the 1960s and 1970s composing for large and small groups, in addition to raising three children who would themselves develop into established musicians. Toward the end of his career, Brubeck was presented many lifetime achievement awards for the work he had done as a composer and performer.

BRUNSWICK. An important **record label** established in the 1910s in Iowa. Brunswick acquired many other record labels throughout the 1920s and 1930s, including **Vocalion**. Artists to record for Brunswick in the 1920s and 1930s included **Fletcher Henderson**, the Original Memphis Five, **Teddy Wilson**, and **Billie Holiday**. Brunswick was sold to **Decca** in the 1940s.

BRUSH. A type of beater used by drummers that consists of a tube containing many thin straight wires that can be fanned out. Many drummers frequently use brushes when playing slower songs because of their timbre and light feeling. Brushes are much softer in volume than **drum** sticks.

BUCKET MUTE. A type of **mute** that resembles a bucket and attaches to the bell of a **brass** instrument. The bucket mute dampens the sound, resulting in a mellower, rounded sound.

BURRELL, KENNETH EARL "KENNY" (1931–). Developing his jazz skills in Detroit, Burrell's career as a jazz **guitar** player began while working in his hometown with many of the musicians who spent time in that area, including pianist **Tommy Flanagan**. Burrell moved to New York in the mid-1950s and found work with **Dizzy Gillespie**, **Hampton Hawes**, and fellow former Detroit musicians **Donald Byrd** and **Thad Jones**. Burrell began to lead his own groups toward the end of the decade, many of which would continue for several years. Burrell transitioned to studio work in the 1960s for a brief period, while also **recording albums** as both a leader and a **sideman**. Burrell became an active educator in the 1970s, teaching for several decades at the University of California, Los Angeles, including assuming the role of chair for the jazz studies program.

BURTON, GARY (1943–). An important vibraphonist, Burton's career began after a brief time studying at the **Berklee College of Music** and a partnership with **George Shearing**. After working with **Stan Getz** in the 1960s, Burton became active as a leader and made a series of important **recordings** during the 1970s with artists including **Pat Metheny**, **John Scofield**, and **Chick Corea**. In addition to playing a variety of ensembles, Burton has frequently recorded in duos with pianists, including Corea and **Makoto Ozone**. Burton became very active in education, joining the faculty at his alma mater for several years before assuming the role of dean of curriculum.

BUTTERFIELD, BILLY (1917–1988). A **trumpet** player, Butterfield performed in Broadway pit orchestras while also working in various touring jazz bands. After attempting to front his own band, Butterfield worked steadily in the 1950s including performances with **Louis Armstrong, Bobby Hackett,** and the **World's Greatest Jazz Band.**

BUTTERFIELD, DON (1923–2006). Primarily a **tuba** player, Butterfield worked mostly as a **studio musician** in New York. Butterfield spent time working with famous jazz musicians including **Charles Mingus,** Teddy Charles, **Bill Evans,** and the **Thad Jones–Mel Lewis** Orchestra.

BYAS, DON (1912–1972). One of the first great tenor saxophonists, and a figure very influential in the development of **Bebop,** Byas received his first professional work in groups led by **Bennie Moten** and **Walter Page.** In the 1930s, he worked with **Lionel Hampton, Buck Clayton,** and Ethel Waters, while developing his own approach to improvisation. The 1940s proved to be an important decade for Byas as he was first hired to fill in for **Lester Young** in the **Count Basie** Orchestra, and later was called to join a small group led by rising **trumpet** star **Dizzy Gillespie.** Along with other **Bebop** jazz musicians at **Minton's Playhouse,** Byas played in **jam sessions** with **Charlie Christian** and **Thelonious Monk,** among others, further developing the new style. Before the decade was over, Byas had worked with many of the great names in jazz, including **Coleman Hawkins, Oscar Pettiford, Max Roach,** and **Charlie Parker,** along with some time spent playing as a duo with bassist **Slam Stewart,** which resulted in a memorable concert at Town Hall in New York City in 1945. Byas lived in the Netherlands during the later years of his career, primarily freelancing or performing as a guest artist with different groups.

BYERS, BILLY (1927–1996). An important arranger of the 1950s and 1960s, Byers contributed **arrangements** to many top touring bands including those of **Benny Goodman, Quincy Jones, Count Basie,** and **Frank Sinatra.** Byers' work was recorded on several labels including **Mercury** and **Verve.**

BYRD, CHARLIE (1925–1999). Considered a very proficient guitarist at a young age, Byrd's career was shaped by his early association with **Django Reinhardt.** Byrd was greatly influenced by Reinhardt's style although Byrd decided to pursue a career in Classical guitar. After spending part of the 1950s working on developing his Classical technique, Byrd decided to apply all he had learned to jazz. Working mostly as a leader, Byrd also did some tours with **Woody Herman** and **Stan Getz** in the 1950s and 1960s. Byrd spent some time in the 1970s performing with the all-guitar group **Great Guitars,** which also featured **Barney Kessel** and **Herb Ellis.** Byrd died due to complications with lung cancer.

BYRD, DONALD(SON) TOUSSAINT L'OUVERTURE, II (1932–).
Byrd's **trumpet** career began while performing in air force bands before
moving to New York in the mid-1950s. Byrd was considered to be highly
reliable because he had none of the addiction problems that plagued many of
the other musicians during the decade. This reliability, in addition to Byrd's
long phrasing and harmonic ideas, led him to work steadily with many of the
top musicians of the 1950s, including **Art Blakey, John Coltrane, Jackie
McLean, Hank Mobley, Horace Silver**, and **Sonny Rollins**. Byrd became
a leader during the 1960s and frequently recorded for **Blue Note** Records.
He was highly educated and had received bachelor's and master's degrees
in music, in addition to a degree in law. Throughout the 1970s and 1980s,
Byrd was an active teacher, in addition to making a number of **Fusion** and
contemporary **albums** with his groups. Byrd experienced a brief resurgence
of his music in the 1980s, although he would primarily work as an educator
for the remainder of his career.

C

CAB JIVERS. *See* CALLOWAY, CAB.

CABLES, GEORGE ANDREW (1944–). An American jazz pianist, George Cables was initially instructed by his mother who was an amateur pianist. At the age of 18, Cables formed a group with **Steve Grossman** and **Billy Cobham** called the Jazz Samaritans. In 1969 he played with **Art Blakey**, **Sonny Rollins**, and **Joe Henderson** (with whom he stayed until 1971). He then played with **Freddie Hubbard** from 1971 to 1976 and recorded with **Woody Shaw**, Joe Chambers, and **Billy Harper** during the same period. He played with **Dexter Gordon** during his return to the United States (1976–1978) and was pianist for **Art Pepper** (1979–1982). He joined the group Bebop and Beyond in 1984 and would rejoin the renamed Bebop and Beyond 2000 in 1998.

CADET. Created in 1965, renamed from the record label **Argo**. *See also* RECORD LABEL.

CADILLAC. English record label and company founded in London in 1973. *See also* RECORD LABEL.

CAFÉ BOHEMIA. Nightclub in New York opened in 1955 by Jimmy Garofalo. It was the location of performances and **recordings** by **Charlie Parker**, **Miles Davis**, **Art Blakey**, and others. *See also* JONES, JOSEPH.

CAFÉ SOCIETY. Opened in 1938, it was the first racially integrated **club** in New York. Many careers in jazz were launched here through the support of John Hammond, a regular visitor to the club, and many of the great figures in jazz performed here. It was here that **Billie Holiday** debuted "Strange Fruit" to great acclaim. A second location was opened in 1940 on 58th Street.

CALIFORNIA RAMBLERS. A White dance band formed by **banjo** player Ray Kitchingman in 1921 and active until 1937. Notable members of the band included Jimmy and **Tommy Dorsey**, Stan King, **Red Nichols**, and Bill

Moore, a **trumpet** player who was the first African-American to work with an all-White band. The band recorded many **albums** under different pseudonyms and was briefly re-formed in the 1970s and 1980s.

CALL AND RESPONSE. Alternating musical phrases in which a musical statement is followed by a musical answer. It can occur in jazz between instrumental sections in an ensemble, between instrumentalists (as in the practice of trading fours), or between a vocalist and instrumentalist. Some forms, such as the **Blues**, are said to be structured as call and response.

CALLENDER, RED (1916–1992). A **bassist** who made his **recording** debut with **Louis Armstrong** in 1937, he spent three years in the Lester and Lee Young band before forming his own trio. He played with **Erroll Garner**, **Charlie Parker**, **Wardell Gray**, **Dexter Gordon**, and eventually **Art Tatum** (1955–1956). In later years Callender switched to playing tuba. His autobiography, *Unfinished Dream*, was published in 1985.

CALLOWAY, CABELL "CAB" (1907–1994). Bandleader, singer, and entertainer. Cab Calloway attended law school briefly before quitting to pursue a career in music. In 1931, his group the Missourians recorded one of his biggest hits, "Minnie the Moocher" (which contained his famous phrase "Hi-De-Hi"), and replaced the band of **Duke Ellington** at the **Cotton Club**, where they performed until 1940. The group, renamed Cab Calloway and his Orchestra, appeared in several films (*The Big Broadcast* 1933, *The Singing Kid* 1936, *Stormy Weather* 1943) and made many **recordings** before finally dissolving in 1948. Calloway's band contained several members who would go on to great fame, including **Dizzy Gillespie**, **Ben Webster**, Chu Berry, and Mario Bauza. After disbanding his **big band** in 1948, Calloway still appeared with the Cab Jivers, a small group. Later in his life, Calloway appeared in *Porgy and Bess* (1950s), *Hello, Dolly!* (1960s), and the movie *The Blues Brothers* (1980).

CALYPSO. A style of dance and song that originated on slave plantations in the Caribbean; it is most associated with the island of Trinidad. Calypsos are duple meter; modern Calypsos are in a major mode, while earlier examples were in a minor mode and slower tempo.

CAMELIA BRASS BAND. A New Orleans **brass band** established around 1917 by Wooden Joe Nicholas and named after the steamer S.S. *Camelia*.

CAMEO. A **record label** of the Cameo Record Corporation, it sold records in Macy's department stores during the 1920s. The company joined **Plaza** in

1929 to form the American Record Corporation. The Cameo label name was dropped in the 1930s.

CANDID. Its catalog contained nearly 40 **albums** including albums by **Don Ellis, Charles Mingus, Cecil Taylor,** and Booker Little. Purchased by the label Barnaby in the 1970s and then later purchased and reactivated by **Black Lion,** many **recordings** have been reissued in CD format, and more recent recordings have been issued by artists including **Dave Liebman** and **Lee Konitz.**

CANDOLI, CONTE (1927–2001). An American **trumpet** player, Conte Candoli got his start at the age of 16 when he joined **Woody Herman**'s First Herd in 1944. He would go on to play with Chubby Jackson (1947–1948), **Stan Kenton** (1948), Charlie Ventura (1949), Herman again (1949–1950), **Charlie Barnet** (1951), and Kenton again (1951–1953). He moved to Chicago and started his own group in 1954 before moving to California where he played with Howard Rumsey's Lighthouse All-Stars (1955). He recorded with Stan Levey (1954–1957) and played and recorded with his brother **Pete Candoli** (1957–1962) and Terry Gibbs (1959–1962). He played with Woody Herman at the **Monterey Jazz Festival** in 1960, toured Europe with **Gerry Mulligan** (1960–1961), played with drummer **Shelly Manne,** and then with Kenton's Los Angeles Neophonic Orchestra (1965–1969). He performed with the group **Supersax** from 1972 throughout the 1980s and performed in the **Doc Severinsen**–led *Tonight Show* band from 1972 to 1992. Candoli continued to tour extensively through the late 1990s before passing away from prostate cancer in 2001.

CANDOLI, PETE (1923–2008). Brother of **Conte Candoli,** he was known as a lead **trumpet** player. He played with many **big bands** during the 1940s including Sonny Dunham, Will Bradley, Ray McKinley, **Benny Goodman, Tommy Dorsey,** Teddy Powell, **Woody Herman,** Boyd Raeburn, Tex Beneke, and Jerry Gray. He moved to Los Angeles and became noted for his studio work and performed with the bands of Les Brown and **Stan Kenton.** He later led a group (1957–1962) with his brother Conte and started a nightclub act with his wife, Edie Adams, in 1972. He continued to perform with his brother into the 1990s.

CAPITOL. American **record label** founded in 1942 by **Johnny Mercer,** Glenn Wallichs, and B. G. Desylva specializing in popular music. Early artists included **Nat "King" Cole,** Peggy Lee, Country singer Tex Williams, and **Stan Kenton.** During the 1950s the label grew as artists such as Dean Martin, **Frank Sinatra,** and guitarist Les Paul were added. In 1956 the label broke into the Rock and Roll market by signing Gene Vincent; later it would sign the Beach Boys and begin a distribution arrangement with the Beatles. After the breakup of the Beatles, its catalog included artists such as Pink Floyd, Merle Haggard, Glen Campbell, Bob Seeger, and Anne Murray. During the 1980s and 1990s, its artists included Duran Duran, Bonnie Raitt, Garth Brooks, the Beastie Boys, and Radiohead. Recent popular artists on Capitol Records include Coldplay and Katy Perry.

CAPP-PIERCE JUGGERNAUT. A **big band** formed in 1975 as the Capp-Pierce Orchestra by Frank Capp and Nat Pierce. The band performed and recorded **Basie**-style big band material and included members such as Bill Berry, **Bobby Shew**, Marshal Royal, **Blue Mitchell**, and **Herb Ellis**.

CARDINAL. **Record label** established in 1920 and notable for issuing **Ethel Waters'** first **recording** in 1921.

CARISI, JOHNNY (1922–1992). A **trumpet** player, then later a composer/arranger, Johnny Carisi played with **Glenn Miller** from late 1942 until Miller's death and then wrote for various **big bands** including Ray McKinley, **Charlie Barnet**, and **Claude Thornhill**. He wrote "Israel" while studying with composer Stefan Wolpe, which would appear on **Miles Davis'** landmark **album** *Birth of the Cool*. During the late 1950s and 1960s, Carisi wrote many small ensemble and chamber pieces, including **arrangements** for **Gil Evans** and trumpeter **Marvin Stamm**. He became a faculty member of the Manhattan School of Music and Queens College CUNY in 1969 and continued to compose and perform until his passing in 1992.

CARLTON, LARRY (1948–). Guitarist. Credits from the 1970s and 1980s include Joni Mitchell, Steely Dan, Michael Jackson, Dolly Parton, **Quincy Jones**, and many others. He was awarded a Grammy in 1981 for composing the theme song of the TV show *Hill Street Blues*. After a long period of rehabilitation due to a gunshot wound he received outside his studio in 1988, Carlton joined the **GRP record label** in 1991 and eventually replaced **Lee Ritenour** in the Smooth Jazz group Fourplay. *See also* GUITAR.

CARMICHAEL, HOAGLAND HOWARD "HOAGY" (1899–1981). A composer, songwriter, and singer. An early friendship with cornetist **Bix Beiderbecke** led him to compose one of his first works, "Riverboat Shuffle," which was recorded by the Wolverines in 1924. He completed a law degree in 1926 but returned to music after he heard a **Red Nichols recording** of his "Washboard Blues." Thereafter he moved to New York and began his career as a songwriter, collaborating with many lyricists including **Johnny Mercer**. His most famous compositions include "Stardust," "Skylark," "Georgia on My Mind," "The Nearness of You," and "Heart and Soul." He won an Academy Award in 1951 for "In the Cool, Cool, Cool of the Evening."

CAROLINA COTTON PICKERS. A band formed in Florida in 1933 from members of the Jenkins orphanage bands.

CARR, IAN (1933–2009). Trumpet player, writer, and teacher. He taught himself to play the trumpet in 1950 and played in many bands throughout the 1960s, 1970s, and 1980s, most notably the band Nucleus, an important and popular **Jazz-Rock** group. His biography of **Miles Davis**, *Miles Davis: A Critical Biography*, is recognized as one of the seminal works on Miles Davis, and he co-authored *Jazz: A Rough Guide*, which is a standard reference text. *See also* ENGLAND.

CARRUTHERS, EARL "JOCK" (1910–1971). A baritone saxophone player, Carruthers played with **Bennie Moten**'s band in 1928 in Kansas City before moving to St. Louis to play with Dewey Jackson and **Fate Marable**, followed by a long membership in the band of **Jimmie Lunceford**. After Lunceford's passing in 1947, Carruthers continued to play in the band before moving back to Kansas City, where he performed with local groups throughout the 1960s.

CARTER, BENNY (1907–2003). Known primarily for his **alto saxophone** playing and also the ease with which he switched between alto and many other instruments, Benny Carter originally started on the **trumpet** and took a few lessons on C-melody saxophone before settling on the alto saxophone. After brief stints in the bands of **Duke Ellington** and Billy Fowler, he worked with **Fletcher Henderson** from 1930 to 1931. Following that he served briefly as musical director of **McKinney's Cotton Pickers**, during which time he also wrote **arrangements** for the bands of **Chick Webb** and **Benny Goodman**, among others. In 1932 he started his own band, which was dissolved in 1934. He moved to Europe and worked in several countries before settling in London as the staff arranger for the BBC Dance Orchestra from 1936 to 1938.

Carter returned to the United States in 1938 to lead his own band at the **Savoy Ballroom** until 1940. He then toured with the band before permanently settling in Los Angeles in 1942. He began to write music for films, including portions of *Panic in the Streets* (1950) and *An American in Paris* (1951) and later for television productions. During the 1950s and 1960s he continued to compose, arrange, and perform, and by the 1970s he was appearing at festivals and nightclubs and making annual tours of Europe and Japan. He was awarded an honorary doctorate from Princeton University in 1974, the Grammy Lifetime Achievement Award in 1987, and his composition "Harlem Renaissance Suite" won the Grammy Award for Best Jazz Composition in 1992. Widely regarded during the **Swing** era as second only to **Johnny Hodges**, Carter was influential in the creation of alto saxophone style before the emergence of **Charlie Parker**. Among his many notable compositions is the jazz standard "When Lights Are Low."

CARTER, BETTY (1929–1998). Born Lillie Mae Jones, Carter was an American jazz singer who grew up in Detroit and got her start **singing** with **Charlie Parker** and **Dizzy Gillespie** during their tours through the city. She eventually landed a spot in **Lionel Hampton**'s band in 1948 where she earned the nickname "Bebop." In 1951 she moved to New York where she worked with artists including Muddy Waters and later headlined tours with **Ray Charles**. In 1971 she founded Bet-Car Productions, her own **record label**. She continued to perform with her own trio through the 1980s and 1990s, and in 1988 she signed with **Verve**, winning a Grammy the following year.

CARTER, RON (1937–). Initially studying cello at age 10 and working toward a career in Classical music, Ron Carter would switch to the **bass** in 1954 and eventually became one of the most recorded jazz bassists of all time. After graduating from the Eastman School of Music in 1959 with a B.M., he joined the **Chico Hamilton** Quintet with **Eric Dolphy** and received an M.M. degree from the Manhattan School of Music. From there he played with many famous musicians including **Cannonball Adderley, Randy Weston, Thelonious Monk, Don Ellis**, and many others before replacing **Paul Chambers** in **Miles Davis**' group in 1963. He remained in Davis' group until 1968, during which time he, along with **Herbie Hancock** and **Tony Williams**, formed one of the most noted **rhythm sections** in jazz history. In addition to his work with Davis, he played with artists including **Sonny Rollins, Freddie Hubbard, Wayne Shorter, McCoy Tyner, Cedar Walton**, and many others. He also worked with vocalists including Lena Horne, Aretha Franklin, and **Helen Merrill**, as well as the Rap group a Tribe Called Quest.

CASTRO-NEVES, (CARLOS) OSCAR (DE) (1940–). A Brazilian guitarist who helped to popularized the Bossa Nova style. He performed in the first concert of Bossa Nova music presented at Carnegie Hall in 1962 and then went on to play with artists including **Dizzy Gillespie, Stan Getz**, and Lalo Schifrin. He moved to Los Angeles in 1967 and wrote, arranged, and toured with the

Paul Winter Consort until 1970. From 1971 through 1981, he was guitarist and musical director for the popular musician Sergio Mendes and also played with **Quincy Jones, Lee Ritenour, Dave Grusin,** and **Ella Fitzgerald,** among others. He has also participated as an arranger or producer in projects for artists including **Toots Thielemans, Joe Henderson,** and Terence Blanchard.

CATALYST. A **record label** and company established in 1975 that recorded until 1977. Artists include **Sonny Stitt,** Frank Foster, and **Ahmad Jamal.** The label reissued **albums** from other countries by artists including **Paul Gonsalves, Carmen McRae,** and **Helen Merrill.**

CATLETT, SID(NEY) (1910–1951). An American jazz drummer, Catlett was known primarily for his work in **Swing** music. His first **gig** was with Darnell Howard in 1928, after which he moved to New York and worked first with **Benny Carter**'s band, then **McKinney's Cotton Pickers, Fletcher Henderson,** and Don Redman. He was the featured drummer in a **big band** led by **Louis Armstrong** from 1938 to 1941 before playing briefly as a member of **Benny Goodman**'s band. He led his own groups during the 1940s, and also played with **Duke Ellington, Ben Webster** (who played in Catlett's quartet), and **Dizzy Gillespie** (**recording** "Salt Peanuts" in 1945) before returning to Armstrong's All Stars from 1947 to 1949. In 1951, Catlett collapsed backstage and died of a heart attack at the Chicago Opera House during a benefit for **"Hot Lips" Page.**

CHALLIS, WILLIAM "BILL" (1904–1994). An American arranger, he got his start as the staff arranger for the Jean Goldkette band. After meeting cornetist **Bix Beiderbecke,** both would move to **Paul Whiteman**'s band in 1927 where Challis wrote much of Whiteman's most jazz-oriented music. His association with Beiderbecke would also lead to writing for **Frankie Trumbauer**'s small group. Challis left Whiteman's band in 1930 and went on to write **arrangements** for **Fletcher Henderson,** the **Dorsey** brothers, and **Artie Shaw,** among others. He remained active as an arranger into the 1960s.

CHALOFF, SERGE (1923–1957). Baritone sax player and one of the first important soloists on the instrument. He played with Boyd Raeburn (1945), **Georgie Auld** (1945–1946), and **Jimmy Dorsey** (1946–1947) before joining **Woody Herman**'s Second Herd and becoming one of the famous "Four Brothers" (1947–1949). His playing was influenced by **Charlie Parker.** He kicked a drug habit in 1950, but the last portion of his life was marred by spinal paralysis, causing him to play his last **recording session,** a reunion of the Four Brothers in 1957, in a wheelchair.

CHAMBERS, PAUL (1935–1969). One of the most well known jazz bassists of the 1950s and 1960s, Paul Chambers grew up in Detroit, starting on the tuba before switching to the **bass**. He toured with Paul Quinichette in 1954 before moving to New York where he played with the **J. J. Johnson–Kai Winding** Quintet (1955), **Bennie Green** (1955), and George Wallington (1955). Thereafter he joined **Miles Davis**, with whom he played from 1955 to 1963. After his time with Davis, he played with pianist **Wynton Kelly** until 1966. An alcoholic and heroin addict, he was nevertheless a popular **sideman** who recorded with artists including **Sonny Rollins, Cannonball Adderley, Freddie Hubbard, Bill Evans,** and **John Coltrane** (who titled his composition "Mr. P.C.," in honor of Chambers), among others. Also known for his bowed solos, Chambers contracted tuberculosis in 1968 and died early in 1969.

CHANGES. Musician's term for the harmonic progression to a song, as in "chord changes." *See also* IMPROVISATION.

CHANNEL. A term for the B section within the form of American popular song (AABA), usually a contrasting harmonic and melodic section. *See also* BRIDGE.

CHARLES, RAY (1930–2004). An American pianist and songwriter, he was also instrumental in the development of Soul music and a prolific force in American popular music. Born in Florida in poverty, Charles contracted glaucoma at the age of five and was blind one year later. He studied music and composition at the St. Augustine School for the Deaf and the Blind and later formed a group and toured around the state of Florida before moving to Seattle in 1947. He signed with **Atlantic** in 1952 and recorded several **albums,** his first trademark performance coming with "I've Got a Woman" in 1955. His unique inflection and interpretation was further realized with successive albums including *What'd I Say* (1959). During his time with Atlantic he also recorded jazz albums with artists including **Milt Jackson** and **David "Fathead" Newman.**

Charles moved to the ABC label in order to gain more creative control over his music, **recording** hits including "Georgia on My Mind" (1960) and "Hit the Road Jack" (1961), followed by a foray into Country music with "Modern Sounds in Country and Western Music" (1962). His momentum was slowed somewhat by a 1965 arrest for heroin possession, after which he took a year off from performing. He would record several other albums of varying styles before returning to jazz in 2000 with an appearance on **Steve Turre's** *In the Spur of the Moment.* After his death from liver disease in 2004, his album

Genius Loves Company was posthumously released and was awarded eight Grammy Awards, and a biopic, *Ray*, was released in 2005 starring Jamie Foxx as the title character, a role for which Foxx won the Academy Award for Best Actor. *See also* BLUES, RHYTHM AND BLUES.

CHARLESTON. A popular dance style of the 1920s, its popularity was aided by a dance song of the same name by **James P. Johnson** and Cecil Mack in 1923. The dance, named after the city of Charleston, South Carolina, where it possibly originated, symbolized the reckless abandon of the "Roaring Twenties" but eventually fell out of favor, and its movements were combined into a newer dance, the Lindy.

CHARLESTON CHASERS. The name given to several different studio dance bands led by **Red Nichols**, Dick Johnson, Phil Napoleon, and **Benny Goodman** that recorded on the **Columbia record label** between 1925 and 1931. At various times the groups included **Tommy Dorsey, Jack Teagarden, Glenn Miller**, and **Gene Krupa**, among others.

CHARLIE PARKER RECORDS. A **record label** and company founded in New York in 1961 by **Charlie Parker**'s widow, Doris Parker, and Aubrey Mayhew. The company was active for about two years, during which time a few of Parker's previously unissued **albums** were released, in addition to new material recorded by artists including **Cecil Taylor, Duke Jordan, Teddy Wilson**, and **Slide Hampton**.

CHART. A jazz musician's term for a printed piece of music.

CHASE. A competition between two or more soloists, where each tries to outplay or outperform the other. Similar in concept to **trading**, but instead of trading a set amount of measures, the soloists would first trade **choruses**, then half choruses, then phrases, and so on. *See also* CUTTING CONTEST.

CHASE, WILLIAM "BILL" (1934–1974). American **trumpet** player, known for his upper register. After studying at Berklee College of Music, Bill Chase played lead trumpet in **Maynard Ferguson**'s **big band** in 1958, recorded an **album** with **Stan Kenton** in 1959, and performed at the **Monterey Jazz Festival** with **Woody Herman**. Chase would stay in Herman's band until 1967, after which he started the **Jazz-Rock** group Chase, containing four trumpets, a **rhythm section**, and a singer. After another brief European tour with Herman's band in 1969, he recorded his band's first album in 1971, the self-titled *Chase*, which contained the hit song "Get It On." Successive albums were not as well received. Chase and three other members of his band died in a plane crash in 1974 during a tour.

CHEATHAM, ALDOLPHUS ANTHONY "DOC" (1905–1997). Known more for his playing later in his life, Doc Cheatham started on playing **trumpet** at the age of 14. He worked in various local bands before moving to Chicago around 1925, where he played with Albert Wynn and subbed for **Louis Armstrong**. He then moved to Philadelphia and played with Wilbur De Paris (1927–1928), then to New York where he performed briefly with **Chick Webb**. After touring Europe with Sam Wooding from 1928 to 1930, he became known more as a lead trumpet player than a soloist and spent time playing in many different bands, including **McKinney's Cotton Pickers** in 1931 and 1932, seven years with the **Cab Calloway** Orchestra from 1932 to 1939, and brief stints with **Teddy Wilson** and then **Benny Carter**. In the 1950s and 1960s, Cheatham worked with various Latin bands and also toured with De Paris, Sammy Price, and **Herbie Mann** before settling down to lead his own band in New York from 1960 to 1965. After a brief stint with Benny Goodman in 1966, Cheatham settled in as a freelance musician, and his soloing became more recognized. He continued to perform at jazz festivals and clubs into the 1990s. In 1991 he appeared with **Wynton Marsalis** at a tribute to Louis Armstrong and in 1996 recorded an **album** with trumpeter Nicholas Payton. A few days after a performance with Payton in 1997, Cheatham died in his sleep due to a stroke.

CHERRY, DON (1936–1995). Generally associated with playing the pocket **trumpet** or **cornet**, Cherry joined **Ornette Coleman**'s group in 1957 and appeared on Coleman's first seven **albums**. Those albums, in addition to the group's celebrated stint at the **Five Spot** Café in New York (starting in 1959), established Cherry at the forefront of the **Avant-Garde** movement. During this time he also recorded with **John Coltrane** (*The Avant-Garde*) in 1960. After leaving Coleman's group, Cherry went on to play with **Sonny Rollins**, **Archie Shepp**, **Steve Lacy**, and **Albert Ayler**. In Europe between 1964 and 1966, Cherry recorded his two most critically successful albums, *Complete Communion* (1965) and *Symphony for Improvisers* (1966). Thereafter, he toured Europe, Africa, and Asia and became known for incorporating non-Western musical elements into his music, writing for and performing with wood flutes, gamelan, and other non-Western instruments. Throughout the 1970s, 1980s, and into the 1990s, he would play with several groups, including Codona, Old and New Dreams (a group dedicated to playing Coleman's music), Nu, and the Multikulti orchestra and quintet. While in Spain in 1995, Cherry died from liver failure caused by hepatitis. *See also* POCKET TRUMPET.

CHIAROSCURO. A **record label** and company established in New York in 1970. During the 1970s, Chiaroscuro issued **albums** by artists including **Earl Hines**, **Mary Lou Williams**, and **Teddy Wilson** and also by some **Free Jazz** musicians. The label was active into the 1990s.

CHICAGO FOOTWARMERS. A **recording** group formed in Chicago in 1927, it also went by the names the Dixieland Thumpers and the State Street Ramblers.

CHICAGO JAZZ. A variation of New Orleans Early Jazz style created by White musicians in and around Chicago during the 1920s. Famous musicians associated with the style include **Benny Goodman**, **Gene Krupa**, **Bix Beiderbecke**, and **Frankie Trumbauer**. Chicago style was characterized by more frenetic rhythms, better instrumental technique, and a focus on the soloist. In contrast with the earlier New Orleans style, **piano** was typically used in place of **banjo**, and the upright bass in place of **tuba**.

CHILDERS, MARION "BUDDY" (1926–2007). A lead **trumpet** player, Buddy Childers got his start at age 16 playing in **Stan Kenton**'s band in 1942. He played with Kenton until 1954, also appearing with numerous other bands including those of **Woody Herman** (1949) and **Tommy Dorsey** (1951–1952). In the 1950s and 1960s, Childers worked as a freelance musician in Los Angeles and spent seven years in Las Vegas (1959–1966). In the 1970s and 1980s, Childers performed with many **big bands**, notably the **Toshiko Akiyoshi–Lew Tabackin** Big Band and **Bob Florence**'s big band. He served as Frank Sinatra Jr.'s musical director starting in 1983 and died from cancer in 2007.

CHILTON, JOHN (1932–). English jazz **trumpet** player and jazz scholar. Chilton formed his own band in 1954, joined Bruce Turner's Jump Band in 1958, and played in a few other groups before becoming musical director for George Melly in 1971. He was noted mainly for his jazz texts, including *Who's Who of Jazz: Storyville to Swing Street*, *Louis: The Louis Armstrong Story*, and biographies of **Sidney Bechet** and **Coleman Hawkins**. *See also* ENGLAND.

CHISHOLM, GEORGE (1915–1997). Scottish trombonist. He was influenced to play the **trombone** by hearing **recordings** of **Jack Teagarden**. In 1937 he played in a **jam session** in London with **Fats Waller**, **Coleman Hawkins**, and **Benny Carter** that helped to start his career. He recorded **albums** with both Carter and Waller in the late 1930s. He joined the

Squadronaires in 1939 and in 1950 was a member of the BBC Radio Show Band. In the late 1950s and 1960s he appeared on the television show *The Black and White Minstrel Show* as a musician and a comic. In the 1960s and 1970s he was a guest soloist with Alex Welsh's orchestra, and in the 1970s and 1980s he appeared with Keith Smith's Hefty Jazz and his own band, the Gentlemen of Jazz. He was awarded the Order of the British Empire (OBE) in 1984 and retired from playing in the 1990s before dying in 1997.

CHIZHIK, LEONID (1947–). A Russian pianist, Leonid Chizhik graduated from the M. I. Glinka State Conservatory in Gorky in 1970. Appearing in various trios and orchestras from the mid-1960s through the 1970s, he was the first pianist in the former Soviet Union to program complete recitals of improvised music. The founder of the Chizhik Jazz Center in Moscow in 1989, he was also director-general of the Moscow Art Center beginning in 1990. He moved to Germany in 1991 to teach piano at the Richard Strauss Konservatorium in Munich and at the Franz Liszt Music Academy in Weimar.

CHOCOLATE DANDIES. Named after a stage show by Noble Sissle and **Eubie Blake**, the Chocolate Dandies were various different **recording** groups who recorded from the late 1920s through the mid-1940s. The most well known group contained the combination of **Benny Carter** and **Coleman Hawkins** and produced some of the most important examples of the **Swing** style.

CHOICE. Record label and company founded in New York in 1972 that issued many **recordings** by solos, duo, and small groups in the **Swing** or **Bop** style. *See also* RECORD LABEL.

CHOPS. A term referring to either the actual embouchure used on a **brass** or woodwind instrument or the facial muscles used to create that embouchure. It may also be used to refer to a musician's technical proficiency, as in "He has great chops."

CHORD PROGRESSION. The harmonic movement from one chord to another, or more generally speaking, a series of chords within a song. Some chord progressions in jazz have become standard, as in the **Blues** or in a turnaround. *See also* CHANGES.

CHORD SYMBOL. The specific notation used to denote the root and quality of a chord in a song. *See also* CHANGES; CHORD PROGRESSION.

CHORUS. In jazz, this refers to performing the harmonic progression to a song once through, either with the melody being performed or with an improvised solo. It is often repeated to allow for more statements of the melody or more improvised solos.

CHRISTENSEN, JON (1943–). A Norwegian jazz percussionist who, early in his career, was the main drummer of choice for American jazz musicians visiting Norway. He went on to perform at festivals with **Dexter Gordon, Phil Woods, Sonny Stitt,** and **Sonny Rollins,** among others. In the 1970s Jon Christensen would record a number of **albums** on the **ECM** label and was central to developing the style that characterized ECM throughout the 1970s, 1980s, and 1990s, drumming in **Keith Jarrett**'s European Quartet and many other groups. *See also* EUROPE.

CHRISTIAN, CHARLIE (1916–1942). An American guitarist in the early Bebop style, Christian grew up poor in Oklahoma City. By 1937 he was experimenting with amplifying his acoustic **guitar,** and in 1939 he was discovered by talent scout John Hammond, who convinced Christian to travel to Los Angeles and audition for **Benny Goodman.** That evening at the Victor Hugo Restaurant in Beverly Hills, Goodman, initially unimpressed with Christian, called for the tune "Rose Room." When it was Christian's turn to solo, he played 25 **choruses** that electrified the audience and convinced Goodman to put him in the group. From 1939 to 1941 he played with Goodman and became an important fixture at the famous **jam sessions** held at **Minton's Playhouse,** which included **Thelonious Monk, Dizzy Gillespie, Charlie Parker,** and **Kenny Clarke.** One of the most influential guitarists in the history of jazz and popular music, Christian's style and lines were incorporated and imitated by guitarists and **Bop** musicians for years afterwards. Christian contracted tuberculosis in 1941 and died in 1942.

CHRISTLIEB, PETER (1945–). An American tenor **saxophonist,** Christlieb briefly played with **Woody Herman** in 1966 before joining **Louie Bellson** in 1967, with whom he would continue to perform for the next 20 years. He was also a member of **Doc Severinsen**'s *Tonight Show* band through 1992, in addition to playing with the bands of **Count Basie, Benny Goodman, Mel Lewis,** and **Bob Florence,** among others. He co-led a group with saxophonist **Warne Marsh,** and in 1978 their **album** *Apogee* was a critical success.

CIRCLE (I). A Free Jazz group founded in 1970 by **Chick Corea, Anthony Braxton, Dave Holland,** and **Barry Altschul.**

CIRCLE (II). A record label and company founded in 1946 with the goal of **recording** the cultural transition from African music to jazz. Several different ensembles and artists were recorded, and in addition several records by **Jelly Roll Morton** were reissued.

CIRCLE (III). A record label and company founded in Germany in 1976 that issued mainly **Free Jazz** and **Bop** records.

CIRCULAR BREATHING. A method used by wind players to continuously play without interrupting the tone to breathe. It is accomplished by breathing through the nose while using the cheeks to continue to push air through the instrument.

CLAMBAKE SEVEN. An octet formed by **Tommy Dorsey** in 1935 that served as a smaller ensemble within his **big band**. The group would perform interludes during the big band's performances and also at **jam sessions** in addition to making several **recordings**. Founded to contrast with the relatively rigid style of big band music of the time, it was an excellent solo vehicle for many of its members until it was disbanded in 1952.

CLARINET. A single-reed woodwind instrument, popular in **Early Jazz** and played by **Benny Goodman, Woody Herman,** and **Artie Shaw,** among others. *See also* BASS CLARINET; BATISTE, ALVIN; DANIELS, EDDIE; DAVERN, KENNY; DODDS, WARREN "BABY"; HUCKO, MICHAEL ANDREW "PEANUTS"; NOONE, JIMMIE; PROCOPE, RUSSELL; RUSSELL, CHARLES ELLSWORTH "PEE WEE"; SWEATMAN, WILBUR.

CLARKE, KENNY (1914–1985). American drummer who was instrumental in the **Bebop** movement. Clarke got his start playing with **Roy Eldridge** in Philadelphia, then moved to New York by way of St. Louis. While in New York he played in the house band at **Minton's Playhouse** and, along with **Thelonious Monk, Charlie Parker, Dizzy Gillespie, Charlie Christian,** and **Bud Powell,** helped lay the foundation for the Bebop style. Central to his playing were moving the time-keeping role on the drum set from the bass drum to the ride **cymbal,** which freed up the snare and bass drum to be used in his trademark "dropping **bombs,**" or adding off-beat accents. After a brief stint in the military, Clarke became a founding member of the **Milt Jackson Quartet** (the forerunner to the **Modern Jazz Quartet**) in 1951, and also made many **recordings** with **Miles Davis,** including the seminal recording *Birth of the Cool*. After his association with the Modern Jazz Quartet ended in 1955, he moved to Paris and performed with Bud Powell's trio, among many other groups. He continued to live and work in **Europe** until his death in 1985.

CLARKE, STANLEY (1951–). Settling on the **bass** guitar only after learning the accordion, **violin**, cello, and **bass**, Stanley Clarke got his first notable jazz **gigs** working first with **Horace Silver**, **Pharoah Sanders**, and **Joe Henderson** during the early 1970s. During a tour with **Stan Getz**, he founded the group **Return to Forever** with pianist **Chick Corea**. It was as a member of this group that Clarke's amazing technique on the bass guitar was recognized, and Clarke was influential in the years before the discovery of bassist **Jaco Pastorius**. After his time in Return to Forever, Clarke has moved mostly away from jazz and into the realm of commercial music.

CLARKE, TERRY (1944–). A Canadian drummer, Terry Clarke worked with various local groups and visiting American musicians until he toured the United States with **alto saxophonist John Handy** from 1965 to 1967. He spent 1967 to 1969 as a member of the Pop group the Fifth Dimension before settling in Toronto in 1970. While in Toronto he freelanced and recorded with many musicians, including **Jim Hall**, Ted Moses, Frank Rosolino, **Chet Baker**, **Blue Mitchell**, **Herb Ellis**, and **Art Pepper**; was a regular member of **Rob McConnell**'s Boss Brass; and also toured internationally with **Oscar Peterson**. In 1985 Clarke moved to New York where he continued to work with Hall, the **Toshiko Akiyoshi** Jazz Orchestra, and **Helen Merrill**, among many others.

CLARKE-BOLAND BIG BAND. Big band formed by **Kenny Clarke** and Francy Boland. The band was based mostly in Europe, **recording** its first **album** in 1961 and disbanding in 1973. *See also* EUROPE.

CLAVE. A rhythmic concept underpinning Salsa and other related jazz styles, the clave holds the rhythm together in Afro-Cuban music. *See* AFRO-CUBAN JAZZ.

CLAXTONOLA RECORDS. A record label and company founded in Iowa City, Iowa, in 1918 and active until 1925. *See also* RECORD LABEL.

CLAYTON, WILBUR DORSEY "BUCK" (1911–1991). A **trumpet** player, Buck Clayton got his start in California in 1934 when he formed a **big band** and played in Shanghai, China, for two years. Upon returning to California in 1936, he was invited to join the **Count Basie** Orchestra to replace "Hot Lips" Page and was a member of Count Basie's band until he was drafted into military service in 1943. During his time with the Basie band, he achieved notoriety for his solo work and also participated in **sessions** with **Lester Young**, **Teddy Wilson**, and **Billie Holiday**. While with Basie he also became an arranger; after his return from military service in

1946 he wrote **arrangements** for Basie, Benny Goodman, and Harry James. In the late 1940s Clayton led his own sextet on a tour through Europe, and in the mid 1950s he recorded some memorable **jam sessions** organized by John Hammond for **Columbia**, in addition to touring with **Mezz Mezzrow** and **Eddie Condon** and appearing at festivals with **Sidney Bechet**, **Coleman Hawkins**, and **J. J. Johnson**. Clayton continued to tour with Condon into the early 1960s, but by the late 1960s, lip problems interfered with his career, and despite surgery he was forced to abandon playing in favor of arranging. He briefly played again during a U.S. State Department tour from 1977 to 1979 but did not play again afterwards. In 1987 he formed his own big band that performed his compositions and arrangements and remained active with the band until a week before his death.

CLEVELAND, JIMMY (1926–2008). A trombonist, he played with his family band until he joined **Lionel Hampton**'s in 1950. After working with Hampton, he went on to play with numerous other leaders including **Dizzy Gillespie**, **Donald Byrd**, **Miles Davis**, **Gil Evans**, **James Moody**, **Gerry Mulligan**, **Oliver Nelson**, and **Wes Montgomery**, among others. After moving to Los Angeles around 1969, Cleveland worked in the band for *The Merv Griffin Show* until 1977 and recorded for **Quincy Jones**. He was one of the most recorded jazz trombonists of the 1950s and 1960s.

CLIMAX. Record label. It issued five Bill Russell/**George Lewis** recordings in 1943.

CLOONEY, ROSEMARY (1928–2002). A vocalist and actress, Rosemary Clooney started **singing** with her sister Betty, eventually landing a spot alongside Tony Pastor, touring and doing one-night shows. Eventually Rosemary would sign with **Columbia** Records in 1950 and go on to make several hits, including "Tenderly," which would later become her theme song. She also began her career as an actress in 1953. She semi-retired in the 1960s but in the 1970s restarted her career and made many popular records on the **Concord** label, many of which were tributes to songwriters including Cole Porter, Harold Arlen, Irving Berlin, and several others. She continued to perform late in her life and was awarded the Lifetime Achievement Award at the Grammys in 2002 before passing away from lung cancer later that same year.

CLOUDS OF JOY. Alternatively known as *Dark Clouds of Joy* or *Twelve Clouds of Joy*, it was a band started by Terrence Holder and later taken over by **Andy Kirk**. The group was active between 1929 and 1948.

CLUBS. Typically refers to a venue that can be a nightclub, bar, restaurant, or any other location that has music. Clubs were central to the evolution of jazz, whether as a performance space or a **jam session** location. *See also* BIRDLAND; FIVE SPOT; MINTON'S PLAYHOUSE; MONROE'S UPTOWN HOUSE; ONYX.

C-MELODY SAXOPHONE. A saxophone pitched in C; notable performers include **Frankie Trumbauer**.

COBB, JIMMY (1929–). Cobb started working locally in Washington, D.C., with **Charlie Rouse, Benny Golson, Billie Holiday**, and others before joining **Earl Bostic** in 1951. Later that year he joined **Wynton Kelly** in the trio that accompanied **Dinah Washington**, a group he would play with until 1956. In 1956 and 1957 he joined the Adderley brother's quintet, and in 1958 he and **Cannonball Adderley** joined **Miles Davis**, during which time they recorded the landmark jazz **album** *Kind of Blue* (1959). Cobb recorded during this period with artists including **John Coltrane, Kenny Dorham, Wayne Shorter, Donald Byrd, Wes Montgomery**, and various others. In 1962 he formed a trio with Wynton Kelly and **Paul Chambers** that would last until Chambers' death in 1969. Thereafter he accompanied **Sarah Vaughan** during the 1970s and appeared with **Nat Adderley** during the 1980s. During the late 1990s he formed his own group, *Jimmy Cobb's Mob*, in New York.

COBBLESTONE. A record label established in New York in 1972, it included **recordings** by artists **Sonny Stitt** and **Jimmy Heath**, among others.

COBHAM, BILLY (1944–). A percussionist born in Panama, Billy Cobham's family moved to New York when he was three years old. By the late 1960s he was playing in **sessions** and performing with **Horace Silver**, among others. In 1969 he formed the **Jazz-Rock** group *Dreams* with **Michael** and **Randy Brecker** and stayed with the group until 1971, also **recording** with **Miles Davis** during this time. After *Dreams*, Cobham joined **John McLaughlin** and his Mahavishnu Orchestra, where he achieved notoriety as a Jazz-Rock drummer.

CODONA. A **Free Jazz**/world music trio formed in 1978 by Collin Walcott, **Don Cherry**, and Naná Vasconcelos. It was active until Walcott's death in 1984.

COKER, JERRY (1932–). A saxophonist and educator, Jerry Coker left Indiana University to tour with **Woody Herman** from 1953 to 1954. He recorded briefly in Paris, in San Francisco, and also with **Mel Lewis** before moving to the West Coast and playing briefly with **Stan Kenton**. After 1960, he became known for his work as an educator and was appointed to several successive university positions and published several jazz education texts.

COLE, NAT "KING" (1919–1965). American pianist and singer, Nat "King" Cole was born in Alabama, and in 1921 his family moved to Chicago, where he learned how to play **piano** by ear from his mother. In 1936 he and his brother joined the tour of the show *Shuffle Along*; he was later stranded in Los Angeles when the show folded. In Los Angeles he formed a trio with Oscar Moore and Wesley Prince; although the members would change, his trio would stay active until 1950. The instrumentation of the trio (piano/**guitar/bass**) would inspire other pianists including **Oscar Peterson** and **Ahmad Jamal** to form similar groups. Gradually adding his vocals to his performances, and after a series of hits including "The Christmas Song" (1946) and "Nature Boy" (1948), Cole completed the transformation from jazz pianist to Pop vocalist with his **recording** of "Mona Lisa" in 1950. He would continue to release a number of successful Pop **albums** before dying from lung cancer.

COLE, RICHIE (1948–). An American alto saxophonist, Richie Cole studied with **Phil Woods** in high school and attended the Berklee College of Music. He joined **Buddy Rich** in 1969, and during the 1970s he played with several **big bands** including **Lionel Hampton**. From 1973 to 1979 he performed with vocalist **Eddie Jefferson**. During the 1980s and 1990s, Cole led his own band named Alto Madness.

COLE, WILLIAM RANDOLPH "COZY" (1909–1981). An American percussionist, in 1930 he recorded with **Jelly Roll Morton** and afterwards played in the **big bands** of Blanche Calloway, **Benny Carter**, and Willie Bryant. He spent 1936 to 1938 with the **Onyx** Club band led by **Stuff Smith** and achieved notoriety as a soloist during a four-year stint with **Cab Calloway** from 1938 to 1942. He studied at Juilliard in the mid-1940s and performed in various groups in the 1940s until replacing **Sid Catlett** in **Louis Armstrong**'s All Stars from 1949 to 1953. In 1954 he opened a drum school with **Gene Krupa**, and during the 1950s he appeared in a number of films. In the late 1950s his **recording** of "Topsy" with **Jack Teagarden** and **Earl Hines** was a surprise Top 40 hit. During the 1960s and 1970s, Cole toured and freelanced before passing away from cancer in 1981.

COLEMAN, EARL (1925–1995). A singer, Earl Coleman started with Billy McShann and **Earl Hines** before he recorded his hit "This Is Always" with **Charlie Parker** in 1947. He would go on to record with notable jazz musicians including **Fats Navarro, Max Roach, Art Farmer**, and **Sonny Rollins**, among others, in addition to a few records later in his life as a leader.

COLEMAN, GEORGE (1935–). Coleman taught himself to play alto saxophone in his teenage years. In the early 1950s he played with B. B. King, and by 1955 he had switched to playing tenor saxophone. In 1958 he joined **Max Roach**'s quintet, and in 1960 he joined **Slide Hampton**'s octet, **recording** with **Lee Morgan, Booker Little**, and others. From 1963 to 1964 he performed with **Miles Davis**; in 1964 he left the group to play with **Elvin Jones**. He also played with **Herbie Hancock** on his **album** *Maiden Voyage* in 1965. Since the 1970s, Coleman has led his own various small groups.

COLEMAN, ORNETTE (1930–). An alto saxophonist, Coleman was instrumental in the development of **Avant-Garde** Jazz. Ornette Coleman's initial influence was **Charlie Parker**. He played with several **Rhythm and Blues (R&B)** bands before a tour with Pee Wee Crayton led him to Los Angeles in 1950. In Los Angeles, Coleman took a job as an elevator operator and studied music theory and harmony textbooks, developing many of the theories and concepts that would later prove controversial. Having difficulty finding people with whom to perform, he was finally discovered by **Red Mitchell** and **Percy Heath**. At the behest of **John Lewis**, Coleman and **Don Cherry** attended the Lenox School of Jazz in 1959, and Coleman's quartet (which included Cherry, **Charlie Haden**, and **Billy Higgins**) began an extended appearance at the **Five Spot** Café in New York. It was during this time at the Five Spot that Coleman recorded some of his most influential **albums**, including *The Shape of Jazz to Come* and *Free Jazz*. These albums, in particular *Free Jazz*, were highly influential in the Avant-Garde movement, but also extremely controversial. Coleman retired in 1962 but returned in 1965 after teaching himself to play the **trumpet** and **violin**. By the end of the 1960s, Coleman was again playing with Cherry, Haden, and other previous band members. In the mid-1970s, Coleman formed the group Prime Time and codified his personal music theory as "harmolodics"—equality of harmony, melody, and rhythm. In 2007 he was awarded both the Pulitzer Prize and the Grammy Lifetime Achievement Award.

COLEMAN, WILLIAM JOHNSON "BILL" (1904–1981). Originally a **clarinet** and **saxophone** player, Bill Coleman switched to the **trumpet** after hearing **Louis Armstrong**. In the 1920s and 1930s Coleman played in various bands, getting his **recording** debut with Lloyd and Cecil Scott in 1927. Coleman recorded with **Fats Waller** while in Teddy Hill's band from 1934 to 1935 and thereafter moved to Paris where he toured with Willie Lewis and performed with his own groups. He returned to New York in 1940 and played with various bands including **Benny Carter, Teddy Wilson, Andy Kirk,** and others, and he recorded with both **Lester Young** and **Coleman Hawkins** in 1943. In 1948 Coleman moved permanently back to France and toured and recorded there for the rest of his life. *See also* FRANCE.

COLLECTIVE IMPROVISATION. A form of **improvisation** where some or all members of the group improvise at the same time and no one voice is more important than another.

COLLETTE, WILLIAM MARCEL "BUDDY" (1921–2010). He began playing the saxophone at the age of 12, but he learned to play other wood-wind instruments and is most known for his **flute** playing. Collette toured with several **big bands** during the early 1940s and led a dance band while serving in the navy during World War II. After he was discharged from the navy, he played with several more bands, including the Stars of Swing and **Benny Carter**. He also worked and recorded with **Charles Mingus**, of whom he was an early teacher. Collette came to prominence in 1955–1956 for his flute playing with **Chico Hamilton**'s quintet. Afterwards he went on to record under his own name and also with **Red Callender, Louie Bellson,** and many others. During the 1960s Collette turned to writing and film scoring, which he continued throughout the 1970s and 1980s, interspersed with appearances with **Thelonious Monk** (1964) and Benny Carter (1978). Collette also founded the record company Legend in 1973. Known also as a teacher, in 1994 he released *A Jazz Audio Biography* and in 2000 published his autobiography *Jazz Generations: A Life in American Music and Society.*

COLLIER, (JAMES) GRAHAM (1937–2011). English bassist, **trumpet** player, and composer. Graham Collier started playing in an army band in 1954, and in 1961 he attended the **Berklee School of Music** where he was the first British student to graduate. After a brief stint as the bassist in the **Tommy Dorsey** Orchestra in 1963, Collier moved to England and formed his own band. The band, Graham Collier Music, performed Collier's own music and contained notable British jazz musicians, including **Kenny Wheeler** and **Mike Gibbs,** among others. Collier would continue to lead his own bands throughout the 1980s and also formed his own record label, **Mosaic** (a different label from the American company). Collier was awarded the Order of the British Empire (OBE) in 1987, and he continued to write music for television, film, the stage, and radio. *See also* ENGLAND; RECORD LABEL.

COLORADO JAZZ PARTY. An annual jazz festival and series of **jam sessions** held in Colorado from 1963 to 1993. Presented by Dick Gibson, the event featured world-class musicians performing together in various combinations. It was also known as the Gibson Jazz Party.

COLTRANE, ALICE (1937–2007). A pianist, Alice Coltrane studied jazz with **Bud Powell** in Paris in 1959. While on tour with Terry Gibbs from 1962 to 1963 she met **John Coltrane**, whom she married in 1965 and with whom she had three children. She replaced **McCoy Tyner** in Coltrane's group in 1966 and played with the band until Coltrane's death in 1967. Following John Coltrane's death, from 1967 to 1972 Alice Coltrane led many groups that included musicians **Pharoah Sanders, Joe Henderson,** and **Roy Haynes,** among others. In 1972 she moved to California and became involved with spiritual and religious concerns, performing less regularly. In 1987 she performed a tribute to John Coltrane with her sons Ravi Coltrane and Oran Coltrane.

COLTRANE, JOHN (1926–1967). Next to **Charlie Parker,** there is no more influential or imitated jazz saxophonist than John Coltrane; next to **Miles Davis,** there is perhaps no more influential figure in jazz. Around the age of 15, Coltrane began playing the alto saxophone, and from 1945 to 1946 he toured with a navy band, followed by tours with King Kolax and Eddie "Cleanhead" Vinson. He recorded with **Dizzy Gillespie** in 1949, playing with his **big band** from 1949 to 1950 and his sextet from 1950 to 1951. Thereafter he played with **Earl Bostic** (1952) and **Johnny Hodges** (1953–1954), during which time he switched permanently to the tenor saxophone.

After spending two weeks with **Jimmy Smith,** Coltrane received and accepted Miles Davis' offer to replace **Sonny Rollins** in his quintet. Coltrane would be in Davis' group on and off until 1960, famously fired in 1957 due to his drug addiction but rehired after kicking his habit in 1958. During this time Coltrane participated in several of Davis' most famous **recordings,** including *Kind of Blue* and *Milestones*; released some of his own recordings as a leader, including *Blue Train* and *Giant Steps*; and had a much celebrated stint with **Thelonious Monk** in 1957.

In 1960, Coltrane left Davis' group and formed his own quartet with **McCoy Tyner, Elvin Jones, Reggie Workman** (until 1961), and then **Jimmy Garrison** on bass. During this time, Coltrane produced many of his finest recordings, notably "My Favorite Things" in 1960, on which Coltrane plays the soprano saxophone, and *A Love Supreme* in 1964, which contained the spiritual message that framed the latter years of his life. As Coltrane ventured deeper into the Avant-Garde during 1965 and 1966, the quartet changed members, adding **Pharoah Sanders**, **Alice Coltrane**, and **Rashied Ali** while losing Tyner and Jones. Coltrane died of liver cancer at the relatively young age of 40.

COLUMBIA. Probably the oldest and longest-lasting name of any **record label**, Columbia's roots extend back as far as the late 1880s, when it was created as a subsidiary of the American Graphophone Company in Washington, D.C. During the 1910s through the 1930s, the Columbia catalog included many noted jazz artists, including the **Original Dixieland Jazz Band**, **Bessie Smith**, **King Oliver**, **Paul Whiteman**, **Jack Teagarden**, **Louis Armstrong**, **Fletcher Henderson**, **Duke Ellington**, and **Benny Goodman**. In 1938, the label was purchased by the **Columbia Broadcasting System (CBS)**. During the 1940s, CBS also counted several **dance bands** among its artists, including the bands of **Woody Herman** and **Count Basie**, and also other artists including **Billie Holiday**. The label signed and recorded a tremendous amount of Rock and Roll and popular music artists throughout the last half of the century but still served as a home for many famous jazz artists including **Miles Davis**, **Thelonious Monk**, and **Wynton Marsalis**. Columbia was purchased by Sony in 1987 but remains active today. *See also* EPIC.

COLUMBIA BROADCASTING SYSTEM (CBS). Record label and company. *See also* COLUMBIA; ELECTRICAL AND MUSICAL INDUSTRIES (EMI).

COMBO. A term that refers to a small jazz ensemble or music group, it is a shortened form of the word *combination*. The term most often applies to a jazz group with more than four members, but less than a traditional **big band**.

COMMODORE. An American record label and company established in 1938 in New York. Artists included **Coleman Hawkins**, **Billie Holiday**, and **Jelly Roll Morton**. *See also* RECORD LABEL.

COMPING. A term used to refer to the harmonic and/or rhythmic accompaniment provided by ensemble members (typically piano, guitar, bass, and drum set) for soloists. The term is short for *accompaniment* or *complement*.

CONCORD. An American record label and company established in 1973 in Concord, California. Artists included older **Swing** musicians such as **Warren Vaché** and Scott Hamilton. *See also* RECORD LABEL.

CONGA. An Afro-Cuban drum with a barrel-shaped shell, played by striking the head with the fingers or the open palm. **Chano Pozo**, playing with **Dizzy**

Gillespie in the late 1940s, was instrumental in introducing the conga to jazz music. *See also* AFRO-CUBAN JAZZ; CLAVE.

CONNIFF, RAY (1916–2002). A trombonist, Ray Conniff played with various dance bands in the 1930s and 1940s including the bands of **Artie Shaw** and Harry James. In the late 1950s Conniff gave up the trombone for arranging. His group, the Ray Conniff Singers, was very successful during the later 1950s and the 1960s.

CONQUEROR. Record label, it began issuing records in 1928 and was discontinued in 1942.

CONTACT. Record label and company founded in 1964 in New York. It released material by artists including **Coleman Hawkins** and **Lester Young**. *See also* RECORD LABEL.

CONTEMPORARY. A record label and company founded in 1951 in Los Angeles by Lester Koenig. Artists included **Art Pepper, Chet Baker, Ornette Coleman, Harold Land, Art Farmer, Sonny Rollins, Cecil Taylor**, and many others.

CONTINENTAL. A record label and company founded in the mid-1940s. Artists included **Cozy Cole** and **Mary Lou Williams**. *See also* RECORD LABEL.

CONTINUUM. A quintet that included **Slide Hampton, Jimmy Heath, Kenny Barron, Ron Carter**, and **Art Taylor**, formed in the late 1970s to play the music of **Tadd Dameron**.

COOK, HERMAN "JUNIOR" (1934–1992). A tenor saxophonist, Junior Cook worked with **Dizzy Gillespie** in 1958 before joining **Horace Silver**'s quintet from 1959 to 1964. Cook and **Blue Mitchell** both left Silver's quintet in 1964 and played together from 1964 to 1969. After teaching at the **Berklee College of Music** he would go on to work with **Freddie Hubbard** from 1973 to 1975 and Louis Hayes from 1975 to 1976. In the 1980s Cook played with **Clifford Jordan** and the **McCoy Tyner big band**, among others. *See also* TENOR SAXOPHONE.

COOL JAZZ. A variation and reaction to the **Bebop** style of the 1940s, Cool Jazz was an attempt to tone down some of the harsher aspects of Bop. Often interchanged with the term **West Coast Jazz**, Cool Jazz emphasized **arrangements** and often demonstrated softer dynamics and articulations using less extremes of register. **Miles Davis' album** *Birth of the Cool* is an oft-cited example. Notable artists associated with Cool Jazz styles include **Gerry Mulligan, Chet Baker**, and **Lee Konitz**. *See also* LIGHTHOUSE CAFÉ.

COPELAND, RAY (1926–1984). Originally a Classical **trumpet** player, Ray Copeland switched to jazz and played with several bands in Manhattan and Brooklyn throughout the late 1940s, including Cecil Scott and **Mercer Ellington**. In the late 1950s, he settled in New York and would work with **Ella Fitzgerald** (1965) and tour with **Thelonious Monk** (1967). During the 1970s he became active as a composer and a jazz educator.

COREA, ARMANDO ANTHONY "CHICK" (1941–). A jazz pianist, Chick Corea got his start playing in several **Latin** bands before joining **Blue Mitchell** in 1964 and later **Stan Getz** in 1967. In 1968, Corea joined **Miles Davis'** band and recorded with Davis on his first **Fusion albums**. Corea and **Dave Holland** left Davis' group in 1970 and formed their own group, **Circle**, with **Barry Altschul** and **Anthony Braxton**, and the group was active into 1971 when Corea founded his band **Return to Forever**. He would re-form the band several more times, and the band would stay active until 1980. During the 1980s, Corea played with his Akoustic Band and his Elektric Band, and during the 1990s and into the 2000s Corea remained an active performer. Several of his compositions, including "Windows" and "Spain," among others, have reached the status of jazz standards.

CORNET. A **brass** instrument with three valves, the cornet was also a predecessor of the modern **trumpet**. The cornet is more conical in construction than the trumpet, and the instrument produces a warmer, darker sound. Many early jazz artists played the cornet, including **Buddy Bolden, Bix Beiderbecke**, and **Louis Armstrong**, who switched to the trumpet in the early 1930s. Eventually improvements in the trumpet helped it surpass the cornet as the more popular instrument of the two. *See also* HANDY, W(ILLIAM) C(HRISTOPHER); OLIVER, JOE; PETIT, BUDDY; SPANIER, MUGGSY; STEWART, REX.

CORYELL, LARRY (1943–). A guitarist originally influenced by Jimi Hendrix and Eric Clapton, Larry Coryell moved to New York in 1965 to pursue a career as a musician and began playing with **Chico Hamilton** and then Free Spirits. After spending time with **Gary Burton** from 1967 to 1968 and **Herbie Mann** in 1968, Coryell formed the group Foreplay in 1969. He performed with this group until 1973 when he formed the **Jazz-Rock**

band Eleventh House with **Randy Brecker**. During the late 1970s, Coryell switched to acoustic guitar and played in many small groups, and also recorded with **Charles Mingus** and **Sonny Rollins**. After a brief hiatus in the early 1980s to deal with alcoholism and drug addiction, in the mid-1980s he was touring with **John McLaughlin** and playing electric guitar again. In the 1990s, Coryell freelanced and led his own groups and continued to record.

COTTON CLUB. A famous nightclub in Harlem, it was notable for showcasing stage shows, bands, and dancers for a White-only clientele. The **Duke Ellington** Orchestra became known through its involvement from 1927 to 1931 as the house band and through radio broadcasts. The bands of both **Fletcher Henderson** and **Cab Calloway** preceded and followed (respectively) Ellington's as house bands. Numerous celebrities, primarily Caucasian, frequented the establishment. *See also* MILLS BLUE RHYTHM BAND.

COUNTSMEN. A name given to several bands in the 1970s and 1980s whose members were former members of the **Count Basie** Orchestra and performed Basie's repertoire.

COURBOIS, PIERRE (1940–). A Dutch percussionist, Pierre Courbois started playing jazz with a **Dixieland** group in Arnhem in the mid-1950s. Throughout the 1960s he played with several groups including the Original Dutch Free Jazz Group and the Free Music Quartet. From 1970 to 1975, Courbois led a **Free Jazz** group called Association PC, and after playing with several other groups, he formed New Association PC in 1984. In 1991 he formed Jubilation PC and in the late 1990s the Pierre Courbois Quintet. *See also* EUROPE.

COVINGTON, WARREN (1921–1999). A trombonist who got his start playing with Isham Jones in 1939, then later worked with Les Brown in 1945 and **Gene Krupa** in 1946. In 1950 he played with **Tommy Dorsey** and took over Dorsey's band following his death in 1958. He toured with the band from 1961 through the 1970s in addition to playing in several studio **big bands** and orchestras.

COWELL, STANLEY (1941–). A pianist, Stanley Cowell moved to New York in 1966 and played with **Max Roach** (1967–1970) and then with the **Bobby Hutcherson–Harold Land** Quintet (1968–1971). In the 1970s he and **Charles Tolliver** co-founded the **record label** Strata-East. During the mid-1970s and 1980s, Cowell performed with the Heath brothers and with **Larry Coryell**. He is currently active as a jazz educator.

CRANE RIVER JAZZ BAND. A jazz band formed in England in 1949. *See also* ENGLAND.

CRANSHAW, BOB (1932–). A **bass** player, Bob Cranshaw was a founding member of **Walter Perkins'** MJT+3 in 1957. In 1960 he moved to New York and by 1962 he began playing with **Sonny Rollins**, with whom Cranshaw would continue to perform throughout the 1990s. In addition to his work with Rollins, Cranshaw has played with any number of famous jazz musicians including **McCoy Tyner, Thelonious Monk, Horace Silver, Lee Morgan, Johnny Hodges, Coleman Hawkins, James Moody,** and **Wes Montgomery,** among many others.

CRAWFORD, HANK (1934–2009). A saxophonist, Hank Crawford began playing in Memphis with artists including B. B. King and Ike Turner in the early 1950s. In 1958 he joined **Ray Charles,** and by 1961 he became the musical director of the group. After leaving Charles' group in 1963, Crawford would record many **Soul Jazz albums** and continue to play in that trademark style for the remainder of his life. *See also* SAXOPHONE.

CREOLE. A **record label** that reissued many early jazz records in the 1950s.

CREOLE BAND. Popular name for many early jazz bands, referencing people of racially mixed backgrounds, typically including French, Spanish, or African.

CRESCENT. Record label that issued **recordings** by **Kid Ory**'s Creole Jazz Band in the mid-1940s.

CRESCENT CITY JAZZERS. A jazz band made up of New Orleans musicians that performed during the 1920s at the Arcadia Ballroom in St. Louis, later changing their name to the **Arcadian Serenaders.** *See also* EARLY JAZZ.

CRISS, WILLIAM "SONNY" (1927–1977). An **alto saxophonist,** Sonny Criss was influenced early on by **Charlie Parker,** with whom he played in 1946 and again in 1948. In the early 1950s, Criss toured with **Jazz at the Philharmonic** and in the mid-1950s he played with **Buddy Rich**'s quintet and led his own groups. Criss moved to **Europe** in 1961 but returned to Los Angeles in 1966 and recorded many **albums.** In 1973 and 1974, Criss toured Europe again, but in 1977 he contracted stomach cancer and committed suicide.

CRISS CROSS JAZZ. Record label and company founded in 1981 in the Netherlands that focuses on **albums** by younger, Bop-oriented jazz musicians. Artists include John Swana, Chris Potter, Seamus Blake, and Mark Turner, among numerous others. *See also* RECORD LABEL.

CROSBY, HARRY LILLIS "BING" (1903–1977). A singer and actor, Bing Crosby was one of the most popular entertainers of the 20th century. He got his start **singing** jazz in 1926 with **Paul Whiteman**, with whom he performed until 1930, when Crosby began his solo career. During the 1930s and into the 1940s, Crosby's career reached near stratospheric levels thanks to radio and film. His most memorable contributions to jazz include partnerships with **Louis Armstrong** and **Johnny Mercer**. Easily the most popular singer of the first half of the 20th century, Crosby's career declined in the 1960s, and he died in Spain while playing golf.

CROUCH, STANLEY (1945–). Originally a drummer, Stanley Crouch began performing **Free Jazz** in 1967 with various groups, performing alongside members that included **Arthur Blythe** and **David Murray**. After moving to New York in 1975, Crouch began a career as a writer and jazz critic, writing for the *Soho Weekly News* and the *Village Voice*. Crouch was also a mentor and advocate of **Wynton Marsalis**.

CRUSADERS. Originally the Modern Jazz Sextet and founded in the 1950s by Wilton Felder, **Joe Sample**, Stix Hooper, Wayne Henderson, and two other musicians, the group moved to Los Angeles and changed their name to the Jazz Crusaders. They made several **Soul Jazz albums** and in 1970 shortened their name to the Crusaders and changed styles to Jazz **Funk**. Henderson would leave the band in 1975, and after the success of their album *Street Life* in 1979, the Crusaders began using vocalists. In 1983, Hooper also left the band, and after 1991 the group completely disbanded. In the mid-1990s the group would reunite again, and various disagreements resulted in there now being two groups—the Crusaders and the Jazz Crusaders featuring Wayne Henderson. *See also* JAZZ CRUSADERS.

CUBER, RONNIE (1941–). Starting on the clarinet at age nine, switching to the **tenor saxophone** and then settling on the **baritone saxophone** his senior year in high school, Ronnie Cuber followed up his appearance at the **Newport Jazz Festival** in 1959 with stints with **Slide Hampton** (1962) and **Maynard Ferguson** (1963–1965). He joined the **George Benson** quartet in 1966, followed by some time with **Lionel Hampton** and then **Woody Herman**. In the late 1960s and early 1970s, Cuber performed with a variety of **Latin** groups and Rock and Soul artists, including Aretha Franklin and Eddie Palmieri. During the 1970s he also started leading his own groups, and he would record with many notable Rock musicians through the mid-1980s including Steely Dan, Billy Joel, Eric Clapton, and others. In the mid-1980s, Cuber joined the NBC *Saturday Night Live* band and continued to lead and record his own groups, and in the 1990s he performed and arranged for the **Mingus** Big Band.

CUBOP. *See* AFRO-CUBAN JAZZ.

CUICA. A Brazilian drum.

CUP MUTE. *See* MUTE.

CUPOL. A **record label** founded in 1947 in Sweden that became a part of the **Columbia Broadcasting System (CBS)** in 1970.

CUT. A term with several meanings, it can refer to a record, a **recording**, or a specific track on a record; to the editing process of a recording; or to one soloist outperforming another soloist.

CUTTING CONTEST. A contest between improvisers, a cutting contest can take place during a performance, a **recording**, or a **jam session**. It can also refer to a **battle of bands**, in which two or more bands alternate performing pieces until a "winner," as determined by those dancers and enthusiasts in attendance, is decided. *See also* IMPROVISATION.

CYMBAL(S). Modern cymbals are circular, concave metal discs, and in jazz they are usually placed on stands around and as part of a **drum set**. Jazz drummers may use any variety of cymbals, but most often they make use of the hi-hat (two cymbals that are operated by a foot pedal), the ride cymbal (generally used to keep time), and the crash cymbal (used to provide extra accent for specific notes). The ride cymbal is generally responsible for maintaining the "**Swing**" pattern and can come in a variety of sizes. The pattern played on a cymbal is sometimes also referred to as the ride pattern due to its ride cymbal roots.

Additionally, there are lesser-used cymbals that players may use for extra effect. A China cymbal is a full-sized cymbal but with the edges turned up and a shallower, raised cup in the middle. The sound produced slightly resembles a high-pitched gong. The zinger cymbal, rarely used in modern times, is a much smaller cymbal that is attached to the bass drum. This cymbal is simultaneously played with the same beater (or mallet) that strikes the bass drum, therefore striking the two instruments at the same time. A cymbal used extensively during the 1920s is the Charleston cymbal, 25 centimeters in diameter and often containing a large cup or bell.

D

DAFFODIL. A record label and company founded in 1973 by **Blossom Dearie**, it remains active today. *See also* RECORD LABEL.

DAMERON, TADLEY EWING "TADD" (1917–1965). A pianist, composer, and arranger, Tadd Dameron played in a few **territory bands** before he landed with Harlan Leonard in 1939, for whose band he penned "Dameron Stomp" and "A La Bridges." He then went on to write for **Jimmie Lunceford, Coleman Hawkins, Count Basie, Billy Eckstine,** and **Sarah Vaughan**, among others, in addition to sitting in on sessions with **Dizzy Gillespie** and **Charlie Parker**. From 1945 to 1947, he wrote **arrangements** for Gillespie's **big band**, and in 1948 he led his own group with **Fats Navarro** and appeared with **Miles Davis**. During the early 1950s he worked with **Clifford Brown** but was sidelined by problems with drugs, which would eventually result in his arrest in 1958. After his release from jail, Dameron continued to write for artists including **Sonny Stitt, Blue Mitchell, Milt Jackson,** and **Benny Goodman**. Many of Dameron's compositions are considered jazz standards, including "Good Bait," "Our Delight," and "Hot House." *See also* DAMERONIA.

DAMERONIA. A group formed in 1982 and led by **Philly Joe Jones** that was dedicated to the music of **Tadd Dameron**. After Jones' death in 1985, the group was led by Don Sickler.

DANCE BAND. The name for bands whose repertoire was primarily dance music; many were active from the late 1910s through the 1940s.

DANIELS, EDDIE (1941–). Originally a tenor and **alto saxophone** player, Eddie Daniels has since become one of the premiere jazz **clarinet** players in the world. After performing at the **Newport Jazz Festival** in 1957, Daniels graduated from Brooklyn College in 1963 and Juilliard in 1966. During his time at the Juilliard School of Music, Daniels was a founding member of the **Thad Jones–Mel Lewis** Orchestra, a group with which he would perform for the next six years. During the 1970s, Daniels played with **Freddie Hubbard,**

Sonny Rollins, Don Patterson, and others, in addition to **recording** under his own name. In 1984 his **album** *Breakthrough* for clarinet and orchestra was a successful foray into **Third Stream** music, and in the 1990s Daniels resumed playing tenor saxophone and led his own quartet.

DANISH RADIO BIG BAND. A Danish **big band** founded in 1964. Led by artists including Ray Pitts, Palle Mikkelborg, and by **Thad Jones** from 1977 to 1978, the band has had several international conductors, including **Stan Kenton**, Frank Foster, **Oliver Nelson**, **Dizzy Gillespie**, **Bob Brookmeyer**, and **Maria Schneider**, among others.

DANISH RADIO JAZZ GROUP. A Danish **big band** founded in 1961, starting as a nine-piece ensemble, it was led by Erik Moseholm, Ray Pitts, and Palle Mikkelborg, among others. The group disbanded in 1986.

DANKWORTH, JOHN (1927–2010). After switching from the **violin** to the **clarinet** to play jazz in a local jazz band, John Dankworth switched to the **alto saxophone** after being strongly influenced by **Charlie Parker**. Dankworth worked on several transatlantic ocean liners in the late 1940s in order to hear jazz in New York, and he became a fixture of the London **Bebop** scene. At the end of 1949 he formed the Johnny Dankworth Seven and three years later founded his own **big band**, performing his own **arrangements** and composi- tions. His band achieved success on the Pop charts with singer **Cleo Laine** (whom he later married) and contained many notable British jazz musicians including **Kenny Wheeler**, Don Rendell, Danny Moss, and Dudley Moore. In the 1960s, Dankworth continued to lead small groups and big bands, and in 1971 he became the musical director for Laine. During the 1980s he led a touring quintet and worked as a guest conductor with several pops orchestras. In 1974, Dankworth was awarded the CBE (commander, Order of the British Empire), and in 2006 he was knighted. *See also* ENGLAND.

DARK CLOUDS OF JOY. The name of two separate Kansas City jazz bands both founded by Terrence Holder, one in 1926 and one in 1929.

DAUNTLESS RECORDS. A **record label** established in the 1960s. Artists included Steve Kuhn and **Toshiko Akiyoshi**.

DAVERN, KENNY (1935–2006). Starting his professional career at the age of 16, by 1954 Kenny Davern was playing **clarinet** with **Jack Teagarden** and Phil Napoleon. In the 1960s, Davern led his own groups, played with the **Dukes of Dixieland** (1962–1963), and also played with **Ruby Braff**, among others. In 1974 he switched from clarinet to **soprano saxophone** and founded the group Soprano Summit with Bob Wilber. That collaboration would last until 1979, and in the early 1980s he founded the Blue Three and switched back to clarinet. Throughout the 1990s, Davern toured and recorded, even reuniting with Wilber in a group named Soprano Reunion.

DAVIS, ARTHUR (1934–2007). Starting first on the **piano** and then the **tuba** (for which he won a national competition), Art Davis switched to the **bass** in 1951. He performed with **Max Roach** and **Dizzy Gillespie** and then had several stints with **John Coltrane**, including **recordings** in 1961 and 1965. During the early 1960s, Davis played with numerous musicians, including **Booker Little, Freddie Hubbard, Clark Terry, Oliver Nelson, Ornette Coleman, Art Blakey, Erroll Garner, Clifford Jordan, McCoy Tyner, Count Basie**, Lena Horne, and countless others. He spent the mid-1960s as a member of several television orchestras, and from 1971 to 1973 he taught at Manhattan Community College before playing with **Thelonious Monk** for a short while. Thereafter, Davis began work on a career in psychology, getting his B.A. from Hunter College in 1973, his M.A. in music in psychology from New York University in 1976, and a Ph.D. in clinical psychology from New York University in 1981. He continued to play music while pursuing his career as a psychologist, participating in many small groups and duos. During the 1990s, Davis played in a quartet with **Herbie Hancock, Marvin "Smitty" Smith**, and Ravi Coltrane. His book *The Arthur Davis Method for Double Bass* (1975) is a popular instructional double bass text.

DAVIS, EDDIE "LOCKJAW" (1922–1986). A self-taught tenor saxophonist, Eddie Davis got his start working in the **big bands** of **Cootie Williams** and Lucky Millinder; after four months with **Louis Armstrong** in 1945, Davis joined the band of **Andy Kirk**, and it was from a title of one of the **recordings** with that band that Davis garnered the nickname "Lockjaw." During 1947–1952, Davis directed **jam sessions** at **Minton's Playhouse** in New York, and in 1952 Davis began working with **Count Basie**, a relationship that would extend through the 1970s. During the mid to late 1970s, Davis co-led a group with **Harry "Sweets" Edison**.

DAVIS, MILES DEWEY (1926–1991). Perhaps the most iconic figure in jazz history, Miles Davis' journey to musical greatness began when his father gave him a **trumpet** at the age of 13. By 1944, Davis moved to New York to study music at Juilliard. His studies were short-lived, and by the end of 1945 he was playing regularly with **Charlie Parker**. By the end of the 1940s,

Davis had played with **Dizzy Gillespie, Benny Carter, Coleman Hawkins, Max Roach**, and many other notable musicians.

In 1949, Davis began what would be a lifelong obsession with musical innovation and change when he and **Gil Evans** collaborated to record the tracks that would later be released as the landmark **album** *Birth of the Cool* and spearhead the **Cool Jazz** style. Davis' burgeoning heroin addiction slowed his career considerably in the early 1950s, but a performance in 1955 at the **Newport Jazz Festival** revived sufficient interest in Davis for him to form his own quintet with Red Garland, **Paul Chambers, Philly Joe Jones**, and **John Coltrane**. Adding **Cannonball Adderley** to the group, Davis recorded *Milestones* in 1958, and his sextet of **Bill Evans, Jimmy Cobb**, Adderley, Coltrane, and Chambers recorded the album *Kind of Blue* in 1959 and introduced **Modal Jazz**. *Kind of Blue* is Davis' best-selling album and is widely regarded as one of the greatest jazz albums ever recorded.

From 1957 to 1960, he continued collaborating with Evans and recorded yet more landmark albums—*Miles Ahead, Porgy and Bess*, and *Sketches of Spain*. Davis formed a second quintet in 1963 with **Herbie Hancock, Ron Carter, Tony Williams**, and a succession of tenor players including **Hank Mobley** and **George Coleman** before **Wayne Shorter** got the job in 1964. This group recorded several more landmark jazz albums including *E.S.P.* and *Miles Smiles*, but by 1968 Davis' attention turned to Rock and Jazz **Fusion**. His albums *In a Silent Way* and *Bitches Brew* were some of the first forays in this genre, which Davis would continue to explore until his retirement in 1975 after a series of personal problems. His health declined due to complications from sickle cell anemia and casual drug use, but in 1981 he returned to music with several new groups and made inroads in **Funk** and Pop music. Two months after a performance of Gil Evans' old **arrangements** at the **Montreux Jazz Festival** in 1991, Davis died due to complications from a stroke.

Davis' skills in developing talent were unparalleled, and a complete list of his sidemen would include many of the best jazz musicians of the last half of the 20th century. In addition to the above-mentioned names, Davis' sidemen included **Wynton Kelly, Chick Corea, Jack DeJohnette, Dave Holland, John McLaughlin, John Scofield, Dave Liebman, Branford Marsalis**, and many, many others. Davis' restless nature meant that he was at the forefront of every innovation in jazz since the 1940s, starting with **Bebop, Cool Jazz, Modal Jazz**, dabbling in the **Avant-Garde, Fusion**, and even Pop. His influence on jazz is immeasurable and is not likely to diminish.

DAVIS, RICHARD (1930–). A Classical and jazz bassist, Richard Davis started in Chicago playing with **Ahmad Jamal** (1953–1954) and then moved to New York while playing with pianist Don Shirley (1954–1956). He toured extensively with **Sarah Vaughan** (1957–1963), and during this time he also joined the **Eric Dolphy–Booker Little** Quintet. Throughout the 1960s he would perform with a variety of other jazz artists, including **Stan Getz, Joe Henderson, Kenny Dorham,** Frank Foster, **Earl Hines,** and **Eddie Daniels,** and he was a founding member of the **Thad Jones–Mel Lewis** Orchestra, with whom he performed from 1966 to 1972. Davis left New York in 1977 to teach at the University of Wisconsin and settled permanently in Madison, Wisconsin. He has continued to tour with various musicians including Jon Faddis, **McCoy Tyner,** Cecil Bridgewater, and others throughout the 1980s and 1990s.

DAVIS, WILLIAM STRETHEN "WILD BILL" (1918–1995). Originally an arranger and a guitarist, Wild Bill Davis played and arranged for Milt Larkin, **Earl Hines,** and **Louis Jordan** from the late 1930s through the 1940s. After playing the piano with Jordan, Davis started playing the **Hammond organ** first as a soloist and then as a leader of his own group. His most successful **arrangement** was "April in Paris," which he arranged for **Count Basie** in 1955. During the 1960s, Davis worked with **Johnny Hodges** and **Ella Fitzgerald,** and in 1969 he joined **Duke Ellington,** also serving as arranger. In the 1970s he worked with various groups including **Lionel Hampton,** and in the 1980s he continued to tour Europe and the United States, performing into the 1990s.

DAVISON, "WILD" BILL (1906–1989). A **cornet** player, Wild Bill Davison worked with various local bands in Chicago before a tragic traffic accident in 1931. As a result of the traffic accident, Frank Teschemacher, a fellow Chicago musician, was killed, and Davis moved to Milwaukee. He would stay in Milwaukee until 1940, when he moved to New York after his career gained momentum through the release of a few **recordings.** While in New York, Davis recorded under his own name and played with **Eddie Condon** starting in 1945; he would continue to play with Condon intermittently until the 1960s. Also in the 1940s, Davison recorded with **Sidney Bechet.** In 1960, Davison moved to the western coast of the United States and appeared at various jazz festivals, including the annual **Colorado Jazz Party,** and he would continue to tour and perform either solo or with various groups until a few weeks before his death.

DAWSON, ALAN (1929–1996). A **drummer,** Alan Dawson played with a few local bands before joining **Lionel Hampton**'s band and touring **Europe** in 1953. Dawson returned to Boston and played with pianist Sabby Lewis (with whom he had played before), and in 1957 he got a job teaching at the **Berklee School of Music**, where he would teach until 1975. Among some of his more noteworthy students are **Tony Williams**, Clifford Jarvis, Harvey Mason, and **Joe LaBarbera**. During this time he stayed in Boston and performed locally and also for jazz musicians passing through, including **Roy Eldridge**, **Phil Woods**, **Coleman Hawkins**, and **Sonny Stitt**, among others. During the 1960s he performed and recorded with Jaki Byard and Booker Ervin, a collaboration that resulted in several well-received **albums**. In 1968, Dawson joined the **Dave Brubeck** Quartet and performed with them until 1976. He also performed annually at the **Colorado Jazz Party** beginning in the 1960s and into the 1980s. Dawson continued to teach privately after leaving Berklee and was still **recording** into the mid-1990s.

DE ANDRADE, DJALMA (1923–1987). A **guitar** player also known by the name Bola Sete, Djalma De Andrade moved from Brazil to the United States in 1959. De Andrade was discovered by **Dizzy Gillespie** and recorded with him in 1962, then worked with **Vince Guaraldi** from 1963 to 1966 before forming his own Brazilian group.

DEARIE, MARGRETE BLOSSOM (1924–2009). A singer, Dearie Blossom got her start when she moved to New York in the mid-1940s and joined the Blue Reys, a vocal group within **Woody Herman**'s band. She moved to Paris and formed her own vocal group, the Blue Stars; their French version of "Lullaby of Birdland" was a hit in the United States. The Blue Stars would later go on to become two other groups, the Double Six of Paris and the Swingle Singers. Blossom moved back to the United States in 1956 and led her own trio in which she also played piano, and in 1973 she founded **Daffodil** Records, a **record label** that released many of her **albums**. *See also* EUROPE.

DECCA. A British **record label** that began issuing **recordings** in 1929 but dates as far back as 1914. The label made Classical releases in England until an American branch was opened in New York in 1924. The American branch issued records by artists including **Louis Armstrong**, **Count Basie**, **Woody Herman**, and **Lionel Hampton**. The label was active through various parent companies until 1999; during that time it released many Classical, Pop, and Rock **albums**.

DECZI, LADISLAV (1938–). A Slovakian **trumpet** player, Ladislav Deczi played with several groups in Europe throughout the 1950s and 1960s, including as the leader of Jazz Cellula. He left Czechoslovakia in 1985 and moved to New York after a brief time in Germany; in New York he and his son founded another Jazz Cellula and recorded.

DEDRICK, LYLE "RUSTY" (1918–2009). A **trumpet** player, Rusty Dedrick started working with Dick Stabile in 1938 and then joined **Red Norvo.** Dedrick left Norvo in 1941 and performed and recorded with **Claude Thornhill** through 1942 and again from 1946 to 1947, in addition to arranging works for the group. During the 1950s and 1960s, Dedrick freelanced in New York including a stint with **Lionel Hampton** in 1970 and 1971. In 1971 he became a faculty member at the Manhattan School of Music, where he would eventually assume the position of director of jazz studies. From 1984 to 1985, he was editor-in-chief of Kendor Music.

DEFUNKT. A **Fusion** group formed in 1978 by **trombone** player Joseph Bowie.

DEJOHNETTE, JACK (1942–). A **drum set** player, Jack DeJohnette performed first with **John Coltrane** in the early 1960s, and after some time in the **Association for the Advancement of Creative Musicians,** he moved to New York in 1966 to replace **Elvin Jones** in Coltrane's group. After Coltrane, DeJohnette played with many other musicians, including the **Charles Lloyd** Quartet, **Thelonious Monk, Freddie Hubbard, Keith Jarrett, Chick Corea, Stan Getz,** and **Bill Evans,** and he also recorded under his own name. In 1969, DeJohnette joined **Miles Davis** for his **album** *Bitches Brew,* and joined the group permanently from 1970 to 1972. In 1971 he formed his own band, Compost, and during the rest of the 1970s he recorded prominently on the **ECM** label with **Kenny Wheeler, John Abercrombie,** and others. He also recorded with his own various groups, including Gateway, Directions, New Directions, and Special Edition. In the 1980s, DeJohnette played with Jarrett's Standards Trio, and in the 1990s he recorded with **Herbie Hancock, Michael Brecker, Pat Metheny,** and others.

DELMARK. A record label and company established in 1953 in St. Louis and first called Delmar. The label was moved to Chicago in 1958 and changed to Delmark. The label issued **Traditional Jazz** by **George Lewis, Earl Hines,** and others, and also had a series of more modern jazz by artists including **Sonny Stitt, Sun Ra,** and **Anthony Braxton,** among others.

DELTA. A **record label** that issued four **recordings** by Kid Rena in the 1940s.

DE LUXE. A record label and company established in 1944. Artists include **Benny Carter** and **Billy Eckstine.** *See also* RECORD LABEL.

DERBY. A **record label** established in 1948 in New York; one of the earliest labels to issue 45 rpm singles. Early releases were mostly **race records**, but by 1953 the catalog was mainly Pop music.

DERBY (MUTE). A type of mute that resembles a felt hat, it is used by trumpet players to quiet the sound of the instrument for effect. *See also* MUTE.

DEUTSCHE GRAMMOPHON. A record label and company established in 1898 in Hanover. Important in the early technology of record production, the company continues to exist today and is the largest and most successful Classical record company in the world. *See also* RECORD LABEL.

DE VILLERS, MICHEL (1926–1992). A French alto and baritone saxophonist, Michel De Villers started playing jazz with a quartet in 1943. From 1946 to 1947 he played and recorded with **Django Reinhardt.** During the 1950s he played with mostly French bands but a few visiting American musicians including **Buck Clayton** and Bill Coleman. He has continued to tour and perform in Europe. *See also* ALTO SAXOPHONE; BARITONE SAXOPHONE; EUROPE; SAXOPHONE.

DE VRIES, LOUIS (1905–1935). A Dutch **trumpet** player who was active in bands in the Netherlands in the 1920s and 1930s. Louis Armstrong considered him the best trumpet player in **Europe**.

DE WEILLE, BENNY (1915–1977). A German **clarinet** player, he recorded with several bands in Europe in the late 1930s and early 1940s. In 1940 he formed the Bar Trio and imitated **Benny Goodman**; the group is regarded as the best example of German **Swing** music. *See also* EUROPE.

DIAL. A record label and company founded in 1946 in Hollywood, it featured many Bop musicians including **Charlie Parker**, **Dizzy Gillespie**, and **Dexter Gordon**, among others. The company also had **recordings** in older styles by artists including **Sidney Bechet**, **Roy Eldridge**, and **Earl Hines.** *See also* RECORD LABEL.

DICKENSON, VIC(TOR) (1906–1984). A trombone player who was self-taught, Victor Dickenson played in **territory bands** before working with

Blanche Calloway, Claude Hopkins, **Benny Carter**, and **Count Basie** in the 1930s and into 1941. He recorded with **Sidney Bechet** in the early 1940s and spent three years as a member of Eddie Haywood's group (1943–1946). During the 1950s he worked with **Bobby Hackett** and **Ruby Braff**, during the 1960s he worked regularly with Eddie Condon, and during the 1970s with the **World's Greatest Jazz Band**. Dickenson continued to be active as a player up until his death.

DI MEOLA, AL (1954–). A guitarist originally inspired by the Beatles, Al Di Meola started playing at the age of nine, and by 1971 he was attending the **Berklee College of Music**. Di Meola left Berklee briefly to join Barry Miles, returned in 1974, and then joined **Chick Corea** in the group **Return to Forever**. He played with Return to Forever until they broke up and then went on tours with **John McLaughlin** and Paco DeLucia in the early 1980s. In 1985 he formed the Al Di Meola Project, and in 1995 he formed Rite of Strings with **Stanley Clarke** and Jean-Luc Ponty. He has continued to record in various settings throughout the 1990s and 2000s.

DIP. Dropping and raising the pitch of a note quickly after the attack, notated by a U symbol above or below the note. This is also referred to as a bend.

DIRECT-TO-DISC RECORDING. A technique used during the 1970s where **recordings** were made directly to discs instead of first to an intermediary medium.

DIRTY DOZEN BRASS BAND. Formed in 1975 in the style of a New Orleans marching band. Containing two **trumpets**, a **tenor saxophone**, a **soprano saxophone**, a **trombone**, a sousaphone, a snare **drum**, and two bass drummers, the group achieved international popularity playing a mix of **Rhythm and Blues (R&B)**, modern jazz, and traditional New Orleans street music. Throughout the years the band has performed with many artists including **Dizzy Gillespie**, **Branford Marsalis**, Dr. John, and David Bowie, among others.

DISCOGRAPHY. A list of **recordings**, arranged either by content, individuals or ensembles, or **record label**.

DISCOVERY. A record label and company formed in 1948 in New York. Artists include **Red Norvo**, **Art Pepper**, **Dizzy Gillespie**, **Cedar Walton**, and others.

DIVA. An all-female **big band** formed in New York in 1993. Notable members include Ingrid Jensen, Virginia Mayhew, and Carol Chaikin. The group is led by drummer Sherri Maricle.

DIXIELAND (JAZZ). A term synonymous with Early Jazz or **Traditional Jazz** styles. The name is derived in part from the **Original Dixieland Jazz Band**. *See also* EARLY JAZZ.

DIXIELAND THUMPERS. A studio group that recorded in 1927, the same members also made up the **Chicago Footwarmers**.

DIXIE STOMPERS. A **Traditional Jazz** group founded in Belgium, it recorded between 1944 and 1958. The group is regarded as the best Belgian Traditional Jazz ensemble.

DIXIE SYNCOPATORS. A group formed by **Joe "King" Oliver** in Chicago in 1925.

DIXON, BILL (1925–2010). A **trumpet** player, he worked in various capacities as a trumpet player and arranger in the late 1940s through the 1950s. In 1961–1963 he led **Free Jazz** groups with **Archie Shepp**, and in 1964 he helped organize the "October Revolution in Jazz" featuring contributions from **Avant-Garde** musicians including **Sun Ra**, John Tchicai, Rowell Rudd, and others. Later that year Dixon helped to organize the **Jazz Composers Guild**, a short-lived organization that counted Sun Ra, Shepp, Tchicai, and **Cecil Taylor** among its founding members. Since then, Dixon has collaborated with dancer Judith Dunn (1965–1983), played with the group Sound Unity (1991), and toured Europe and the United States. Beginning in 1968 he also taught at Bennington College.

DODDS, JOHNNY (1892–1940). One of the best **clarinet** players in the early New Orleans style, Johnny Dodds started playing at age 17 and was mostly self-taught. From 1912 to 1918 he played with **Kid Ory**, toured with **Fate Marable** from 1918 to 1919, and then in 1920 he moved to Chicago to join **King Oliver**. After leaving Oliver's band in 1923, he played with **Freddy Keppard** and a year later took over the band as leader. He directed the band for six years and worked in Chicago with his brother, **Baby Dodds**, in addition to appearing on **recordings** with **Louis Armstrong's Hot Five** and **Hot Seven** and on recordings with **Jelly Roll Morton**. Dodds suffered a heart attack in 1939 and died the following year.

DODDS, WARREN "BABY" (1898–1959). A **drummer**, Baby Dodds is considered to be the exemplar of the New Orleans **Early Jazz** style. His first **gigs** were with **Bunk Johnson**, Willie Hightower, Papa Celestin, and then three years (1918–1821) with **Fate Marable**. He joined **King Oliver** in 1922 and moved to Chicago in 1923 where he would remain for approximately 20 years. During this time he recorded with **Louis Armstrong** and **Jelly Roll Morton** in addition to playing in groups with his brother, clarinetist **Johnny Dodds**. During the 1940s he played with **Jimmie Noone**, Bunk Johnson again, **Sidney Bechet**, and **Mezz Mezzrow**. Among his more famous pupils were **Gene Krupa** and **Dave Tough**.

DODGION, JERRY (1932–). An **alto saxophonist, tenor saxophonist,** and **flute** player, Jerry Dodgion started his career playing with **Gerald Wilson** from 1953 to 1955. He then toured with **Red Norvo** from 1958 to 1961 and played in several of **Benny Goodman**'s groups. From 1961 to 1967 he played regularly with **Oliver Nelson's big bands**, and in 1965 he was an original member of the **Thad Jones–Mel Lewis** Orchestra, with whom he played through 1979. He also played with Duke Pearson, **Count Basie**, and others. In the 1980s he played with Astrud Gilberto and **Dizzy Gillespie**'s big band, and in 1991 he was an original member of the Carnegie Hall Jazz Band. He has also played with the American Jazz Orchestra and the Lincoln Center Jazz Orchestra. In the mid-1990s he led his own group comprised of five saxophones, and a **rhythm section** named Jerry Dodgion's New York Saxophones. He is currently leading his own group named "The Joy of Sax."

DOIT. A glissando, rising from the end of a note to an indeterminate pitch.

DOLPHY, ERIC (1928–1964). A saxophonist, bass clarinetist, and flutist, Eric Dolphy started playing with Roy Porter from 1948 to 1950. In the early 1950s, Dolphy was in the military, in 1958 he joined **Chico Hamilton**, and from 1959 to 1960 he played with **Charles Mingus**. During the early 1960s, Dolphy played with many different artists, including **John Coltrane**, **John Lewis**, and **Booker Little** in a group he led, in addition to continuing to play with Mingus. Eric Dolphy died of a heart attack caused by diabetes in 1964.

DOMINO. A **record label** launched in 1924 and active into the early 1930s.

DONALDSON, LOU (1926–). Originally starting on **clarinet** at the age of 15, Lou Donaldson later switched to the **alto saxophone** and in 1952 made his first records with **Milt Jackson** and **Thelonious Monk**. He also led several small groups from 1952 to 1953 with such notable sidemen as **Blue Mitchell**, **Clifford Brown**, **Horace Silver**, **Art Blakey**, and **Philly Joe Jones**. In 1954 he performed with a group that directly preceded Blakey's **Jazz Messengers** on the **Blue Note album** *A Night at Birdland*. Donaldson has led his own groups ever since, venturing into the **Soul Jazz** and Jazz **Funk** styles.

DORHAM, McKINLEY HOWARD "KENNY" (1924–1972). A trumpet player, Kenny Dorham (originally named Kinny but eventually known as Kenny) received his first trumpet as a gift from his sister in 1939. He worked first with Milt Larkin's **big band** before a brief stint in the army. In 1944 he moved to New York and was a participant in the **jam sessions** at **Milton's Playhouse**; he also played in **Dizzy Gillespie**'s **Bebop big bands** and in the band of **Billy Eckstine**. In 1947, Dorham played with **Lionel Hampton**, and in 1948 he replaced **Miles Davis** in **Charlie Parker**'s quintet. He was a founding member of **Art Blakey**'s **Jazz Messengers** in 1954, and in 1956 he led his own group known as the Jazz Prophets. He left that group to join **Max Roach** after the unfortunate death of **Clifford Brown**, and he would play with Roach from 1956 to 1958. In 1962, Dorham led a quintet with **Joe Henderson** and in 1967 co-led a big band with Henderson that was later revived by Henderson in the 1990s. One of his most famous compositions, "Blue Bossa," is now considered a jazz standard.

DOROUGH, BOB (1923–). A songwriter, singer, and pianist, some of Dorough's earliest work was as an accompanist to boxer Sugar Ray Robinson in New York while Robinson was working as an entertainer. He spent some time in Paris in the mid-1950s and after returning to the United States in the late 1950s worked with various groups, the most notable of which was the **Miles Davis** sextet in 1962. From 1972 to 1996 he wrote the music for the PBS television program *Schoolhouse Rock*, and he has continued to tour and lead groups. Among his more famous compositions is the jazz standard "Devil May Care."

DORSEY, JIMMY (1904–1957). A clarinetist and alto saxophonist, Jimmy Dorsey started on the **trumpet** before switching to reeds in 1915. In 1924 he played with the California Ramblers, and from 1925 to 1934 he freelanced and recorded with **Paul Whiteman**, **Frankie Trumbauer**, **Red Nichols**, and **Bix Beiderbecke**. In 1934 he and his brother, **Tommy Dorsey**, founded the Dorsey Brothers Orchestra and would play together until 1935 when an argument on the bandstand resulted in Tommy leaving the group to form his own. From then on, Jimmy led the orchestra himself, and in the early 1940s he had several hits with vocalists Helen O'Connell and Bob Eberly. Dorsey would continue to lead various bands until in 1953 when he and his brother re-formed the Dorsey Brothers Orchestra. The Dorsey brothers performed together until Tommy died in 1956; Jimmy followed shortly thereafter. *See also* BANDLEADER; BIG BAND.

DORSEY, TOMMY (1905–1956). A **trombone** player and **bandleader,** Tommy Dorsey started on the **trumpet** before switching to the trombone. From 1926 to 1934, Dorsey played in bands led by **Paul Whiteman** and Jean Goldkette, many times with his brother, saxophonist **Jimmy Dorsey.** In 1934 he and his brother formed the Dorsey Brothers Orchestra, which would last until 1935, when the brothers broke up and went their separate ways. Tommy Dorsey took over a band led by Joe Haymes. Dorsey's orchestra employed many excellent instrumentalists and arrangers, including **Sy Oliver, Buddy Rich, Gene Krupa,** and **Charlie Shavers,** and notable singers including Dick Haymes and **Frank Sinatra.** The band had a string of hits throughout the 1940s, including "I'm Getting Sentimental Over You," "Marie," and "Song of India," but fell upon hard times as the **Swing** era drew to a close in the early 1950s. Tommy reunited with his brother Jimmy in 1953 to re-form the Dorsey Brothers Orchestra, a group he would co-lead until he choked to death in his sleep in 1956. *See also* BANDLEADER; BIG BAND; CLAM-BAKE SEVEN.

DOUBLE BASS. *See* BASS.

DOUBLE MUTE. A **mute,** similar in appearance to two straight mutes, where one sits within the other. Also known as a clear-tone, solo-tone, or mega mute.

DOUBLE SIX (OF PARIS). A sextet formed in 1959, it got its name from the practice of overlapping two separate **recordings,** making the group sound as if it contained 12 members. The group recorded music by **Quincy Jones** and later **Dizzy Gillespie** before disbanding in 1966.

DOUBLE-TIME (I). A **record label** and company founded by Jamey Aebersold in Indiana in 1995. Artists include **Dave Liebman, Rufus Reid, Bobby Shew,** Kenny Werner, and many others.

DOUBLE-TIME (II). The practice of playing twice as fast as a previously established tempo. A soloist can also play double-time by playing rhythmically twice as fast as the accompaniment.

DOWNBEAT. In jazz, the downbeat is most commonly referred to as the first beat in the measure, or it can also refer to the strong beats in a measure.

DOWNBEAT MAGAZINE. One of the foremost journals in jazz, the magazine was formed in 1934 by Albert Lipschultz and is still popular today. It is well known for record reviews, interviews, annual artist polls, and industry updates.

DRAG (or DRAGGING). Playing behind the beat, unintentionally or intentionally for musical effect. It can also refer to a rudiment of percussion technique.

DREAMLAND CAFÉ. A nightclub in Chicago, it was also known as the Dreamland Ballroom in the 1910s and early 1920s. Performers included **Freddie Keppard, Cab Calloway, Louis Armstrong**, and many others.

DREAMS. One of the early **Jazz-Rock** bands, Dreams recorded two **albums** for **Columbia** in the early 1970s. The group included, at various times, such musicians as **Billy Cobham, Michael Brecker** and **Randy Brecker**, and **John Abercrombie**.

DREW, KENNY (1928–1993). A pianist, Kenny Drew began playing at the age of five. He made his first **recording** in 1949 with **Howard McGhee**. In the early 1950s, he worked with **Sonny Stitt, Lester Young, Charlie Parker, Coleman Hawkins, Miles Davis, Sonny Rollins, Art Blakey, Dexter Gordon**, and **Clifford Brown**, among others. In the late 1950s, Drew continued to play with some of the biggest names in jazz, including **Dinah Washington, Buddy Rich, John Coltrane** (on his **album** *Blue Train*), **Art Farmer, Chet Baker**, and many more. In 1961, Drew moved to Paris, and in 1964 he moved to Copenhagen, Denmark. He recorded extensively for **SteepleChase**, formed a successful duo with **Niels-Henning Ørsted Pedersen**, and continued to play actively until his death in 1993.

D'RIVERA, PAQUITO (1948–). A saxophonist, clarinetist, and **bandleader**, Paquito D'Rivera was studying at the conservatory in Havana when he met **Chucho Valdés**. D'Rivera and Valdés would go on to form the Cuban group **Irakere** and were signed by **Columbia** Records in 1979. In 1980, D'Rivera defected to the United States during a tour of Spain and immediately moved to New York, where he played with **Dizzy Gillespie, McCoy Tyner**, and others, and formed his own group. He recorded with artists including Tito Puente and **Lionel Hampton**, and he was a founding member of Dizzy Gillespie's

United Nations Orchestra in 1988, a group he led during much of the 1990s. In 1996, D'Rivera was awarded a Grammy for his **album** *Portraits of Cuba*, and he continues to perform and record. *See also* ORQUESTA CUBANA DE MÚSICA MODERNA.

DROP. A glissando downward from the end of a note.

DRUMS. *See* DRUM SET.

DRUM SET. The name for the central percussion instrument in jazz, usually a kit that contains a minimum of a **bass drum**, snare drum, suspended (**ride**) **cymbal**, crash cymbal, and hi-hat cymbal. The basic layout of the **drum set** was standardized in the 1940s during the **Bebop** era but can be varied by individual drummers according to their preference. Famous jazz drummers include **Gene Krupa, Art Blakey, Philly Joe Jones, Tony Williams, Max Roach**, and many others. *See also* ANTOLINI, CHARLY; BELLSON, LOUIE; DODDS, BABY; ERSKINE, PETER; FOSTER, AL; HAMILTON, JEFF; JONES, ELVIN; JONES, HAROLD; KRUPA, GENE; MANNE, SHELLY; MOSES, BOB; MUHAMMAD, IDRIS; PERSIP, CHARLIE; RICH, BUDDY; WASHINGTON, KENNY.

DUKE, GEORGE (1946–). A keyboardist and record producer, George Duke accompanied musicians including **Dizzy Gillespie** and **Kenny Dorham** from 1965 to 1967 as pianist at the Half Note. In the late 1960s he also worked with **Don Ellis, Gerald Wilson**, and **Bobby Hutcherson** before he joined Jean-Luc Ponty and began playing electric piano. He played with **Cannonball Adderley** from 1971 to 1972 around stints with Frank Zappa in 1970 and 1973 to 1975. In 1975 he also co-led a group with **Billy Cobham** and formed a **Funk** band with **Stanley Clarke** named the Clarke-Duke Project, and in the late 1970s he began working as a record producer. Since then he has played mostly **Rhythm and Blues (R&B)** and produced Pop projects.

DUKES OF DIXIELAND. A group formed by **trumpet** player Frank **Assunto** and his brother, trombonist Fred Assunto, in 1949. From 1958 to 1960 the group recorded a few **albums** with **Louis Armstrong** and in the early 1960s had a few other successful albums. After Frank died in 1974, the band underwent several leadership changes, and a version of the band continued to play into the 1990s.

DUNBAR, TED (1937–1998). A guitarist, Ted Dunbar began subbing for **Wes Montgomery** in 1962–1963 while working as a pharmacist across the street from an Indiana club where Montgomery played. In the early 1960s in Dallas, Dunbar worked with musicians including **David "Fathead" Newman**, Red Garland, and others before moving to New York in 1966 with **Billy Harper**. During the 1970s, Dunbar played with many notable musicians including **Gil Evans, Tony Williams, McCoy Tyner, Sonny Rollins, Ron Carter, Roy Haynes**, and many others. In 1972, Dunbar became a faculty member at Livingston College, Rutgers, where guitarist Kevin Eubanks would eventually number among his students. He resumed **recording** in 1989 and was the author of several books on jazz harmony and guitar.

DUTCH SWING COLLEGE (DSC). A Dutch group formed in 1945 and active into the 1990s. The group has performed with many visiting American jazz musicians and recorded with notable musicians including **Sidney Bechet** and **Teddy Wilson**.

DUTREY, HONORÉ (1894–1935). A trombonist, Honoré Dutrey worked with many New Orleans bands before joining the U.S. Navy in 1917. During his time in service, Dutrey suffered carbide poisoning, which damaged his lungs. He was eventually able to resume playing, and in the early 1920s he worked with **King Oliver** in Chicago. In the mid-1920s he led his own band and played with **Louis Armstrong** and **Johnny Dodds** and retired at the end of the 1920s.

DUVIVIER, GEORGE (1920–1985). Originally a Classical violinist, George Duvivier switched to the string **bass** sometime around 1937. By 1940 he was working with **Coleman Hawkins**, and in 1944 he became the arranger for **Jimmie Lunceford** and later for **Sy Oliver**. In the 1950s he played with Lena Horne, **Louie Bellson**, and **Bud Powell**, among others, in addition to doing studio work. During the 1960s, Duvivier continued to play with Powell and also appeared with **Shelly Manne, Eric Dolphy, Benny Goodman**, and **Ben Webster**. Throughout the 1970s and the 1980s Duvivier made appearances at the **Colorado Jazz Party** and worked with **Benny Carter, Hank Jones** and **Warren Vaché**.

E

EAGLE BAND. A New Orleans–based **Early Jazz** band that was popular in the early 1900s. The Eagle Band was initially founded by the **trumpet** legend **Buddy Bolden**. After Bolden left the band, the trumpet chair was passed down to many of the great Early Jazz trumpet legends including **Freddie Keppard** and **King Joe Oliver**. Other future jazz artists such as **Sidney Bechet**, **Bunk Johnson**, and **Baby Dodds** were a part of the group as well. The group temporarily folded in 1917 but performed several times in the 1920s. In the 1960s, an Early Jazz tribute group used the name Eagle Band for touring purposes.

EARLY JAZZ. A term used interchangeably with **Traditional Jazz**, Early Jazz can refer to the **New Orleans** or **Chicago** styles popular during the 1910s and 1920s. Also referred to as **Dixieland**, the music is most often performed with a **front line** consisting of **clarinet, trumpet**, and **trombone**, and a **rhythm section** of **piano** or **banjo, bass** or **tuba**, and **drum set**. Significant Early Jazz groups include **Louis Armstrong**'s **Hot Five** and **Hot Seven**, and the Creole Jazz Band. *See also* BECHET, SIDNEY; BEIDERBECKE BIX; EUROPE, JAMES REESE; MORTON, JELLY ROLL; OLIVER, JOE "KING"; ORY, KID; VACHÉ, WARREN; YOUNG, TRUMMY.

EAST COAST JAZZ. Another name for the **Hard Bop** and **Soul** styles that were developed during the 1950s and 1960s. East Coast Jazz was a term used to counter the idea of **West Coast** or **Cool Jazz** that was taking place during the same time. Rarely were the Hard Bop or Soul Jazz styles referred to as East Coast Jazz, and the term never had the impact that musicians who coined the term hoped it would.

EAST WEST. An American **record label** founded by Atlantic Records in 1957, now owned by Warner Music Group.

EAST WIND (I). Established in 1974, East Wind was a Japan-based **record label** that recorded mostly Japanese jazz musicians. *See also* JAPAN.

EAST WIND (II). A Connecticut-based **record label**, founded in 1984 that was dedicated to **recording** and preserving jazz music made in Russia or by Russian musicians.

ECHO EFFECT. A device used oftentimes as a pedal to simulate or create echoes to the sound. This can be established by digital means or by using a tape loop to create an echo effect.

ECKSTINE, WILLIAM CLARENCE "BILLY" (1914–1993). Eckstine took up **singing** in his early teens, and after a brief attempt at playing football that ended up in a broken collarbone, he decided to pursue a singing career. After relocating from Pittsburgh to Chicago, Eckstine's unique and robust voice helped him secure work, most notably with the **Earl Hines** Orchestra, one of the top groups of the day. Other musicians performing with the group at this time included **Dizzy Gillespie** and **Charlie Parker**. Eckstine stayed with the group from 1939 to 1943 until he was encouraged by his peers to start his own band. Gillespie and Parker followed Eckstine in his new endeavor and were joined later by many other future jazz stars including **Dexter Gordon**, **Miles Davis**, **Kenny Dorham**, **Sonny Stitt**, and **Art Blakey**. The band was very successful, and Eckstine quickly became one of the most popular singers of the 1940s. Eckstine recorded several **albums** during this time, including *Blowing the Blues Away* (1953, Swingtime); *Airmail Special* (1945, Drive Archive); and *Mister B and the Band* (1946, Savoy).

After the band folded in 1947, Eckstine was signed by MGM to record albums of **ballads**. The majority of Eckstine's **recordings** after the 1940s focused on his ballad singing and utilized strings instead of only a band. Although his contract with MGM expired during the 1950s, Eckstine continued to perform in this manner for the remainder of his career. He was joined by **Sarah Vaughan** (another Earl Hines alumnus) during the 1960s for a few recordings. *See also* BANDLEADER.

ECM. Founded by producer Manfred Eicher, ECM has been one of the most influential jazz labels since its creation in 1969. Primarily **recording** European **Free Jazz** and **Fusion** artists, ECM greatly influenced the jazz world with recordings such as **Keith Jarrett**'s *The Koln Concert* (1975, ECM) and **Jan Garbarek**'s *Witchi-Tai-To* (1972, ECM). ECM has a catalog of over 600 **albums** in addition to having a Japanese affiliate, Japo.

ECONOMY HALL. A jazz club in New Orleans. Located just outside of the French Quarter, Economy Hall was founded before the 1900s. *See also* CLUBS.

EDDIE CONDON'S. A jazz club run by guitarist Eddie Condon in New York from the mid-1940s until 1967. Condon had secured a record deal with **Columbia** Records, and many of the artists that performed at the club were recorded live. Included among these artists were **Early Jazz** musicians such as **Wild Bill Davison**, Budd Freeman, and **Pee Wee Russell**. *See also* CLUBS.

EDISON. A **record label** created by Thomas Alva Edison in the early 1900s. Edison's **recordings** were made on both cylinders and vertically cut discs which were known as Edison Diamond Discs. The significance of this company is that it was one of the very first recording companies. Edison recorded only a few jazz tunes. Edison Records closed in 1929.

EDISON, HARRY "SWEETS" (1915–1999). Originally from Columbus, Ohio, Edison picked up the **trumpet** while living in Cleveland in 1927. He began to play professionally soon after and relocated to St. Louis to pursue further musical opportunities. After several years in St. Louis, Edison moved to New York and was quickly picked up by **Count Basie** to perform in his **big band**. Edison remained with the group until 1950. Edison freelanced with many groups during the 1950s and 1960s including **Jazz at the Philharmonic**, Count Basie's big band, and the **Nelson Riddle** orchestra. Edison also recorded several of his own **albums** that included dates with tenor saxophonist **Eddie "Lockjaw" Davis**: *Jawbreakers* (1962, Original Jazz Classics) and *Just Friends* (1975, Black and Blue). Edison continued to perform both as a soloist and in big bands throughout the 1980s and 1990s.

EDISON-BELL. A London-based **record label** that primarily distributed American records to England. Created in the early 1890s, Edison-Bell worked with American partner labels including Emerson and Paramount to distribute dance band and **Early Jazz recordings** to the United Kingdom. Records of **Fletcher Henderson** and **Louis Armstrong** were notable items released by Edison-Bell. *See also* ENGLAND.

EDWARDS, TEDDY (1924–2003). Edwards, like many of his peers, was born into a family of musicians. By the age of 12, he had chosen to focus on the alto saxophone. In 1936, he began touring with a variety of bands from the Detroit area until his family relocated to Florida. At the age of 20, Edwards was invited to join Roy Milton's band in Los Angeles, a location Edwards would make home for the majority of his career. **Trumpet** player **Howard McGhee** heard Edwards in Los Angeles and asked him to join his small group to play tenor saxophone. Edwards dedicated the rest of his career to performing on the tenor saxophone and became quite active in the Los Angeles jazz scene. Equally adept in both **big band** and small-group settings, Edwards worked as a leader and with a variety of groups including ones led by **Max Roach**, **Benny Carter**, **Benny Goodman**, Howard Rumsey, **Gerald Wilson**, and Bill Berry. Edwards recorded as a leader many times during the 1960s, including the releases *Teddy's Ready* (1960, Original Jazz Classics) and *Together Again* (1961, Contemporary). The latter featured former bandmate Howard McGhee. Edwards continued performing late in his life and was still **recording** into the late 1990s.

EIGHTS. A term referring to when members of the ensemble alternate improvising over eight-measure sections of a song. Often, eights are traded between a **front line** player and the drummer. *See also* FOURS; TWOS.

ELDRIDGE, (DAVID) ROY (1911–1989). Born in Pittsburgh, Pennsylvania, Eldridge received his formal training playing with different touring bands in the 1920s. Eldridge moved to New York in 1930 and was hired by **Fletcher Henderson** several years later. Eldridge's style was highly influential to rising star **Dizzy Gillespie**, and he is often referred to as being the musical link between **Louis Armstrong** and Gillespie.

In the 1940s, Eldridge played with **Gene Krupa** and **Artie Shaw** until he was hired for several tours with **Norman Granz**'s **Jazz at the Philharmonic**. Eldridge continued to play with several of his bandmates from Jazz at the Philharmonic during the 1960s including **Ella Fitzgerald** and **Coleman Hawkins**. Eldridge, also known as "Little Jazz," continued to play until late in his life, including sessions as a leader and frequent appearances as a **sideman**.

ELECTRICAL AND MUSICAL INDUSTRIES (EMI). The result of the merging of two of the leading **recording** companies of the early 20th century, Electrical and Musical Industries (EMI) became one of the most significant recording companies ever. EMI acquired many start-up companies from a variety of music genres and is most famously known for producing many of the Beatles most popular **albums**. EMI is important to jazz because it acquired many important jazz labels, including jazz's signature label, **Blue Note** Records, in the 1980s.

ELECTRICAL RECORDING. The process of capturing sound through the use of electrical signals. Electrical **recording** was a very important breakthrough of the early 1920s and provided recording companies with a much more accurate method of capturing sound. Electrical recording was the most prominent means of capturing sound for several decades until the development of digital recording.

ELECTRIC BASS (GUITAR). A member of the guitar family, it is used as a replacement for the acoustic bass. An electric bass guitar has four strings (like its acoustic counterpart) but has greater flexibility with amplification and sound production. The electric bass guitar was created in 1951 by Leo Fender and has several different variations including the six-string bass guitar and the fretless guitar. Significant jazz performers of the electric bass include John Patitucci, **Jaco Pastorius**, and **Marcus Miller**. *See also* SWALLOW, STEVE.

ELECTRIC GUITAR. The electric counterpart to the acoustic guitar. The electric guitar matches the acoustic guitar in its string setup and tuning and features knobs that allow the user to alter the tone and volume of the instrument. There are two major forms of the electric guitar, the solid-body and hollow-body. There have been several important jazz innovators of the electric guitar including **Charlie Christian** and Les Paul. Other important jazz guitarists include, **Kenny Burrell**, **Jim Hall**, **Wes Montgomery**, and **John Scofield**. *See also* ELECTRIC BASS (GUITAR).

ELECTRIC PIANO. The electric **piano** is a member of the keyboard family. Its primary function is to serve as an electric reproduction of an acoustic piano. Electric pianos offer the user significantly fewer features such as patches or synthesized sounds in comparison to most electronic keyboards. *See also* ELECTRONIC KEYBOARDS.

ELECTROLA. A German subsidiary of the **Gramophone Company**, it was created in the 1920s. Electrola was included as part of the **Columbia/** Gramophone merger that resulted in the creation of **Electrical and Musical Industries (EMI)** in the 1920s. Electrola was responsible for issuing RCA Victor **albums** in Germany and in the 1980s reissued many **Blue Note** albums from several decades prior.

ELECTRONIC KEYBOARDS. An electronic instrument with keys arranged like a piano that is often equipped with a multitude of synthesized sounds that allow the user to mimic other instruments or other sounds. Electronic keyboards became popular in the 1970s when the **Fusion** movement was taking place. Famous pianists to utilize electronic keyboards include **Herbie Hancock**, **Chick Corea**, and **Joe Zawinul**. *See also* ELECTRIC PIANO.

ELEKTRA MUSICIAN. A record label formed in the 1980s by future **Blue Note** president Bruce Lundvall. Elektra Musician was dedicated to **recording** all forms of jazz and signed several major artists including pianist **Bill Evans**, **John McLaughlin**, **Woody Shaw**, **Dexter Gordon**, and **McCoy Tyner**. The label became less organized when Lundvall left for Blue Note in 1985, and it was eventually merged with Warner and Atlantic.

ELEMENTS. A **Fusion** and world music group created by **Pat Metheny** Group alumnus Mark Egan. The group took the official name Elements in 1983 and recorded several **albums** during the next decade including *Elements* (1982, Antilles); *Illumination* (1987, Novus); and *Spirit River* (1990, Novus).

ELIAS, ELIANE (1960–). Elias began her musical career as a pianist during her childhood in Brazil and toured with groups from the region when she was in her late teens. On the recommendation of bassist **Eddie Gomez**, she moved to New York at the age of 20. She freelanced with several groups including **Steps Ahead** and developed a repertoire for the group's **trumpet** player, **Randy Brecker**. Elias and Brecker were married for a short while and had a child, which limited Elias' availability for touring during the next several years. During the late 1980s and most of the next few decades, Elias toured and recorded with her groups. Elias signed a contract with **Blue Note** Records in 1989 and recorded a series of **albums** for the label that include *Fantasia* (1992, Blue Note) and *Solos & Duets* (1994, Blue Note).

ELLINGTON, EDWARD KENNEDY "DUKE" (1899–1974). Ellington studied **piano** as a youth and began playing professionally by the age of 17. He was hired by several groups during the 1920s, most notably the band led by **Elmer Snowden**. Included in the group were many musicians who became important to Ellington including **Bubber Miley**, **Otto Hardwick**, **Sonny Greer**, and **"Tricky" Sam Nanton**. After a few years, Ellington assumed control of the ensemble and in 1927 began a famous residency at the **Cotton Club** in New York. During this time, Ellington continued to add musicians to his band, the most significant addition being alto saxophonist **Johnny Hodges**, who would play a vital role in the Ellington sound.

During the 1930s, Ellington had many popular hits and had one of the most popular working units in the nation. Toward the end of the decade, Ellington hired several influential musicians, including **Ben Webster** and **Billy Stray-horn**, the latter of whom would also become a vital arranger and composer for Ellington. Throughout the 1940s, Ellington presented concerts around the world and continued to compose both large- and small-scale works.

During the 1950s, Ellington's band continued to work, and Ellington was asked to write several movie scores and completed jazz renditions of Peter Tchaikovsky's *Nutcracker* ballet and a suite based on works by William Shakespeare. Ellington also expanded and worked in smaller groups with **Charles Mingus, Max Roach**, and **John Coltrane** in the 1960s. Throughout the next decade and a half, Ellington would be a revered figure in jazz, and much of his work was religion related. He is considered today to be the most prolific and greatest jazz composer. Ellington's son, **Mercer**, would take control of Ellington's orchestra after Ellington died.

ELLINGTON, MERCER KENNEDY (1919–1996). Ellington's musical training started early with his father, the great **big band** leader and composer, **Duke Ellington**. In his early twenties, Ellington attempted to run his own band but was never able to fully escape his father's shadow despite having reputable musicians such as **Dizzy Gillespie, Carmen McRae**, and **Kenny Dorham** in the band. After several failed attempts at being a **bandleader**, Ellington spent time as a manager for groups, primarily the **big band** led by **Cootie Williams** during the 1940s and 1950s. Ellington received the opportunity to join his father's band in a similar capacity in the 1960s and remained with it until his father's death in 1974, at which point he took over complete bandleading duties for the Duke Ellington Orchestra. Ellington would remain in this capacity well into the 1990s. In addition to his bandleading, Ellington played **trumpet** and was a composer, most notably contributing "Things Ain't What They Used to Be" to the jazz repertoire. Ellington also recorded several **albums** with the Duke Ellington Orchestra including *Digital Duke* (1987, **GRP**).

ELLINGTON, RAY (1915–1985). Born in London, Ellington participated in several English military bands during the 1930s and 1940s and became an important element in the British **Bebop** scene during the late 1940s. He led his own quartet for many years, touring, **recording**, and participating in British radio broadcasts of the late 1940s and 1950s. Ellington's career was further heightened with his participation in *The Goon Show*, a radio program for which he sang, acted, and performed. After the program ended, Ellington's popularity diminished, although he was a regular in many London jazz clubs until his death.

ELLIS, DON(ALD) (1934–1978). Upon graduating from Boston University, Ellis established himself quickly as an innovative composer and capable **trumpet** player. In the 1950s, Ellis was hired by several cutting-edge groups including those of **Charles Mingus** and **George Russell**. Ellis made several **recordings** as a leader in the early 1960s that showcased his small-group playing, including *How Time Passes* (1960, Candid) and *Out of Nowhere* (1961, Candid).

Toward the mid-1960s, Ellis shifted his musical interests to leading a **big band** and began a very unique style of composition. Frequently, Ellis would make use of a variety of instruments including African percussion, doubling of instruments that were not typically doubled (such as the acoustic **bass**), and a variety of electronic instruments. Ellis would also make use of a variety of atypical time meters and had a grasp on the **Free Jazz** movement that was taking place. Until his death, Ellis made recordings with his big band for many **albums** considered to be classics, including *Don Ellis at Monterey* (1966, **Pacific** Jazz); *Don Ellis at Fillmore* (1970, **Columbia**); and *Tears of Joy* (1971, Columbia).

ELLIS, HERB(ERT) (1921–2010). Playing **guitar** since the age of seven, Ellis attended college in his home state of Texas before beginning work with the famous Casa Loma Orchestra. Ellis primarily freelanced in the 1940s, most notably with **Jimmy Dorsey**. Ellis received a tremendous popularity boost when he was officially made a member of the **Oscar Peterson** trio in the 1950s. Ellis left Peterson in the late 1950s and began accompanying vocalists, including **Ella Fitzgerald** and Julie London. Ellis resided in Los Angeles during this time and worked regularly as a **studio musician** to accompany his regular playing.

The 1970s brought Ellis an opportunity to share his guitar abilities with several of his guitar-playing peers, and he played in groups with **Charlie Byrd**, **Barney Kessel**, and **Joe Pass**. Ellis continued to freelance and record with a variety of artists, in addition to branching out and leading **sessions** under his own name. The **Great Guitars** group that included Byrd and Kessel continued to play well into the 1990s, and Ellis continued to play regularly into the 2000s.

EMARCY. A **record label** founded in 1954 that released several significant **albums** by **trumpet** player **Clifford Brown**.

EMERSON. A **record label** founded by Victor Emerson. Emerson recorded several jazz artists during its nine-year existence from the late 1910s to the 1920s. Included among recorded artists were **Eubie Blake** and **Bessie Smith**.

ENGELS, JOHN, JR. (1935–). Born in the Netherlands, Engels received his first big break as a drummer playing with **Mary Lou Williams**. Engels was frequently hired by a variety of European-based jazz bands including ones led by Harry Pohl, Cees Singer, and Louis Van Dijk. Engels was also regularly called to play for touring American musicians. **Zoot Sims, James Moody, Thad Jones, Lew Tabackin, Jimmy Knepper,** and **Art Farmer** were all musicians who performed with Engels. *See also* DRUM SET; EUROPE.

ENGLAND. The jazz scene in England was very focused on dance music during the 1910s after the spreading of various dance styles by Vernon and Irene Castle in **Europe**. England remained this way from the 1920s to the 1930s and never really developed a familiarity with the **Dixieland** or **New Orleans Jazz** styles during this period. One of Great Britain's first jazz **bandleaders, George Webb,** was highly influential in the country and was an important figure in the establishment of jazz. Jazz, or at least jazz that was of a different variety than dance band music, is said to have made its first true appearance in the country in 1943. Native Englishmen began to develop the British jazz scene as additional jazz styles became prominent.

Toward the end of the 1940s, saxophonist **John Dankworth** pioneered jazz small groups in England and was responsible for helping shape a new modern sound in England. Another significant figure in the development of English jazz was musician and entrepreneur Ronnie Scott, a pivotal jazz figure whose **club**, Ronnie Scott's, remains an important performance venue for musicians across the globe. Scott is credited with helping to convince saxophonist **Dexter Gordon** to relocate to Europe in the 1960s. Several prominent jazz musicians moved from England to the United States including **Victor Feldman** and **George Shearing**, and many left their mark in the 1950s and 1960s.

Jazz continued to flourish during the 1970s and 1980s in Europe thanks in large part to several individuals including John Taylor, **Kenny Wheeler** (who is originally from Canada), and Evan Parker. American jazz vocalists **Mark Murphy** and **Jon Hendricks** relocated to England in the 1960s and 1970s when they discovered that they could work much more frequently than in the United States.

ENJA. A record label founded in Germany during the early 1970s. Founders Mathias Winckelmann and Horst Weber were responsible for the creation of the label and frequently recorded jazz artists. The label expanded and had an operations center in New York along with a studio in Munich. Enja released **albums** recorded by **Tommy Flanagan, Elvin Jones, Albert Mangelsdorff, John Scofield,** and **Woody Shaw**. Enja remained active for several decades. *See also* EUROPE; RECORD LABEL.

EP. Acronym for "extended play," EP is a type of record released during the 1950s that was shorter in duration than an LP. *See* EXTENDED-PLAY DISC.

EPIC. Only in existence for approximately 10 years, the Epic **record label** was used by **Columbia** Records to release **recordings** of jazz artists during the 1950s and early 1960s. Artists recorded on the Epic label include **Horace Silver, Art Blakey, Slide Hampton**, Mose Allison, and **Lester Young**.

ERICSON, ROLF (1922–1997). Drawing inspiration from **Louis Armstrong**, Swedish-born **trumpet** player Ericson moved to the United States after touring with several Swedish bands. Ericson lived in New York and Los Angeles for a collective three years, playing with several jazz bands including the **Woody Herman** Orchestra. Ericson spent parts of the next two decades performing in the United States and Sweden. During this time, Ericson was either involved with his groups or working with established jazz legends including Harry James, **Tommy Dorsey, Charlie Parker, Benny Goodman**, and **Duke Ellington**. Ericson led his own groups in Germany for most of the 1970s and 1980s before moving back to the United States again for several years until a green card issue forced him back to Sweden, where he remained until his death.

ERSKINE, PETER (1954–). A drummer since he was a young child, Erskine is another successful product of the **Stan Kenton** summer jazz camps. As a teenager, Erskine played with Kenton in the 1970s before working with trumpeter **Maynard Ferguson** and the **Fusion** supergroup Weather Report. Erskine spent much of the 1980s working with several Fusion-inspired groups including **Steps Ahead** and groups led by fellow Weather Report member **Jaco Pastorius**. Erskine has toured and recorded with a who's who of jazz greats, including **Gary Peacock, Gary Burton**, Joey Calderazzo, **Jan Garbarek**, and **Eddie Gomez**. In the 2000s, Erskine founded a steady working trio featuring Allan Pasqua, in addition to serving on the faculty at the University of Southern California. Erskine is a highly regarded educator and has written several texts on jazz drumming. *See also* DRUM SET.

ERWIN, GEORGE "PEE WEE" (1913–1981). A **Swing** era **trumpet** prodigy, Erwin's career was highlighted by performances in the 1930s with bands led by **Benny Goodman, Glenn Miller**, and **Ray Noble**. He played with **Tommy Dorsey** in 1937–1939 and then led his own **big band** from 1941 to 1942. He became active in radio and television work as a staff **studio musician** for the **Columbia Broadcasting System (CBS)**. Erwin led groups in the 1970s dedicated primarily to music of the Swing era and toured frequently in the United States and Europe.

ESP-DISK. A New York–based **record label** active in the 1960s and 1970s that made several significant **recordings** of **Free Jazz** artists that include **Albert Ayler, Ornette Coleman,** Henry Grimes, and Sunny Murray. The label was later used for reissuing, primary releasing **albums** of pianist **Bud Powell** late in his career.

ESQUIRE. A British-based **record label** that was active from 1941 to the late 1960s that primarily documented the roots of early British jazz. English jazz icons **John Dankworth** and Ronnie Scott were documented on the Esquire label. *See also* ENGLAND.

EUREKA BRASS BAND. An important New Orleans–based **brass band** that at different times was led by **George Lewis** and Willie Wilson. The Eureka Brass Band was actively working from 1920 to 1975 and is considered to be important toward the preservation of the New Orleans Brass Band tradition.

EUROPE. Before spreading to America, the **dance band** craze that led to the **Swing** era started in Europe. **France** and **England** were two of the areas visited by dancers Vernon and Irene Castle who sparked a tremendous following. With the development of **recording** technology, Europeans were able to hear American jazz musicians in the 1910s before musicians were able to tour frequently overseas. Jazz bands such as those of **Paul Whiteman** and Will Marion Cook visited Europe toward the end of the 1910s and then constantly throughout the 1920s and 1930s. In many cases, members of these touring groups found Europe's love for jazz inspiring and elected to remain there. Clarinetist and soprano saxophonist **Sidney Bechet** was one of the first musicians to purchase a home overseas after he elected to stay in France following a tour with Cook's band.

The European jazz scene before the war was very sparse and existed mostly in Western European countries. With the exception of France, jazz was actively recorded or performed in public in very few countries. Most of the music was very informal. Musicians played in dance-style groups that performed for private parties or other social gatherings. Touring bands from the United States were groups that focused on a variety of styles that were becoming popular in the United States. These groups ranged from dance and popular music groups like the Paul Whiteman Orchestra, New Orleans jazz bands like **King Oliver**'s Creole Jazz Band, and a variety of American military bands and orchestras. In the 1930s, only France had an established jazz scene with icons like Sidney Bechet, **Django Reinhardt**, and **Stéphane Grappelli**.

Throughout the 1920s and 1930s, a steady stream of musicians left the United States for Europe in hopes of escaping the racial problems that existed in the United States, artistically and economically. Musicians would continue to pursue this self-exile for the next four decades. Citing a variety of issues, including racial issues, educational issues, lack of teaching opportunities, and the uncompromising capital nature of America's recording scene, musicians like **Ben Webster** would end up spending major parts of their careers overseas.

Following the end of World War II, Europe continued to be a prime spot for escaping jazz musicians. Rising jazz stars such as **Dizzy Gillespie** and **Billy Eckstine** were able to tour frequently, and many boasted about how much better the conditions were for musicians compared to being on the road in the United States. During the 1940s, a number of Americans defected, including saxophonists **Don Byas** and **James Moody** and drummer **Kenny Clarke**. All of these musicians made significant marks on the jazz scene in various countries and would become influential musicians on the global scale.

In the late 1950s through modern day, jazz has developed into a highly artistic music in Europe, more so perhaps than in America. Many musicians who left the United States point to Europe as being much more receptive, respectful, and understanding of jazz in comparison to the United States. Throughout the 1960s, 1970s, and 1980s, **Free Jazz** and creative music took precedence in the European jazz scene, including inspiring numerous jazz festivals in Switzerland, Germany, and Italy that featured all forms of jazz.

EUROPE, JAMES REESE (1881–1919). A highly influential leader of military and **dance bands**, Europe made his mark in the early 1900s. Considered one of the first jazz band leaders, Europe frequently performed concerts and helped break racial boundaries by using groups that were racially mixed. One of Europe's first big breaks occurred when he directed a 125-piece orchestra of African-Americans at Carnegie Hall in 1912. Europe is also credited with being associated with Vernon and Irene Castle, a pioneering dance group who helped spark the popularity of dance bands. Through his popularity with this group, Europe was signed to a record deal in 1913, the first African-American led orchestra conductor to do so. Europe is also credited as being highly influential toward the development of **Ragtime** and its transition into **Early Jazz** and **Stride**. Europe died after being stabbed by a band member.

EUROPEAN JAZZ FEDERATION. An influential jazz organization founded to unite separate countries in jazz education efforts. Founded in

1969, the European Jazz Federation became known as the **International Jazz Federation** in 1977.

EVANS, GIL (1912–1988). Evans led bands at the early age of 21, playing piano until he was hired by several groups, most notably **Claude Thornhill**, to serve as arranger. Evans was a pioneer for arranging works for jazz **big band** that would include additional instruments less common in jazz, including the tuba and **French horn**. He would also produce compositions that weren't dependent on outstanding soloists but focused instead on the **arrangement**. Evans' arrangements caught the ear of **Miles Davis**, and the two collaborated on a number of projects for **Columbia** including *Miles Ahead* (1957), *Porgy and Bess* (1958), *Birth of the Cool* (1950), and *Sketches of Spain* (1960). The relationship between Davis and Evans would last almost a decade.

Evans continued practicing new concepts in orchestration with his own groups throughout the 1960s, 1970s, and 1980s. Evans further expanded the instrumentation of his band and frequently used electronic instruments and synthesizers in his later years. He incorporated popular music from the 1970s and 1980s into arrangements for his group, including compositions by Sting and Jimi Hendrix. Evans' groups with Davis and with his own projects featured many top-notch musicians including **Elvin Jones**, **Ron Carter**, and **Steve Lacy**.

EVANS, WILLIAM JOHN "BILL" (1929–1980). Evans' career would turn out to be among the most influential of any jazz musician. He was born in New Jersey and studied **piano** during his college years. After serving in the army, Evans relocated to New York to continue his education while also performing. Between 1956 and 1960, Evans met, played with, and recorded with **Charles Mingus**, **Miles Davis**, and **Paul Motian**. Considered to be a focal point of the first major Miles Davis quintet, Evans' playing was captured on several **recordings** of the group. After Evans left Davis' group, he began a solo career highlighted by his first trio featuring drummer Paul Motian and prodigious bassist **Scott LaFaro**.

Evans would primarily play in the trio setting for the remainder of his career. Focusing on developing rich harmony while also exploring new ways to play tunes, Evans' influence was great on the next generation of pianists, including **Herbie Hancock** and **Keith Jarrett**. Evans' sensibilities continue to be highly influential to current pianists Brad Mehldau and Fred Hersch.

From the 1960s to 1980, Evans' trios featured fluctuating personnel. Bassists that played in Evans' groups include **Eddie Gomez**, **Gary Peacock**, **Chuck Israels**, and Marc Johnson. Evans' career was marked with several difficult time periods, including the suicide of his older brother Harry in 1979. Evans' playing is often described as melancholy, despite the advanced level of harmony constructed in much of his playing.

EVERYBODY'S. A short-lived **record label** based out of New York in 1925, Everybody's distributed **albums** recorded by other New York companies and was responsible primarily for the release of one of **Duke Ellington**'s first albums.

EXCELLOS FIVE. A **Traditional Jazz** band, based out of Brussels and led by Robert Kierberg in the 1920s.

EXCELSIOR BRASS BAND. A highly influential early New Orleans jazz group founded in the late 1890s. The Excelsior Brass Band played a diverse repertoire of music ranging from marches to dance music and was an important group in the development of the **brass band** style. Led by Theogene Bacquet, the group remained active until the 1930s.

EXCLUSIVE. A record label founded in Los Angeles, Exclusive Records released a few **albums** during the 1940s that included several **recordings** of tenor saxophonist **Lucky Thompson**. *See also* RECORD LABEL.

EXPERIMENTAL BAND. A group founded by **Muhal Richard Abrams** that is considered to be the precursor to the highly influential Chicago-based **Association for the Advancement of Creative Musicians (AACM).**

EXTENDED CHORD. A term describing chords that include notes, sometimes diatonic, that are considered extensions to the preexisting harmony.

EXTENDED-PLAY DISC. An important development in **recording** technology, the extended-play disc was recorded at 45 rpm and allowed jazz performances to be longer than previous LPs. An extended-play disc was generally used when an artist wanted to release only a few tracks instead of a full **album**. *See also* EP.

FAIRE DU BOEUF. The French term meaning to participate in a **jam session** or a performance where the musicians are playing together for more casual purposes instead of more refined rehearsed purposes. *See also* EUROPE; FRANCE.

FAKE BOOK. A source used by jazz and Pop musicians to reference popular songs used in each genre. The books contain the chord **changes** (harmonic progression) for many different songs, and often the melody. Through use of the fake book, the musician can improvise and harmonize during the performance by referencing the tune in the fake book as needed. Fake books have been in existence for several decades and are frequently used in **jam sessions** in which there are tunes being played that are not commonly known by all of the musicians performing.

FAMOUS. A **record label** founded in New York that was in existence for four years. The Famous label was used to distribute records from Paramount.

FAMOUS DOOR (I). A jazz club located on **52nd Street** in New York City, it featured artists including Sarah Vaughan and Count Basie, and inspired many other clubs in other cities.

FAMOUS DOOR (II). The Famous Door **record label** was founded by Harry Lim during the 1970s. Famous Door included records by **Bill Watrous**, Mundell Lowe, **Dave McKenna**, and **Charlie Ventura**.

FANTASY. Partially owned by pianist **Dave Brubeck**, the Fantasy label was originally created to document **recordings** of its owner, Brubeck. During the 1960s, the label expanded to cover several genres and was involved in production with Pop artists Joan Baez and Creedence Clearwater Revival. Fantasy teamed with several significant jazz labels in the 1970s and 1980s, and many **albums** originally released on the Fantasy label were reissued on the Original Jazz Classics label. *See also* RECORD LABEL.

FARLOW, TALMADGE HOLT "TAL" (1921–1998). Farlow began his professional career as a **guitar** player working in New York during the mid- to late 1940s. During this time, he worked with several small groups including those led by Buddy DeFranco and **Red Norvo**. In the 1950s, Farlow did little touring but did begin to lead groups under his own name. After getting married in the latter part of the decade, Farlow did not perform regularly again until the 1970s, when he began performing and **recording** regularly and working with his former bandmates. For most of his career, he was involved with groups that did not include a **drum set**. Farlow is credited with being highly influential for his fluent technique and ability to play fast.

FARMER, ARTHUR "ART" (1928–1999). Growing up in Phoenix, Arizona, Farmer played many instruments while growing up until settling on the **trumpet** in high school. Farmer and his brother, Addison, would frequently spend time with many of the musicians in touring bands that stopped in Phoenix. Farmer moved to Los Angeles at age 17 to begin working regularly in bands led by **Benny Carter**, **Gerald Wilson**, and Jay McShann.

After associations with **Teddy Edwards** and **Hampton Hawes**, Farmer moved to New York. In the 1950s, Farmer worked with many of the leading talents in jazz including **Charles Mingus**, **Horace Silver**, and **Gerry Mulligan**, often choosing to play **flugelhorn** instead of trumpet. Farmer also began playing regularly with tenor saxophonist **Benny Golson** in the Jazztet, a **Hard Bop** group founded by the two of them. The Jazztet would play on and off again for the next few decades.

During the 1960s, Farmer began actively leading and touring with his own groups and eventually moved to Vienna where he would remain active for the remainder of his career. Farmer kept a working group in both Europe and the United States and was frequently touring both. In the late 1980s, Farmer experienced a slight resurgence in his popularity and was involved with groups that included both up-and-coming musicians and more veteran players. Included in these groups were Geoff Keezer, Lewis Nash, **Cedar Walton**, **Billy Higgins**, and **Slide Hampton**. Farmer continued to be an active performer until his death.

FARRELL, JO(SEPH) (1937–1986). Born in Chicago into a family of musicians, he became devoted to the tenor saxophone at the age of 13. Farrell studied music in college before moving to New York in the late 1950s. During the 1960s, Farrell remained active as a performer in jazz and as a **studio musician**. He was hired by several significant jazz musicians during this time including **Chick Corea**, **Charles Mingus**, **Horace Silver**, **Maynard Ferguson**, and **Slide Hampton**.

In the 1970s, Farrell recorded as a leader although he never toured much under his own name. Farrell relocated to Los Angeles and continued working in **recording** studios and playing with the **Fusion** supergroup **Return to Forever** in 1972–1973. His life was frequently up and down, and he struggled with several narcotic and alcohol addictions, which led to his career declining in the 1980s. Farrell only did a handful of tours and recordings before his death due to bone cancer.

FEATHER, LEONARD (1914–1994). Feather's career in jazz was very diverse. He worked as a composer, arranger, and producer, but most notably as a significant jazz author and historian. Born and educated in England, Feather moved to the United States during World War II. He wrote for several American magazines including *Esquire* and played an active role in fighting bias in music polls against African-Americans.

In the 1950s, Feather composed several popular songs for **Dinah Washington** and Louis Jordan, in addition to composing several jazz songs that would become staples in the jazz canon. One of Feather's greatest contributions was working for *DownBeat* magazine, a relationship that would last for almost four decades. Feather was also the author of several books and in the 1960s would also write regularly for the *Los Angeles Times*. He worked briefly in education in the 1970s and 1980s, teaching at several universities.

FEED. An alternate term for the accompanying of a soloist. *See also* COMPING.

FELDMAN, VICTOR STANLEY (1934–1987). Feldman's career started in England as a drummer and eventually as a vibraphonist playing with several English groups in the 1940s. Feldman moved to the United States in the 1950s and worked with many of the premier **West Coast Jazz** musicians including Howard Rumsey, **Leroy Vinnegar**, and Frank Rosolino. In the 1960s, Feldman played with **Cannonball Adderley**, **Benny Goodman**, and **Miles Davis**, in addition to contributing the song "Seven Steps to Heaven" to the jazz standard repertoire. Much of the 1970s and 1980s he spent working with musicians in a variety of genres including Joni Mitchell and Steely Dan, in addition to jazz masters **J. J. Johnson** and **Art Pepper.** Feldman died due to complications of an asthma attack.

FELSTED. An English **record label** founded in July 1954 to distribute American records for the British Decca label. Felsted was also active in **Japan** and released **albums** by **Coleman Hawkins** and **Buster Bailey**, among others.

FELT MUTE. A type of **mute** that acts as a dampener for **brass** instruments, making them softer and mellower. A felt mute is made out of felt and is generally used in place of a **bucket mute** or a **hat**.

FERGUSON, MAYNARD (1928–2006). Ferguson's prolific career began after moving from Canada to the United States in the 1940s to work in the **trumpet** sections of **Jimmy Dorsey, Charlie Barnet**, and **Stan Kenton**. Ferguson began leading his own bands in the middle of the 1950s, and many great jazz musicians got their start either serving as arrangers for the band or as performers in it. Musicians who worked with Ferguson included **Slide Hampton, Don Sebesky, Wayne Shorter, Joe Farrell**, Rufus Jones, and **Ronnie Cuber**.

During the 1960s, Ferguson led several types of groups ranging from **big bands** to small ensembles. For a while, Ferguson lived in India and England until returning to New York in the 1970s. Ferguson remained very active touring during these years and further enhanced his reputation as a stellar high-note player and soloist. Ferguson's style switched slightly during this decade as he began to incorporate popular music into his group's repertoire. Ferguson maintained groups in this style for the next two decades while also working with a more mainstream group named the Big Bop Nouveau. Ferguson was performing regularly until his death.

FESTIVAL. A generic term used to describe the grouped performances and events surrounding a gathering of like-minded enthusiasts. *See also* JAZZ FESTIVAL.

FESTIVAL INTERNATIONAL DE JAZZ DE MONTREAL. Also known as the Montreal Jazz **Festival**, this festival has been active for over three decades and was founded in 1980. The Montreal festival annually hires a diverse array of musicians, sometimes including musicians considered to be outside the jazz realm. Famous jazz musicians who have played the Canadian festival include **Wynton Marsalis, Cecil Taylor, Art Blakey**, and **Bobby McFerrin**. In the 1960s and 1970s, the festival typically limited participating artists to those of North America, but it has since expanded involvement to musicians from across the globe. *See also* JAZZ FESTIVAL.

FIDELITY. A **recording** term that refers to the quality of a recording and the ability to reflect sounds as they would be heard in real life.

52ND STREET. A term used in reference to 52nd Street in New York City where many significant jazz clubs were located during the 1930s and 1940s.

FILL. A term used to describe the space between melodic phrases that a drummer plays so as to maintain musical momentum. Fills in **big band** writing often exist as opportunities for the drummer to play material to either answer a melodic statement previously played by the band or to prepare for material that follows.

FINEGAN, BILL (1917–2008). Finegan served as an arranger for several touring bands of the 1930s, most notably with **Tommy Dorsey** and **Glenn Miller**. Finegan co-led a group with **Eddie Sauter** for most of the 1950s. Finegan spent much of the next several decades contributing **arrangements** to the Glenn Miller reunion orchestra and to the band of **Mel Lewis**.

FINNISH JAZZ FEDERATION. An organization formed in Finland in the 1960s with the intention of presenting jazz performances, educational events, and jazz publications. The Finnish Jazz Federation was one of the organizations to join the **International Jazz Federation** and has been active for over three decades.

FIREHOUSE FIVE PLUS TWO. A Los Angeles–based **Traditional Jazz** group comprised of **studio musicians** that was formed in the 1940s. The Firehouse Five Plus Two never toured regularly but remained active into the 1970s.

FISCHER, CLARE (1928–2012). Fischer studied many instruments while young, eventually settling on **piano**. He attended Michigan State University where he received a bachelor of music and a master of music. Fischer gained experience as a composer and pianist working with bands in his native Michigan until being drafted by the U.S. Army in 1952. He played **alto saxophone** and then served as a music arranger for the U.S. Military Academy Band in West Point, New York. Following his military service, Fischer began arranging for the popular vocal group, the Hi-Los. Fischer's arranging talents led him to work writing for **Dizzy Gillespie, Cal Tjader, Donald Byrd**, and **George Shearing**. He began performing and **recording** with his own groups in 1962, appearing with **Bud Shank** and **Joe Pass**, among others. In the mid-1970s, Fischer formed his **Latin Jazz** group, Salsa Picante, to great acclaim. He worked throughout the 1970s and 1980s as a pianist and keyboardist. Fischer became an in-demand writer for artists of all styles, working with artists including Michael Jackson**, João Gilberto**, Chaka Kahn, Prince, and **Branford Marsalis**.

FITZGERALD, ELLA (1917–1996). A rags-to-riches story, vocalist Fitzgerald grew up an orphan, but her talents were recognized at the age of 14 at a youth talent contest held at the **Apollo** Theater in New York. Fitzgerald was soon working in New York with the **Chick Webb** band until his death, after which Fitzgerald assumed leadership of the band. Her rendition of "A Tisket, A Tasket" remained on the Pop charts for 17 weeks. Her vocal **scat** style was reminiscent of an instrumentalist, and she was revolutionary in her approach to soloing. Fitzgerald's popularity boomed in the 1940s.

During her career, Fitzgerald made very popular songbook **albums** of the music of Cole Porter, Duke Ellington, the Gershwins, Johnny Mercer, Irving Berlin, and Rodgers and Hart. She performed with the greatest names in jazz, including **Louis Armstrong, Duke Ellington, Dizzy Gillespie, Count Basie, Nat "King" Cole, Frank Sinatra**, and **Benny Goodman**. Fitzgerald found great support from producer **Norman Granz** and was featured in his **Jazz at the Philharmonic** concerts. She won 13 Grammy Awards and was the most popular jazz vocalist in the world for many years.

FIVE PENNIES. An Early Jazz group founded by **Red Nichols** that was also the name of a motion picture made in the 1950s about Nichols' life.

FIVE SPOT. An important jazz club in New York that was used in several live **recordings** during the 1950s and 1960s. Among the significant artists to play on live recordings of performances at the Five Spot were **Thelonious Monk, Eric Dolphy**, and **John Coltrane**. *See also* HIGGINS, BILLY.

FLAG WAVER. A term to describe a musical piece used as the finale of a performance in which the band usually plays material that is at a brisk tempo and/or is placed in the upper registers of their respective instruments. The flag waver is considered to be an important part of the set as it is designed to impress and excite the audience.

FLANAGAN, TOMMY (1930–2001). One of the many musicians from the Detroit area on the jazz scene, Flanagan found work at an early age as a pianist. At the age of 17, he worked with rising stars **Milt Jackson** and **Kenny Burrell** until having to serve in the military in 1953. Flanagan moved to New York in the 1950s and recorded with legions of great jazz musicians including **J. J. Johnson, John Coltrane, Donald Byrd**, Kenny Burrell, **Elvin Jones**, and **Coleman Hawkins**.

In the 1960s, Flanagan would begin several relationships as a musical director for vocalists including **Ella Fitzgerald** and **Tony Bennett**. Flanagan would reestablish a solo career in the 1980s and lead several **recording sessions** and tours, working with musicians including Joe Chambers, Peter Washington, and Lewis Nash. He died in 2001 and maintains a legacy as a highly lyrical player. *See also* PIANO.

FLANGER. An electronic sound production technique of playing two versions of the same passage while slightly altering the pitch of one. Not common, it is used primarily by guitarists.

FLARE. A term used to describe a musical cue made by the band that signifies the final **chorus** or few bars of a solo. It is frequently used by New Orleans Jazz musicians.

FLIP. A term used to describe a type of note ornamentation in which the performer plays a note, then slurs to any note above, followed by an immediate return to the original note. Each instrument has different methods for executing a flip.

FLORENCE, BOB (1932–2008). Florence began his career as an arranger and pianist at the age of 21 while living in his hometown of Los Angeles. Florence gained recognition for many of his **arrangements**, and they were used by many popular **big bands** including those led by Harry James, **Louie Bellson**, Frank Capp, **Stan Kenton**, **Buddy Rich**, and **Count Basie**. Florence's popularity blossomed during the 1950s and 1960s and resulted in him writing music for many studio and television **sessions**.

Florence began leading a big band full time in the 1970s. Assisted by fellow composer and arranger **Bill Holman**, Florence filled his band with many of Los Angeles's first-call musicians. He would also play piano in the group that was called the Bob Florence Limited Edition. Florence died due to complications from pneumonia. *See also* BANDLEADER.

FLORES, CHUCK (1935–). A drummer, Flores performed on the West Coast with musicians including **Shorty Rogers**, **Art Pepper**, and **Bud Shank**. In addition to being an in-demand small-group drummer, Flores was a part of several **big bands**, including those led by **Maynard Ferguson**, **Woody Herman**, and **Toshiko Akiyoshi**. Flores started leading his own groups in the 1970s, ranging from a quartet to a quintet, featuring **trumpet** player Bob Summers and saxophonist Bobby Militello. Flores has a highly influential musician for the Hispanic music community and has also been very active as an educator.

FLUGELHORN. A member of the **trumpet** family, the flugelhorn has less compact tubing and a larger bell. The instrument is frequently used to achieve a mellower, less articulate sound. Many trumpeters also play the flugelhorn. Significant flugelhorn performers have included **Clark Terry**, **Art Farmer**, **Chuck Mangione**, and **Chet Baker**. *See also* ROGERS, SHORTY.

FLUTE. A member of the woodwind family consisting of a metal tube with various holes that can be covered by pads controlled by keys. The flute is held parallel to the ground, and air is blown into and over the mouthpiece. The flute is a common although not regular instrument in jazz and many times is used as an alternate instrument for saxophonists. **James Moody** and **Frank Wess** are two important saxophonists to use the flute as a solo instrument. Significant jazz flutists include **Herbie Mann** and **Hubert Laws**.

FLYING DUTCHMAN. Founded by Bob Thiele, the Flying Dutchman label recorded and issues **albums** from 1969 to the mid-1980s. Artists to record or have albums released on the Flying Dutchman include **Louis Armstrong**, **Ornette Coleman**, and Bud Freeman. *See also* RECORD LABEL.

FONTANA, CARL (1928–2003). Originally from Louisiana, Fontana attended college in his home state at Louisiana State University until he was called to play **trombone** with the **Woody Herman** band. Fontana was an innovator of the doodle tonguing technique, which is used by some trombonists to play at quicker tempos. He gained much recognition for this in the 1950s and toured with several **big bands**, including ones led by **Lionel Hampton** and **Stan Kenton**.

Fontana settled in Las Vegas in the 1960s and was there for most of the remainder of his career. Becoming a staple of the music scene there, Fontana recorded many live **albums** with guest musicians including Pete Christlieb and fellow trombonist Andy Martin. Fontana would do some touring in the 1970s with the supergroup **Supersax** in addition to his own group. He died due to complications with Alzheimer's disease.

FORENINGEN NORSKE JAZZMUSIKERE. Norwegian-based jazz organization founded in the late 1970s that served as a union for jazz musicians.

FORMAN, BRUCE (1956–). Based out of San Francisco, Forman learned **guitar** and **saxophone** while in high school. In the late 1970s, he received his first big break touring with alto saxophonist **Richie Cole**. Forman connected with many of the top San Francisco jazz musicians including vibraphonist **Bobby Hutcherson** and pianist **George Cables**. Forman worked as a leader for most of the 1990s and 2000s in addition to performances under the leadership of drummer Eddie Marshall. He has become a staple in the music education scene and has worked extensively for the **Monterey Jazz Festival**'s education programs in addition to serving on the faculty at the University of Southern California.

FORMS. A term used to describe the construction of songs in terms of sections. Often, sections within the form are marked by different letters. AABA is an example of a song form in which the same melodic material is played two times in a row (AA) followed by new material, also known as the **bridge** or B, followed by a reprisal of the original material (A). An example of AABA form is the song "I've Got Rhythm" which is frequently used by jazz musicians.

FORREST, JIMMY (1920–1980). Forrest was a saxophonist as a youth, changing his preference from **alto saxophone** to tenor. Forrest connected with many of the bands in his native city of St. Louis until he turned 18 and left to work with several touring bands. Forrest made the move to New York City in the early 1940s and played with several notable groups, including bands led by Jay McShann and **Andy Kirk**. Throughout the 1950s and 1960s, Forrest was a first-call substitute musician for many of the top bands. He worked with both **Duke Ellington** and **Count Basie** in this capacity. Forrest also spent several years working with **trumpet** legend **Harry "Sweets" Edison** toward the end of the 1950s.

FORTUNE, CORNELIUS "SONNY" (1939–). One of the many jazz musicians who grew up in the Philadelphia music scene, Fortune was a relatively late bloomer and did not get his first big break until the late 1960s when he was hired by **Elvin Jones** and Mongo Santamaría. An **alto saxophone** player, Fortune found steady work during the 1970s working with **McCoy Tyner** and **Miles Davis** off and on and also working as a leader. Fortune would continue to work with Jones throughout the 1980s and 1990s in addition to frequently serving as a **sideman** for many artists, including **Oliver Nelson** and **Pharoah Sanders**.

FOSTER, ALOYSIUS "AL" (1944–). Foster took up the **drum set** at the age of 10 and was working professionally by the age of 16. His first **recording** experience came on a **session** led by **Blue Mitchell** in the 1960s, and he was regularly used as a drummer for several house bands in New York because of his availability, due to his lack of desire to tour and leave his family. Foster would work for several years with **Miles Davis** in the 1970s and was also the primary drummer for the Great Quartet, a group made up of jazz superstars **Freddie Hubbard**, **McCoy Tyner**, and **Ron Carter**.

Foster would record, tour, and perform regularly during the 1980s and 1990s, working with a wide range of artists including **Mike Stern**, Chris Potter, **Jimmy Heath**, Joe Lovano, Kenny Werner, and Roy Hargrove. Foster remains very active as both a leader and a **sideman**, touring and recording frequently.

FOSTER, GARY (1936–). Born in Kansas, Foster studied music for several years in Missouri and Kansas before moving to Los Angeles to pursue studio work. He was very active both as a jazz **saxophone** performer and **studio musician**, and he worked with many of the Los Angeles–based bands including a band led by **Clare Fischer**. Foster recorded as a leader in the 1980s and has remained very active as a performer and clinician during the decades since.

FOUNTAIN, PETE (1930–). Fountain learned **clarinet** before turning 10 and played in **Dixieland** bands in his hometown of New Orleans, Louisiana. He began forming his own groups in the 1950s, including the Basin Street Six, and Pete Fountain and the Three Coins. The majority of Fountain's career was spent in New Orleans despite several sabbaticals to cities including Chicago and Los Angeles. In addition to his Dixieland ventures, Fountain made several appearances with television orchestras including the host bands for the *Lawrence Welk Show* and the NBC *Tonight Show*. The majority of Fountain's work during the 1980s and 1990s was spent leading his groups in New Orleans in addition to performance tours of the United States and Europe.

FOURS. A term used to describe when a soloist **trades** four measures of solo or melodic material with either another instrumentalist or a member of the **rhythm section**. Often, a soloist will trade fours with the drummer toward the end of a solo section, prior to playing the final melody. *See also* CUTTING CONTEST; EIGHTS; TWOS.

(THE) FOUR SOUNDS. A group that served as the precursor to the group **the Three Sounds**, co-founded by Bill Dowdy in 1956. *See also* HARRIS, GENE.

FOURTH WAY. A San Francisco group that specialized in using electronic instruments and developing the **Jazz-Rock** style. Musicians to have played in the Fourth Way include Michael White, **Ron McClure**, and Eddie Marshall.

FOWLKES, CHARLIE (1916–1980). A multi-instrumentalist as a youth, Fowlkes spent the majority of his career as a baritone saxophonist. He freelanced for several years during the 1940s until landing the **baritone saxophone** chair with **Count Basie's** **big band**. He spent much of his career with Basie despite a brief sabbatical during the late 1960s and early 1970s.

FRANCE. The French jazz scene is credited as being highly influenced by several visiting American artists. After the dance craze was started in the United States by Vernon and Irene Castle in the 1910s and after the migration of artists and writers to Paris in the 1920s, France's art scene flourished. Soprano saxophonist **Sidney Bechet** became a highly influential figure in the music scene in Paris during the 1920s (and made the switch from clarinet to soprano saxophone while residing overseas). Despite some legal problems and eventually moving back to America for a brief time (where he worked briefly as a tailor), Bechet had a resurgence of popularity in the 1950s in Paris, and his legacy remains very important.

Toward the late 1920s and 1930s, guitarist **Django Reinhardt** and violinist **Stéphane Grappelli** started an influential quartet that was inspired both by **New Orleans Jazz** and gypsy music from the French countryside. Reinhardt, along with Bechet, became an influential figure in France and in the development of a unique style of jazz music. France was not as influenced by the **Bebop** craze that took place in the United States during the 1940s and in **England** during the 1950s. **Dixieland**, **New Orleans** style, and the hybrid gypsy music of Reinhardt became major styles that would remain prominent in France for many years. France would also openly accept jazz as art music in later decades and featured many annual **jazz festivals**.

FREEDOM. A division of the **Black Lion** record label, Freedom primarily reissued **albums** that had been previously released on Black Lion, before being purchased by Arista records.

FREE JAZZ. A significant jazz style developed in the 1950s by artists including **Ornette Coleman** and **Cecil Taylor**. Free Jazz, which is also referred to as **Avant-Garde** Jazz, can be a style of spontaneous composition/performance, or to play using different sets of rules that dictate what (or when) each musician plays, or can have all of the musicians play loosely off melodic material written prior to the performance. Free Jazz rose in the 1950s, although a specific year has not been determined. Some performers, such as **Lennie Tristano** and **Lee Konitz**, are credited with playing Free Jazz before the style was formalized later in the decade. Free Jazz continues to be an important part of improvisation today and is still frequently heard. *See also* ABRAMS, MUHAL RICHARD; AYLER, ALBERT; BLEY, CARLA; HADEN, CHARLIE; LYONS, JIMMY; MANGELSDORFF, ALBERT; PEACOCK, GARY; RUSSELL, GEORGE; SANDERS, PHAROAH; SHEPP, ARCHIE; SUN RA; ULMER, JAMES "BLOOD."

FREEMAN, EARLE LAVON "VON" (1923–). One of Chicago's true jazz legends, Freeman's career began working with several touring bands and house bands in Chicago. He began leading his own groups in the 1950s that included musicians such as pianists **Ahmad Jamal**, **Muhal Richard Abrams**, and Andrew Hill. Freeman explored a variety of performance styles in the 1960s and 1970s, including performances with Blues and show bands. In the 1980s, Freeman began **recording** more as a leader and was used as a **sideman** with groups led by Steve Coleman, Greg Osby, and **Johnny Griffin**.

FREEMAN, EARL LAVON "CHICO" (1949–). Freeman is the son of Chicago **tenor saxophone** legend **Lavon "Von" Freeman** and grew up playing **trumpet** after being inspired by **Miles Davis**. While attending Northwestern University, Freeman decided to switch to the tenor saxophone, which he would play for the remainder of his career. Freeman was associated with many of the jazz musicians affiliated with the Chicago jazz scene including **Muhal Richard Abrams** and **Don Pullen**. In the 1980s, Freeman had brief associations with Cecil McBee and **Jack DeJohnette**, in addition to leading his own groups. Freeman served on the faculty at the New School in New York during the 2000s.

FREE MUSIC PRODUCTION (FMP). A German company formed in the 1960s that was responsible for promoting and **recording** German jazz for several decades. The FMP released many **albums** it recorded in addition to setting up several **jazz festivals**. The FMP has been affiliated with many German jazz musicians and groups including **Peter Brötzmann**, Gunther Christmann, and Ulrich Gumpert.

FRENCH HORN. A valved **brass** instrument, pitched in between a **trumpet** and a **trombone**, it has tubing and a large bell that faces away from the player. Frequently used in orchestras and wind ensembles, the difficulty of performing the instrument makes it rarely used as a solo instrument in jazz. Vincent Chauncey and **Julius Watkins** are two French horn players who have frequently been recorded on jazz **albums**. *See also* SCHULLER, GUNTHER.

FRESH SOUND. A **record label** founded in Spain, Fresh Sound was one of the few record labels founded during the 1980s that strictly reissued **albums** that had been recorded decades prior. It also goes by the name Fresh Sound New Talent.

FRIARS SOCIETY ORCHESTRA. Another name for the popular **Early Jazz** group the **New Orleans Rhythm Kings**.

FRIESEN, DAVID (1942–). Friesen's first performance experience as a bassist came while serving in the military in the early 1960s. Friesen established himself playing on the west coast of the United States in Washington and California along with musicians including **Marian McPartland, Woody Shaw**, and saxophonist **Joe Henderson**. Friesen was a first-call bassist for many top musicians during the 1970s and 1980s, working with **Stan Getz, Art Farmer, Mal Waldron, Dave Liebman**, and **John Scofield**. Friesen remained on the West Coast and continued to freelance during the 1990s and 2000s. *See also* BASS.

FRISELL, WILLIAM "BILL" (1951–). Born in Baltimore, Maryland, and raised in Colorado, Frisell moved around much as a young man. During the 1970s and 1980s, Frisell lived in Massachusetts, Belgium, and Seattle, while developing a reputation as an outstanding and unique jazz **guitar** player. His first few big breaks came while he was living in Europe **recording** as a **sideman** on several dates for the **ECM** label followed by a several-decade apprenticeship in groups led by drummer **Paul Motian**.

Frisell began working as a leader in the late 1980s and recorded in a variety of settings. Working with **Free Jazz** and **Avant-Garde** artists such as a Jim Zorn and Wayne Horvitz, Frisell developed an eclectic guitar style that would be one of his artistic trademarks. He also frequently teamed up with guitarists considered to be more **Straight-Ahead** artists such as **John Scofield** and Robben Ford. Frisell's groups would range from duos to quartets, quintets, and larger groups that would often feature eclectic instrumentation such as cello and **synthesizer**. Frisell continued to record in a variety of styles including solo guitar and music that incorporated **Blues** and American Folk music.

FRISHBERG, DAVID (1933–). A journalism major at the University of Minnesota, Frishberg's true love was playing jazz piano, and after serving a term in the air force, he moved to New York City to pursue his dream. He was hired by several significant jazz artists during the late 1950s, including trombonist **Kai Winding** and vocalist **Carmen McRae**. He would serve as a **sideman** for most of the 1960s working with **Bob Brookmeyer, Roy Eldridge**, and **Zoot Sims**, among others. In the early 1970s, Frishberg moved to Los Angeles and began leading his own groups while also working with California-based musicians Bill Berry, **Jack Sheldon**, and Richie Kamuca. For much of the 1990s and 2000s, Frishberg would work solely as a leader on the U.S. western coast in addition to doing some touring and **recording**.

FRONT LINE. A term used to describe the instrumentalists who play with a group, usually responsible for the melody. **Miles Davis'** early and late quintets featured a front line of **trumpet** and **tenor saxophone**.

FUKUMURA, HIROSHI (1949–). A trombonist originally from Japan, Fukumura attended school in the United States until relocating to Japan where he worked frequently with alto saxophonist **Sadao Watanabe**. *See also* JAPAN.

FULLER, CURTIS DUBOIS (1934–). Fuller played several instruments as a youth until he chose the **trombone** during his time in the military in the early 1950s. Fuller was one of the many jazz musicians who first made their mark in Detroit before eventually involving themselves in the New York scene. During the 1950s, Fuller played with many of the top names in jazz including **John Coltrane, Paul Chambers, Dizzy Gillespie, Donald Byrd,** and **Jackie McLean**.

One of Fuller's most important musical associations came when he was hired to be the third member of the **front line** for **Art Blakey**'s **Jazz Messengers** in the early 1960s. Fuller remained with the group for several years until he resumed working as a **sideman** and leader in New York. He has recorded as a leader several times, including a well-known date with fellow trombonist **Slide Hampton**. In addition to his time with the Jazz Messengers, Fuller also spent time working with the **Hard Bop** group the Jazztet that was co-led by **trumpet** player **Art Farmer** and tenor saxophonist **Benny Golson**.

During much of the 1970s, 1980s, and 1990s, Fuller worked as a leader in addition to playing in many tribute bands. He continues to work as a leader despite having struggled with several health-related issues.

FUNK. A style of music with early roots in jazz that drew heavily upon the Soul, **Blues**, and **Rhythm and Blues (R&B)** traditions. Funk is different from other styles because of its reliance on straight quarter notes and rhythms that are syncopated to the 16th-note level. Many Funk bands use **brass** and **saxophones** to provide rhythmic background support. James Brown and Kool and the Gang represent two significant Funk groups. Funk is not a jazz-specific style but rather another source music that jazz drew upon in the later decades. *See also* FUSION.

FUSION. A style of jazz created in the late 1960s and early 1970s in which musicians drew from and then combined a variety of sources. Fusion often used electronic instruments and was frequently modally based. **Rhythm and Blues (R&B)** and **Funk** music elements were used frequently in early Fusion music, as well as music from other countries, most significantly Brazil. Influential Fusion groups included **Return to Forever**, Weather Report, and **Miles Davis**' late 1960s groups. *See also* FUNK; LORBER, JEFF; WATANABE, KAZUMI.

G

GADD, STEVE (1945–). A drummer, Steve Gadd started learning to play at the age of three, and at age 11 he sat in with **Dizzy Gillespie**. His first professional **gig** was with **Chuck Mangione** (1971–1972) after which Gadd moved to New York where he picked up studio work and joined **Chick Corea**'s **Return to Forever**. During the 1970s and the 1980s, Gadd worked with a variety of popular music artists such as Steely Dan and Stevie Wonder, and jazz artists including Corea, **Eddie Gomez**, and the Manhattan Jazz Quintet. He also formed his own group in 1986 named Gadd's Gang that included Jon Faddis and **Ronnie Cuber**, among others. Gadd continues to record and tour with many popular artists.

GALAXIE DREAM BAND. A group formed by German vibes player Gunter Hampel in 1972.

GALAXY. A **record label** founded in 1964 in Berkeley, California. Artists it recorded include **Sonny Stitt, Milt Jackson, Chet Baker, Nat Adderley, Roy Haynes, Philly Joe Jones**, and others.

GALBRAITH, (JOSEPH) BARRY (1919–1983). A guitarist, Barry Galbraith got his start when he moved to New York in 1941. During his time there he played with **Art Tatum, Red Norvo**, and others before joining **Claude Thornhill**'s band from 1941 to 1942 and again from 1946 to 1947. During the 1950s and 1960s, Galbraith spent his time as a **studio musician**, playing with notable musicians including **Benny Goodman, Tal Farlow, Helen Merrill, Coleman Hawkins, Phil Woods, Billie Holiday, Eric Dolphy, Gil Evans, Stan Kenton**, and many others, finishing the 1960s with a stint in the **Thad Jones–Mel Lewis** Orchestra in 1969. During the 1970s Galbraith focused on teaching and published his *Barry Galbraith Guitar Study Series* in 1982. *See also* GUITAR.

GALE, ERIC (1938–1994). A guitarist, Eric Gale started playing when he was 12 and spent his formative years playing in various **Rhythm and Blues (R&B)** groups. In the 1960s he played with **Jimmy Smith, David "Fathead"**

Newman, **Clark Terry**, **Sonny Stitt**, Aretha Franklin, and others, and in 1970 he became the guitarist for the CTI label. During the 1970s he also recorded **albums** under his own name, played with **Stanley Turrentine**, and formed the group Stuff with **Steve Gadd**. He continued to play throughout the 1980s and 1990s before passing away from lung cancer.

GALPER, HAL (1938–). A pianist, Hal Galper was trained classically before attending the **Berklee College of Music** from 1955 to 1958. Galper moved to Boston in 1959, and into the early 1960s his activities included performances with Sam Rivers, **Tony Williams**, and **Chet Baker**. He moved to New York in 1967 and worked as a freelance musician with **Phil Woods**, **Donald Byrd**, **Stan Getz**, **Chuck Mangione**, Anita O'Day, **Bobby Hutcherson**, **Harold Land**, and others. From 1973 to 1975 he played **electric piano** with **Cannonball Adderley**, and in the later 1970s he established his own quintet with **Randy Brecker**, **Michael Brecker**, Wayne Dockery, and Billy Hart. Galper joined Phil Woods on a permanent basis in 1980, playing in his quintet through 1990. During the 1990s, Galper recorded with Tim Hagans and Jerry Bergonzi.

GANELIN, VYACHESLAV SHEVELEVICH (1944–). A Russian pianist, Vyacheslav Ganelin started playing in dance bands in the early 1960s before forming his own trio in 1964. In 1969 he and Vladimir Tarasov founded the Ganelin Trio, changing the name to the G-T-Ch Trio after being joined by Vladimir Chekasin in 1971. The group toured the world and performed **Free Jazz** before disbanding in 1987. Ganelin immigrated to Israel in 1987 where he taught and led his own groups.

GARANYAN, GEORGY ARAMOVICH (1934–2010). A Russian alto saxophonist, Georgy Garanyan taught himself to play before leading an octet in the mid-1950s. From 1958 to 1966 he was the soloist and arranger for Oleg Lundstrem, and he also toured and led his own quintet. He continued to lead various orchestras during the 1970s and wrote music for many films. In 1991 he formed the Moscow Big Band, and in 1998 he became the conductor of the Georgy Garanian Municipal Big Band Moskva-Krasnodar. He continues to record, tour, and lead his own various small groups. *See also* SAXOPHONE.

GARBAREK, JAN (1947–). A tenor saxophonist and soprano saxophonist, Jan Garbarek taught himself to play both instruments after hearing **John Coltrane** on the radio. In 1965 he was discovered by **George Russell**, with whom he would make his first **recording** the next year. He continued to perform with Russell during the early 1970s and formed his own trio in 1973.

Garbarek joined **Keith Jarrett**'s quartet in 1977 and later continued to tour with his own groups. His **album** *Officium* was a success on both the jazz and Classical charts in 1993, and in 1995 *Visible World* was also a hit. *See also* SAXOPHONE.

GARCIA, RUSS(ELL) (1916–2011). A **trumpet** player and composer, Garcia studied composition first at San Francisco State College and later at Westlake College in Los Angeles. Although he played in a few **dance bands** and recorded West Coast–style jazz **albums** as a leader from 1955 to 1957, he is known more for his compositions and **arrangements**. Garcia has arranged for Buddy DeFranco, **Charlie Barnet**, **Roy Eldridge**, **Johnny Hodges**, Ray Brown, and **Stan Kenton**, in addition to composing **Third Stream** pieces and for television and film. *See also* WEST COAST JAZZ.

GARNER, ERROLL LOUIS (1921–1977). A pianist, Erroll Garner taught himself to play the **piano** and never learned to read music. Garner spent his early years playing in his hometown of Pittsburgh, Pennsylvania, before moving to New York in 1944, where he regularly subbed for **Art Tatum** before joining **Slam Stewart**'s trio in 1945. Thereafter he formed his own trio, which included **bass** and **drum set**, and he would perform in this format or as a soloist for the rest of his life. Garner developed a completely unique and individual style that was aided by his own virtuosic technique. He is also known for composing the well-known **ballad** "Misty."

GARRISON, ARV(IN) CHARLES (1922–1960). A self-taught guitarist, Garrison started leading his own groups in 1941. In 1946 he recorded **albums** with **Dizzy Gillespie** and **Charlie Parker** before touring with his wife, bassist Vivien Garry. During the 1950s, Garrison continued to perform in his hometown of Toledo, Ohio. *See also* GUITAR.

GARRISON, JIMMY (1934–1976). A bassist, Jimmy Garrison began his career when he and **Philly Joe Jones** moved to New York in 1958. Garrison played with several musicians, including **Benny Golson**, **Elvin Jones**, **Lennie Tristano**, and **Stan Getz** before joining **Ornette Coleman**'s group in 1961. Later in 1961 he joined **John Coltrane**'s quartet and played with Coltrane until his death in 1967. After Coltrane's death, Garrison performed with Jones, **Archie Shepp**, and **Alice Coltrane**, and he taught at Bennington College and Wesleyan University. Garrison died from lung cancer. *See also* BASS.

GAZELL. A **record label** formed in 1949 in Stockholm, Sweden, that released many Swedish jazz **albums** during the 1950s. The label was purchased by Sonet; in 1986 it was re-formed with some of the original catalog. Sonet also released new jazz and non-jazz albums.

GELLER, HERB(ERT) (1928–). A saxophonist, Herb Geller played with Joe Venuti in Los Angeles before moving to New York in 1949. While in New York, Geller played and recorded with **Claude Thornhill** in 1950, but by 1951 Geller married and moved back to Los Angeles. During the 1950s, Geller performed with **Billy May, Chet Baker, Maynard Ferguson, Bill Holman, Benny Goodman**, and **Louie Bellson** before moving to Germany in 1962. From 1965 to 1994, Geller performed, composed, and arranged for the Norddeutscher Rundfunk or NDR, in addition to doing radio work, composing, and performing with various other European groups. *See also* EUROPE.

GENE NORMAN PRESENTS. A label founded by Gene Norman in 1953, also known as GNP or GNP-Crescendo. Artists include **Clifford Brown, Max Roach, Dizzy Gillespie**, and **Lionel Hampton**, among others. *See also* RECORD LABEL.

GENNETT. A record label and company that began issuing records in 1917 that was active until 1934. Artists included the New Orleans Jazz Band, the **New Orleans Rhythm Kings, King Oliver**, and **Jelly Roll Morton**, among others. *See also* RECORD LABEL.

GEORGIA WASHBOARD STOMPERS. A name also used by the members of the **Washboard Rhythm Kings**, the group featured spirited vocals, horns, a washboard player, and occasionally kazoo, in addition to traditional instruments including **guitar, trumpet**, and **clarinet**.

GETZ, STAN (1927–1991). A tenor saxophonist, Stan Getz played several other instruments before settling on the tenor at the age of 15. By the age of 16 he was already touring with **Jack Teagarden**, and he played with a string of **big bands** including **Stan Kenton, Jimmy Dorsey**, and **Benny Goodman** before joining **Woody Herman** and becoming a member of Herman's famous reed section, the Four Brothers. In 1949 he formed his own groups and spent the 1950s performing and touring despite a drug habit. Getz spent 1958 to 1960 in Europe, and in 1962, after moving back to the United States, Getz and **Charlie Byrd** helped to inspire the **Bossa Nova** craze. His **recordings** from this period are some of his most famous, including the Grammy-winning *Getz/Gilberto*, with the classic rendition of "The Girl from Ipanema," featuring **Astrud Gilberto**. Getz continued to lead small groups throughout the 1960s, 1970s, and 1980s in a variety of different styles and was active up until his death in 1991 from cancer.

GHB. A **record label** and subsidiary of **Jazzology** founded in 1954.

GHOST BAND. The name given to a band that continues to perform after its leader/founder is deceased. Examples include the still-active bands of **Glenn Miller**, **Count Basie**, and **Duke Ellington**.

GHOST(ED) NOTE. A stylistic interpretation in jazz where a note is implied through various techniques rather than physically sounded.

GIBBS, MICHAEL "MIKE" (1937–). Originally born in Rhodesia (now Zimbabwe), Mike Gibbs started playing the **trombone** at age 17 before moving to the United States in 1959 to study music, studying with **George Russell** and **J. J. Johnson**. In 1965 Gibbs moved to England and performed with **Graham Collier** and **John Dankworth** and established a reputation as a composer and arranger. From 1974 to 1953, Gibbs was composer-in-residence at the **Berklee School of Music**, during which time he continued to perform and also to work as a record producer. After resigning from Berklee in 1983, Gibbs moved back to England in 1985 and worked with Dankworth, **Pat Metheny**, and **John McLaughlin**. Gibbs directed the Creative Jazz Orchestra during the 1990s and recorded with **John Scofield**. *See also* EUROPE.

GIG. The term used as a noun for a performance or engagement, or as a verb referring to performing at an engagement.

GILBERTO, ASTRUD (1940–). A Brazilian singer, she is most known for her **singing** on "The Girl from Ipanema," which she recorded in 1963 with **Stan Getz, João Gilberto** (then her husband), and Antônio Carlos Jobim. She recorded several **albums** in the **Bossa Nova** style throughout her career. In the early 1980s she performed in New York with **Jerry Dodgion**, and throughout the 1990s she continued to tour in groups that included her son, Marcelo Gilberto (a bass player).

GILBERTO, JOÃO (1931–). A Brazilian singer and **guitar** player, João Gilberto moved to Rio de Janeiro at age 18 and soon began working with Antônio Carlos Jobim. In 1962, Gilberto moved to New York and the year after began collaborating with **Stan Getz**, resulting in the **album** *Getz/Gilberto*, the iconic album of the **Bossa Nova** craze that swept the United States and the world in the early 1960s. From the late 1960s to the early 1970s, Gilberto resided in Mexico before moving back to the United States, where he continues to perform and record.

GILLESPIE, JOHN "DIZZY" (1917–1993). John Birks Gillespie started playing the **trombone** before switching to the **trumpet** at the age of 12. Largely self-taught, Gillespie received a scholarship to an agricultural school in North Carolina, but in 1935 he dropped out of school and moved to Philadelphia to play music. While in Philadelphia, he got his first **gig** with Frankie Fairfax's band, and his antics earned him the nickname Dizzy. It was in this band that Dizzy also began to imitate the playing of fellow trumpeter **Roy Eldridge**, learning the style from fellow **sideman Charlie Shavers**.

Gillespie moved to New York in 1937 and took Eldridge's spot in Teddy Hill's band, due in part to his skillful imitation of Eldridge's style. In 1939, Gillespie joined **Cab Calloway**'s band and met trumpeter Mario Bauza, a friendship that would help to shape Gillespie's later experiments in **Afro-Cuban Jazz**. Gillespie met **Charlie Parker** in 1940 and was soon participating in the storied **jam sessions** at **Minton's Playhouse** in New York, the early proving grounds of the **Bebop** style. Gillespie's antics eventually led to Calloway dismissing him from his band in 1941, and through the rest of the early 1940s, Gillespie would continue to perfect his new Bebop style in his own groups or in groups led by Lucky Millinder or **Earl Hines**.

In 1944, Gillespie joined **Billy Eckstine**'s band, and then in 1945 he formed a quintet with Parker that produced seminal Bebop **albums** that introduced the entire world to this new form of jazz. Also in 1945, he formed his first **big band**, a short-lived venture that would lead to him forming a much more successful big band in 1946. That orchestra would introduce **Chano Pozo** and with it the Afro-Cuban Jazz style with songs like "Manteca" and "Cubana Be/Cubana Bop." Work would continue with that band until 1950 when the orchestra was forced to disband, but Gillespie would go on to play with small groups throughout the early 1950s, including contests with his former idol Eldridge and records with **J. J. Johnson** and a young **John Coltrane**. Also during the 1950s, another defining incident in his life occurred—according to one story, in 1953 a dancer tripped over Gillespie's trumpet at a party. The bell was bent upward at an angle, and Gillespie had to finish the gig; much to his surprise he discovered he liked the change. The angle allowed him to hear himself better and allowed him to project his sound to the audience while he was leaning down to read music, and soon he had a trumpet designed that included the bent bell. It became his signature instrument for the rest of his life.

In 1956, President Dwight D. Eisenhower asked Gillespie to lead a jazz band on a State Department–sponsored tour of Africa, the Middle East, and Asia. The tour was successful, and another tour was organized to South America. Both bands contained many excellent young jazz musicians, including **Lee Morgan, Wynton Kelly, Benny Golson**, and others. Through the 1960s, Gillespie continued to lead his own small groups, and in the early 1970s, Gillespie toured with the Giants of Jazz. Gillespie appeared at **jazz festivals** throughout the 1980s, playing with young trumpet players Jon Faddis and **Wynton Marsalis**. Gillespie continued to play until 1992.

As a creator of the Bebop style, Gillespie was not only influential for his playing, but also his teaching. He was known as a great teacher of the music, and he helped to pass the new style on to many other musicians throughout his life. His influence on jazz ranks with **Louis Armstrong** and places him among the greatest musicians in jazz history.

GILMORE, STEVE (1943–). Although he studied briefly with Ray Brown, Steve Gilmore largely taught himself to play the **bass** around the age of 12. By the age of 14, he was working professionally and got his first notable professional job performing with **Ira Sullivan** in 1967. During the 1970s, Gilmore also played with Al Cohn and **Zoot Sims**, **Richie Cole**, and the **Thad Jones–Mel Lewis** Orchestra, and in 1974 he began an association with **Phil Woods**. Gilmore has been a mainstay of Woods' quintet ever since, although he has performed and recorded with a few other artists including **Tom Harrell**, **Hal Galper**, and **Dave Liebman**.

GILT-EDGE. A **record label** founded in 1944 in Los Angeles. Most of the catalog contained records by Cecil Gant.

GITLER, IRA (1928–). A writer, Ira Gitler attended the University of Missouri and Columbia University before working at **Prestige** Records from 1950 to 1955. He is known for *The Encyclopedia of Jazz* of which he was the assistant writer with Leonard Feather, in addition to *The Encyclopedia of Jazz in the Sixties*, *The Encyclopedia of Jazz in the Seventies*, *The Biographical Encyclopedia of Jazz*, and writing for several publications including *DownBeat*, *Jazz Times*, and others.

GIUFFRE, JIMMY (1921–2008). A clarinetist, saxophonist, composer, and arranger, Jimmy Giuffre started writing music for Boyd Raeburn before he joined **Jimmy Dorsey** in 1947 as a composer and performer. Later that year Giuffre composed and arranged "Four Brothers" for the **Woody Herman** band to feature the reed section, and in 1949 he joined the band as a performer. During the 1950s, Giuffre played with Howard Rumsey, **Shorty Rogers** and his Giants, and formed his own group (which would later include **Bob Brookmeyer**), in addition to teaching at the Lenox School of Jazz. In the 1960s, Giuffre began to move toward **Free Jazz** with his trio that included **Paul Bley** and **Steve Swallow**. He would perform with various versions of this group throughout the 1970s, incorporating world music into his performances. In the 1980s, Giuffre began performing on soprano saxophone, **flute**, and bass flute and continued to tour with various groups, sometimes playing **Bebop** but eventually shifting to electronic instruments after being influenced by the band Weather Report. During the 1990s he continued to play and taught for a time at the New England Conservatory of Music, but he was eventually forced to retire due to Parkinson's disease. *See also* SAXOPHONE.

GLEASON, RALPH (1917–1975). A writer, Ralph Gleason founded one of the first jazz periodicals in the United States, *Jazz Information*, in 1939, and wrote for *DownBeat* magazine from 1948 to 1961. From 1950 until his death in 1975, Gleason wrote about jazz and popular music for the *San Francisco Chronicle*, and in 1967 he was a founder of the magazine *Rolling Stone*. He was also a founding member of the **Monterey Jazz Festival** in 1958.

GLISS(ANDO). A quick, sliding movement either before a pitch, after a pitch, or most commonly between pitches in a musical passage.

GLOBE UNITY ORCHESTRA. A **big band** formed in Germany in 1966 by Alexander Von Schlippenbach to perform his piece "Globe Unity." The band continued to tour throughout the 1970s and 1980s and performed a varied repertoire, including standards, compositions by members of the band, and free improvisations. Among the members of the band were **Kenny Wheeler**, **Steve Lacy**, and many others.

GLOW, BERNIE (1926–1982). A lead **trumpet** player, Bernie Glow began playing the trumpet at the age of nine. Glow played with **Artie Shaw** from 1945 to 1946, Boyd Raeburn in 1947, and **Woody Herman** from 1947 to 1950. From the 1950s on he was primarily a **studio musician, recording** with **Benny Goodman, Bob Brookmeyer, Miles Davis** and **Gil Evans, Dizzy Gillespie**, and several others.

GNP. *See* GENE NORMAN PRESENTS.

GOLD, HARRY (1907–2005). A **bandleader**, tenor saxophonist, and bass saxophonist, Harry Gold played with a few British jazz bands before joining Oscar Rabin in 1939. Gold formed a small group within Rabin's band named the Pieces of Eight that was a very successful **Dixieland** group. Gold eventually relinquished leadership of the band in 1957 but continued to play with the group while he worked freelance with other bandleaders. In 1975 he revived the band, toured internationally, and made several more **recordings**. The band disbanded in 1991, but Gold continued to perform until shortly before his death. *See also* EARLY JAZZ; ENGLAND; SAXOPHONE.

GOLDENE SIEBEN. A band formed in 1934 in Berlin with some of the best musicians in the city. Die Goldene Sieben recorded many **albums** for the **Electrola** label, made several radio broadcasts, and even appeared on film, but was contractually prohibited from performing in public.

GOLSON, BENNY (1929–). Golson started playing the **tenor saxophone** at the age of 14, and in 1951 he worked with Bullmoose Jackson. While in Jackson's band, he met **Tadd Dameron**, who would greatly influence Golson's writing style. From 1953 to 1954, Golson played with Dameron's band, then played with **Lionel Hampton** and **Earl Bostic** before landing in **Dizzy Gillespie**'s **big band** from 1956 to 1958. After Gillespie's band, Golson played with **Art Blakey** and his **Jazz Messengers** from 1958 to 1959, then led many of his own groups before he and **Art Farmer** formed the **Jazztet** in 1962. From the mid-1960s to the mid-1970s, Golson rarely played and focused on writing and arranging music for film and television. In the late 1970s and 1980s, he resumed performing more frequently, leading his own groups and performing in several reunions with Blakey and with the Jazztet. Golson continued to play in various reunion bands throughout the 1990s in addition to continuing to lead his own groups. He is known for some of his compositions including "I Remember Clifford," "Whisper Not," "Stablemates," and "Killer Joe," which have all achieved status as jazz standards.

GOMEZ, EDDIE (1944–). A bassist, Eddie Gomez started playing **bass** at the age of 11 after moving to New York from Puerto Rico. He performed with **Marian McPartland** from 1963 to 1966 and toured briefly with Gary McFarland, in addition to **recording** with **Gerry Mulligan**. Gomez left Mulligan's group to play in pianist **Bill Evans**' trio, a group with whom Gomez would record and perform until 1977. Gomez then performed with the bands **Steps Ahead**, New Directions, and Special Edition, in addition to playing with **Chick Corea** and many others. In the 1980s, Gomez was a member of the Manhattan Jazz Quintet and also Gadd's Gang, and has remained an active performer since.

GONSALVES, PAUL (1920–1974). A tenor saxophonist, Paul Gonsalves performed in a couple bands before he joined **Count Basie**'s band in 1946. Gonsalves played with Basie until 1949 and then joined **Dizzy Gillespie**'s **big band** until 1950. From 1950 on, Gonsalves performed with the **Duke Ellington** big band, and it was with this band that Gonsalves made his claim to fame—a 27-chorus **Blues** solo on "Diminuendo and Crescendo in Blue" at the 1956 **Newport Jazz Festival** that elevated him to stardom and helped to resurrect Ellington's career. Gonzalves continued to play with Ellington and was a regularly featured soloist in the band, and he also recorded as a **sideman** with musicians including **Sonny Stitt** and **Eddie "Lockjaw" Davis**.

GOODMAN, BENJAMIN DAVID "BENNY" (1909–1986). From a poor family in Chicago, Benny Goodman was pushed to take up a musical instrument by his parents, and by 1919 he was receiving formal training from Classical clarinetist Franz Schoepp. In 1925, Goodman moved to Los Angeles to play with **Ben Pollack**, and then he settled in New York in 1928. While in New York he worked with **Red Nichols** and **Paul Whiteman**. In 1934, Goodman formed his first **big band** for an extended appearance at Billy Rose's Music Hall. The **gig** dried up after a few months, but Goodman managed to land a spot on the NBC Radio Show *Let's Dance*, which allowed Goodman to feature his band performing **arrangements** by **Fletcher Henderson**. When the show ended, Goodman took the band on tour, the beginning of which was not promising despite the band's popularity. However, the band's final performance at the Palomar Ballroom in Los Angeles on August 21, 1935, caused a sensation and marked the beginning of the Swing era in the United States.

Goodman performed and toured with his band into 1936, and during this time he also started a trio that featured himself, **Gene Krupa**, and **Teddy Wilson**. Although this was not the first racially integrated group in jazz, Goodman's immense popularity made it the most visible. He later expanded the group to a quartet with the addition of **Lionel Hampton**, and his band contained some of the best musicians of the time, including Harry James, Ziggy Elman, Vernon Brown, and others. Goodman was soon labeled the "King of Swing" after a successful performance at Carnegie Hall in 1938, and he also began performing Classical music, including works by Wolfgang Mozart, and *Contrast*, a piece Goodman commissioned from Béla Bartók. Illness forced him to disband the group in 1940, but he re-formed the group a few months later, including increasing his quartet to a septet and adding **guitar** player **Charlie Christian**.

Goodman continued to perform throughout the duration of World War II, and by 1947 the final version of his traveling band had begun to concede territory to the **Bebop** movement as his band now included **Fats Navarro** and Doug Mettome. After disbanding the group in 1949, Goodman continued to lead various small groups and tour internationally, notably with tours to South America, the Soviet Union, and **Japan**. Goodman would spend the 1960s and 1970s touring with bands and having various reunion concerts with Krupa, Wilson, and Hampton.

GOOD TIME JAZZ. A record label and company founded in 1949 in Los Angeles. Later acquired by **Fantasy**, artists included **Jelly Roll Morton**, **Willie "the Lion" Smith**, **Bunk Johnson**, and **Kid Ory**, among others. *See also* RECORD LABEL.

GOODWIN, BILL (1942–). A primarily self-taught drummer, Bill Goodwin started playing the **drum set** at the age of 13. His first professional experience was with Charles Lloyd in 1959; thereafter he played with many musicians including **Bud Shank**, Frank Rosolino, **Art Pepper, George Shearing, Gary Burton, Toshiko Akiyoshi, Stan Getz, Gerry Mulligan**, and others. From 1974 through the present day, Goodwin has been a member of **Phil Woods'** band, and from 1979 he has also worked as a producer for Woods, **Tom Harrell**, and others.

GOOFUS. A type of keyboard harmonica, it is mainly a novelty instrument. Air is blown through a tube while the keyboard itself is laid flat. Jazz musicians who have played the goofus include Adrian Rollini and **Don Redman**. *See also* GOOFUS FIVE.

GOOFUS FIVE. A band led by Adrian Rollini in the 1920s that included the **goofus** in some of their pieces.

GORDON, DEXTER (1923–1990). A **tenor saxophone** player, Gordon got his start playing with **Lionel Hampton** from 1940 to 1943, and his first experience as a leader on a **recording session** was with **Nat "King" Cole** playing the **piano**. He worked briefly in 1944 for **Fletcher Henderson, Louis Armstrong**, and **Billy Eckstine**, and by then he was starting to become recognized as an important figure in the new **Bebop** style. Dexter spent the next few years alternating on the east and west coasts of the United States and recording a series of records with **Wardell Gray**, the two of them "dueling" on the saxophone. His career was sidelined during the early 1950s due to narcotic addiction, and his output during the 1950s was sporadic. In 1962 a successful tour of Europe led to Gordon moving there for the next 14 years, performing at **jazz festivals** and touring extensively. In 1976 he decided to return to the

United States, and for his first performance back at the **Village Vanguard** in New York, there were lines of eager fans around the block. Gordon also appeared in the film *Round Midnight* in 1986, for which he was nominated for an Academy Award. *See also* CUTTING CONTEST; EUROPE.

GOYENS, AL(PHONSE) (1920–). A **trumpet** player, baritone saxophonist, and **bandleader**, Goyens led his own band from 1946 to 1958, which included **Don Byas, Kenny Clarke,** and others. After 1958, Goyens toured and performed with an international orchestra, and in the early 1990s he played and arranged for the Brussels **Big Band**. *See also* EUROPE.

GOYKOVICH, DUSKO (1931–). A **trumpet** player, Dusko Goykovich graduated from the Academy of Music in Belgrade in 1953 and performed in Germany before attending the **Berklee School of Music** from 1961 to 1963. After Berklee, he played with **Maynard Ferguson** and **Woody Herman** before moving back to Germany. While in Germany, Goykovich performed with the **Clarke**-Boland Big Band from 1968 to 1973, and in the mid-1970s he co-led a band with **Slide Hampton**. In the 1980s and 1990s, Goykovich continued to lead his own groups and record.

GOZZO, CONRAD JOSEPH (1922–1964). A **lead** trumpet player, Conrad Gozzo studied **trumpet** from his father and eventually replaced one of his father's other students in Isham Jones' **big band** in 1938. Gozzo spent time with the bands of **Claude Thornhill, Benny Goodman, Artie Shaw,** Goodman again, and then **Woody Herman**. From 1947 to 1951 he performed on Bob Crosby's radio broadcasts and with **Jerry Gray**. He spent the rest of the 1950s as a **studio musician** and made **recordings** with Herman, **Shorty Rogers, Stan Kenton,** Goodman, and many others.

GRAHAM, BILL (1918–). An alto and **baritone saxophone** player, Bill Graham played with **Count Basie,** Lucky Millinder, and Erskine Hawkins from 1945 to 1946. From 1946 to 1953, Graham toured and recorded with **Dizzy Gillespie,** from 1955 to 1957 with Count Basie, and in 1958 with **Duke Ellington** on his **album** *Black, Brown and Beige*. From the 1960s on, Graham quit touring and became a public school teacher in New York.

GRAMAVISION. A **record label** and company established in 1979 in Katonah, New York. Artists include John Carter, Anthony Davis, **John Scofield,** and Medeski Martin & Wood, and current artists including **Bill Frisell** and Ron Miles.

GRAMERCY FIVE. A group formed by **Artie Shaw** in 1940 as a small group within his **big band** and named after the Gramercy telephone exchange in New York. The group recorded several successful **albums** in the 1940s with a band that included **Roy Eldridge** on **trumpet**.

GRAMOPHONE COMPANY. Record company established in 1898 in London. The company was established by Trevor Williams and William Barry Owen, agents of Emile Berliner—the inventor of the disc gramophone. The company was merged in 1931 with **Columbia International** to form **Electrical and Musical Industries (EMI)**. *See also* RECORD LABEL.

GRANDE PARADE DU JAZZ. A **jazz festival** founded by **George Wein** and held annually from 1974 to 1993 in Nice, France. Artists included **Art Blakey** and the **Jazz Messengers**, the **Preservation Hall Jazz Band**, **Count Basie**, the **Thad Jones–Mel Lewis** Orchestra, **Buddy Rich**, and many others. In 1994, it was replaced by the Nice Music Festival.

GRANZ, NORMAN (1918–2001). A concert promoter and jazz filmmaker, Norman Granz made the film *Jammin' the Blues* in 1944, which is still considered as one of the best short films on jazz ever made. Granz established the Jazz at the Philharmonic series in 1944. He also established the record company **Verve** in 1956 and the record company **Pablo** in 1973, which he continued to manage in the 1980s. Granz also became manager for some of the artists he promoted, including **Ella Fitzgerald** and **Oscar Peterson**. *See also* RECORD LABEL.

GRAPPELLI, STÉPHANE (1908–1997). An important early innovator of the jazz **violin**, Grappelli was mostly self-taught until formally attending the Paris Conservatory from 1924 to 1928. In 1934 he was a founding member of the **Quintette du Hot Club de France** with **Django Reinhardt**; Grappelli would stay with the group until 1939 when he moved to England. While in England, Grappelli worked with **George Shearing**, but in the 1950s his career slowed. A revived interest in jazz violin caused in part by the **album** *Violin Summit* (1966) with Grappelli, Jean-Luc Ponty, **Stuff Smith**, and Svend Asmussen helped breathe life back into his career, and his performances and records from the 1970s remain definitive examples of jazz violin style. He remained active into the 1990s.

GRAY, JERRY (1915–1976). A composer, arranger, and **bandleader**, Jerry Gray experienced early success with his version of "Begin the Beguine" for

Artie Shaw's band in 1938. Gray was the chief arranger for **Glenn Miller** from 1939 to 1945 and took over the band from 1945 to 1946 after Miller's disappearance. Among his hits from his time with Miller's band are "Pennsylvania 6–5000" and "A String of Pearls." Gray led his own radio show in Hollywood from 1946 to 1952, and during the rest of the 1950s he was a freelance arranger and director, writing for films including *The Glenn Miller Story* (1954). He continued to write and arrange during the 1970s until his death in 1976.

GRAY, WARDELL (1921–1955). A tenor **saxophone** player, Gray played with **Earl Hines** in 1943 and joined **Billy Eckstine**'s band in 1944. He moved to Los Angeles and became known for several **jam sessions** with **Dexter Gordon** that resulted in the **album** *The Chase* in 1947, followed shortly after by a **recording** with **Charlie Parker**. Gray then spent some time in **Benny Goodman**'s short-lived **Bebop big band**, and played with **Louie Bellson** from 1952 to 1953. Gray died under somewhat unusual circumstances, possibly related to his drug addiction.

GREAT GUITARS. A quintet formed by guitarists **Barney Kessel**, **Charlie Byrd**, and **Herb Ellis** in 1974.

GREAT JAZZ TRIO. A group formed by **Hank Jones** in 1967. Members of the group changed regularly and at one time included **Ron Carter**, **Tony Williams**, **Shelly Manne**, and **George Duvivier**, among others.

GREEN, BENNIE (1923–1977). A **trombone** player, Bennie Green got his start playing with **Earl Hines** in 1942, with whom he would continue to perform off and on during the 1950s. Green also played with **Charlie Ventura** in the late 1940s. Green worked as a leader throughout the 1950s and 1960s, employing at various times **Paul Chambers**, **Elvin Jones**, and Sonny Clark, in addition to working with a group co-led by **Gene Ammons** and **Sonny Stitt**. In 1969, Green also performed with **Duke Ellington** for one of Ellington's sacred concerts. Following that, Green settled in Las Vegas and worked primarily in hotel and casino house bands.

GREEN, CHARLIE (1900–1936). A trombonist, Charlie Green worked with several **brass bands** before joining **Fletcher Henderson** in 1924 with whom he continued to perform off and on. Green also accompanied **Bessie Smith** on several of her **recordings** during this period, in addition to appearing on recordings with **Louis Armstrong**, **Fats Waller**, **James P. Johnson**, and others. From 1929 through the early 1930s, Green performed with **Benny**

Green and also with **Chick Webb**. Green froze to death after being locked out of his residence in New York.

GREEN, FREDDIE (1911–1987). A guitarist, Freddie Green originally started on **banjo** before switching to **guitar** and playing with **Kenny Clarke** in 1936. On the recommendation of John Hammond, Green (who later would spell his last name "Greene") was hired by **Count Basie** in 1937. Green would continue to perform with Basie for the next 47 years, forming an essential part of Basie's early All-American Rhythm Section along with Basie, bassist **Walter Page**, and drummer Jo Jones. Green also contributed to the band as a composer and arranger. Included among his compositions are "Down for Double," "Right On," and "Corner Pocket." After Basie's death in 1984, Green recorded with other groups, including **Manhattan Transfer**.

GREEN, GRANT (1935–1979). A **guitar** player, Grant Green was largely self-taught and spent his early years playing Gospel music and with **Rhythm and Blues (R&B)** bands. In 1960, Green moved to New York and helped establish the **organ** trio instrumentation of guitar, organ, and **drum set**. Green recorded many **albums** during the 1960s with artists including **Lou Donaldson, Stanley Turrentine, Hank Mobley, Lee Morgan, McCoy Tyner, Herbie Hancock**, and many others. Green took a break from music in the mid- to late 1960s but resumed playing in the 1970s, although his drug addiction somewhat limited his output.

GREEN, URBIE (1926–). A **trombone** player, Green played in a wartime draft band before joining **Gene Krupa** from 1947 to 1950. From 1950 to 1953, Green played with **Woody Herman**, and in the mid-1950s Green joined **Benny Goodman**, sometimes leading the band when Goodman was unable. Green also worked as a **bandleader** during the late 1950s, and he took over **Tommy Dorsey**'s orchestra following Dorsey's death in 1966. He continued to play during the 1990s, **recording** an **album** with his son and Chris Potter in 1995.

GREENE, BOB (1922–). A **piano** player and **bandleader**, Bob Greene got his start playing with **Baby Dodds** before **recording** with Conrad Janis, Sidney DeParis, and Johnny Wiggs in the early 1950s. He worked as a writer for radio documentaries and wrote speeches for Lyndon Johnson and Robert Kennedy, and after Kennedy's assassination in 1968, he returned to playing jazz as his profession. In 1969 he performed a tribute to **Jelly Roll Morton**, and by 1971 he was leading a re-creation of Morton's **Red Hot Peppers**. The band stayed active during the 1990s and toured extensively, including in the United States, South America, and **Europe**.

GREER, SONNY (1895–1982). A drummer, Sonny Greer met **Duke Ellington** in 1919 while working as a member of the orchestra at the Howard Theatre in Washington, D.C. In 1922 he became a member of **Elmer Snowden**'s Washingtonians, the group that became Ellington's orchestra. He was instrumental in developing the "jungle sounds" that made Ellington's run at the **Cotton Club** in New York such a success. Greer played with Ellington through 1951 before he was asked to leave the band. Afterwards, Greer freelanced with many musicians including ex-Ellington band members **Johnny Hodges**, Tyree Glenn, and J. C. Higginbotham. Greer led his own bands throughout the 1960s and was active in the 1970s and early 1980s until his death.

GREY, AL(BERT) THORNTON (1925–2000). A trombonist, Al Grey started playing with U.S. Navy bands during World War II. After appearing with **Benny Carter** (1945–1946) and **Jimmie Lunceford** (1946–1947), Grey joined **Lionel Hampton** from 1948 to 1953. During his time with Hampton, Grey began to solo with a plunger **mute**, an ability for which he became renowned. Grey played with **Dizzy Gillespie** from 1956 to 1957 before joining **Count Basie** from 1957 to 1961, and again from 1964 to 1966 and 1971 to 1977. In between his stints with Basie's band, Grey led his own groups with sidemen including **Herbie Hancock, Donald Byrd, Bobby Hutcherson,** and others. After leaving Basie for the final time in 1977, Grey led a quintet with **Jimmy Forrest** until Forrest was too ill to perform; the quintet continued with Buddy Tate through 1987 until Tate had a heart attack. From 1988 into the 1990s, Grey led his own group named Al Grey and His Musical Sons, which featured his son and the sons of many other famous jazz musicians. Grey also co-authored a book with his son Mike Grey on plunger technique for **trumpet** and trombone. *See also* TROMBONE.

GRIFFIN, JOHNNY (1928–2008). A **tenor saxophone** player, Johnny Griffin got his start right out of high school, playing with **Lionel Hampton**'s **big band** from 1945 to 1947. Griffin then played with Joe Morris from 1947 to 1950, and during that time he also performed with **Philly Joe Jones**, Arnett Cobb, and others, in addition to playing regularly with **Thelonious Monk** and **Bud Powell**. He spent 1951 to 1953 in the U.S. Army, moved to Chicago for a few years, and then joined **Art Blakey**'s **Jazz Messengers** for a few months in 1957, followed by a few months in Monk's quartet. Griffin would earn the nickname "tough tenor" while leading a group with **Eddie "Lockjaw" Davis** from 1960 to 1962 through enthusiastic improvisatory competition between the two men. In 1963, Griffin moved to Paris and continued to perform with musicians including **Art Taylor, Kenny Clarke,** and **Bud Powell**. Griffin performed with the Clarke-Boland Big Band from 1967 to 1969. During most of the 1970s, Griffin lived in the Netherlands and toured **Europe** and the United States. During the 1980s, Griffin led his own groups, and in 1992 he performed with the Phillip Morris Superband.

GROFÉ, FERDE (1892–1972). A composer and arranger, Ferde Grofé studied in Germany as a child and arranged for a couple of jazz bands before being hired by **Paul Whiteman** in 1920. Grofé's **arrangement** of George Gershwin's "Rhapsody in Blue" was so successful that it encouraged Whiteman to expand into the symphonic jazz genre. Grofé's other successful works include "Mississippi" and "The Grand Canyon Suite." Grofé left Whiteman in the early 1930s and led his own band in addition to working as an arranger and conductor, and throughout the remainder of his life Grofé also wrote many pieces for symphony and for concert band. Because of the success of his arrangements and the popularity of Whiteman's band, Grofé was very influential in the development of jazz arranging for much of the 1920s and 1930s.

GROOVE. Used in jazz, it is a term that can refer to the beat or feel of the music. Music that is "in the groove" generally feels good or is enjoyable to listen to, while music that does not "groove" lacks those qualities. Similar to the use of the term *swing*, it is generally employed as part of an opinion and as such is difficult to define.

GROSSMAN, STEVE (1951–). A **soprano** and **tenor saxophone** player, Steve Grossman was already living in New York, leading his own groups, and even playing with **Elvin Jones** at the young age of 16. By 1968 he was playing with the Jazz Samaritans, a group that included **George Cables** and **Lenny White**, and by 1969 he recorded with **Miles Davis**. The next year, Grossman replaced **Wayne Shorter** in Davis' group. In 1971 he played with **Lonnie Smith**'s quintet, from 1971 to 1973 he again played with Jones, and in 1975 he was a founding member of Gene Perla's Stone Alliance. During the 1980s, Grossman led his own groups and performed with musicians including **Cedar Walton** and **Tom Harrell**, and from the 1990s, despite moving to Bologna, Italy, Grossman returned frequently to the United States to perform and record.

GROWL. A musical effect employed mostly by **brass** players, woodwind players, and vocalists. On brass and woodwind instruments, the effect can be created by actually "growling" through the throat while playing, by using a technique known as "flutter-tonguing" (similar to the effect of rolling the letter *r* in speech), or by some combination of the two techniques. The growl effect was popularized by brass players such as **Bubber Miley, Tricky Sam Nanton,** and **Cootie Williams,** each as members of the **Duke Ellington** Orchestra and all using a **plunger mute** in combination with the growl technique.

GRP (GRUSIN-ROSEN PRODUCTIONS). A **record label** founded in 1978 by **Dave Grusin** and Larry Rosen. During the 1990s, GRP reissued many old **albums** from the Impulse! label. Artists recorded under the GRP label include **Dizzy Gillespie, Arturo Sandoval, Michael Brecker, Chick Corea, Billy Cobham,** and Dave Grusin himself.

GRUSIN, DAVE (1934–). A pianist, composer, and record producer, Dave Grusin graduated from the University of Colorado before he was hired by Andy Williams to be the pianist and musical director for his band, a job Grusin held from 1959 to 1964. Grusin also played with **Benny Goodman** and **Thad Jones** during this time, but most importantly he began a long Academy Award–winning career of writing music for television and films. During the 1970s he recorded with singers **Sarah Vaughan** and **Carmen McRae,** and in 1978 he founded the **GRP** record label with drummer Larry Rosen. He managed the label until 1994 while continuing to arrange music for television and film. Grusin has been nominated for many Academy Awards and won an Oscar in 1989 for his work on *The Milagro Beanfield War.*

GRYCE, GIGI (1925–1983). An alto **saxophone** player and composer, Gigi Gryce started playing in local bands during the late 1940s. Gryce studied composition at the Boston Conservatory in 1948 and then in Paris with Arthur Honegger and Nadia Boulanger. After moving to New York in 1952, Gryce performed and wrote for **Max Roach, Tadd Dameron,** and **Clifford Brown,** and then he joined **Lionel Hampton's** band that toured **Europe** in 1953. In 1954 he performed in groups with **Art Farmer, Donald Byrd,** and **Art Blakey.** In the late 1950s, Gryce led his own groups, but during the 1960s and 1970s, Gryce taught public school in New York. Gryce composed many Classical pieces; among his well-known jazz compositions are "Minority" and "Nica's Tempo."

GUARALDI, VINCE(NT) ANTHONY (1928–1976). A **piano** player and composer, Guaraldi played with **Cal Tjader, Bill Harris, Georgie Auld, Sonny Criss, Woody Herman,** Frank Rosolino, and **Conte Candoli** during the 1950s, and by the 1960s he was working as a leader in addition to composing. In 1962, Guaraldi won the Grammy Award for Best Original

Jazz Composition for his song "Cast Your Fate to the Wind," but he remains best known for composing the music to the popular Charlie Brown *Peanuts* cartoon.

GUARDSMAN. Record label established in 1914 in London. The label lasted until 1928; notable musicians included **Fletcher Henderson**.

GUARNIERI, JOHNNY (1917–1985). A **piano** player, Johnny Guarnieri met **Art Tatum, Fats Waller, James P. Johnson**, and **Willie "the Lion" Smith** early in his life, all of whom would be influential on his style. From 1939 through the early 1940s, Guarnieri played for a time with **Benny Goodman** and then joined **Artie Shaw**'s **Gramercy Five**, where he played harpsichord. He played at the famous **jam sessions** at **Minton's Playhouse** in Harlem during the early 1940s and also played during that time with **Charlie Christian** as a member of Goodman's small group. After spending 1942–1943 with **Jimmy Dorsey**'s orchestra, Guarnieri spent the rest of the 1940s playing and **recording** with a variety of artists including **Cozy Cole, Lester Young, Ben Webster, Coleman Hawkins, Roy Eldridge**, and **Louis Armstrong**. During the 1950s and 1960s, he appeared in several television shows including *The Today Show, Art Ford's Jazz Party*, and *After Hours*. From the 1960s on, he spent most of his time as a house pianist for hotels in Los Angeles and Hollywood, touring rarely.

GUILD. A record company founded in 1945 in New York City. The company only lasted one year but is noteworthy for being the first company to record both **Dizzy Gillespie** and **Charlie Parker** together. *See also* RECORD LABEL.

GUITAR. An instrument in the lute family, the modern guitar has a fret board and six strings (although some guitars have more than six strings). Famous jazz guitarists include **Wes Montgomery, Django Reinhardt, Charlie Christian, Jim Hall**, and **Joe Pass**. *See also* ABERCROMBIE, JOHN; ELECTRIC GUITAR; ELECTRIC BASS (GUITAR); ELLIS, HERB; JORDAN, STANLEY; METHENY, PAT; POWELL, BADEN; RITENOUR, LEE; SCOFIELD, JOHN; STERN, MIKE; TOWNER, RALPH.

GUTBUCKET. In jazz, a term referring to an uninhibited or reckless style of performance.

GUY, JOE (1920–1962). A **trumpet** player, Joe Guy got his start playing in Teddy Hill's orchestra in 1937. Guy went on to perform as the principal soloist in **Coleman Hawkins' big band** from 1939 to 1940, and in 1941 he became a fixture at the **jam sessions** at **Minton's Playhouse,** performing regularly with **Thelonious Monk, Kenny Clarke,** and **Charlie Christian.** Guy played with **Cootie Williams** in 1942, and from 1945 to 1947 he was **Billie Holiday**'s manager and love interest. Guy disappeared from the New York jazz scene before passing away in the early 1960s.

H

HACKETT, BOBBY (1915–1976). A cornetist and guitarist, Bobby Hackett played in a trio with **Pee Wee Russell** and Teddy Roy and even led his own band for a short while before moving to New York in 1936. Hackett gained notoriety when he performed with **Benny Goodman** at a Carnegie Hall concert in 1938, and he spent the rest of the 1930s leading his own bands and also playing with Horace Heidt. From 1941 to 1942 he played with **Glenn Miller**, in 1943 for the NBC Orchestra, from 1946 with the ABC Orchestra, and in 1947 in concert with **Louis Armstrong**. During the 1950s, Hackett worked mostly as a **studio musician**. In addition, he recorded a series of **albums** with the comedian Jackie Gleason, some albums with **Jack Teagarden**, and continued to lead his own bands. During the 1960s, Hackett again played with Goodman, led the Glenn Miller memorial band, and toured with singer **Tony Bennett**. In 1972 he played in the **World's Greatest Jazz Band** and again with Goodman in 1973–1974 and 1976. *See also* CORNET; GUITAR.

HADEN, CHARLIE (1937–). A **bass** player, Haden started playing early as a member of the Haden family band where he sang and played **piano**. After moving to Los Angeles in the mid-1950s, Haden played with **Art Pepper, Paul Bley**, and **Hampton Hawes**. Haden met **Ornette Coleman** while playing with Bley, and the two began playing together in 1958, eventually moving to New York in 1959 for their celebrated stint at the **Five Spot**. Drug problems interrupted Haden's career, but he was playing again in 1964 with Denny Zeitlin's trio, **Archie Shepp**, and again with Coleman in 1966. He played with **Keith Jarrett** from 1967 to 1976, in 1969 formed the Liberation Music Orchestra, and in 1976 formed his group Old and New Dreams with **Don Cherry, Dewey Redman**, and Ed Blackwell. During the 1980s and 1990s, Haden continued to perform with the Liberation Music Orchestra, led his own group Quartet West, and played with **Pat Metheny, Michael Brecker, Chet Baker, Joe Henderson, Tom Harrell**, Joe Lovano, and many others. He remains an active performer today. *See also* FREE JAZZ.

HAHN, JERRY DONALD (1940–). A **guitar** player, Jerry Hahn played in local bands before joining John Handy's band in 1964, in which he played electric guitar. After **recording** an **album** with **Jack DeJohnette** and touring with the Fifth Dimension, Hahn joined **Gary Burton**'s group from 1968 to 1969. In 1972, Hahn taught at Wichita State University, and during the 1990s he recorded with **Dave Liebman**, **Art Lande**, and others.

HAIG, AL(LAN) WARREN (1922–1982). A pianist, Al Haig was stationed in New York with the U.S. Coast Guard during the early 1940s, and in 1945 he recorded many classic **Bebop sessions** with **Charlie Parker** and **Dizzy Gillespie**. Haig toured with Parker from 1948 to 1950 and then with **Stan Getz** until 1951. Haig was absent from the jazz scene until he was rediscovered during the 1970s, after which he toured extensively and worked as a solo act or leading a trio. *See also* PIANO.

HAKIM, SADIQ (1919–1983). A pianist, Sadiq Hakim got his first notable **gig** with **Ben Webster** from 1944 to 1945. In 1945 he played in **recording sessions** with **Charlie Parker** and **Dizzy Gillespie** for the **Savoy** record label, and from 1946 to 1948 Hakim played with **Lester Young**. From 1951 to 1954, Hakim played with **James Moody** and from 1956 to 1960 with Buddy Tate. In 1966 he moved to Montreal, Canada, where he worked in nightclubs, and he toured Japan from 1979 to 1980.

HALF-VALVE. A technique used with valved **brass** instruments where the valves are not completely depressed when producing a tone, resulting in a restrained tone. It is mostly used for effects.

HALL, JIM (1930–). A guitarist, Jim Hall got his first **gig** in Los Angeles as a member of **Chico Hamilton**'s quintet from 1955 to 1956. From 1956 to 1959 he was a member of **Jimmy Giuffre**'s trio, and during the late 1950s and early 1960s he also played with **Bill Evans, Ben Webster, Ella Fitzgerald**, Paul Desmond, **Lee Konitz, Sonny Rollins, Art Farmer**, and others. Starting in 1962, Hall also began leading his own trios, which at various times included **Tommy Flanagan, Percy Heath, Ron Carter, Red Mitchell**, and Colin Bailey. During the late 1960s and early 1970s he made some duo **recordings** with Evans and Carter, in addition to working with Desmond, Mitchell, and **Bob Brookmeyer**. During the 1980s he performed with **George Shearing** and violinist Itzhak Perlman in addition to Carter. From the mid-1980s into the 1990s he led a quartet with sidemen including Steve LaSpina, Bill Stewart, Terry Clarke, Larry Goldings, Chris Potter, and others. Additionally, Hall performed with Rollins, **John Scofield, Pat Metheny**, and Joe Lovano. *See also* ELECTRIC GUITAR; GUITAR; SIDEMAN.

HAMILTON, FORESTOM "CHICO" (1921–). A drummer and bandleader, Hamilton was already playing with noted jazz musicians including **Illinois Jacquet, Charles Mingus, Dexter Gordon**, and Ernie Royal before he had finished high school. From 1940 to 1941, Hamilton played with **Lionel Hampton, Lester Young, Duke Ellington**, and others before joining the U.S. Army in 1942. After leaving the army he played in bands led by **Jimmy Mundy** and **Count Basie** and worked with **Ella Fitzgerald**, then from 1948 to 1955 he worked with Lena Horne. In 1952 he also appeared in **Gerry Mulligan**'s piano-less quartet and performed with **Wardell Gray**. In 1955, Hamilton formed his own group that would remain active with different personnel and instrumentation throughout the 1970s. Among his many sidemen with this group were **Jim Hall, Eric Dolphy, Ron Carter, Buddy Collette**, and others. The group originally consisted of **guitar, bass, drum set**, woodwinds, and a cello; the cello was ultimately replaced by **trumpet/ trombone**. During the late 1960s, Hamilton led a septet with two alto saxophones and two trombones, and during the 1970s and 1980s he led **Jazz-Rock** groups, including his group Euphoria. He continued to perform and record during the 1990s and 2000s.

HAMILTON, JEFF (1953–). A drummer and **bandleader**, Jeff Hamilton got his first **gigs** in the mid-1970s with the bands of **Tommy Dorsey** and **Lionel Hampton**. From 1975 to 1977, Hamilton played in a trio with **Monty Alexander** and John Clayton, and in 1977–1978 with **Woody Herman**. From 1978 to 1983, Hamilton played in the group L.A. 4 with Ray Brown, Laurindo Almeida, and **Bud Shank**. In 1984 he co-founded the Clayton-Hamilton Jazz Orchestra with John and Jeff Clayton, and the group continues to perform. During the mid-1980s, Hamilton also played with **Ella Fitzgerald, Count Basie**'s orchestra, Brown's own jazz trio, **Bill Holman**, and others. During the 1990s he was a member of **Oscar Peterson**'s trio in addition to leading his own trio and performing with vocalist Diana Krall. *See also* DRUM SET; BIG BAND.

HAMILTON, JIMMY (1917–1994). A **clarinet** and **tenor saxophone** player, Jimmy Hamilton got his start working in the early 1940s with Lucky Millinder, **Jimmy Mundy, Teddy Wilson**, and **Benny Carter**. From 1943 to 1968, Hamilton was a member of **Duke Ellington**'s orchestra as the featured clarinet soloist, after which he moved to St. Croix where he continued to perform and teach. In the 1980s, Hamilton played with **Mercer Ellington**, in the group Spacemen (which consisted of fellow Ellington band members including **Clark Terry**), and the Clarinet Summit.

HAMMER, JAN (1948–). A keyboardist, Jan Hammer studied at the Prague Conservatory before immigrating to the United States in 1968 after the Russian invasion of Czechoslovakia. During the early 1970s, Hammer worked with **Sarah Vaughan** and **Elvin Jones** before joining the Mahavishnu Orchestra in 1971. From 1973 to 1975 he played with **Billy Cobham** in the group Spectrum, and during the late 1970s and 1980s he led his own groups and played with Jeff Beck and **Al Di Meola**. Since then he has been active as a composer for film and television; most notable was his Grammy Award–winning work for the 1980s TV hit, *Miami Vice.*

HAMMOND, JOHNNY (1933–1997). An organist, Johnny Hammond imitated **Bud Powell** and **Art Tatum** early in his training before switching to the **Hammond organ** and forming his own group in Cleveland in 1957. After playing with **Nancy Wilson** in 1958, Hammond recorded many **Soul Jazz albums** from 1959 to 1970. During the 1970s and 1980s, Hammond continued to record and utilize other electronic keyboards, but during the 1990s he switched back to the Hammond B3 organ after its resurgence in popularity during the 1990s. *See also* ORGAN.

HAMMOND ORGAN. An electronic **organ** that is popular in jazz music. The most famous model played by jazz musicians is the B3. Popular jazz organists include **Jimmy Smith**, **Johnny Hammond**, and Joey DeFrancesco, among others.

HAMPTON, LIONEL (1908–2002). A drummer, vibraphonist, and **bandleader,** Lionel Hampton played drums in local bands and accompanied and recorded with **Louis Armstrong** in 1930–1931. After switching to **vibraphone,** Hampton was heard by **Benny Goodman**, who hired him for a **recording session** with **Teddy Wilson** and **Gene Krupa**. The group, known as the Benny Goodman Quartet, was enormously successful. Hampton would continue to play in Goodman's groups through 1940, even taking over on drums after Krupa's departure. During his time with Goodman, Hampton also made several notable "all-star" small-group recordings.

Starting in 1940, Hampton began to lead his own **big band**, which became immensely popular; among his many sidemen were **Illinois Jacquet, Dexter Gordon, Fats Navarro, Clifford Brown, Clark Terry, Art Farmer, Cat Anderson, Charles Mingus, Wes Montgomery, Dinah Washington,** Aretha Franklin, and others. Hampton and his band would continue to tour throughout the world into the early 1960s, in addition to playing with other great jazz artists including **Stan Getz, Oscar Peterson,** and **Art Tatum**. During the 1960s and 1970s, Hampton participated in Benny Goodman reunion groups, big band reunions, and also played with small groups, and during the 1980s and 1990s he again led his big band. *See also* DRUM SET; SIDEMAN.

HAMPTON, LOCKSLEY WELLINGTON "SLIDE" (1932–). A composer, arranger, **bandleader**, and **trombone** player, Slide Hampton was working as a trombonist and arranger for a **Rhythm and Blues (R&B)** band when he moved to New York and joined **Lionel Hampton**'s band from 1955 to 1957. From 1958 to 1959, Hampton played and wrote for **Maynard Ferguson**, and during the 1960s he led his own octet with **Freddie Hubbard, Booker Little, George Coleman**, and others. During this time he also worked as the musical director for R&B singer Lloyd Price. He moved to **Europe** after touring there with **Woody Herman** in 1968, where he led various bands and worked as a soloist. Hampton returned to the United States in 1977, and since then he has led the World of Trombones (a nine-piece trombone ensemble with **rhythm section**), the Manhattan Composer's Orchestra, and the Collective Black Artists Orchestra. During the 1980s he also played with Continuum, a group dedicated to the music of **Tadd Dameron** and consisting of **Jimmy Heath, Kenny Barron, Ron Carter**, and **Art Taylor**, in addition to performing and directing **Dizzy Gillespie**'s United Nations Orchestra. During the 1990s he continued to perform and lead a group called the Jazzmasters, which included Jon Faddis, Roy Hargrove, Claudio Roditi, **Steve Turre**, and others. Hampton is the recipient of two Grammy Awards and was recognized in 2005 by the National Endowment for the Arts (NEA) with the NEA Jazz Masters Award.

HANCOCK, HERBIE (1940–). A pianist and composer, Herbie Hancock had already played with **Coleman Hawkins** and **Lee Morgan** before he moved to New York and recorded with **Donald Byrd** in 1961. In 1962 he recorded his debut **album** as a leader that featured "Watermelon Man," one of his most popular compositions. Hancock played with **Eric Dolphy** from 1962 to 1963, and from 1963 to 1968 he played in one of **Miles Davis**' most famous groups along with **Tony Williams** and **Ron Carter**. While with Davis, Hancock continued to work as a **sideman** with other groups and led his own groups, **recording** some of his most famous tunes including "Cantaloupe Island," "Dolphin Dance," "Maiden Voyage," and "Speak Like a Child."

After leaving Davis in 1968, Hancock formed his own group and participated in Davis' albums *In a Silent Way* and *Bitches Brew*. In 1973 he released the album *Headhunters*, which contained his **Funk** composition "Chameleon." During the middle to late 1970s, Hancock continued to lead his **Fusion** group, and he also led his group **V.S.O.P.** with **trumpet** player **Freddie Hubbard**, in addition to playing as a duo with **Chick Corea**.

During the 1980s, Hancock achieved commercial success with the song "Rockit" and won an Academy Award for his score to the film *Round Midnight*, while continuing to perform with artists including Carter, Williams, **Michael Brecker, Pat Metheny**, and many others. During the 1990s, Hancock won a Grammy Award for his tribute album to George Gershwin, and during the 2000s his album *Directions in Music: Live at Massey Hall* with Brecker and Roy Hargrove received a Grammy Award. His album *River: The Joni Letters* won a Grammy Award for Album of the Year—the second jazz album to ever receive that award. *See also* ELECTRIC PIANO; PIANO; SYNTHESIZER.

HANDY, JOHN (1900–1971). A saxophonist and clarinetist, John Handy played clarinet in local bands before moving to New Orleans in 1918, where he played in bands led by Tom Albert and Charlie Love. In 1928, Handy switched to the **alto saxophone**, and in 1932 he formed the Louisiana Shakers with his brother Sylvester. During the 1930s, Handy played with Lee Collins, Jim Robinson, and others; in 1938 with Charlie Creath; in the 1940s with the Young Tuxedo Brass Band; and during the 1950s with Kid Clayton. During the 1960s he toured and performed with the Preservation Hall Jazz Band. *See also* CLARINET; SAXOPHONE.

HANDY, W(ILLIAM) C(HRISTOPHER) (1873–1958). A **cornet** player and composer, W. C. Handy played in a **brass band** and toured the South with minstrel shows during the 1890s and early 1900s. From 1903 he led his own band, the Memphis Orchestra, eventually moving to New York City in 1917, where he set up his own music publishing company. He continued to play throughout the 1920s and 1930s, notably with **Jelly Roll Morton**. Known as "the Father of the Blues," among his most famous compositions is "St. Louis Blues."

HANNA, JAKE (1931–2010). A drummer, Hanna got his first notable **gigs** in 1956 with Buddy Morrow, then spent the rest of the 1950s playing with **Toshiko Akiyoshi, Woody Herman**, and **Maynard Ferguson**. From 1959 to 1961 he played with **Marian McPartland**, then briefly with **Bobby Hackett, Duke Ellington**, Harry James, and Herb Pomeroy before rejoining Herman's band from 1962 to 1964. From 1965 to 1975, Hanna was the drummer for Merv Griffin's television show, and in 1972 he was a founding member of the group Supersax. From 1975, Hanna led a group with **Carl Fontana** and from 1976 performed with Rosemary Clooney. From the mid-1970s and into the 1990s, Hanna was the drummer for the **Concord record label** and therefore recorded with numerous artists including **Harry Edison, Tal Farlow, Joe Pass, Teddy Wilson, Snooky Young**, and many others.

HANNA, ROLAND P. (1932–2002). A pianist, Roland Hanna took leave from the Juilliard School in 1955 to play with **Benny Goodman**. During the late 1950s, Hanna played with **Coleman Hawkins, Charles Mingus,** and **Sarah Vaughan**. From 1963 to 1966, Hanna led his own group in New York, and from 1967 to 1974, he was a regular member of the **Thad Jones–Mel Lewis** Orchestra. During the 1970s he also played with the New York Jazz Sextet and the New York Jazz Quartet. During the 1980s, Hanna was a member of **Mingus Dynasty**, and from 1986 to 1992 he was a member of the Lincoln Center Jazz Orchestra. Hanna continued to tour throughout the 1990s as a soloist and with his own trio.

HARD BOP. A style of jazz from the 1950s, related to **Bebop**. Hard Bop is generally more soulful and returns to a more **Blues**-influenced idiom. Famous jazz musicians associated with Hard Bop include **Clifford Brown, Art Blakey, Horace Silver**, and **Cannonball Adderley**. *See also* MOBLEY, HANK; MORGAN, LEE; BYRD, DONALD.

HARDEE, JOHN (1918–1984). A tenor saxophonist, John Hardee played with Tiny Grimes in New York after his discharge from the military in 1946. From 1946 to 1948, Hardee led his own band, and during the rest of the 1940s he recorded with **Earl Bostic**, Lucky Millinder, and others. Eventually moving to Wichita and then Dallas to pursue a career in music education, Hardee continued to play and lead his own bands into the 1970s. *See also* SAXOPHONE; TENOR SAXOPHONE.

HARDING, LAVERE "BUSTER" (1917–1965). A pianist and arranger, Buster Harding moved to New York in 1938, and from 1939 to 1940 he performed and arranged for **Teddy Wilson**'s band. During the 1940s, Harding arranged for many **bandleaders**, including **Cab Calloway, Artie Shaw, Count Basie, Benny Goodman, Coleman Hawkins, Tommy Dorsey, Glenn Miller**, and others. During the 1950s he arranged for **Dizzy Gillespie** and **Billie Holiday**. *See also* BIG BAND; PIANO.

HARDMAN, BILL (1933–1990). A **trumpet** player, Bill Hardman played with **Tadd Dameron** while in high school. During the 1950s, Hardman played with Tiny Bradshaw, **Jackie McLean, Charles Mingus, Art Blakey**'s **Jazz Messengers, Horace Silver**, and **Lou Donaldson** (with whom he would play until 1966). During the late 1960s, Hardman played with both Mingus and Blakey again, and during the 1970s he led the Brass Company and played briefly with **Mel Lewis**. During the 1980s he led a group with Junior Cook and performed with **Cedar Walton, Sonny Stitt**, and at a Jazz Messengers Reunion.

HARDWICK(E), OTTO (1904–1970). An alto saxophonist, Otto Hardwick was a friend of **Duke Ellington** when the two were young. Hardwick was an original member of Ellington's orchestra and moved with him to New York City in 1923, staying with the band until 1928. He then played with Noble Sissle, **Chick Webb**, and in a band that included **Fats Waller** before rejoining Ellington in 1932. Co-author of Ellington's "Sophisticated Lady," Hardwick played with Ellington until 1945 before retiring from music.

HARLEM BLUES AND JAZZ BAND. A band formed in 1972. Members included **Doc Cheatham**, George James, Clyde Bernhardt, and others. The group recorded and toured into the 1990s.

HARLEM HAMFATS. A group formed in the 1930s and active until 1939. The band's style was an early predecessor to **Rhythm and Blues (R&B)**. Members included **trumpet** player Ann Cooper, one of a small number of female wind players to be recorded during the **Swing** era.

HARLEM KIDDIES. A Danish group formed in 1940 that was active into the 1950s.

HARLEQUIN. A **record label** formed in 1981 in England, still in existence today. It features reissues of music of the 1920s and jazz from the 1950s and 1960s. Prominent releases included the "Jazz and Hot Dance" series of records.

HARMOGRAPH. A **record label** established in 1921 in St. Louis that was active until 1925.

HARMOLODIC THEORY. A term coined by saxophonist **Ornette Coleman** used to describe the theory behind his playing. The precise musical meaning of the term is unclear at best, but the term is apparently a combination of the words *harmony*, *movement*, and *melody*.

HARMONICA. Also known as the mouth organ and mouth harp, it is rarely utilized in jazz.

HARMONY (I). A musical term that refers to either the sounding of two or more pitches at once, chords, or chord progressions.

HARMONY (II). A **record label** established in 1925. Artists included **Fletcher Henderson** (whose band recorded under the name Dixie Stompers).

HARP. Another term for **harmonica.**

HARPER, BILLY (1943–). A saxophonist, Billy Harper played in local bands before moving to New York in 1966 and then working with **Gil Evans** from 1967 to 1976. During his extensive time with Evans, Harper also played with **Art Blakey's Jazz Messengers** from 1967 to 1970, with **Lee Morgan** from 1969 to 1971, a long stint with the **Thad Jones–Mel Lewis** Orchestra from 1969 to 1977, briefly with **Elvin Jones** in 1970, with **Donald Byrd** from 1970 to 1972, and then as part of a long-standing relationship with **Max Roach** from 1970 to 1978. Harper started leading his own groups in the mid-1970s.

HARRELL, TOM (1946–). A **trumpet** and **flugelhorn** player, Tom Harrell got his first gig touring with **Stan Kenton** in 1969, followed by a stint with **Woody Herman** from 1970 to 1971. Harrell played with **Horace Silver** from 1973 to 1977, and at other times in the 1970s played with **Cecil Payne, Bill Evans,** Bob Berg, and in **Chuck Israel's** National Jazz Ensemble. From 1979 to 1981, Harrell played with **Lee Konitz,** during the early 1980s with the **Mel Lewis** Orchestra, and from 1984 to 1989 with **Phil Woods.** Harrell formed his own group in 1989 with Joe Lovano and continues to perform and tour. Harrell was diagnosed with a form of schizophrenia while in college and requires powerful medication in order to function and perform.

HARRIS, BARRY DOYLE (1929–). A pianist, Barry Harris performed with **Miles Davis, Sonny Stitt, Max Roach,** and others while growing up in Detroit. Harris played with Roach briefly in 1956 and then briefly with **Cannonball Adderley** in 1960 before moving to New York. While in New York, Harris led his own groups and played with **Yusef Lateef, Dexter Gordon, Hank Mobley,** and others. From 1965 to 1969, Harris worked with **Coleman Hawkins,** and since has led his own groups and been extremely active as a teacher. *See also* PIANO.

HARRIS, BILL (1916–1973). A trombonist, Bill Harris got his first important gig with Ray McKinley in 1942. Harris then played with **Benny Goodman** from 1943 to 1944 before joining **Woody Herman's** orchestra, with whom he would play off and on from 1944 to 1959. Harris played briefly with **Jack Teagarden** during the early 1960s. *See also* TROMBONE.

HARRIS, EDDIE (1934–1996). A saxophonist, Eddie Harris played piano with **Gene Ammons,** and after finishing his military service in 1961, he had a huge hit with his performance of the theme from the movie *Exodus.* During the late 1960s, Harris played the electronic **saxophone**, and his composition "Freedom Jazz Dance" was a hit for **Miles Davis**. Harris also continued to lead his own groups and play with artists including **Cedar Walton, Ron Carter**, and others. During the early 1970s he switched to performing Rock music, but by the late 1970s and into the 1990s he was again playing with jazz musicians including **Jimmy Smith, Horace Silver**, and **John Scofield**, among others.

HARRIS, GENE (1933–2000). A pianist and **bandleader**, Gene Harris played early in an army band before forming the groups that would become the "Three Sounds" with Andy Simpkins and Bill Dowdy in 1956. The group was together in various forms throughout the 1970s, eventually playing music in a **Jazz-Rock** style. Harris briefly retired from performing from 1977 to 1980 before returning to music during the 1980s and 1990s, playing with **Benny Carter**, Ray Brown, and others, and assembling the Philip Morris Super Band in the late 1980s. *See also* (THE) FOUR SOUNDS.

HARRISON, DONALD "DUCK" (1960–). A saxophonist, Harrison studied at the **Berklee College of Music** from 1979 to 1980 before playing with **Roy Haynes** from 1980 to 1981. Harrison and Terrence Blanchard both joined **Art Blakey**'s Jazz Messengers from 1982 to 1986, and went on to form their own quintet in the mid-1980s. During the 1990s, Harrison led his own quartet in addition to performing with the all-star band Chartbusters, with **Randy Brecker**, Nicholas Payton, and others. *See also* SAXOPHONE.

HARRISON, JIMMY (1900–1931). A **trombone** player, Jimmy Harrison was self-taught and played in minstrel shows early in his life. Harrison played with Sam Wooding, Charlie Johnson, June Clark, and **James P. Johnson** before moving to New York in 1923 and playing with Fess Williams and then Charlie Smith. After working with **Elmer Snowden** and **Duke Ellington** during the mid-1920s, Harrison joined **Fletcher Henderson**'s band from 1927 to 1930 before dying from a stomach ailment.

HART, BILLY (1940–). A drummer, Billy Hart got his first gig with Shirley Horn from 1961 to 1964. During the rest of the 1960s, Hart played with **Jimmy Smith, Wes Montgomery, Eddie Harris, Marian McPartland**, and others. During the 1970s, Hart played with **Herbie Hancock, McCoy Tyner**, and **Stan Getz**, in addition to performing as a **sideman** with **Miles Davis, Clark Terry**, and many others. During the 1980s and 1990s, Hart performed with **Mingus Dynasty**, the groups Quest and Great Friends, Joe Lovano, **Tom Harrell**, Clark Terry, **Lee Konitz, Larry Coryell**, and many others. *See also* DRUM SET.

HARTMAN, JOHNNY (1932–1983). A singer and pianist, Johnny Hartman got his first **gig** after World War II **singing** with **Earl Hines**. Hartman then sang with **Dizzy Gillespie** from 1947 to 1949 and **Erroll Garner** in 1949 before launching a successful solo career. During the 1960s he also performed and recorded with **John Coltrane**, and during the 1980s with **Roland Hanna**.

HAT. A kind of **mute**, also known as the **derby** mute.

HAT HUT. A **record label** and company established in 1974 in Switzerland and still in existence. Additional labels within the company include hat ART and hatOLOGY, which is comprised primarily of jazz and improvised music. In addition to new **recordings,** Hat Hut releases reissues. Artists include **Steve Lacy, Max Roach, Cecil Taylor,** and others.

HAWES, HAMPTON (1928–1977). A pianist, Hampton Hawes played with **Dexter Gordon** and **Wardell Gray** in the 1940s before playing with **Howard McGhee** and **Charlie Parker** from 1950 to 1951. During the 1950s, Hawes played with **Shorty Rogers,** spent some time in the army, and then led his own group with **Red Mitchell.** In 1958, Hawes was arrested for narcotics possession and spent the next five years in jail before being pardoned by President John F. Kennedy in 1963. During the rest of the 1960s, Hawes played with **Harold Land, Jackie McLean,** Mitchell, **Jimmy Garrison,** and Leroy Vinnegar, and appeared in **Jon Hendricks'** *Evolution of the Blues* and also in the TV series *Jazz on Stage.* Hawes continued to play during the 1970s, performing with **Kenny Clarke, Gene Ammons,** and others. *See also* PIANO.

HAWKINS, COLEMAN (1904–1969). A **tenor saxophone** player, Coleman Hawkins studied harmony and composition before his first tour with Mamie Smith's Jazz Hounds from 1922 to 1923. Hawkins moved to New York City in 1923, and after freelancing for a short time he played with **Fletcher Henderson,** with whom he would remain for 10 years (1924–1934). From 1934 to 1939 he performed and toured in **Europe,** playing with local groups and also with **Django Reinhardt** and **Benny Carter.**

Hawkins formed a nine-piece group upon his return to New York in 1939 and days later recorded his famous version of "Body and Soul," which was a huge hit. In 1940, Hawkins formed his own **big band,** and then from 1941 to 1943 he led his own small groups. By 1944 his group included many musicians who would be at the forefront of the emerging **Bebop** style, including **Dizzy Gillespie** and **Thelonious Monk,** and later **Miles Davis, Fats Navarro, J. J. Johnson, Howard McGhee,** and others.

He continued to lead his own groups through the rest of the decade, in addition to playing in **Jazz at the Philharmonic**. During the late 1950s, Hawkins played with Monk and with **Roy Eldridge**, and during the 1960s he performed with **Duke Ellington, Oscar Peterson**, and **Sonny Rollins**, among others, and he also appeared on television and in movies. The first influential tenor saxophonist, Hawkins' playing continually evolved, and he is regarded as one of the first jazz masters.

HAYES, EDWARD BRIAN "TUBBY" (1935–1973). A **saxophone** player, Tubby Hayes played with groups in **England** during the 1950s in addition to leading some of his own bands. During the 1960s, Hayes led his own **big band** and toured the United States several times, in addition to appearing in **Europe** with **Duke Ellington** in 1964. A successful performer on many other instruments in addition to the saxophone, Hayes was very influential in the British jazz scene.

HAYNES, ROY OWEN (1925–). A drummer, Roy Haynes played in Boston-area **Swing** bands before joining Luis Russell from 1945 to 1947. During the rest of the 1940s and early 1950s, Haynes played with **Lester Young, Miles Davis, Charlie Parker, Bud Powell, Stan Getz**, and others, in addition to leading his own groups featuring **Kenny Dorham** and **Sonny Rollins**. From 1953 to 1958 he played with **Sarah Vaughan**, and during the late 1950s he performed with **George Shearing, Eric Dolphy, Thelonious Monk**, and others. During the 1960s, he led his own group, was **Elvin Jones'** substitute in **John Coltrane**'s group, and performed with Getz and **Gary Burton**. In 1969 he played with his group Hip Ensemble in a **Jazz-Rock** style, and during the 1970s he played with **Hank Jones, Art Pepper, Dizzy Gillespie**, Burton, and others. In 1981, Haynes joined **Chick Corea**'s group, Trio Music, and during the 1980s and 1990s he continued to lead his own groups in addition to performing with **Donald Harrison, Pat Metheny, Dave Holland**, and many others. *See also* DRUM SET.

HEAD. In jazz, it is the term for the melody to a song or tune.

HEAD ARRANGEMENT (HEAD CHART). A term for an **arrangement** of a song that is worked out by the musicians but generally not written down; it can also refer to a very simple arrangement of a song.

HEARD, J(AMES) C(HARLES) (1917–1988). A drummer, J. C. Heard performed on tours with **Norman Granz**'s **Jazz at the Philharmonic**. Known as a versatile performer, he played in **Swing, Bebop**, and **Blues** settings. Over his career, he performed with **Erroll Garner, Teddy Wilson, Coleman Hawkins**, and many more.

HEARD, JOHN WILLIAM (1938–). A **bass** player, John Heard worked early with Tommy Turrentine and then with **Al Jarreau**, with whom he played from 1966 to 1968. During the rest of the 1960s, Heard also worked with **Sonny Rollins** and **Wes Montgomery** before moving to Los Angeles in 1969. Heard played with violinist Jean-Luc Ponty in 1969, and during the 1970s he performed with John Collins, **Ahmad Jamal, Count Basie, Toshiko Akiyoshi, Louie Bellson, Oscar Peterson, Blue Mitchell, Joe Henderson**, and others. During the 1980s, Heard performed with **Pharoah Sanders, Clark Terry, Tal Farlow, Eddie "Lockjaw" Davis, Buddy Montgomery**, and others before retiring for a time to focus on painting and sculpting. Heard resumed his musical career in the 1990s, playing with Jamal, **Benny Carter**, and others.

HEATH, ALBERT "TOOTIE" (1935–). A drummer, Albert "Tootie" Heath worked with **John Coltrane** in the early 1950s before following his brothers **Percy Heath** and **Jimmy Heath** to New York City in 1957. Heath then worked with **J. J. Johnson, Cedar Walton**, and later with the **Jazztet**, in addition to **recording** with **Nat Adderley, Kenny Dorham**, and others. Heath moved to Europe from 1965 to 1968 and while there played with **Dexter Gordon, Coleman Hawkins, Joe Henderson**, and others. Heath returned to the United States in 1968 and played with **Herbie Hancock** from 1968 to 1969 and **Yusef Lateef** from 1970 to 1974 before joining his brothers as part of the Heath Brothers group in 1975. From 1978 until the mid-1980s, Heath worked mostly as a teacher, but he resumed his playing career and since has performed with the Jazztet, **Tal Farlow**, the **Modern Jazz Quartet**, and reunion concerts with his brothers. *See also* DRUM SET.

HEATH, JIMMY (1926–). A saxophonist, **flute** player, composer, and arranger, Jimmy Heath toured with Nat Towles before forming his own **big band** in 1946, which at various times counted **John Coltrane** and **Benny Golson** among its members. In 1947, Heath and his brother **Percy Heath** moved to New York City and played with **Howard McGhee** from 1947 to 1948. Heath played with **Dizzy Gillespie** from 1949 to 1950, **Kenny Dorham** in 1953, and **Miles Davis** from 1953 to 1955. During the 1960s, Heath played with **Donald Byrd** and **Art Farmer**, in addition to leading his own groups that usually featured one or more of his brothers. During the 1970s, Heath played again with Farmer and led his own group with his brothers **Percy** and **Tootie Heath**. From 1982, Heath led another quartet and later his own big band. Heath reunited with his brothers in 1997, in addition to performing in a group with **Slide Hampton** and Jon Faddis. Heath also had a productive career as a composer, arranger, and teacher. *See also* SAXOPHONE.

HEATH, PERCY (1923–2005). A bassist, Percy Heath played with Red Garland early before moving to New York City with his brother **Jimmy Heath** and playing with **Howard McGhee** from 1947 to 1948. During the early 1950s, Heath played with **Miles Davis, Stan Getz, Fats Navarro, Charlie Parker, Dizzy Gillespie, Sonny Rollins, Thelonious Monk, Horace Silver, Clifford Brown**, and many others. In 1951, Heath joined **Milt Jackson**'s quartet, and in 1952 the group became the **Modern Jazz Quartet** (MJQ). Heath played with the MJQ until it disbanded in 1975, and then he resumed playing with his brothers Jimmy and **Tootie Heath**. During the 1980s and 1990s, Heath continued to make appearances with the re-formed MJQ in addition to playing with his brothers. *See also* BASS.

HEATH, TED (1900–1969). An English **trombone** player and **bandleader**, Ted Heath played with many English **dance bands** before leading his own **big band** in 1944. The band was featured in radio broadcasts and gave regular Sunday concerts at the London Palladium. Heath's band was popular in **England** into the 1950s and appeared in film and television, in addition to several tours of the United States.

HEFTI, NEAL (1922–2008). A **trumpet** player, composer, and arranger, Neal Hefti had already written music for Nat Towles and **Earl Hines** before joining **Charlie Barnet**'s band as a member of the trumpet section in the early 1940s. Hefti's career as an arranger took off after his stint with the **Woody Herman** band from 1944 to 1945, where he composed many popular **arrangements** including "The Good Earth" and "Wildroot." During the rest of the 1940s he also wrote for Harry James and composed "Repetition," featuring **Charlie Parker**. During the 1950s, Hefti led his own **big band** and worked for **Count Basie**, composing many popular songs including "Li'l Darlin'" and "Cute." From the 1960s onward, Hefti worked as a composer for film and television. Among his most popular works in the commercial field is the theme from the television show, *Batman*.

HEMPHILL, JULIUS (1938–1995). A saxophonist, **flute** player, and composer, Julius Hemphill worked with **Blues** bands and Ike and Tina Turner before forming the **World Saxophone Quartet** in 1976 with **Oliver Lake, David Murray**, and Hamiet Bluiett. Hemphill remained with the group through 1989 in addition to leading many of his own groups. *See also* SAXOPHONE.

HENDERSON, BILL (1926–). A vocalist, Bill Henderson moved to New York in the 1950s and in 1958 recorded with **Horace Silver**. During the 1960s, Henderson worked with **Ramsey Lewis, Oscar Peterson,** and **Count Basie** before moving to Los Angeles to pursue a career as an actor, although he continued to sing occasionally.

HENDERSON, EDDIE (1940–). A **trumpet** player, Eddie Henderson took early lessons from **Louis Armstrong** and received his M.D. from Howard University in 1968. After his graduation, he played with **John Handy** and **Philly Joe Jones** in 1968. During the 1970s, Henderson played with **Herbie Hancock,** briefly with **Art Blakey's Jazz Messengers,** and led his own groups, which leaned toward **Jazz-Rock** by the end of the decade. He practiced general medicine from 1975 to 1985 part time in a small San Francisco clinic. During the 1980s he played with **Billy Harper, Kenny Barron, David Friesen,** and **John Hicks,** and during the 1990s with **Mulgrew Miller, McCoy Tyner's big band,** and many others.

HENDERSON, FLETCHER HAMILTON, JR. (1897–1952). A **bandleader,** composer, and arranger, Henderson moved to New York in 1920 and worked as a song plugger for the Harry Pace–**W. C. Handy** music publishing company. Soon thereafter he worked as a manager for Pace's Swan record company, putting together bands and performing with **Ethel Waters,** and in this way Henderson began to lead his own bands.

He first led a band at the Club Alabam in 1924, and then achieved fame leading his band at the Roseland Ballroom from 1924 to 1934. Early on, **Don Redman** and Henderson worked out the basics of the band's **arrangements,** which would in turn influence many other bands throughout the **Swing** era. **Louis Armstrong** was an early featured soloist in the band, and other band members over the years included **Jimmy Harrison, Benny Carter, Coleman Hawkins, Roy Eldridge, Ben Webster,** and **Sid Catlett.**

Starting in 1934, Henderson began selling his arrangements to **Benny Goodman,** who in turn was instrumental in the rise in popularity of Swing music, and from 1939 to 1941 he stopped leading his band entirely and worked as Goodman's staff arranger. During the 1940s, Henderson continued to lead his band on and off, and during the late 1940s he was again working as an accompanist for Waters. In 1950, Henderson suffered a stroke, and he died in 1952.

HENDERSON, HORACE W. (1904–1988). A pianist, arranger, and **bandleader,** Horace Henderson led his band, the Collegians, during the early 1920s. Members of the band included **Rex Stewart** and **Benny Carter,** and later, when the band was reorganized and renamed the Stompers in the late 1920s, **Roy Eldridge**. In 1931, Henderson worked as a pianist and arranger for **Don Redman**, and from 1933 to 1936 he worked as the arranger for his brother **Fletcher Henderson**. From 1937 he resumed leading his own bands, which he continued to lead until his service in the army during World War II. During the mid-1940s, Henderson arranged for the **big bands** of **Jimmie Lunceford**, **Tommy Dorsey**, and others, and from 1945 to 1947 he worked as pianist and musical director for Lena Horne. Thereafter, from the late 1940s all the way into the 1980s, Henderson led many different groups in Chicago, Minneapolis, Denver, and Colorado Springs.

HENDERSON, JOE (1937–2001). A **tenor saxophonist** and composer, Joe Henderson played with **Sonny Stitt** and led his own groups before moving to New York in 1962 and working with **Brother Jack McDuff**. From 1962 to 1963 he worked with **Kenny Dorham**, from 1964 to 1966 with **Horace Silver**, and from 1969 to 1970 with **Herbie Hancock**, in addition to forming his own **big band** in 1967. Henderson mostly led his own groups from the 1970s onward and was also involved in music education. Among his more famous compositions are "Recordame," "Black Narcissus," and "Inner Urge."

HENDRICKS, JON (1921–). A singer, Jon Hendricks worked early with **Art Tatum** and **Charlie Parker** before moving to New York in 1952. While in New York he recorded a vocal version of "Four Brothers" with **Dave Lambert**, and soon with the addition of **Annie Ross** they formed the trio of Lambert, Hendricks, and Ross. The group was active until 1964 and toured with **Count Basie**. In 1968, Hendricks moved to London and began touring in **Europe** and Africa before returning to the United States in 1972. Hendricks worked as a jazz critic for the *San Francisco Chronicle* and also put on the very successful *Evolution of the Blues* (which he had originally premiered in 1960). Hendricks has continued to perform with his wife and children, in addition to **Bobby McFerrin**, **Manhattan Transfer**, **Al Jarreau**, and others. *See also* LAMBERT, HENDRICKS, AND ROSS.

HEP. Record label and company established in 1974 in Edinburgh. Artists included **Fletcher Henderson**, **Don Redman**, **Andy Kirk**, Boyd Raeburn, and others. *See also* RECORD LABEL.

HERMAN, WOODROW CHARLES "WOODY" (1913–1987). A **bandleader**, clarinetist, and saxophonist, Woody Herman formed his first band with sidemen from Isham Jones' band after it disbanded in 1936. Herman would lead this band in various guises until 1944 when it became known as Herman's Herd, which included **Pete Candoli, Neal Hefti,** Bill Harris, Billy Bauer, **Dave Tough,** Ralph Burns, and later **Shorty Rogers, Conrad Gozzo,** and **Red Norvo.** The band was successful, but Herman was forced to disband the group in 1946, re-forming it in 1947 as the Second Herd, also known as the Four Brothers band for its saxophone section that included **Herbie Steward** (later Al Cohn), **Stan Getz, Zoot Simms,** and **Serge Chaloff.** In 1949, Herman was forced to disband the group again but re-formed it shortly thereafter as the Third Herd, and counted **Red Rodney, Carl Fontana, Kai Winding, Jake Hanna,** and later **Bob Brookmeyer** among its members. The band continued to stay active throughout the 1960s and 1970s, again employing some of the best musicians in the business, including **Bill Chase,** Phil Wilson, **Cecil Payne,** and many others, and continued to stay active after Herman's death. *See also* CLARINET; SAXOPHONE.

HEYWOOD, EDDIE (1915–1989). A pianist, **bandleader,** and composer, Eddie Heywood worked freelance in New York in the late 1930s before working with **Benny Carter** and **Don Redman.** From 1941 onward, Heywood led his own groups, which included **Doc Cheatham** and **Vic Dickenson,** and recorded with **Billie Holiday.** In the mid-1940s, Heywood also performed with **Coleman Hawkins** and **Sid Catlett,** and his band had a hit in 1944 with its version of "Begin the Beguine." Heywood was forced to stop playing from 1947 to 1950 due to paralysis in his hands, but he resumed playing with his trio in 1951. During this time, Heywood also worked as a composer and had a hit with his composition "Canadian Sunset." His paralysis worsened during the 1960s, and he turned more toward composing and arranging.

HIBBLER, AL(BERT) (1915–2001). A singer, Al Hibbler sang with local bands before working with Jay McShann in 1942. From 1943 to 1951, Hibbler worked with **Duke Ellington,** and during the early 1950s he also sang with **Count Basie, Gerald Wilson,** and others, in addition to having a few hit songs of his own, including "Unchained Melody." He continued to sing on his own during the 1950s, 1960s, and 1970s, including a notable **session** with **Rahsaan Roland Kirk** in 1972.

HICKS, JOHN (1941–2006). A pianist, John Hicks worked as a **freelance** musician with **Chick Corea, Kenny Dorham, Lou Donaldson, Tony Williams,** and many others before joining **Art Blakey's Jazz Messengers** from 1964 to 1965. During the rest of the 1960s, Hicks worked with **Betty Carter** and then **Woody Herman,** in addition to performing with **Freddie Hubbard, Hank Mobley, Lee Morgan,** Anita O'Day, **Slide Hampton,** and others. Starting in the 1970s, Hicks began leading his own bands, in addition to working with Blakey, **Woody Shaw**, Charles Tolliver, **Oliver Lake**, **Lester Bowie**, Carter, and others. During the 1980s, Hicks played with **Pharoah Sanders, Bobby Watson, Mingus Dynasty, Branford Marsalis, Wynton Marsalis, Eddie Henderson**, and others, in addition to leading his own **big band**.

HIFIJAZZ. Record company established in 1956 in Hollywood. The company primarily released jazz, and the music of the jazz released was of a light and unsophisticated level. **Albums** from the HiFijazz were later released on the Everest label. **King Pleasure** and **Bill Holman** recorded on HiFijazz. *See also* RECORD LABEL.

HIGGINBOTHAM, J. C. (1906–1973). A trombonist, Higginbotham worked in **territory bands** until moving to New York City in 1928 and joining Luis Russell's orchestra. Higginbotham remained with Russell until 1931, joined **Fletcher Henderson**'s group from 1931 to 1933, played with the **Mills Blue Rhythm Band** from 1934 to 1936, and from 1937 to 1940 he again played in Russell's group under **Louis Armstrong**'s direction. From 1940 to 1947, Higginbotham played with **Red Allen**, led his own groups during the 1950s in addition to playing occasionally with Allen, and toured during the 1960s. *See also* TROMBONE.

HIGGINS, BILLY (1936–2001). A drummer, Billy Higgins worked in **Rhythm and Blues (R&B)** bands before playing with **Don Cherry, Dexter Gordon**, James Clay, and others. In 1957, Higgins recorded with **Red Mitchell**, and in 1958, Higgins joined **Ornette Coleman** and **Charlie Haden**, with whom he would play in Los Angeles and later during Coleman's stint at the **Five Spot** in New York City. In 1960, Higgins played with **Thelonious Monk** and with **John Coltrane**, and from 1962 to 1963 with **Sonny Rollins**. During the 1960s, Higgins also performed with **Hank Mobley, Lee Morgan, Herbie Hancock, Blue Mitchell, Donald Byrd**, Coleman, and others. During the 1970s, Higgins worked with **Cedar Walton** (with whom he would work into the 1990s), **Milt Jackson, George Coleman**, and others. During the 1980s and onward, Higgins played with **Pat Metheny, Slide Hampton**, Haden's Quartet West, and others. Higgins continued to play into the 1990s until he retired for a time due to his health, resuming again in the late 1990s. *See also* DRUM SET.

HINES, EARL KENNETH "FATHA" (1903–1983). A **piano** player and **bandleader**, Earl Hines was working professionally by 1918, and during the early 1920s he made his first **recording** with singer Lois Deppe. In 1923 he moved to Chicago where he played with Carroll Dickerson from 1925 to 1926, and he worked briefly as musical director for **Louis Armstrong**. Hines joined **Jimmie Noone** from 1927 to 1928 and during this time also recorded with Armstrong. From 1928 to 1947, Hines led his own **big band**, which at various times included **Charlie Parker, Dizzy Gillespie, Wardell Gray, Bennie Green, Billy Eckstine, Sarah Vaughan**, and many others. After disbanding the group in 1947, Hines played with Louis Armstrong's All Stars from 1948 to 1951, and from 1952 to the late 1950s he led small groups and toured. Hines was inactive until 1964 when his popularity surged after a series of concerts in New York City. Thereafter Hines continued to tour and remained active into the 1980s. Hines' linear approach to the right hand on the **piano** was known as **"trumpet** style," and his playing has been highly influential to many other jazz pianists. *See also* STRIDE.

HINTON, MILTON "MILT" (1910–2000). A bassist, Milt Hinton played **tuba** before switching to **bass** in the 1920s. Hinton's first professional **gigs** in the late 1920s were with Tiny Parham and **Freddie Keppard**. During the early 1930s, Minton played with Eddie South and Zutty Singleton, in addition to performing with **Art Tatum, Fate Marable**, Erskine Tate, and others. From 1936 to 1951, Hinton played in **Cab Calloway**'s orchestra; during this time he also performed with **Billie Holiday, Lionel Hampton**, and others. After leaving Calloway's band, Hinton played briefly with **Count Basie** before joining **Louis Armstrong** during the early 1950s. From the mid-1950s and into the 1970s, Hinton freelanced and performed with many artists, including **Ben Webster, Coleman Hawkins, Paul Gonsalves, Sonny Stitt, Hank Jones**, Jay McShann, and many others, in addition to tours with Paul Anka and **Bing Crosby** during the 1970s and 1980s. Hinton is well known for his expertise in the **slap bass** style of playing. He continued to play into the 1990s.

HIRT, AL(OIS) MAXWELL (1922–1999). A **trumpet** player and **bandleader**, Al Hirt served as a bugler in the U.S. Army during World War II. After his discharge, Hirt played in several **Swing** bands, including those led by **Tommy Dorsey**, Ray McKinley, and Horace Heidt. During the mid-1950s, he led his own groups, and by the 1960s he was a best-selling artist. During the 1960s he had several **albums** in the *Billboard* Top 10, and he remained active into the 1990s. Among his hits is included "Java."

HIS MASTER'S VOICE (HMV). A **record label** that dates back to 1899 that issued many early jazz **recordings**. Since the 1960s the label has mainly released Classical music. The label spawned a popular chain of over 400 stores.

HIT OF THE WEEK. Record label established in 1930 in New York. **Recordings** were not made of shellac but out of paper and resin instead, sold in many different locations including newsstands and record stores. The label did not turn a profit and became defunct in 1932.

HODGES, JOHNNY (1907–1970). A **saxophone** player, Johnny Hodges took lessons with **Sidney Bechet** and then later replaced Bechet in a band led by **Willie "the Lion" Smith** in 1924. During the 1920s, Hodges would play with Bechet and **Chick Webb** before joining **Duke Ellington's** orchestra in 1928. Hodges played with Ellington from 1928 to 1951 in addition to playing with **Lionel Hampton, Teddy Wilson, Earl Hines,** and others. Hodges left Ellington's band in 1951 and formed his own band, which had a hit with "Castle Rock." He then rejoined Ellington's band in 1955 and remained a member of the orchestra, in addition to playing with **Billy Strayhorn, Wild Bill Davis, Oliver Nelson,** and others. His emotional bends and scoops, along with his full saxophone sound, was a mainstay of the Ellington Orchestra.

HOGGARD, JAY (1954–). A vibraphonist, Jay Hoggard was originally a philosophy major in college before switching to music. Hoggard toured **Europe** with university groups and spent a summer in Africa before moving to New York in 1977. During the 1970s, Hoggard played with **Kenny Burrell,** Sam Rivers, **Chico Freeman, Cecil Taylor,** and many others, and from the late 1970s onward he has led his own groups. *See also* VIBRAPHONE.

HOHENBERGER, KURT (1908–1979). A German **trumpet** player and **bandleader,** Kurt Hohenberger played in many European groups during the 1930s and 1940s, and from the late 1930s, he led his own bands before retiring from music in the 1950s. *See also* EUROPE.

HOLDSWORTH, ALLAN (1946–). A **guitar** player, Holdsworth performed with **Fusion** groups in **England,** including **Ian Carr's** group Nucleus and the group Soft Machine, before moving to the United States and joining **Tony Williams** in his group Lifetime during the mid-1970s. During the early 1980s, Holdsworth led his own group, IOU, and since has performed solo in addition to playing with Gordon Beck and others.

HOLIDAY, BILLIE (1915–1959). A vocalist, Billie Holiday (born Elenora Fagan) began **singing** in clubs in Brooklyn and Harlem in the early 1930s before **recording** with **Benny Goodman** in 1933. Holiday sang with **Teddy Wilson** from 1935 to 1939, in addition to working with **Count Basie** and **Artie Shaw.** From 1936 to 1942, Holiday recorded as the leader of her own groups, and these recordings, combined with her work with Wilson and **Lester Young**, are some of her most popular and enduring. Holiday became extremely popular in the early 1940s, her career even venturing into film with the movie *New Orleans*, in which she appeared with **Louis Armstrong**. In 1947, Holiday, who counted heroin among her vices, was jailed on drug charges; she would be arrested for possession several more times, and in the early 1950s she lost her cabaret card. She continued to record during the 1950s, but by then her hard life had taken a toll on her voice. Holiday's interpretive style and relaxed phrasing has enshrined her as one of the greatest jazz vocalists.

HOLLAND, DAVE (1946–). A bassist, Dave Holland started playing the bass in 1963 and, after being heard by **Miles Davis**, moved to the United States from London, England, in 1968. Holland played with Davis from 1968 to 1970, appearing on Davis' forays into Jazz **Fusion**: *In a Silent Way* and *Bitches Brew*. From 1970 to 1971, Holland played in the group Circle, which he formed with **Chick Corea** and **Anthony Braxton**. During the 1970s, Holland performed with Braxton, Sam Rivers, **Stan Getz**, and **Jack DeJohnette**, and since the 1980s he has led his own groups that have featured **Kenny Wheeler**, **Marvin "Smitty" Smith**, Steve Coleman, and later **John Scofield** and Joe Lovano. *See also* BASS; CIRCLE (I); EUROPE.

HOLLEY, MAJOR QUINCY, JR. (1924–1990). A **bass** player, Major Holley first played **tuba** but switched to bass during his time playing in U.S. Navy bands in the early 1940s. After his discharge from the navy, Holley played with **Dexter Gordon** and **Wardell Gray** on the western coast of the United States before moving to Detroit, where he played with **Charlie Parker**, **Ella Fitzgerald**, **Art Tatum**, **Coleman Hawkins**, and many others. In 1950 he recorded with **Oscar Peterson** before moving to London in 1951. While in London he spent time playing with the BBC Orchestra from 1954 to 1956.

During the late 1950s, Holley joined **Woody Herman** and eventually returned to the United States for good, and from 1959 to 1960 he played with Al Cohn and **Zoot Simms**. During the early to mid-1960s, Holley played in a quintet with Hawkins and **Roy Eldridge**, and in 1964 he played with **Duke Ellington**. From 1967 to 1970 he taught at the **Berklee School of Music**, and from the 1970s onward Holley played in pit orchestras, television and radio studios, and with **James Moody**, **Marian McPartland**, the Kings of Jazz, **Lee Konitz**, **Eddie "Lockjaw" Davis**, **Roland Hanna**, and many others.

HOLMAN, BILL (1927–). A saxophonist, **bandleader**, and composer, Bill Holman studied jazz in college before joining **Charlie Barnet** in the early

1950s. In 1952 he joined the band of **Stan Kenton**, for whom he would write **arrangements** into the 1970s. During the 1950s, Holman also played with **Shorty Rogers, Mel Lewis**, and **Conte Candoli**, among others. Holman eventually abandoned performing in the 1960s, and in addition to writing for television, he has written music for **Maynard Ferguson, Count Basie, Buddy Rich, Doc Severinsen, Louie Bellson, Gerry Mulligan**, and many others. Since 1975, Holman has led his own **big band** that performs mostly his own arrangements.

HONK. A technique used on the **saxophone** where a loud note is sounded in the lower or middle register. It is typically used more as an effect than as a part of normal performance.

HOOPER, LES (1940–). A **piano** player and composer, he worked as a composer of radio and television music in Chicago during the 1960s. In the 1970s, Hooper formed a **big band**, and the subsequent **album** was the recipient of a few Grammy nominations. He has continued to write music for film, television, and advertising, and to compose and arrange music for both big bands and small groups.

HORIZON. A **record label** formed in 1975 in Los Angeles. Artists include **Thad Jones, Mel Lewis, Ornette Coleman**, and others. After 1977, no new **recordings** were made; however the label reissued recordings through 1989 on compact disc and cassette.

HORN. In jazz parlance, horn can refer to any of the wind instruments present in a typical jazz ensemble: **saxophone, trombone**, or **trumpet**.

HORN, PAUL (1930–). A saxophonist, clarinetist, and **flute** player, Paul Horn played with **Chico Hamilton** from 1956 to 1958, and during the early 1960s he led his own groups in addition to doing Hollywood studio work. In 1965 he appeared as the principal soloist in Lalo Schifrin's *Jazz Suite on Mass Texts*, and in 1966 he played with **Tony Bennett**. Horn went to India in 1967, China in 1979, and the Soviet Union in 1983, and in 1970 he moved to Victoria, British Columbia, where he established his own group, presented a weekly television show, and wrote music for films. He has recorded as a soloist at the Taj Mahal in India and at the Great Pyramids of Cheops near Cairo, Egypt. *See also* STUDIO MUSICIAN; SAXOPHONE.

HOT. A term applied to jazz music that implies vigor, intensity, and excitement. The term has been used as a descriptor of a style of jazz itself ("hot" jazz), a style of solo, and as a part of many bands' names (the **Hot Five, Jelly Roll Morton**'s Red Hot Peppers, etc.).

HOT CLUB DE FRANCE. An organization established in Paris in 1932 that was devoted to the preservation and promotion of **Traditional Jazz** styles. The **Quintette du Hot Club de France**, which included guitarist **Django Reinhardt**, was formed as a result of the club's activities. The club rejected modern forms of jazz. In 2000, there existed 17 affiliated clubs in **France**. *See also* CLUBS.

HOT FIVE/HOT SEVEN. The name given to groups led by **Louis Armstrong** during the mid- to late 1920s. The original Hot Five included Armstrong, **Kid Ory, Johnny Dodds, Johnny St. Cyr**, and **Lil Armstrong**. The group expanded to be known as the Hot Seven with the addition of Pete Briggs and **Baby Dodds**. The groups also included **Earl Hines**, Zutty Singleton, and others during this time. The resultant **recordings** are considered among the most significant in **Early Jazz**. *See also* CHICAGO JAZZ; DIXIELAND.

HOT JAZZ. *See* HOT.

HOT RECORD SOCIETY (HRS). A **record label** established in 1937 in New York. It primarily recorded small jazz groups of the late **Swing** era. **Recording** stopped in 1946, although the material was purchased and released by the **Riverside** label in the 1960s.

HOWARD, PAUL LEROY (1895–1980). A saxophonist and clarinetist, Paul Howard also doubled occasionally on **cornet** and got his first job with Wood Wilson's Syncopaters in 1916. During the early 1920s, Howard played with both **King Oliver** and **Jelly Roll Morton**, and in 1924 he formed his own group known as the Quality Serenaders, which lasted through the 1920s and at one time included **Lionel Hampton**. During the 1930s, Howard played with Ed Garland, Hampton, Eddie Barfield, and Charlie Echols, and from 1939 to 1953 he led his own band in California and also served as financial secretary for the musicians' union. *See also* CLARINET; SAXOPHONE.

HUBBARD, FREDDIE (1938–2008). A virtuosic **trumpet** player, Freddie Hubbard also played mellophone, **French horn**, and **tuba**; led local groups; and recorded with the Montgomery brothers before moving to New York in 1958. From 1958 to 1961, Hubbard played with many musicians, including **Philly Joe Jones, Sonny Rollins, Slide Hampton, J. J. Johnson**, and

Quincy Jones, and in 1961 he joined **Art Blakey**'s **Jazz Messengers**. He played with Blakey until 1964, played with **Max Roach** from 1964 to 1965, and appeared on **recordings** with **Herbie Hancock, Ornette Coleman, John Coltrane**, and others. Hubbard worked primarily as a leader during the next 20 years, and from 1976 to 1979 he performed with Hancock, **Ron Carter, Wayne Shorter**, and **Tony Williams** in the group **V.S.O.P.** Lip problems eventually curtailed his playing during the 1990s. *See also* HARD BOP; MONTGOMERY, BUDDY; MONTGOMERY, WES.

HUCKO, MICHAEL ANDREW "PEANUTS" (1918–2003). A saxophonist and clarinetist, Peanuts Hucko played **tenor saxophone** in bands led by Jack Jenney, Will Bradley, Joe Marsala, and others before joining **Glenn Miller**'s Army Air Force Band as lead alto saxophonist and clarinet soloist. After World War II, Hucko performed with **Benny Goodman** and then Ray McKinley before joining Eddie Condon from 1947 to 1950. During the late 1950s, Hucko played with Goodman, **Jack Teagarden, Earl Hines**, and **Louis Armstrong**'s All Stars, in addition to television studio work that continued into the 1960s. During the 1970s, Hucko worked on the Lawrence Welk show and led the Glenn Miller Orchestra (1974) before settling in Denver. From the 1980s he continued to perform and tour as a soloist and with his own groups. *See also* CLARINET; SAXOPHONE.

HUGHES, WILLIAM HENRY "BILL" (1930–). A trombonist, Bill Hughes played with **Andy Kirk** and **Frank Wess** before joining **Count Basie**'s orchestra from 1953 to 1957. Hughes did not play from 1957 to 1963, but from 1963 onward he played in Basie's band.

HUMPHREY, RALPH (1944–). A drummer, Ralph Humphrey played with **Don Ellis**'s orchestra from 1968 to 1973. From 1973 to 1974 he worked with Frank Zappa, and from then on he has worked as a freelance musician and teacher.

HUTCHERSON, BOBBY (1941–). A vibraphonist, Bobby Hutcherson was inspired to play the **vibraphone** after hearing **recordings** of **Milt Jackson**. During the 1960s, Hutcherson played with **Jackie McLean, Eric Dolphy, Archie Shepp, Hank Mobley, Dexter Gordon**, Gil Fuller, **Lee Morgan, Joe Henderson**, and many others in addition to making recordings as a leader. From 1967 to 1971, Hutcherson led a group with **Harold Land**, and from 1971 he has resided in San Francisco. He has since continued to freelance and tour, playing at times with Land, **McCoy Tyner, Woody Shaw, Freddie Hubbard**, and many others. *See also* VIBRAPHONE.

HYMAN, RICHARD "DICK" (1927–). A keyboardist and composer, Dick Hyman played with **Charlie Parker, Dizzy Gillespie,** and **Lester Young** during the late 1940s and joined **Benny Goodman** in 1950. From the 1950s, Hyman worked as a **studio musician** in addition to being active as a composer and arranger for **Count Basie, Doc Severinsen,** and others. From the 1970s, Hyman played with **Ruby Braff** and toured with the New York Jazz Repertory Company, where he recreated music by **Fats Waller, Jelly Roll Morton, James P. Johnson, Louis Armstrong,** and others. Hyman has also worked extensively as a composer for television and film.

I

IBRAHIM, ABDULLAH (1934–). Born in South Africa, Ibrahim used the name Dollar Brand while making a name for himself as a **pianist** in the 1950s. Ibrahim relocated to Zurich, Switzerland, where he had a momentous encounter with pianist and **bandleader Duke Ellington**. Ellington landed a record contract for Ibrahim that resulted in several **albums**. Ibrahim moved to New York in the mid-1960s and continued his career primarily as a leader of his own groups in addition to a brief tour with **Elvin Jones**. Ibrahim always remained vested in music from his native country and moved back to South Africa in 1971. His desire to bring jazz there got him exiled in 1976 when he attempted to start a **jazz festival**. In the 1980s, Ibrahim formed the group Ekaya and recorded the self-titled album *Ekaya* (1983, Ekapa). Ibrahim continued to lead his own groups into the 1990s and 2000s, dedicating many works to regions of South Africa.

IMPERIAL. Founded in Los Angeles in 1946, Imperial was a **record label** that made a few jazz **recordings**. Despite their limited jazz output, Imperial did still have significant recordings of tenor saxophonist **Harold Land** and **trumpet** player Erskine Hawkins.

IMPERIAL ORCHESTRA. Created by Manuel Perez in the early part of the 1900s, the Imperial Orchestra was a **dance band** located in the New Orleans area. Despite a solid run of almost 12 years, the Imperial Orchestra disbanded in 1912.

IMPROVISATION. A practice of creating music, either by harmonic, melodic, or rhythmic means at the moment it is being performed. Improvisation is a signature attribute of jazz and is at the heart of many of its compositions. Many songs from the jazz repertoire provide the improviser a lead sheet or **chart** that includes a melody and a set of chord **changes**. Common practice is that the soloist or improviser performs the melody followed by an improvisation over the chord changes associated with the melody. Especially in small-group performances, much of the material is improvised including interpretations of the melody, accompaniment behind both the melody and the soloist(s), and from the soloist themselves. *See also* BLOW; CHORD PROGRESSION; COLLECTIVE IMPROVISATION; COMPING; CUTTING CONTEST; EIGHTS; FOURS; SCAT; TWOS.

INCUS. Based in London and founded in 1970 by creative and **Free Jazz** musicians Tony Oxley, Derek Bailey, and Evan Parker, Incus produced records of creative music for almost three decades. In addition to dates led by the founders of the company, Incus also recorded other English jazz heroes including John Surman. Incus was also responsible for several creative music festivals that included guests **Steve Lacy** and John Zorn. *See also* ENGLAND; RECORD LABEL.

INNER CITY. A diverse New York–based jazz **record label** formed in 1976 that split its effort between reissuing **albums** from labels from other countries including East Wind and Enja and also making new **recordings**. The label was shut down in 1980 due to a legal dispute, despite having released a recording that won Record Label of the Year in 1979.

INSIDE. A reference to one's ability to improvise within the existing harmonic structure of a song. Inside is often considered to be a response to the 1960s movement of playing outside of the given harmony. *See also* IMPROVISATION; OUTSIDE.

INSTITUTE OF JAZZ STUDIES. An archive housed at the State University of New Jersey, Rutgers, that contains an extensive jazz record and book collection. The collection thrives on donations and inspired an academic jazz journal for many years. The Institute of Jazz Studies was founded in 1952 by Marshall Stearns.

INSTITUT FÜR JAZZFORSCHUNG. Formed in 1969 and housed in Graz, Austria, the Institut für Jazzforschung was created as a research institute to be paired with the University in Graz. The institute inspired research in many different jazz-related fields and leads conventions and also an academic journal, both inspired by jazz studies.

INTERNATIONAL ASSOCIATION OF JAZZ RECORD COLLECTORS (IAJRC). A group of jazz **recording** enthusiasts. The IAJRC meets with the intention of exchanging rare or unpublished recordings. To help promote both the group and many of the recordings that the group discovered, the IAJRC created a record label with the same name to distribute many of these recordings. Included in these recordings are previously unreleased works by **Miles Davis** and **Stan Getz**. The IAJRC was founded in Pittsburg, Pennsylvania, in the mid-1960s and continues to meet regularly. *See also* EUROPE; RECORD LABEL.

INTERNATIONALE GESELLSCHAFT FÜR JAZZFORSCHUNG. Also known as the International Society for Jazz Research, the Internationale Gesellschaft für Jazzforschung was founded along with the **Institut für Jazzforschung** in Graz, Austria. This group meets several times a year and has published the jazz magazine *Jazzforschung* since the group's inception in 1969. *See also* EUROPE.

INTERNATIONAL JAZZ FEDERATION (IJF). Officially named the International Jazz Federation in 1977, this group had earlier been known as the European Jazz Federation during its beginnings in the 1960s. After being recognized by the International Music Council, the International Jazz Federation created offices in several major international cities including London, Warsaw, and eventually New York. Several country-specific jazz groups were formed from their ties with the International Jazz Federation including groups in Paris and Israel. Several periodicals were published by the International Jazz Federation during its existence.

INTERNATIONAL JAZZ JAMBOREE FESTIVAL. Founded by the Polska Federacja Jazzowa in the late 1950s, the International Jazz Jamboree Festival (also known as just the Jazz Jamboree) is one of the world's longest-running **jazz festivals**. Located in Warsaw, Poland, the festival began as a four-day event but has since expanded to over a week. **Duke Ellington** and **Dizzy Gillespie** are among the jazz legends who have performed at the Jazz Jamboree over the half century of its existence. *See also* EUROPE.

INTERNATIONAL NEW JAZZ FESTIVAL MOERS. Inspired by **Free Jazz** and creative music, Burkhard Hennen founded the International New Jazz Festival Moers in Moers, Germany. Over the next two decades the festival continued to draw consistently larger crowds growing to over 40,000 in the late 1990s. In 1974, three years after the festival began, Hennen spearheaded the creation of a **record label**, Moers Music, to document many of the performances from the festival. Despite substantial growth of the festival over several decades, the festival was hit with economic problems during the late part of the 2000s and had to shorten its duration to three days. Notable artists to perform at the festival include **Albert Mangelsdorff** and **Anthony Braxton**. *See also* JAZZ FESTIVAL.

INTERNATIONAL SWEETHEARTS OF RHYTHM. A 17-piece **big band** comprised of all women, the International Sweethearts of Rhythm was founded in the late 1930s and was in existence for an entire decade. The majority of their work came from touring and performing on radio broadcasts during World War II. *International Sweethearts of Rhythm* (1946, Rosetta) was one of the few **recordings** made by the group. Notable members include Viola Burnside, Ernestine Davis, and vocalist Anna Mae Winburn.

INTRODUCTION (INTRO). A term used to designate the opening material of a piece that prepares the listener for the primary melodic material of the work. Intros are commonly used for many jazz standards and songs from the Great American Songbook.

IRAKERE. Founded in 1973 by several budding Cuban jazz stars, Irakere instantly became a leading **Afro-Cuban Jazz** group. Original members include pianist **Chucho Valdés**, clarinetist and saxophonist **Paquito D'Rivera**, and **trumpet** player **Arturo Sandoval**. A performance at the 1978 **Newport Jazz Festival** gained Irakere a following in the United States and a record deal with the **Columbia Broadcasting System (CBS)** that spawned one of their first **albums** *Irakere* (1979, CBS). D'Rivera and Sandoval both left in the 1980s, but Valdés maintained the group during the next two decades. The group was very influential and innovative toward the development of the fusion of modern, post-Bop jazz and Afro-Cuban rhythms. In addition to touring, the group continued to record new material throughout the next two decades. *See also* CLARINET; ORQUESTA CUBANA DE MÚSICA MODERNA; PIANO; SAXOPHONE.

IRWIN, DENNIS (1951–2008). Born in Alabama, Irwin began his musical career at the age of nine when he took up the **clarinet**. He continued his clarinet studies throughout high school and attended North Texas State University to study music. After one year, he was convinced by others he should take up playing double **bass**. Irwin began gigging steadily in Texas over the next few years working primarily with many vocalists including Ann Hampton Calloway and **Mose Allison**. After moving to New York in the mid-1970s, Irwin developed a strong reputation and was a first-call bass player for groups led by **Art Blakey**, the **Mel Lewis** Orchestra, **Stan Getz**, and **Chet Baker**. Irwin maintained a steady professional working relationship with Joe Lovano and **John Scofield** that began in the 1970s when he hosted **jam sessions** at his loft in New York. Irwin recorded and toured with both musicians until his death.

ISRAELS, CHUCK (1936–). Born into a musical family, Israels learned several instruments growing up, including cello and **guitar**, before settling on **bass**. After spending a year at the Massachusetts Institute of Technology studying engineering, Israels transferred to Brandeis University to study music. He soon made connections in New York and was actively performing with many groups. Toward the end of the 1950s, Israels was hired by many leading musicians including **John Coltrane** and **Cecil Taylor**. After the death of **Scott LaFaro** in 1961, **Bill Evans** hired Israels for the bass chair in his trio. Israels stayed with Evans for five years. In the 1970s, Israels started the National Jazz Ensemble which was in existence for almost five years and was dedicated to performing music of jazz masters that included **Jelly Roll Morton** and **Duke Ellington**. The National Jazz Ensemble recorded one **album**, *National Jazz Ensemble* (1996, Chiaroscuro). Israels became less active as a performer over the next two decades and became a faculty member at Western Washington University.

ISSUE NUMBER. An identification system used by **recording** companies to label discs in the companies' catalog of records. An issue number was also used by other record companies that sold or reviewed records. The issue number contained information regarding what style of disc was made (long-play, extended-play, etc.). The issue number was made extinct with the creation of tape recordings. *See also* RECORD LABEL.

J

JACKIE AND ROY. A popular vocal jazz duo made up of Jackie Cain and Roy Kral, formed in the 1940s. The married couple recorded **albums** for a number of companies and appeared in concert regularly throughout the United States. In addition to their performances, Jackie and Roy hosted their own television show in Chicago and made appearances in television commercials.

JACKSON, GREIG "CHUBBY" (1918–2003). Born in New York, Jackson took up the **bass** as a teenager and was substituting for influential bassist **Oscar Pettiford** in the 1940s. Jackson worked with **Woody Herman, Conte Candoli, Neal Hefti**, and **Charlie Ventura** during the 1940s, many of whom he would work with again during the 1950s. Jackson worked as a leader during the 1960s and 1970s, while living in different places across the country including Los Angeles, Miami, and Las Vegas. Jackson's career experienced a brief resurgence during the 1980s while working with **Lionel Hampton**, but he was forced into retirement in the 1990s due to health-related issues.

JACKSON, MILTON "MILT" (1923–1999). Among the major jazz figures to move from Detroit to New York, vibraphonist Jackson quickly became involved with the **Bebop** scene and worked with **Dizzy Gillespie, Charlie Parker**, and **Woody Herman** during the mid- to late 1940s. In the 1950s, Jackson started leading his own groups, which included **sidemen John Lewis** and Connie Kay. Jackson's quartet would turn into the popular jazz group the **Modern Jazz Quartet**, and Jackson would perform with them for the greater part of the next decade. Jackson appeared as a sideman on **albums** by artists such as **John Coltrane, Coleman Hawkins**, and **Ray Charles**. Jackson would experience a resurgence toward the end of his career and recorded a **big band** album featuring the Los Angeles based Clayton-Hamilton Orchestra. *See also* VIBRAPHONE.

JACQUET, JEAN BAPTISTE "ILLINOIS" (1922–2004). Jacquet played **saxophone** with touring bands as a teenager before being hired by vibraphonist **Lionel Hampton**. He achieved a high level of fame for his solo on "Flying

Home" that was recorded with the Hampton band, and he used his popularity to start his own groups. Despite a brief stay with the **Count Basie** band in the 1940s, he would primarily lead his own groups for the remainder of his career, performing at festivals across the world. Jacquet was also invited to tour with the **Norman Granz** group **Jazz at the Philharmonic** during the late 1950s. He served a three-year artist-in-residence term at Harvard University and was awarded an honorary doctorate from the Juilliard School of Music. *See also* APOLLO THEATER.

JAMAL, AHMAD (1930–). Born Frederick Russell Jones and originally from Pittsburgh, Jamal began playing professional **piano** as a teenager and started touring with his own groups when he was 20. He primarily led a trio and would often substitute **guitar** in place of drums. He was considered highly influential to **Miles Davis**, who would refer piano players in his group to reference Jamal's stylings. "Poinciana" is considered to be one of Jamal's finest recorded tracks.

Jamal attempted several non-music related ventures in the early 1960s and briefly did not play. Throughout the 1970s and 1980s, Jamal experimented with a variety of sounds including using electronics, strings, and additional percussion in his groups. Jamal continues to perform and tour.

JAMES, ROBERT "BOB" (1939–). Keyboardist James worked with a variety of **Straight-Ahead** jazz groups in the 1960s, including ones led by **Sarah Vaughan**, **Quincy Jones**, **Freddie Hubbard**, **Stanley Turrentine**, and **Ron Carter**. James began doing studio work in the 1970s and was also performing with Pop acts. Toward the end of the 1980s, James became affiliated with the Contemporary or **Smooth Jazz** movements taking place and founded the group Fourplay. James continued to tour, record, and write well into the 2000s.

JAM SESSION (JAM). A term that describes impromptu performances given by musicians both in public and private formats. Jam sessions have been an important part of jazz culture and oftentimes provide musicians opportunities to perform with other musicians with whom they would not normally play. Jam sessions also play a vital role for aspiring musicians, in that they give young musicians performance opportunities with older or established musicians that they would not otherwise have. *See also* CUTTING CONTEST; IMPROVISATION; MINTON'S PLAYHOUSE; MONROE'S UPTOWN HOUSE.

JAPAN. Prior to World War II, jazz had brief periods of popularity in Japan. Dance halls grew steadily throughout the 1920s, and the creation of **dance**

bands continued to rise. Dance bands frequently performed in Japan during this time and were often playing music that was copied from American records. Japan had fully assimilated Western music notation. Regions like Osaka developed into cultural meccas that featured an active nightlife that became receptive to other styles of jazz. **Dixieland** and **New Orleans Jazz** styles became prevalent, and groups imitated **recordings** of American groups such as those led by **Jelly Roll Morton** and **King Oliver**.

In the 1930s, the government took action to prohibit jazz, with one of the primary objectives being to significantly reduce the American elements performed. Composers and arrangers in Japan used Folk or Pop music from their native country as melodic material instead of American-based compositions. In 1937, Japan took significant strides toward prohibiting jazz performances. Government officials had specific regulations musicians were required to follow, including restrictions on the number of times a drummer could hit certain **cymbals**. Wartime was also especially harmful toward the development of jazz in Japan because many established groups disbanded. Musicians were needed to serve the country in other capacities, and many groups that stopped playing were never re-formed.

At the conclusion of the war and into the American occupation of Japan during the 1940s and 1950s, jazz began to steadily gain a stronger following. The government switched its stance on jazz music, and Japanese musicians were very interested in providing American soldiers with the music they enjoyed. Some historians credit this time as a critical period for Japan and the growth of jazz there. The desire to make music satisfactory to Americans versus creating more original interpretations of jazz was considered a harmful process. Critics of Japanese jazz maintain that too much of the music composed lacks creativity and many times is just imitative of music previously heard on records or from visiting musicians.

Many local jazz musicians began moving to the United States in the 1960s. Two of Japan's most prominent jazz musicians, **Toshiko Akiyoshi** and **Sadao Watanabe**, have both had successful careers in both Japan and America. Akiyoshi developed a successful piano career in Japan before leading her own **big band** for several decades in New York from the 1970s onward. Watanabe, a saxophonist, has primarily focused on **Bebop** and **Fusion** for brief periods of time.

Despite occasional debate from critics on the approach Japanese musicians take to create and develop jazz, Japan has played an important role in the survival of jazz. Japan remains a prominent region for musicians from America to visit, and the Blue Note club in Japan remains one of the most active spots for touring jazz artists. Stylistically, the use of Folk music from Japan remains prevalent in many works of jazz today, most notably many of the groups led by the late drummer **Elvin Jones**. *See also* OKOSHI, TIGER; OZONE, MAKOTO.

JARREAU, ALWYN "AL" (1940–). After earning a degree in psychology and unhappily practicing it for several years in San Francisco, Jarreau decided to pursue a career in **singing**. Jarreau's first big break occurred when he was hired by pianist **George Duke**, which then led to a contract with Warner Bros. While he has worked some in the jazz genre, Jarreau's greatest claim to fame was as a Soul and **Rhythm and Blues (R&B)** singer. Jarreau won multiple Grammy Awards and continued to sing and record into the 2000s. *See also* SCAT.

JARRETT, KEITH (1945–). Deemed a virtuoso, Jarrett was considered a proficient pianist at a young age and began experimenting with composition and **improvisation**, in addition to his Classical piano studies, before becoming a teenager. Jarrett moved from his hometown of Allentown, Pennsylvania, to Boston, Massachusetts, to attend the popular **Berklee School of Music** in the early 1960s, but he did not finish and instead relocated to New York several years later. During the late 1960s, he established himself working first with **Art Blakey** and the **Jazz Messengers** and then with rising tenor saxophonist **Charles Lloyd**.

Performances with Lloyd resulted in a popularity boost for Jarrett who would soon be hired by **Miles Davis** to play **electric piano** in his band, an instrument Jarrett played only with Davis and swore to never play again after leaving the group. While working with Davis, Jarrett began to record frequently as a leader and worked with many musicians including bassist **Charlie Haden** and drummer **Paul Motian**. During the 1970s, Jarrett was influential in the development of the **ECM** record label. He would record on ECM for the next four decades.

Toward the end of the 1970s, Jarrett formed a working relationship with bassist **Gary Peacock** and drummer **Jack DeJohnette**, both of whom he would record and tour with for the greater part of the next four decades. Jarrett's trio would become highly influential to the next wave of jazz pianists, most significantly through his melodic development and his building of introductions to songs. Jarrett cemented his place in the history of jazz with many of these trio **recordings**. His solo piano performances of original and completely improvised compositions are considered to be landmark recordings. *See also* PIANO.

JASPAR, BOBBY (1926–1963). Born in Belgium, Jaspar worked in Europe as a flutist and tenor saxophonist in the 1950s including performances with pianist Henri Renaud before moving to New York in 1956. Jaspar played with several of the top jazz musicians during the late 1950s, including trombonist **J. J. Johnson, Miles Davis**, and **Donald Byrd**. Like many musicians of the era, Jaspar dealt with substance abuse, which led to his death from complications from heart surgery. *See also* EUROPE; FLUTE.

JAZZ AND PEOPLE'S MOVEMENT. Founded in the 1970s, the Jazz and People's Movement was created to bring awareness of African-American related music to the mass media. Important members of the organization include Andrew Cyrille, **Rashied Ali, Billy Harper**, and **Freddie Hubbard**.

JAZZ ARTISTS GUILD. A group founded in 1960 by **Max Roach** and **Charles Mingus**, among others, with the intention of forming opposition to festivals that had become commercially oriented. The influence of the Jazz Artists Guild was seen in other groups, such as the **Association for the Advancement of Creative Musicians**, that focused on increasing awareness of lesser-known artists. *See also* JAZZ FESTIVAL.

JAZZ AT THE PHILHARMONIC (JATP). Created as a group for a series of performances in concert halls in Los Angeles by **Norman Granz**, Jazz at the Philharmonic became an important touring group for over a decade. Comprised of musicians such as **Roy Eldridge, Dizzy Gillespie, Charlie Parker, Stan Getz, Lester Young, Oscar Peterson, Gene Krupa**, and **Buddy Rich**, the JATP provided an important forum for important and influential jazz musicians to be heard in settings that garnered them public acclaim. Many of the concerts were recorded and, over time, released by many of the record labels affiliated with Granz. The JATP was popular in both the United States and Europe and ceased touring in the late 1960s. *See also* EUROPE.

JAZZ BROTHERS. An **Art Blakey**–inspired group founded in the early 1960s by **trumpet** player and **flugelhorn** player **Chuck Mangione**.

JAZZ CARDINALS. Founded by **Trumpet** King **Freddie Keppard** in the 1920s, the Jazz Cardinals were a Chicago-based **Early Jazz** group that recorded several times for Paramount. Other members of the Jazz Cardinals included Eddie Vincent and **Johnny Dodds**. *See also* CHICAGO JAZZ.

JAZZ CENTRE SOCIETY. The Jazz Centre Society was founded in the late 1960s in **England** to help create more work for jazz musicians. The group expanded its reach from London to most of Great Britain. In existence for a little under 20 years, it had to shut down in the mid-1980s due to financial problems. *See also* EUROPE.

JAZZ COMPOSERS GUILD. A precursor to the **Jazz Composers Orchestra Association**, the Jazz Composers Guild, formed by **Bill Dixon** in 1964, was in existence for a little over a year during the mid-1960s with the intention of promoting **Free Jazz** independently of its other stylistic peers. Important members of the Jazz Composers Guild included Mike Mantley and **Carla Bley**, among others.

JAZZ COMPOSERS ORCHESTRA ASSOCIATION (JCOA). Formed in New York out of the remains of the **Jazz Composers Guild**, the Jazz Composers Orchestra Association was created in the mid-1960s to present opportunities for **Free Jazz** and creative musicians to compose music for large ensembles. The ensemble remained in existence for a little over a decade and gave many public performances in addition to **recording** several times.

JAZZ COMPOSERS WORKSHOP. A group formed by **Charles Mingus** in the 1950s with the intention of **recording** and performing new works.

JAZZCORE. A style of jazz that fuses many modern music elements including hard-core Rock, Metal, and Punk music with jazz instrumentation and improvisation. Jazzcore distinguishes itself from these other musical styles in that many times the instrumentation includes **saxophone** or **trumpet** in addition to **electric guitar** and **drums**.

JAZZ CRUSADERS. Founded by a group of friends in college, originally under the name the Modern Jazz Sextet, the name Jazz Crusaders was adopted when the group moved to Los Angeles in the 1960s and began **recording**. The Jazz Crusaders was one of the first groups to explore **Jazz-Rock** and **Soul Jazz**. Important members of the Jazz Crusaders included pianist **Joe Sample**, guitarist **Larry Carlton**, and trombonist Wayne Henderson. The group shortened their name to the Crusaders in 1971.

JAZZFEST BERLIN. Originally known as the Berliner Jazztage, the Jazzfest Berlin was founded in the early 1960s in Germany and remained an important organization for German musicians. The Jazzfest Berlin has hosted performances from a variety of artists during its several-decade run, including **Herbie Hancock, Don Cherry, Lee Konitz**, Victor Lewis, and **Peter Brötzmann**. Unlike some of its **jazz festival** peers, the Jazzfest Berlin is generously sponsored by the government and often takes place in the best venues in Berlin. *See also* EUROPE.

JAZZ FESTIVAL. Jazz festivals can range from one day to several weeks or months and typically feature many groups performing during the duration of the event. Festivals such as the **Monterey Jazz Festival** feature multiple performances each day on three to five different stages. Due to associated expenses, festivals frequently require the support of several sponsors. Significant jazz festivals include the **Montreux International Jazz Festival**, the **Newport Jazz Festival**, and the Monterey Jazz Festival, among many others. *See also* FESTIVAL INTERNATIONAL DE JAZZ DE MONTREAL; GRANDE PARADE DU JAZZ; INTERNATIONAL JAZZ JAMBOREE FESTIVAL; INTERNATIONAL NEW JAZZ FESTIVAL MOERS; JVC GRANDE PARADE DU JAZZ NICE; JVC JAZZ FESTIVAL NEW YORK; MOLDE INTERNATIONAL JAZZ FESTIVAL; NEW ORLEANS JAZZ & HERITAGE FESTIVAL; NORTH SEA JAZZ FESTIVAL; PORI INTERNATIONAL JAZZ FESTIVAL; SACRAMENTO DIXIELAND JUBILEE.

JAZZ INSTITUTE OF CHICAGO (JIC). Created in the late 1960s as an organization to help preserve the roots of jazz, the Jazz Institute of Chicago sponsors festivals, concerts, and public events to bring awareness to jazz.

JAZZKERHO BREAK. The most popular jazz organization in Finland, the Jazzkerho Break was created in 1968 with the purpose of creating concerts and increasing the popularity of jazz in Finland. The Jazzkerho Break, or "Jazz Society Break," released **albums**, newsletters, and worked with several other organizations to sponsor events until the 1990s.

JAZZLINE. Formed by two prominent 1950s and 1960s musicians, Duke Pearson and Dave Bailey with help from Fred Norsworthy, the Jazzline **record label** initially reissued albums in the 1960s. **Albums** by Walter Bishop, Pearson, and **Freddie Hubbard** were released under the label. In the 1980s, another company started a record label under the same name in Germany, and both reissued jazz albums in addition to releasing new material. The label is no longer active.

JAZZ MESSENGERS. A popular **Hard Bop** group co-founded by pianist **Horace Silver** and drummer **Art Blakey** in the 1950s that remained in existence until Blakey's death in the 1990s. Silver and Blakey eventually split, and the name "Jazz Messengers" was briefly associated with Silver's groups before it came under the sole ownership of Blakey. The **front line** for the Jazz Messengers was frequently **saxophone** and **trumpet** (although at times **trombone** was used as well) accompanied by a **rhythm section**. The Jazz Messengers was a highly influential group whose members often went on to have strong solo careers. Influential musicians to spend time playing in the Jazz Messengers include **Lee Morgan**, **Wayne Shorter**, **Freddie Hubbard**, **Hank Mobley**, **Clifford Brown**, **Curtis Fuller**, **Bobby Watson**, and **Wynton Marsalis**.

JAZZMOBILE. A program sponsored by the Harlem Cultural Council that was created by **Billy Taylor** in the mid-1960s. The Jazzmobile presented concerts in urban centers by bringing a portable stage to areas of metropolitan New York. The Jazzmobile program was in existence for a little over a decade and included educational outreach projects as part of its objective. Musicians to participate in the Jazzmobile included **Jimmy Heath, Thad Jones, Herbie Hancock, Dizzy Gillespie**, and **Art Blakey**.

JAZZOLOGY. A **Traditional Jazz record label** founded in the late 1940s that initially focused on music recorded in or originating from Chicago. Jazzology and its sister label, **GHB**, were founded by the same owner, George Buck. Jazzology acquired several labels, including **Circle**, Southland, Paramount, and Lang-Worth. Jazzology remained active for several decades and into the 1980s. *See also* RECORD LABEL.

JAZZ RECORD. A short-lived **record label** created in 1946 by Art Hodes who, after less than a year of operations, sold the company to the **Jazzology** label.

JAZZ-ROCK. A style of jazz similar to **Fusion** and popular in the 1960s that blends elements of popular music, **Funk**, and styles of jazz like **Soul Jazz** and **Hard Bop**. Jazz-Rock is defined by the rhythmic pulse contained in the **rhythm section** and the use of jazz **improvisation** or jazz-influenced writing. Oftentimes Jazz-Rock is very difficult to separate from Jazz Fusion. Pianist Jeff Lorber is a notated performer of the Jazz-Rock style.

JAZZ SERVICES. A jazz education and awareness program created in **England** in the 1980s. Jazz Services provided youth the opportunity to learn and listen to jazz, in addition to promoting English musicians and concerts. *See also* ENGLAND.

JAZZ SOCIETY (I). Founded in the early 1950s, the Jazz Society **record label** was created in France to reissue "**hot jazz**" **albums** from the 1920s and 1930s.

JAZZ SOCIETY (II). Founded by Carl Hallstrom, the second incarnation of the Jazz Society **record label** was created in 1970 in Stockholm, Sweden, with the intention of reissuing **albums** by 1930s jazz masters including **Duke Ellington** and **Count Basie**.

JAZZTET. A **Hard Bop** group co-founded by **Art Farmer** and **Benny Golson** in the mid-1950s. Additional members of the Jazztet included trombonist

JOHNSON, ALBERT J. "BUDD" • 189

Curtis Fuller and a young McCoy Tyner. While the Jazztet was only active for a few years in the 1950s and 1960s, Farmer and Golson formed a reunion version of the group in the 1980s. Some of the music of the Jazztet overlapped Golson's time with the **Jazz Messengers**, and songs like "Whisper Not" were recorded with both groups. *See also* COMBO.

JAZZTONE. Created by the traditionally Classical-oriented label Concert Hall Society, Jazztone was a **record label** established in the mid-1950s to provide customers with a mail-order option for receiving **albums** instead of purchasing them at stores. The label folded after two years, although albums recorded by the company were reissued by other companies during the 1970s.

JAZZ WEST. A small **record label** founded in 1954 by Herbert Kimmel that put out **albums** by **Jack Sheldon** and **Kenny Drew**. Jazz West would eventually be purchased and have reissues released by **Blue Note** Records.

JEFFERSON, EDDIE (1918–1979). Jefferson worked as both a tap dancer and a vocalist throughout the late 1930s and 1940s. Credited with developing the idea of **vocalese**, Jefferson was one of the first vocalists to apply syllables or lyrics to improvised jazz solos that had been recorded previously. Jefferson was highly influential to the group **Lambert, Hendricks, and Ross**, and in the 1960s and 1970s he recorded vocalese of solos by **Lester Young** and **Coleman Hawkins**. Jefferson was infrequently used as a **sideman**, although he did tour with **Richie Cole** and Roy Brooks in the 1970s, before being involved in an incident outside a club in Detroit where he was shot and killed.

JOHANSSON, JAN (1931–1968). Originally from Sweden, Johansson began his career working in Sweden contributing **arrangements** and playing **piano** for several local groups. He worked with one of **Stan Getz**'s European quartets for a few years in the late 1950s, in addition to working with the European rendition of **Jazz at the Philharmonic**. Before dying at the age of 37, Johansson served as the principal arranger and composer for several popular groups in Sweden. *See also* EUROPE.

JOHNSON, ALBERT J. "BUDD" (1910–1984). Coming from a family of musicians, Johnson took up the **tenor saxophone** as a youth and moved to Kansas City at the age of 18 to pursue work in **territory bands**. Throughout the 1930s and 1940s, Johnson's tenor saxophone playing was heard with many popular bands including **Earl Hines**, **Louis Armstrong**, **Fletcher Henderson**, **Woody Herman**, **Don Redman**, **Dizzy Gillespie**, and **Billy Eckstine**.

In the 1950s, Johnson alternated between leading his own groups and free-lancing with other artists including **Benny Goodman**, **Quincy Jones**, **Gil Evans**, and **Earl Hines**. Johnson would become more actively involved with education during the last few years of his life, including teaching at the State University of New York, Stonybrook campus.

JOHNSON, GUS, JR. (1913–2000). A drummer, bassist, and vocalist, Johnson played primarily **drum set** for the majority of his career. Born in Texas, Johnson moved to Kansas City to catch on with the **territory band** craze that was happening. Johnson worked with Jay McShann and Lloyd Hunter during the 1930s before working with **Eddie Vinson**, **Buck Clayton**, and **Earl Hines** in the 1940s. Johnson was given the drum seat in **Count Basie**'s band in the 1950s but was forced to give it up due to health problems.

Johnson would remain very popular among **Swing** era musicians throughout the 1950s and 1960s, working with **Rex Stewart**, **Coleman Hawkins**, **Roy Eldridge**, **Ben Webster**, **Woody Herman**, and Al Cohn. Johnson worked with the **World's Greatest Jazz Band** in the 1970s, in addition to freelancing with a variety of groups and living in Colorado. Health problems continued to hurt Johnson, and despite attempting to continue his career, he steadily cut down on performances until he officially retired in 1990.

JOHNSON, JAMES LEWIS "J. J." (1924–2001). One of the most influential jazz trombonists of all time, Johnson's career started in his hometown of Indianapolis, Indiana, before he migrated to New York following tours with **Illinois Jacquet**, **Count Basie**, and **Benny Carter**. Johnson's **Bebop** prowess on the trombone led him to be used frequently by many of the top musicians including **Charlie Parker**, **Miles Davis**, and **Bud Powell**.

Like some of his musical counterparts (most notably **trumpet** player **Kenny Dorham**), Johnson was forced into taking a day job for part of the early 1950s and did not prominently reenter the jazz scene until he formed the popular trombone group Jay and Kai, with **Kai Winding**. Johnson became an important composer and performer during the decade when he landed a multi-record deal with **Columbia**, in addition to having large-scale works recorded and performed live at various **jazz festivals**. Johnson's writing of the time was considered to be in the **Third Stream** style.

Johnson was also notable in that he primarily led his own groups for the next decades. Rarely having to record as a **sideman** or freelance, Johnson led several popular quartets and quintets during the 1960s, 1970s, and 1980s. For a brief period in the 1970s, Johnson was actively involved in composition and as a **studio musician**, and he assisted on the soundtrack for *Across 110th Street*. Johnson's health deteriorated in his final years, which caused him to stop performing in the late 1990s. Johnson died from a self-inflicted gunshot wound.

JOHNSON, JAMES OSIE (1923–1966). He was an important freelance drummer for most of the 1940s, 1950s, and 1960s, who performed with many notable **Swing** era musicians including **Illinois Jacquet**, **Bennie Green**, **Johnny Hodges**, **Pee Wee Russell**, and **Coleman Hawkins**. *See also* DRUM SET.

JOHNSON, JAMES P(RICE) (1894–1955). As a young man of 14, Johnson was tutored on **piano** by many of New York's finest musicians, including **Eubie Blake**. In his early twenties, he worked frequently as an accompanist for dancers in the segregated sections of New York and became an influential composer and performer.

Johnson was important in the development of the **Stride** Piano style, and his compositions were made available to the public via the use of **piano rolls**. Named the "Father of Stride Piano," contemporaries **Fats Waller** and Blake frequently performed Johnson's music during the 1920s, and Johnson's work became increasingly larger in scope. Toward the end of the decade, Johnson also wrote an opera, two-piano pieces, and had many of his works orchestrated for symphony orchestra.

Johnson's health began to decline in the 1940s, and he incurred several strokes. By the 1950s, he was forced to retire from performing. Many of Johnson's pieces still remain in the solo jazz canon including "Carolina Shout" and "The Charleston." Johnson's influence can be heard in the performances and compositions of his contemporaries and other performers like **Duke Ellington** and **Teddy Wilson**.

JOHNSON, PLAS JOHN, JR. (1931–). Playing in New Orleans–inspired bands as a teenager, Johnson found his calling as a tenor saxophonist. Johnson moved from Louisiana to the western coast of the United States where he found work as a **studio musician** in Los Angeles in the mid-1950s. Primarily working in recording studios and not touring, Johnson was on **albums** led by Rosemary Clooney, **Nat "King" Cole**, Etta James, B. B. King, and Diana Ross. One of Johnson's biggest claims to fame was his playing being featured on the soundtrack for the *Pink Panther* movies. Johnson did less studio work in the 1970s and 1980s and played in Los Angeles with musicians like Bill Berry, **Carl Fontana**, **Herb Ellis**, and Ray Brown.

JOHNSON, REGINALD "REGGIE" (1940–). Johnson was an important **Avant-Garde bassist** during the 1960s who worked with many of the most important **Free Jazz** musicians. Johnson's resume included dates and tours with **Archie Shepp, Rahsaan Roland Kirk**, and **Stanley Cowell**. Over the next few years, Johnson did substantial work with **Straight-Ahead** artists including **Art Blakey, Kenny Burrell, Blue Mitchell**, and **Tom Harrell**.

JOHNSON, WILLIE GARY "BUNK" (1889?–1949). Johnson is a significant figure in the development of **Early Jazz** and was one of the first musicians to work with **trumpet** legend **Buddy Bolden** in the New Orleans area. Johnson developed his own trumpet sound that was inspired by Bolden but remained individual and was used in Early Jazz groups such as the **Eagle** and Superior bands and **Henry Allen**'s Brass Band. After spending much of the 1920s working in show bands and minstrel groups, Johnson was forced into a brief retirement in the 1930s due to health problems. Johnson resumed his career toward the end of the 1930s and worked with many touring groups, including the **Yerba Buena Jazz Band** and **Sidney Bechet**, before suffering from complications from a stroke in 1948.

JONES, ELVIN RAY (1927–2004). The youngest member and arguably the most famous of the Jones brothers, Elvin Jones took up the drums in high school and always had a unique fascination with rhythm. After playing in the Detroit area as a teenager, Jones moved to New York and found work quickly with artists including **J. J. Johnson, Sonny Rollins**, and fellow Michigan musician **Donald Byrd**. While playing with these groups, he was heard by tenor saxophonist **John Coltrane** who invited Jones to join him on tour. This group would work regularly during the 1960s, with Jones providing exemplary rhythmic support in Coltrane's quartets.

Along with **McCoy Tyner** and **Jimmy Garrison**, Jones' playing with Coltrane helped redefine the role of the drummer in small-group playing while also helping to develop a new, more interactive style of playing behind a soloist. After his time with Coltrane, he led his own groups for the next three decades. Joe Farrell, **David Liebman**, Eric Lewis, Nicholas Payton, and **Wynton Marsalis** all toured or played with Jones during his three-decade run as a **bandleader**. Jones suffered from a heart condition, which led to his death in 2004. He remains an important figure in jazz and a huge influence on drummers of all genres.

JONES, ETTA (1928–2001). Jones sang as a teenager and got work with the assistance of **Leonard Feather** in the 1940s. Much of her career was geared toward **Soul Jazz** and **Rhythm and Blues (R&B)** audiences, both of which she embraced. Jones performed frequently with her husband, tenor saxophonist Houston Person.

JONES, HAROLD (1940–). Jones was one of many musicians who originated from the Indianapolis area. A drummer, he worked with musicians including **Wes Montgomery** and **Freddie Hubbard**, who both came from that area. Jones primarily freelanced throughout the next few decades and worked with **Count Basie, Sarah Vaughan, Gene Harris**, Natalie Cole, and **Marian McPartland**. *See also* DRUM SET.

JONES, HENRY "HANK" (1918–2010). A pianist, he was the oldest of the famous Jones family of musicians. His career lasted almost seven decades and included performances with many of the greatest musicians in jazz. He moved to New York while in his late twenties and found work playing **Bebop** with **Charlie Parker, Coleman Hawkins, Benny Goodman**, and **Jazz at the Philharmonic**. Jones also found steady work as a **studio musician** and worked for the **Columbia Broadcasting System (CBS)** for almost two decades, doing little touring.

In the 1970s he founded the **Great Jazz Trio** with **Ron Carter** and **Tony Williams**, although the personnel would change over the years. Jones primarily worked in trio settings during the 1980s, although he did significant work along with other pianists in duo settings. The Great Jazz Trio also often featured other artists as they toured and were very popular at many **jazz festivals** worldwide. Jones played in New York **clubs** for a majority of the 1990s and worked in several groups that featured tenor saxophonist Joe Lovano in the 2000s. Fellow pianist Geoff Keezer gathered many top pianists, including **Kenny Barron** and **Chick Corea**, to record a tribute **album** to Jones in the early 2000s.

JONES, JOSEPH "PHILLY JOE" (1923–1985). Like many of his contemporaries, Jones' career started after he served time in the military in the 1940s. Jones worked in the Philadelphia area in the 1940s before moving to New York. He served a term working as the house drummer for the club **Café Society** where he played with many top-touring musicians, including **Dexter Gordon** and **Dizzy Gillespie**. Jones bounced around cities for a few years, playing engagements in Washington, D.C.; Philadelphia; and New York again in the 1950s. During his second tenure in New York, he became acquainted with **Tadd Dameron** and **Miles Davis**, both of whom would use him frequently during the 1950s. He was given the nickname "Philly" to identify him over the older Jo Jones, the great **Count Basie** Orchestra drummer.

His work with Miles Davis proved to be some of the most important playing of the decade. Jones, along with Red Garland and **Paul Chambers**, comprised the first **rhythm section** of Davis' many great quartets. Because he frequently had to deal with his personal addictions, Davis fired him in 1959. Jones primarily freelanced for the rest of his career including spending several periods working with **Bill Evans** and **Hank Mobley**. In the 1980s, he formed a tribute group to **Tadd Dameron**, *Dameronia*.

JONES, QUINCY (1933–). Prior to becoming one of the most influential producers and entertainment entrepreneurs ever, Jones was a **trumpet** player and jazz arranger. After attending several universities including the Schillinger House of Music (later renamed the **Berklee School of Music**) in the early 1950s, Jones worked with **Clifford Brown, Count Basie, Lionel Hampton**, and **Dizzy Gillespie**, as both a trumpeter and arranger. Jones moved to **France** in 1957, where he continued to study music in addition to working as a conductor and arranger.

Jones returned to the United States in the 1960s and began working as a producer and director for **Mercury** Records while continuing to compose and conduct. From this point in his career, Jones abandoned most jazz-related music and focused on his own compositions until he met and worked with Michael Jackson in Hollywood in the 1970s. Jackson and Jones forged a dynamic relationship, and Jones was highly influential in the success of many of Jackson's records. Jones' legacy is in being a racial pioneer, in that he was able to work his way higher into the **recording** industry than any African-American before him, and of his work as a composer and producer.

JONES, THADDEUS JOSEPH "THAD" (1923–1986). The middle child of the Jones family, Thad Jones first played **cornet** in groups led by his older brother, **Hank Jones**, until he served time in the military. In the 1950s, Jones worked with several **big bands**, most notably groups led by **Charles Mingus** and **Count Basie**. With the Basie band, Jones made his mark in the jazz world as a soloist, arranger, and composer. Jones led several small-group **sessions** during the late 1950s and early 1960s until he left Basie's band to form his own big band, co-led with drummer **Mel Lewis**.

The Thad Jones–Mel Lewis Orchestra remained a working unit from its inception in the mid-1960s until 1979, when Jones left to pursue his own ventures. During their decade and a half together, the group was one of the top working big bands, powered by Jones' compositions. "Tip Toe," "Little Pixie," and "A Child Is Born," are examples of Jones' standout big band writing, and much of the music written during this period remains active in the music world today. Jones was put in charge of the Count Basie orchestra in the mid-1980s before having to leave the group for health reasons.

JONES AND COLLINS ASTORIA HOT EIGHT. A group founded in the late 1920s in New Orleans. The group was not in existence very long and only made one **recording**, in 1929. Members of the ensemble include Nat Story, Louis Nelson, Theodore Purnell, and Joe Strode.

JONES-SMITH INC. A group led by **Count Basie** that had to record under a name not affiliated with Basie to avoid complications with existing record contracts. Jones-Smith Inc. members included his 1930s **big band rhythm section** of **Walter Page** and Jo Jones, in addition to tenor saxophonist **Lester Young.**

JORDAN, CLIFFORD LACONIA, JR. (1931–1993). Jordan took up the **tenor saxophone** while in high school in Chicago, Illinois. He worked with **Max Roach** and **Sonny Stitt** while in his early twenties before he moved to New York to pursue work with **Horace Silver, J. J. Johnson**, and **Kenny Dorham**. Jordan rejoined Roach for most of the 1960s, and the two toured the United States and **Europe** in addition to some performances with **Charles Mingus**. Jordan became a leader in the late 1960s and for most of the 1970s, and formed the group that would eventually become known as Eastern Rebellion, with **Cedar Walton** and **Billy Higgins**. Jordan primarily freelanced throughout the 1980s and early 1990s, working in a variety of groups ranging from duos to a **big band** he led in the early 1990s.

JORDAN, DUKE (1922–2006). Jordan's career has primarily been as a first-call pianist for **recording sessions** and tours, although some time was spent focusing on leading groups under his own name. Born in New York, Jordan found success early on in New York playing in groups around town, some led by **Charlie Parker** and **Miles Davis**. In the late 1940s and early 1950s, Jordan found work with **Sonny Stitt, Coleman Hawkins**, and **Stan Getz**. Jordan's most famous pairing was with baritone saxophonist **Cecil Payne**, with whom he worked on and off for several decades. He took several years off to work as a cab driver before resuming his performance career in the 1970s. During the 1980s and 1990s, Jordan worked frequently as a **sideman** with **Clark Terry, Charles McPherson**, and Dannie Richmond. Jordan's composition, "Jordu," remains an important work in the jazz canon. *See also* JORDAN, SHEILA; PIANO.

JORDAN, LOUIS (1908–1975). Primarily a **Rhythm and Blues (R&B)** tenor saxophonist, Jordan starred in jazz groups led by **Chick Webb** and **Fats Waller** early in his career. Jordon became a leader in the 1950s and led a popular group, the Tympany Five. Many future jazz stars passed through his groups, including Idrees Sulieman, Paul Quinichette, Shadow Wilson, and **Wild Bill Davis**. *See also* TENOR SAXOPHONE.

JORDAN, SHEILA (1928–). Jordan developed her vocal style while living in New York in the 1940s when she studied the music of **Charlie Parker** and put vocalese to many of his solos. She was briefly married to **Duke Jordan** in the 1950s while still mastering the **Bebop** style. Jordan was affiliated with several jazz pioneers throughout the 1950s and 1960s, including **Lennie Tristano**, **George Russell**, and Roswell Rudd. Jordan's vocal style changed during each different era, experimenting with **Free Jazz** and incorporating a more modern approach to her work.

Jordan maintained a day job from the late 1960s until the 1980s, although she continued to work in a variety of jazz groups that toured and recorded frequently. Jordan's breadth of performances included a duo with **bass** player Harvie Swartz, and in front of a **big band** led by George Gruntz. Jordan continues to be an influential vocalist due to her diversity of repertoire and unique ability to adapt to different genres.

JORDAN, STANLEY (1959–). Jordan has been an active jazz guitarist since he was in high school. He was educated at the prestigious Princeton University in the late 1970s before working with jazz greats **Dizzy Gillespie** and **Benny Carter**. Throughout the 1980s and 1990s, Jordan gained a strong following from a variety of musicians including **Al Di Meola**, Omar Hakim, and **Kenny Burrell**, who were all very interested in Jordan's technique, which consisted of him tapping the guitar strings instead of plucking them. Using the tapping technique allowed Jordan to play two lines simultaneously and/or accompany himself. *See also* GUITAR.

JUG BAND. Primarily a Folk ensemble, the jug band was a popular type of group among African-Americans during the 1920s. In addition to traditional instruments, jug bands contained a musician playing a jug that sounded bass notes and acted as a percussion instrument. Not common to jazz, the jug band played an influential role in Folk music that was important to the development of jazz.

JUMP. A style of jazz very similar to **Swing** that was considered to be very high energy and was performed for crowds that enjoyed being very active. Jump was very popular in the 1940s and had departed from its jazz roots and become more Pop music influenced in the 1950s.

JVC GRANDE PARADE DU JAZZ NICE. An important festival created by **George Wein** in the 1970s in Nice, France. Throughout the 1980s and early 1990s, the festival became a multicultural festival that included music from across the globe and not strictly jazz. The festival name was changed to the Nice Music Festival in 1993. *See also* JAZZ FESTIVAL.

JVC JAZZ FESTIVAL NEW YORK. This is the name the famous **Newport Jazz Festival** adopted when **George Wein** took charge in 1986. After a brief period in which the Newport Jazz Festival took on the name of its sponsor, Kool, the Japanese Victor Corporation (JVC) took over promoting and sponsoring the festival for the next several decades.

KAMINSKY, MAX (1908–1994). Kaminsky's career as a **trumpet** player began in 1920, and he reached popular status around the Boston area by the time he was 20. Kaminsky was hired by many **big bands** and small-group leaders throughout the early 1930s including groups led by **Joe Venuti, Tommy Dorsey,** Bud Freeman, and **Artie Shaw.** Kaminsky's career was primarily as a freelancer, which was the case for most of the 1940s. On several occasions, he attempted to lead his own big band, but for a variety of reasons these ventures never lasted for more than a year or two. His career was given a boost when he was hired to tour with **Jack Teagarden** and **Earl Hines** in the late 1950s. Kaminsky's career settled significantly in the following decades, and he worked primarily as a freelance musician with big bands in New York.

KANSAS CITY FIVE. A popular name used by several Kansas City jazz quintets, including groups led by **Elmer Snowden,** Eddie Durham, and **Buck Clayton.**

KANSAS CITY JAZZ. The term used to describe the style of jazz that was being played by **territory bands.** Kansas City Jazz was considered to be a melting pot of a variety of jazz styles, and the bands that worked there included elements of **Ragtime,** early **Blues,** and **Swing** music. Notable bands from the region included those of **Buck Clayton, Bennie Moten, Andy Kirk,** and most importantly, **Count Basie.** Many important jazz musicians came out of this area including **Ben Webster, Coleman Hawkins,** and **Charlie Parker.**

KANSAS CITY ROCKETS. A **big band** founded in Kansas City by previous members of the **big band** led by **Bennie Moten.** The group frequently toured and played in Chicago during its six-year existence from 1931 to 1937.

KANSAS CITY SEVEN. A septet led by **Count Basie** in the 1940s and 1950s. The majority of Basie's career featured him fronting a **big band** with the exception of the brief hiatuses he would take to lead the Kansas City Seven.

KANSAS CITY SIX. A group that grew out of the Kansas City Five and was often made up of members from **Count Basie**'s **big band**. The Kansas City Six was active from the late 1930s into the 1960s, and sometimes the group was augmented to include a seventh musician. Members of the Kansas City Six include Eddie Durham, **Buck Clayton**, Jo Jones, **Dicky Wells**, and **Lester Young**. Members rotated frequently, however, and the group went through several personnel changes during its existence.

KELLAWAY, ROGER (1939–). Kellaway developed as a pianist and bassist while still a teenager and studied both instruments and composition at New England Conservatory in the late 1950s. Kellaway developed a reputation as an outstanding pianist and accompanist and was hired by several groups in the 1960s, including ones led by **Sonny Rollins, Bob Brookmeyer, Kai Winding**, and **Wes Montgomery**. **Trumpet** player and composer **Don Ellis** hired Kellaway to join his revolutionary **big band** in Los Angeles. Kellaway quickly settled in Los Angeles and found work as a pianist and as a movie score composer contributing to films such as *A Star Is Born* and *The Paper Lion*.

Kellaway was frequently hired by vocalists as both an accompanist and musical director, and he worked with Mark Murphy, Bobby Darin, Joni Mitchell, and Helen Merrill. Much of the next few decades was dedicated to composition, and Kellaway wrote for a variety of ensembles, but he especially enjoyed writing for strings. Trumpeter Claudio Roditi, clarinetist and saxophonist **Eddie Daniels**, and cellist Yo-Yo Ma were all involved with projects that Kellaway did involving strings. Despite his focus on composition, Kellaway continued to perform frequently as a jazz soloist throughout the 1980s and 1990s.

KELLY, WYNTON (1931–1971). Kelly's family moved from Jamaica to New York in 1935, and Kelly found work as a pianist almost 10 years later at the age of 15. Kelly was considered very prodigious, and between 1948 and 1956 he worked with many of jazz's rising stars including tenor players **Eddie Vinson, Eddie "Lockjaw" Davis**, and **Lester Young**; Bebop trumpet innovator **Dizzy Gillespie**; and bassist **Charles Mingus**. After Kelly established his own trio in the late 1950s, he was hired to replace Bill Evans in **Miles Davis'** groups. Kelly's **rhythm section** mates from the Davis group decided to depart with Kelly to work in a trio format, sometimes featuring an added instrumentalist. Kelly died at the age of 39 due to complications from a heart attack.

KENTON, STAN(LEY) (1911–1979). Unlike most jazz musicians, Kenton rarely served as a **sideman** or apprentice to anyone and was very ambitious in the 1930s about starting his own **big band**. Kenton did not gain recognition regarding his band until the early 1940s and with the **album** *Artistry in Rhythm* (1948, Capitol). Similar to **bandleaders** like **Woody Herman** and **Count Basie**, much of Kenton's fame was attributed to the work of his arrangers and bandmates. Arrangers that came through Kenton's band included Pete Rugolo, **Neal Hefti**, and William Russo, who were featuring soloists that included **Lee Konitz, Art Pepper**, and **Shorty Rogers**.

In the 1950s, Kenton attempted to experiment with newer music and helped create the style known as **Third Stream**. Included in this style was the work "City of Glass" by composer Bob Graettinger that was completely unique to the current jazz scene. Kenton experimented with band sizes that ranged from 17 to 43 pieces and would sometimes include mellophones and a string section.

Kenton also did much work in terms of education and was responsible for helping to develop some of the first summer jazz camps. These camps or clinics were usually housed on university campuses and were influential in the spreading of jazz. Kenton was very adept at changing with the times and was not afraid to embrace the **Fusion** Jazz movement that took place during the 1970s. He continued to lead a band until his death in 1979. *See also* FERGUSON, MAYNARD; HOLMAN, BILL; RUSSO, WILLIAM "BILL."

KENTUCKY CLUB. The Kentucky Club in New York was home to many jazz stars including **Elmer Snowden, Billie Holiday**, and **Duke Ellington**. The club's original name was the Hollywood Club.

KEPPARD, FREDDIE (1890–1933). Keppard was an important figure in the early New Orleans jazz scene and was part of the **Trumpet** King lineage that took place in the region. Keppard studied several instruments as a youth but eventually decided on pursuing a career as a cornet player. Keppard was an important member of several key New Orleans jazz ensembles that included the Olympia Orchestra and the Original Creole Orchestra. Following another trumpet figurehead, **"King" Joe Oliver**, Keppard moved to Chicago in the early 1920s. Keppard was an active performer until 1928, at which point health problems forced him into retirement.

KESSEL, BARNEY (1923–2004). Kessel took up the **guitar** before the age of 12 and was playing professionally in California before the age of 20. Kessel's popularity skyrocketed during the late 1940s and early 1950s, and he participated in much studio work and was also a first-call guitarist for many of the local Los Angeles **big bands**. In 1952, Kessel was hired by rising jazz pianist **Oscar Peterson** to participate in a multimonth tour, and the two would continue an on-and-off-again relationship for the next few decades. Kessel recorded many **albums** under his own name and became a **bandleader** during the late 1950s. Toward the end of the 1960s, Kessel's popularity reached an all-time high, and he formed a group, the **Great Guitars**, with two of his established contemporaries—**Herb Ellis** and **Charlie Byrd**. Kessel participated in this group in addition to leading groups well into the 1980s. Kessel suffered a stroke in the early 1990s and eventually was forced to retire from playing but remained an active teacher until his death.

KEYNOTE. A **record label** founded in New York that published many important **recordings** of jazz musicians made in the early 1940s. Included in these recordings were significant dates led by **Lester Young**, **Coleman Hawkins**, and **Earl Hines**. The label was only in existence for eight years but captured two of the earliest recordings made of jazz pioneer Lennie Tristano.

KEYSTONE KORNER. A significant jazz club in the San Francisco Bay area that featured many of California's top musicians, in addition to touring groups. **Freddie Hubbard** and **Joe Henderson** made several significant live **recordings** of their groups at the Keystone Korner.

KICK. A term used by **bandleaders** and drummers to signify a specific beat or rhythm that needs to be accented by the drums. Oftentimes the drummer will use the bass (or "kick") drum to mark the given beat or phrase.

KING. The King record company purchased many labels during its existence and distributed many records recorded by the Bethlehem, De Luxe, and Queen labels. King Records was in business from 1944 until the 1970s. *See also* RECORD LABEL.

KING JAZZ. A **record label** founded in 1945 that primarily issued records that had been recorded by other companies. Vogue and Storyville both had records released under the King Jazz label.

KING PLEASURE (1922–1981). A vocalist originally from Cincinnati, Pleasure (born as Clarence Beeks) was innovative through the use of taking transcribed instrumental solo **improvisations** and adding lyrics to them. Pleasure had several hits in the 1940s and garnered recognition for his lyrics to **Charlie Parker**'s composition "Parker's Mood." Despite reaching a moderate level of success and influencing many other performers, Pleasure fell into anonymity in the 1950s and did not perform actively. *See also* VOCALESE.

KIRBY, JOHN (1908–1952). Kirby was very interested in trombone at the age of 16, but after an incident in which his instrument was stolen, he elected to switch first to the tuba and then the acoustic bass. His prowess for the bass became well known in New York, and he played with a variety of **bandleaders** in the 1930s including saxophonist **Benny Carter**, drummer **Chick Webb**, and **Fletcher Henderson**. Kirby formed his own group, a sextet comprised of top musicians of the day, including **Charlie Shavers, Buster Bailey**, and **Russell Procope**. The sextet is credited for being a predecessor to **West Coast Jazz** and was one of the top jazz groups from 1938 to 1942. Kirby would continue to lead the group throughout the 1940s but had to deal with a variety of issues including alcoholism. The sextet's popularity lessened during the end of the decade, and Kirby attempted planned comebacks with the group several times before he died.

KIRK, ANDREW "ANDY" (1898–1992). Kirk was born in Cincinnati but raised in Colorado where he developed his appreciation for music. He studied both bass saxophone and bass and was hired by several local touring bands. Kirk moved to Texas in the late 1920s and after several frustrating experiences with **bandleaders** decided to start his own group called Andy Kirk and His **Clouds of Joy**. Kirk's band was considered to be one of the most prominent groups of the 1930s and featured many legendary musicians including pianist **Mary Lou Williams, Ben Webster**, and **Lester Young**. Kirk famously traded Webster to **Fletcher Henderson** for rising jazz star Lester Young in 1933. Kirk's band became famous during the 1930s and 1940s, and the list of jazz performers to play with Kirk grew and included **trumpet** player **Howard McGhee** and saxophonists Jimmy Forrest and **Eddie "Lockjaw" Davis**.

Kirk's popularity reached its peak in the early 1940s, and the band disbanded at the end of the decade. He continued to work on the commercial side of things until he decided to pursue a career in hotel management and, later, real estate. Kirk was never totally removed from music, however, and he took several opportunities to lead bands as he got older, eventually taking a job with the New York American Federation of Musicians.

KIRK, RAHSAAN ROLAND (1936–1977). Despite suffering from blindness as a child, Kirk learned to play several instruments while growing up including bugle, **trumpet**, manzello, stritch, **clarinet**, and both the C-melody and tenor **saxophones**. Kirk found his calling with the tenor saxophone although he did manage to incorporate numerous instruments into his performances many years later. He became a **bandleader** early in his career and did several tours of Europe in the early 1960s in addition to working with

Charles Mingus. His groups included many of the more prominent musicians of the 1960s, including George Gruntz, Tete Montoliu, **Niels-Henning Ørsted Pedersen**, and Harold Mabern. While his playing was considered to be **Avant-Garde**, it captured a variety of styles, and he was an active participant in promoting jazz, especially the works of African-American composers. Many of his performances involved him playing multiple instruments simultaneously.

KIRKLAND, KENNETH "KENNY" (1955–1998). Considered to be one of the "Young Lions" of jazz during the 1980s, Kirkland received his training from the Manhattan School of Music and played early in his career with **John Scofield** and **Dave Liebman**. Kirkland made a name for himself by playing with both **Branford** and **Wynton Marsalis** in the 1980s and 1990s. He served as the pianist for Wynton Marsalis' quintets and quartets before serving as Branford Marsalis' pianist for the majority of his career. When Branford was hired to direct the NBC *Tonight Show* band, Kirkland followed and was the band's pianist from 1992 to 1994. Kirkland's career was also boosted through several tours with the Pop star Sting. Kirkland died at the age of 43.

KLACTO. A short-lived 1960s **record label** that was inspired by and featured the music of **Charlie Parker**.

KLEIN, EMMANUEL "MANNY" (1908–1994). Born in New York, **trumpet** player Klein received his first break when he subbed for **Bix Beiderbecke** in the **Paul Whiteman** Orchestra. Klein would develop a reputation as a standout **lead** trumpet player and soloist and worked primarily for Los Angeles–based studios while also touring and **recording** with many Los Angeles–based **big bands**. Although the majority of his recording work was in studios for television and movies, Klein consistently played with bands based out of Southern California until his death.

KLEMMER, JOHN (1946–). Klemmer was born in Chicago and began playing **tenor saxophone** after attempting to play the **guitar** and **alto saxophone**. Working with dance bands in the 1960s in addition to attending the summer camps led by composer/**bandleader Stan Kenton**, Klemmer developed much of his musical training hands-on. Along with many other musicians, Klemmer followed bandleader **Don Ellis** west to participate in Ellis' revolutionary groups. In the 1970s, Klemmer served primarily as a **bandleader** and did much **recording** of **Avant-Garde** Jazz and also more Fusion-based projects. Klemmer suffered from a variety of illnesses in the early 1980s and was forced into taking several long, multiyear sabbaticals from playing.

KLINK, AL(BERT) (1915–1991). Klink most famously served as second tenor in the **Glenn Miller** band. Klink's career as a tenor saxophonist included tours and **recordings** with many of the 1930s' and 1940s' most popular groups, including the Glenn Miller Orchestra and the bands of **Benny Goodman** and **Tommy Dorsey**.

KLUGH, EARL (1954–). Klugh's career began while he was still a teenager when he started **recording** as a leader. Considered a prodigious guitarist, Klugh recorded with many of his guitar contemporaries during the 1970s including **George Benson** and Chet Atkins. Klugh's style bounced between Fusion and smoother, more Pop-related ventures. Klugh continued to be a leader throughout the 1980s and 1990s, working on projects that contained elements of jazz and various other styles including Country music and **Rhythm and Blues (R&B)**. *See also* GUITAR.

KNEPPER, JAMES "JIMMY" (1927–2003). Knepper's career began in his native Los Angeles working as a trombonist for many of the local **big bands**. Knepper attempted to formally study music several times at a variety of universities in Texas and California but never completed a degree. In the 1950s, Knepper received several of his first big breaks by touring and **recording** with **Art Pepper, Stan Kenton, Woody Herman, Claude Thornhill**, and most notably, **Charles Mingus,** with whom he achieved his highest level of success. Knepper continued his relationship with Mingus into the 1960s and worked with a variety of other artists for extended periods including the **Mel Lewis–Thad Jones** Orchestra, **Lee Konitz,** and **Gil Evans**. Despite never branching out as a solo artist, Knepper was constantly in demand as a trombonist for a variety of groups in the 1970s and 1980s, including several Charles Mingus tribute groups as well as groups that included past members of Mingus' ensembles.

KOLLER, HANS (1921–2003). Formally trained at the Academy of Music in Vienna before World War II, Koller's career as a jazz saxophonist was put on hold until after the events of the war. Koller relocated to Germany and became one of the country's most popular saxophonists. In the 1950s, he performed with several touring jazz acts that came through the country including **Dizzy Gillespie** and **Lee Konitz**. Koller never moved to the United States and instead remained an important force in European jazz during the 1950s and 1960s. He relocated back home to Vienna in 1970 and continued to be an active performer and jazz educator until he retired in 1995. The Austrian government elected to honor him by naming one of their top awards for performers after him.

KONITZ, LEE (1927–). Originally from Chicago, Konitz's playing was considered to be very fresh and inspired the start of many different jazz movements. In the late 1940s, Konitz played alto saxophone with **Claude Thornhill** and was shortly thereafter hired by **Miles Davis** to participate in the *Birth of the Cool* **recordings**. Konitz's style was very distinctive, and he was one of the first musicians to inspire the **West Coast Jazz** or **Cool Jazz** style. Konitz soon paired up with pianist **Lennie Tristano** in the 1950s, and the two of them, along with Warne Marsh, would develop a new system of **improvisation** that helped bridge the gap between **Free Jazz** and **Bebop**. Konitz would also tour with **Stan Kenton** and several other groups during the 1950s.

Konitz would begin recording prominently as a leader toward the end of the 1950s and continued on for the next few decades, making many significant contributions to jazz. He is credited with being one of the first alto saxophonists to develop a style and sound that was different from that of **Charlie Parker**. Konitz would work with **Paul Bley** in the early 1960s followed by working with Marsh again in the 1970s. Konitz led his own nonet in the late 1970s and the 1980s. Konitz was also very influential in shaping what is now considered to be the European jazz sound and has inspired countless musicians. Prominently involved in teaching, Konitz remains active through not only performing but also acting as a jazz educator at summer camps and as guest artist around the world.

KONOPASEK, JAN (1931–). Born in Czechoslovakia, Konopasek was an important baritone saxophonist from Eastern **Europe**. In addition to playing with many of Europe's most influential jazz musicians, including **Hans Koller** and Klaus Doldinger, Konopasek worked with many touring American musicians, such as **Oliver Nelson** and **Stan Kenton**. Konopasek briefly attended the **Berklee School of Music** in Boston, Massachusetts, and eventually moved to the United States. Despite catching on with several touring **big bands**, most notably those of **Woody Herman** and **Buddy Rich**, Konopasek never officially made the United States his home and alternated living between the United States and his native Prague.

KRAL, ROY (1921–2002). Kral worked as a pianist in Chicago during his early twenties playing in various groups. After meeting his future wife, vocalist and bandmate Jacqueline Cain, Kral's reputation began to grow with the popular group they spearheaded: Jackie and Roy. The two kept the group active for several decades and never did much work apart. Kral gained some recognition as a composer and wrote music for several commercials while the couple lived in New York during the 1960s. Kral's contribution to the group was significant, and he remains an influential person in the development of vocal jazz.

KRAZY KAT. Primarily a **Rhythm and Blues** label, Krazy Kat recorded and released some jazz records by Joe Davis. *See also* RECORD LABEL.

KRESS, CARL (1907–1965). Kress began his life as a musician first on **piano** before eventually settling on **guitar**. Before turning 20 years of age, he had already made it as a professional guitarist working with rising **bandleader Paul Whiteman** in the mid-1920s. Kress had a style that was very popular, and he was hired by many groups in the Chicago area including those of **Frankie Trumbauer, Jimmy Dorsey**, and **Miff Mole**. After working for several years as a touring musician, he worked mostly as a **studio musician** for the remainder of his career, with the exception of a performing duo that he maintained with George Barnes.

KRUPA, (EU)GENE (1909–1973). Growing up in Chicago in the early part of the 20th century, Krupa absorbed much of the music that was going on and was inspired by the drumming of early jazz masters **Baby Dodds** and Zutty Singleton. He achieved success early working on and **recording** with local bands at the age of 18. He continued to do so until he had one of his first big national breaks, touring with clarinetist **Benny Goodman** in 1934. The work with Goodman inspired Krupa to lead his own band, which he attempted to do several times, the first of which took place in 1938.

During the 1940s, Krupa once again worked for Goodman until he was hired to be the regular drummer of the **Jazz at the Philharmonic** group, a relationship that lasted well into the 1950s. Krupa would mix engagements leading his own groups with playing as a member of other groups during the 1960s, most notably reuniting with Goodman to participate in Goodman's quartet. Krupa struggled with a variety of health concerns in the 1970s, and his playing drastically declined until his death. His playing style was especially innovative in that he helped to transform the **drum set** into a solo instrument.

KUSTBANDET. A Swedish **big band** that grew out of a smaller group, Kustbandet was dedicated to preserving music from the **Swing** era. Kustbandet was formed in the early 1960s, and much of its repertoire was pulled from the bands of **Fletcher Henderson** and **Duke Ellington**.

L

LABARBERA, JOE (1948–). Trained initially by his father and later by legendary teacher **Alan Dawson**, LaBarbera had a more sporadic career than his brothers. Like his older brother Pat, Joe LaBarbera attended the **Berklee College of Music**. Army service briefly interrupted LaBarbera's career in the late 1960s, but it was quickly put back on track in the 1970s when he was hired by **Chuck Mangione** and **John Scofield**. LaBarbera resided in New York during the 1970s and 1980s and was working with a variety of groups, most notably with innovative pianist **Bill Evans**. During the 1980s, LaBarbera also worked with singer **Tony Bennett** and many musicians associated with **West Coast Jazz** including **Conte Candoli** and **Bud Shank**. *See also* LABARBERA, PAT.

LABARBERA, PAT (1944–). The oldest brother in a family of musicians, LaBarbera chose to pursue a career playing the **tenor saxophone**. LaBarbera was well educated, attending the **Berklee School of Music** in 1964, and was hired shortly after leaving the school by **Buddy Rich**. After several years of touring with Rich's **big band**, LaBarbera decided to settle in Canada, where he would remain active both as a performer and educator, overseeing several jazz camps and serving on the faculty of many universities. His claim to fame ended up being his role in **Elvin Jones'** groups in which he was a member beginning in 1975. LaBarbera's career alternated between leading his groups and working with Jones. He is also a highly respected educator and has had several texts published, in addition to being a participant in many **recording sessions**. *See also* LABARBERA, JOE.

LABEL. *See* RECORD LABEL.

LACY, STEVE (1934–2004). Primarily playing the **soprano saxophone**, Lacy made a name for himself by developing an eclectic style and working with **Avant-Garde** musicians, in addition to **Straight-Ahead** musicians. Lacy had an on-and-off-again relationship with both **Gil Evans** and **Thelonious Monk** throughout the 1950s and 1960s. Lacy studied **Dixieland** as a youth but was willing to experiment with a variety of styles and was hired by artists including **Cecil Taylor** and **Ornette Coleman**. Lacy was very popular in **Europe** during the 1960s and worked with many of the top European musicians including Enrico Rava and Johnny Dyani.

Lacy developed a sterling reputation as a composer into the 1970s and wrote for a variety of groups that included the use of electronics, strings, and voice. Lacy also never gave up his love for the music of Monk and worked in collaboration with pianist **Mal Waldron** on a series of projects based on Monk's music. Throughout the 1980s and 1990s, Lacy worked with musicians from many different countries including players from India, Japan, and South America. Lacy continued to develop his compositional prowess during the 1990s and wrote for **big band**, in addition to writing an improvised opera.

LADNIER, THOMAS "TOMMY" (1900–1939). Ladnier learned **trumpet** as a teenager and moved to Chicago from Louisiana before turning 18 to pursue a career in music. Ladnier was very popular during the 1920s and worked with many leading Chicago bands, most notably the group led by jazz icon **King Oliver**. Ladnier was also the lead soloist with **Fletcher Henderson** for two years before virtually disappearing from the jazz scene in the 1930s. Despite **recording** with soprano saxophonist **Sidney Bechet** in the late 1930s, very little of Ladnier's playing was recorded before his early death.

LAFARO, SCOTT (1936–1961). A late bloomer on the **bass**, LaFaro did not pick up the instrument until he was already in college at Ithaca Conservatory. He was a very adept musician, however, and two years later he was already working in touring groups that brought him to Los Angeles, where he was heard by **West Coast** trumpeter **Chet Baker**, who used him in his group for a few years. After a visit to Chicago, he was hired by **Sonny Rollins** for a period of time until he decided a change was needed and he relocated to New York. LaFaro's life was cut drastically short, but he made a few significant **recordings** with pianist **Bill Evans** before his early passing. LaFaro was an important figure in the development of the walking bass and helped establish a new style of playing that allowed the bass player to focus more on creating melodic lines. LaFaro died as a result of a car accident.

LAFITTE, DENIS FERNAND "GUY" (1927–1998). Born in **France**, Lafitte was an influential tenor saxophonist in the French jazz scene and was frequently hired by touring American bands. Lafitte ran several groups during the course of his career, in addition to constant freelancing. Highlights of Lafitte's career include being awarded the Prix Django Reinhardt and performing with **Duke Ellington** in the 1960s.

L.A. FOUR. A popular jazz quartet formed in 1974. In existence for a little over 10 years, the L.A. Four toured and recorded in Los Angeles frequently. At various times members of the L.A. Four included **Bud Shank**, Ray Brown, Chuck Person, **Shelly Manne**, and **Jeff Hamilton**.

LAINE, CLEMENTINA "CLEO" (1927–). Laine hails from Middlesex, England, and developed a reputation for being a standout vocalist in any genre. Laine married English jazz artist **John Dankworth** in 1958 and worked in a variety of venues including theater and performances with her husband's groups. Laine's diversity has brought her many accolades, the most notable being several Grammy nominations for Classical, jazz, and even Pop records.

LAKE, OLIVER EUGENE (1942–). Lake's early career was established by his passion for teaching and his willingness to dedicate himself to racial awareness. After living and teaching in St. Louis for several years, Lake formed the Black Artists Group (BAG) and attempted to bring the group's message to France. **Avant-Garde** trumpeter **Lester Bowie** was a part of the group that Lake brought overseas. Lake returned to the United States in 1974 to pursue new musical ventures. Along with **David Murray** and Hamiet Bluiett, Lake founded the **World Saxophone Quartet**, a group that has remained active for several decades. Lake's saxophone style always leaned toward the Avant-Garde despite attempts to venture into Reggae and other popular music. Many of Lake's musical associations were with musicians of similar intentions and styles, including Andrew Cyrille, **Anthony Braxton**, Fred Hopkins, and, later, Geri Allen. Lake continued to work in Avant-Garde settings throughout the 1990s and 2000s.

LAMBERT, DAVID "DAVE" (1917–1966). Lambert initially entered the music scene in the late 1930s as a drummer but was hired by several bands to sing vocals. **Gene Krupa** and Harry James were **bandleaders** who employed Lambert's vocal talents during the 1940s. Toward the end of the decade, after a brief association with **Charlie Parker**, Lambert began studio work and met fellow vocalist **Jon Hendricks**. Hendricks and Lambert maintained a close musical relationship throughout the 1950s and 1960s with the creation of the leading vocal jazz group **Lambert, Hendricks, and Ross**. Lambert's career and life were tragically cut short when he was involved in a fatal car accident.

LAMBERT, HENDRICKS, AND ROSS. Founded by three vocalists in 1957, **Dave Lambert, Jon Hendricks**, and **Annie Ross**, the trio would be a leading and innovative vocal jazz group for decades. The group helped define the **vocalese** style in which the singers would put words or syllables to famous improvised jazz solos. The group stayed in its original context from 1957 to 1962, until Ross decided to leave. Although she was replaced, the group was never the same and ended two years later.

LAMOND, DONALD DOUGLAS "DON" (1920–2003). Lamond studied drums at the Peabody Conservatory and worked primarily as a **Swing**-style drummer during the 1940s. He worked with several significant jazz musicians in the late 1940s, including **Woody Herman**, **Red Norvo**, and **Charlie Parker**. Lamond had several one-year relationships with many significant artists in the 1950s, including **Stan Getz**, **Marian McPartland**, and **Sonny Stitt**. Lamond freelanced for most of the 1950s and 1960s. In the 1970s, he moved to Florida, where he would lead his own band and freelance with other groups that toured through the area.

LAND, HAROLD (1928–2001). Although he was born in Houston, Texas, Land grew up and received his first musical training in San Diego, California. He favored the tenor **saxophone**, and at the age of 28 he moved to Los Angeles to join the rising jazz group led by **Clifford Brown** and **Max Roach**. Land's association with this group was influential to his career, and he left the group only for family reasons. Land pursued a solo career after leaving the Brown-Roach Quintet, in addition to freelancing with musicians who came through the Los Angeles area. During the 1960s and 1970s, Land worked with groups led by **Slide Hampton** and **Blue Mitchell**, and he maintained a steady working relationship with fellow California-based musician, vibraphonist **Bobby Hutcherson**. Land was a member of the jazz supergroup the Timeless All-Stars, which also featured Hutcherson, in addition to **Billy Higgins**, **Buster Williams**, and **Cedar Walton**. Land continued to record, tour, and perform until his passing in 2001.

LANDE, ART (1947–). Lande made his mark on the modern piano jazz scene through innovations that took place during his early days working as a pianist in San Francisco. He worked with many of the jazz musicians living in the San Francisco Bay area, including **Joe Henderson** and **Bobby Hutcherson**. Lande started leading his own groups in the mid-1970s, most notably forming the group Rubisa Patrol, which included Mark Isham, Bill Douglas, and **Paul McCandless**. Lande would continue to maintain working relationships with these musicians for the next several decades in a variety of different contexts. Lande and McCandless formed an especially deep connection and would work together as a duo, with a vocalist, and with a variety of other groups.

Lande also left his stamp on the world of jazz education, first serving on faculty for a jazz school in Switzerland, followed by periods of time at the Cornish School of the Arts, Naropa Institute, and University of Colorado at Boulder. The majority of Lande's career in the 1990s and 2000s was spent working in Colorado, forming various groups including the Russian Dragon Band and the Boy-Girl Band. Lande has recorded many **albums** in both solo and group format and is considered an important figure in the development of the modern solo piano.

LANDMARK. Created by noted jazz historian and author Orrin Keepnews, Landmark records made several substantial releases in the 1980s, including **albums** by **Mulgrew Miller** and **Donald Byrd**. Landmark also did some re-issuing of previously released albums until it was sold to Muse records. *See also* RECORD LABEL.

LANG, EDDIE (1902–1933). Lang grew up with popular jazz violinist **Joe Venuti** and studied guitar in the early 1920s. After moving to New York, Lang's popularity grew substantially, and he was hired by many of the popular touring bands including Jean Goldkette and **Paul Whiteman**. Lang was an important figure in the creation and popularity of the guitar in jazz.

LANG-WORTH. Founded before World War II, Lang-Worth records was established to record **albums** that would be aired on radio stations. Focusing on **Early Jazz**, Lang-Worth primarily recorded and issued album by stars of the 1930s, including **John Kirby, Jimmie Lunceford,** and **Fats Waller**. The label was eventually sold to the **Jazzology record label**.

LAPORTA, JOHN (1920–2004). LaPorta's career was largely defined as an educator at the **Berklee College of Music** from the late 1950s into the 1980s. LaPorta made his mark as a saxophonist with **Woody Herman** and **Charles Mingus** before pursuing a bachelor's degree in clarinet performance and a master's degree in music education. LaPorta's tenure at Berklee was marked with numerous awards and involvement in many of jazz's premier educational organizations. In addition to education and remaining active as a jazz performer, LaPorta also had a significant Classical career primarily working with the Boston Pops.

LAROCCA, NICK (1889–1961). LaRocca was one of the many **Early Jazz** musicians who made the pilgrimage from New Orleans to Chicago during the late 1910s. LaRocca was famously involved in the **Original Dixieland Jazz Band,** which is credited as being the first jazz group to be captured on record. The group was under fire because the band was made up of all White musicians, and jazz was considered to be primarily an African-American based music. A **cornet** player, he continued to play with the Original Dixieland Jazz Band until it disbanded in the late 1930s, then relocated back to his home in New Orleans where he essentially retired from music. *See also* CHICAGO JAZZ.

LATEEF, YUSEF (1920–). Lateef (originally named William Emanual Huddleston) is originally from Detroit, Michigan. He began his career playing **alto saxophone** before ultimately switching to tenor. He achieved a mild level of success in the 1940s working with bands led by **Roy Eldridge** and **Dizzy Gillespie**. Due to some family issues and his desire to return to school, Lateef took time off in the 1950s to study **flute** and composition. Lateef was one of the few musicians to convert to the Islamic faith during the civil rights movement.

Lateef would resume his performance career after moving to New York and would play with **Charles Mingus** and **Cannonball Adderley** until eventually stepping out on his own as a leader. The majority of Lateef's work during the 1970s and 1980s was as a **leader** and composer. Lateef not only wrote jazz pieces but also composed larger works that featured flute and other instruments. Lateef continues to play regularly and has also been an active teacher.

LATIN JAZZ. A style of jazz similar to **Afro-Cuban Jazz**, in which Latin American music is fused with jazz. The usual constant for indentifying Latin Jazz will be the presence of Latin American rhythms and jazz-inspired improvisation. It is common for jazz musicians to use Latin rhythms in compositions like **Dizzy Gillespie**'s "A Night in Tunisia." Latin Jazz sometimes serves as a generic term to describe music that is influenced by many South American and Central American cultures, including music from Brazil. *See also* IRAKERE.

LAWS, HUBERT (1939–). Laws was a very strong flutist who had success with several groups before attending the prestigious Juilliard School of Music in the 1960s. His career after school was a mix of Classical and jazz-related ventures, many of which were connected to his brother, **Ronnie Laws**, a saxophonist. Hubert Laws was featured with several New York–based symphonies and orchestras in addition to **recording** several jazz **albums**. He is considered an innovator because of the recognition and fluidity he brought to the **flute** as a solo instrument.

LAWS, RONALD "RONNIE" (1950–). Laws began playing saxophone professionally at the age of 21. Relocating from Houston to Los Angeles, he found work playing with jazz artists including Walter Bishop Jr. and **Kenny Burrell**, and Pop-related music with Earth, Wind and Fire, and **Quincy Jones**. Laws stepped out as a **bandleader** in the 1980s and was considered to be a contemporary **Smooth Jazz** soloist. *See also* LAWS, HUBERT.

LAY BACK. A style of phrasing in which the performer purposefully plays behind where the beat is felt, in order to establish a dragging or rather sluggish feeling.

LAY OUT. This term refers to purposefully not playing during a portion, or all, of a piece. It is common for a specific accompanist to lay out on specific solos to achieve a special effect. For example, a saxophone player in a quartet might ask the pianist to "lay out" for the first chorus of his solo so that he can interact more with the bassist and drummer.

LEAD. A reference to whoever is the principal player in a section, whoever has the primary melodic line, or whoever is responsible for cueing or coordinating the other members of the section. In a traditional **big band** setup, the first **trumpet** and the first alto are often referred to as lead trumpet and lead alto because they frequently have the primary melodic material for most pieces.

LEADER. A term used to describe whoever is responsible for directing a group in performance. The term can sometimes also imply that the person serves as musical director for a group, but this is not always the case. Leaders can also be performers with the band. Some of the most famous leaders in jazz include **Count Basie, Duke Ellington**, and **Stan Kenton**. *See also* BANDLEADER.

LEADERS. An **Avant-Garde** Jazz group formed in the mid-1980s that included Arthur Blythe, **Chico Freeman, Don Cherry**, and Cecil McBee. The group was in existence for almost 10 years before breaking up in 1994 after doing several tours and **recording** a live video.

LEAD SHEET. Very common to jazz and other popular music, a lead sheet provides the performers with a copy of the melody and chord changes to the song they are playing. Most **fake books** are made up with lead sheets of songs from the Great American Songbook, in addition to the jazz standards. Some lead sheets will also provide the performers with some of the **rhythm section** figures that are played on the original version of the song.

LEE, WILLIAM "BILL" (1928–). Bass player Lee made his mark in the 1940s and 1950s by working with a variety of top-flight musicians in Chicago and New York, including **Johnny Griffin, George Coleman, Clifford Jordan**, Vernel Fournier, **Philly Joe Jones**, and **Phineas Newborn**. Lee never stepped out as a **leader** but was frequently used as a **sideman** for the majority of his career. His son, Spike Lee, would end up being a highly influential filmmaker, and the two collaborated several times on movie projects.

LEE, WILLIAM (1952–). One of the first jazz musicians to play the electric bass as his primary instrument, Lee had great success playing in the 1970s with the **Brecker** Brothers, **Billy Cobham, Sonny Stitt, George Benson**, and **Bob James**. Lee became a highly utilized **session** player and made numerous **recordings** throughout the next few decades, eventually landing a position with the house band for the NBC show *Late Night with David Letterman*.

LEVALLET, DIDIER (1944–). Levallet, a **bass** player born in Arcy-sur-Cure, **France**, he was used frequently by house bands in Paris, in addition to working with many touring American jazz musicians. Being fluent in many jazz styles, Lavallet was adept in playing **Bebop** and **Hard Bop** but made significant strides in more creative, **Avant-Garde** styles during the 1970s and 1980s. Groups led or influenced by Lavallet varied in size from a quintet to a **big band** and sometimes involved the use of stringed instruments. He contributed greatly to the French jazz scene with the creation of the Association pour le Développement de la Musique Improvisée (ADMI), a group focused on spreading jazz and presenting concerts.

LEVEY, STAN (1926–2005). Born in Philadelphia, Levey's career was peaking as a late teenager when he was working with **Dizzy Gillespie, Coleman Hawkins**, and **Thelonious Monk** before turning 19 years of age. Levey relocated to New York to play with these musicians and continued to play with a who's who of jazz throughout the 1940s. Artists who performed with him included **Charlie Parker, Art Tatum, Stan Kenton, George Shearing**, and **Stan Getz**. Levey opted for a change of scenery in the mid-1950s and moved to California. He capitalized on the studio and commercial scene in Los Angeles while also working steadily as a **sideman** for many **West Coast Jazz** innovators including **Art Pepper, Chet Baker**, Frank Rosolino, and Howard Rumsey. However, music lost its appeal for Levey during the late 1960s and early 1970s, and he opted instead for a career as a photographer.

LEVIEV, MILCHO (1937–). Leviev's greatest contributions to jazz include his **piano** playing, composition, and his influence on the Bulgarian jazz scene. Before leaving his native Bulgaria in the 1970s, Leviev worked as a leader of many groups, for which he wrote compositions. After moving to the United States, Leviev worked with many **Fusion** artists including John Klemmer and **Billy Cobham**. Leviev also started his own Fusion band, Free Flight, although the group was not received with high praise. Leviev showed his diversity in working with other genres of jazz, including performances with **Art Pepper** and **Charlie Haden**.

LEVINE, MARK (1938–). A significant contributor to the San Francisco jazz scene as well as the development of the **Latin Jazz** scene, pianist Levine made his mark playing with touring groups led by **Woody Shaw, Joe Henderson**, and Mongo Santamaría. In addition to playing, he has also been a highly influential teacher and has published several significant jazz and piano texts.

LEWIS, GEORGE (I) (1900–1968). Lewis was an important clarinetist in the New Orleans region. He played with many of the early New Orleans jazz groups, including the **Olympia** Orchestra and the **Eureka Brass Band** in the 1920s. In the 1940s, after suffering from some dental problems, he began actively playing again and moved back to New Orleans after spending part of the last decade in New York. Lewis led his own groups in New Orleans and remained an important figure in the preservation of the **Early Jazz** tradition.

LEWIS, GEORGE (II) (1952–). Lewis took up the **trombone** before the age of 10 and spent much of high school mimicking the **tenor saxophone** solos previously played by jazz masters. Lewis completed a music degree at Yale University and returned to Chicago, where he would become a leading figure for several of the movements going on there. An active member of the **Association for the Advancement of Creative Musicians (AACM)**, Lewis was influenced by several of its members, including **Lester Bowie** and **Muhal Richard Abrams**.

LEWIS, JOHN (AARON) (1920–2001). Despite growing up in rural New Mexico, Lewis moved to New York in his twenties and got his first big break when he was hired to play with **Dizzy Gillespie**. Lewis had his academic life interrupted several times during the 1940s and 1950s when he was invited to tour with Gillespie and other jazz artists. Lewis completed a master's degree in the early 1950s and resumed playing shortly thereafter when hired by **Charlie Parker, Miles Davis**, and **Ella Fitzgerald**.

Lewis' biggest accomplishment was his affiliation with vibraphonist **Milt Jackson** and the formation of the **Modern Jazz Quartet** (MJQ). The MJQ was a formidable jazz group for almost five decades and recorded many **albums**. Lewis would be hired to serve as music director for the **Monterey Jazz Festival** for almost two decades starting in 1958. Lewis was also an active teacher and served on the faculty of several schools in addition to working as a director for summer camps sponsored by the Lenox School of Jazz.

In the 1980s, Lewis resigned from his post at the Monterey Jazz Festival to continue to make a living primarily as a performer. He was also a distinguished composer who wrote for **big band**, in addition to his small groups and the MJQ. *See also* THIRD STREAM; VIBRAPHONE.

LEWIS, MEADE (ANDERSON) "LUX" (1905–1964). An important innovator of the **Boogie Woogie** piano style, Lewis spent the majority of his career in Chicago. Lewis played with Joe Turner, **Charlie Christian**, and Edmond Hall during the 1930s and 1940s. Lewis recorded several popular hits, including the song "Honky Tonk Train Blues." Lewis died in 1964 in an automobile accident.

LEWIS, MELVIN "MEL" (1929–1990). Lewis made his professional debut as a drummer at the age of 13 when he filled in for musicians who had been drafted to serve in World War II. Lewis first caught on as a **big band** drummer with Boyd Raeburn, Tex Beneke, and **Stan Kenton** in the late 1940s and 1950s. Lewis was equally adept at small-group playing and worked extensively with groups led by Frank Rosolino, **Hampton Hawes**, and **Bill Holman**. Lewis would spend much of the late 1950s and early 1960s working with musicians who defined the **West Coast Jazz** scene including **Art Pepper**, Stu Williamson, **Bill Perkins**, and Pepper Adams, among others.

After several tours with jazz icons **Gerry Mulligan** and **Dizzy Gillespie**, Lewis relocated to New York and started his own group with the help of **trumpet** player and composer **Thad Jones**: the Thad Jones–Mel Lewis Orchestra. The orchestra gained much popularity and was made up of many of the top jazz musicians. Jones broke away from the orchestra in the late 1970s and left sole leadership to Lewis. During the 1980s, Lewis filled the orchestra with many rising jazz stars including Dick Oatts, Ralph Lalama, **Tom Harrell**, Joe Lovano, Kenny Werner, and **Jim McNeely**. The band would continue to work after Lewis' passing and became known as the **Village Vanguard** Orchestra and would continue to play many of Lewis' and Jones' pieces.

Lewis was also a fully capable small-group player and played with many artists in the 1980s including Warne Marsh, **Gil Evans**, and Jon Faddis. He had a section of the University of Missouri Library named in honor of him.

LEWIS, RAMSEY (1935–). Born and educated in Chicago, Lewis entered the professional world leading his own groups at the age of 15. He was involved with a quartet featuring Wallace Burton for almost 15 years that garnered much national recognition. Lewis gained further recognition in the 1970s by changing his style to a more popular electronic, contemporary sound, for which he received some criticism. Lewis recorded frequently and is one of the rare jazz musicians to make numerous appearances on the *Billboard* charts. Lewis had several television programs in the 1980s and continues to be a key element to the creation of the BET Jazz channel.

LIBERTY. A **record label** founded in 1933 and owned by the Liberty Music Shop in New York. The Liberty Music Shop label did very little **recording** and primarily released **albums** recorded by **ARC**.

LICK. A term used to describe a specific phrase or sequence of notes. Learning specific licks or patterns as a developing jazz musician is a primary educational tool for learning to play over certain **chord** progressions.

LIEBMAN, DAVID "DAVE" (1946–). Liebman's youth was spent studying with two significant jazz artists, learning theory with **Lennie Tristano** and saxophone with **Charles Lloyd**. During the 1970s, Liebman would play both tenor and soprano saxophones with several important groups, including the groups of **Elvin Jones** and **Miles Davis**. Liebman would also focus on leading his own groups, most notably starting the group Lookout Farm in the mid-1970s. The pianist from that group, Richie Bierach, would work with Liebman frequently throughout the next few decades, including duo projects and larger works.

Throughout the 1980s, Liebman balanced freelance work with artists including Elvin Jones and **Wayne Shorter**, while continuing to lead his own groups. Liebman started the Dave Liebman Group in the early 1990s, a group with members that included guitarist Vic Juris, pianist Phil Markowitz, and drummer Jamey Haddad. Frequently working as a **sideman** for most of the 2000s, Liebman also took a greater interest in education and is the author of several important jazz texts. *See also* SOPRANO SAXOPHONE.

LIGHTHOUSE CAFÉ. Located in Hermosa Beach, California, the Lighthouse was a popular jazz **club** during the 1950s that featured West Coast musicians, including **Shorty Rogers, Miles Davis, Chet Baker**, Howard Rumsey, and the "Lighthouse All-Stars." Rumsey maintained a weekly engagement there for several years.

LIMELIGHT. A **record label** in the 1960s that released **albums** recorded during the same time by artists including **Art Blakey, Rahsaan Roland Kirk,** and **Dizzy Gillespie.** Albums released on the label were eventually reissued during the 1970s.

LINCOLN, ABBEY (1930–2010). Vocalist Lincoln (born Anna Marie Wooldridge) made her initial mark on the jazz scene during the 1950s and 1960s while working with **Sonny Rollins, Thelonious Monk, Benny Carter,** and her husband for most of the 1960s, **Max Roach.** Lincoln was very active in the civil rights movement along with Roach, and she used her popularity to work in films toward the end of the 1960s and 1970s. Lincoln resumed her jazz career in the late 1980s and worked with **Stan Getz,** in addition to working as a leader.

LINDBERG, NILS (1933–). Born in Uppsala, Sweden, Lindberg was a very prominent composer and pianist during the 1950s and 1960s. Lindberg played with **Duke Ellington**'s orchestra in the 1970s but was primarily considered to be a composer who wrote in a variety of jazz-influenced styles.

LINDSTROM. An important company created in Europe by Carl Lindstrom that recorded much material released on the popular **record labels** Odeon and Parlophone. After a successful run and expansion into the American record business, Lindstrom was sold to record powerhouse **Columbia** in the mid-1920s.

LINDSTROM, ERIK (1922–). A Finnish bass player who was considered a first-call bassist in his native country.

LIP. A term used by musicians to describe the process of altering one's pitch by making adjustments with the embouchure to sharpen or flatten a note. Frequently **brass** players are asked to lip a note up or down for intonation or effect.

LISTON, MELBA (1926–1999). Liston's first professional experience as a trombonist came when her family moved to Los Angeles and she began working with local bands including the band of **Gerald Wilson.** Throughout the 1940s, Liston steadily picked up work as an arranger and trombonist, playing with groups led by **Dexter Gordon, Dizzy Gillespie,** and **Billie Holiday.**

In the 1950s, Liston spent time working as an actress before resuming her jazz career by developing a steadily working relationship with pianist Randy Weston. Liston would work on and off with Weston for several decades and became an important contributor to many of his groups. Liston also worked with **Quincy Jones**, **Charles Mingus**, and **Clark Terry** during the 1960s, while also continuing her career with Weston. For most of the 1970s and 1980s, Liston led her own groups and contributed **arrangements** for various Pop acts. In 1985, she suffered a stroke, which would greatly limit her performing career, although she continued be an active arranger and composer until her death.

LITTLE, BOOKER (1938–1961). Considered the heir apparent to **Clifford Brown**, Little's life was tragically cut short, but not before he left his mark on the jazz world. Little learned to play the **trumpet** when he was a teenager and worked with **Phineas Newborn**, **Johnny Griffin**, and **Max Roach** during the 1950s. Little's most substantial work took place in the early 1960s, when he formed a quintet with **Mal Waldron** and **Free Jazz** pioneer **Eric Dolphy**. Little worked briefly with **John Coltrane** before passing away due to complications from uremia.

LITTLE CHICKS. A small-group version of **Chick Webb**'s famous band during the 1930s, although sometimes Webb was not included in the group. Members of Little Chicks included Wayman Carer, Teddy McRae, and **Louis Jordan**.

LLOYD, CHARLES (1938–). Part of the Memphis school of musicians, Lloyd grew up around jazz musicians Frank Strozier, **Booker Little**, and **Phineas Newborn**. Lloyd relocated to California to pursue college, during which time he met many West Coast Jazz musicians including **Harold Land**, **Gerald Wilson**, and **Chico Hamilton**, with whom he had his first professional performance experience. After a short tenure with **Cannonball Adderley**, Lloyd began to lead his own groups, which used many rising jazz stars including **Herbie Hancock**, **Keith Jarrett**, and **Jack DeJohnette**.

After several years of successful touring, Lloyd was forced to take time off due to complications from health problems. Lloyd made several appearances during the 1980s but did not resume playing full time until the end of the decade and into the 1990s. Lloyd led several different groups and maintained a quartet of European musicians that included Bobo Stenson. Lloyd began to record for **ECM** in the 1990s and has recorded in a variety of contexts since then.

LOCKE, EDWARD "EDDIE" (1930–). An important **Early Jazz** drummer who came to prominence during the 1950s. He was associated primarily with **Coleman Hawkins** but spent time working with several other groups, including those of **Duke Ellington** and **Kenny Burrell**. Locke spent most of the 1970s working with **Roy Eldridge** before freelancing and leading his own groups during the 1980s and 1990s.

LOCKWOOD, DIDIER (1956–). A violinist, Lockwood was one of **France**'s top jazz musicians during the 1970s and worked with many American artists who were touring France during that time. Lockwood performed with **Straight-Ahead** jazz artists in addition to working with **Fusion** and popular music groups. He worked primarily as a **leader** during the 1980s and spent time performing and **recording** in New York with musicians including Michel Petrucciani, John Blake, **Dave Liebman**, and **Mike Stern**.

LONDON JAZZ COMPOSERS ORCHESTRA (LJCO). A culmination of work by several people (most notably Buddy Guy), the London Jazz Composers Orchestra was created in the 1970s as an opportunity for British composers to write creative music for a large ensemble. The LJCO included a majority of English musicians such as **Kenny Wheeler**, Evan Parker, Derek Bailey, and Tony Oxley. In addition to playing music written by members of the band, the LJCO also did collaborative projects with other musicians and groups, including **Anthony Braxton** and the BBC Symphony Orchestra.

LOOSE TUBES. A large English ensemble that was founded, in part, by **Graham Collier**. Loose Tubes frequently played concerts and made public appearances during the 1980s. Members of the group included Steve Berry, Django Bates, and Eddie Parker. Loose Tubes only remained active for six years, but did record two **albums**. *See also* ENGLAND.

LORBER, JEFF (1952–). Lorber studied **piano** and keyboards at the **Berklee School of Music** in Boston before moving to the western coast of the United States in the early 1970s. After living in Portland for several years, Lorber relocated to Los Angeles and quickly became engaged in the **Fusion** scene. The majority of Lorber's playing in the 1980s was with Fusion and contemporary groups and artists like Kenny G and Eric Marienthal. Lorber spent most of the 1990s working with Contemporary and **Rhythm and Blues (R&B)** artists.

LOUISIANA FIVE. Only in existence for two years, the Louisiana Five was a **Traditional Jazz** group formed in 1918. Despite their short existence, the group recorded many times but were not as popular as their Traditional Jazz peers, the **Original Dixieland Jazz Band**.

LUNCEFORD, JAMES MELVIN "JIMMIE" (1902–1947). Lunceford developed his acumen for bandleading at a young age, running groups as a teenager before being involved with many of the top **bandleaders** of the 1920s. Working with musicians such as Ed Wilcox and Willie Smith, Lunceford formed the beginnings of his orchestra in the early 1930s. The Jimmie Lunceford Orchestra became one of the most popular touring bands of the 1930s and recorded frequently.

In the late 1930s, Lunceford's orchestra went through several personnel changes, and **Gerald Wilson** joined the band and assisted with arranging duties. Other famous musicians to pass through Lunceford's orchestra included **George Duvivier, Tadd Dameron,** and **Snooky Young.** Lunceford's tendency to not pay his musicians properly resulted in many of them leaving during the 1940s, although Lunceford managed to keep the orchestra active.

LYONS, JAMES LIPPINCOTT "JIMMY" (1916–1994). Founder of the **Monterey Jazz Festival** in 1958, he got his start in radio broadcasting.

LYONS, JIMMY (1933–1986). Born in New Jersey, Lyons had strong ties to New York and grew up learning jazz and **saxophone** from jazz masters including Elmo Hope and **Bud Powell.** Lyons strongly connected with the **Free Jazz** movement that began in the late 1950s and worked with **Cecil Taylor.** When Lyons was not working with Taylor, he relied on work outside of music to support himself for most of the 1960s. He became involved in music education during the 1970s and remained in education for the remainder of his life, in addition to working with Taylor or leading his own groups.

M

MABERN, HAROLD, JR. (1936–). Originally a drummer, Harold Mabern switched to **piano** and got his first **gig** with Walter Perkins and the group MJT+3 after moving to Chicago in 1954. After moving to New York in 1959, he performed with a series of notable musicians including **Harry "Sweets" Edison, Lionel Hampton, Art Farmer** and **Benny Golson**'s Jazztet, **Donald Byrd, Miles Davis, J. J. Johnson, Wes Montgomery**, and **Lee Morgan**'s final group. During the 1970s, Mabern began teaching at William Patterson College in addition to continuing to play with musicians including **Freddie Hubbard, Roy Haynes, Hank Mobley, Clark Terry**, and others. During the 1980s he was a regular member of **George Coleman**'s quartet and in the early 1990s participated in the 100 Gold Fingers of Jazz.

MACERO, ATTILIO JOSEPH "TEO" (1925–2008). A composer and record producer, Teo Macero's first notable **gig** was playing **tenor saxophone** in **Charles Mingus**' first Jazz Composers Workshop in 1953. Macero won Guggenheim Awards for composition in 1957 and 1958, and in 1957 he became a producer for **Columbia** Records. During his time with Columbia, Macero worked on many notable **albums** by artists including **Duke Ellington, Thelonious Monk, Stan Getz, Dave Brubeck**, and many others. He also supervised some of **Miles Davis**' most important records, including *Kind of Blue* (1959), *In a Silent Way* (1969), and *Bitches Brew* (1969). In 1975, Macero left Columbia Records to form his own label, Teo Productions. He wrote music for television and film, and during the 1980s he returned to saxophone playing, continuing to perform and record until his death.

MAGNUSSON, BOB (1947–). Originally working on the **French horn**, Bob Magnusson switched to the double **bass** in 1967 and got his start with **Buddy Rich**'s **big band**. Magnusson later played with artists including **Sarah Vaughan, Art Pepper**, and **Benny Golson**, among others. From 1979 to 1982 he issued **albums** with the group Road Work Ahead, and during the early 1990s he performed with **Bobby Shew**'s quintet.

MAGPIE. A record label and company formed in 1929 and in business throughout the 1930s. Important albums released included the series Piano Blues, which was a collection of the work of various pianists.

MAIDEN, WILLIAM "WILLIE" (1928–1976). A composer and **saxophone** player, Willie Maiden started playing the saxophone at the age of 11. From 1952 to 1966, he composed music for **Maynard Ferguson's big band** and was a tenor saxophone soloist in the band from 1956. Maiden worked with **Charlie Barnet** before becoming composer, arranger, and baritone saxophonist for **Stan Kenton** from 1969 to 1973. From 1973 to 1974 he taught composition at the University of Maine at Augusta. *See also* BARITONE SAXOPHONE; TENOR SAXOPHONE.

MAINIERI, MICHAEL "MIKE" (1938–). Mike Mainieri started playing the **vibraphone** at age 10, and by the age of 14 he was touring with **Paul Whiteman**. From 1956 to 1962 he played with **Buddy Rich**, and afterwards he worked with musicians including **Billie Holiday**, **Benny Goodman**, **Coleman Hawkins**, and **Wes Montgomery**. In the late 1960s, Mainieri led the Fusion group White Elephant, and in 1979 he formed the Fusion group **Steps Ahead**, whose notable members include **Steve Gadd** and **Michael Brecker**. Mainieri also invented the synthivibe, essentially an electronic vibraphone. In 1992, Mainieri started his own label, NYC Records, for which he also recorded.

MAINSTREAM JAZZ. A term commonly used to apply to modern jazz that is improvised over a chord progression, as opposed to **Free Jazz** or **Avant-Garde** Jazz. The term was originally used in the 1950s and also refers to the style that musicians from the 1920s and 1930s played in later decades. **Trumpet** player **Buck Clayton** is considered to be a prominent player in this style. *See also* STRAIGHT-AHEAD JAZZ.

MAKOWICZ, ADAM (1940–). Originally Polish, Makowicz studied Classical **piano** before becoming interested in jazz. During the early 1960s he formed Jazz Darings, one of the first **Free Jazz** groups in **Europe**. He continued to play the piano in Europe until he made his American debut in 1977 as an unaccompanied soloist. By 1978 he had moved to New York, and in 1986 he became an American citizen. Heavily influenced by **Art Tatum**, he has recorded several **albums** of the American songbook and tours most often as a solo pianist.

MALONE, THOMAS "BONES" (1947–). A trombonist, Malone started playing with **Woody Herman** in 1969 before playing with Duke Pearson,

Louie Bellson, Doc Severinsen, and **Billy Cobham**. From 1973 to 1988, Malone was an arranger for the **Gil Evans** Orchestra, and from 1975 to 1985 he was a performer and arranger for the NBC *Saturday Night Live* band. He has also led his own septet, which has included such notable musicians as Jon Faddis, Ryan Kisor, **Bill Evans**, and others.

MANCE, JULIAN CLIFFORD "JUNIOR" (1928–). A pianist, Junior Mance learned how to play **piano** from his father and started playing professionally at the age of 10. His first important **gig** was with **Gene Ammons**, followed later by performances with **Lester Young**. Mance was drafted in 1951 and played in a U.S. Army band with **Nat Adderley**, his brother **Cannonball Adderley**, and **Curtis Fuller**. After his army service, he became the pianist for the Bee Hive jazz **club** in Chicago, where he played with many notable musicians including **Eddie "Lockjaw" Davis, Charlie Parker, Coleman Hawkins, Lester Young,** and **Sonny Stitt**. Mance was **Dinah Washington**'s accompanist from 1954 to 1956, worked with the Adderley brothers again from 1956 to 1958, and played with **Dizzy Gillespie** from 1958 to 1961. Thereafter, he performed mostly with his own trios whose members have included **Billy Cobham** and **Shelly Manne**. Mance has taught at the New School since the late 1980s and appeared in the 100 Gold Fingers of Jazz tour.

MANDEL, JOHNNY (1925–). A composer, **trumpet** player, and **trombonist**, Johnny Mandel started playing with Boyd Raeburn in 1945, followed by stints of varying length in the bands of **Jimmy Dorsey, Buddy Rich,** and **Woody Herman**. Mandel composed music for **Artie Shaw** and later for **Count Basie**'s orchestra during the 1950s before moving to Los Angeles and starting a career composing for TV and film. Among his most notable jazz compositions are "Emily," "A Time for Love," and "The Shadow of Your Smile," for which he won both a Grammy and an Academy Award.

MANGELSDORFF, ALBERT (1928–2005). A German trombonist, Albert Mangelsdorff first played **violin** and then **guitar** before settling on the **trombone** at the age of 20. Mangelsdorff performed with several European bands to some acclaim during the 1950s and gained some notoriety in 1958 when he performed with Marshall Brown's International Youth Band at the **Newport Jazz Festival**. In 1961 he led a jazz quintet that was popular in Europe throughout the 1960s, and in 1962 he recorded with **John Lewis**. During the late 1960s, Mangelsdorff became associated with **Free Jazz** when he joined the Globe Unity Orchestra, and in 1975 he joined the **United Jazz and Rock Ensemble**. During the late 1970s he performed with Michael Portal in addition to **recording albums** with **Elvin Jones, Jaco Pastorius,** and others. In

1981 he was a founding member of the French/German Jazz Ensemble, and in 1995 he became director of Jazzfest Berlin. Mangelsdorff was a highly regarded trombonist and a master of the technique of **multiphonics** (playing/humming several notes at once). *See also* UNION DEUTSCHER JAZZ-MUSIKER.

MANGIONE, CHARLES "CHUCK" (1940–). While a young man, Chuck Mangione was introduced to many jazz musicians by his father, including **Horace Silver, Art Blakey, Kai Winding,** and **Dizzy Gillespie,** who gave Mangione a **trumpet** in the early 1950s. Mangione attended the Eastman School of Music in the early 1960s and played in a **Hard Bop** group with his brother, pianist Gap Mangione. In 1965 he performed with the **big bands** of **Woody Herman** and **Maynard Ferguson,** and from 1965 to 1967 he performed with Art Blakey. In 1968, Mangione formed his own quartet, and by the 1970s he had recorded many popular **albums,** including the soundtrack to the film *Children of Sanchez* and *Feels So Good* (1977), which sold over two million copies. Mangione switched to playing the flugelhorn exclusively and toured extensively during the 1980s, and after a break from playing during the 1990s, he reunited with his old band in 1997 for a comeback tour.

MANHATTAN TRANSFER. A vocal group, Manhattan Transfer was originally formed in 1969 by Tim Hauser and then re-formed in 1972. Consistently one of the most popular vocal groups in jazz, they encompass many styles and have won multiple Grammy Awards, including Best Jazz **Fusion** Performance for their version of Weather Report's "Birdland" (1980) and Best Jazz Vocal Performance for their **album** *Vocalese* (1985). *See also* GREEN, FREDDIE; VOCALESE.

MANN, HERBIE (1930–2003). A flutist and record producer, Herbie Mann started out playing in a U.S. Army band in the early 1950s. In the late 1950s he formed his Afro-Jazz Sextet and participated in State Department–sponsored tours of Africa, and during the early 1960s he toured Brazil and Japan. During the late 1960s his musical interests broadened to include more world music styles, and in 1973 he formed his group Family of Mann, which performed many of these styles. Throughout the 1970s, Mann experimented with **Fusion** and Rock, and in 1981 he formed his own record company, Herbie Mann Music. In the early 1990s he formed another **record label,** Kokopelli, for which he also recorded. Mann was one of the most popular and accomplished flutists in the jazz idiom.

MANNE, SHELDON "SHELLY" (1920–1984). A drummer, Shelly Manne started playing saxophone but switched to the drums when he was 18. He played with various groups in New York City, participating in **Coleman Hawkins' recording** of "The Man I Love" in 1943, before playing with **Stan Kenton** from 1946 to 1952. In the 1950s, Manne moved to Los Angeles and became an important figure in **West Coast Jazz**. He worked with Howard Rumsey's Lighthouse All-Stars from 1951 to 1953, **Shorty Rogers** from 1953 to 1954, and then recorded with artists including **Art Pepper, Jimmy Giuffre, Teddy Edwards**, and **Lennie Niehaus**, among others. From 1955 onward, Manne led his own group, which included **Leroy Vinnegar, Bill Holman**, and **Conte Candoli** at various times, and ran his own jazz club, Shelly's Manne-Hole, from 1960 to 1974. In 1974 he recorded with **Bill Evans** before joining the group L.A. 4 with Ray Brown from 1974 to 1977. In 1980 he appeared with **Benny Carter** in the Gentlemen of **Swing** and in a Bop group with **Dizzy Gillespie, Cedar Walton, Eddie Gomez**, and others.

MANOR. A **record label** established in the mid-1940s in Newark, New Jersey. Artists include **Jimmie Lunceford, Coleman Hawkins, Dizzy Gillespie**, and **Sid Catlett**, among others. The name was later changed to ARCO, which was discontinued in 1950.

MANZELLO. A form of the instrument saxello, used by **Roland Kirk**.

MARABLE, FATE (1890–1947). A pianist, Fate Marable began playing in riverboat bands in 1907. In 1918 he formed a band named the Jazz Syncopaters (later Fate Marable and his Jazz Maniacs) that included **Louis Armstrong, Johnny Dodds**, and **Baby Dodds**, among others. In later years his band would also feature **Henry "Red" Allen** and **Jimmy Blanton**, along with many other talented musicians, and his band acquired a reputation as a jazz school for talented new musicians. Marable continued to lead bands until 1941; thereafter he performed at various St. Louis clubs until his death in 1947.

MARATHON. A record label active in 1928, artists include Rosa Henderson and Jackson and his Southern Stompers.

MARIA, TANIA (1948–). A Brazilian singer and pianist, Tania Maria moved to Paris in 1974 and recorded several **albums** in the Brazilian style. In 1975 she appeared at the **Newport Jazz Festival** with **Sarah Vaughan**, and in 1982 she recorded the successful album *Come with Me*. During the 1980s she performed with Eddie Duran, Steve Thornton, Don Alias, **Eddie Gomez**, and Michel Petrucciani, and she continued to record into the 1990s.

MARIANO, CHARLES "CHARLIE" (1923–2009). An alto saxophonist and student at the **Berklee School of Music** in Boston, Massachusetts,

Charlie Mariano played with groups in Boston before joining **Stan Kenton**'s orchestra from 1953 to 1955. He played with **Shelly Manne** from 1955 to 1958, again with Kenton from 1958 to 1959, and in 1959 he married **Toshiko Akiyoshi** and started a group with her. The group was together for seven years; during this time Mariano resided mostly in Japan. During the 1960s, Mariano also led his own **Jazz-Rock** group and played with **Charles Mingus**. Mariano traveled extensively during the 1970s exploring world music (he spent four months in India learning the *nagasuram*), and in 1975 he was a founding member of the United Jazz and Rock Ensemble, with which he performed until 1993. From 1975 to 1980 he played with Eberhard Weber, and during the 1980s and 1990s he continued to lead his own groups.

MARIMBA. An African name for a xylophone with calabash resonators, probably introduced into Latin America by African slaves.

MARMAROSA, MICHAEL "DODO" (1925–2002). A pianist who originally studied Classical piano, Marmarosa got his start playing with local bands in Pittsburgh, Pennsylvania. He was playing with the **Gene Krupa** band from 1942 to 1943 and thereafter played with **Tommy Dorsey** (1944) and **Artie Shaw** (1944–1945) before moving to Los Angeles and becoming the house pianist for the Atomic record label. During his time with Atomic, he recorded with Sam Galliard, whose sidemen included **Charlie Parker** and **Dizzy Gillespie**. In the late 1940s he also recorded with Boyd Raeburn, **Wardell Gray**, and **Lionel Hampton**, as well as on some important **recording sessions** with Parker. He played again with Shaw from 1949 to 1950 before basically retiring from music in 1954 due to personal and family problems.

MARSALIS, BRANFORD (1960–). A saxophonist, brother of **Wynton Marsalis**, Branford Marsalis was educated at the **Berklee College of Music** before starting out with **Art Blakey**'s **Jazz Messengers** in 1981. He toured with **Clark Terry** and spent some time in his brother's band in addition to **recording** with musicians including **Miles Davis** and **Dizzy Gillespie**. In 1983 he toured with **V.S.O.P.** II, which included his brother, **Ron Carter**, **Herbie Hancock**, and **Tony Williams**, and in 1985 he began a long-lasting relationship with the Rock artist Sting. During the rest of the 1980s, he recorded many **albums** with his own groups in styles varying from **Funk**, Rock, and **Bebop**, to Soul. In the 1990s, he worked as the leader of the NBC *Tonight Show* band; he left the show in 1995 and in 1998 became a producer for **Columbia** Records.

MARSALIS, ELLIS (1934–). Originally from New Orleans, Marsalis first began his musical career on **saxophone** before switching to **piano**. Highly prominent in the New Orleans jazz scene during the 1950s and 1960s, Marsalis was influential to many of the musicians working in the area. Marsalis fathered six children, including jazz icons Branford and Wynton, both of whom have credited their father with helping them develop into top-flight musicians. In addition to performing, Marsalis has remained very active as a teacher and educator and was awarded an NEA Jazz Masters award in 2011. *See also* MARSALIS, BRANFORD; MARSALIS, WYNTON.

MARSALIS, WYNTON (1961–). A **trumpet** player, Wynton Marsalis was already well versed in both jazz and Classical styles when he left Juilliard in 1980 to join **Art Blakey's Jazz Messengers**. He played in **Herbie Hancock's** first **V.S.O.P.** group in 1981 and from 1982 to 1985 led his own group with his brother **Branford Marsalis, Kenny Kirkland**, Charles Fambrough, and Jeff "Tain" Watts. He also played with Hancock's V.S.O.P. II group in 1983, and in 1984 he became the first musician ever to win a Grammy Award in both Classical and jazz categories. In 1987, Marsalis was co-founder of Jazz at Lincoln Center, and he continued to record **albums** with groups under his own name. Of particular note is *Blood on the Fields*, Marsalis' Pulitzer Prize–winning oratorio on the subject of slavery. Marsalis continues to tour and lead the Lincoln Center Jazz Orchestra.

MARSH, WARNE (1927–1987). A tenor saxophonist, Warne Marsh began playing professionally in 1944, spent some time in Los Angeles touring with **Buddy Rich**, and then in 1948 moved to New York and became a student and **sideman** of pianist **Lennie Tristano**. He spent the rest of the 1950s leading his own groups or working with Tristano and **Lee Konitz**. During the 1960s he moved to the West Coast, working as a private teacher in Pasadena, California. From 1972 to 1977 he played in the group Supersax, and during the rest of the 1970s and early 1980s he continued to lead his own groups and tour.

MARSH LABORATORIES. A **record label** established in Chicago in 1922 by O. B. Marsh that was active until 1936. The label recorded **sessions** of **Jelly Roll Morton** prior to his work with **Victor** records.

MARTINO, PAT (1944–). An **electric guitar** player, Pat Martino started his career performing with saxophonists Willis Jackson, Red Holloway, and **Sonny Stitt** before becoming a member of **organ** trios led by **Jack McDuff,** Don Patterson, **Jimmy Smith**, and **Jimmy McGriff**, among others. Beginning in the late 1960s, Martino led his own bands with notable sidemen including **Cedar Walton, Billy Hart,** and **Billy Higgins,** and during the 1970s he became interested in the work of Classical composers including Karlheinz

Stockhausen and Elliot Carter. Martino suffered a seizure in 1980 that resulted in memory loss, and he was therefore not able to resume playing until 1984. He began **recording** again in 1987 and maintains a busy performance schedule.

MASEKELA, HUGH (RAMOPOLO) (1939–). A South African **trumpet** player, Hugh Masekela received early inspiration from **recordings** of **Duke Ellington, Count Basie,** and **Cab Calloway** before seeing the movie *Young Man with a Horn* and deciding to play the trumpet. In 1959 he was a member of the Jazz Epistles, the first all-Black jazz band to record an LP in South Africa, and in 1961 he immigrated to the United States where he remained for 30 years. He recorded several successful **albums** including *Grazin' in the Grass* in 1968, and in the 1970s he recorded with Herb Alpert. During the 1980s he performed in Paul Simon's *Graceland* tour, and in 1991 he returned to South Africa, where his song "Bring Him Back Home" became the anthem for Nelson Mandela's international tour.

MASON, HARVEY (1947–). A drummer, Harvey Mason took lessons early and purchased his first **drum set** at the age of 16. Mason studied at the **Berklee School of Music** and New England Conservatory before touring with **Erroll Garner** (1969) and then **George Shearing** (1970–1971). During the 1970s, Mason was a **studio musician** in Los Angeles, where he worked with musicians including **Quincy Jones, Herbie Hancock, Donald Byrd, Freddie Hubbard, Gerry Mulligan, Duke Ellington, Gunther Schuller,** and others. In the 1990s Mason was a member of the group Fourplay, along with **Lee Ritenour**. He is active as a studio musician, playing **recording sessions** for numerous film projects.

MASTER (I). A term applied to the original **recording** media that is used to generate further copies.

MASTER (II). A **record label** founded by Irving Mills in 1936. Artists include **Duke Ellington** and Helen Oakley.

MASTER JAZZ RECORDINGS. A **record label** established in 1967 that put out **mainstream jazz**. Artists include **Earl Hines** and Buddy Tate, and the label also published the Master Jazz Piano series.

MASTERSOUNDS. A quartet formed in 1957 by **Buddy Montgomery** and Monk Montgomery with Richie Crabtree and Benny Barth and modeled after the **Modern Jazz Quartet**. The group was active until 1961 and reunited briefly in 1965.

MATTHEWS, DAVE (1911–). An alto and **tenor saxophonist** and arranger, Dave Matthews was educated at Oklahoma University and the Chicago Musical College. During the middle to late 1930s, he played saxophone in the bands of **Ben Pollack, Jimmy Dorsey**, and **Benny Goodman** before joining the Harry James band in 1939, for whom he wrote his **arrangement** of "Two O'Clock Jump." After leaving James' band in 1941, Matthews played with the bands of Hal McIntyre, **Woody Herman, Stan Kenton**, and **Charlie Barnet**, writing arrangements for each of them. He also led his own band during the last half of the 1940s and then spent the next several decades as an arranger.

MAUPIN, BENNIE (1940–). A **saxophonist** and bass **clarinet** player, Bennie Maupin studied at the Detroit Institute for Musical Arts before moving to New York in 1963. During the middle to late 1960s, he worked with Marion Brown, **Pharoah Sanders, Roy Haynes**, and **Horace Silver**. From 1968 to 1974 he worked with **Jack DeJohnette** and played bass clarinet on **Miles Davis'** album *Bitches Brew* (1969). During the late 1960s, Maupin also performed with **McCoy Tyner, Chick Corea**, and **Lee Morgan**, and in the 1970s he worked with **Herbie Hancock**, performing on the album *Headhunters*, in addition to **recording** with **Woody Shaw**. During the 1980s, Maupin did not perform as much, and in 1992 he recorded a reunion with Hancock.

MAXWELL, JAMES "JIMMY" (1917–2002). A **trumpet** player, Jimmy Maxwell started playing at the age of four. Maxwell spent the 1930s performing with **Gil Evans, Jimmy Dorsey**, Maxine Sullivan, and Skinny Enis before joining **Benny Goodman** from 1939 to 1943. After his time with Goodman, Maxwell joined the **Columbia Broadcasting System (CBS)** staff orchestra and performed and recorded for radio and television for the next 30 years. He also performed with **Woody Herman, Count Basie, Duke Ellington, Oliver Nelson**, and **Gerry Mulligan**, and he toured the Soviet Union with Goodman in 1962. He was a member of the NBC *Tonight Show* orchestra from 1965 to 1973 and a performer in various other bands throughout the 1970s.

MAY, WILLIAM "BILLY" (1916–2004). A composer, arranger, and **trumpet** player, Billy May got his start playing and writing **arrangements** for **Charlie Barnet** from 1938 to 1940. May played and arranged for **Glenn Miller**, Les Brown, and **Woody Herman** before moving to Hollywood in 1944. He formed his own studio band in 1951, and then he began arranging for singers including **Frank Sinatra** and **Ella Fitzgerald** in addition to writing music for film and television.

MAYS, WILLIAM "BILL" (1944–). A pianist, Bill Mays got his start as the accompanist for **Sarah Vaughan** from 1972 to 1973 and then **Al Jarreau** in 1975. From 1975 to 1983 he played with **Bobby Shew, Bud Shank,** Howard Roberts, **Shelly Manne, Bob Magnusson,** and **Benny Golson** in addition to leading his own groups. In 1984 he moved to New York City where he continued to lead his own groups; during this time he also played with the Bob Mintzer Big Band and the **Mel Lewis** Orchestra and became active as a composer and arranger.

M-BASE. A term used to describe both the style and members of a collective school of musical thought in the 1980s. Believing in the importance of creative expression, the idea of M-base was created by several musicians, most notably Steve Coleman, Graham Haynes, and **Greg Osby**. These musicians worked frequently with each other throughout the late 1980s and 1990s, often **recording** music that was considered to be highly different from that of mainstream jazz. One of the important concepts to the development of this musical philosophy is the importance of music as an expression of life experience. Musicians that adhere to the M-base approach include Jason Moran, Robin Eubanks, and Geri Allen.

M'BOOM. A percussion ensemble formed in 1970 by **Max Roach** that eventually was a group of 10 band members. Between them, the members of the group play close to 100 percussion instruments. The group recorded several **albums** and continues to perform today.

McCANDLESS, PAUL (1947–). A jazz double-reedist, clarinetist, and saxophonist, Paul McCandless played in Classical groups and jazz **clubs** before joining Paul Winter's Winter Consort from 1968 to 1973. In 1970 he and three other members of that group formed the group Oregon. In the 1980s, McCandless played with the group Gallery, the **Jaco Pastorius Big Band, David Friesen, Art Lande,** Eberhard Weber, and **Carla Bley,** among others. During the 1990s he worked with Béla Fleck and the Flecktones in addition to leading his own groups. He remains active as a performer today.

McCANN, LESLIE COLEMAN "LES" (1935–). A pianist and singer, Les McCann spent time in the navy, where a victory in a talent contest earned him a spot on the *Ed Sullivan Show* in 1956. McCann moved to Los Angeles and formed his own trio with which he recorded many **albums** from 1960 to 1964, and in the late 1960s his live duet with **Eddie Harris** at the **Montreux Jazz Festival** was very successful. During the rest of the 1960s and 1970s, he performed with a wide variety of artists including **Art Pepper,**

Coleman Hawkins, Stanley Turrentine, Johnny Griffin, Paul Chambers, Blue Mitchell, and many others. In the 1970s, McCann switched primarily to electronic keyboards and by the end of the decade had moved from jazz to Rhythm and Blues (R&B) and Soul music. He reunited with Harris in 1986 and performed with him again in Montreux in 1994, but a stroke in 1995 caused problems with his right hand; from then on he regularly hired a second pianist to play with him.

McCLURE, RONALD DIX "RON" (1941–). A bass player and composer, Ron McClure studied at the Hartt School of Music before getting his first gig with Buddy Rich from 1963 to 1964. He then played with Chet Baker, Herbie Mann, Maynard Ferguson, Wynton Kelly, and Wes Montgomery before joining Charles Lloyd from 1966 to 1969. After touring the world with Lloyd, McClure started the group Fourth Way in San Francisco in 1970. During the rest of the 1970s, McClure played with Bobby Hutcherson, Joe Henderson, Freddie Hubbard, Sarah Vaughan, Jack DeJohnette, Thelonious Monk, Keith Jarrett, Baker, Dave Liebman, and Tony Bennett, among others. In the 1980s, McClure played in the quartet Quest with Liebman and Billy Hart, in addition to working with Lee Konitz, Michel Petrucciani, and others. During the 1990s and onward, he has continued to work as a freelance musician and as a leader of his own groups.

McCONNELL, ROBERT MURRAY GORDON "ROB" (1935–2010). A Canadian valve trombonist, Rob McConnell got his start performing with Maynard Ferguson in New York in 1964. After returning to Toronto, he became a studio musician in addition to playing with Phil Nimmons from 1965 to 1969. In 1968, McConnell formed the first version of his Boss Brass—a 16-piece studio band without saxophones. Later he expanded the band to 22 members by adding a saxophone section. McConnell was the primary arranger for the group and received several Grammy Awards.

McCURDY, ROY WALTER, JR. (1936–). A drummer, Roy McCurdy studied at the Eastman School of Music and got his first gig playing and recording with Chuck Mangione and Gap Mangione in the Jazz Brothers from 1960 to 1961. Following that, he played with Art Farmer and Benny Golson in the Jazztet, Betty Carter, and Sonny Rollins before beginning a long stint with Cannonball Adderley from 1965 to 1975, which included separate sessions with Nat Adderley and Joe Zawinul. After Cannonball Adderley's death in 1975, he moved to Los Angeles and worked with Kenny Rankin, Nancy Wilson, Ella Fitzgerald, Freddie Hubbard, Stanley Turrentine, Clark Terry, Sarah Vaughan, and others. McCurdy is active as a private teacher and clinician.

McDUFF, EUGENE "BROTHER JACK" (1926–2001). An organist who was primarily self-taught, Brother Jack McDuff actually started as a bassist in a group with Denny Zeitlin and Joe Farrell. After playing piano with **Johnny Griffin** and **Max Roach** in Chicago in the 1950s, he switched to **organ** and formed his own group in 1959. His group, at times known as Jack McDuff's Heating System, variously included **Joe Henderson**, **George Benson**, **Jimmy Forrest**, and **Pat Martino**, among others. During the 1960s and 1970s he recorded and toured extensively, and during the 1990s his career experienced a revival, including performances with Roy Hargrove and Joey DeFrancesco.

McFARLAND, GARY (1933–1971). A vibraphonist, composer, arranger, and **bandleader**, Gary McFarland learned the **vibraphone** while in the army. McFarland spent time at the **Berklee School of Music** from 1959 to 1960 and then moved to New York City and became known as a composer. His works were performed by numerous artists including **John Lewis**, the **Modern Jazz Quartet**, **Gerry Mulligan**, Anita O'Day, and **Bill Evans**. During the mid-1960s, McFarland toured with his own group but increasingly turned to composing commercial music. He died at the young age of 38 from a heart attack.

McFERRIN, BOBBY (1950–). A pianist and vocalist, Bobby McFerrin studied first at Juilliard and then at Sacramento State College. He started working as a pianist, accompanist, and singer in the 1970s, but in 1977 he switched to **singing** exclusively. He performed with **Jon Hendricks** in 1979, but an unaccompanied performance at the 1981 Kool Aid Jazz Festival launched McFerrin into the spotlight. During the early 1980s he worked with **George Benson**, **Dizzy Gillespie**, **Wayne Shorter**, **Herbie Hancock**, and others, in addition to performing at festivals, including the 1982 Kool Aid Festival where he was introduced as one of the "Young Lions." In 1985 and 1986, McFerrin won the Grammy Award for Best Male Jazz Vocalist, and his **recording** of "Don't Worry, Be Happy" in 1989 remains wildly popular today, in addition to winning the Grammy Awards for Record and Song of the Year. During the 1990s he focused more on composition, and in addition to performances with Hancock and **Chick Corea**, he formed and toured with the 12-person a cappella group Voicestra and served as creative chair for the St. Paul Chamber Orchestra from 1994 to 1998.

McGHEE, HOWARD (1918–1987). A **trumpet** player, Howard McGhee worked in the Midwest with many **territory bands** during the 1930s before ending up with **Lionel Hampton** in 1941. He then performed with a string of bands including those led by **Andy Kirk**, **Charlie Barnet**, **Count Basie**,

Georgie Auld, and **Billy Eckstine** before joining **Coleman Hawkins** from 1944 to 1945. Then based in California, McGhee led several groups and participated in some notable **recordings** with **Charlie Parker**. From 1945 to 1948 he toured with **Jazz at the Philharmonic** in addition to leading his own groups. During the early 1950s, McGhee continued to tour, but his career was sidelined for most of the decade due to his heroin addiction. In 1960, McGhee returned to playing and appeared with **Woody Herman**; he went on to appear with **Duke Ellington, J. J. Johnson, Sonny Stitt, George Coleman, Shelly Manne**, and **Teddy Wilson**, and he started his own **big band** in the mid-1960s. During the 1970s he played at many European festivals, but a heart ailment eventually limited his playing ability.

McGRIFF, JAMES "JIMMY" (1936–2008). An organist and **bandleader**, Jimmy McGriff attended the Juilliard School in addition to studying with **Jimmy Smith** and others. In 1962 he formed his own **organ** trio, and his single, "I Got a Woman," was a *Billboard* hit. Thereafter, he recorded many albums and backed a succession of singers, and during the 1970s he played in **Buddy Rich**'s band.

McKENNA, DAVID "DAVE" (1930–2008). A pianist from a musical family, Dave McKenna had already formed his own trio in the mid-1940s before playing in the Boston area with Boots Mussulli. He played with Charlie Ventura and then joined **Woody Herman** from 1950 to 1951 before he was drafted to serve during the Korean War. After his time in the army he rejoined Ventura and spent the rest of the 1950s playing with **Gene Krupa, Stan Getz, Zoot Sims, Buddy Morrow, Bobby Hackett**, and **Buddy Rich**. In the early to mid-1960s he was on the staff of ABC, and in the late 1960s he moved back to Boston, where he played solo piano in area restaurants and bars. From then on he also made appearances at festivals or on television.

McKIBBON, ALFRED "AL" (1919–2005). A double bassist, Al McKibbon moved to New York City in 1943 and started working with Lucky Millinder, Tab Smith, **Coleman Hawkins, Dizzy Gillespie**, and **Miles Davis** (on the *Birth of the Cool* **sessions**). During the 1950s, McKibbon played with **Thelonious Monk, Earl Hines**, and **Johnny Hodges**, but he spent most of the decade (1951–1958) with **George Shearing**. In 1959 he played with **Cal Tjader**, and in the 1960s he was working as a freelance musician on the West Coast, serving in the staff groups of both **Columbia Broadcasting System (CBS)** and NBC. In 1971–1972 he played with the Giants of Jazz, and during the rest of the 1970s and 1980s he continued to freelance before returning to New York City in 1990 to work in musicals. *See also* BASS.

McKINNEY'S COTTON PICKERS. Led by drummer Williams McKinney, the group began **recording** with Victor in 1928. The 11-piece group featured **arrangements** by **Don Redman** and was originally based in Detroit before relocating to New York City. Although the band's personnel changed regularly, it at times included such figures **as Coleman Hawkins, James P. Johnson, Benny Carter**, and **Fats Waller**. The group disbanded in 1934.

McLAUGHLIN, JOHN (1942–). An English guitarist, John McLaughlin started playing **piano** before switching to **guitar**, where an interest in technically challenging flamenco styles gave way to jazz. McLaughlin played in several **Blues** bands in London during the early 1960s and later began playing jazz with John Surman and **Dave Holland**. McLaughlin moved to New York City in 1969 to play with **Tony Williams** in the band Lifetime and then with **Miles Davis** from 1969 to 1971; he figured prominently in Davis' **albums** *Bitches Brew* and *In a Silent Way*.

In 1971 he formed his own **Fusion** group, the Mahavishnu Orchestra, which included members **Billy Cobham** and Jean-Luc Ponty. He formed the group Shakti with the Indian violinist L. Shankar and played an acoustic guitar he designed that was based on an Indian vina, and during the late 1970s McLaughlin made some **recordings** with acoustic guitar. In the mid-1980s he re-formed the Mahavishnu Orchestra and recorded with Davis on his album *You're Under Arrest*. In 1985 he performed a guitar concerto composed for him by Mike Gibbs with the Los Angeles Philharmonic, and in 1990 he performed his own piece, *Mediterranean Concerto*, with the Scottish National Orchestra. He continues to record and tour.

McLEAN, JOHN LENWOOD "JACKIE" (1932–2006). A saxophonist, Jackie McLean started playing alto at the age of 15, and by 1948–1949 he was playing with **Sonny Rollins** and practicing with **Bud Powell**. McLean played with **Miles Davis** off and on from 1949 to 1953, and during the mid-1950s he played with **Charles Mingus** and **Art Blakey**'s **Jazz Messengers**. After his cabaret card was revoked in the late 1950s due to complications from his heroin addiction, McLean toured with his own groups and recorded as a **sideman** with notable musicians including Sonny Clark, **Donald Byrd, Lee Morgan**, and **Hank Mobley**, among others. In 1965 he toured Japan with his own quintet, and in 1968 he started teaching at the Hartt School of Music, becoming head of the African American Music Department in 1972. He continued to tour and lead groups into the 1990s.

McNAIR, HAROLD (1931–1971). A Jamaican saxophonist and flutist, Harold McNair worked in the Caribbean and then New York before playing with **Kenny Clarke** and **Quincy Jones** in Europe. During the 1960s he also recorded with artists including **Zoot Sims** and **Philly Joe Jones** before passing away from lung cancer in 1971.

McNEELY, JAMES "JIM" (1949–). A pianist, Jim McNeely graduated from the University of Illinois in 1975 and moved to New York City where he played with Ted Curson and then **Chet Baker**. He then began a long-standing engagement with the **Thad Jones–Mel Lewis** Orchestra and its successor, the Mel Lewis Orchestra, which lasted from 1978 to 1984. During the early 1980s, he also played with **Stan Getz** (1981–1985), **Bob Brookmeyer** (1981–1983), and led his own groups. From 1984 to 1989 he played with **Joe Henderson,** and from 1990 to 1995 he was the pianist for **Phil Woods**. McNeely rejoined the newly named Vanguard Jazz Orchestra in 1996, a group with whom he serves as pianist and composer-in-residence. From 1998 to 2003 he was also the conductor of the Danish Radio Orchestra. He continues to freelance, lead his own groups, and serve as a clinician. *See also* VILLAGE VANGUARD.

McPARTLAND, JAMES "JIMMY" (1907–1991). A **cornet** player, Jimmy McPartland was a founding member of the **Austin High School Gang** and at the age of 17 succeeded **Bix Beiderbecke** in the Wolverines. During the 1920s, McPartland performed with several groups including Art Kassel and **Ben Pollack**, and he made several **recordings** that became emblematic of the **Chicago Jazz** style. In the late 1920s and the 1930s, McPartland led his own groups and performed with others in New York and Chicago, including a yearlong stint with **Jack Teagarden** in the early 1940s. In 1942, McPartland was drafted into military service as an infantryman, and it was during this time that he met his wife Marian Turner, who became **Marian McPartland** when they wed in 1945. He continued to tour and perform throughout the 1950s, 1960s, 1970s, and 1980s, including a particularly memorable tribute to Beiderbecke in 1975 at Carnegie Hall.

McPARTLAND, MARIAN (MARGARET) (1918–). An English pianist, Marian McPartland started playing the piano at a young age and discovered jazz at the age of 14. Thereafter she performed as part of a four-piano group for a few years before the Second World War, when she toured and performed for British and American troops and met and married her husband, **Jimmy McPartland**. They moved to the United States in 1946, and McPartland began leading her own groups throughout the 1950s, 1960s, and 1970s, employing sidemen including **Steve Swallow, Eddie Gomez, Billy Hart,** and **Dave Holland**. She became involved in education during this time and wrote several articles about jazz musicians. In 1969 she formed her own **record label**, Halcyon, and in 1979 she debuted her radio show, *Marian McPartland's Piano Jazz*, on National Public Radio (NPR), which is still running as of this writing.

McPHERSON, CHARLES (1939–). An alto saxophonist, Charles McPherson started playing at the age of 13 and in just a few years was studying and performing professionally with **Barry Harris**. McPherson moved to New York in 1959 and on **Yusef Lateef**'s recommendation soon joined **Charles Mingus'** Jazz Workshop, with whom he would perform off and on through 1974. During the 1960s he also recorded with Harris and **Art Farmer**, among others. During the 1970s he was primarily a freelance musician, and during the 1980s he led the group Uptown Express, which included **trumpet** player **Tom Harrell**. In the 1990s he also appeared several times for Jazz at Lincoln Center. Influenced strongly by **Charlie Parker**, McPherson also played portions of the soundtrack to the Parker biopic *Bird*.

McRAE, CARMEN (1922–1994). A jazz singer, Carmen McRae's career began 1944 **singing** with **Benny Carter**. Thereafter she performed with bands led by **Mercer Ellington, Count Basie**, and **Charlie Barnet**, and in the early 1950s she was the intermission singer and pianist at **Minton's Playhouse** in New York. In the mid-1950s she signed with the **Decca** label and issued several **recordings**, and she toured with small groups all the way through the 1980s. She was forced to stop singing after experiencing respiratory failure following a performance at the **Blue Note** in New York in 1991.

MEDALLION. A **record label** established in Cincinnati in 1919. Artists included the Louisiana Five and **Eubie Blake**.

MEHLDAU, BRAD (1970–). A pianist, Mehldau was already winning awards for his playing by the time he attended the New School in New York and studied with **Junior Mance**, Kenny Werner, Fred Hersch, and **Jimmy Cobb**, the latter of whom he began performing with in the early 1990s. During the 1990s he played with Joshua Redman and **Toots Thielemans**, among others, and formed his own trio with Larry Grenadier and Jorge Rossy. During the 2000s, Mehldau has achieved notoriety for his attempts to perform Pop music in a jazz style; he has recorded songs by popular artists including the Beatles, Nick Drake, and Radiohead.

MELLOPHONE. A **brass** instrument with valves that is usually pitched in the keys of F or E. Although not commonly used in jazz, it was used by **Stan Kenton** in his Neophonic Jazz Orchestra.

MELOTONE. A **record label** established in 1930 that offered inexpensive records during the Great Depression and was a label that also released **race records**. Melotone released a variety of musical styles, including jazz, **Blues**, dance music, and Country, before disbanding in 1938.

MENGELBERG, MISHA (1935–). A Dutch pianist known for his association with the Avant-Garde, Misha Mengelberg has performed with artists including **Eric Dolphy**, **Steve Lacy**, and **George Lewis**.

MENZA, DONALD JOSEPH "DON" (1936–). A tenor saxophonist, Don Menza also taught himself to compose during his time in the Seventh Army Jazz Band, a band that included other notable musicians **Cedar Walton**, **Eddie Harris**, and **Don Ellis**. During the 1960s he performed with **Maynard Ferguson** (1960–1962) and **Stan Kenton** (1962) before eventually moving to Europe from 1964 to 1968 and working as a freelance and **studio musician**. Upon his return to the United States in 1968, Menza joined **Buddy Rich**'s **big band**, and after a short stint with **Elvin Jones** he joined **Louie Bellson**, whom he would perform with and compose for through 1994. In the 1970s he also performed with **Woody Herman** and led his own big band, in addition to leading small groups that included sidemen such as Frank Rosolino, Chuck Findley, and **Shelly Manne**. During the 1980s and 1990s he continued to perform in several big bands and toured extensively.

MERCER, JOHNNY (1909–1979). A composer and lyricist, Johnny Mercer moved to New York to work as an actor, but by the 1930s he had become known as an outstanding vocalist for his work with **Paul Whiteman**, **Benny Goodman**, **Bing Crosby**, and others. A prolific lyricist and songwriter with over 1,000 songs to his credit, Mercer was also a four-time Academy Award winner. Among his most famous songs are the jazz standards "I'm an Old Cowhand," "I Thought about You," "I Remember You," "I'm Old Fashioned," and many others.

MERCURY. A record company established in 1945 in New York. Jazz artists with **albums** released by the label include Jay McShann, **Cootie Williams**, and **Buddy Rich**. A subsidiary label, **EmArcy**, also released jazz albums by notable artists including **Clifford Brown**, **Sarah Vaughan**, and **Dinah Washington**. *See also* RECORD LABEL.

MERITT (I). A **record label** active from 1925 to 1929 and founded in Kansas City.

MERITT (II). A **record label** established in 1979, known for reissuing Early Jazz records by artists including **Duke Ellington**.

MERRILL, HELEN (1930–). A vocalist, Helen Merrill got her start **singing** with **Charlie Parker, Miles Davis**, and **Bud Powell** during the late 1940s. During the 1950s she sang with **Clifford Brown, Gil Evans**, and others before moving to **Europe** in 1959 and touring during the early 1960s. By the mid-1960s, Merrill had settled in **Japan**, performing with **Teddy Wilson** and **Gary Peacock**. During the 1970s she made her way back to New York City by way of Chicago and recorded with Evans, **Steve Lacy, Art Farmer**, and others. During the 1980s and 1990s, she continued to tour with artists including **Ron Carter** and **Wayne Shorter**.

METCALF, LOUIS (1905–1981). A **trumpet** player, Louis Metcalf got his start playing with Charlie Creath in St. Louis. During the 1920s, Metcalf performed with a number of noted jazz artists including **Jelly Roll Morton, King Oliver, Sidney Bechet**, and **Duke Ellington**, among others. During the 1930s he toured and performed with **Billie Holiday**, and during the 1940s he led his own band based out of Montreal. From the 1950s onward, he worked primarily in New York City clubs.

METHENY, PAT(RICK) BRUCE (1954–). A guitarist, Pat Metheny was a guitar instructor at the University of Miami and the Berklee School of Music before touring with **Gary Burton** from 1974 to 1977. After his time with Burton, Metheny formed a group with Lyle Mays, a keyboardist with whom Metheny has had a long-standing musical partnership. Other musicians who have played in Metheny's groups over the years have included **Jack De-Johnette, Michael Brecker, Charlie Haden**, and many others. Metheny has also performed and recorded with **Sonny Rollins, Ornette Coleman** (during the 1980s), and Joshua Redman (during the 1990s).

METROJAZZ. A **record label** established in 1958. Artists include **Sonny Rollins, Teddy Edwards**, Pepper Adams, **Thad Jones**, and many others.

METRONOME. Well-known magazine published from 1881 to 1961. The magazine featured jazz articles by such writers as **Leonard Feather** and Barry Ulanov.

METRONOME ALL-STARS. A series of bands put together and recorded by *Metronome* magazine from 1939 to 1956. The members of the groups were determined by an annual poll in the magazine, and artists recorded include **Benny Goodman, Gene Krupa, Nat "King" Cole, Dizzy Gillespie, Fats Navarro, Miles Davis,** and **Billy Eckstine.**

MEZZROW, MEZZ (1899–1972). A clarinetist, Mezz Mezzrow (born Milton Mesirow) played early on with the **Austin High School Gang** in Chicago. In the late 1920s he moved to New York and recorded with **Eddie Condon,** and during the 1930s and 1940s he recorded with **Sidney Bechet** and in 1937 formed one of the first interracial bands. In the 1950s, Mezzrow moved to Europe and continued to play into the 1960s.

MIDDLEBROOKS, WILFRED (ROLAND) (1933–2008). A bassist, Wilfred Middlebrooks played with **Eric Dolphy, Mel Lewis, Billy Higgins,** and others during the 1950s. From 1958 to 1963 he toured with **Ella Fitzgerald;** after leaving her group in 1963, Middlebrooks worked as a freelance musician for the rest of his life. *See also* BASS.

MIDNITE FOLLIES ORCHESTRA. An orchestra formed in Great Britain in 1978 that primarily performed music from the 1920s and 1930s.

MILES, BUTCH (1944–). A drummer, Butch Miles (born Charles Thorton Jr.) got his start as the drummer for **Mel Tormé** from 1972 to 1974. During the rest of the 1970s, Miles performed with the **Count Basie** Orchestra and also for a time with **Dave Brubeck.** From the 1980s onward, Miles has led his own groups and worked as a **sideman** with various artists including **Woody Herman, Zoot Simms, Clark Terry, Gerry Mulligan,** and others.

MILESTONE. A **record label** established in 1966 in New York City. Artists include **Joe Henderson, McCoy Tyner, Sonny Rollins,** and others.

MILEY, JAMES WESLEY "BUBBER" (1903–1932). A **trumpeter,** Bubber Miley played with Mamie Smith before joining **Elmer Snowden's** Washingtonians in 1923, which soon thereafter came under **Duke Ellington's** leadership. Known for his unique sound with the plunger mute, Miley stayed with Ellington until 1929. He performed with Noble Sissle and in the last part of his life led his own orchestra before contracting tuberculosis and dying in 1932. *See also* MUTE.

MILLER, (ALTON) GLENN (1904–1944). A trombonist and **bandleader,** Glenn Miller briefly attended the University of Colorado and freelanced as a trombonist and arranger for several years before forming his own band in 1937. A series of radio broadcasts in 1939 led to immense popularity for his orchestra, and from 1939 to 1942 his band had a series of hits that included "Moonlight Serenade," "Pennsylvania 6–5000," "Chattanooga Choo Choo," and "In the Mood." In 1942, Miller disbanded his group and joined the U.S. Army. He served as leader of the Army Air Force Band, and in 1944 an aircraft in which he was riding disappeared over the English Channel.

MILLER, MARCUS (1959–). A bassist, Marcus Miller worked as a **studio musician** in New York during the late 1970s before joining **Miles Davis** in 1980. Miller worked with Davis throughout the 1980s in addition to working with **David Sanborn**, **McCoy Tyner**, Kevin Eubanks, **Steve Gadd**, and many others. During the 1990s and onward he continued to work as a studio musician.

MILLER, MULGREW (1955–). A pianist, Miller was inspired to play jazz after hearing **Oscar Peterson** and landing his first notable jazz **gig** with **Mercer Ellington** from 1977 to 1980. From 1980 to 1983, Miller played with **Woody Shaw**, and from 1983 to 1986 with **Art Blakey's Jazz Messengers** in addition to freelance work. Miller played with **Tony Williams'** quintet from 1986 to 1992 and after 1992 has led his own groups.

MILLS, IRVING (1884–1985). A music publisher, singer, lyricist, composer, and promoter, Irving Mills formed a music publishing company with his brother in 1919 that was eventually known as Mills Music Inc. In 1926 he became the manager for **Duke Ellington's** orchestra, and at various other times he promoted the bands of **Cab Calloway**, **Fletcher Henderson**, **Jimmie Lunceford**, and others. A noted lyricist, Mills contributed the lyrics for several jazz standards including "Sophisticated Lady" and "It Don't Mean a Thing if It Ain't Got That Swing." In 1931 he fronted a band that eventually became known as the **Mills Blue Rhythm Band**. Mills was also a founder of the **Master** and **Variety** record labels and continued to work actively up to the 1960s.

MILLS BLUE RHYTHM BAND. A **big band** originally formed in 1929 by Willie Lynch as the Blue Rhythm Band, the Mills Blue Rhythm Band got its new name when **Irving Mills** became its manager in 1931. In the beginning, Mills used the band to play at the **Cotton Club** when the other bands of **Duke Ellington** and **Cab Calloway** were unavailable to play, but it later became an important band in its own right before disbanding in 1938.

MILLS BROTHERS. A vocal quintet consisting of Herbert Mills, Harry Mills, Donald Mills, and their brother John Mills Jr., or later their father,

John Mills Sr., the group recorded with **Duke Ellington** in 1932 and **Benny Carter** in 1940 and had a huge hit with their song "Paper Doll" in 1943. Known for the ability to interpret standard songs of the day into great **Swing** numbers with accurate harmonies, they continued to enjoy varying levels of success and performed into the 1980s.

MINGUS, CHARLES (1922–1979). A bassist, Charles Mingus first played the trombone and cello before starting on the bass at the age of 16. Mingus played with **Kid Ory, Louis Armstrong**, and **Lionel Hampton** during the 1940s, but his time with **Red Norvo** from 1950 to 1951 brought him to the national spotlight. During the early 1950s, Mingus played with artists including **Charlie Parker, Miles Davis, Dizzy Gillespie, Thelonious Monk, Duke Ellington**, and many others, including a notable performance at Massey Hall in Toronto with Parker, Gillespie, **Bud Powell**, and **Max Roach**.

In 1952, Mingus formed the Debut record label, and after contributing compositions to the Jazz Composers Workshop from 1953 to 1955, he formed his own workshop in 1955. In his workshop ensemble, Mingus performed with sidemen including **Eric Dolphy, Jimmy Knepper, Rahsaan Roland Kirk**, Dannie Richmond, and many others. During the 1960s, Mingus wrote some of his most intricate compositions including "The Black Saint and the Sinner Lady" and "Meditations on Integration," but the late 1960s saw Mingus retreat from public life. After receiving a Guggenheim fellowship in 1971, a reinvigorated Mingus returned to playing and writing music. Mingus became ill with amyotrophic lateral sclerosis (ALS), also known as Lou Gehrig's disease, in late 1977 and died two years later. Following his death, **Mingus Dynasty** was formed to perform his compositions. The Mingus Big Band continues to perform to this day, and in 1989 **Gunther Schuller** reconstructed and conducted Mingus' unfinished orchestral piece, "Epitaph."

MINGUS DYNASTY. A tribute group dedicated to performing the compositions of **Charles Mingus** formed in 1979 by Mingus' widow, Sue Mingus. Originally a small group consisting of some of Mingus' sidemen, the group recorded a few **albums** and achieved notable success during the late 1980s and early 1990s, but it was eventually surpassed by the Mingus Big Band.

MINTON'S PLAYHOUSE. A nightclub in New York and home to many of the famous **Bebop jam sessions** of the 1930s and 1940s. Minton's, along with **Monroe's Uptown House**, are considered the sites of the origination of **Bebop**. *See also* GILLESPIE, JOHN "DIZZY"; MONK, THELONIOUS; PARKER, CHARLIE.

MISSOURIANS. Originally named the Syncopaters, the Missourians was a **big band** formed in the early 1920s by Wilson Robinson. In 1924 the band became one of the house bands at the **Cotton Club** in New York City, and later one of the house bands at the **Savoy Ballroom**. In 1930, **Cab Calloway** assumed leadership of the band, and it was thereafter known as the Cab Calloway Orchestra.

MITCHELL, BLUE (1930–1979). A **trumpet** player, Mitchell (full name Richard Allen Mitchell) got his start playing in the **Rhythm and Blues (R&B)** bands of Paul Williams and Earl Bostic during the early 1950s before joining the **Horace Silver** quintet from 1958 to 1964. After Silver disbanded the group in 1964, Mitchell formed his own group with most of the same personnel and **Chick Corea** on piano. From 1969 to 1971, Mitchell toured with **Ray Charles** and from 1971 to 1973 with John Mayall. From 1974 until his death, he resided in Los Angeles and freelanced with musicians including **Mel Tormé**, Lena Horne, **Bill Holman**, **Louie Bellson**, and **Harold Land**, among others.

MITCHELL, GEORGE (1899–1972). A cornetist, George Mitchell toured Canada and the west before he settled in Chicago in the early 1920s. While in Chicago, Mitchell worked with **Jimmie Noone**, **Lil Armstrong**, **Jelly Roll Morton**, and **Earl Hines**, among others. After leaving Hines in 1931, Mitchell retired from music and became a bank teller.

MITCHELL, KEITH MOORE "RED" (1927–1992). A bassist, Red Mitchell first played piano and alto saxophone before switching to the bass. From the late 1940s to the early 1950s, Mitchell performed with Chubby Jackson, Charlie Ventura, and **Woody Herman** before a battle with tuberculosis forced him to stop playing for a while. In 1952 he replaced **Charles Mingus** in **Red Norvo**'s group, and in 1954 he played with **Gerry Mulligan**. From 1954 to 1968, Mitchell resided in Los Angeles and performed with **Hampton Hawes**, **Billie Holiday**, **Ornette Coleman**, **Frank Sinatra**, Mulligan, and others, in addition to being the bassist for the MGM Studio Orchestra (1959–1968). From 1968 to 1992, Mitchell resided in Stockholm, Sweden, where he performed with visiting American musicians and with European musicians including the **Radiojazzgruppen**. Mitchell is known for his practice of tuning the strings of his bass to the interval of a fifth.

MITCHELL, WILLIE MELVIN "BILLY" (1926–2001). A tenor saxophone player, Billy Mitchell got his start playing with Lucky Millinder in

New York City in 1948. Thereafter followed appearances with **Jimmie Lunceford**, Gil Fuller, and **Woody Herman** before Mitchell moved to Detroit and led a quintet featuring **Thad Jones** and **Elvin Jones** from 1950 to 1953. Mitchell played with **Dizzy Gillespie** from 1956 to 1957 and **Count Basie** from 1958 to 1961 before leaving to form his own group with **Al Grey** from 1962 to 1964. Mitchell was then musical director for Stevie Wonder before rejoining Basie from 1966 to 1967. During the 1970s and onward, Mitchell resided in the New York area where he performed, did studio work, and worked as a teacher.

MOBLEY, HENRY "HANK" (1930–1986). A tenor saxophonist, Hank Mobley played in a few house bands and **Rhythm and Blues (R&B)** bands before joining **Max Roach** from 1951 to 1953. In 1954, Mobley performed with **Duke Ellington, Tadd Dameron,** and **Dizzy Gillespie** before becoming a founding member of **Art Blakey**'s **Jazz Messengers**, with whom he performed until 1956. From 1956 to 1957, Mobley performed with **Horace Silver** and spent the rest of the 1950s playing with various artists including **Thelonious Monk.** During the 1960s, Mobley freelanced or led his own groups and played with many noted jazz musicians including **Miles Davis, Lee Morgan, Billy Higgins,** and **Philly Joe Jones.** From 1970 to 1972, Mobley was co-leader of a group with **Cedar Walton,** but thereafter persistent health problems forced him to limit his playing.

MODAL JAZZ. A term used to describe a style of jazz based upon a limited number of modes and scales. Among the first proponents of modal jazz were **Miles Davis** and **John Coltrane.** The **album** *Kind of Blue* (1959, **Columbia**) is considered a landmark Modal Jazz album. Examples of songs in the Modal Jazz style include "Impressions" and "So What?"

MODERN JAZZ QUARTET. A jazz group originally formed in 1951 by **Milt Jackson, John Lewis, Kenny Clarke,** and Ray Brown, all of whom were previously members of **Dizzy Gillespie**'s **big band.** In 1952, **Percy Heath** replaced Brown and in 1955 Connie Kay replaced Clarke, and the band continued with those personnel until disbanding in 1974. A reunion tour in 1981 reignited interest in the group, and they continued to get together for a few months every year until 1997. The group's repertoire varied between conventional Bop, **Cool Jazz,** and even **Third Stream** works composed by **Gunther Schuller.** *See also* ROKER, MICKEY.

MODES. A musical term for ordering scales based on starting them on different pitches of the scales.

MOLDE INTERNATIONAL JAZZ FESTIVAL. An annual **jazz festival** located in Molde, Norway, since 1961.

MOLE, IRVING MILFRED "MIFF" (1898–1961). While based in New York, trombonist Miff Mole recorded during the early 1920s with many jazz groups including the Original Memphis Five and artists including **Frankie Trumbauer**. In the mid-1920s, Mole performed with **Red Nichols** in addition to leading some of his own groups. Mole spent the 1930s as a member of the NBC Orchestra and was with the band of **Paul Whiteman** from 1938 to 1940. During the early 1940s, Mole played with **Benny Goodman** and led his own groups, but by the 1950s poor health forced him to stop performing.

MONK, THELONIOUS SPHERE (1917–1982). A pianist, Thelonious Monk started playing at the age of six. From 1941 to 1942 he was the pianist in the celebrated house band at **Minton's Playhouse** and became instrumental in the development of **Bebop**. Through the rest of the early to mid-1940s, Monk performed with Lucky Millinder, **Coleman Hawkins**, and **Dizzy Gillespie** before he started forming his own groups in 1947. During the 1950s, Monk played with **Charlie Parker, Sonny Rollins, Miles Davis**, and **Art Blakey**. In 1957 his group played regularly at the **Five Spot** in New York and included **John Coltrane**. During the 1960s, Monk toured internationally and formed a quartet that included **Charlie Rouse**, John Ore, and Frankie Dunlop. From 1971 to 1972, Monk toured with the Giants of Jazz, a group that included Gillespie, **Sonny Stitt, Kai Winding, Al McKibbon**, and Blakey, and until the mid-1970s he continued to perform and lead groups including one with his own son, T. S. Monk, on **drums**. From the mid-1970s onward, Monk lived in seclusion and did not perform publicly again before his death from a stroke in 1982. Monk has a noted place in jazz history for his role in the development of Bebop and also as a composer; among his more famous compositions are "Round Midnight," "Well You Needn't," "Straight, No Chaser," and "Ruby, My Dear."

MONROE'S UPTOWN HOUSE. Also referred to as "Monroe's," this was a nightclub in New York, one of two principal nightclubs associated with the early development of **Bebop**. *See also* MINTON'S PLAYHOUSE.

MONTEREY JAZZ FESTIVAL. An annual jazz festival held in Monterey, California, since 1958. The festival was created as a nonprofit corporation with the intention of supporting jazz education. This festival has since grown to become one of the leading jazz festivals in the United States and is held each year in September. The festival, which is the longest-running jazz festival in the world, was co-founded by **Jimmy Lyons** and **Ralph Gleason**.

MONTGOMERY, CHARLES "BUDDY" (1930–2009). A pianist, vibraphonist, and brother of guitarist **Wes Montgomery**, Buddy Montgomery got his start when he formed a group with **Slide Hampton** in Indianapolis. After a stint in the army from 1951 to 1954, Montgomery formed several groups with his brothers through the rest of the 1950s, including the Montgomery-Johnson Quintet and the Mastersounds. In the early 1960s he played **vibraphone** briefly with **Miles Davis** before forming the Montgomery Brothers Quintet. He spent the rest of the 1960s freelancing in New York before moving to Milwaukee in 1969 where he played piano and taught. Montgomery eventually moved to Oakland, California, in the 1980s and founded the Oakland Jazz Alliance in 1986.

MONTGOMERY, JOHN LESLIE "WES" (1923–1968). A **guitarist**, Wes Montgomery was inspired by **Charlie Christian** and started playing seriously in 1943. A self-taught player, Montgomery toured with **Lionel Hampton** from 1948 to 1950 before returning to Indianapolis. From the middle to late 1950s he recorded with his brothers in several different groups, and by the early 1960s his increasing popularity meant he was now **recording** and performing with many important jazz musicians, including **Milt Jackson**, **John Coltrane**, **Ron Carter**, **Philly Joe Jones**, **Wynton Kelly**, and many others. In the mid-1960s he also began recording with orchestras and large jazz ensembles, and he won a Grammy Award for his hit "Goin' Out of My Head" before dying rather suddenly from a heart attack. Montgomery's solos were known for his practice of playing single-note lines, octaves, and finally building to chords.

MONTREUX INTERNATIONAL JAZZ FESTIVAL. An annual **jazz festival** held in Montreux, Switzerland since 1967.

MOODY, JAMES (1925–2010). A saxophonist, clarinetist, and flutist, James Moody got his start playing with **Dizzy Gillespie** from 1946 to 1948. Moody moved to Europe in 1948 and performed with **Miles Davis**, **Tadd Dameron**, **Kenny Clarke**, and **Coleman Hawkins**, among others. In 1949 he recorded "I'm in the Mood for Love," which later became a hit. During the 1950s and into the 1960s, Moody led his own groups, and in the 1960s he performed extensively with Gillespie. He continued to lead groups into the 1970s before joining the band at the Hilton Hotel in Las Vegas where he spent several years backing shows by stars including Bill Cosby and **Tony Bennett**. His relationship with Gillespie continued throughout the 1980s, and Moody was a founding member of Gillespie's United Nations Orchestra in 1988. During the 1990s, Moody was nominated for a Grammy Award and performed with groups including **Lionel Hampton**'s Golden Men of Jazz and Tito Puente, and he continued to remain active as a clinician and teacher.

MOORE, FREDDIE (1900–1992). A drummer, Freddie Moore started playing at the age of 12 and worked in many traveling shows before joining Charlie Creath in 1927. During this time he also led his own band before joining **Wilbur Sweatman** from 1928 to 1931. He toured with **King Oliver** from 1931 to 1932 and spent most of the rest of the decade leading his own trio. In the mid-1940s he continued to lead his own groups and was performing with **Sidney Bechet** and Art Hodes, among others. During the 1950s he performed and toured, including a stint with **Mezz Mezzrow** from 1954 to 1955. He would continue to freelance into the 1980s, performing with **Roy Eldridge** among others, but by the mid-1980s he was unable to play the full **drum set** and was forced to switch to washboard.

MOORE, MICHAEL WATSON (1945–). A bassist, Michael Moore started playing at the age of 15 and performed in Cincinnati and with Woody Evans at the Playboy Club before going on tour with **Woody Herman** in 1967. In 1968, Moore moved to New York City, and during the 1970s he played with **Marian McPartland**, James Brown, **Freddie Hubbard**, **Bill Evans**, **Bob Brookmeyer**, **Chet Baker**, **Stan Getz**, **Gerry Mulligan**, Gene Bertoncini, and many others. He continued to play in the 1980s and moved to Great Britain from 1989 to 1992. During the 1990s he played with **Phil Woods**, **Rufus Reid**, Bill Charlap, and others.

MOREIRA, AIRTO (1941–). Breaking into the Brazilian music scene by playing drums with Brazilian pianist/flautist Hermeto Pascoal, Airto developed a great appreciation for Brazilian percussion as a result of his touring. After moving to America in 1968, Airto was quickly swept into the **Fusion** movement and performed and recorded with many leaders of the Fusion era including **Miles Davis** (*Bitches Brew* 1969, **Columbia**); Weather Report (*Weather Report* 1971, Columbia); and **Return to Forever** (*Return to Forever* 1972, **ECM**; *Light as a Feather* 1972, Polydor). He moved to Berkeley, California, in 1973 and led his own groups in addition to performing with many noted jazz musicians, including **Herbie Hancock**, **Gil Evans**, **Freddie Hubbard**, **Keith Jarrett**, **Al Di Meola**, George Duke, and as a percussionist with the Fusion/Rock group Santana. Airto assisted as a composer and performer on several film scores, including *Last Tango in Paris* and *Apocalypse Now*. In addition to being a popular **sideman**, Airto tours and leads a band with his wife, Brazilian vocalist **Flora Purim**. *See also* LATIN JAZZ.

MORELL, MARTY (1944–). A drummer and vibraphonist, Marty Morell played in a group with Al Cohn and **Zoot Simms** in 1966 before joining pianist **Bill Evans'** trio from 1968 to 1974. Morell moved to Toronto in 1974 where he led his own Latin bands, worked as a **studio musician**, and also played percussion with **Rob McConnell's** Boss Brass (from 1978 to 1981).

MORELLO, JOE (1928–2011). A drummer, Joe Morello played in groups with fellow high school student **Phil Woods** before moving to New York in 1952. During the 1950s he played with **Stan Kenton, Marian McPartland** (1953–1956), Woods, **Tal Farlow**, and others. From 1956 to 1967 he played in the **Dave Brubeck** Quartet, with whom he gained great recognition. From 1967 onward he worked primarily as a teacher and drum instructor for Ludwig Drum Corporation, and he continued to play occasionally with McPartland, Brubeck and others.

MORGAN, FRANK (1933–2007). An alto and soprano saxophonist, Frank Morgan started playing professionally in 1948, and after winning a talent contest he worked with **Lionel Hampton**. During the early 1950s he played with **Wardell Gray**, Teddy Charles, **Kenny Clarke**, and others before releasing an **album** under his own name in 1955. Morgan would then spend many of the following years in jail due to his heroin addiction; while in jail he participated in bands along with other inmates including **Art Pepper**. Morgan resumed playing in the 1970s and released an album in 1985. He released many more albums to much acclaim and continued to perform and tour with notable musicians including **Art Farmer, Cedar Walton**, and others. Known for his **Bebop** technique, Frank Morgan died from colon cancer in 2007.

MORGAN, HAROLD LANSFORD "LANNY" (1934–). An alto saxophonist, flutist, and clarinetist, Lanny Morgan worked with **Charlie Barnet, Bob Florence**, and others before touring with **Maynard Ferguson** from 1960 to 1966. Morgan moved to Los Angeles and during the 1970s he freelanced with **Bill Holman**, Bill Berry, and others in addition to joining the group **Supersax**. Morgan continued to play during the 1980s and 1990s, appearing with Natalie Cole in 1992, in addition to leading his own groups and working as a teacher and clinician.

MORGAN, LEE (1938–1972). A **trumpet** player, Lee Morgan began playing professionally at the age of 15 and joined **Dizzy Gillespie's** orchestra from 1956 to 1958, in addition to **recording** with **John Coltrane, Hank Mobley**, and others. From 1958 to 1961, Morgan played with **Art Blakey's Jazz Messengers**. During the early to mid-1960s he played with **Jimmy Heath**

and then again with Blakey, and then he led his own groups and freelanced for the remainder of his life. Morgan was shot by a jealous female acquaintance at the Slugs nightclub in New York where his quintet was performing. Morgan is also known for his hit composition "The Sidewinder." *See also* HARD BOP.

MORGAN, RUSS (1904–1969). A **trombonist** and arranger, Russ Morgan toured with Paul Specht and worked as an arranger before joining Jean Goldkette as music director and arranger in 1926. For the rest of the 1920s and throughout the 1930s, Morgan arranged for many of the bands of the day, including **Fletcher Henderson, Louis Armstrong, Chick Webb**, and others. Starting in 1935, Morgan led a band that had many hits throughout the 1940s. During the 1950s, Morgan had his own television show, and he continued to lead his own band throughout the 1960s until his death from a stroke in 1969.

MORRISSEY, RICHARD EDWIN "DICK" (1940–2000). A British **tenor saxophonist**, Dick Morrissey performed with several English groups throughout the 1960s and recorded many **albums** as a leader. Morrissey was a founding member and co-leader of the **Jazz-Rock** group "If" from 1970 to 1974 and worked a time for the Average White Band. From 1976 to 1985, he co-led the Jazz-**Funk** group Morrissey-Mullen with Jim Mullen, in addition to working with mainstream artists. Poor health eventually forced Morrissey to stop performing. *See also* ENGLAND.

MORROW, BUDDY (1919–2010). A **trombonist**, Buddy Morrow (born Muni Zudekoff) started playing at the age of 12 and moved to New York in 1934. During the middle to late 1930s, Morrow performed and recorded with **Artie Shaw, Tommy Dorsey, Paul Whiteman**, and others. During the 1940s he played with Bob Crosby, Lee Wiley, Red McKenzie, and **Jimmy Dorsey** before leading his own band from 1945 to 1946. He worked as a **studio musician** for the rest of the 1940s, and in the 1950s he achieved some success leading a band that performed Morrow's versions of **Rhythm and Blues (R&B)** tunes. During the 1960s he returned to studio work, and from 1976 into the 1990s he led the **Tommy Dorsey** ghost band. *See also* BANDLEADER.

MORROW, GEORGE (1925–1992). A **bassist**, George Morrow served in the military from 1943 to 1946 before performing with **Teddy Edwards, Charlie Parker**, and others in Los Angeles. From 1948 to 1953, Morrow lived in San Francisco and regularly appeared at Bop City, where he performed with **Dexter Gordon, Billie Holiday, Wardell Gray**, and others. From 1954 to 1956, he played in the **Clifford Brown–Max Roach** Quintet, for which he is best known, and after Brown's death in 1956, he continued to perform in Roach's group until 1958. He played with **Chet Baker, Sonny Rollins,** and others before becoming the bassist for Anita O'Day from 1958 to 1975. He moved to Florida in 1976 and worked in the band at Disney World.

MORTON, FERDINAND "JELLY ROLL" (1885–1941). Born Ferdinand Joseph LaMothe, Morton was a pianist, composer, and **bandleader.** He started playing piano in bordellos in New Orleans' **Storyville** district in 1902. Throughout the rest of the 1900s and the 1910s, Morton played in various locations across the United States in addition to being a gambler and pool hustler, moving to Los Angeles in 1917. Morton moved to Chicago in 1922 and made his first **recordings** in 1923, and from 1926 to 1930 he made some of his most famous recordings as the leader of Jelly Roll Morton's Red Hot Peppers, a group that included **Johnny Dodds, Baby Dodds, Kid Ory,** Omer Simeon, and **George Mitchell.** His career dwindled in the 1930s, although Morton continued to play intermittently, and by 1937 he was running a nightclub in Washington, D.C. A brief revival of interest in **Early Jazz** led to some recordings in 1939–1940, but Morton died a few months after moving to California in 1941. An extremely controversial figure in jazz who once even claimed to have invented it, Morton was one of the earliest and most important jazz composers. *See also* RAGTIME; STRIDE.

MORTON, HENRY "BENNY" (1907–1985). A trombonist, Benny Morton played around New York City before working with **Fletcher Henderson** from 1926 to 1928. He spent the rest of the 1920s and the 1930s working with **Chick Webb, Don Redman,** and **Count Basie,** and during the early to mid-1940s he played with Joe Sullivan, **Teddy Wilson,** Edmond Hall, and others. Morton led his own band in 1946 before working in Broadway pit orchestras, and in the 1950s and 1960s he was active as a studio and freelance musician. During the late 1960s and early 1970s, he toured and performed with the Saints and Sinners, the **World's Greatest Jazz Band,** and others.

MOSAIC (I). A **record label** established by **Graham Collier** in 1974 in London with a catalog of primarily English musicians.

MOSAIC (II). A **record label** established in 1982 in Santa Monica, California. The catalog included reissues of **Thelonious Monk, Charlie Parker,** and others.

MOSCA, SAL(VATORE) JOSEPH (1927–2007). A gifted pianist, Sal Mosca was a student of **Lennie Tristano** during the late 1940s and into the 1950s. From 1949 to 1965, Mosca played with **Lee Konitz,** and during the

1970s he performed with Konitz and **Warne Marsh**, performing in the Lennie Tristano Memorial Concert in 1979. During the 1980s he worked primarily as a teacher. He was relatively inactive after 1992.

MOSES, BOB (1948–). A **drum set** player, Bob Moses started playing at the age of 10 and was largely self-taught. In 1966 he formed the **Jazz-Rock** group Free Spirits with **Larry Coryell** and worked with **Rahsaan Roland Kirk** and **Gary Burton**. After leaving Burton's group in 1968, Moses worked as a freelance musician in New York City before forming the trio Open Sky with **Dave Liebman**. During the 1970s he played in **Jack De-Johnette**'s group Compost, in addition to working with Burton, **Mike Gibbs**, **Pat Metheny**, **Steve Swallow**, and others. From 1979 to 1982 he played with Emily Kuhn and **Sheila Jordan**, and in 1985 he moved to Boston to teach at the New England Conservatory. In 1987 he formed his own group, Mozamba, and during the 1990s he performed with many Latin musicians, in addition to some time with the group Plunge.

MOTEN, BENNIE (1894–1935). A pianist and **bandleader**, Bennie Moten studied with pupils of Scott Joplin before leading his own **Ragtime** trio from 1918 to 1922. His group continued to record throughout the 1920s, and eventually his band included **Hot Lips Page**, **Ben Webster**, **Lester Young**, **Buster Smith**, and **Count Basie** and was one of the best **big bands** in the Midwest if not the entire country. Moten died during a tonsillectomy, and eventually the members of his band re-formed under Count Basie.

MOTEN, BENNY (1916–1977). A bassist, Benny Moten played in local bands before moving to New York City and playing with **Hot Lips Page** in 1941. Moten worked with **Red Allen** for the rest of the 1940s and spent a brief time with Eddie South before working with **Stuff Smith** from 1950 to 1951. During the 1950s, Moten worked with Ivory Joe Hunter, Arnett Cobb, **Ella Fitzgerald**, Wilbur de Paris, and **Roy Eldridge**, among others. From the 1960s on, Moten worked as a freelance musician in New York City.

MOTIAN, STEPHEN "PAUL" (1931–2011). A drummer, Paul Motian studied music at the Manhattan School of Music after his discharge from the navy in 1954. Starting in 1955 and throughout the rest of the 1950s, Motian performed with a variety of musicians including **Gil Evans**, **Thelonious Monk**, Tony Scott, **Stan Getz**, **Lennie Tristano**, **Coleman Hawkins**, **Roy Eldridge**, **Bill Evans**, and many others. In 1959 he joined Evans' trio on a permanent basis, and it was during his time with this group (1959–1964) that Motian really became recognized. After a short stint with **Paul Bley**, Motian went on to play with **Keith Jarrett** off and on from 1966 to 1977. Motian became a member of the **Jazz Composers Guild** in 1964, recorded with **Charlie Haden**'s Liberation Music Orchestra in 1969, and starting in 1972, Motian also led his own groups. From 1980 to 1985 he played in a quintet with Joe Lovano and **Bill Frisell**, and from the late 1980s into the 1990s he led his own trios with Haden, Geri Allen, and others. During the 1980s and 1990s, Motian also worked as a **sideman** with artists including **Tom Harrell**, Frisell, Lovano, and others. In 1992, Motian formed his Electric Bebop Band, which included Joshua Redman, Chris Potter, **Steve Swallow**, and others.

MOUND CITY BLOWERS. Originally a novelty group formed in 1924 by Red McKenzie, the Mound City Blowers eventually expanded to 10 players and at times included **Eddie Condon, Jack Teagarden, Glenn Miller, Coleman Hawkins, Gene Krupa**, and others.

MPS (MUSIK PRODUKTION SCHWARZWALD). **Record label** and company formed in 1968 in Germany. Artists include **Albert Mangelsdorff**, **Oscar Peterson**, and others.

MRAZ, GEORGE (1944–). A bassist, George Mraz played **alto saxophone** and **violin** before studying **bass** at the Prague Conservatory. In 1968, Mraz moved to the United States and studied at the **Berklee School of Music**, then played with **Dizzy Gillespie, Oscar Peterson**, and **Ella Fitzgerald**. From 1972 to 1976 he played with the **Thad Jones–Mel Lewis** Orchestra in New York, and during the rest of the 1970s he appeared at various times with **Stan Getz**, Pepper Adams, **Art Pepper, Zoot Simms, John Scofield**, and others. In 1977 he also began playing with **Tommy Flanagan**, and from 1977 into the 1980s he performed with the New York Jazz Quartet. During the 1980s he played with **Hank Jones, Chet Baker, Warne Marsh, Carmen McRae**, and the group Quest, and during the 1990s Mraz has also played with **Phil Woods, Slide Hampton**, Jerry Bergonzi, Rick Margitza, and many other musicians. He remains an active performer today.

MUHAMMAD, IDRIS (1939–). A drummer, Idris Muhammad started playing at the age of eight. Muhammad worked with various Soul artists, including performing **Soul Jazz** with **Lou Donaldson** from 1965 to 1967. From 1969 to 1973, Muhammad was drummer for the Broadway musical *Hair*, and during the rest of the 1970s he played with various Soul Jazz artists. From 1978 to 1979 he performed with **John Griffin**, and from 1980 on, he has performed with **Pharoah Sanders**. During the 1990s he performed with many artists including **Ahmad Jamal, Lee Konitz, Stanley Turrentine**, and others. *See also* DRUM SET.

MULLIGAN, GERRY (1927–1996). A baritone saxophonist and arranger, Gerry Mulligan moved to New York City in 1946 and got his start there arranging music for **Gene Krupa** from 1946 to 1947. In 1947, while working as arranger for **Claude Thornhill**, Mulligan met **Gil Evans**, and from 1948 to 1950, Mulligan and Evans worked with **Miles Davis** on the "Birth of the Cool" project. Mulligan recorded with his own "tentet" in 1951 and also arranged for **Stan Kenton** before moving to Los Angeles in 1952. While there, Mulligan formed a piano-less quartet with **Chet Baker** that was very successful; Baker was replaced in 1953 by **Bob Brookmeyer**. In 1960 he formed his 13-piece Concert Jazz Band, and from 1968 to 1972 he played with **Dave Brubeck**. Throughout the 1970s, 1980s, and 1990s, Mulligan continued to lead various small groups and **big bands**. *See also* BARITONE SAXOPHONE, COOL JAZZ, WEST COAST JAZZ.

MULTIPHONICS. A technique whereby a normally monophonic instrument is heard to produce two different pitches, such as when a **brass** player plays a note while **singing** a different pitch.

MUNDY, JAMES "JIMMY" (1907–1983). An arranger, Jimmy Mundy was playing saxophone in a band with drummer Tommy Myles in 1932 when **Earl Hines** heard one of his compositions and offered him a job. During the 1930s and 1940s, Mundy's **arrangements** could be heard in many of the popular bands of the day, including the bands of **Benny Goodman**, **Gene Krupa**, Harry James, **Artie Shaw**, **Count Basie**, **Buddy Rich**, and **Paul Whiteman**, among others. During the 1950s, Mundy continued to arrange for large orchestras. Among his more famous arrangements are "Sing, Sing, Sing," "Solo Flight," and "Feather Merchant."

MURPHY, MARK HOWE (1932–). A singer, Mark Murphy got his start **singing** and accompanying himself on piano in New York City bars during the 1950s. During the late 1950s and 1960s, Murphy toured the United States, and in 1962 he appeared on the television show *Jazz Scene USA*. From 1963 to 1973, Murphy resided in London and toured **Europe**, and in 1973 he moved back to the United States after **recording** with **Michael Brecker** and **Randy Brecker** in 1972. Known for his **scat** singing and **vocalese**, Murphy's career resurged when his version of "Milestones" was revived during the **Acid Jazz** movement of the late 1980s. He continues to perform mostly as a freelance soloist.

MURPHY, SPUD (1908–2005). A composer and arranger, Spud Murphy was playing woodwinds in various bands before he began arranging in the early 1930s for **bandleaders** including Austin Wylie, Jan Garber, Mal Hallet, and others. Born in Berlin to Serbian immigrants, his given name was Miko Stefanovic. From 1935 to 1937 he worked as an arranger for **Benny Goodman**, Glen Gray, and **Tommy Dorsey**. From 1938 he led various bands that played his compositions, which later would venture into **Third Stream**. Murphy also developed and taught his own 12-tone system and was active until his death in 2005.

MURPHY, TURK (1915–1987). A trombonist and **bandleader**, Melvin "Turk" Murphy played in the **Yerba Buena Jazz Band** before enlisting in the armed forces during the Second World War. Upon his discharge, Murphy played in groups led by Lu Watters, and in the late 1940s, Murphy left to form his own band based out of San Francisco. The band played at Easy Street and then Earthquake McGoon's in addition to touring and **recording**. Murphy was active until 1987.

MURRAY, DAVID (1955–). A tenor saxophonist, David Murray moved to New York in 1975 and later formed the **World Saxophone Quartet**. During the early 1980s, Murray worked with **Jack DeJohnette** in his group Special Edition and with John Carter in the group Clarinet Summit. Murray has also led his own small and large groups throughout the 1980s and 1990s.

MURRAY DONALD LEROY (1904–1929). A clarinetist and saxophonist, Don Murray started playing with the **New Orleans Rhythm Kings** in 1923. Throughout the rest of the 1920s, Murray played with Jean Goldkette, **Bix Beiderbecke, Frankie Trumbauer**, and others before suffering an alcohol-related death in 1929.

MUSE. A **record label** established in 1972 in New York that issued primarily modern jazz recordings. Artists include **Sonny Stitt, Woody Shaw**, and many others. The label was sold in 1996.

MUSICRAFT. A **record label** founded in 1937 in New York and only active into the late 1940s. Artists included **Teddy Wilson, Duke Ellington**, and **Dizzy Gillespie**, among many others.

MUTE. A piece of equipment added to a musical instrument that muffles the instrument or changes its sound. Common mutes used in jazz include the Harmon mute, the cup mute, the felt mute, the **plunger** mute, and the **hat** (or "**bucket** mute"). The **practice mute**, though not intended for performance settings, is also common.

N

NANCE, RAY (1913–1976). A **trumpeter**, violinist, and vocalist, Ray Nance led groups in the Chicago area during the 1930s and played in bands led by **Earl Hines** and **Horace Henderson**. In 1940, Nance joined **Duke Ellington**'s orchestra, with whom he would remain until 1963, with a break to lead his own group in 1944. After his time with Ellington, Nance continued to lead his own small groups, including one notable septet that included Tiny Grimes, **J. C. Higginbotham**, **Slam Stewart**, and others. Nance contributed many important solos to the Ellington repertoire, notably his solo on "Take the 'A' Train" in 1941. *See also* VIOLIN.

NANTON, JOE "TRICKY SAM" (1904–1946). A trombonist, Joseph "Tricky Sam" Nanton played with **Elmer Snowden** and a few other bands before joining **Duke Ellington** in 1926. Nanton remained with Ellington virtually until his death, having successfully transferred **trumpeter Bubber Miley**'s distinctive **plunger** mute **growl** sound to the **trombone**, occasionally with a sound that was highly imitative and evocative of the human voice.

NASH, RICHARD TAYLOR "DICK" (1928–). A **trombone** player, Dick Nash played with Sam Donahue, Glen Gray, Tex Beneke, and others during the late 1940s, and during the Korean War he played in military bands. From the late 1950s, Nash has enjoyed a very successful career as a **studio musician**.

NATIONAL. A **record label** established in 1944 in New York. Artists include **Charlie Ventura**, **Billy Eckstine**, and others.

NATIONAL ASSOCIATION OF JAZZ EDUCATORS (NAJE). The precursor to the International Association of Jazz Educators (IAJE), the National Association of Jazz Educators was formed in 1968. The group became the International Association of Jazz Educators in 1989 and remained active until 2008.

NATIONAL JAZZ SERVICE ORGANIZATION (NJSO). An organization based in Washington, D.C., that was founded in 1984 by **David Baker**, **Donald Byrd**, and others. The organization focuses on the development and support of jazz and is no longer in existence.

NATIONAL YOUTH JAZZ ORCHESTRA. A group formed in London in 1965 by British educator Bill Ashton. The group remains active today and is open by audition to musicians under the age of 25. The repertoire is drawn from British composers (who are usually former members of the band), and the group performs regularly.

NAVARRO, THEODORE "FATS" (1923–1950). A **trumpet** player, Fats Navarro toured with bands right out of high school, eventually landing with **Andy Kirk** from 1943 to 1944. In 1945, Navarro joined **Billy Eckstine**'s band, ably replacing **Dizzy Gillespie**. Navarro left the band in 1946 and spent the rest of his short life performing with **Tadd Dameron**, **Bud Powell**, **Coleman Hawkins**, **Eddie "Lockjaw" Davis**, **Charlie Parker**, and other leading musicians of the **Bebop** movement. Extremely influential to a young **Clifford Brown**, Navarro died from a combination of tuberculosis and drug addiction.

NELSON, DAVE (1905–1946). A **trumpet** player, pianist, composer, and arranger, Dave Nelson was the nephew of **King Joe Oliver**, and during the 1920s he played with **Ma Rainey**, **Jelly Roll Morton**, **Jimmie Noone**, and others before joining Oliver's band for a short stint in 1930. Thereafter, Nelson led his own groups and during the 1940s worked as an arranger for Lewis Publishing before passing away from a heart attack.

NELSON, LOUIS "BIG EYE" (1885–1949). A clarinetist, "Big Eye" Louis Nelson worked with many bands in New Orleans before World War I, including the Imperial Orchestra, the Golden Rule Orchestra, the Imperial Band, and the Superior Orchestra. At one time reputed to have played bass with **Buddy Bolden**, Nelson also played with **King Oliver** and **Jelly Roll Morton** before moving to Chicago in the mid-1910s to play with **Freddie Keppard**. Nelson moved back to New Orleans in 1918 and worked with John Robichaux until 1925, and he led his own groups during the 1930s and 1940s.

NELSON, OLIVER (1932–1975). A saxophonist and composer, Oliver Nelson played with the Jeter-Pillars Orchestra and with George Hudson in the late 1940s and spent the early part of the 1950s in a military band. After leaving the military, Nelson went to college and then moved to New York in 1958, working briefly with **Louie Bellson**. In the early 1960s, Nelson played with **Eric Dolphy**, **Duke Ellington**, **Eddie "Lockjaw" Davis**, **Wild Bill Da-**

vison, and **Quincy Jones,** and he recorded what is probably his most famous **album,** *Blues and the Abstract Truth* (1961), which featured his composition, "Stolen Moments." In 1967, Nelson moved to the West Coast, and he continued to lead groups and tour, in addition to writing for TV and film, before dying of a heart attack in 1975.

NESTICO, SAMUEL "SAMMY" (1924–). A composer and arranger, Sammy Nestico arranged music for military bands for 15 years before he became the arranger for **Count Basie** in 1967, and the **albums** upon which his music appeared won several Grammy Awards. Nestico has since worked as a composer and arranger for television and film, and he has been active in the area of jazz education in addition to continuing to write and publish **big band** music. He is also the author of the textbook *The Complete Arranger* (1994) and remains an active composer and arranger.

NEWBORN, PHINEAS, JR. (1931–1989). A pianist and composer, Phineas Newborn played in a **Rhythm and Blues (R&B)** band run by his father during the 1940s before playing with **Lionel Hampton** in 1950 and again in 1952. After serving in the military during the mid-1950s, Newborn began leading his own groups and performed with **Charles Mingus, Roy Haynes,** and others. He continued to play into the 1960s, but starting in the middle of the decade his career began to give way to bouts of mental illness and alcoholism, and he played and recorded only sporadically for the rest of his life.

NEW BLACK EAGLE JAZZ BAND. A group formed in 1971 that performs traditional, New Orleans style jazz. The group continued to perform and tour into the 1990s.

NEW HOT PLAYERS. A jazz group formed in Switzerland during the 1930s and active in Europe in various guises into the 1950s.

NEWMAN, DAVID "FATHEAD" (1933–2009). A saxophonist, David "Fathead" Newman played in groups with **Cedar Walton** and **Ornette Coleman** while he was a teenager before joining **Ray Charles** from 1954 to 1964. After his time with Charles, Newman spent a few years in Dallas, Texas, before moving to New York in 1966. During the 1970s, Newman worked again with Charles for a year before spending 1972 to 1974 with **Herbie Mann.** Newman continued to record and lead his own groups into the 1990s.

NEWMAN, JOSEPH "JOE" (1922–1992). A **trumpet** player and composer, Joe Newman played in college **big bands** until joining **Lionel Hampton** in 1941. Newman then spent the rest of the decade alternating between playing with **Count Basie** and **Illinois Jacquet**. Newman rejoined Basie in 1952 and played with the band until 1961, and from the 1960s Newman toured with **Benny Goodman** and led his own groups.

NEW ORLEANS FOOTWARMERS. A group formed in 1932 and led by **Sidney Bechet** that was active into the 1940s.

NEW ORLEANS JAZZ. A genre of jazz that developed in New Orleans around the turn of the 20th century. Typical instrumentation included **cornet, clarinet, trombone, banjo, tuba** (or **bass**), and **drums**. New Orleans style jazz went through a revival during the 1940s and 1950s and is still performed today. Important musicians of the New Orleans Jazz style include **King Oliver, Louis Armstrong, Jelly Roll Morton**, and many others. *See also* EARLY JAZZ; ORIGINAL DIXIELAND JAZZ BAND; ORIGINAL MEMPHIS FIVE; TRADITIONAL JAZZ.

NEW ORLEANS JAZZ & HERITAGE FESTIVAL. A **festival** founded in 1968, and held annually since, that showcases many different styles of jazz.

NEW ORLEANS JAZZ CLUB. An organization established in 1948 by members and fans of the New Orleans jazz scene. The organization has published a journal titled *Second Line* since 1950.

NEW ORLEANS RHYTHM KINGS (NORK). A band formed in 1922 by George Brunies, Elmer Schoebel, and others in Chicago. The group recorded several excellent **albums** and was one of the leading bands in Chicago before disbanding in 1925.

NEW ORLEANS WANDERERS. A group formed in 1926 that included **Lil Hardin, Johnny Dodds, Kid Ory, Johnny St. Cyr**, and others. The group was formed for a two-day **recording session** and was never active again.

NEWPORT JAZZ FESTIVAL. A **jazz festival** founded in 1954 that was held annually in Newport, Rhode Island, before moving to New York from 1971. Long directed by **George Wein**, it was brought back to Newport in 1981. Many significant jazz performances occurred at the Newport festival.

NEW YORK ART QUARTET. A group founded in 1964 that was active until 1966 and performed music in the **Free Jazz** style. The group's members included Roswell Rudd, John Tchicai, Don Moore, and J. C. Moses. *See also* NEW YORK CONTEMPORARY FIVE.

NEW YORK CONTEMPORARY FIVE. A group active from 1963 to 1964 that was formed by **Don Cherry, Archie Shepp**, John Tchicai, Don Moore, and J. C. Moses. *See also* NEW YORK ART QUARTET.

NEW YORKERS. A band that was active from 1927 to 1929 that included **Dave Tough**. The group recorded and toured **Europe** and is credited with bringing **Chicago Jazz** to Europe.

NEW YORK JAZZ QUARTET. A group formed in 1972 by **Roland Hanna, Ron Carter, Billy Cobham**, and **Hubert Laws**. Later members included **Frank Wess, Ben Riley**, and **George Mraz**, and the group played together until 1982.

NEW YORK JAZZ SEXTET. A group consisting of **Art Farmer, James Moody, Albert "Tootie" Heath**, Tom McIntosh, **Tommy Flanagan**, and **Richard Davis** that recorded in the mid-1960s. The name was also used by a group led by **Roland Hanna** that eventually became the **New York Jazz Quartet**.

NEW YORK SAXOPHONE QUARTET. A group formed in 1959 that performs a mix of **French** Classical music and jazz. The group is dedicated to commissioning new works for the saxophone ensemble and performs contemporary cutting-edge music.

NICHOLAS, ALBERT (1900–1973). A clarinetist, Nicholas Albert concluded military service in 1919 and during the 1920s and 1930s had several stints working with **King Oliver**, Luis Russell, **Chick Webb**, and others before joining **Louis Armstrong** from 1937 to 1939. During the 1940s, Nicholas played with Zutty Singleton, **John Kirby, Jelly Roll Morton, Baby Dodds, Wild Bill Davison, Kid Ory, Sidney Bechet**, and others. During the 1950s, Nicholas also played with **Rex Stewart** and settled in Paris in 1953, remaining in **Europe** and touring and performing until his death.

NICHOLAS BROTHERS. The Nicholas Brothers consisted of Fayard and Harold Nicholas, a duo who worked as singers and tap dancers. The group became well known working at the **Cotton Club** during the 1930s, performing with **Cab Calloway, Duke Ellington, Jimmie Lunceford**, and others. Their career expanded to Broadway and film, but they eventually moved to **Europe** to find a more racially open-minded audience. They split briefly but later reunited and continued to appear together.

NICHOLS, ERNEST LORING "RED" (1905–1965). A cornetist and **bandleader,** Red Nichols moved to New York in the mid-1920s and worked with **Paul Whiteman,** played in Broadway orchestras, and recorded extensively with his own groups, most famously Red Nichols and His Five Pennies. Among the more famous sidemen in his group were **Miff Mole, Jimmy Dorsey, Benny Goodman, Jack Teagarden, Glenn Miller, Artie Shaw,** among others. Nichols continued to lead bands both big and small into the 1940s, and a 1959 biographical film titled *The Five Pennies* sparked a renewed interest in his career late in his life.

NIEHAUS, LENNIE (1929–). A saxophonist, composer, and arranger, Lennie Niehaus played in **Stan Kenton**'s **big band** during the 1950s, with a two-year interruption owing to military service. From the 1960s he has continued to perform but has worked mostly as a composer and arranger, writing jazz music and also music for television and film. Additionally, he works as an educator and pedagogue.

NIEWOOD, GERRY (1943–2009). A saxophonist, Gerry Niewood moved to New York and joined **Chuck Mangione**'s band from 1968 to 1976. After leaving Mangione's group, Niewood played with the **Thad Jones–Mel Lewis** Orchestra briefly before joining **Chuck Israel**'s National Jazz Ensemble in 1976. Niewood worked with **Dave Matthews** from 1977 through 1986 and appeared with **Gerry Mulligan** in 1979. During the 1980s and on, Niewood mostly led his own groups and freelanced. Niewood died in a plane crash on the way to play a concert with Mangione.

NIMMONS, PHIL(IP) RISTA (1923–). A clarinetist, composer, and **bandleader,** Phil Nimmons studied at Juilliard in the 1940s and formed a band for the Canadian Broadcasting Corporation in 1953. The band, under the names of Nimmons 'n' Nine or Nimmons 'n' Nine Plus Six, appeared frequently on Canadian television and toured widely until disbanding in 1980. Nimmons is considered one of the preeminent figures in Canadian jazz.

NISTICO, SAL(VATORE) (1940–1991). A saxophonist, Sal Nistico was a cousin of **Sammy Nestico.** Nistico played with **Rhythm and Blues (R&B)** groups before joining **Chuck Mangione**'s Gap Brothers band from 1959 to 1961. Nistico then played with **Woody Herman** from 1962 to 1965, **Count Basie** in 1965 and again in 1967, and again with Herman from 1968 to 1970. During the 1970s, Nistico appeared with **Don Ellis, Slide Hampton,** Herman, **Buddy Rich, Chuck Israel**'s National Jazz Ensemble, and others, in addition to leading his own groups. Nistico remained active in the 1980s, **recording** with **Johnny Griffin** as well as with his own groups.

NOBLE, RAY (1903–1978). A composer, arranger, and **bandleader**, Ray Noble was a staff arranger at HMV Records during the early 1930s and led the company's New Mayfair Orchestra with much success. Noble moved to the United States and led a group at the Rainbow Room in New York City that included **Glenn Miller, Claude Thornhill, Charlie Spivak**, and others from 1935 to 1937. Thereafter, Noble worked in California as a radio personality in addition to leading his own bands. Among Noble's most famous compositions is his tune "Cherokee," which was the theme song for **Charlie Barnet**'s band, the basis for **Charlie Parker**'s hit "Koko," and is also generally regarded as a measuring stick of a **Bebop** improviser's technical dexterity.

NOONE, JIMMIE (1895–1944). A clarinetist and **bandleader**, Jimmie Noone replaced **Sidney Bechet** in **Freddie Keppard**'s band from 1913 to 1914. After his time with Keppard, Noone formed the Young Olympia Band and played with **Kid Ory**. From 1917 to 1918, Noone toured with Keppard, and in 1918, Noone and **King Oliver** both moved to Chicago and played with Bill Johnson. From 1920 to 1926, Noone played with Doc Cook's Dreamland Orchestra, and from 1926 on, Noone led his own groups, which at one point included **Earl Hines** on piano. In the 1940s, Noone benefited from the revival of interest in **New Orleans Jazz** and **Dixieland**, performing and **recording** with Ory, **Jack Teagarden**, and others.

NORDSKOG. A **record label** established in 1921 in Santa Monica, it was the first company to release a record of an African-American ensemble from New Orleans. Artists included **Kid Ory**. The label went bankrupt in 1923.

NORSK JAZZFORBUND. A group founded in Norway in 1965 that helped to foster the development of jazz in that country.

NORTH SEA JAZZ FESTIVAL. A **jazz festival** held annually in The Hague since 1976 and still in existence today.

NORVO, KENNETH "RED" (1908–1999). A vibraphonist, Red Norvo played in a marimba band before being hired by **Paul Whiteman**, with whom he played until 1932. While with Whiteman, Norvo met and married Mildred Bailey, and from 1936 they co-led an orchestra in New York. In the mid-1940s, Norvo played with **Benny Goodman, Dizzy Gillespie**, and **Charlie Parker** before joining **Woody Herman** in 1946. From 1947 on, he led groups, which included at various times **Charles Mingus, Tal Farlow**, Jimmy Raney, **Dick Hyman**, and others. *See also* VIBRAPHONE.

NOTATION. The practice of writing down music for performers using established conventions. Jazz notation specifically differs from regular notation in that during improvised sections, the music does not contain written pitches for the instrumentalist to play, but rather a series of slashes with chord symbols placed above them to show the soloist the harmony that the accompaniment is playing. *See also* CHANGES; IMPROVISATION.

NOTO, SAM (1930–). A **trumpet** player, Sam Noto played with **Stan Kenton** from 1953 to 1958 and rounded out the decade with appearances with **Louie Bellson** and **Woody Herman**. During the 1960s he played with **Count Basie** in addition to leading his own groups. From 1969 to 1975, Noto worked in Las Vegas show bands, and from 1975 to 1982 he played with **Rob McConnell**'s Boss Brass. Noto has continued to lead groups and play in show bands.

NUCLEUS. A highly influential English Fusion band formed by **Ian Carr** in 1969. The group was active in the 1980s, and there have been sporadic reunions since, including 2005 and 2007.

O

OBOE. A double-reed member of the woodwind family. Not common to jazz, the oboe is used in some **Third Stream** and modern jazz compositions. Groups such as Orchestra U.S.A. and the Gil Evans Orchestra make use of the oboe in their compositions. Significant jazz oboists have included **Paul McCandless** of the jazz group **Oregon**, and Charles Pillow.

ODEON. A German **record label** founded in 1903, Odeon was acquired by several companies throughout the early 1900s and eventually ended up becoming a division of **Electrical and Musical Industries (EMI)** records. Odeon was considered to be the German division of EMI. Odeon developed a reputation for making records of various types of world music and having distribution that spread across the globe. The United States and British markets were not targets of Odeon, and most **albums** that were recorded on Odeon were distributed in the United States under the **OKeh** or **Columbia** labels that were also associated with EMI.

O'FARRILL, ARTURO "CHICO" (1921–2001). Originally from Havana, Cuba, O'Farrill studied jazz and **big band** writing in both Havana and Florida before moving to New York. In his early twenties, O'Farrill caught on both with the **Bebop** movement spearheaded by **Charlie Parker** and **Dizzy Gillespie** and with the **Afro-Cuban**, Afro-Latin movements that were sweeping the big band scene. Groups led by Gillespie, Machito, and eventually O'Farrill himself were developing big band works fusing Afro-Cuban rhythms and melodies with Bebop-style **improvisation**. O'Farrill found himself as one of the fathers of this movement and was a very popular big band composer and arranger. In the 1950s, O'Farrill's groups became a staple in New York, performing regularly until O'Farrill decided to relocate to Mexico City, Mexico.

O'Farrill's popularity did not lessen when he left the United States, and he kept busy by arranging and composing for many popular jazz players including **trumpeter Art Farmer, Count Basie, Gerry Mulligan,** and **Stan Getz**. In 1965, O'Farrill returned to the United States and New York where he would reside for many years. For the next three decades, O'Farrill would freelance as an arranger, musical director, and producer for various groups in New York. Most notably, he contributed to projects led by Jazz at Lincoln Center and Dizzy Gillespie's Dream Band, and he recorded his own band on the **album** *Pure Emotion* (1995, Milestone).

OFFBEAT. A term used to describe any rhythmic figures that do not occur on a downbeat, or the first part of the beat. Consecutive offbeats are the core of **syncopation**, which is also a very important element of the **Ragtime** style.

OGUN RECORDS. A British **record label** dedicated to **Free Jazz** and other creative music, founded in 1973. The label produced and recorded many **albums** over the next three decades by both British and South American artists. Trevor Watts, Evan Parker, and Ogun founder Harry Miller's group Isipingo all recorded on this label.

OKEH. Focusing on African-American music, Otto Heinemann founded OKeh records in 1916. Heinemann produced "Crazy Blues" by Mamie Smith in 1920, which proved to be a major hit for the label. With the release of "Crazy Blues," OKeh started the genre of race music or **race records**, which were **recordings** targeted toward African-Americans. OKeh recorded jazz and **Blues** music primarily in the 1920s and was sold to **Columbia** Records in 1926. OKeh was weakened during the Great Depression and struggled through most of the 1930s. The label would be revived during each of the next few decades, focusing on different and new genres of music. OKeh focused on **Rhythm and Blues (R&B)** during the 1940s through the mid-1960s with hits by artists like Johnny Ray and Chuck Willis until the label officially shut down in 1970. **Epic** Records issued several Rap albums under the OKeh name in the 1990s. *See also* RECORD LABEL.

OKOSHI, TORU "TIGER" (1950–). A native of Japan, Okoshi began his professional **trumpet** career performing in groups in his native country until he was 22. After becoming a U.S. citizen in 1972, he attended the **Berklee College of Music** in Boston and became quickly engulfed in the music scene there. He freelanced and toured with several artists in the late 1970s, including **Gary Burton, Buddy Rich, Dave Liebman,** and **George Russell.** Okoshi recorded several **albums** in the 1980s including *Tiger's Baku* (1981, JVC) and *Face to Face* (1989, JVC). He continued to freelance in the 1980s with artists including **Mike Stern** and **Bill Frisell** until he accepted a teaching position at his alma mater, the Berklee College of Music. *See also* JAPAN.

OLD AND NEW DREAMS. Inspired by their work with **Ornette Coleman, sidemen** from Coleman's first jazz **recordings** put together the Old and New

Dreams Quartet to perform music Coleman had written during his early **Free Jazz sessions**. Trumpeter **Don Cherry**, saxophonist **Dewey Redman**, bassist **Charlie Haden**, and drummer Ed Blackwell established the group in 1976 in honor of Coleman's music and also to celebrate acoustic music during a period in which electronics were being used by most **mainstream jazz** groups. Old and New Dreams performed well into the 1980s before disbanding except for reunion concerts.

OLIVER, JOE "KING" (1885–1938). Oliver played **trombone** professionally in bands around New Orleans in the early 1900s but did not make a splash on the scene until he switched to **cornet** in 1905. From 1905 to 1917, Oliver steadily gained popularity and became highly influential in the New Orleans dance band scene. Oliver led or co-led many of the top groups in the area and worked with musicians such as **Kid Ory** and Richard Jones. Ory is credited with giving Oliver the "King" title, a nickname that was given to trumpeters who were considered to be the top trumpet player of their time. Oliver decided to relocate to Chicago in 1918 and was influential in inspiring other musicians to follow his lead and move from New Orleans. In 1923, Oliver had assembled the first variation of his Creole Jazz Band that included **Lil Hardin**, **Louis Armstrong**, **Johnny Dodds**, and **Baby Dodds**. The Creole Jazz Band's popularity soared, and they are credited as being one of the first and most popular jazz bands on the planet. During this time, he recorded "Dippermouth Blues" (1923, Gennett), which includes one of his most famous solos.

The band enjoyed a very popular but short run until it disbanded in 1927 so that the members could pursue solo careers. Oliver relocated to New York and began to tour nationwide during the early 1930s. Due to dental problems, Oliver's playing dropped off, and despite organizing tours for his band, he did not play regularly. He had two **recording sessions**, *New York Sessions* (1930, Bluebird) and *King Oliver* (1931, Classics) that document some of his final performances. Oliver's dental problems worsened throughout the 1930s, and in 1936 he decided to permanently retire from playing. He took a job as a janitor in Georgia and remained in the position until his passing two years later. *See also* DIXIE SYNCOPATERS.

OLIVER, MELVIN JAMES "SY" (1910–1988). Oliver was born in Battle Creek, Michigan, but his family relocated to Zanesville, Ohio, where he began studying jazz. Oliver established himself first as a **trumpet** player playing with local groups, eventually touring with midwestern bands before he began to focus on arranging. The leader of one of these touring bands, Zack Whyte, is credited with giving Oliver his nickname of "Sy," which is shorthand for psychology but has no relation to Oliver. Oliver gave some of his **arrangements** to **big band** leader **Jimmie Lunceford**, who then hired him to both perform and arrange for his band. Lunceford reached his highest level of popularity while Oliver was contributing arrangements that included "My Blue Heaven" and "Organ Grinder Swing."

Oliver was lured away from Lunceford (and held off an early musical retirement) by **Tommy Dorsey,** who offered him a significant raise over what he had been earning previously. Oliver was hired as the staff arranger for Dorsey and took a several-decade hiatus from playing trumpet. Dorsey's hits "On the Sunny Side of the Street" and "Opus 1" were both penned by him. After army service and the end of the war in the 1940s, he freelanced for several decades working both as a **bandleader** and as a commission-based composer and arranger. He had one **album** of music released, *Oliver's Twist & Easy Walker* (1962, Mobile Fidelity) that featured seldom-recorded trumpeter **Charlie Shavers**. Oliver resumed trumpet playing in the 1960s and 1970s when he led his own **big band** for several years, continuing to write well into the 1980s.

OLYMPIA BRASS BAND. A New Orleans–based **brass band** established in 1962. In addition to touring and **recording** in Europe, the Olympia Brass Band was a staple in New Orleans, performing at venues such as Preservation Hall.

OLYMPIA ORCHESTRA. A dance band led by **trumpet** pioneer **Freddie Keppard** in New Orleans. The band played regularly while Keppard was in charge, but when leadership was handed off to A. J. Piron so that Keppard could further pursue his solo career, the band quickly faded and eventually disbanded. This happened despite the presence of rising jazz star **King Joe Oliver** taking over the trumpet chair for Keppard. The band was in existence from 1904 to 1914.

100 CLUB. A **club** located at 100 Oxford Street, London, that presented live jazz. The 100 Club, which also operated as the Feldman **Swing** Club during its creation in the early 1940s, featured many British jazz acts as well as touring jazz stars like **Louis Armstrong**. The club eventually gave up on jazz and focused on other styles of music, most notably Rock and more popular music.

ONWARD BRASS BAND (I). Formed in 1886 with a partner group, the Onward String Band, the Onward Brass Band was created to perform for public events such as picnics or parades. Cornetist Joseph Othello Lainez initially led the group until he developed health problems and was replaced by Manuel Perez. Perez would run the band into the 1920s, including changing the name to the Imperial Brass Band. The Onward Brass Band featured a larger instrumentation than most **brass band** groups that would follow, with 10 to 12 members.

ONWARD BRASS BAND (II). A New Orleans-based **brass band** inspired by the group with the same name that had pioneered the brass band tradition in New Orleans in the early 1900s. In 1960, Paul Barbarin organized and led the group until his death in 1969, at which time the leadership reins were giving to Louis Cottrell Jr. The group became significantly less active with the passing of Cottrell in 1978, but did perform throughout the next decade.

ONYX (I). A **record label** founded by Don Schlitten with the intention of producing **albums** of previously unreleased material from the 1940s and earlier. **Charlie Parker, Art Tatum, Charlie Shavers**, and **Teddy Edwards** were all artists who had material freshly released through the Onyx label. In 1978, two years after Onyx was created, the label merged with the **Muse** label also owned by Schlitten. Eventually both Muse and Onyx were absorbed into the Xanadu catalog.

ONYX (II). It was a nightclub in New York, in business between 1928 and the late 1940s. Founded by bootleggers during prohibition, the Onyx Club was a popular stop for **Bebop** musicians and was frequented by **Charlie Parker** and **Dizzy Gillespie**, among others. *See also* SPIRITS OF RHYTHM.

OPEN (I). A term used to inform the player to remove any **mute** or effect that is being used on their instrument.

OPEN (II). A term used in most improvised music to dictate a section of music in which there is an infinite number of measures until the section changes or the song progresses. In jazz, most sections that feature soloists are usually referred to as "open" and rely on the soloist or conductor to cue or indicate the next section. *See also* VAMP.

ORCHESTRA U.S.A. An influential **Third Stream** ensemble founded by pianist **John Lewis** in 1962. Orchestra U.S.A. was created by combining the instruments of a typical jazz **big band** with woodwind and string sections. **Gunther Schuller** and Harold Farberman contributed **arrangements**, as did other rising composers such as **Benny Golson, Jimmy Giuffre**, and Gary McFarland. The group only lasted three years but recorded several times.

OREGON. A jazz group established in 1970 that focused on playing creative improvised music that was influenced by many genres. Each member played more than one instrument, and the group performed works that ranged in style from Classical chamber works to jazz quartet pieces. Reedist **Paul McCandless**, bassist Glen Moore, guitarist and multi-instrumentalist Ralph Towner, and percussionist Collin Walcott created Oregon after all had previous worked as part of the Paul Winter Consort. Oregon continued to play off and on again for the next three decades and recorded several **albums**.

ORGAN. An instrument that is similar to the **piano** in terms of setup and key placement but is sounded by air traveling through pipes to achieve a deep ringing effect. The organ was originally created in the early 1600s and was only built in churches that could not only handle the size of the massive instrument but were also sympathetic to the acoustics necessary to handle the big sound. The traditional pipe organ is almost never used in jazz, but several of its variations have become commonplace including the **Hammond** B3 organ. The Hammond B3 organ was made famous in the early 1960s by keyboardists **Jimmy Smith** and **Lonnie Smith** because of its unique sound and the ability of the player to also walk bass lines in addition to accompanying or soloing. Famous **Hammond** B3 **recordings** include *Back at the Chicken Shack* (**Blue Note**, 1960).

ORIGINAL CREOLE BAND. One of the first touring jazz bands, the Original Creole Band formed in 1908 to tour Los Angeles and other cities in Southern California and Arizona. The group started with five members but over the next several years included more instruments and toured extensively in Chicago and the eastern coast of the United States. **Trumpet** player **Freddie Keppard** was asked to tour with the band and left his own group, the **Olympia Orchestra**, in 1914 to pursue an opportunity to tour and play with the Original Creole Band. Keppard proved to be an important member of the band and had the final say when the band was offered a record deal to sign with **Victor** in 1916. Due to fears that people would "steal" his style, Keppard declined the record contract, which would have made the Original Creole Band the first jazz group to record an **album**. After five years of touring, the group stopped in 1917. Different variations of the group popped up in both New York and Chicago, with the Chicago version still featuring Keppard until his chair was passed along to **Joe "King" Oliver**.

ORIGINAL DIXIELAND JAZZ BAND. An all-White jazz group that is credited with making the first jazz **recording**, which took place in 1917 for **Victor** Records. The Original Dixieland Jazz Band was made up of five Chicago-based musicians: cornetist **Nick LaRocca**, clarinetist **Larry Shields**, trombonist Eddie Edwards, drummer Tony Sbarbaro, and pianist Henry Ragas. Their initial recording sold incredibly well, and their popularity was very high for a few years until other groups were able to record and develop similar followings. There is some controversy with the Original Dixieland Jazz Band in that the group proclaimed that they were vital toward the creation of **New Orleans Jazz** and were often at odds with African-American musicians who did not receive equal credit for their work in the development of the style. The group was inducted into the Grammy Hall of Fame in 2006.

ORIGINAL MEMPHIS FIVE. A **Traditional Jazz** group founded in 1917. Led by **trumpeter** Phil Napoleon and pianist Frank Signorelli, the group played on and off for several decades and into the 1950s. The group was very popular in the 1920s and recorded many times in addition to playing regularly in New York. Programming was especially important to the group, and often their performances were very carefully planned out. The name "Original Memphis Five" was used as a generic name for groups led by both Napoleon and Signorelli in the 1950s when the original group performed sparingly.

ORIGINAL NEW ORLEANS JAZZ BAND (I). The first group to use the name "Original New Orleans Jazz Band" was led by trombonist and **trumpet** player Merritt Brunies. No **recordings** were made of this group, and they only played together for two years, from 1916 to 1918, before disbanding.

ORIGINAL NEW ORLEANS JAZZ BAND (II). The second group to use the title "Original New Orleans Jazz Band" was more successful than the first. Pianist Jimmy Durante formed the second version of this group in 1918 with the intention of presenting material similar to the **Original Dixieland Jazz Band**. The group had two **recording sessions,** *Ole Miss/Ja-Da* (1918, **OKeh**) and *Ja-Da/He's Had No Lovin' for a Long Time* (1919, Gennett). Durante ditched the moniker "Original New Orleans Jazz Band" in 1920 and continued to run the group under his own name. *See also* EARLY JAZZ; TRADITIONAL JAZZ.

ORIGINAL NIGHTHAWK ORCHESTRA. A **Traditional Jazz** group led by Carleton Coon and Joe Sanders in the 1920s. The Original Nighthawk Orchestra is considered an abbreviated version of the group's original name, the Coon-Sanders Original Nighthawk Orchestra.

ORIGINAL TEDDIES. A **Swing** band formed in Switzerland by Teddy Stauffer in 1929. The group did not perform regularly throughout the 1930s but did find steady work in 1939 and again in 1941 when **sideman** Eddie Brunner took charge.

ORIGINAL TUXEDO ORCHESTRA. Another name for the Tuxedo Brass Band, the Original Tuxedo Orchestra was founded in New Orleans as both a **brass band** and dance orchestra in 1917. Co-led by Papa Celestin and trombonist William Ridgley, the group performed regularly at the Tuxedo Dance Hall in New Orleans before breaking up in 1925. Celestin continued to record **albums** under the name "Tuxedo Jazz Orchestra" into the late 1920s and early 1930s.

ORIOLE (I). A short-lived **record label** in the 1920s that was sold exclusively by McCrory's department stores and quickly sold to the **Plaza** group. Plaza used the Oriole label to distribute records that it otherwise would not have. When Plaza was purchased by the **American Record Company**, it became a dime-store label until its termination in 1938.

ORIOLE (II). A London-based **record label** that primarily issued **race records**. Oriole drew from the catalogs of **Vocalion**, Ultraphon, and later the **Mercury** label. Artists to have records distributed by the Oriole label include Adelaide Hall, Joe Turner, and **trumpet** player Freddy Taylor. Oriole also distributed reissues of 1940s and 1950s records originally recorded by **Savoy** records.

ORQUESTA CUBANA DE MÚSICA MODERNA. A predecessor to the **Afro-Cuban** supergroup **Irakere**, Orquesta Cubana de Música Moderna was created in 1967. **Paquito D'Rivera, Arturo Sandoval**, and **Chucho Valdés** led the group until 1973 when the same members pursued a new direction and formed Irakere.

ØRSTED PEDERSEN, NIELS-HENNING (1946–2005). Pedersen was born in Denmark and played music at a young age. He first took up **piano** but changed to the acoustic **bass** in his early teens. At the age of 14 he was playing bass at a high level, which led him to **recording** as a professional and performing with local bands. Pedersen was hired by the famous Montmartre Club in Copenhagen, where he served as an important member of the house band. Almost every touring musician who visited the club used Pedersen, and he quickly developed a sterling reputation among American jazz musicians. Pedersen was used by many pianists and had short touring stints with jazz legends **Bill Evans** in the 1960s and **Oscar Peterson** in the 1970s and 1980s. Pedersen had famously turned down an opportunity to serve as **Count Basie**'s bassist to continue to work as the Montmatre Club bassist.

Pedersen's career included working with **Straight-Ahead** jazz musicians such as **Kenny Dorham** and **Dexter Gordon**, but he also spent time working with artists affiliated with the **Avant-Garde** and **Free Jazz** movements, including **Albert Ayler, Archie Shepp,** and **Anthony Braxton**. Pedersen recorded a few live **albums** for the **SteepleChase** label in the 1970s but primarily worked as a **sideman**. In 1991, Pedersen was awarded the Nordisk Rads Musikpris for a lifetime of excellence. Pedersen succumbed to heart failure in 2005.

ORY, EDWARD "KID" (1886–1973). Ory was raised in the Louisiana countryside and moved to New Orleans in the early 1910s to pursue a musical career on **trombone** and **banjo**. Much of Ory's success was built on his trombone playing and his ability to lead a band. Up until 1919, many of Ory's bands were considered to be the finest **dance bands** and **Swing** bands in New Orleans, and many famous musicians worked in his groups, including trumpeters **Joe "King" Oliver** and **Louis Armstrong**. Ory relocated to California, commuting between San Francisco and Los Angeles where he continued to lead and perform in dance bands. Several trips were made to perform and record in Chicago with many of jazz's top groups, including King Oliver's Creole Jazz Band and Louis Armstrong's **Hot Five**. In the 1930s, Ory tired of the business and retired to pursue other interests.

During World War II, he regained an interest in playing and landed a performance opportunity on the Orson Welles radio broadcasts. Ory led his own **Traditional Jazz** and **Dixieland** groups in the 1940s and 1950s, touring the United States and sometimes overseas. In 1966, Ory had a change of heart again and decided to retire once more. After retiring, he moved to Hawaii where he lived for the remainder of his life. Ory was important to jazz as an ambassador and a **bandleader**, and he was one of the first and most influential trombonists of the Swing era.

OSTINATO. A repeated figure, rhythmically, melodically, or harmonically, that occurs while other elements of a composition are changing. Ostinatos are usually seen in jazz as alternatives to improvised **comping** during a **solo** section.

OUT CHORUS. A term to cue or alert performers that the last chorus of a given section is or is about to take place.

OUTSIDE. A slang term used to describe when a soloist elects to improvise outside of a song's harmonic movement. Much of the music categorized as **Free Jazz** as well as much modern music features **improvisation** that moves outside the harmonic framework of the piece.

OWENS, JIMMY (1943–). A New York native, Owens took up the **trumpet** at the age of 10 and studied with jazz trumpeter **Donald Byrd** and

Classical trumpet technician Carmine Caruso. Owens began playing professionally in New York–based bands led by **Thad Jones**, **Slide Hampton**, **Maynard Ferguson**, and **Gerry Mulligan**, all before his 24th birthday. During the late 1960s and early 1970s, Owens added short stints with **Duke Ellington**, **Count Basie**, **Billy Taylor**, and **Billy Cobham**. The Collective Black Artists was co-founded by Owens in 1969 before he pursued a degree in business administration from the University of Massachusetts. Owens was a major contributor to the Jazzmobile program that was put on in the 1970s. As a teacher, Owens has served on faculty for several schools, including Oberlin University and in the Jazz and Contemporary Music Program at the New School in New York.

OWL. A French **record label** that was founded in 1975. Owl focused on producing new **recordings** of jazz artists such as **Lee Konitz**, **Gil Evans**, **Dave Liebman**, and **Steve Lacy**.

OZONE, MAKOTO (1961–). Ozone was born in Kobe, Japan, and took up the **piano** at a very young age. When Ozone turned 12, he became enamored with the playing of **Oscar Peterson** after witnessing a live concert and began to transcribe Peterson's solos. At the age of 19, Ozone moved to Boston, Massachusetts, to attend the prestigious **Berklee College of Music**. Ozone was quickly welcomed into the jazz scene for performance opportunities with artists such as **Gary Burton** and Phil Wilson, and by 1982 he was already a faculty member for the school. *Makoto Ozone* (1981, **Columbia**) was Ozone's first **album**, recorded after his first year at Berklee, and was produced by Gary Burton. Throughout the 1980s, Ozone would tour, often in a trio format in addition to doing some freelancing with other artists like Burton.

Ozone faced work permit problems in 1989 and moved back to Japan where he immediately signed a deal with the JVC **record label**. Ozone would continue to perform short tours and festival dates in the United States during the 1990s in addition to **recording** albums for **Verve** and JVC. During this time, Ozone also displayed his appreciation for Classical music and performed Classical works in both solo piano and symphony settings. In the 2000s, Ozone continued to add to his discography by continuing to put out well-reviewed albums, bringing his total output to 32 recordings while continuing to tour the world in both jazz and Classical settings. *See also* JAPAN.

P

PABLO. Founded by jazz producer **Norman Granz** in 1973, Pablo Records was a very successful **record label** with two additional divisions: Pablo Live and Pablo Today. Granz lined up musicians with whom he had previously worked during his association with the **Verve** label. Included among these artists were **Oscar Peterson** and **Ella Fitzgerald**. The Pablo Live label distributed many **albums** recorded at the **Montreux International Jazz Festival**. Pablo Records was successful into the 1980s and was active in reissuing albums from companies previously affiliated with Granz. Pablo was purchased by **Fantasy** records in the late 1980s and was reprinted as part of the Original Jazz Classics series.

PACIFIC. A **record label** started in Los Angeles, Pacific Jazz became an important label for **recording** and preserving the beginnings of the **West Coast Jazz** style. The founder of Pacific Jazz, Richard Bock, did an exceptional job at locating talent and was the first to record solo **albums** for artists like **Chet Baker, Jim Hall, Art Pepper, Joe Pass,** and **Wes Montgomery**. Bock expanded the label to include world music in 1958, but this was not as successful as his previous jazz ventures. As jazz became less popular, Bock sold the label to **Liberty** Records in 1965. The label was passed from Liberty to **Electrical and Musical Industries (EMI)** to **Capitol** and eventually ended up in the hands of **Blue Note** Records in the 1990s. Many of the albums were reissued through Blue Note. *See also* RECORD LABEL.

PAGE, ORAN THADDEUS "HOT LIPS" (1908–1954). Page tried several instruments before deciding on the **trumpet** at the age of 12. During his late teenage years, Page began performing with bands in his native Texas before catching on with touring acts booked through the Theater Owners Booking Association. His first big break took place when he was hired for **Walter Page**'s Blue Devils, although prior bands he played with featured famous singers **Bessie Smith** and **Ma Rainey**. In 1930, Page began performing with a **big band** led by **Bennie Moten** in Kansas City for three years until he left to join a band led by Moten's pianist, **Count Basie**. Page's time with Basie lasted about a year before he returned to Kansas City to resume playing with

Moten's group. Page left Moten again in 1936 to pursue what was to be an unsuccessful solo career.

Artie Shaw hired Page to perform as a trumpet soloist and singer for his big band in 1941, but the relationship lasted only a few months due in part to the racial bias Shaw experienced for hiring an African-American musician. Eddie Condon, Page's next employer, experienced a similar bias when he recruited Page for his band. For the remainder of his career, Page would never remain with one band or group for very long. He maintained a solo career working as a guest soloist with groups in **Europe** in addition to working with American groups led by **Don Redman** and Pearl Bailey. Page's style was credited as being highly bluesy and is considered to be one of the leading voices for the development of the **Rhythm and Blues** style.

PAGE, WALTER SYLVESTER (1900–1957). Born in Missouri, Page was considered to be a vital contributor to the **bass** during the **Swing** era, further developing the **walking bass** style that was taking place during that era. Page performed mostly in Kansas City for his whole musical career. He played with **Bennie Moten** during the early 1920s until he started his own band, the **Blue Devils**. The Blue Devils and Moten's band were competitors in the Kansas City area, and oftentimes Moten would lure players from the Blue Devils to join his band. Eventually both bands folded, and Page was asked to serve as bassist for **Count Basie's big band,** becoming one of the members of what was to be known as the "All American Rhythm Section," along with guitarist **Freddie Green**, drummer Jo Jones, and Basie. Page remained with Basie for the remainder of his career and until his death in 1957. *See also* JONES-SMITH INC.

PAICH, MARTY (1925–1995). Beginning his jazz career as a pianist, Paich enlisted in the military at the age of 18 and became a staff arranger for the Air Force Band. After being released in 1946, Paich went on to continue studying arranging at the Los Angeles Conservatory of Music and Arts. Paich's career would be a combination of playing piano, composing, and arranging music, music that was often at the forefront of the **West Coast Jazz** scene. Throughout the 1950s, Paich wrote for groups led by **Shelly Manne, Shorty Rogers**, Peggy Lee, **Mel Tormé**, and most notably for **Art Pepper** on the **album** *Modern Jazz Classics* (1959, Original Jazz Classics). Paich recorded several albums under his own name, some of them featuring his **arrangements** such as the album *I Get a Boot Out of You* (1959, Warner Bros.) and others featuring his piano playing such as *Marty Paich Trio* (1957, V.S.O.P.).

Paich arranged for many singers throughout the 1960s and 1970s, including **recording** dates for **Ella Fitzgerald**, Sammy Davis Jr., **Sarah Vaughan**, and

Ray Charles. Often Paich also served as conductor for these dates, and he developed a sterling reputation as a top jazz conductor. Paich eventually began to move away from jazz dates and wrote music for movies and television.

PALO ALTO. Based in the California city with the same name, Palo Alto Records began in 1981 and existed for four years before the **record label** shut down. Created to make new **recordings** of San Francisco area musicians, Palo Alto made several successful records during its short existence. San Francisco–based jazz historian Herb Wong was an influential member of the company and helped determine which artists should be recorded.

PALOMAR BALLROOM. A famous venue in Los Angeles that was home to many local bands in addition to being a popular venue for touring acts. It was also the site of the **Benny Goodman** Orchestra's hugely successful appearance with his band in 1938. The Palomar was destroyed by a fire in late 1939.

PANACHORD. A British-based **record label** that issued **albums** similar to the U.S.-based **Melotone**. Panachord was founded in 1931 and was used primarily for distribution rather than **recording**. Recordings from **Decca**, **Brunswick**, and the **American Record Company** were distributed by Panachord during its existence. A subsidiary of Panachord in Denmark released albums recorded by Dutch Decca, many of which were jazz recordings of American artists who had relocated to **Europe**. Panachord was discontinued in 1939.

PARADOX. A **record label** founded in New York that was in existence for four years, from 1948 to 1952. The majority of Paradox's **recordings** were of **Traditional Jazz** artists and were acquired by the Chimes Music Shop label and eventually the **Jazztone** label to be presented as reissues.

PARAMOUNT. A Wisconsin-based **record label** that served as the primary distributor for New York Recording Laboratories. Paramount began releasing **race records** during a 10-year period from 1922 to 1932 before the company closed its doors after collaborating with the **American Record Corporation** and **Plaza**. Artists who had records on Paramount include Blind Lemon Jefferson, **Ma Rainey**, **King Oliver**, **Fletcher Henderson**, and the Original Memphis Five.

PARAMOUNTORKESTERN. A highly influential **Traditional Jazz** group from Sweden that was formed in 1926. Swedish violinist Folke Andersson founded the group and helped them make approximately 100 records before breaking up in 1930.

PARAPHERNALIA. A jazz quintet founded in Great Britain by baritone saxophonist Barbara Thompson, made up of violinist Billy Thompson, pianist Peter Lerner, bassist Dave Ball, and drummer Jon Hiseman. *See also* ENGLAND.

PARIS, JACKIE (1926–2004). Paris got his start performing as a dancer and a singer as a teenager in New York before his jazz career took a brief hiatus due to a stint in the military during World War II. Paris's career took off after his return from the army in 1946, and during the next 10 years he toured and recorded with many of the leading jazz artists of the time including **Charlie Parker** and **Lionel Hampton**. His career as a jazz **sideman** was never truly fulfilled, and often he was booked as a lounge singer in resorts instead of in jazz clubs. Despite continuing to record with other mainstream jazz artists such as **Charles Mingus** and **Donald Byrd** in the 1950s and 1960s, Paris' career was mostly of the crooner variety, and the majority of his **recordings** were **ballads**.

PARKER, CHARLIE "BIRD" (1920–1955). One of the most influential jazz musicians of all time, alto saxophonist Parker became a seminal figure in the creation and history of **Bebop**. Born in Kansas City, Parker took up the **alto saxophone** at the age of 11 and began playing locally, absorbing much from the touring musicians who originated in the city, including **Count Basie**. **Bandleader** Jay McShann hired Parker in the late 1930s for a brief period, and after a tour to New York, Parker decided to relocate there. During the early part of the 1940s, Parker played in impromptu **jam sessions** that included future stars **Dizzy Gillespie** and **Thelonious Monk**.

Recording was banned in 1942 for two years due to complications with the musicians union, which prohibited the early days of Bebop from being recorded. However, shortly after the ban was lifted, Gillespie and Parker became very active in recording. Throughout the next few years, Parker would dominate the jazz scene, leading many different quintets through the 1940s and early 1950s. Parker's playing was incredibly fast and creative, a perfect match for the Bebop style.

Many of Parker's groups included future jazz stars including **Max Roach**, **Miles Davis**, **Kenny Dorham**, **Bud Powell**, and **Chet Baker**. Parker dealt with extreme addiction problems that resulted in him taking several breaks from playing as well as a stint in prison. Parker died at the age of 35 from a variety of symptoms, the majority of which were tied to his heroin addiction. Parker's influence was enormous, and most saxophonists (especially alto saxophonists) who followed were largely indebted to his style. *See also* IMPROVISATION; MINTON'S PLAYHOUSE.

PARKER, LEO (1925–1962). Initially an alto saxophonist, Parker was already a consummate performer, **recording** with **Coleman Hawkins** at the age of 19. In order to maintain a steady **gig** with vocalist **Billy Eckstine**, he switched to **baritone saxophone**. This change of instrument proved vital to Parker's career, and he became one of the leading voices on the instrument. Throughout the 1940s, he played with **Bebop** disciples **Charlie Parker** and **Dizzy Gillespie** in addition to being a regular performer with groups led by **Illinois Jacquet**. Before Parker died, he was signed by **Blue Note** and released several records for the label including *Let Me Tell You 'bout It* (1961, Blue Note) and *Rollin' with Leo* (1961, Blue Note). *See also* SAXOPHONE.

PARLOPHONE. A British **record label** that primarily reissued or released **albums** recorded on the Lindstrom and **OKeh** labels beginning in the 1920s. Parlophone presented several series of **recordings** in 1929 and 1932 that were specifically for jazz called the New Rhythm Style Series. After 1934, Parlophone also used records from the **American Record Company** and **Brunswick**. **Electrical and Musical Industries (EMI)** records acquired the company in 1931 and began distribution of Parlophone Records in other countries including Eastern **Europe** and Australia. Parlaphone was used until the 1960s to distribute albums recorded on other labels until jazz was deemed to be no longer profitable. *See also* ENGLAND.

PASS, JOE (1929–1994). Pass was a standout guitarist while still in high school after beginning a professional career at the age of 13. After being offered several jobs, he dropped out of school to pursue work as a professional musician but wasn't ready to handle the 1940s jazz scene. Pass succumbed to heroin addiction for almost a decade, and his inability to stay clean resulted in him bouncing between prisons and rehabilitation centers. His flawless technique and approach to **improvisation** were not lost during this period, and in the early 1960s, after managing to break his addiction, he was signed to the **Blue Note** label, **recording** both *The Complete "Catch Me" Sessions* (1963, Blue Note) and *Joy Spring* (1964, Blue Note).

Pass became very popular for the duration of the 1960s and 1970s, both as a **sideman** and leader. Accompanying artists like **Sarah Vaughan** and **Ella Fitzgerald** in addition to becoming a steady performer in **Oscar Peterson**'s groups, Pass became one of the most influential guitarists of his time. Pass, like his protégé **Stanley Jordan**, was a prodigious finger picker and was able to maximize his ability to perform as a soloist with no accompaniment. The record label **Pablo** signed Pass and released records that were considered to be some of the most important jazz **guitar albums** ever made, including *Virtuoso, Volume 1* (1973, Pablo) and *We'll Be Together Again* (1983, Pablo).

Pass' record output from 1975 to 1990 included over 20 live concert albums in **solo**, duet, quartet, and quintet settings. Pass continued to tour until he died. His legacy lives on with his many recordings and a wealth of instructional materials that cover his famous technique and his advanced improvisational material.

PASSPORT. A German jazz quartet that was one the first European groups to catch on to the Fusion and **Jazz Rock** phase that had transpired in the United States. Passport was founded by Klaus Doldinger in 1970, although it did not formally go by the name "Passport" until a year later. The group had success during the 1970s playing in Germany and also touring overseas. Passport went through a style transformation in the 1980s that focused more on Pop styles than **improvisation**.

PASTORIUS, JACO (1951–1987). Born in Norristown, Pennsylvania, Pastorius made his mark on the modern music scene through the fretless **electric bass**. In the early 1970s, Pastorius received his first break when he was hired to be the **bass** player with **Fusion** supergroup Weather Report. Using the group as a launching pad to display his highly developed bass technique, Pastorius was hired by several other major musical artists including vocalist Joni Mitchell, Rock group **Blood, Sweat and Tears**, and Jazz **Fusion** guitarist **Pat Metheny**. Pastorius also recorded a self-titled **album** *Jaco Pastorius* (1975, **Epic**) that received wide acclaim.

Pastorius continued to freelance into the 1980s while also starting his own band, Word Of Mouth, which recorded the self-titled album *Word Of Mouth* (1981, Warner Bros.). A variety of problems, including drug addiction, set Pastorius back during the middle portion of the decade and led to his early death. Beaten outside of a nightclub in Fort Lauderdale, Florida, Pastorius never recovered from the head wounds he suffered.

PAYNE, BENJAMIN "BENNIE" (1907–1986). Payne was a pianist and vocalist who began his career in his native city of Philadelphia at the age of 19. After receiving tutelage from the great pianist **Fats Waller**, Payne toured and played with various musical revues across the United States and **Europe**. In 1931, Payne was hired by **Cab Calloway**, a musical relationship that would last over a decade. Payne was included on many of Calloway's **recordings** and movie appearances. After completing some military service, Payne did little work as a **sideman** and instead focused on becoming a **leader** of his own group. Payne relocated to the Los Angeles area in the 1950s where he continued his own groups in addition to continuing work as a pianist and musical director for revues and cabaret shows.

PAYNE, CECIL McKENZIE (1922–2007). Payne's musical career took its first big steps at the age of 21 when he enlisted in the military. Payne played **clarinet** with military bands but was quick to change back to the **saxophone** upon his discharge in 1946. Early in his career, Payne played both **alto** and **baritone saxophones** and was hired to do both by many of jazz's leading artists. **J. J. Johnson** hired him to record on alto, while his baritone saxophone playing was featured in groups led by Clarence Briggs, **Dizzy Gillespie**, and **James Moody**. In the 1950s, Payne primarily freelanced but also toured with several groups including tenor saxophonist **Illinois Jacquet**. He recorded his first two **albums** as a **leader**, *Patterns* (1956, Savoy) and *Night at the Five Spot* (1957, Signal), during this decade. In addition to his work as a saxophonist, Payne assisted his father in running the family's real estate business.

Payne continued to be a very active **sideman** throughout the 1960s and performed with **Kenny Drew**, Machito, **Lionel Hampton**, **Randy Weston**, **Woody Herman**, and **Count Basie**. The next decade was a defining one for Payne as he began to lead more of his own groups, **recording** two albums for the Muse label in addition to touring with **Benny Carter** and fellow baritone saxophonist Nick Brignola. During the 1980s, Payne was a featured member of many tribute groups including **Dameronia**, a reunion **big band** led by Illinois Jacquet and Dizzy Gillespie. Payne shared his vast experience with the next generation of jazz musicians by starting the group Bebop Generation in the 1990s that featured veteran, established musicians, as well as up-and-coming ones, such as Eric Alexander and Joe Farnsworth. Payne would continue to be a leader and sideman over the course of the next two decades until his death.

PAYNE, PERCIVAL "SONNY" (1926–1979). Beginning his career at the age of 18 working as a **drum set** player with musicians such as **Hot Lips Page** and Earl Bostic, Payne's popularity quickly caught on in his hometown of New York City. Throughout the 1940s he would record and tour with many groups including those led by Erskine Hawkins, Earl Bostic, and Tiny Grimes. Payne's defining moment came in 1955 when he was hired to fill in for **Gus Johnson** in **Count Basie**'s **big band**. He would perform with Basie's group off and on for the next two decades and would also appear on many of Basie's most popular **albums**, including *April in Paris* (1956, Verve) and *Atomic Mr. Basie* (1957, Roulette). Despite a brief sabbatical to perform with **Frank Sinatra** in the mid-1960s, Payne served as Basie's primary drummer until he took over the drum chair in Harry James' big band. Before his death, Payne had one more go-round with Basie's band before finishing his career with James.

PAZ. An English **Fusion** group founded by vibraphonist Dick Crouch in 1972. Paz made use of electronic instruments as well as a broad use of eclectic percussion. **Albums** recorded by the group Paz include *Look Inside* (1983, Paladin) and *Dancing in the Park* (1997, Turret).

PEACOCK, GARY (1935–). Peacock began as a pianist in various elementary and secondary schools that he attended while his family moved across the northwestern United States. At the age of 19, he joined the army and performed in various military bands until an accident caused the band's **bass** player to lose the ability to walk. Peacock began studying the bass and made it his instrument of choice. After being discharged, Peacock moved to Los Angeles and was hired by musicians **Bud Shank, Art Pepper, Dexter Gordon**, and **Harold Land**. After moving to New York in 1962, Peacock's popularity soared, and he was highly in demand by many of the cutting-edge **Free Jazz** musicians including **Paul Motian, Albert Ayler, Don Cherry,** and **Archie Shepp**.

Peacock suffered from several health problems in the mid-1960s that caused him to play significantly less than he had previously. Until 1977, Peacock played sparingly and used the time to study Eastern religion and biology. The year 1977 was important for Peacock as he recorded his first two solo **albums** on **ECM**, *Tales of Another* (1977, **ECM**) and *December Poems* (1977, ECM). *Tales of Another* was a significant album in that it marked the first **recording** of what would become the **Keith Jarrett** trio, featuring pianist Jarrett and drummer **Jack DeJohnette**. This trio would begin to tour steadily from 1983 throughout the next several decades, recording many times on the ECM label under Jarrett's name. Peacock continues to freelance with former bandmates Motian and **Paul Bley** in addition to teaching and offering workshops on meditation.

PEACOCK'S PROGRESSIVE JAZZ. A division of the Houston-based Peacock **record label** dedicated to **recording** jazz **albums**. Peacock's Progressive Jazz was not a success and was only in existence from 1958 to 1959. **Betty Carter** and Sonny Criss recorded the only two albums to be released on the label.

PEPPER, HUR EDWARD "ART" (1925–1982). Born in California, Pepper's professional **alto saxophone** career began in the early 1950s when he was hired by **bandleader Stan Kenton**. After spending several years on tour, Pepper left the band to begin a solo career that resulted in many acclaimed records toward the end of the 1950s. These **recordings** featured **sidemen** including **Gerry Mulligan, Paul Chambers**, and Red Garland. Dealing with drug addiction, Pepper faced both the legal and the health problems that commonly follow, and several years of his career involved little to no music. In the late 1960s, Pepper experimented with playing the tenor saxophone before being hired to play alto again with **Buddy Rich**. Pepper regained a lot of his popularity toward the end of the 1970s, working in self-led groups until his death in 1982.

PERFECT. A division of the American Pathe **record label**. Perfect was established to sell similar records to what was being released on American Pathe, but for a cheaper cost. American Pathe was purchased by the American Record Corporation, and Perfect was converted into a dime-store label until it was discontinued in 1938.

PERKINS, BILL (1924–2003). After moving to Santa Barbara from Chile, Perkins took up the **clarinet** and **piano** while still a teenager. He soon switched to **tenor saxophone** and began studying the instrument seriously after a military stint during World War II. His career took off in the late 1940s when he was hired by several Los Angeles area bands including groups led by Jerry Wald and **Woody Herman**. He was highly influenced by **Lester Young** and was one of the leading voices in **West Coast Jazz**. In 1953, Perkins began an on-and-off-again working relationship with **Stan Kenton** and remained an important soloist for the group until 1959. He expanded his skill set to include composition, arranging, and working as a **recording** engineer. During the 1960s he served in all of these capacities, both with his own groups and other projects with which he was involved.

In 1968, Perkins was hired by **Doc Severinsen** to play **baritone saxophone** in the NBC *Tonight Show* band. Perkins would be affiliated with the band until Doc Severinsen's band was replaced in 1992. During this period, he would regularly freelance with many small groups in California including groups led by **Shorty Rogers**, Frank Strazzeri, James Clay, and **Bud Shank**. Perkins died in 2003 due to complications with cancer. *See also* BIG BAND.

PERSIP, CHARLIE "CHARLI" (1929–). Persip grew up in New Jersey where he learned to play the **drum set**. At the age of 24, Persip was given an opportunity to play with **Tadd Dameron**, which very quickly gained him recognition that resulted in a touring and **recording** opportunity with **Dizzy Gillespie**. Persip was Gillespie's drummer for five years and was featured on several recordings including the Gillespie classic *Sonny Side Up* (1957, **Verve**). Persip started his own solo career in the late 1950s, recording *Charli Persip and the Jazz Statesmen* (1960, WEA), which featured a young **Freddie Hubbard**.

Throughout the 1960s, Persip continued to lead his own groups while also playing with groups led by **Gil Evans**, **Gene Ammons**, and **Don Ellis**. Persip was an important member of the group that started the Jazzmobile in New York. He played well in many styles. In the late 1960s, he toured with singer **Billy Eckstine**, and in the 1970s he played with **Free Jazz** pioneers **Archie Shepp** and **Rahsaan Roland Kirk**. Persip continued to freelance throughout the 1980s and 1990s and also became more involved in education when he was hired as a faculty member for the Jazz and Contemporary Music Program at the New School in New York City.

PETERSON, OSCAR (1925–2007). A very influential jazz musician, Canadian-born Oscar Peterson was a prodigious pianist as a youth, winning many competitions. He was influenced by many of the **Stride** and **Swing** pianists and worked professionally in Canada before being recruited to participate in **Jazz at the Philharmonic (JATP)** groups in the late 1940s. For most of the 1950s, Peterson combined working with JATP and leading his own trios, which received great acclaim. Peterson's groups during this time frequently used **guitar** in the place of drums, although toward the end of the 1950s, Peterson returned to using a drummer, most frequently Ed Thigpen.

Peterson continued to lead trios in the 1960s and 1970s while also appearing on other **recordings** as a **sideman**. During this time, Peterson recorded with many jazz legends including **Joe Pass**, **Dizzy Gillespie**, **Clark Terry**, and Sam Jones. Peterson is often credited with having an especially strong and functional left hand, the mark of a great pianist. He worked steadily in the 1980s but was halted after suffering a stroke in the early 1990s. While Peterson resumed his career afterwards, the stroke caused some physical damage, and Peterson's flashy and strong technique was never the same. Peterson remained active performing and touring until his death in 2007.

PETIT, BUDDY (1895–1931). Petit (born Joseph Crawford) was a Louisiana native who made a career both as a **bandleader** and **cornet** player in the New Orleans area. Petit started the Young Olympians and was also **Freddie Keppard**'s replacement in the Young Olympia Band. Despite touring with many leading jazz musicians of the 1910s and 1920s, like **Jelly Roll Morton** and **Sidney Bechet**, no **recordings** exist of Petit. Passing away at an early age, the mystery about Petit's musical ability and technique has added to his legacy.

PETRUCCIANI, MICHEL (1962–1999). Born into a family of jazz musicians, Petrucciani decided to take up **piano** at the age of four instead of **guitar** or **drums** like the others in his family. Petrucciani grew up in **France**, and his career blossomed at a young age; he was featured in concerts with **Kenny Clarke** and **Clark Terry** before turning 18. Petrucciani's popularity grew, and he toured with **Lee Konitz** and **Charles Lloyd** before his own solo career took off. Throughout the 1980s, Petrucciani led a trio that included Jean-Francois Jenny-Clark, Aldo Romano, Palle Danielson, Eliot Zigmund, Andy McKee, and **Gary Peacock**. Petrucciani was included as a **sideman** in a group featuring **Jim Hall** and **Wayne Shorter** at the **Montreux Jazz Festival**.

In the 1990s, Petrucciani relocated to New York and continued to record. Several of Petrucciani's most popular **albums** include *Power of Three* (1986, Blue Note) and *Pianism* (1985, Blue Note). Petrucciani suffered from osteogenesis imperfecta, which contributed (along with a serious bout of pneumonia) to his early passing.

PETTIFORD, OSCAR (1922–1960). Pettiford was born into a very successful musical family where he learned to play many instruments until he settled on the double **bass**. At the age of 20, Pettiford was hired by **Charlie Barnet**. Pettiford stayed with Barnet for one year during which the group visited New York. Pettiford decided to permanently relocate there. **Clubs** such as **Minton's Playhouse** and the **Onyx** Club became major hot spots for the emerging jazz scene, and Pettiford worked quickly to start playing in both venues with artists like **Thelonious Monk, Budd Johnson, Dizzy Gillespie, Roy Eldridge**, and **Lester Young**. Pettiford became **Coleman Hawkins'** bass player of choice and was called to tour with Hawkins on the West Coast. From the mid-1940s to the beginning of the next decade, Pettiford continued to work with a who's who of emerging and established musicians, including **Duke Ellington, J. C. Heard, George Shearing, Fats Navarro, Dexter Gordon**, and **Bud Powell**.

After suffering a serious arm injury, Pettiford spent time learning the cello, which he pioneered as a jazz instrument. After spending a year to recover from his broken arm, Pettiford regained his original form and picked up touring with the finest jazz musicians. During the 1950s, Pettiford recorded and toured with **Horace Silver, Kenny Clarke, Phineas Newborn, Charlie Shavers**, and **Cannonball Adderley**. Pettiford garnered several record deals during this time and recorded many classic **albums** for the **Bethlehem** label that include *Another One* (1955, Bethlehem) and *Oscar Pettiford Modern Quintet* (1954, Bethlehem).

Pettiford was one of the first jazz musicians to permanently relocate to **Europe**, moving to Copenhagen in 1959. He served as bassist for the **Stan Getz** quartet that played at the Jazzhus Montmartre club until his unfortunate early death as a result of complications from fracturing his skull in a car crash.

Pettiford's legacy will be always be strong as he was one of the first bassists to be embraced during the **Bebop** era and provided a style to be copied by bass players for years to come. *See also* EUROPE.

PHASE SHIFTER. An effects controller that alters the sound produced on an instrument (typically **electric guitar**) and applies it over the original sound. Another effects device, the **flanger**, is very similar.

PHILLIPS, FLIP (1915–2001). Highly influenced by a **recording** of **Frankie Trumbauer**, Phillips (born Phillip Edward Filipelli) fell in love with jazz and the saxophone at the age of 11. Phillips' professional career began at the age of 19 playing clarinet, with his first big break coming when he was hired for a short stint with **Benny Goodman** in 1942. After touring with **Woody Herman** for a time, Phillips played with **Jazz at the Philharmonic** for almost 11 years, finishing in 1957. Phillips maintained a period of retirement in Florida for almost 12 years until being hired again by Herman. The majority of his playing during the next decade would consist of numerous performances with Herman's Thundering Herd. Many of Phillips' best solo recordings came out during this time and include *Flipenstein* (1981, Progressive) and *The Claw: Live at the Floating Jazz Festival* (1986, Chiaroscuro). Phillips continued to play well into his seventies and celebrated his 80th birthday with a performance in 1995.

PHOENIX JAZZ. Established in New Jersey, Phoenix Jazz Records was founded by Bob Porter in 1972 with the intention of reissuing important jazz **recordings** that had been disregarded by smaller labels. Porter acquired little-known **albums** of music by **Bud Powell**, **Dizzy Gillespie**, **Coleman Hawkins**, **Billie Holiday**, and **Charlie Parker** and rereleased them on the Phoenix Jazz Label. Phoenix Jazz Records stopped distribution in the 1990s. *See also* RECORD LABEL.

PIANO (I). A marking in music to designate that the volume of the passage or piece is to be played softly.

PIANO (II). An instrument that was developed after the harpsichord around 1698 that sounds by pressing keys that are attached to small hammers or mallets that strike keys hidden inside the body of the instrument. Originally known as the pianoforte, the piano is typically made up of 88 keys that are arranged in a set order of white and black keys. The piano comes in many different sizes, with the grand piano being the largest and the upright piano being the smallest and most compact. The setup for the piano is also the inspiration for the electronic keyboards that were developed in the 20th century.

The piano has played a pivotal role in jazz and has a strong lineage dating back to the early 1900s and the development of **Ragtime**—a precursor to jazz. The Ragtime piano style evolved into the **Boogie-Woogie** and **Stride** styles, which paved the way for modern pianists. Important pianists in jazz include **Scott Joplin, Jelly Roll Morton, James P. Johnson, Art Tatum, Bud Powell, Oscar Peterson, Bill Evans, McCoy Tyner, Herbie Hancock, Chick Corea**, and **Brad Mehldau**. *See also* ELECTRIC PIANO; ELIAS, ELIANE; JARRETT, KEITH; JORDAN, DUKE; PIERCE, NATHANIEL; TATUM, ART; TRISTANO, LENNIE; WALLER, FATS.

PIANO(LA) ROLL. An invention of the early 1900s that allowed pianists to record what they were playing onto paper rolls by making perforations. These rolls could then be played back through the **piano** without requiring a pianist. *See also* JOHNSON, JAMES P(RICE); QRS; WALLER, FATS.

PICCOLO. Generally referring to a small member of the **flute** family that sounds higher than a normal flute, the term *piccolo* can also be used to describe any such instrument that sounds higher than the normal instrument would (e.g., piccolo **trumpet**).

PICKUP GROUP. A set of musicians who have not played together much and are often assembled for only one or two performances. Pickup groups are common for artists who travel by themselves from city to city and need to assemble a band for a particular performance or set of **gigs**. **Louis Armstrong** in particular used many pickup groups during the 1930s and 1940s while he was touring without a band.

PIERCE, NATHANIEL (1925–1992). Pianist Nat Pierce moved to Boston in the 1940s to study at the New England Conservatory while also playing in many of the local **jam sessions**. Pierce was hired frequently both as a pianist and an arranger for many groups during the 1950s including **Woody Herman, Count Basie, Ella Fitzgerald**, Paul Quinichette, **Phil Woods, Bob Brookmeyer, Pee Wee Russell**, and **Quincy Jones**. The television program *The Sound of Jazz*, which featured jazz legends like **Coleman Hawkins** and **Lester Young**, was solely arranged by Pierce. Pierce would spend much of the 1970s working with vocalists and settled for serving as an accompanist and musical director for singers **Carmen McRae** and Anita O'Day, in addition to **recording** frequently as a **sideman** for the Concord label. *See also* PIANO.

PLAZA MUSIC COMPANY. A **record label** founded in 1922 that created several labels including Banner, **Regal**, Domino, Oriole, Conqueror,

Jewel, and Homestead. Plaza was bought along with **Cameo** and Pathe by the American Record Corporation in 1929.

PLOP. A form of ornamentation using a gliss or lip bend to attack the beginning of a note. The plop is the opposite of a fall, in which a gliss or lip bend would be used at the end of a note.

PLUNGER. A standard or slightly smaller toilet plunger that is used as a **mute** for **brass** instruments. The plunger allows the performer to bend the pitch of a note by slowly opening or closing the gap between the plunger and the bell of the instrument, and can be used to perform abstract sounds not usually achieved by the instrument. Some **big band** passages call for brass sections to use plungers to create a wide dynamic and unique sound shape. **Clark Terry, Al Grey, Bubber Miley**, and **"Tricky" Sam Nanton** are all considered experts at using the plunger in improvisational settings.

POCKET CORNET. A smaller version of a **cornet** that reduces the size by more compactly wrapping the tubing around a smaller bell than is traditionally associated with the cornet. **Don Cherry** is the most notable performer to use the pocket cornet. *See also* POCKET TRUMPET.

POCKET TRUMPET. Slang for **pocket cornet**. Both instruments are identical in their manufacturing. The pocket cornet is made of the same amount of tubing as the traditional **trumpet**, but the tubing is wrapped in such a way as to make the instruments half the size of an ordinary trumpet (or **cornet**). *See also* CHERRY, DON.

POLISH JAZZ SOCIETY. A jazz society that evolved in Poland from the Federation of Polish Jazz Clubs and the Polish Jazz Federation, the Polish Jazz Society is a prominent body in Polish music. Founded and led by Jan Byrczek in 1967, the group has produced many concerts, publishes a Polish jazz journal, and has started a **piano** competition. The Polish Jazz Society helped pave the way for other major jazz organizations in terms of developing structure as well as presenting events.

POLLACK, BEN (1903–1971). Pollack had a brief career as a drummer in Chicago until he gained recognition as a **bandleader** toward the middle part of the 1920s. Pollack led bands from 1928 to the 1940s until he decided to explore other business ventures, leaving the music profession. His bands were often successful, and many future jazz stars including **Benny Goodman, Jack Teagarden,** and **Glenn Miller** were participants in his groups.

PONOMAREV, VALERY (1943–). Inspired by **Clifford Brown,** Ponomarev fell in love with jazz while living as a youth in Russia. After several professional touring experiences, Ponomarev decided to relocate to the United States at the age of 30. He toured for several years with **Art Blakey** beginning in 1977 and was granted U.S. citizenship two years later. After his apprenticeship, Ponomarev primarily freelanced while also **recording** several **albums** under his own name. Ponomarev was a featured soloist with **Lee Konitz,** Frank Foster, and Pepper Adams and has played in many **Hard Bop** groups including ones led by Hard Bop pioneers Junior Cook and **Benny Golson.**

POPULAR SONG FORM. The name given to songs that have a common form or **chord progression.** Many of these songs would be the basis for jazz standards during the 1940s and 1950s. The song form could range from being basic such as a song with an AABA form (two of the same sections repeated [AA], a new section [B], and finally a repeat once again of the first section [A]). In some cases a popular song form could be even more specific, such as the use of George Gershwin's harmonic progression to "I've Got Rhythm," which is the basis for hundreds of jazz compositions.

PORCINO, AL (1925–). Born in New York, Porcino began his professional career as a **trumpet** player at the age of 18 by playing in many of the top bands that were touring during the 1940s, including those led by **Tommy Dorsey, Louis Prima,** and **Gene Krupa.** Porcino maintained an on-and-off-again relationship with the bands led by **Woody Herman** and **Stan Kenton** and worked with both bands frequently. After relocating to Los Angeles in the later part of the 1950s, Porcino formed his own group, the Jazz Wave Orchestra, while continuing to freelance with **big bands.**

Porcino continued to be a first-call trumpeter for any touring band, and in the 1960s he toured and recorded with both the **Buddy Rich** Big Band and the **Thad Jones–Mel Lewis** Orchestra. After a stint with **Mel Tormé** in the early 1970s, Porcino relocated to Germany where he once again led a big band. Porcino all but abandoned freelancing in 1980 and instead focused on his own band and accompanying guest artists who traveled to Germany.

PORI INTERNATIONAL JAZZ FESTIVAL. A **jazz festival** founded in Pori, Finland. The festival has grown in stature since beginning in 1966 and matured from a three-day festival to a 10-day festival by the year 2000. Major artists like **Benny Goodman, Freddie Hubbard,** and the **Dirty Dozen Brass Band** have made appearances at the festival throughout the years. The festival has now been in existence for 47 years and has become popular among jazz and Pop music enthusiasts.

PORTENA JAZZ BAND. Founded by Argentinian pianist Ignacio Romero, the Portena Jazz Band was a 10-piece ensemble that toured **Europe** and Russia in addition to playing in its native Argentina. The group was a highly influential group in Argentina and is considered to be one of the nation's finest **Early** and **Traditional Jazz** bands. The band continues to perform and record.

POTTER, CHARLES "TOMMY" (1918–1988). Potter, along with **Oscar Pettiford**, was one of the front-runners of bass during the **Bebop** era. After apprenticeships with **Trummy Young** and **Billy Eckstine**, Potter was hired by **Charlie Parker** during the late 1940s and was a part of many of Parker's famous Dial and Savoy **recording sessions**. During the 1950s and 1960s, Potter worked with many of the leading jazz musicians including performances and recordings with **Bud Powell, Max Roach, Stan Getz**, Dizzy Reece, Al Cohn, and **Harry "Sweets" Edison**. Potter never had much of a solo career but continued to freelance throughout the remainder of his life.

POWELL, BADEN (1937–2000). Powell began a prolific career as a **guitar** player at an early age, touring with many of Brazil's famous singers in addition to starting a solo career. Originally from Rio de Janeiro, Powell dropped out of school to tour Brazil and was recorded on broadcasts for Brazil's Radio Nacional. He was heard playing at the Bar Plaza in Rio by leading Brazilian artists such as Antônio Carlos Jobim and quickly became associated with the **Bossa Nova** movement. Powell also developed a reputation as a composer, which was further heightened during his collaborations with the poet Vinicius de Moraes. De Moraes wrote lyrics for many of Powell's compositions including "Canto de Ossanha," "Canto do Xango," and "Tristeza e Solidao."

Powell was also very interested in music from Northeast Brazil that included the use of African and Brazilian folklore. This fusion of styles became known as Afro-Samba. De Moraes and Baden split in the early 1960s, and Powell moved to **France** to pursue new opportunities. In addition to being a Bossa Nova icon in France, Powell also became a prominent **studio musician**. In 1966, he recorded his first **album** as a leader, *Tristeza on Guitar*, and was recorded on the soundtrack to the French film *A Man and a Woman*. Throughout the remainder of the 1960s and into the 1970s, Powell freelanced and toured with many musicians including **Stan Getz** and **Stéphane Grappelli**. In 1984, he moved to Germany for five years until returning home to Rio de Janeiro in 1989, where he remained until his death. During the last years of his life, Powell continued to tour and record and solidified his reputation as one of Brazil's finest and most influential guitarists.

POWELL, EARL RUDOLPH "BUD" (1924–1966). Originally from New York, Powell would develop into one of **Bebop**'s finest musicians. During the 1930s, Powell studied Classical piano in addition to learning the solos of popular **Stride** pianists. Powell began to work into the music scene in the 1940s, most notably working with **Cootie Williams**.

Powell's career took off in the latter half of the 1940s, when he performed with several significant Bebop figures, including **Dexter Gordon, J. J. Johnson**, and **Sonny Stitt**. Influenced by **Charlie Parker**, Bud Powell is credited with being the first pianist to fully embrace the Bebop language. Powell suffered from mental illness, which led to his placement in a mental facility in the late 1940s. He battled mental illness for many years and was institutionalized again at times during the 1950s. Musicians had enormous respect for Powell, and he frequently led groups in the 1950s in addition to serving as a **sideman** with artists including **Cannonball Adderley** and **Art Blakey**. Toward the end of the decade, Powell relocated to **France** where he would work for much of the remainder of his career. Powell died after contracting tuberculosis. *See also* POWELL, RICHIE.

POWELL, RICHIE (1931–1956). A native of New York and brother of established jazz icon **Bud Powell**, Richie Powell studied music both in college and with pianist **Mary Lou Williams**. Powell's big break came when he was invited to join the **Clifford Brown–Max Roach** Quintet, a highly influential supergroup of the early 1950s. Powell was involved in the same fatal automobile accident that resulted in the death of Clifford Brown.

POZO, CHANO (1915–1948). A Cuban immigrant, Pozo was a singer and percussionist rooted in the **Afro-Cuban** tradition. In collaboration with **Dizzy Gillespie**, Pozo was an important early voice toward the fusing of Afro-Cuban and jazz styles. Unfortunately, Pozo was murdered in Harlem before he could make the most of his pairing with Gillespie.

PRACTICE MUTE. A **mute** designed to block the majority of sound coming out of the instrument so that a player can practice quietly. Most practice mutes emit very little sound from the instrument.

PRESERVATION HALL. A historic venue in New Orleans that was home to many **brass bands**. It was founded by Larry Borenstein in 1961 as a performance space to accompany his previously established art studio. It now serves to protect and honor **New Orleans Jazz**. *See also* PRESERVATION HALL JAZZ BAND.

PRESERVATION HALL JAZZ BAND. A jazz band established in New Orleans in 1963. The Preservation Hall Jazz Band has had fluctuating personnel that included trombonist George Lewis, **trumpeter** De De Pierce, pianist Billy Pierce, and drummer Alonzo Stewart. Despite constant personnel changes, The Preservation Hall Jazz Band remains active and has toured throughout the 1980s, 1990s, and 2000s. *See also* DRUM SET; EARLY JAZZ; PIANO; PRESERVATION HALL.

PRESS ROLL. A type of drum rudiment in which each of the drumsticks roll simultaneously. *See also* DRUM SET.

PRESTIGE. A **record label** founded on the idea of **recording** ambitious music of the top musicians of the day, Prestige recorded many **albums** that are now considered to be classics. Included in their catalog are recordings by **Miles Davis**, **John Coltrane**, and **Sonny Rollins**. Toward the end of the 1950s, Prestige decided to change the direction of their recordings and limited the number of artists who recorded on the label. In the early 1970s, Fantasy Records purchased the rights to all Prestige recordings and has since reissued many of these classic recordings.

PREVIN, ANDRE (1929–). After his family immigrated from Germany to the United States, Previn was encouraged to study the **piano**. As a teenager, Previn found work playing jazz **gigs** and also began taking work as an arranger. During the 1950s, Previn recorded frequently including the **albums** *Jazz: King Size* (1958, Original Jazz Classics) and *Double Play!* (1957, Original Jazz Classics). Previn's interest in jazz and composition lessened during the next few years, and he found himself more interested in Classical music and conducting. He garnered great reviews as a conductor and was hired by the London Symphony in addition to serving as a guest conductor for other American orchestras. Previn recorded some jazz dates during the 1980s and 1990s and toured, most often in a trio setting.

PRICE, SAMMY (1908–1992). Price was born in Texas and played **piano** with many of the touring bands from Texas during the late 1920s and early 1930s. He worked as both an accompanist and arranger for many vocalists, and after relocating to New York, he began playing a steady set of solo piano **gigs**. Throughout his career, he bounced between several different music genres including **Rhythm and Blues (R&B)** and Gospel. Price recorded several **albums** including *Barrelhouse and Blues* (1969, Black Lion) and *Paradise Valley Duets* (1988, Parkwood).

PRIESTER, JULIAN (1935–). Priester learned **trombone** as a teenager and began his professional career playing with **Rhythm and Blues (R&B)** bands in the 1950s. In 1956, he was hired by **Lionel Hampton**, later by **Dinah Washington**, and eventually by **Max Roach** after Priester moved to New York. Priester's association with Roach introduced him to many up-and-coming musicians including **Booker Little** and **Eric Dolphy**. Priester recorded frequently during the 1960s and was on **albums** led by **Freddie Hubbard**, **Blue Mitchell**, and **Stanley Turrentine**. Priester eventually moved away from New York and spent a brief time in San Francisco before settling in the Seattle area. He joined the faculty of the Cornish College of the Arts where he continues to teach. Priester did record several label albums under his own name including *Keep Swinging* (1960, Original Jazz Classics) and *Polorization* (1977, **ECM**).

PRIMA, LOUIS (1911–1978). Raised in New Orleans, Prima studied **singing** and **trumpet**. He lived in New Orleans for many years before relocating to New York in 1935. Prima led both small and **big bands** and made homes in Chicago and Los Angeles over the next several decades. Prima was known for his raspy voice and was very popular among mainstream listeners. Prima's popularity as a singer landed him a role in the Walt Disney movie *The Jungle Book*. In 1975, Prima suffered from a brain tumor that led to his death. *See also* BANDLEADER.

PRIME TIME. Group formed by **Ornette Coleman** in the 1970s, Prime Time was Coleman's response to **Fusion** and used electronic instruments. *Dancing in Your Head* (1975, A&M) was one of the group's few **recordings**.

PRINCE OF DARKNESS. A nickname given to **Miles Davis** that is also the name of one of his compositions.

PROCOPE, RUSSELL (1908–1981). Originally from New York, Procope took up the **clarinet** and **saxophone** during the late 1910s and began his professional career playing with **Jelly Roll Morton** a decade later. Procope performed with many of the top bands of the 1930s including those of **Fletcher Henderson, Benny Carter**, and **Chick Webb**. After a stint in the military during World War II, Procope joined **Duke Ellington**'s orchestra and remained a member of the group until the 1970s. Procope did some freelancing and recorded a solo **album**, *The Persuasive Sax of Russell Procope* (1956, Dot), while serving as a **sideman** to Ellington. After Ellington's death, Procope continued to freelance in New York until his death in 1981.

PROGRESSIVE. Founded by Gus Statiras, Progressive was a **record label** that had limited success in releasing jazz **albums** in the 1950s. Saxophonist Al Cohn and pianist George Wallington both had several albums recorded and released on the label, but the majority of the other **recordings** made on the label were eventually issued on Savoy. A Japanese company, Baybridge, purchased some of the recordings and issued them during the 1970s.

PROGRESSIVE JAZZ. A term used in the 1950s referring to the desire of **big band** leaders to perform more advanced, dissonant, and complex music. Progressive Jazz featured less improvisation than all other forms of big band writing of this era. **Stan Kenton**'s orchestra was at the forefront of the Progressive Jazz movement. Arrangers Bob Graettinger and Pete Rugolo, along with Kenton, were proponents of Progressive Jazz.

PULLEN, DON (1941–1995). Pullen, like many jazz musicians, was raised in a family of musicians and took up the **piano** at the age of eight. He was accepted at Johnson C. Smith University to study medicine. In 1963, Pullen gave up medicine and dedicated himself to jazz full time. Pullen performed with leading **Free Jazz** artists including **Muhal Richard Abrams** and Milfred Graves, in addition to performing regularly as an organist with more mainstream styles of music.

In the 1970s, Pullen's style caught on with many of jazz's leading voices, and he performed with **Art Blakey**, **Charles Mingus**, Sam Rivers, and **David Murray** at different junctures. Pullen's solo career also took off at this time, and he began to record solo **albums**, including *Capricorn* (1975, **Black Saint**) and *Healing Force* (1976, Black Saint). Toward the end of 1979, Pullen formed a quartet with George Adams that developed a huge following, especially in **Europe**. The group recorded several albums including *The Sixth Sense* (1985, Black Saint) and his debut album for the **Blue Note** label, *Breakthrough* (1986, Blue Note). The drummer for the group, Dannie Richmond, died in 1988, and the group disbanded shortly thereafter. Pullen freelanced with artists including **John Scofield** and Maceo Parker until he died in 1995.

PUNK JAZZ. A term used to describe the hybrid style of combining jazz **improvisation** and harmonic styling with the rhythms, **grooves**, and form structures associated with Punk music found in **England** and New York. Jazz artists that have been associated with Punk Jazz include John Zorn.

PURIM, FLORA (1942–). Purim began her professional career as a singer in Sao Paulo with her future husband, **Airto Moreira**. After moving several times, Purim relocated to New York where she was quickly hired by musicians, including **Stan Getz** and **Gil Evans**, who were interested in exploring Brazilian music. Along with Airto, Purim was a founding member of **Chick Corea**'s group **Return to Forever**, a group she participated in during the early 1970s. Purim began a solo career shortly after leaving Corea's group that included a brief period of touring without her husband. Despite extensive touring during the 1990s and 2000s, Purim recorded very little after 1987. *Humble People* (1985, Concord) and *Butterfly Dreams* (1973, Original Jazz Classics) highlight her solo **albums**.

PURITAN. A **record label** formed in 1920 that issued **albums** recorded by several companies including the Bridgeport Die & Machine Company (BD&M). The label distributed albums depending on where the original material was recorded and was divided when BD&M broke away and created the Puretone label. Puritan was abandoned in 1927 when the remaining companies began to use other labels.

QRS. Founded in 1900, QRS was created as a partner business for a **piano** company to manufacture **piano rolls**. QRS served as an important component toward preserving the **Stride, Ragtime,** and **Early Jazz** piano styles when it made piano rolls of famous pianists including **James P. Johnson** and **Fats Waller.**

QUINTETTE DE HOT CLUB DE FRANCE. A jazz group affiliated with the popular 1930s French jazz club, the **Hot Club de France**. Violinist **Stéphane Grappelli** and guitarist **Django Reinhardt** played prominent roles in the creation of the group, which lasted until 1949. Despite occasional absences of Grappelli and Reinhardt, they remained the only consistent members in the group, as other positions in the group were filled by several different musicians. The Quintette du Hot Club de France was a pioneering group for jazz and helped establish **France** as a leader of jazz music.

R

RACE RECORD. A term used for records that were targeted at African-American listeners. Several companies would create subsidiary labels that released race records. Record companies changed the name from race records to **Rhythm and Blues (R&B)** records in the late 1940s. Rhythm and Blues eventually became a style and was no longer considered to be a type of race record. *See also* OKEH; RECORD LABEL.

RADIOJAZZGRUPPEN. A European nonet that was created in the early 1960s in Denmark by Erik Moseholm. The band lasted over two decades and had several leaders including Lars Togeby. *See also* EUROPE; RIEL, ALEX.

RAGTIME. A style of music pioneered in the late 1890s that was based upon highly syncopated rhythms. At first, Ragtime was primarily a **piano** music that was worked into **brass bands** and other instrumental groups. Frequently, musicians would "rag" a particular song by changing straight eighth-note rhythms to more syncopated figures. Ragtime is considered the main predecessor to jazz because of the similarities between syncopated figures and **Swing** eighth-note figures. Pianist Scott Joplin wrote many Ragtime compositions, including two Ragtime operas. "Maple Leaf Rag" and "The Entertainer" are two of Joplin's most famous Ragtime compositions. *See also* BLAKE, EUBIE; EUROPE, JAMES REESE; MORTON, FERDINAND "JELLY ROLL"; MOTEN, BENNIE; OFFBEAT; SYNCOPATION; WALLER, THEODORE "FATS."

RAINEY, CHUCK (1940–). A **bass** player, Rainey got his start playing in **Rhythm and Blues (R&B)** bands in his native Ohio in the 1960s. After moving to New York in 1964, Rainey found work with musicians including Jerome Richardson, **Gato Barbieri**, and **Gene Ammons**. Rainey relocated to Los Angeles during the 1970s, where he would continue working with **Straight-Ahead** jazz artists such as **Donald Byrd** while working more frequently with **Fusion** groups and leading his own bands. Throughout the 1980s and 1990s, he primarily led his own groups, in addition to becoming increasingly more active as a teacher. He remains an active performer and clinician.

RAINEY, MA (1886–1939). Rainey began **singing** as a teenager in the 1890s before she began actively touring with minstrel shows. She was to become influential in the development of the **Blues** and vocal Blues styles and was frequently recorded during the early 1920s. Despite her great popularity, Rainey retired from performing in 1935, several years before her death.

RAMBLERS. A 1920s **big band** founded in Denmark that achieved fame by **recording** with American touring musicians. The band remained active well into the 1990s, although the ensemble name changed several times, finally settling on the VARA Dance Orchestra.

RAMIREZ, ROGER "RAM" (1913–1994). Working in the 1930s with amateur bands followed by professional experiences with **Rex Stewart** and **Sid Catlett**, pianist Ramirez's early career was very active. In the 1940s, Ramirez found work with **Ella Fitzgerald**, **Charlie Barnet**, and John Kirby before primarily working as a solo pianist. After spending a greater part of the 1950s still working as a soloist, Rainey worked with **Blues** groups for the remainder of his career.

RAMPART. A short-lived **record label** in the late 1940s that released **recordings** of **Early Jazz** American and European bands until 1952. Notable musicians to have **albums** released on this label include Bob Wilber.

RCA VICTOR. One of the first phonograph companies and **record labels**, RCA Victor remains an important label for the reissue of **Early Jazz** and **Swing albums**. RCA Victor is credited with releasing the very first jazz on record, a release of the **Original Dixieland Jazz Band**. Throughout the 1920s and 1930s, RCA Victor released albums by almost every top band of the time, including bands led by **Duke Ellington**, **Paul Whiteman**, **Glenn Miller**, **Tommy Dorsey**, **Benny Goodman**, and **Lionel Hampton**. RCA Victor's productivity lessened throughout the 1950s and 1960s, and the company was eventually sold in 1986 to General Electric. *See also* RECORD LABELS.

RECORDING. A term to describe the process of capturing live sound or the product of capturing the sound. Recording has been prominent since the beginning of the 20th century and incredibly important for the preservation of all music created in that century. The **Original Dixieland Jazz Band** made the first recording of a jazz group in 1917.

RECORD LABEL. In the early 1900s the **recording** industry boomed with the development of records and accessible devices on which they could be played. During this time, three major companies primarily controlled the record industry, **Edison, Victor,** and **Columbia.** The development of independent labels played a significant role in the distribution of jazz and helped to establish its popularity in the 1920s. Many of these independent labels like **Blue Note** Records, **Verve** Records, and Impulse Records helped distribute, maintain, and preserve the jazz spirit for decades to come. Due to the advent of recording, jazz was spread worldwide and not just in American cities accessible to touring musicians. Once the music was heard overseas, it opened the door for musicians looking to pursue performance opportunities across the world.

It is important to distinguish between recording companies and record labels. Recording companies complete the actual recording process. Record labels are responsible for distribution of the recording. Many of the large companies like Columbia act as both a recording company and record label due to their huge financial capacity. Many smaller record labels founded in the 1910s and 1920s acted only as an outlet for musicians to have their recordings distributed. For this reason, record labels were frequently acquired by one of the larger companies (such as Columbia) who saw in the small labels a competing business that was without the financial or recording resources to match the big labels. In modern times, musicians frequently record their **album** at a venue that has no relation to a record label and then hope to find a company to distribute the product.

Another significant development in the history of record labels and jazz is the development of "**race records**" or a "race series" presented by a record label. From 1921 to the early 1940s, record companies released specific recordings targeted toward the African-American communities in certain regions. The record label **OKeh** was created for this purpose. In some cases, existing labels like Victor would create a subsidiary label such as **Bluebird** to release these race records. Many companies no longer released "race records" after the Great Depression. The companies that did remain active selling them eventually changed the name of these types of recordings to **Rhythm and Blues,** which in the 1950s would be shortened to R&B.

The first big record companies were all impacted by jazz. The **Edison** label suffered greatly from a lack of jazz in its catalog. The company determined jazz to be unsatisfactory and chose not to sell it, a decision that left the company bankrupt after only a few decades. The Victor Company was quite popular and responsible for releasing the first-ever jazz recording in 1917, two sides by the **Original Dixieland Jazz Band.** In the 1920s the label was purchased by the Radio Corporation of America (**RCA**) and released discs under the RCA Victor label. RCA Victor was also quick to pick up the abandoned **Brunswick** label from Columbia in 1940, a move that netted it the **Glenn Miller Swing** era hit "Chattanooga Choo Choo." Nowadays RCA Victor primarily serves as a label used for reissues of early Swing music.

Of the big three recording companies, Columbia has remained the most active and dominant for over a century. The record label Columbia was purchased several times, most notably by **Electrical and Musical Industries (EMI)** in the early 1930s and again by the American Radio Corporation (ARC) in 1934. Recordings would continue to be released on Columbia for many decades, and it is credited with signing **Miles Davis** in the mid-1950s to a deal that would run through the remainder of his life and result in many of his most famous recordings.

The rise of independent labels began in the 1910s and remains an important venue to this day for aspiring musicians wishing to be heard. The Brunswick label was very successful early on and created the subsidiary label **Vocalion**. Brunswick was purchased by ARC (in addition to several other significant independent labels including **OKeh** and Pathe) around the time Columbia was acquired by ARC. Eventually, Brunswick was dropped by ARC and as previously mentioned picked up by RCA Victor. Other significant labels of the 1920s and 1930s include United Artists (responsible for releasing a **Paul Whiteman** disc that was the first to reach one million copies sold), Black Swan, **Decca** Grammaphone, and **Blue Note** Records (founded in 1939 as a **Dixieland/Early Jazz** revival label). In the 1940s, independent labels further blossomed with the creation of the **Mercury**, Chess, and **Fantasy** labels.

Several significant jazz record labels came into prominence during the 1950s: the aforementioned Blue Note label, **Verve**, and **Pacific**. In addition to Columbia, these labels produced many of the classic recordings of bands led by artists such as **Ornette Coleman**, **Art Blakey**, **John Coltrane**, and **Oscar Peterson**. Impulse records, created in the 1960s, was largely responsible for documenting many of John Coltrane's later live performances and capturing much of the music made by **Avant-Garde** Jazz musicians.

As jazz became less popular toward the end of the 1960s, many labels were bought and sold to larger companies for the primary purpose of reissuing older records. Both the Blue Note and Pacific labels were sold to the **Liberty** label during the late 1960s. The rise of European-based labels like **SteepleChase** and **ECM** took place in the 1970s and documented the jazz movement that was taking place overseas. Labels like Columbia would continue to release jazz albums well into the 1980s and were responsible for important recordings made by **Dexter Gordon** and **Wynton Marsalis** that helped spark the acoustic revival in jazz. Blue Note experienced a resurgence of production in the 1990s and 2000s thanks in large part to crossover artists like Norah Jones, who were able to blend a popular sound and style with strong jazz influences.

Today, with the ability to record and distribute records no longer held only by large companies, many individual musicians are able to do recording and distribution on their own. The development of online marketplaces such as iTunes and Artist Share has also provided musicians with the ability to produce their own music, but has at the same time led to the unfortunate slow death of the importance and relevance of the record labels. *See also* BLACK SAINT.

RED HOT PEPPERS. The name for a **Traditional** and **Early Jazz** group founded by pianist **Jelly Roll Morton**. Included in the group were trombonist **Kid Ory** and drummer **Baby Dodds**. The Red Hot Peppers remained in existence from 1926 to 1930.

REDMAN, DONALD (1900–1964). Developing first as an alto saxophonist, Redman broke into the music scene in the 1920s by working with **Fletcher Henderson**. After spending several years performing and arranging for Henderson, Redman took work arranging for several other groups until starting his own group in the 1930s. His tenure as a **bandleader** was short in comparison to many of his peers during this same time, as the band disbanded after about 10 years.

In the 1940s, Redman was in demand as an arranger and found work writing for bands led by **Count Basie** and **Tommy Dorsey**. After periods arranging for Basie and Dorsey, Redman moved to **Europe** and wrote for a variety of groups including a new band he formed. Redman would primarily work overseas before returning to New York shortly before his passing in 1964. Considered to be the premier arranger of his day, Redman is held in high regard for his arranging and orchestration abilities.

REDMAN, WALTER DEWEY (1931–2006). Originally from Texas, Redman played several instruments before settling on the **tenor saxophone** while studying in college. Redman's early career was marked by time spent in education and army service before moving to San Francisco, where he decided to play jazz professionally. Another relocation, this time to New York, resulted in Redman's big break, playing with **Free Jazz** pioneers **Charlie Haden** and **Ornette Coleman**. During the late 1960s, while working with Haden and Coleman, Redman freelanced with other groups in addition to leading his own groups.

Redman attracted many of the top musicians and formed a quartet in the mid-1970s that included Keith Jarrett and Ed Blackwell called Old and New Dreams. Redman worked frequently as a **leader** during the 1980s and 1990s, most notably playing with Joe Lovano, **Paul Motian**, Anthony Cox, and

Elvin Jones. Redman's son, Joshua, developed into one of the premier jazz musicians during the 1990s. Redman succumbed to liver failure in 2006.

RED ONION JAZZ BABIES. A group created by the **record label** Gennett that featured jazz stars **Louis Armstrong** and **Sidney Bechet** in the mid-1920s. Red Onion Jazz Babies never officially toured and only recorded four times.

REED SECTION. A term used to describe the woodwind players in an ensemble. In a traditional **big band** setting, the **saxophone** section is commonly referred to as the reed section. *See also* ALTO SAXOPHONE; BARITONE SAXOPHONE; CLARINET; FLUTE; OBOE; SOPRANO SAXOPHONE; TENOR SAXOPHONE.

REGAL. A commonly used **record label** name. Three different companies took the Regal name to distribute **albums**. The **Plaza** music company maintained a record label called Regal for almost 10 years until Plaza was sold to ABC. Several overseas **Columbia Broadcasting System (CBS)** affiliates in the 1920s operated labels named Regal that distributed jazz until the mid-1930s. In the 1940s, a record company assumed the name Regal and released albums by **Cab Calloway** under the same name. This company closed its doors in 1951.

REGAL-ZONOPHONE. A merger of two **Electrical and Musical Industries (EMI)** record labels that intended to release **albums** recorded by **Columbia**'s 1920s **Regal record label** and EMI's "cheap" label, **Zonophone**. Regal-Zonophone released few jazz records with the exception of reissues from the 1920s.

REGINA. A short-lived **record label** in New York that released **albums** by **Charlie Mariano** and **Roger Kellaway** in the 1960s.

REGIS. A **record label** founded by the Regic Record Company that lasted a year and a half before being consolidated with another label, Manor. Regis primarily distributed jazz and Gospel **albums**.

REID, RUFUS (1944–). Initially interested in the **trumpet**, Reid worked with military bands after graduating from high school and before permanently changing to the **bass**. During the 1960s, Reid moved to several cities including Sacramento, Seattle, and Chicago, where he found regular work as a jazz bassist. In Chicago, he worked with **Sonny Stitt**, **Dizzy Gillespie**, **Kenny Dorham**, **Lee Konitz**, **Bobby Hutcherson**, and **Freddie Hubbard**.

Reid relocated to New York in the mid-1970s and found work with **Thad Jones**, **Dexter Gordon**, and **Henry Threadgill**. During the 1980s, Reid was an in-demand **sideman** and toured and recorded with many jazz legends including **Bob Brookmeyer**, **Jack DeJohnette**, Harold Danko, **Art Farmer**, **Stan Getz**, and **J. J. Johnson**. Reid became a more active **leader** during the 1990s and established a regular group along with drummer Akira Tana, in addition to remaining one of New York's busiest bass players.

REINHARDT, JEAN BAPTISTE "DJANGO" (1910–1953). One of **France**'s most important musicians and a highly influential guitarist, Reinhardt grew up with Gypsies before moving to Paris in the late 1920s. Reinhardt established himself working in cafés during the 1930s, including establishing an important relationship with violinist **Stéphane Grappelli**. Throughout the 1930s, Reinhardt became increasingly active as a composer and wrote several pieces that became important works of the decade. He would play with many touring American artists like **Benny Carter** and **Coleman Hawkins** before being invited, at **Duke Ellington**'s expense, to visit the United States. Reinhardt's time overseas was not as promising as expected, and he soon resumed his career in France. Reinhardt's legacy and playing style is still present in guitarists today, and several books and motion pictures have been made about his life.

RELEASE. Another word for the **bridge** or the middle material of a song. Commonly, it is the B section of the AABA song form.

RENA RAMA. Founded by prominent Swedish musicians Bobo Stenson and Palle Danielsson, Rena Rama was a popular European quartet that remained active from 1972 to 1993. The group toured frequently and made several **albums**. Rena Rama's personnel remained fairly constant with the exception of the **drum set** player, which changed frequently.

RENAUD, HENRI (1925–2002). Raised as both a Classical and jazz musician in **France**, Renaud's career as a pianist flourished when he moved to Paris to work in various jazz groups. In addition to working as a leader, Renaud frequently accompanied touring American artists including **Don Byas** and **Roy Eldridge**. In the 1950s, Renaud led his own groups that often were the same groups providing the accompaniment for the Americans. Renaud was also active with the Vogue label and recorded **albums** with many famous jazzmen, eventually being hired to run the French jazz affiliate for Columbia Broadcast Systems. Renaud did only a little playing during the 1970s and 1980s before having a small comeback with various French groups and his own groups. *See also* PIANO.

REPRISE. A **record label** that recorded its founder, **Frank Sinatra**, in addition to several major jazz artists during the 1960s. Reprise also recorded dates with **Duke Ellington, Bud Powell, Dizzy Gillespie**, and **Don Ellis**, as well as several **albums** that featured Sinatra with **Count Basie**. In the late 1960s, the label gave up on jazz and primarily recorded Pop music. Several reissues were made of albums recorded on Reprise in the 1990s.

RETURN TO FOREVER. A highly influential **Fusion** and **Jazz-Rock** group that was founded in the early 1970s. Formed by **Chick Corea** with the help of **Stanley Clarke, Airto**, and **Lenny White**, Return to Forever was one of the top working groups of the 1970s. The band also included tenor saxophonist Joe Farrell and vocalist **Flora Purim** and remained in existence for 12 years. The group saw several personnel changes during its existence and made varied use of electronics and percussion.

REVELATION. Created in Los Angeles in the 1960s, the Revelation **record label** produced many jazz **albums** during its existence. Revelation recorded and distributed albums by musicians including Carmell Jones, **Clare Fischer, Gary Foster**, and **Warne Marsh**.

REVOLUTIONARY ENSEMBLE. Founded by violinist Leroy Jenkins, the Revolutionary Ensemble was a trio in existence for most of the 1970s. The group featured **violin**, bass, and drums in addition to a wide range of percussion instruments that the band members played. The Revolutionary Ensemble never reached a high level of fame and did little **recording**.

RHYTHMAKERS. A group comprised of Billy Banks, **Henry "Red" Allen, Pee Wee Russell**, and Zutty Singleton, among others, it was created just for **recording**. Rhythmakers did several recording **sessions** in which some of the personnel shifted. The recordings were quite popular, and the group also went by the name the Chicago Rhythm Kings. All of the recording sessions were done in 1932.

RHYTHM AND BLUES (R&B). A style of music developed in the 1940s intended to reach a mostly African-American listening audience that included much of the music that had previously been recorded and sold as **race records**. A name given to replace the politically incorrect "race records," Rhythm and Blues developed into a musical style that remained prominent in the 1950s and 1960s before being renamed "Soul." Early R&B performers embraced the **Blues** tradition of the 1930s while breaking away from the typical **Swing** rhythms in accompaniment, choosing instead to favor more shuffle- and **groove**-oriented stylings. Prominent early R&B artists included Wynonie Harris and Roy Hawkins. **Nat "King" Cole**, Joe Turner, and **Eddie "Cleanhead" Vinson** are jazz musicians who frequently crossed over into R&B-inspired or styled music.

In the 1980s, record companies created a new genre, Contemporary Rhythm and Blues, in order to market artists who played a fusion of styles including traditional Rhythm and Blues with **Funk** and 1970s-era influenced accompaniment. In the 1990s and 2000s, R&B expanded to include music by artists from other genres including Hip-hop, Rap, and Pop, and has remained a primarily vocal music. Artists such as Mary J. Blige and R Kelly are considered modern Rhythm and Blues artists. Great Britain developed its own unique strain of R&B based on singers of the Motown and Disco eras fused with Britain's own Punk and Rock music. R&B remains a popular form of music and is incorporated by numerous jazz artists including **Herbie Hancock** and Roy Hargrove. *See also* JORDAN, LOUIS.

RHYTHM SECTION. A term used to describe the pianist, bassist, and drummer of an ensemble. Occasionally a **guitar** will be added or used in place of the **piano**, and a percussionist can also be added. *See also* BASS; DRUM SET; VIBRAPHONE.

RIALTO. A Chicago-based **record label** that released several significant **albums** of **Jelly Roll Morton** during the 1920s.

RICH, BERNARD "BUDDY" (1917–1987). Considered to be a child prodigy, Rich was performing professionally at the age of 11. After working with various professional musicians in the late 1930s and the 1940s including **Artie Shaw, Benny Goodman**, and **Tommy Dorsey**, Rich began leading his own groups in addition to working with the **Jazz at the Philharmonic** groups that were currently touring. Rich worked with **trumpeter** Harry James for 13 years until he decided to permanently pursue **bandleading**, which he would do for the remainder of his career. Equally skilled at both large- and small-group playing, Rich would dissolve his band in the 1970s to pursue small-group opportunities. Rich was known as a powerful and dazzling drummer who frequently led high-caliber bands.

RICHARDSON, JEROME (1920–2000). Richardson grew up in California and took up the **alto saxophone** while a youth. Throughout the late 1930s and 1940s, Richardson forged the beginnings of his career working with musicians like **Lionel Hampton, Jimmie Lunceford**, and **Marshal Royal**. Richardson relocated to New York in the mid-1950s and worked with **Oscar**

Pettiford, in addition to beginning to lead his own groups. Richardson was a savvy multi-instrumentalist and was frequently used for **recording sessions**, specifically large ensemble recordings. Richardson was an original member of the **Thad Jones–Mel Lewis** Orchestra and played with the group until he relocated to California in the 1970s. Throughout the 1980s and 1990s, Richardson performed in **big bands** on the West Coast and in New York in addition to playing on many small-group recording sessions.

RIDDLE, NELSON (1921–1985). Riddle entered the music business as a trombonist before getting work as an arranger for bands led by **Tommy Dorsey** and Bob Crosby. In the 1950s, Riddle retired from professional playing to pursue arranging work, specifically for various studio orchestras. He served several roles during the 1960s and 1970s, including working as a musical director and composer for motion picture and television. Of all Riddle's work, he received the most acclaim for his work with **Frank Sinatra**, with whom he made many significant **albums**.

RIDE-OUT. An **Early Jazz** term used in reference to the final chorus of a song.

RIDLEY, LARRY (1937–). Inspired by Ray Brown, Ridley took up the **bass** and worked frequently with fellow Indianapolis musicians **Wes Montgomery** and **Freddie Hubbard** while still a teenager. Ridley spent most of the 1960s establishing himself by performing with musicians including **Horace Silver**, **Lee Morgan**, **Slide Hampton**, Red Garland, and **Jackie McLean** before pursuing a music education degree in 1971. Ridley would continue to work professionally in the 1970s while also becoming increasingly more active in education. Working with **Philly Joe Jones**, **Chet Baker**, **Cedar Walton**, and **Lucky Thompson**, Ridley would remain a first-call bassist throughout the 1980s and 1990s, in addition to remaining a prominent educator.

RIEL, ALEX (1940–). Born in Denmark, Riel became one of his country's most important drummers and worked with many popular European and American musicians during his career. Riel spent time studying jazz in the United States at the **Berklee School of Music** in the 1960s before resuming his career overseas. Riel worked with **Radiojazzgruppen**, Jesper Lundgaard, **Don Byas**, **Dexter Gordon**, and Ken McIntyre, among others, throughout the 1970s and 1980s. *See also* EUROPE.

RIFF. A term used to describe a short phrase that is often repeated. During the **Swing** era, riffs were commonly made up by instrumental sections in a **big band** and played in support of soloists.

RILEY, BEN(JAMIN) (1933–). Riley studied drums while serving time in the air force during the 1950s before playing with many of the famous musicians of that decade, including **Randy Weston, Stan Getz, Junior Mance, Johnny Griffin, Ahmad Jamal, Sonny Rollins,** and Ray Bryant. Riley's most famous musical association was a three-year tenure with influential pianist **Thelonious Monk.** Riley continued to work steadily during the 1970s with a variety of groups and performers, most notably the group **Sphere,** which he co-led with the members of the ensemble that included **Kenny Barron** and **Buster Williams.** Riley has continued to freelance since the 1980s with musicians including Ray Drummond, Claudio Roditi, and **Barry Harris** and regularly performs today.

RIM SHOT. A technique used by drummers to achieve a sharp loud sound from the snare drum by hitting across the drum. *See also* DRUM SET; PRESS ROLL.

RISTIC. An English **record label** that was used to distribute **Early** and **Traditional Jazz albums** between the 1950s and 1970s.

RITENOUR, LEE (1952–). Guitarist Ritenour received his first professional experiences working with Sergio Mendes before focusing on a career doing studio work. Ritenour primarily led his own groups in the 1980s and 1990s that were considered to be **Fusion** or **Jazz-Rock** inspired groups. The most notable of all these groups was the contemporary group Fourplay that Ritenour founded along with keyboardist **Bob James.** Ritenour continues to work as a performer and educator.

RIVERSIDE. Founded in New York in 1953 by Orrin Keepnews, the Riverside **record label** released many important **albums** by artists including **Thelonious Monk, Bill Evans,** and **Cannonball Adderley.** The label was only in existence for 11 years but acquired many **recordings** from other labels, which it then later reissued. The Riverside label was purchased by **Fantasy** in the 1970s.

ROACH, MAXWELL "MAX" (1924–2007). In the 1940s, drummer Max Roach became one of the most influential drummers of the decade and was considered the equivalent to peers **Charlie Parker** and **Dizzy Gillespie.** Roach was constantly working with them in the 1940s in addition to a brief period working with **Miles Davis** and **Coleman Hawkins.** In the 1950s, Roach would form one of jazz's most popular and imitated groups: the **Clifford Brown**–Max Roach Quintet. Roach's musical relationship with Brown was very strong, and the two had a significant run until Brown's death in

1956. Much of the material they worked on was recorded on classic **albums** released on the **EmArcy record label**.

After Brown's death, he continued to lead quintets, most notably one featuring the next rising trumpet player, **Booker Little**. Roach became increasingly more active in the civil rights movement, and several of his albums during the early 1960s were representative of this. He focused his work on other musical exploits for most of the decade and well into the 1970s. Later in the 1970s, Roach worked with **Free Jazz** stars **Anthony Braxton, Archie Shepp**, and **Cecil Taylor**, in addition to founding his own group, the percussion-only ensemble **M'Boom**, which included fellow drummer Joe Chambers.

Roach primarily led his own groups late in his career in addition to furthering his interest in composition. M'Boom continued to work regularly in the 1990s and 2000s. Roach also became a more active educator and lecturer before he died.

RODNEY, RED (1927–1994). Born Robert Roland Chudnick, Rodney found his first professional work as a **trumpet** player filling in for musicians who had been called in to serve in the military while he was still a teenager. In the 1940s, Rodney worked with **Jimmy Dorsey, Gene Krupa, Claude Thornhill**, and **Woody Herman** before being hired to work in **Charlie Parker's** quintet. Rodney's career for most of the 1950s, 1960s, and 1970s was on and off again due to complications with drug addiction and health problems. Rodney suffered a stroke in the 1970s that caused significant damage.

In the mid-1970s, Rodney worked more frequently and started leading his own groups, most notably a quintet with tenor saxophonist **Ira Sullivan**. The 1980s and early 1990s remained Rodney's most popular years, and his groups were often in high demand. Rodney died in 1994 due to complications with lung cancer.

ROGERS, MILTON "SHORTY" (1924–1994). Rogers' career as a **trumpet** player began when he was a teenager and worked with **Red Norvo** and **Woody Herman** during the 1940s. The 1950s was a breakout decade for Rogers in which he performed with several popular artists, including **Stan Kenton** and **Art Pepper**, while also working extensively on composition both in jazz form and with motion picture soundtracks. Rogers would develop into an important figure during the 1950s, most notably as a **West Coast Jazz**–styled soloist and as a **bandleader** for his own groups. Rogers continued to be active as a performer and composer throughout the remainder of his life and was an innovator in the use of the **flugelhorn** as a solo instrument.

ROKER, MICKEY (1932–). A staple in the Philadelphia music scene, Roker worked with many of the musicians from the area before they became famous, including **McCoy Tyner**, **Lee Morgan**, and **Kenny Barron**. He performed extensively with pianist Junior Mance's trio and Duke Pearson's **big band** in the 1960s, in addition to freelancing with other musicians. **Dizzy Gillespie** hired Roker in the 1970s to fill the **drum set** chair in his groups until he was hired to play with Ray Brown in the 1980s. Roker retired from touring in the 1990s and worked primarily in Philadelphia, with some occasional touring. For a brief period during the 1990s, he was affiliated with the **Modern Jazz Quartet** and **Milt Jackson.**

ROLL. A technique used by drummers in which they beat very rapidly on a given drum or **cymbal** by alternating drumstick hits. There are a variety of different rolls that a drummer uses that can be referred to as a drum roll or a **press roll**. *See also* DRUM SET.

ROLLINS, THEODORE "SONNY" (1930–). In the first decade of Rollins' professional career, he would develop into one of the most influential tenor saxophonists and jazz musicians ever. Rollins was surrounded by jazz musicians as a youth and worked with **Jackie McLean** and **Kenny Drew** before he turned 18. In the late 1940s and 1950s, Rollins was hired by many jazz luminaries including **Thelonious Monk** and **Miles Davis**, and his style encouraged **Max Roach** to replace **Harold Land** with Rollins in the famous **Clifford Brown–Max Roach** Quintet. Rollins' tenure with the group raised his popularity to new heights, and after Brown's passing, Rollins began leading his own groups.

During the middle to late 1950s, Rollins supplanted every other saxophonist in terms of popularity and released many classic **albums**. Rollins improvised with a freer sense of rhythm than had previously been explored and was also considered to be a master of developing variations of themes. Tracks like "Blue 7" exemplify Rollins' ability to improvise using a theme. Rollins worked frequently with former bandmate Max Roach during this time and also worked with other jazz musicians, including **John Coltrane** and **Kenny Dorham.**

In the 1960s, Rollins split the decade working with several different musical styles and groups. The first part of the decade was spent working with a quartet that featured guitarist **Jim Hall** instead of a **piano**. Inspiration for this group came after Rollins had spent an extended period of time not performing, choosing instead to practice, most famously on a bridge in New York. Rollins explored playing **Free Jazz** for a period during the middle to later part of the decade before once again taking a sabbatical in the late 1960s and early 1970s.

Throughout the later 1970s and the 1980s, Rollins began working regularly again leading his own groups. For brief periods of time, Rollins explored commercial music and also used electronic instruments, but he ended up working primarily with **Straight-Ahead** jazz groups for the remainder of the 1990s and 2000s. Rollins remains an important icon to jazz musicians and is considered to be one of the greatest improvisers of all time.

ROSS, ANNEBELLE "ANNIE" (1930–). Born in **England**, Ross' family moved to Los Angeles when she was 13, where she learned to sing from her aunt. Ross toured as a cabaret singer and recorded several **albums** of jazz vocals in the 1950s. Seeking to further the **vocalese** style, Ross helped pioneer the style that led to an invitation to join a new group with **Dave Lambert** and **Jon Hendricks**. This group, named **Lambert, Hendricks, and Ross**, would be an influential vocal group from the mid-1950s to the early 1960s, **recording** many albums of popular jazz songs. Ross left the group to relocate to **Europe** where she would lead small groups in her own name for the next few decades. In addition to **singing**, Ross also worked in the television and movie industries during the 1970s, 1980s, and 1990s.

ROULETTE. Created in 1957, the Roulette **record label** made several significant **recordings** of jazz musicians in the late 1950s, including **Count Basie, Joe Williams, Maynard Ferguson,** and **Jack Teagarden.** Roulette remained active until it was purchased in 1989 by **Electrical and Musical Industries (EMI).**

ROUSE, CHARLIE (1924–1988). A tenor saxophonist, Rouse was a prominent **big band** player during the 1940s working with bands led by **Billy Eckstine** and **Dizzy Gillespie** before spending time working with **Rhythm and Blues** bands. In the 1950s, he freelanced with musicians like **Oscar Pettiford** and **Julius Watkins** before being hired to work in a quartet headed by **Thelonious Monk.** This association lasted a little more than a decade and ended in 1970. Rouse pursued other interests in the 1970s and was an original member of the group **Sphere,** which also included **Kenny Barron** and former Monk bandmate Ben Riley. Rouse freelanced with several groups during the 1980s before passing away due to lung cancer.

ROWLES, JIMMIE (1918–1996). Born in Spokane, Washington, Rowles' career was brought to life when he moved south to California and began working as a pianist with groups there. Rowles' career combined spending years serving as an accompanist for vocalists including Peggy Lee, **Billie Holiday**, **Ella Fitzgerald**, and **Sarah Vaughan** in addition to working with leading **West Coast Jazz** groups led by performers like **Zoot Sims**, Al Cohn, and **Dexter Gordon**. Rowles spent many years working in studios in Hollywood in addition to the freelance work he did performing with different groups.

ROYAL, ERNIE (1921–1983). The **trumpet**-playing brother of **saxophonist Marshall Royal**, Ernie Royal began working professionally in the late 1930s with groups led by Britt Woodman and **Lionel Hampton**. Royal played a significant role in the desegregation of musicians when he became the first African-American to work regularly with clarinetist **Benny Goodman**. Royal semi-retired from playing in the mid-1950s and took a job as a writer for the American Broadcasting Company. He was considered a very good **lead** trumpet player and freelanced frequently with artists like **Quincy Jones** and **Gil Evans** after he left his writing job in 1972.

ROYAL, MARSHALL (1912–1995). The older brother of trumpeter **Ernie Royal**, saxophonist Marshall Royal got his start in Los Angeles working in various **clubs** and several **big bands**. Royal spent time working in studios in addition to playing with bands led by **Lionel Hampton** and Eddie Heywood. Royal's big break came in the 1950s when he was hired to be the lead alto in **Count Basie**'s big band. Shortly after being hired into the band, Royal also became the musical director for the ensemble, which lasted until the 1970s when he decided to relocate to Los Angeles and work with big bands there. Royal would primarily lead his own groups, usually small groups, for the remainder of his career. Royal was regarded highly by his peers, and many of his later touring groups featured jazz stars including **Frank Wess** and **Harry "Sweets" Edison**.

ROYAL ROOST. A club in New York that was popular during the 1940s and 1950s, the Royal Roost also had a **record label** named after it. The record label Royal Roost released several **albums** by significant jazzmen including **Sonny Stitt**, **Johnny Smith**, and **Bud Powell**. The label remained active from the early 1950s through 1971.

RUGOLO, PETE (1915–2011). Receiving formal composition lessons from Darius Milhaud, Rugolo's career was defined by successfully writing **charts** for many artists during the 1950s. **Miles Davis**, **Stan Kenton**, **Mel Tormé**, and **Nat "King" Cole** all employed Rugolo's services during the 1940s and 1950s, which helped him develop his reputation as an outstanding composer and arranger. After writing for several vocalists including **Billy Eckstine**,

Rugolo retired from jazz composition to focus on studio work for television and motion pictures.

RUSHING, JAMES ANDREW "JIMMY" (1903–1972). Rushing's career as a vocalist took off in the 1920s when we was invited to sing with many of the preeminent groups in jazz including those led by **Jelly Roll Morton**, **Walter Page**, and **Bennie Moten**. After spending a brief part of the 1930s with **Count Basie**, Rushing primarily led groups on his own and was known for being an outstanding jazz and **Blues** singer. Rushing would tour with Basie again later in his career but made his mark on the jazz world on his own. Rushing's hit "Everyday I Have the Blues" has been used and imitated by many singers over the decades.

RUSSELL, CHARLES ELLSWORTH "PEE WEE" (1906–1969). One of the few musicians to have the **clarinet** as their primary instrument, Russell's professional career began playing in groups led by **Jack Teagarden** and **Bix Beiderbecke** before turning 21. Russell would develop into one of the leading **Dixieland** musicians of the 1950s and 1960s, leading groups on his own in addition to working with established musicians like Eddie Condon and Bobby Hackett. Russell suffered from problems with addiction, which led to a liver condition that would result in his passing in 1969.

RUSSELL, DILLON "CURLY" (1917–1986). A prominent **bass** player during the 1950s, Russell's most famous **recordings** were those made with **Art Blakey**'s group, which featured **Clifford Brown**. Russell was a very popular bassist during the 1950s, working with musicians like **Stan Getz**, **Miles Davis**, and **Coleman Hawkins**, in addition to his dates with Blakey. Russell pursued a career in other genres of music in the late 1950s.

RUSSELL, GEORGE (1923–2009). A compositional pioneer of **Free Jazz** and **Third Stream** music, Russell's career began writing for **Straight-Ahead** groups led by **Dizzy Gillespie** and Buddy DeFranco. Russell was always seen as a forward thinker and developed his own theory on musical construction, referred to as the Lydian Chromatic Concept of Tonal Organization, which he applied to his works in the 1950s. Russell recorded with his own groups several times during the 1950s recording primarily as a pianist. Russell was affiliated with many of the top musical thinkers during the late 1950s and early 1960s, including **Carla Bley**, **Don Ellis**, and **Eric Dolphy**, and wrote for similar-minded artists.

Russell became increasingly involved in education during the end of the 1960s in addition to exploring new sounds that included the use of electronics. Signed by **Blue Note** Records in the 1980s, Russell experienced a brief resurgence, and his music became increasingly more popular in **England**. Russell continued to compose and record in the 1990s and 2000s.

RUSSO, WILLIAM "BILL" (1928–2003). Russo broke into the jazz scene as a **trombone** player with **Stan Kenton** in the early 1950s, but his career flourished when Kenton began playing his compositions and **arrangements**. Russo's music was an important part of the **Third Stream** sound that Kenton developed during the 1950s, which then inspired Russo to start his own groups. Throughout the 1960s and 1970s, he was active as a composer, conductor, and leader for a variety of groups that were working in **Europe** and also spent time writing for motion pictures and television. Russo wrote several texts on approaches to arranging for jazz ensemble and continued to lead bands into the 1990s.

S

SACKVILLE. Record label established in 1968 in Toronto. Artists include Frank Rosolino, **Doc Cheatham, Archie Shepp,** and others.

SACRAMENTO DIXIELAND JUBILEE. A **jazz festival** held every year in Sacramento, California, since 1974. The name has since changed to Sacramento Jazz Jubilee to allow for the inclusion of other jazz styles, and today it is named the Sacramento Music Festival.

ST. CYR, JOHNNY (1890–1966). A guitarist and **banjo** player, Johnny St. Cyr led some of his own groups before playing in a group led by **Freddie Keppard.** From 1914 to 1917, St. Cyr played with **Kid Ory** in addition to local marching bands. From 1918 to 1920 he worked with **Fate Marable,** briefly in 1923 with **King Oliver,** and then from 1924 to 1929 with Doc Cook. During this time, St. Cyr recorded as a member of **Louis Armstrong**'s **Hot Five** and **Hot Seven** (1925–1927), and also with **Jelly Roll Morton,** in addition to accompanying **Jimmie Noone.** When the Great Depression hit, St. Cyr returned to New Orleans to work as a plasterer while still continuing to play with a number of groups. St. Cyr moved to Los Angeles in 1955 and from 1961 led his own group at Disneyland, the Young Men from New Orleans.

SAINTS AND SINNERS. A **Dixieland** band formed in 1960 that was active until 1970.

SAMBA. A Brazilian style of music in duple meter with a quick tempo and syncopated rhythms that is associated with popular Brazilian dance. Numerous jazz standards incorporate the Samba style.

SAMPLE, JOSEPH "JOE" (1939–). A pianist, Joe Sample was a founding member of the **Jazz Crusaders** while still in high school. Sample would play with the group, which eventually became known simply as the **Crusaders,** until 1987. In addition, during the late 1960s, Sample worked with **Bobby Hutcherson** and **Harold Land,** and during the 1970s as a member of the group L.A. Express. During the 1990s, Sample formed a group known as the Soul Collective and also played in the group Legends.

SAMPSON, EDGAR (1907–1973). A multi-instrumentalist, composer, and arranger, Edgar Sampson played **saxophone** in many bands during the 1920s, including a brief stint with **Duke Ellington**. During the 1930s, Sampson played with **Fletcher Henderson, Rex Stewart,** and **Chick Webb,** and it was during this time that he began to compose and arrange works for **big band,** contributing to the bands of **Benny Goodman, Artie Shaw, Teddy Wilson,** and others. Sampson continued to play from the 1940s on, leading his own big band from 1949 to 1951 and leading small groups from the late 1950s through the early 1960s, in addition to writing music for such varied artists as Tito Puente.

SANBORN, DAVID (1945–). A saxophonist, David Sanborn has worked for many popular Rock and **Rhythm and Blues (R&B)** groups including David Bowie, **Stevie Wonder,** James Taylor, and others. Sanborn has also played with **Gil Evans** and with the **Brecker** Brothers, in addition to leading his own groups and **recording** his own **albums,** many of which have won Grammy Awards.

SANDERS, PHAROAH (1940–). A saxophonist, Pharoah Sanders moved to New York in 1962 and started playing with **Billy Higgins, Don Cherry,** and **Sun Ra.** From 1965 to 1967, Sanders also worked with **John Coltrane,** and after Coltrane's death, he worked with the Jazz Composer's Orchestra and led his own small group before moving back to California in the early 1970s. Sanders has since mainly led his own groups, and his **recordings** have spanned a variety of styles including **Swing,** Disco, **Avant-Garde, Bebop,** and **Rhythm and Blues (R&B).** During the 1990s, Sanders recorded with **Steve Turre,** Wallace Roney, and others.

SANDOVAL, ARTURO (1949–). A **trumpet** player, Arturo Sandoval played in groups in Cuba and was a founding member of the **Orquesta Cubana de Música Moderna,** which became the group **Irakere.** It was through this group that Sandoval met **Dizzy Gillespie,** who would later hire Sandoval to play in his United Nations Band. While touring with that group in 1990, Sandoval defected to the United States and has continued to lead his own groups and work as a **sideman.** Sandoval has performed a wide range of music, from Classical music with the National Symphony Orchestra, to Latin music with **Paquito D'Rivera** and Tito Puente, to jazz and **Bebop** with varied groups including the **GRP** All-Star Big Band,

Woody Herman, Stan Getz, Herbie Hancock and others, and Pop music with various popular artists.

SANTAMARÍA, MONGO (1922–2003). A percussionist, Mongo Santamaría was first inspired by Chano Pozo and moved to New York in the late 1940s. From 1951 to 1957, Santamaría played with Tito Puente, from 1957 to 1961 with Cal Tjader, and from 1961 on he led his own groups that included such notable sidemen as Chick Corea and Hubert Laws. Santamaría scored a Top 10 hit with his version of Herbie Hancock's "Watermelon Man" in 1962.

SAUTER, EDDIE (1914–1981). A composer and arranger, Eddie Sauter arranged music for Red Norvo's groups during the 1930s. From the late 1930s on, Sauter wrote music for Benny Goodman, Artie Shaw, Woody Herman, Tommy Dorsey, Ray McKinley, and others. During the 1950s, Sauter led his own big band and later arranged music for Stan Getz.

SAVOY BALLROOM. The Savoy Ballroom opened in 1926 and was located on Lenox Avenue in Harlem. The Savoy was one of the first racially integrated public places in the country. Boasting two stages, it was the scene of numerous occasions of battling bands in which each band performed, the winner being determined by the public. Major bands that performed there include the Chick Webb Orchestra and the Benny Goodman Orchestra, and later, Bebop greats Dizzy Gillespie, Charlie Parker, and others. It is memorialized by the jazz classic of Edgar Sampson, "Stompin' at the Savoy." See also BATTLE OF BANDS.

SAXOPHONE. A family of reed instruments (soprano, alto, tenor, and baritone) utilized prominently in jazz. Important jazz saxophone players include Coleman Hawkins, Lester Young, Charlie Parker, John Coltrane, Gerry Mulligan, and many others. See also ALTO SAXOPHONE; BARITONE SAXOPHONE; HONK; SOPRANO SAXOPHONE; TENOR SAXOPHONE.

SCAT. A style of vocal improvisation in which a vocalist uses nonsensical syllables to create a solo. Originally attributed to Louis Armstrong, the style has since been adopted by many jazz vocalists, notably Ella Fitzgerald, Betty Carter, and Sarah Vaughan, among others. See also JEFFERSON, EDDIE; MURPHY, MARK; TORMÉ, MEL; VOCALESE.

SCHNEIDER, MARIA (1960–). A composer and bandleader, Maria Schneider was first apprenticed to Gil Evans and Bob Brookmeyer. While studying with Brookmeyer, Schneider wrote music for the **Mel Lewis** Orchestra. Schneider founded a band with John Fedchock in 1988, and in 1991 she was the recipient of the Gil Evans Fellowship Award. From 1993, Schneider has led her own **big band** in New York City and has been the recipient of two Grammy Awards and nine Grammy Award nominations.

SCHULLER, GUNTHER (1925–). An educator, writer, composer, and conductor, Gunther Schuller first became interested in jazz after hearing **Duke Ellington**. In 1949, Schuller played **French horn** on **Miles Davis'** *Birth of the Cool*, and during the 1950s he wrote music for the **Modern Jazz Quartet**. Since then, Schuller has been active in the **Third Stream** genre, a term he invented to describe the intersection of jazz and Classical music. Schuller is the author of several texts on jazz history, including *Early Jazz: Its Roots and Musical Development* and *The Swing Era: The Development of Jazz, 1930–1945*.

SCOFIELD, JOHN (1951–). A guitarist, John Scofield first achieved jazz notoriety performing with **Gerry Mulligan** and **Chet Baker** in 1974. Scofield went on to perform with **Billy Cobham, Charles Mingus,** Jay McShann, **Ron Carter, Lee Konitz, Steve Swallow,** and others during the remainder of the 1970s. Scofield joined **Miles Davis** from 1982 to 1985, and from 1985, Scofield has led his own groups, which have included Joe Lovano, **Dennis Irwin, Randy Brecker, Dave Holland,** and others. *See also* ELECTRIC GUITAR; GUITAR.

SCOOP. A musical technique where the performer starts a note under the pitch and bends it up to the correct pitch.

SCOTT, TOM (1948–). A saxophonist and composer, Tom Scott formed the group L.A. Express in 1973, and over the years his sidemen in the group have included **Steve Gadd** and **Joe Sample**. In addition to leading his own groups, Scott has performed or recorded with **Gerry Mulligan, Tony Williams, Woody Herman,** and the **GRP** Big Band. Scott has been extremely active as composer for television and film, with credits including *Conquest of the Planet of the Apes*, *Beretta*, and many others.

SEBESKY, DON (1937–). A trombonist, composer, and arranger, Don Sebesky played with **Kai Winding, Claude Thornhill, Maynard Ferguson,** and in **Tommy Dorsey**'s band during the 1950s. During the late 1950s, Sebesky worked as a composer and arranger for Ferguson, **Stan Kenton,** and **Gerry Mulligan**. From the 1960s on, Sebesky has worked mostly as a composer and arranger, writing music for **Wes Montgomery, Buddy Rich, Freddie Hubbard**, and others, in addition to his own **big band**. He has since become more active in education and lecturing, and he published a popular book on jazz arranging, *The Contemporary Arranger*.

SESSION. In jazz vernacular, a term used to describe any time when musicians get together to play, as in a **jam session** or **recording** session.

SET. In jazz vernacular, a term used to describe the collection of tunes to be played at a performance, or also to describe a portion of a performance usually split up by breaks.

SEVERINSEN, CARL "DOC" (1927–). A **trumpet** player and **bandleader**, Doc Severinsen played in the bands of **Charlie Barnet**, Sam Donahue, and **Tommy Dorsey** during the late 1940s. From 1949, Severinsen worked as a **studio musician**, and in 1962 he became assistant conductor of the NBC *Tonight Show* band, taking over complete leadership in 1967. Severinsen remained with the show until 1992 and since has been active as a guest artist and conductor with symphony orchestras, led his own groups, and performed in reunion shows with other members of the *Tonight Show* band. He was touring as recently as 2012.

SHAKE. An instrumental technique where the pitch of a note is moved rapidly back and forth to a higher one; this can be accomplished in the same manner as a trill or, on a **brass** instrument, with very rapid lip trills (using either a quick lip slur or actually shaking the instrument).

SHAKTI. A Fusion band formed by **John McLaughlin** in 1973. The band mixed jazz with the music of India and was mainly active during the 1970s, with reunion performances in 1985 and 1997.

SHANK, CLIFFORD EVERETT "BUD" (1926–2009). A saxophonist and flutist, Bud Shank played with **Charlie Barnet** on the West Coast from 1946 to 1948, and then with **Stan Kenton** from 1950 to 1952. His career was briefly interrupted when he was drafted in 1952, but upon his return to Los Angeles he played with Howard Rumsey's Lighthouse All-Stars from 1953 to 1955, in addition to **recording** with **Gerry Mulligan** and **Chet Baker**. From 1956 he led his own group and freelanced in the Los Angeles area, and in 1974 he formed the group L.A. Four with Ray Brown; later sidemen would include **Jeff Hamilton**. During the 1980s, Shank played with Baker, **Shorty Rogers**, and in a reunion of the Lighthouse All-Stars, in addition to leading his own groups throughout the 1990s.

SHARON, RALPH (1923–). A pianist and arranger, Ralph Sharon worked with **Ted Heath** during the late 1940s before moving to the United States in 1953. During the 1950s, Sharon played with **Charles Mingus, Kenny Clarke, Milt Hinton**, and others before becoming the musical director for **Tony Bennett** in 1956, a post which he held for more than 40 years. Sharon also worked as an accompanist for **Rosemary Clooney** and **Mel Tormé**, in addition to leading his own groups.

SHAUGHNESSY, ED(WIN THOMAS) (1929–). A drummer, Ed Shaughnessy worked with **George Shearing, Jack Teagarden, Charlie Ventura**, and others during the late 1940s. During the 1950s, Shaughnessy played with **Zoot Sims, Roy Eldridge, Charles Mingus, Duke Ellington, Benny Goodman, Tommy Dorsey**, among others, in addition to working for the **Columbia Broadcasting System (CBS)**. During the 1960s, Shaughnessy played with **Count Basie, Oliver Nelson, Clark Terry, Johnny Hodges**, and many others, and in 1964 he joined the NBC *Tonight Show* band. Shaughnessy has continued to play in bands led by **Doc Severinsen** after the *Tonight Show* band was replaced in 1992, in addition to leading his own groups and working as a teacher.

SHAVERS, CHARLIE (1917–1971). A **trumpet** player, Charlie Shavers played while still young in a trumpet section with **Dizzy Gillespie**. During the late 1930s, Shavers played with Lucky Millinder before achieving notoriety with **John Kirby** in 1937. Shavers left Kirby's group in 1944 and became the featured trumpet soloist in **Tommy Dorsey**'s band, a position that he would hold intermittently into the 1950s. During the 1950s and 1960s, Shavers also played with **Benny Goodman, Louie Bellson, Frank Sinatra**, and **Jazz at the Philharmonic**, in addition to leading his own groups.

SHAW, ARTIE (1910–2004). A clarinetist, **bandleader**, and composer, Artie Shaw played in bands in Connecticut and Cleveland before moving to New York in 1929. Shaw played regularly at **jam sessions** during the early 1930s and recorded with **Teddy Wilson** before quitting music from 1934 to 1935. Shaw formed a short-lived group in the mid-1930s with the instrumentation of a string quartet, **rhythm section**, and clarinet, but by 1937 he had disbanded the group and formed a more traditional **big band**. Members of his band included **Buddy Rich, Billie Holiday**, and **Georgie Auld**, and in 1938 the band had a huge hit with "Begin the Beguine"; other hits, including "Moonglow" and "Stardust," followed.

Shaw disbanded the group in 1939, and in 1940 he recorded his hit "Frenesi" with a studio orchestra. He formed his group **Gramercy Five** and re-formed his big band with an additional string section shortly thereafter, only to disband the groups again after a few months. During World War II, Shaw led a group for the U.S. Navy, and in 1944 he formed a new band that featured **Roy Eldridge**. Shaw continued to found and then disband groups throughout the rest of the 1940s and 1950s, finally retiring permanently from playing music in 1954. Shaw worked as a writer and educator through the rest of the 1950s, 1960s, and 1970s, and in 1983 he again organized a big band which was nominally led by clarinetist **Dick Johnson**, although Shaw occasionally appeared as conductor.

SHAW, ARVELL (1923–2002). A bassist, Arvell Shaw played with **Fate Marable** in 1942 before his career was interrupted by military service. After leaving the service in 1945, Shaw began a long association with **Louis Armstrong** that would last intermittently until 1971. In addition to his time with Armstrong, Shaw played with **Benny Goodman**, **Sidney Bechet**, **Coleman Hawkins**, and others during the 1950s, and **Teddy Wilson**, **Wild Bill Davison**, and others during the 1960s. During the 1970s, Shaw worked with **Earl Hines** and others, and from the 1980s he worked in pit orchestras on Broadway, in addition to appearing with **Lionel Hampton**'s Golden Men of Jazz and in Keith Smith's "The Wonderful World of Louis Armstrong" tour.

SHAW, WOODY (1944–1989). A **trumpet** player, Woody Shaw worked with **Eric Dolphy** in 1963 before moving to Europe for a few years, where he worked with **Bud Powell**, **Kenny Clarke**, and others. Shaw returned to the United States in 1965, joining **Horace Silver** and later **McCoy Tyner** and **Max Roach**. During the 1970s, Shaw played with **Art Blakey**'s **Jazz Messengers** in addition to leading his own bands which included **Joe Henderson**, **Bobby Hutcherson**, and others, and featured **Dexter Gordon** during his homecoming tour in 1976. Shaw continued to lead his own groups in the 1980s, but problems related to drug addiction haunted him until his untimely death in 1989.

SHEARING, GEORGE (1919–2011). A Canadian pianist, George Shearing was born blind and was inspired to play jazz by **recordings** of **Fats Waller**, **Teddy Wilson**, and **Art Tatum**. Shearing moved to the United States in 1947 and led his own quintet using guitar, **vibraphones**, **bass**, and **drums**; sidemen in the groups included **Cal Tjader**, **Joe Pass**, and Israel Crosby. Shearing continued to lead the quintet until 1967, thereafter appearing with trios and duos, as soloist, and also with singers including **Carmen McRae** and **Mel Tormé**. Shearing is known for his distinctive "locked hands" style and also for his popular composition "Lullaby of Birdland."

SHELDON, JACK (1931–). A **trumpet** player and vocalist, Jack Sheldon played with many of the best jazz musicians on the West Coast during the 1950s, including Howard Rumsey's Lighthouse All-Stars, **Art Pepper, Wardell Gray, Dexter Gordon, Jimmy Giuffre, Stan Kenton**, and others. From 1959 to 1960, Sheldon worked with **Benny Goodman**, but during the 1960s his career turned to stand-up comedy and acting. During the 1970s and 1980s, Sheldon led his own small groups in addition to playing in bands led by Bill Berry, Goodman, and **Woody Herman**, and from the 1990s, he has led his own **big band**. He continues to perform today.

SHEPP, ARCHIE (1937–). A saxophonist, Archie Shepp moved to New York in 1959 and joined **Cecil Taylor** from 1960 to 1961. During the early to mid-1960s, Shepp played with **Bill Dixon, Don Cherry** (in the group New York Contemporary Five), and **John Coltrane** before leading his own groups from 1965 on. Originally an advocate of **Free Jazz**, Shepp has since broadened his stylistic horizons to include more conventional ideas.

SHEROCK, CLARENCE "SHORTY" (1915–1980). A **trumpet** and **cornet** player, Shorty Sherock played with **Ben Pollack** before joining **Jimmy Dorsey** during the late 1930s. From the late 1930s through the mid-1940s, Sherock played with **Gene Krupa, Tommy Dorsey**, and Horace Heidt, and during the mid-1940s, Sherock led his own band in addition to performing with **Jazz at the Philharmonic**. From the 1950s on, Sherock worked freelance and as a **studio musician**, and he was active until 1979.

SHEW, BOBBY (1941–). A **trumpet** player, Bobby Shew played with the bands of **Tommy Dorsey, Woody Herman, Benny Goodman**, and **Buddy Rich** during the middle to late 1960s. After several years playing trumpet in Las Vegas, Shew moved to Los Angeles and began work as a **studio musician**, also working as a member of the **Toshiko Akiyoshi–Lew Tabackin** Big Band and other bands led by **Louie Bellson, Don Menza, Ed Shaughnessy**, and others. From the 1980s, Shew has appeared primarily in small-group settings, and he has remained active as a clinician and educator.

SHIELDS, LARRY (1893–1953). A **clarinet** player, Larry Shields joined **Nick LaRocca**'s band at the young age of 15. From 1916 to 1921, he played in the **Original Dixieland Jazz Band** and participated in the first jazz **recording** in 1917. Shields later played with **Paul Whiteman**, and during the 1930s he re-formed the Original Dixieland Jazz Band with different members for various tours and performances.

SHIHAB, SAHIB (1925–1989). A saxophonist, Sahib Shihab played with **Fletcher Henderson** and **Roy Eldridge** during the mid-1940s. From 1947 into the 1950s, Shihab played with **Art Blakey, Thelonious Monk, Tadd Dameron, Dizzy Gillespie, John Coltrane,** and others. Shihab settled in Europe after touring there with **Quincy Jones** from 1959 to 1960, writing a jazz ballet in 1965 based on "The Red Shoes." Shihab continued to perform until his death in 1989.

SHORTER, WAYNE (1933–). A saxophonist and composer, Wayne Shorter played with **Horace Silver** before his burgeoning career was interrupted by military service in 1956. After returning from service, Shorter played with **Maynard Ferguson** before joining **Art Blakey's Jazz Messengers** from 1959 to 1964. Shorter joined **Miles Davis** from 1964 to 1970, and in 1970, Shorter and **Joe Zawinul** founded the group Weather Report, with which he performed into the 1980s. During the 1970s, Shorter also performed with **Herbie Hancock** and **Freddie Hubbard** in Hancock's **V.S.O.P.** Since the mid-1980s, Shorter has led various small groups. Among Shorter's well-known compositions are the tunes "E.S.P.," "Footprints," and "Nefertiti." He continues to perform in concert and at **jazz festivals.**

SHOUT. In jazz parlance, the section of music for **big band** that features the entire band playing together, typically in the same rhythms and led by trumpets in the upper register.

SHUFFLE. A specific rhythmic style associated with jazz and **Blues** where eighth notes are played in more of a dotted eighth–sixteenth note feel as opposed to the eighth-note triplet feel of **Swing.**

SIDEMAN. A term used to describe the musician(s) who are not **leading** or fronting a group. Frequently, musicians will assume sideman roles before they begin leading their own groups. Significant sidemen in the history of jazz include performers who apprenticed with a given musician for several years before then developing into an important artist. Musicians such as **John Coltrane** and **Cannonball Adderley** each spent several years as a sideman working under **Miles Davis** before fronting their own bands. Many **rhythm section** players, including **Paul Chambers, Hank Jones, Freddie Green, Sonny Payne,** and Walter Davis worked primarily as sidemen throughout most of their careers.

SILVER, HORACE (1928–). A pianist and composer, Horace Silver's first **gig** was with **Stan Getz** from 1950 to 1951. Silver then moved to New

York and during the 1950s played with **Art Blakey, Coleman Hawkins, Lou Donaldson, Lester Young,** and others, co-leading the **Jazz Messengers** with Blakey before forming his own quintet in 1956. Silver has continued to lead his own groups with sidemen over the years that have included **Blue Mitchell, Art Farmer, Joe Henderson, Tom Harrell, Woody Shaw, Hank Mobley,** and Randy and Michael **Brecker,** and he was active through the 1990s. Also a noted composer, Silver's most famous jazz compositions include "The Preacher," "Song for My Father," and "Peace." *See also* HARD BOP; SOUL JAZZ.

SIMMONS, JOHN (1918–1979). A bassist, John Simmons originally played **trumpet** but switched later to the bass. Simmons's first **gigs** were with **Nat "King" Cole** during the 1930s, and he recorded with **Teddy Wilson** in 1937. During the 1940s, Simmons worked with a number of musicians, among them **Roy Eldridge, Benny Goodman, Louis Armstrong, Duke Ellington, Hot Lips Page, Billie Holiday, Coleman Hawkins, Ben Webster, Benny Carter, Thelonious Monk,** and many others. During the 1950s, Simmons played with **Sonny Stitt, Eddie "Lockjaw" Davis, Louie Bellson, Buddy Rich, Art Tatum, Maynard Ferguson,** and **Harry Edison** before illness interrupted his career in the 1960s.

SIMS, ZOOT (1925–1985). A saxophonist and **bandleader,** John "Zoot" Sims worked early in a few bands, including **Benny Goodman**'s, before his career was interrupted by military service from 1944 to 1946. After leaving the army, Sims played again with Goodman before achieving fame as a member of the Four Brothers saxophone section in **Woody Herman**'s band, with whom he would perform from 1947 to 1949. Sims spent the rest of 1949–1950 with **Artie Shaw,** and during the 1950s, Sims played with Goodman, **Roy Eldridge, Stan Kenton,** and **Gerry Mulligan,** and co-led a group with Al Cohn. During the 1960s and 1970s, Sims continued to perform on and off with Goodman and Herman, in addition to leading his own groups. Sims was active into the 1980s.

SINATRA, FRANK (1915–1998). A singer and actor, Frank Sinatra was inspired to sing after hearing **Bing Crosby** in 1933, and in 1935 he was awarded first prize in the Major Bowes Amateur Hour as a member of the group Hoboken Four. Sinatra toured with the group briefly and appeared on radio for the next few years until he joined Harry James from 1939 to 1940. Sinatra then joined **Tommy Dorsey** from 1940 to 1942, during which time he became extremely popular, with hits including "Imagination," "Violets for Your Furs," and "Polka Dots and Moonbeams."

By 1943, Sinatra decided to capitalize on his popularity by quitting Dorsey's band to pursue a solo career, which was wildly successful for the next several years as he made several records and appeared in many films. A lull in his popularity in the early 1950s was averted after his Academy Award–winning appearance in the film *From Here to Eternity*. His **recording** career was resurrected soon after, signing with **Capitol** Records in 1953 and making several extremely successful **albums** during the 1950s including *In the Wee Small Hours* (1955), *Songs for Swingin' Lovers* (1956), and *Come Fly with Me* (1958). During the 1960s he continued to make hit records, in addition to forming his own record label, **Reprise**, on which he recorded with **Count Basie** and **Duke Ellington**. Sinatra briefly retired in 1971 but resumed touring in 1973 and was active until 1995. An extremely popular singer, Sinatra transcended music and moved to the realm of cultural icon.

SINGING. The act of creating a melody using one's voice as the instrument. In jazz, popular or important singers and vocalists are numerous, including **Louis Armstrong**, **Betty Carter**, **Ella Fitzgerald**, **Billie Holiday**, and Diana Krall. *See also* BENSON, GEORGE; BEY, ANDY; CALLOWAY, CAB; CLOONEY, ROSEMARY; ECKSTINE, WILLIAM "BILLY"; GILBERTO, ASTRUD; HARTMAN, JOHNNY; HENDRICKS, JON; JARREAU, AL; McFERRIN, BOBBY; McRAE, CARMEN; MILLS BROTHERS; MERRILL, HELEN; MURPHY, MARK; PRIMA, LOUIS; RAINEY, MA; ROSS, ANNEBELLE "ANNIE"; RUSHING, JIMMY; SCAT; SINATRA, FRANK; SMITH, BESSIE; TORMÉ, MEL; VAUGHAN, SARAH; VOCALESE; WASHINGTON, DINAH; WATERS, ETHEL; WILLIAMS, JOE.

SITAR. An instrument in the lute family that is fretted and associated with India and South Asia. It has been incorporated into jazz at times by **Miles Davis**, **John Scofield**, and others.

SIT IN. In jazz parlance, a term that refers to a musician performing with a group of which he/she is not a regular member, including impromptu performances.

SLAP BASS. This term can refer to either pulling the strings of a double **bass** extremely hard (causing the strings to "slap" back to the instrument), or to the practice of actually "slapping" the bass with the thumb or hand while plucking the strings with other fingers. **Milt Hinton** is considered to have been one of the masters of this technique.

SMEAR. An instrumental technique involving bending the pitch of a note downward and then back to the original pitch.

SMITH, BESSIE (1894–1937). A singer, Bessie Smith began **singing** in the same minstrel show as **Ma Rainey** during the early 1910s. In 1923, she had a hit with "Downhearted Blues" and almost immediately became one of the most popular **Blues** singers of the time. From 1923 on, she recorded with a number of artists including **Louis Armstrong**, **James P. Johnson**, **Fletcher Henderson**, and many others, but her career was eventually curtailed by the advent of the Great Depression. Often referred to as "Empress of the Blues," Smith attempted a comeback during the 1930s that featured a **recording session** with **Jack Teagarden** and **Benny Goodman** before dying as the result of a car accident in 1937.

SMITH, CHARLIE (1927–1966). A drummer, Charlie Smith worked with **Ella Fitzgerald** in 1948. During the late 1940s and the 1950s, Smith played with **George Shearing**, **Benny Goodman**, **Oscar Peterson**, **Artie Shaw**, **Charlie Parker**, and **Dizzy Gillespie**, among others. During the 1960s, Smith worked mostly as a composer and educator.

SMITH, CLADYS "JABBO" (1908–1991). A **trumpeter** and a singer, Jabbo Smith played in bands in Philadelphia and New York during the 1920s, and in 1927 he recorded with **Duke Ellington** on his piece "Black and Tan Fantasy." For the rest of the 1920s, Smith played with **James P. Johnson** and **Fats Waller**, moving to Chicago in 1928. In Chicago, Smith played with **Earl Hines** and led his own bands, making several noteworthy records with his group the Rhythm Aces. Smith continued to perform until briefly retiring in Milwaukee, and then came out of retirement during the 1960s and continued to perform into the 1980s.

SMITH, HENRY "BUSTER" (1904–1991). A clarinetist, saxophonist, and arranger, Buster Smith played in groups in Texas before joining **Walter Page**'s **territory band** in Oklahoma in 1925. During the middle to late 1920s, the band included many musicians who would later go on to play with **Bennie Moten**, including **Count Basie** and **Hot Lips Page**. In 1931, Smith assumed leadership of the band, now known as the 13 Original Blue Devils, featuring saxophonist **Lester Young**. In 1933, Smith disbanded the group and moved to Kansas City where he joined Moten's band and later, after Moten's death, joined Basie's band. Smith remained in Kansas City after Basie took his band to New York in the late 1930s, eventually forming his own group that would feature **Charlie Parker**. In 1938, Smith moved to New York and worked as an arranger for Basie, **Benny Carter**, and others. He moved to Dallas in 1942 and continued to play, later on **bass** and **piano**, well into the 1980s. Smith is recognized as an early influence on Parker.

SMITH, JIMMY (1925–2005). An organist, Jimmy Smith started playing the Hammond B3 organ in 1953, and by 1955 he had formed his own trio and was **recording albums** for **Blue Note** Records. Over the years, Smith recorded with a wide variety of sidemen, including Donald Bailey, **Kenny Burrell, Stanley Turrentine, Lee Morgan, Lou Donaldson, Wes Montgomery**, and others. Smith continued playing into the 2000s and is generally viewed as perhaps the most influential jazz organist to ever play the instrument. *See also* HAMMOND ORGAN; ORGAN.

SMITH, JOHNNY (1922–). A guitarist, Johnny Smith was a **studio musician** during the late 1940s and early 1950s before he formed a group and recorded the critically acclaimed **album** *Moonlight in Vermont* with **Stan Getz** in 1952. Smith continued to lead groups and record throughout the 1950s, including playing under the name Sir Jonathon Gasser on the album *Jazz Studio* in 1953 with **Bennie Green** and **Kenny Clarke**. Smith moved to Colorado Springs, Colorado, during the 1960s and became the owner of a music store.

SMITH, LONNIE LISTON (1940–). A pianist, Lonnie Liston Smith moved to New York in 1962 and started working with **Betty Carter**. During the rest of the 1960s and into the 1970s, Smith worked with **Max Roach, Roland Kirk, Art Blakey, Joe Williams, Pharoah Sanders**, and others before landing with **Miles Davis** in 1973. He recorded two CDs with Davis, *On the Corner* and *Big Fun*. After leaving Davis' group, Smith formed the group Cosmic Echoes with his brother in 1974, a group that performed into the 1990s. He remains active as a performer at **jazz festivals** and jazz clubs worldwide.

SMITH, MARVIN "SMITTY" (1961–). A drummer, Marvin "Smitty" Smith played in the bands of **Jon Hendricks**, Frank Foster, Kevin Eubanks, and others during the 1980s, in addition to freelance appearances with **Slide Hampton, Bobby Watson, Archie Shepp**, Terrence Blanchard, **Branford Marsalis**, Ray Brown, **Ron Carter, Sonny Rollins**, the Jazztet, and many others. Smith joined the NBC *Tonight Show* band led by Eubanks in 1995 and has remained active as a **studio musician** since then.

SMITH, PINE TOP (1904–1929). A pianist, Clarence "Pine Top" Smith was discovered during the 1920s and recorded **albums** in the late 1920s in Chicago. Of those **recordings**, "Pine Top's Boogie-Woogie" is his best known, simultaneously naming and popularizing the genre of **Boogie-Woogie**. Smith died from a gunshot wound from a stray bullet.

SMITH, RUSSELL (1890–1966). A **trumpet** player, Russell Smith moved to New York in 1910, and from 1925 to 1941 he was the **lead** trumpet player for the band of **Fletcher Henderson**. During this time, Smith also played with **Benny Carter** and **Horace Henderson**. After leaving Fletcher Henderson's group, Smith played with **Cab Calloway** from 1941 to 1946 and **Noble Sissle** from 1946 to 1950. Smith resided in California from the 1950s until his death, working primarily as a teacher.

SMITH, STUFF (1909–1967). A singer and **violin** player, Hezekiah "Stuff" Smith worked with many bands, including a brief stint with **Jelly Roll Morton**, before forming his own band in the mid-1930s that included **Cozy Cole** and performed regularly at the **Onyx** Club in New York. Forced to disband the group due to bankruptcy, Smith re-formed other groups and even took over **Fats Waller**'s band for a short time in the early 1940s after Waller died. During the 1940s and early 1950s, Smith's career was seemingly in decline before being revived by a group of records released in 1957. Smith continued to play and tour throughout most of the 1960s, eventually residing in **Europe**.

SMITH, WILLIE "THE LION" (1887–1973). A **pianist**, Willie "the Lion" Smith earned his nickname as a soldier during World War I. Although well known to fellow musicians including **Fats Waller** and **Duke Ellington**, Smith toiled in relative obscurity in New York until the mid-1930s, when **Decca** released a series of **albums** that displayed his mastery of the **Stride** technique. Smith continued to lead groups, record, perform, and tour into the early 1970s.

SMOOTH JAZZ. A term used to describe a style of jazz that combines jazz-influenced phrasing and improvising with adult/contemporary Pop music styles. Smooth jazz rarely spotlights improvisation, instead focusing on melodic material that was inspired or taken directly from Pop music in these genres. This style became prominent in the late 1970s. Smooth jazz artists include saxophonists Kenny G and **David Sanborn**, and guitarist **George Benson**, who had commercial success with releases including "This Masquerade" and "Breezin'."

SNOWDEN, ELMER (1900–1973). A banjoist, saxophonist, and **bandleader**, Elmer Snowden moved to New York in 1923 and formed the **Washingtonians**, a band that also featured **Duke Ellington** and **Bubber Miley**. Ellington soon became the leader of the group, and it formed the nucleus of his own very successful orchestra. Snowden continued to lead his own bands during the 1920s and 1930s and employed many great jazz musicians including **Jimmie Lunceford, Count Basie, Rex Stewart, Benny Carter, Chick Webb, Roy Eldridge, Sid Catlett,** and many others. Snowden continued to lead bands throughout the 1940s, 1950s, and 1960s, although he retired from music for a bit during the 1950s and worked as a parking lot attendant. *See also* BANJO.

SOCIETY BAND. A term applied to dance bands that were typically employed by wealthy patrons. Society bands generally performed a lighter, less aggressive **Swing** style.

SOLO. See IMPROVISATION.

SOLOFF, LEW(IS) MICHAEL (1944–). A **trumpet** player, Lew Soloff graduated from the Eastman School of Music in 1965 and spent the next few years working with many musicians in New York including **Gil Evans, Maynard Ferguson, Joe Henderson** (in his rehearsal **big band**), **Slide Hampton, Chuck Mangione,** Machito, Tito Puente, and others. In 1968, Soloff replaced **Randy Brecker** in the group **Blood, Sweat and Tears,** with whom he would play until 1973. During the 1970s, Soloff played with the **Thad Jones–Mel Lewis** Orchestra and the Gil Evans Orchestra, freelanced and recorded with **Stanley Turrentine** and **Sonny Stitt,** and co-led a group with Jon Faddis. During the 1980s and 1990s, Soloff played with the Manhattan Jazz Quintet, the Manhattan Jazz Orchestra, the Carnegie Hall Jazz Band, the Lincoln Center Jazz Band, and the **Mingus** Big Band. He remains active as an educator and performer.

SONET. Record **label** founded in 1956. Artists include **Zoot Sims, Warne Marsh, Archie Shepp, Benny Carter,** and others.

SOPH, ED(WARD B.) (1945–). A drummer, Ed Soph toured with **Stan Kenton** during his summers while a student at North Texas State University during the 1960s, and after graduation he played **drum set** with **Woody Herman** from 1968 to 1971. Soph moved to New York in 1971 and spent the 1970s working freelance and also with **Bill Watrous, Clark Terry,** and **Dave Liebman.** Soph has taught at the University of North Texas since the 1980s.

SOPRANO SAXOPHONE. An instrument in the **saxophone** family, pitched in the key of B♭ and above the **alto saxophone.** Notable performers include **John Coltrane, Sidney Bechet, Branford Marsalis,** and **David Liebman.**

SOPRANO SUMMIT. Group formed by Bob Wilbur and **Kenny Davern** in 1972 that was active until 1979.

SOUL JAZZ. A style of jazz that became prominent in the early 1960s and is sometimes considered synonymous with **Hard Bop**. Soul Jazz is considered to be a style that emphasizes the **groove**, or rhythmic pulse, that is occurring behind the melody. Often this pulse is more of a straight eighth-note feel that is reminiscent of similar pulses found in Gospel, **Rhythm and Blues (R&B)**, and **Blues** music. Groups like the **Jazz Crusaders** are credited with performing in the Soul Jazz style. *See also* TURRENTINE, STANLEY.

SOUL NOTE. A **record label** founded in 1979. Artists include **Art Farmer**, **Paul Motian**, and others.

SPANIER, FRANCIS JOSEPH JULIAN "MUGGSY" (1906–1967). A **cornet** player, Muggsy Spanier's first **gig** was with Elmer Schoebel in 1920. During the 1920s, Spanier played in various bands, and by 1929 he was working with Ted Lewis, with whom he played until 1936, when he left to join **Ben Pollack**. Spanier formed his own bands from the late 1930s on, including the **Ragtime** Band. During the 1940s, he played with **Sidney Bechet**, Bob Crosby, **Miff Mole**, and others. During the 1950s, he appeared with **Earl Hines**, retiring from music in 1964.

SPHERE. A **Thelonious Monk** tribute band formed in 1982 by **Charlie Rouse** that was active until 1988. *See also* BARRON, KENNY; RILEY, BEN.

SPIKES' SEVEN PODS OF PEPPER. A name used by **Kid Ory**'s Original Creole Jazz Band during **recordings** in the early 1920s.

SPIRITS OF RHYTHM. A band formed in 1929 by Wilbur Daniels, Douglas Daniels, and Leo Watson. All three played the tiple, a **guitar**-like instrument, and the band, which expanded to include guitar and percussion during the 1930s, performed frequently at the **Onyx** nightclub.

SPIVAK, CHARLIE (1907–1982). A **trumpet** player and **bandleader**, Charlie Spivak worked with Paul Specht during the 1920s. During the 1930s, Spivak played with **Ben Pollack**, the **Dorsey** brothers, **Ray Noble**, and Bob Crosby, in addition to working as a **studio musician**. During the 1940s, Spivak led his own band, which was bankrolled by **Glenn Miller**, and after that group disbanded he led another band into the 1950s.

SPONTANEOUS MUSIC ENSEMBLE. A group formed in Great Britain in 1965. Members included **Kenny Wheeler** and **Dave Holland**, and the group was primarily associated with Free Jazz.

SPOTLITE. A **record label** and company established in 1968. Artists include **Charlie Parker** (reissues of the **sessions** on **Dial**) and **Art Pepper**, among many others.

SPROLES, VICTOR (1927–). A bassist, Victor Sproles played with **Coleman Hawkins, Ira Sullivan, Charlie Parker, Wardell Gray, Lester Young, Dexter Gordon, Stan Getz, Sun Ra, Eddie "Lockjaw" Davis**, and others during the 1950s. During the 1960s, Sproles played with **Carmen McRae**, **Art Blakey**'s **Jazz Messengers**, and **Lee Morgan**. Sproles continued to perform and record into the 1980s. *See also* BASS.

SPYRO GYRA. A **Jazz-Rock** Fusion group founded in 1974 by Jay Beckenstein and Jeremy Wall. Among their many successful **albums** is *Morning Dance* (1979). The group remains active into the 2010s.

SQUADRONAIRES. The name given to the Royal Air Force's **dance band** formed in 1940. After World War II, the group continued to play, eventually becoming a civilian group that remained active until 1964.

STAMM, MARVIN (1939–). A **trumpet** player, Marvin Stamm had his first notable **gigs** with **Stan Kenton** during the early 1960s. Stamm then played with **Woody Herman**, the **Thad Jones–Mel Lewis** Orchestra, Duke Pearson, **Chick Corea**, and others in addition to working as a **studio musician**. During the 1970s, Stamm led his own groups and worked with **Benny Goodman** and **Frank Sinatra**, and during the 1980s he was a founding member of the Bob Mintzer **Big Band** and appeared with the American Jazz Orchestra and with George Gruntz. During the 1990s, Stamm played with **Maria Schneider** and **Louie Bellson**, and since then he has regularly toured and played with a variety of groups, often accompanied by **Bill Mays** on piano.

STARR, KAY (1922–). A vocalist, Kay Starr sang with **Glenn Miller** and Bob Crosby during the late 1930s, but she achieved fame when she sang with **Charlie Barnet** from 1943 to 1945. During this time she also sang with the Capitol Jazzmen, which included **Coleman Hawkins, Benny Carter, Nat "King" Cole**, and **Max Roach**. From 1948, Starr worked on her own or as **leader** of a group, **singing** mostly Pop music, but she has occasionally worked with jazz musicians, including **Ben Webster** and **Count Basie**.

STATE STREET RAMBLERS. A name given to many different bands that recorded during the late 1920s; the groups at times included **Johnny Dodds, Baby Dodds,** and others.

STEEPLECHASE. A **record label** established in 1972 in Copenhagen by Nils Winther. Many American expatriates who lost contracts with other labels chose to record on SteepleChase. Artists include **Dexter Gordon, Paul Bley,** Andy LaVerne, and others. The label is still active today.

STEPS AHEAD. A **Fusion** group formed in 1979 by **Mike Mainieri** that included **Michael Brecker, Eddie Gomez,** and **Peter Erskine.** The group underwent many personnel changes but continued to perform into the 1990s. *See also* ELIAS, ELIANE; STERN, MIKE.

STERN, MIKE (1953–). A guitarist, Mike Stern was a student of **Pat Metheny** during the early 1970s, who helped get Stern his first **gig** with **Blood, Sweat and Tears** in 1974. During the 1980s, Stern played with **Billy Cobham, Miles Davis, Jaco Pastorius, David Sanborn,** and **Steps Ahead.** During the 1990s, Stern led his own groups and played with the **Brecker Brothers** and **Joe Henderson,** and from the 2000s on, he has led his own groups and continues to tour and record. *See also* ELECTRIC GUITAR; GUITAR.

STEWARD, HERBIE (1926–). A **tenor saxophone** player, Herbie Steward got his first notable **big band gig** with **Artie Shaw** from 1944 to 1946. In 1947, Steward was an original member of **Woody Herman**'s Four Brothers, and during the late 1940s to early 1950s, Steward played with Shaw, **Tommy Dorsey, Claude Thornhill,** and Harry James. In the mid-1950s, Steward moved to Las Vegas and in the 1970s to San Francisco, freelancing and playing at **jazz festivals.**

STEWART, REX (1907–1967). A cornetist, Rex Stewart moved to New York in 1921 and worked with **Elmer Snowden** from 1924 to 1925. Stewart played briefly with **Fletcher Henderson** in 1926, with **Horace Henderson** from 1926 to 1928, and then returned to Fletcher's band from 1928 to 1933. Stewart then joined **Duke Ellington**'s band in 1934, playing in the group until 1945 and co-composing several Ellington pieces including "Boy Meets Horn." After leaving Ellington's group, Stewart worked in **Europe** for a time (at one point as a chef), and during the 1950s he organized some Fletcher Henderson reunion groups in addition to writing books and articles about jazz.

STEWART, SLAM (1914–1987). A bassist and **bandleader**, Leroy Eliot "Slam" Stewart effected his trademark **solo** style of using a bow to play a solo and also humming the same melody one octave above. During the late 1930s and early 1940s, Stewart worked in a duo with Slim Gaillard, becoming famous for their hit "Flat Foot Floogee." Stewart then joined **Art Tatum** and played with him on and off from 1943 to 1950, in addition to working with **Benny Goodman, Erroll Garner, Dizzy Gillespie**, and others. During the 1950s, Stewart continued to work, appearing with **Roy Eldridge** and others, and during the 1960s and 1970s, he toured in addition to working as a teacher.

STICHTING JAZZ EN GEÏMPROVISEERDE MUZIEK IN NEDERLAND. A group active from 1965 to 1997 that promoted and developed jazz in the Netherlands.

STITT, EDWARD "SONNY" (1924–1982). A saxophonist, Sonny Stitt emerged during the heyday of the **Bebop** movement, playing with **Billy Eckstine**'s band in 1944 where he met other like-minded musicians including **Fats Navarro, Dexter Gordon**, and **Art Blakey**. During 1946, Stitt played with **Dizzy Gillespie**, and in 1947 he also played with **Miles Davis** and **Charlie Parker**. In the early 1950s, Stitt co-led a group with **Gene Ammons**, and during the rest of the 1950s he led his own groups and played in **Jazz at the Philharmonic**. During the 1960s, he played with Davis and later **Clark Terry**, and during the 1970s he appeared with the Giants of Jazz. Stitt continued to play until a few days before his death.

STOCK ARRANGEMENT. A simple, basic, and easily readable published composition made widely available.

STOMP. In Early Jazz, a stomp was a song that involved a dance or dance steps. It can also be used to refer to counting off a band's performance, as in to "stomp off."

STOP-TIME. A musical technique where the band plays only on specific downbeats or **lays out** (stops playing) entirely in order to accentuate a particular soloist or **solo** section in a song.

STORYVILLE (I). A section of the city of New Orleans famous during the early part of the 20th century as a breeding ground for **Early Jazz**.

STORYVILLE (II). A **record label** formed in 1951 in Boston. Artists include **Sidney Bechet, Zoot Sims, Lee Konitz**, and others.

STRAIGHT-AHEAD. In jazz parlance, "Straight-Ahead" refers to **Bebop** and post-Bebop styles, but excludes **Fusion, Free Jazz,** and their offshoots. Musicians who play in a Straight-Ahead style usually are very familiar with the jazz tradition and choose to play in a simple, noncomplex manner. Musicians associated with the Straight-Ahead style include **Kenny Dorham, Hank Mobley, Clifford Brown, Sonny Rollins,** and scores of others. *See also* MAINSTREAM JAZZ.

STRAYHORN, WILLIAM THOMAS "BILLY" (1915–1967). A pianist, composer, and arranger, Billy Strayhorn was primarily interested in Classical music before he heard **Duke Ellington**'s band. Strayhorn contrived to meet Ellington, and after Ellington heard Strayhorn's music the two began a long musical partnership that would last until Strayhorn's death. Among Strayhorn's many famous compositions are "Take the 'A' Train," "Lush Life," "Satin Doll," "Chelsea Bridge," and countless others, many of which also credit Ellington as co-composer.

STRETCH OUT. A jazz term meaning that a soloist plays a solo of indeterminate and exceptional length.

STRIDE. A style of **piano** playing made popular during the 1920s and 1930s where the intervals in the accompaniment in the left hand span more than an octave, causing the performer to "stride" across the keyboard. Among the best-known Stride Piano players are **James P. Johnson, Willie "the Lion" Smith,** and **Fats Waller.** *See also* BASIE, WILLIAM "COUNT"; BLAKE, EUBIE; EUROPE, JAMES REESE; HINES, EARL KENNETH "FATHA"; MORTON, FERDINAND "JELLY ROLL"; PETERSON, OSCAR; POWELL, EARL RUDOLPH "BUD"; QRS; WEATHERFORD, TEDDY; WILLIAMS, CLARENCE.

STUDIO MUSICIAN. Also known as a **session** musician, a **studio musician** is any musician whose primary source of income comes from **recording**, usually as part of a film or television orchestra.

SUBSTITUTE CHORD. A chord used in the place of another chord. The substitution can be planned and orchestrated in a song or spontaneous on the part of the soloist or accompaniment, and it usually follows specific harmonic conventions.

SUBTONE. An instrumental technique on reed instruments; the performer attempts to eliminate the overtones of a particular pitch. This produces a softer, warmer tone and is used most often in the lower register.

SULLIVAN, IRA (1931–). A **trumpet** player and saxophonist, Ira Sullivan played in a house band in Chicago in the early 1950s that backed **Charlie Parker, Lester Young, Wardell Gray, Roy Eldridge, Sonny Stitt,** and many others. Sullivan played briefly with **Art Blakey** in New York in 1956, but his performing career slowed down after he moved to Florida in the 1960s. From the 1970s, he has been active primarily as an educator.

SULLIVAN, JOSEPH "JOE" (1906–1971). A pianist and composer, Joe Sullivan made his record debut in 1927 with Red McKenzie and Eddie Condon's Chicagoans. Sullivan moved to New York in 1928 and from the late 1920s and throughout the 1930s worked with **Red Nichols** and **Bing Crosby.** During the 1940s, Sullivan worked as a soloist in addition to working with Condon. From the 1960s on, he both led his own groups and worked as a soloist.

SULLIVAN, MAXINE (1911–1987). A singer, Maxine Sullivan recorded her first hit, "Loch Lomond," with **Claude Thornhill** in 1937. During the late 1930s and early 1940s, she worked with her first husband, **John Kirby,** and during the 1940s she also worked as an actress. Known for her jazz interpretations of folk songs, her career experienced a revival during the 1970s when she toured with the **World's Greatest Jazz Band.**

SUN RA (1914–1993). Born Herman Bourke Blount but calling himself Sun Ra, he was a pianist, composer, arranger, and **bandleader.** Sun Ra worked first with **Fletcher Henderson** during the mid-1940s. During the 1950s, he formed his own band, the Myth-Science or Solar Arkestra, which started out in a somewhat traditional **Bebop** style but by the 1960s was the most experimental group in jazz. Although Sun Ra's vision of reality was quite unique, as in his belief that he came to Earth from outer space, his groups developed a large following over the years, and the stylistic variety and technical abilities of his groups have been critically acclaimed.

SUPERBONE. An instrument that is a combination of **trumpet** and **trombone,** invented by trumpeter **Maynard Ferguson.**

SUPERSAX. A group founded in 1972 that usually consists of five saxophones, a **trumpet,** and a **rhythm section.** Originally, the group performed complete harmonized transcriptions of **Charlie Parker** solos, and in later years the repertoire expanded to include the solos of **Bud Powell** and **John Coltrane** as well. Notable members of the group include **Warne Marsh, Conte Candoli, Blue Mitchell, Carl Fontana,** and others. *See also* MORGAN, LANNY.

SURMAN, JOHN (1944–). A British saxophonist, John Surman played in groups throughout **Europe** that included **Dave Holland, John McLaughlin,** and **Albert Mangelsdorff** during the 1960s and 1970s. From the 1980s on, Surman has played with **Jack DeJohnette, Paul Bley, Bill Frisell,** and in the **Gil Evans** orchestra, in addition to leading his own groups.

SUTTON, RALPH EARL (1922–2001). A pianist, Ralph Sutton played with **Jack Teagarden** both before and after World War II. From 1948 to 1956, Sutton was the pianist in varying capacities at Eddie Condon's club in New York. During the 1960s, Sutton worked mostly as a soloist, with the exception of an appearance with Bob Crosby in 1966. Sutton continued to tour in addition to making local appearances in Colorado.

SWALLOW, STEVE (1940–). A bassist and composer, Steve Swallow moved to New York in 1960 and played with **Paul Bley**. During the 1960s, Swallow played with Bley, **Benny Goodman, Art Farmer,** and **Stan Getz,** and in 1968 he began a long association with **Gary Burton**. During the 1970s, Swallow performed with **Art Lande,** led his own groups and worked as a professor at the **Berklee School of Music**. During the 1980s, Swallow played with **Carla Bley** and also **John Scofield,** and during the 1990s he played with **Paul Motian** and many others. *See also* ELECTRIC BASS.

SWARTZ, HARVIE (1948–). A bassist and pianist, Harvie Swartz graduated from the **Berklee School of Music** and then spent the 1970s playing with the **Thad Jones–Mel Lewis** Orchestra, **Gil Evans, Stan Getz, Lee Konitz,** and **Eddie Daniels,** and from 1973 he had a long-standing association with **Sheila Jordan**. From the 1980s, Swartz led his own groups and worked as an educator, and in recent years he has played with **Chick Corea, Michael Brecker,** Ingrid Jensen, and many others. Since the early 2000s, he is known as, and works under the name of, Harvie S.

SWEATMAN, WILBUR (1882–1961). A clarinetist, **bandleader,** and composer, Wilbur Sweatman worked in minstrel shows during the early 1900s and formed a band in 1902. Sweatman continued to lead bands during the 1910s and 1920s, **recording** some early jazz **albums** and employing musicians including **Freddie Keppard, Duke Ellington,** and others. Known for his ability to play three **clarinets** at the same time, Sweatman retired as a performer to focus on a career as a booking agent, music publisher, and publicist.

SWING (I). An elusive term, swing can refer to the specific rhythms played during a jazz performance, it can refer to the "feel" of a jazz performance, and it can even refer to the quality of the jazz performance.

SWING (II). A genre within jazz that rose to prominence during the 1930s. Although it is also associated with the **dance band** craze of the same time period, it is not exclusive to that definition, as the Swing period also brought a greater focus on **improvisation**. Important Swing musicians include **Coleman Hawkins** and **Roy Eldridge**, and **bandleaders Benny Goodman, Glenn Miller**, and **Fletcher Henderson**, among others. *See also* ALLEN, HENRY "RED"; BASIE, WILLIAM "COUNT"; HODGES, JOHNNY; WEBSTER, BEN.

SYMPHONIC JAZZ. A term applied to attempts during the 1920s to move jazz from dance halls, bars, and other places of ill repute to concert-style settings, championed by, among others, the **bandleader Paul Whiteman**. A direct forerunner to both **Third Stream** and **Cool Jazz**, early examples of symphonic jazz include George Gershwin's "Rhapsody in Blue" and **Duke Ellington**'s "The Blue Bells of Harlem."

SYNCOPATION. An important stylistic element in jazz music, syncopation occurs when rhythmic accents are placed on weak beats or weak parts of the beat.

SYNTHESIZER. An electronic keyboard that synthesizes the sounds of other instruments or entirely new sounds. Popular especially in Jazz **Fusion**, synthesizers have been employed by many important jazz keyboardists including **Chick Corea, Herbie Hancock**, and others. *See also* ELECTRIC PIANO.

T

TABACKIN, LEW(IS) BARRY (1940–). A saxophonist and **flute** player, Lew Tabackin moved to New York in 1965 and worked as a freelance musician with **Cab Calloway, Maynard Ferguson, Buddy Morrow, Clark Terry**, the **Thad Jones–Mel Lewis** Orchestra, **Joe Henderson**, and others. During the late 1960s, Tabackin played in a group with **Donald Byrd** and **Elvin Jones**, led his own small groups, and met and married **Toshiko Akiyoshi**. In 1970, Akiyoshi and Tabackin formed a small group together, in 1973 they formed a **big band** together, and from 1972 to 1983 Tabackin played in Los Angeles with the NBC *Tonight Show* band. Tabackin was extremely involved with his big band into the 1980s; the band has been very popular and was nominated for several Grammy Awards. During the 1980s, Tabackin also worked with **Dave Holland**, and from the 1990s he has led and toured with his own small groups. He remained principal soloist with the Toshiko Akiyoshi Orchestra until 2003, at which time he began working primarily as a small-group **leader**.

TAG. A musical statement added to the end of a piece. The term can also refer to repeating the last few measures of a song, deliberately not resolving the harmonic progression, and allowing for some additional short **solos** before the piece ends.

TAILGATE (TROMBONE). In Early Jazz, the term referred to trombone players in early New Orleans bands who, when riding through the city and playing music on wagon beds, would have to stand at the rear of the wagon (the tailgate) in order to allow for sufficient freedom of motion for their slide. In musical terms, tailgate trombone refers to idiomatic trombone figures, slides, and glissandi that were popularized by the **Dixieland** style. *See also* EARLY JAZZ; YOUNG, TRUMMY.

TAKE. A term from the **recording** industry, a take usually refers to a complete recorded performance of a song.

343

TATE, GRADY (1932–). A singer and percussionist, Grady Tate played with **Wild Bill Davis** in the early 1960s before moving to New York in 1962. During the 1960s, Tate played with **Quincy Jones, Duke Ellington, Count Basie, Bill Evans, Eddie "Lockjaw" Davis,** Duke Pearson, **Jimmy Smith, Stan Getz, Donald Byrd, Nat Adderley, Oscar Peterson, Peggy Lee, Ella Fitzgerald, Ray Charles,** and many others, and from 1968 to 1974, Tate was a member of the NBC *Tonight Show* band. During the 1970s, he played with **Zoot Sims, Benny Carter, Earl Hines,** and others, and he has continued to freelance since then, at times also working as a singer. In addition to performing, Tate has spent time teaching, most notably as a faculty member at Howard University.

TATUM, ART (1909–1956). A pianist, Art Tatum suffered from total blindness in one eye and partial blindness in the other. Primarily self-taught, Tatum cited **Fats Waller** as an early influence and already had his first professional **gigs** by 1926. Having played on the radio and in **clubs,** he moved to New York in 1932 and spent the rest of the 1930s playing in clubs, leading his own groups, and making solo and group records that were popular in jazz circles. In the late 1930s, his international reputation was such that he was able to tour **England,** and by the 1940s he was working in a group with **Slam Stewart** and Tiny Grimes, although he continued to perform primarily as a soloist. During the 1950s, an association with record producer **Norman Granz** yielded some records that featured Tatum with other artists of the day, including **Ben Webster, Roy Eldridge, Benny Carter, Lionel Hampton, Buddy Rich,** and others.

An enormously talented and technically proficient pianist, his place in jazz history is difficult to quantify because of his seeming transcendence of style and genre. His amazing facility on the piano inspired other instrumentalists to new heights on their own instruments, and his harmonic ideas and advancements influenced many who came after him.

TAYLOR, ART(HUR), JR. (1929–1995). A drummer, Art Taylor played as a teenager in local groups with **Sonny Rollins** and **Jackie McLean.** During the 1950s, Taylor played with **Coleman Hawkins, Bud Powell, Art Farmer, Donald Byrd, Miles Davis, Thelonious Monk, John Coltrane,** and others, in addition to leading his own groups. During the 1960s, Taylor moved to **Europe** and toured and performed with **Dexter Gordon** and **Johnny Griffin.** Taylor moved back to the United States in the 1980s, led his own groups, hosted a radio show, and published a collection of interviews with jazz musicians over the years—*Notes and Tones* (revised version 1993, original 1977).

TAYLOR, BILLY (I) (1906–1986). A **bass** and **tuba** player, Billy Taylor moved to New York in 1924, and during the rest of the 1920s he worked with **Elmer Snowden**, Charlie Johnson, **Duke Ellington**, and **McKinney's Cotton Pickers** (until 1931). During the 1930s, Taylor worked with Johnson and **Fats Waller** before playing with Ellington's band from 1935 to 1940, the engagement for which he is perhaps best known. During the 1940s, Taylor played with **Coleman Hawkins** and **Red Allen** before moving primarily to studio work in 1942, although he continued to freelance in New York.

TAYLOR, BILLY (II) (1921–2010). A pianist and composer, Billy Taylor moved to New York in 1944 and got his first **gig** with **Ben Webster**. During the rest of the 1940s, Taylor played with **Dizzy Gillespie, Slam Stewart, Stuff Smith,** and others in addition to leading his own group from 1948 to 1950. During the 1950s, Taylor worked with **Artie Shaw** as a member of the **Gramercy Five**, became the house pianist at **Birdland**, led his own groups, and developed an increasing interest in jazz education. During the 1960s, his performing career diminished, giving way to a career as a jazz disc jockey and in education. During the 1970s and 1980s, Taylor expanded his work to include television. Taylor was awarded many honorary degrees, and among his most popular compositions is "I Wish I Knew How It Would Feel to Be Free," an important piece of the civil rights era.

TAYLOR, CECIL (1929–). A pianist, Cecil Taylor played with **Hot Lips Page** and **Johnny Hodges** during the early 1950s before forming a quintet with **Steve Lacy** and others, making his first record in 1955. During the late 1950s, Taylor's group had a regular engagement at the **Five Spot** in New York City, and during the 1960s, Taylor's group included **Jimmy Lyons** (with whom he would perform often throughout the 1980s), Sunny Murray, and Henry Grimes. Taylor worked only intermittently for most of the 1960s with groups that included **Albert Ayler, Archie Shepp,** and others, and in the early 1970s he accepted a few brief positions teaching at universities but quit those jobs in frustration and resumed his playing career. During the late 1970s and 1980s, he had some successful partnerships with **Max Roach,** and he has since enjoyed renewed popularity and interest. Over the course of his career, Taylor has been a leading performer of the **Avant-Garde** style, and he continues to record and perform frequently, most notably at the **Village Vanguard** in 2010.

TEAGARDEN, WELDON LEO "JACK" (1905–1964). A **trombone** player and **bandleader**, Jack Teagarden had his first **gig** in New York with **Ben Pollack** from 1928 to 1933. During his time with Pollack, Teagarden also played with **Louis Armstrong**, Eddie Condon, and others, and from 1933 to 1938, Teagarden played with **Paul Whiteman**. Teagarden formed a **big band** in 1939 that lasted until 1946, when he was forced to declare bankruptcy. Teagarden joined Armstrong's All Stars from 1947 to 1951, and from then until his death he led small groups that featured his brother Charles and his sister Norma. He was an exceptionally talented trombonist whose command of the instrument was so complete that an argument can be made for him as one of the greatest jazz trombonists of all time.

TEMPO. A musical term for the speed of the beat in a piece of music, typically measured in beats per minute (bpm), which can be tied to written instructions (i.e., "fast **swing**," "slow **shuffle**," etc.).

TENOR SAXOPHONE. A member of the **saxophone** family and pitched in the key of B♭, it is perhaps the most popular wind instrument in jazz. Popularized by **Coleman Hawkins** and **Lester Young**, subsequent jazz tenor players are almost too numerous to name, although some of the most important include **John Coltrane**, **Wayne Shorter**, **Joe Henderson**, and **Sonny Rollins**. *See also* BRECKER, MICHAEL; GETZ, STAN; HAWKINS, COLEMAN; HENDERSON, JOE; JOHNSON, ALBERT J. "BUDD"; JOHNSON, PLAS JOHN, JR.; JORDAN, CLIFFORD; LOVANO, JOE; MOBLEY, HENRY "HANK"; WEBSTER, BEN.

TERRITORY BAND. The name given to local, touring dance bands that rose up across the midwestern, western, and southern sections of the United States during the 1920s and 1930s. Some of the territory bands would later grow to national prominence, as was the case with **Bennie Moten**'s (later **Count Basie**'s) band.

TERRY, CLARK (1920–). A **trumpet** and **flugelhorn** player, Terry played in a U.S. Navy band during World War II, and after his discharge he had brief stints with **Lionel Hampton, Charlie Barnet, Charlie Ventura,** and others before joining **Count Basie** from 1948 to 1951. In 1951, Terry joined **Duke Ellington**'s orchestra and remained with the group until 1959. During the 1960s, Terry worked as a **studio musician**, played in **Doc Severinsen**'s *Tonight Show* band, led his own small groups and a **big band**, and recorded **albums** with **Oscar Peterson, Bob Brookmeyer, J. J. Johnson**, and many others. Terry switched to the flugelhorn during the 1970s, and he has continued to be active as a clinician and performer, leading his own groups (included the Spacemen during the 1990s), playing with Peterson, and appearing with Hampton's Golden Men of Jazz. Recently, health concerns have limited his performance activity.

THEATER OWNER'S BOOKING ASSOCIATION (TOBA). A group founded by theater owners in the early 1920s in order to manage the appearances of performers, it eventually expanded to included theaters in many major cities. A number of important musicians started their careers on the TOBA circuit, including **Ma Rainey, Bessie Smith, Bennie Moten,** and others.

THEME. The melody of a piece of music, or the defining musical statement of a phrase.

THIELEMANS, JEAN-BAPTISTE "TOOTS" (1922–). A Belgian guitarist, harmonica player, composer, and noted whistler, Toots Thielemans played with **Benny Goodman** in **Europe** in 1950 before immigrating to the United States in 1951. Thielemans played with **George Shearing** from 1953 to 1959, and from 1959 he has led his own groups, touring and appearing in the United States and Europe. His 1961 performance of his own composition "Bluesette" featured him playing **guitar** and whistling. During the 1970s and 1980s, Thielemans continued to tour and play, appearing with **Oscar Peterson, Dizzy Gillespie,** and **Paquito D'Rivera.**

THIGPEN, ED(MUND) LEONARD (1930–2010). A drummer, Ed Thigpen played with **Cootie Williams** in New York during the early 1950s and then performed with **Dinah Washington, Johnny Hodges, Lennie Tristano, Bud Powell,** and others before joining **Billy Taylor**'s group from 1956 to 1959. From 1959 to 1965, Thigpen was the drummer in **Oscar Peterson**'s trio, and from 1965 to 1972 (excepting a brief interruption in 1967) he played with **Ella Fitzgerald.** In 1972, Thigpen moved to **Europe** and thereafter appeared with visiting American musicians in addition to making trips back to the United States to perform and record.

THIRD STREAM. A term first used by **Gunther Schuller** to describe a style of music that combines elements of both jazz and Classical music. Composers who embraced this style include Robert Graettinger, **Red Norvo, Dave Grusin,** Jimmy Giuffre, **Gil Evans,** and **Steve Lacy.** *See also* JOHNSON, JAMES LEWIS "J. J."; RUSSELL, GEORGE; RUSSO, WILLIAM "BILL"; THORNHILL, CLAUDE.

THOMPSON, DON(ALD) WINSTON (1940–). A bassist, pianist, and vibraphonist, Don Thompson toured North America with John Handy during the mid-1960s, and from 1969 to 1993 he was a member of **Rob McConnell**'s Boss Brass. During the 1970s, he played with Paul Desmond and later with **Jim Hall,** with whom he appeared from 1975 to 1982. During the 1980s, Thompson played with **George Shearing,** and while residing in Canada he accompanied many visiting musicians including **Slide Hampton** and **Clark Terry**. Thompson has also appeared on **recordings** by **Dave Liebman** and **Kenny Wheeler**.

THOMPSON, ELI "LUCKY" (1924–2005). A saxophonist, Lucky Thompson moved to New York in 1943 and over the next few years appeared with **Lionel Hampton, Billy Eckstine,** and **Count Basie**. Thompson relocated to the West Coast in 1946 and recorded many **albums**, worked with **Dizzy Gillespie** and **Charlie Parker**, and led his own groups. Thompson moved back to New York in 1948 and led his own groups, and in 1954 he recorded with **Miles Davis** on the album *Walkin'*. In 1956, Thompson played with **Stan Kenton**, and from 1958 through the early 1960s, Thompson resided in **Europe**. During the 1970s, he worked as a teacher before he became disgusted with music and retired, vanishing from the public eye. During the 1990s, he was found in Seattle, homeless and indigent, and was put up in a nursing home by local residents.

THORNHILL, CLAUDE (1909–1965). A pianist, composer, arranger, and **bandleader**, Claude Thornhill played with **Benny Goodman, Billie Holiday, Paul Whiteman**, and others during the late 1930s. In 1940, Thornhill formed his own band, for which **Gil Evans** and Thornhill himself wrote and arranged music, which lasted until 1942 when Thornhill joined the U.S. Navy. After World War II he re-formed his band and continued to perform and lead groups into the 1950s. Thornhill's symphonic style of mixing different timbres and using non-jazz instruments such as the **French horn** and bass clarinet influenced Evans, **Gerry Mulligan**, and many other subsequent jazz composers.

THREADGILL, HENRY (1944–). A saxophonist, composer, and **bandleader**, Henry Threadgill was a member of **Richard Abram**'s Experimental Band and the **Association for the Advancement of Creative Musicians** during the 1960s. In the 1970s, he formed his trio Reflection, which later became Air, and he has continued to lead his own small groups and large ensembles.

(THE) THREE SOUNDS. An instrumental group formed in 1957 by **Gene Harris**, Bill Dowdy, and Andy Simpkins. The group produced several **albums** for the **Blue Note** label during the late 1950s and into the 1960s, and its debut album, *Introducing the Three Sounds*, was extremely successful. Throughout the years the group also backed soloists including **Stanley Turrentine, Sonny Stitt, Miles Davis**, and **Lou Donaldson**.

THREE T'S. A group formed by the brothers Charlie and **Jack Teagarden** and **Frankie Trumbauer** that played in New York in 1936.

TIBERI, FRANK (1928–). A saxophonist, Frank Tiberi played in many groups, including those of **Benny Goodman, Urbie Green, Dizzy Gillespie,** and others throughout the 1950s and 1960s. In 1969, Tiberi joined the **Woody Herman** Orchestra, a group with which he continues to appear to this day, and when Herman died in 1987, Tiberi took over musical leadership of the group.

TIMBALES. A Latin percussion instrument that consists of a pair of two differently pitched drums, usually placed on the same stand with a cowbell. Noted timbaleros in jazz include Tito Puente.

TIME. In music, the time can refer to the time signature of a piece of music (e.g., 4/4 time), and it can also refer to the act of playing music with a steady beat. In addition, in jazz, time can refer to the rhythmic feel or tempo of a performance.

TIMELESS RECORDS. A **record label** founded in 1975 in the Netherlands. Artists include **Cedar Walton, Archie Shepp, Art Blakey,** and **Pharoah Sanders.**

TIMMONS, BOBBY (1934–1974). A pianist, Bobby Timmons moved to New York in 1954 and played with **Kenny Dorham, Chet Baker, Sonny Stitt, Maynard Ferguson, Art Blakey,** and **Cannonball Adderley** during the middle to late 1950s. During the 1960s, Timmons played again with Blakey in addition to leading his own groups, but alcoholism ultimately derailed his career and resulted in his death from cirrhosis in 1974. Among his best-known compositions is the **Hard Bop** classic "Moanin'."

TIZOL, JUAN (1900–1984). A Puerto Rican valve trombonist and composer, Juan Tizol moved to the United States in 1920 and joined **Duke Ellington**'s orchestra in 1929. Tizol spent the next 30 years alternating between Ellington's group and that of Harry James—playing with Ellington until 1944, James from 1944 to 1951, Ellington from 1951 to 1953, James from 1953 to 1960, and a final stint with Ellington from 1960 to 1961. Tizol retired from music in 1961. Among his best-known compositions are "Caravan" and "Perdido."

TJADER, CALLEN RADCLIFFE "CAL", JR. (1925–1982). A vibraphonist, percussionist, composer, and **bandleader,** Cal Tjader had his first

gig playing with **Dave Brubeck** from 1949 to 1951. During the 1950s, Tjader played with **George Shearing** and then led his own groups. Over the years, Tjader added a Latin and Afro-Cuban influence to his music, using percussionists in his group such as **Mongo Santamaría**.

TOLLIVER, CHARLES (1942–). A **trumpet** player, Charles Tolliver worked with many musicians during the 1960s including **Jackie McLean, Art Blakey, Sonny Rollins, Gerald Wilson**, and **Max Roach**. From 1969 he led his own group, Music Inc., and in 1971 he co-founded the record label Strata-East Records. He continues to perform and record with his groups.

TOMPKINS, ROSS (1938–2006). A pianist, keyboardist, and composer, Tompkins played with **Kai Winding, Roy Eldridge, Eric Dolphy, Bob Brookmeyer, Clark Terry, Bobby Hackett**, and others during the 1960s. From 1972 to 1992, Tompkins worked with the NBC *Tonight Show* band, and during that time, Tompkins also played with **Louie Bellson, Snooky Young, Zoot Sims**, and many others. From 1992 on, Tompkins worked primarily as a freelance musician. He worked as a clinician for the **Monterey Jazz Festival** education programs in the 2000s.

TOM-TOM. A type of drum that is an important part of the jazz **drum set**. A typical setup would include at least two differently pitched tom-toms, but often three.

TORMÉ, MELVIN HOWARD "MEL" (1925–1999). A vocalist and composer, Mel Tormé's group, the Mel-Tones, sang with **Artie Shaw** during the 1940s, but from 1947 Tormé worked primarily as a solo act. An outstanding improviser, Tormé performed many jazz standards and worked often with a jazz **rhythm section** as a backing group, including collaboration with **George Shearing**. Among his best-known compositions is the classic "The Christmas Song," which he co-authored with Robert Wells. *See also* IMPROVISATION; SCAT; SINGING.

TOUGH, DAVE (1907–1948). A drummer, Dave Tough was an important member of the famous and highly influential **Austin High School Gang** in Chicago during the 1920s. Tough worked in bands in Chicago until leaving for Europe from 1927 to 1929, where he played with **Mezz Mezzrow**. Alcoholism interrupted his career during the mid-1930s, but by 1936, Tough was performing with **Tommy Dorsey**, with whom he performed until 1938 and again in 1939. In 1938, Tough replaced **Gene Krupa** in **Benny Goodman**'s band, and then later played with **Jack Teagarden** before ill health interrupted his career. During the 1940s, Tough played with **Artie Shaw** and then, after going through another bout of alcoholic illness, with **Woody Herman** from 1944 to 1945. Tough did short stints with **Charlie Ventura** and **Eddie Condon** thereafter, but he died in 1948 after he fell and fractured his skull while walking home.

TOUSSAINT, JEAN (1957–). Originally from the Virgin Islands, saxophonist Jean Toussaint studied at the **Berklee College of Music** and played for a time with Wallace Roney before he joined **Art Blakey**'s **Jazz Messengers** in 1982. Toussaint played with Blakey until 1986, and during that time he also performed with many other musicians including **Wynton Marsalis**. Toussaint moved to London in 1987 where he has taught, led his own groups, and performed with **Max Roach** and **Cedar Walton**, in addition to local British musicians. He continues to perform to this day. *See also* ENGLAND.

TOWNER, RALPH (1940–). A guitarist, Ralph Towner moved to New York in 1968 and worked with a few jazz groups before he achieved notoriety playing with the group Weather Report in 1971. During the 1970s, Towner was a co-founder of the group **Oregon**, led a group called Solstice, appeared with **Gary Burton** from 1974 to 1975, and also appeared with **John Abercrombie**. Towner has continued to lead his own groups.

TRACEY, STANLEY WILLIAM "STAN" (1926–). A pianist, composer, and arranger, Tracey worked as a house pianist in London and performed with visiting American musicians including **Zoot Sims, Sonny Rollins, Dexter Gordon, Freddie Hubbard**, and others during the 1960s. During the mid-1960s, Tracey began leading his own groups and **big bands** in **England** and also became a notable composer—"Under Milkwood" being one of his best-known compositions. He still performs regularly.

TRACK. In the **recording** industry, a track can refer to a song on an **album**, or it can also refer to the separate channels often employed when recording groups with multiple members.

TRADE. In jazz parlance, to trade means that two or more improvising soloists alternate playing choruses or smaller sections of a song, sometimes in apparent competition with each other. *See also* CHASE; CUTTING CONTEST; EIGHTS; FOURS; TWOS.

TRADITIONAL JAZZ. A term used that applies to the genre of jazz popularized in New Orleans before the **Swing** era. During the Swing era, a revival of Traditional Jazz was led by several musicians including **Jimmie Noone** and **Sidney Bechet**. Traditional Jazz remains a very popular art form and is the focus of many **jazz festivals**, including the **Sacramento Dixieland Jubilee**. It is also referred to as Trad Jazz. *See also* DIXIELAND.

TRANSCRIPTION. In music, transcription can refer to the act of notating a musical performance; in jazz, this typically entails notating recorded improvised solos. This term also refers to the resultant work.

TRANSITION (I). A musical term referring to a section of music that serves as a **bridge**, or connector, between two larger sections, and often involves a modulation.

TRANSITION (II). A **record label** established in 1955. Artists include **Sun Ra** and **Donald Byrd**. The label was acquired by **United Artists** in 1958.

TRIANGLE. A **record label** active in the 1920s. Artists include **Jelly Roll Morton** and **Fletcher Henderson**.

TRISTANO, LEONARD "LENNIE" (1919–1978). A pianist, composer, and educator, Lennie Tristano was blind from an early age. Tristano worked as a teacher in Chicago in the mid-1940s and counted **Lee Konitz** and **Bill Russo** among his students. In 1946, Tristano moved to New York where he began working with **Charlie Parker** and **Dizzy Gillespie**. Tristano continued to teach (**Warne Marsh** being another prominent student), and in the early 1950s he opened a jazz school, one of the first of its kind. The school remained open until 1956, from which time Tristano worked primarily as a private teacher, performing rarely. Tristano predated the **Free Jazz** movement of the late 1950s and 1960s as an early experimenter in the genre, and he was also known for his experimentation with **recording** techniques such as overdubbing. Tristano was also highly influential as one of the first teachers of jazz, with many of his students having long and successful careers.

TROMBONE. A **brass** instrument, typically in the tenor or bass range, that relies on a slide to change pitches within partials. Famous jazz trombonists include **Tommy Dorsey**, **Jack Teagarden**, Frank Rosolino, **Slide Hampton**, **Glenn Miller**, and many others. *See also* ANDERSON, RAY; JOHNSON, JAMES LEWIS "J. J."; MOLE, IRVING MILFRED "MIFF"; ORY, KID; SUPERBONE; TRUMBAUER, FRANKIE; WINDING, KAI.

TRUMBAUER, FRANKIE (1901–1956). A saxophonist and **bandleader**, Frankie Trumbauer was one of the few performers of the C-melody **saxo-**

phone. Trumbauer was already a bandleader in his teens, and during the early 1920s he worked with several different bands in the Midwest before he met **Bix Beiderbecke** while working as musical director for Jean Goldkette in 1925. During his stint with **Paul Whiteman**, Trumbauer made a series of **recordings** with a band featuring Beiderbecke, made from 1929 to 1936. From 1937 to 1939, Trumbauer led his own bands, but by the 1940s he had basically retired from music.

TRUMPET. A **brass** instrument usually pitched in the key of B♭ and operated with piston valves. The trumpet is similar to a **cornet**, although the trumpet features a cylindrical bore where a cornet features a conical bore. Important jazz trumpet players include **Louis Armstrong, Roy Eldridge, Miles Davis, Dizzy Gillespie, Clifford Brown, Freddie Hubbard, Maynard Ferguson**, and many others. *See also* ALLEN, HENRY "RED"; BAKER, CHET; BEIDERBECKE, LEON "BIX"; BRECKER, RANDY; CANDOLI, PETE; CLAYTON, BUCK; ELDRIDGE, ROY; FLUGELHORN; HARRELL, TOM; HUBBARD, FREDDIE; JAMES, HARRY; LITTLE, BOOKER; NAVARRO, FATS; ROGERS, SHORTY; SEVERINSEN, CARL "DOC"; SHAW, WOODY; SHEW, BOBBY.

TUBA. A large instrument pitched in the bass range and used often in early New Orleans–style jazz, occasionally in the form of the sousaphone. *See also* BARBER, JOHN WILLIAM "BILL"; BUTTERFIELD, DON.

TUNÇBOYACIYAN, ARTO (1957–). Born in Turkey, Tunçboyaciyan began his career as a percussionist at a young age playing in a band with his older brother Onno. Tunçboyaciyan developed a reputation as a capable **sideman** and played throughout Europe until 1981, at which time he moved to New York City. Throughout the 1980s he worked almost entirely as a sideman with many groups including ones led by Ed Schuller, Gust William Tsilis, and fellow Armenian musician Armen Donelian. His first solo **album**, *Virgin Land* (1989, Keytone), was released in 1989, although he did not achieve much acclaim as a **bandleader** until 2000.

During the 1990s, his reputation as a standout percussionist grew among jazz musicians, and he was used on **recording sessions** by Arthur Blythe, Bob Berg, Jay Anderson, **Oregon**, and saxophonist Bill Evans. His brother Onno died in 1996, a major event in Tunçboyaciyan's life that resulted in much of Arto's work being dedicated in Onno's memory.

TURNAROUND. A jazz term for a harmonic progression used to return to the original key of the piece.

TURNER, JOE (I) (1907–1990). A pianist, Joe Turner moved to New York in 1925 and worked with **Benny Carter** and **Louis Armstrong**. During the 1930s, Turner toured **Europe** as a soloist, and during the 1940s he played with **Sy Oliver** and **Rex Stewart** before returning to Europe, where he remained for the rest of his life.

TURNER, JOE (II) (1911–1985). A singer, "Big" Joe Turner started working with pianist Pete Johnson as a teenager and was touring with Kansas City bands led by **Bennie Moten, Count Basie**, and others during the late 1920s and into the 1930s. Turner moved to New York in 1936 and had a notable performance with Johnson in 1938 at a Carnegie Hall concert entitled *From Spirituals to Swing*. Turner toured and performed during the 1940s, employing accompanists including **Art Tatum, Willie "the Lion" Smith**, and others, but by the 1950s his style changed to include the new **Rhythm and Blues (R&B)** sounds that were becoming popular. During this time he recorded one of his best **albums**, *The Boss of the Blues*, featuring Johnson on **piano** and including many songs in the Kansas City **Blues** style of his youth.

TURRE, STEVE (1948–). A trombonist, Steve Turre played with an eclectic mix of groups during the early 1970s, from jazz groups such as those led by **Rahsaan Roland Kirk, Art Blakey, Thad Jones–Mel Lewis, Woody Shaw**, and others, to popular non-jazz acts including Santana, Van Morrison, and **Ray Charles**. From the middle to late 1970s, Turre played with Kirk, **Chico Hamilton, Slide Hampton, Cedar Walton**, and others, in addition to leading his own groups. During the 1980s, Turre played with Shaw, joined the NBC *Saturday Night Live* band, and appeared with **Dizzy Gillespie**'s United Nations Orchestra. In the 1990s, Turre continued to lead his own groups and played with the Carnegie Hall Jazz Band, the **Mingus** Big Band, and many other groups. He remains active performing today.

TURRENTINE, STANLEY (1934–2000). A saxophonist, Turrentine played with **Ray Charles, Earl Bostic, Tadd Dameron**, and **Max Roach** during the 1950s. From 1960 onward, Turrentine principally led his own groups, which at times included **Jimmy Smith**, and his **recordings** serve as excellent examples of the **Soul Jazz** style. Among his most famous compositions is his tune "Sugar."

TWELVE CLOUDS OF JOY. A name used by **Andy Kirk** for his bands from 1929 to 1948.

TWO-BEAT. A musical term that applies to accenting beats 1 and 3 of a four-beat measure.

TWOS. In jazz parlance, the term refers to trading two-measure phrases with another soloist. *See also* CHASE; CUTTING CONTEST; EIGHTS; FOURS; TRADE.

TYNER, McCOY (1938–). While still in high school, pianist McCoy Tyner led his own groups, which included **Lee Morgan**. In 1959, he worked with the Jazztet led by **Benny Golson** and **Art Farmer**. Tyner became famous as the pianist in **John Coltrane**'s groups from 1960 to 1965, and during the same time he also recorded as a leader in groups featuring Morgan, **Joe Henderson**, and others. In 1967, he played with **Art Blakey**'s **Jazz Messengers**, and from 1967 he led his own groups, which included sidemen **Thad Jones**, **Woody Shaw**, **Wayne Shorter**, Henderson, and others. During the 1970s, Tyner played with the Milestone Jazzstars and led his own groups, and during the 1980s he continued to lead his own groups in addition to appearing with **Freddie Hubbard**, **Sonny Rollins**, and others. In the 1990s, Tyner at times added soloists to his trios including **Eddie Henderson** and **Michael Brecker**. Tyner is noted for his use of the intervals of a fourth and a fifth in his harmonies and **comping**.

U

ULMER, JAMES "BLOOD" (1942–). Ulmer learned to play **guitar** as a teenager and played with a variety of groups throughout his early career including **Rhythm and Blues (R&B)** and Soul groups in the Pittsburgh area. Ulmer teamed up with organist Big John Patton in Detroit and went with him to New York to record several **albums** for **Blue Note** Records, including *Accent on the Blues* (1969, Blue Note), and decided to bring his own band to New York. After several successful months of working in New York, Ulmer decided to permanently relocate there and was hired by a variety of different musicians including **Rashied Ali**, **Art Blakey**, and most importantly, **Ornette Coleman**. Ulmer became an important member of Coleman's groups during the 1970s and 1980s and was highly influenced by Coleman's approach to **Free Jazz**. Throughout the next three decades, Ulmer would work as a **sideman** in groups like the Music Revelation Ensemble and Phalanx, and he would lead his own groups which at times included horns and sometimes worked as a trio. Ulmer has recorded as a leader several times, including *America: Do You Remember the Love?* (1986, Blue Note) and *Black Rock* (1982, Columbia).

UNION DEUTSCHER JAZZMUSIKER. A jazz organization based in Germany and founded in the early 1970s with the intention of establishing a reputable jazz presence in Germany. The Union Deutscher Jazzmusiker created its own performance ensemble, the German-French Jazz Ensemble, and was affiliated with several other jazz groups including the **International Jazz Federation**. **Free Jazz** trombonist **Albert Mangelsdorff** was a highly influential member of the Union Deutscher Jazzmusiker. *See also* EUROPE.

UNITED. Created by Lew Simpkins, the United Recording Company was in existence for six years: between 1951 and 1957. The **record label** produced very few jazz records, the biggest hit being an **album** by **Jimmy Forrest** called *Night Train* (1951, **United Artists**).

UNITED ARTISTS. Created in 1958 as a **record label** offshoot of the United Artists motion picture company, the United Artists record label produced many classic jazz **recordings** during the late 1950s and 1960s. Artists to record for United Artists included **John Coltrane, Duke Ellington, Kenny Dorham, Billie Holiday,** and **Oliver Nelson.** The **Thad Jones–Mel Lewis** Orchestra recorded several **albums** for the Solid State label, which was a subsidiary of the United Artists label. These recordings were reissued on the Mosaic box set *The Complete Solid State Recording of the Thad Jones–Mel Lewis Big Band* (1970, Mosaic). United Artists was acquired by **Electrical and Musical Industries (EMI)** music in the 1980s, and EMI has since then reissued many of the classic recordings made during that time.

UNITED HOT CLUBS OF AMERICA. A short-lived **record label** during the late 1930s and early 1940s founded by Milt Gabler that issued **albums** from other companies including **Vocalion** and **Commodore.**

UNITED JAZZ AND ROCK ENSEMBLE. Founded by Wolfgang Dauner and made popular by recurring television appearances, the United Jazz and Rock Ensemble was created in 1975. Members changed throughout the years but included many jazz legends such as trombonist **Albert Mangelsdorff,** trumpeters **Kenny Wheeler** and **Ian Carr,** bassists Dave King and Eberhard Weber, and saxophonist **Charlie Mariano.**

UPCHURCH, PHIL (1941–). Originally from Chicago, Upchurch began his professional **guitar** career as a teenager playing and recording with **Rhythm and Blues (R&B)** groups. Despite having great success in the R&B genre including a Top 40 hit with his own group, Upchurch began **recording** with jazz artists including **Jimmy Smith** and **Brother Jack McDuff,** and touring with **Quincy Jones** and **Cannonball Adderley.** Upchurch recorded many **albums** in a variety of styles throughout the 1970s and 1980s. In the early 1980s, Upchurch relocated to Los Angeles and began to focus primarily on studio work instead of touring, while also leading his own groups.

UP TEMPO. A term used by jazz musicians to describe the tempo of a song that is considered to be fast, often performed at over 240 beats per minute.

URBANIAK, MICHAL (1943–). Originally from Warsaw, Poland, Urbaniak would spend much of his formative years learning **violin** with many different jazz groups across Eastern Europe until receiving a scholarship to study at the **Berklee College Of Music** in 1971. Urbaniak was proficient in both Classical and jazz settings and created a very reputable following in **Europe.** After spending several years in Boston at the Berklee College, Urbaniak moved to New York and began experimenting with **Free Jazz** and electronic music, eventually forming his own band, Fusion. Fusion recorded one **album** *Fusion* (1975, Columbia). During the 1980s, Urbaniak worked with many top jazz musicians including **John Abercrombie, Kenny Kirkland, Steve Gadd, Archie Shepp,** and **Miles Davis.** Urbaniak recorded for several labels during this decade, producing albums such as *Take Good Care of My Heart* (1984, **SteepleChase**) and *Cinemode* (1988, Rykodisc). Urbaniak is credited with being a proficient violinist in a variety of jazz settings ranging from **Straight-Ahead** to **Free Jazz.**

URSO, PHILIP (1925–2008). Born in Jersey City, New Jersey, Urso took up the **clarinet** at a young age, changing to **tenor saxophone** at the age of 13. Urso moved to New York at the age of 22 and played with several bands during the late 1940s, including groups led by Elliot Lawrence, **Woody Herman,** and **Jimmy Dorsey.** One of Urso's first major breaks came when he was invited to play with **Miles Davis** in 1952. Urso and valve trombonist **Bob Brookmeyer** led a quintet featuring jazz stars **Horace Silver, Kenny Clarke,** and **Percy Heath,** which recorded the **album** *Urso-Brookmeyer Quintet* (1954, Savoy). Urso recorded two albums under his own name, *Philosophy of Urso* (1954, Savoy) and *Sentimental Journey* (1956, Regent). Despite his growing popularity, Urso elected to withdraw from any major visibility and moved to Denver, Colorado, in the late 1950s. Urso would play locally and not record much as a leader.

URTREGER, RENÉ (1934–). A pianist at the age of four, Urtreger honed his technique studying Classical music while growing up in **France.** Urtreger began his professional jazz career at the age of 19 playing with American jazz musicians who were on tour in Europe. He played regularly in **Europe** for most of the 1950s, including regular engagements with **Kenny Clarke** in Paris. Urtreger's playing was not captured on many **recordings;** however, he was documented on the **Miles Davis** recording *Ascenseur Pour L'échafaud* (1957, Fontana). Urtreger was a first-call pianist for musicians touring through Paris and bolstered his resume during the late 1950s and early 1960s by working with **Stan Getz, Chet Baker, Lester Young,** and **Dexter Gordon.**

Urtreger's relationship with Clarke was of special importance, and Urtreger continued to tour and perform with Clarke in the 1960s. Urtreger took a sabbatical from performing for many years but did make guest appearances when musicians of note toured through France. Urtreger reemerged as a solo artist when he decided to return to performing jazz full time in the late 1970s. During his resurgence, Urtreger toured and recorded in both solo and small-group settings. Urtreger continues to play professionally although he still has not had a significant recording output.

V

VACHÉ, WARREN, JR. (1951–). A **trumpet** player styled in the **Dixie-land** tradition, Vaché received his first big break at the age of 25 when he was hired to perform with legendary clarinetist **Benny Goodman**. Throughout the 1970s and 1980s, Vaché was a featured soloist with many groups that thrived playing **Traditional Jazz**, including ones led by **Woody Herman** and Eddie Condon in addition to a group with Scott Hamilton that Vaché co-led. After the 1980s, Vaché began leading his own groups and recorded several **albums**. Vaché also performed some **Bebop**-related material, although the majority of his groups and **recordings** focused on **Early Jazz**.

VALDÉS, CHUCHO (1941–). Learning from his father, Bebo Valdés, Chucho Valdés (Born Jesús Dionisio Valdés in Quivicán, Cuba) learned **piano** at a very young age but did not establish himself as a prominent fig-ure in his native Cuba until the end of the 1960s. Along with several other prominent musicians, Valdés first established the **Orquesta Cubana** de **Música Moderna** in the late 1960s, a group that would turn into the **Latin Jazz** iconic group, **Irakere**. Valdés teamed up with several other prominent Cuban musicians to form this group that included **Paquito D'Rivera** and **Arturo Sandoval**. In the early 1980s, Valdés became the primary leader for this group and was responsible for many of its **recordings**. Unlike many of his fellow Cuban bandmates, Valdés never defected to the United States but constantly received work visas to perform, tour, and teach in the U.S. during the 1990s and 2000s. During these two decades, Valdés continued to tour with Irakere less and began working more as a **sideman** and with his own Latin Jazz groups that ranged from piano trios to quintets with **trumpet**, **saxophone**, and sometimes percussion.

VALIDE. An alternate name for a **superbone** or a **trombone** that has both a slide and valves.

VAMP. A term referring to a repeated phrase or section of a song that func-tions as an introduction, interlude, or ending. *See also* OPEN.

VAN EPS, GEORGE (1913–1998). Van Eps received early musical training from his siblings and became a proficient **guitar** and **banjo** player before reaching his teenage years. In 1924, Van Eps began playing professionally and throughout the next two decades would catch on with many major touring jazz acts, including those led by **Benny Goodman** and **Ray Noble**. Van Eps is credited with being an innovator on guitar by including a seventh string on the instrument to be used for playing bass notes. Van Eps primarily worked as a freelance musician but was also an established writer and had several books published on guitar technique. His innovations for the guitar are still used today by guitarists like Charlie Hunter, who also employs the use of an extra string for the same purpose that Van Eps included his.

VAN HA TRIO. A Belgian jazz trio that often served as a host band for touring American musicians. The trio was made up of Roger Van Haverbeke, Tony Bauwens, and Freddy Rottier. The group has remained active since its formation in the 1960s.

VARIETY (I). A short-lived **record label** that distributed discs recorded in the mid-1920s by the Cameo Record Company.

VARIETY (II). Founded by **Irving Mills** in 1937, the Variety **record label** only lasted a year. Several **recordings** were released on Variety including ones comprised of members of the **Duke Ellington** Orchestra.

VARSITY. A **record label** founded by Eli Oberstein for the purpose of releasing cheaper records. The majority of releases by Varsity were either commercial jazz or **race records** made in the 1930s.

VAUGHAN, SARAH (1924–1990). Unlike many of the musicians from her era, Vaughan was not born into a musical family. She received **piano** and voice training and began her professional career at a young age. During the early 1940s, Vaughan won an award for best young talent at the **Apollo Theater** in Harlem, New York; was featured with **Earl "Fatha" Hines' big band**; and soon after was hired by vocalist **Billy Eckstine** to perform with his big band. Vaughan's popularity soared, and she was hired in 1949 by **Columbia** Records to record exclusively for five years. The majority of the records she made were either popular music or **ballad** based, and her talents for interpreting jazz music were not fully maximized while with Columbia.

After her record contract was up, Vaughan spent a good deal of time working with a variety of jazz musicians including **Clifford Brown, Count Basie,** and **Cannonball Adderley,** and she also recorded several albums under her own name. During the 1960s, her jazz output again decreased, but she would make several concert and television appearances with famous jazz artists **Dizzy Gillespie, Maynard Ferguson,** and **Herbie Hancock.** Vaughan's legacy will always be strong because of her striking vocal style and command of standards.

VAULT. Around for less than a decade after being founded in 1965, Vault Records did little **recording** but did capture a few important jazz musicians, most notably a young **Gary Burton.** *See also* RECORD LABEL.

V-DISC. Created by the U.S. armed services in 1943, V-Disc was created with the intention of creating **recordings** for the army. Eventually music was distributed to all departments of the military. Many classic jazz musicians were captured on V-Disc recordings including **Louis Armstrong, Glenn Miller,** and **Coleman Hawkins.** The label was dropped several years after World War II ended. *See also* RECORD LABEL.

VELVET TONE. A **record label** founded by **Columbia** to release **race records** from 1926 to 1932.

VENTURA, CHARLIE (1916–1992). Ventura began playing **saxophone** as a teenager and focused on **tenor saxophone** after being highly influenced by **Coleman Hawkins.** He was hired by drummer **Gene Krupa** in 1942 and remained in Krupa's band for several years until electing to pursue a solo career. Ventura experimented with a **big band** that quickly dwindled down to an octet. The group adopted the name "Bop for the People" and was an important launching pad for several significant jazz musicians including **Conte Candoli, Dave McKenna, Kai Winding, Bennie Green,** and **Ed Shaughnessy.** Ventura also included several of his brothers, Ben, Ernie, and Peter, in these groups. Bop for the People disbanded in the early 1950s, and Ventura continued to maintain a steady solo career.

Ventura made several different cities home throughout the next few decades, including Minneapolis, Denver, Las Vegas, and eventually Fort Lauderdale. Complications with a variety of illnesses and dental problems forced Ventura to stop playing in the mid-1970s. Ventura succumbed to cancer in 1992.

VENTURA, RAY(MOND) (1908–1979). A French pianist, Ray Ventura played a prominent role in the development of jazz as a popular music in France during the 1930s. Ventura was a **sideman** for a brief time during the 1920s until he formed his own groups that were extremely popular until

World War II. Ventura did some touring in the 1940s but mostly led local groups in Paris. *See also* FRANCE.

VENUTI, GIUSEPPE "JOE" (1903–1978). Born in Philadelphia, Venuti was a highly influential violinist during the 1920s and 1930s. His first major musical relationship was with guitarist **Eddie Lang**, with whom Venuti recorded on and off again for several years until Lang's early death. **Big band** leader and composer Jean Goldkette hired Venuti for several tours in the early 1930s, and Venuti's popularity spread. Throughout the remainder of the decade, Venuti played and recorded with many influential musicians including **Bix Beiderbecke, Frankie Trumbauer, Tommy Dorsey, Jack Teagarden,** and **Paul Whiteman.**

After Venuti's surge of touring, his popularity became slightly subdued after the 1940s, while primarily leading his own groups. Venuti served as a **studio musician** in Los Angeles in the mid-1940s and continued to freelance and tour. He experienced a brief resurgence in the 1960s after a performance at the Dirk Gibson **Colorado Jazz Party** and into the 1970s when he recorded with many of his admirers including **Ross Tompkins, Marian McPartland, Dave McKenna,** and **Scott Hamilton.** At the end of the decade, Venuti succumbed to several serious health issues and died at the age of 74.

VERSE. A section of music in which the melodic material stays constant but the words or lyrics change. Almost all music taken from the Great American Songbook and used as a jazz standard contain a section that would be considered a verse.

VERVE. Founded by jazz producer and engineer **Norman Granz,** Verve Records would become a highly influential and important jazz label after its creation in 1956. Previous Granz projects from other labels were reissued on the Verve label, resulting in a catalog of music featuring **Charlie Parker, Dizzy Gillespie, Lester Young,** and **Ella Fitzgerald.** Granz sold the company in 1960, and Verve moved in several new directions during the 1970s, including expanding to include Folk music in its repertoire. In the 1980s, Verve began producing jazz records again including **albums** by **Joe Henderson, Stan Getz,** and **Betty Carter.** The label was consolidated by its parent company along with several other jazz labels in 1998. *See also* RECORD LABEL.

VIBES. *See* VIBRAPHONE.

VIBRAPHONE. Similar to a marimba or **xylophone,** the vibraphone is the most commonly used instrument of the pitched percussion family. With its tones set up in a similar fashion to a **piano,** the vibraphone is made up of pitched metal bars that are struck with mallets. The vibraphone has an electric motor that controls the amount of sustain of each note so that it is a more effective accompanying instrument. Significant jazz vibraphonists include **Lionel Hampton, Bobby Hutcherson, Milt Jackson, Gary Burton**, and Stefon Harris. *See also* MAINIERI, MIKE; TJADER, CAL.

VICTOR. One of the oldest known **record labels**, Victor was established in 1900. Victor was responsible for releasing the first jazz **recording** in 1917 in a recording of the **Original Dixieland Jazz Band**. Throughout the 1920s, Victor would add to its jazz catalog and record **big bands** led by **Paul Whiteman** and **Duke Ellington**. Victor remained at the forefront of recorded jazz in the 1930s and produced discs by **Glenn Miller, Benny Goodman, Artie Shaw**, and **Lionel Hampton**. Victor dwindled in the 1940s and was eventually slowed down considerably when the market for jazz dried up. Victor was purchased by a German company in 1986, at which point it served only as a label for reissues.

VIENNA ART ORCHESTRA. Founded in 1977 by three European jazz musicians, Mathias Rüegg, Wolfgang Puschnig, and Woody Schabata; Rüegg served as the primary **leader** for the orchestra. The group was very influential in the development of jazz in Austria and constantly promoted jazz music. The Vienna Art Orchestra featured concerts that focused on a variety of composers including **Ornette Coleman, Duke Ellington, Charles Mingus**, and **Jelly Roll Morton**. Many jazz musicians performed with the group, among them **Art Farmer** and **Betty Carter**. Working together for over 20 years, the Vienna Art Orchestra suffered few personnel changes during its existence and was at its height during the late 1990s. *See also* EUROPE.

VILLAGE GATE. A jazz club in New York that was popular during the 1950s. Pianist **Horace Silver** made a notable **recording** of one of his groups at the Village Gate.

VILLAGE VANGUARD. First opened in 1935, the New York **club** began featuring all jazz in 1957. Along with **Birdland**, the Village Vanguard remains one of jazz's most historic clubs in New York. The Village Vanguard has featured nearly every important jazz performer since the 1950s. **John Coltrane, Brad Mehldau**, and **Wynton Marsalis** are some of the musicians who have recorded multidisc live performances of their sets from the venue. *See also* JONES, THAD; McNEELY, JIM; WILDER, JOE.

VINNEGAR, LEROY (1928–1999). Originally from Indianapolis, Indiana, Vinnegar made his first mark on the Chicago jazz scene as the house **bass**

player for the Bee Hive Jazz Club. Accompanying many touring musicians, Vinnegar performed with many of the top working musicians of the 1950s, including **Charlie Parker, Lester Young, Sonny Stitt,** and **Johnny Griffin.** Vinnegar was encouraged to relocate to California in 1954, at which point he became a regular with drummer **Shelly Manne'**s groups. Throughout the remainder of the 1950s, he played with many **West Coast Jazz** stars including **Herb Geller, Dexter Gordon, Conte Candoli, Art Pepper,** and **Chet Baker.** Toward the end of the 1950s, he was hired by **tenor saxophone** legend **Ben Webster,** and the two would work together for the better part of a decade.

Vinnegar continued his working relationship with Webster while also freelancing with many of the musicians based out of Los Angeles. He was the original bass player for the Jazz **Fusion** group, the **Jazz Crusaders,** and also did commercial and studio work in the late 1960s. Vinnegar suffered from a variety of health problems in the 1980s, which led to his relocating to Portland, Oregon, for quality-of-life reasons. Until Vinnegar's passing in 1999, he primarily led his own trio and continued to tour and record.

VINSON, EDDIE "CLEANHEAD" (1917–1988). Despite coming from a lineage of musicians, Vinson did not familiarize himself with an instrument until he was 17, at which point he took up the **alto saxophone.** Vinson quickly made his mark and within a year was playing as a member of touring bands, most notably one led by tenor saxophonist **Illinois Jacquet.** Vinson relocated to New York in the late 1930s and was hired to be a vocalist and saxophonist with **Cootie Williams** for several years. Vinson began leading his own groups toward the later part of that decade, and many young musicians, such as Red Garland and **John Coltrane,** were at one time members of his groups.

Vinson's style flipped between **Straight-Ahead** Jazz, **Blues,** and early **Rhythm and Blues (R&B),** and he was very popular in all genres. He was signed to a deal with King Records that prominently featured R&B artists, though many of his **recordings** were jazz based. His popularity dwindled in the 1950s, but he continued to record and perform with many of the top jazz talent including **Wynton Kelly, Count Basie,** and **Cannonball Adderley.** Vinson experienced a slight resurgence in the late 1960s and 1970s when several of his concerts in **Europe** with Jay McShann received acclaim. Vinson would continue to record and tour, primarily in Europe, until his death in 1988.

VIOLIN. A member of the string family, the violin was developed from the medieval instrument the viol. Like the viola, cello, and **bass,** the violin features four strings tuned a fourth apart, and it is the top voice of all stringed instruments. The violin is rarely used in jazz despite several virtuosos who have become proficient jazz soloists, including **Stéphane Grappelli** and Regina Carter. *See also* NANCE, RAY; SMITH, STUFF; URBANIAK, MICHAL; VENUTI, JOE.

VOCALESE. A vocal style of applying text or syllables to previously improvised jazz solos. The vocal group **Lambert, Hendricks, and Ross** were very influential to the common use of vocalese. Other artists like Joni Mitchell, Kurt Elling, and the New York Voices make full use of vocalese when they perform classic jazz songs. *See also* JEFFERSON, EDDIE; JORDAN, SHEILA; MANHATTAN TRANSFER.

VOCALION. A **record label** in New York that was a pioneer in releasing vertical-cut records. Vocalion recorded several important jazz groups in the 1920s and 1930s, including the **Original Dixieland Jazz Band**, **Billie Holiday**, and **Duke Ellington**. Vocalion was fused with several other labels during its existence and was associated with jazz labels **OKeh** and **Bluebird**. Despite surviving on reissues throughout the 1960s, Vocalion was shut down in 1969.

VOGUE. Record label based out of **France** in the late 1940s that made several significant **recordings** of touring American jazz musicians including **Clifford Brown**, **Art Farmer**, and **Sidney Bechet**. Despite being purchased several times, the Vogue record label name lasted well into the 1980s.

VOICING. A term that describes the order and position of notes one uses when playing chords or writing chords to be played by instrumentalists. Voicing can refer to how a pianist plays a chord, or how he arranges notes in both or one of his hands.

VON OHLEN, JOHN (1941–). Originally from Indianapolis, Indiana, Von Ohlen attempted to learn several instruments as a youth, and upon entering college, he was undecided about pursuing **trombone** or **drum set**. Despite being accepted to and attending the prestigious North Texas State University, he dropped out before completing a year and worked as both a trombonist and drummer until eventually deciding on drums. Toward the end of the 1960s, Von Ohlen received his big break playing and **recording** with the bands of **Woody Herman** and **Stan Kenton**. In the late 1970s, he began leading his own groups, first in Indianapolis, Indiana, and then in Cincinnati, Ohio. Von Ohlen led both small groups and **big bands** and developed a reputation as a very diversified and distinguished performer.

V.S.O.P. (I). Name of a band fronted by **Herbie Hancock, Tony Williams, Ron Carter, Wayne Shorter,** and **Freddie Hubbard.** The band did a few tours and made several live **recordings** in the late 1970s and 1980s. Shorter and Hubbard were replaced by **Wynton** and **Branford Marsalis** for several years until the group disbanded.

V.S.O.P. (II). A short-lived **record label** created to release **Columbia Broadcasting System (CBS)** records of **Louis Armstrong** in the 1980s.

W

WAITS, FREDDIE (1943–1989). Waits' career began as a **Rhythm and Blues (R&B)** drummer in the late 1950s before working with several Detroit-based musicians, including bassist Cecil McBee. Waits played with a variety of musicians after moving to New York in 1965, including **McCoy Tyner, Sir Roland Hanna,** and **Cedar Walton.** Waits toured with Pop acts during the latter part of the 1960s and early 1970s before resuming his jazz career playing with the **Duke Ellington** Orchestra led by **Mercer Ellington.** Waits did not become a **leader** until the late 1970s and primarily led a percussion-only group. In the 1980s and 1990s, most of Waits' contributions would come as a **sideman,** performing in a variety of settings that included **big band,** with vocalists, playing **Straight-Ahead** small-group jazz, and playing **Free Jazz.**

WALDRON, MALCOLM EARL "MAL" (1926–2002). Born in New York, Waldron first studied Classical **piano** before focusing on jazz while attending college. Waldron was frequently employed by leading musicians of the 1950s, including **Charles Mingus,** Ike Quebec, **John Coltrane, Frank Wess,** and **Max Roach.** In the 1960s, Waldron worked with young jazz stars **Eric Dolphy** and **Booker Little** in a quintet.

After suffering several health problems in the early part of the 1960s, Waldron worked for several years in France and for a while in Japan. Much of the two decades was spent working as a **sideman** and **leading** his own trio. Waldron would participate in tribute groups for the Dolphy/Little quintet he was a part of during the 1980s, while also working with many of the same musicians with which he was affiliated during the 1950s. Waldron continued to tour and record until his death in 2002.

WALKING BASS. A style of bass playing that became very important in the development of jazz. Similar to the drumming technique of playing a bass drum on every beat, walking bass involves the bassist playing every beat of every measure, while outlining inversions of **chords** and/or scales. Walking bass was preceded by a style in which the bassist merely played the root of the chord for the duration of the chord. *See also* BASS; PAGE, WALTER.

WALLER, THEODORE "FATS" (1904–1943). Studying with early **piano** icon **James P. Johnson**, Waller began his professional career as a late teenager and was **recording** by the age of 18. Equally adept as a composer and a performer, Waller had pieces performed and recorded by the **Fletcher Henderson** orchestra and also wrote a musical. "Honeysuckle Rose" and "Ain't Misbehavin'" are two of Waller's compositions that remain an important part of the jazz canon. Primarily a **leader**, Waller also served as a **sideman** in a variety of groups, most notably in a pit orchestra for a Broadway show that also featured jazz **trumpet** star **Louis Armstrong**.

Waller toured during much of the 1930s in addition to participating in several radio broadcasts. During the decade, Waller was one of the most popular working musicians and was frequently featured in films. Despite taking a break during World War II, Waller recorded in both **Europe** and Los Angeles, most notably on several **albums** featuring drumming legend Zutty Singleton and alto saxophonist **Benny Carter**. Waller died due to complications with pneumonia. *See also* STRIDE.

WALRATH, JACK ARTHUR (1946–). Walrath studied **trumpet** at the **Berklee School of Music** in the mid-1960s and began working professionally on the west coast of the United States after graduating. Hired by both jazz and Pop acts, Walrath freelanced with several artists including Glenn Ferris and **Ray Charles** for several years until he relocated to New York. Walrath was adept in several jazz styles, and for the latter part of the 1970s and most of the 1980s, he worked as a **sideman** with groups led by **Charli Persip**, Dannie Richmond, **Joe Morello**, and Sam Rivers. During the 1980s, Walrath also began to lead his own groups, usually quintets or sextets, and was often active as a composer and arranger.

WALTON, CEDAR (1934–). After studying **piano** at the University of Denver, Walton relocated to New York at the age of 21 to play jazz professionally. Despite a brief hiatus while he served in the U.S. Army, Walton connected with several top-flight musicians toward the end of the 1950s and worked with trumpeter **Kenny Dorham** and tenor saxophonist **John Coltrane** before being hired to replace **Bobby Timmons** in the **Hard Bop** group, **Art Blakey** and the **Jazz Messengers**. Walton was a first-call pianist for many groups in the late 1960s and worked with **Joe Henderson, Lee Morgan,** and **Hank Mobley**, among others.

Walton also began leading groups in the 1960s and formed the basic quartet that would result in one of the top jazz groups of the 1980s: Eastern Rebellion. Eastern Rebellion was made up of **Billy Higgins**, Sam Jones, or David Williams on **bass**, and several **saxophone** players including **Clifford**

Jordon, **George Coleman**, and Bob Berg at different times. Walton spent much of the 1980s touring with this group or his own trio. Walton is credited with contributing several songs to the jazz repertoire including "Bolivia" and "Fantasy in D."

WARE, WILBUR (1923–1979). Ware came to prominence as a bassist during the 1940s while working with **Roy Eldridge** and **Sonny Stitt**, before substance abuse slightly derailed his career. In the 1950s, Ware resumed performing and appeared with **Clifford Brown** and **Johnny Griffin** before he became a staple at the Beehive Jazz Club in Chicago. He worked with **Art Blakey**, **Stan Getz**, and **Cannonball Adderley**, in addition to leading his own groups for the latter part of the 1950s and early 1960s. Ware adopted the **Free Jazz** movement and worked with **Archie Shepp** in the 1960s, continuing his association with many of the musicians he had worked with in the 1950s, such as **Thelonious Monk** and **Sonny Rollins**.

WARREN, EARLE (1914–1994). Based out of the Midwest, Warren's career was hallmarked by his tenure as lead alto with the **Count Basie** band. Warren's time with Basie began in 1937 and lasted the better part of the next three decades. He lived in **Europe** for several years during the 1980s and spent time working on tributes to Count Basie. Warren is generally remembered as being important for helping shape the Basie band's sound, rather than as a soloist.

WARREN, EDWARD "BUTCH" (1939–). Born in Washington, D.C., Warren made his mark playing **bass** in New York–based groups and on **recordings** with **Straight-Ahead** artists including **Kenny Dorham**, Sonny Clark, and **Dexter Gordon**. Warren spent some of the 1960s working with Pop groups and doing studio **sessions** and returned to playing jazz during the 1970s.

WASHBOARD BAND. The name for a group of musicians that included a washboard among the instruments used in the group. Several groups were considered to be washboard bands, and oftentimes they would feature strings or singers. The **Washboard Rhythm Kings** were an example of a washboard band.

WASHBOARD RHYTHM KINGS. Another name for the Alabama Washboard Stompers, the Washboard Rhythm Kings were based out of both New Jersey and Philadelphia. The band was popular during the 1930s, and several other groups have since used the name Washboard Rhythm Kings. *See also* WASHBOARD BAND.

WASHINGTON, DINAH (1924–1963). Born Ruth Lee Jones, Washington had her name changed in the 1940s after her first big break **singing** with the **Lionel Hampton** band. Washington was known as a master interpreter of styles and would record songs in many different genres including Pop, **Rhythm and Blues (R&B)**, **Blues**, and jazz. Washington worked with several important jazz musicians in the 1950s including **Clifford Brown** and **Cannonball Adderley** before she died from a drug overdose in 1963.

WASHINGTON, GEORGE (1907–). Washington served as a trombonist with many of the touring bands of the 1930s including **Benny Carter** and **Don Redman**. Despite several tours with bands during the 1940s and 1950s, most of Washington's career was spent working as a **studio musician** on the West Coast.

WASHINGTON, GROVER, JR. (1943–1999). Washington's early **saxophone** career was marked by service in the military, followed by several apprenticeships with groups based on the use of the Hammond B3 organ. Washington became a **bandleader** in the 1970s and primarily played what would be considered **Soul Jazz** or Contemporary Jazz. Washington made several *Billboard* Top 100 hits, most notably his classic "Mister Magic." Most of Washington's **recordings** were made while a leader, but he did some side work in the 1990s prior to his death. *See also* HAMMOND ORGAN.

WASHINGTON, KENNY (1958–). Coming from a musical family, Washington took up the **drums** at a young age and was working with **Lee Konitz** at the age of 19. Well respected by older musicians, Washington played with many jazz greats during the 1980s and 1990s including **Johnny Griffin**, **Cedar Walton**, **Ron Carter**, and **Milt Jackson**. Washington worked with both **big bands** and small groups in the late 1980s and 1990s. He ended up one of the most recorded jazz drummers of the 1990s, despite rarely leading groups on his own.

WASHINGTONIANS. A precursor to the **Duke Ellington** Orchestra, **Elmer Snowden** started the group in the early 1920s, with Ellington taking leadership shortly thereafter. The group would eventually assume Ellington's name in the late 1920s.

WATANABE, KAZUMI (1953–). Watanabe served a role as an important **Fusion** guitarist during the 1970s, working primarily in his home country of **Japan** until he became involved with several American artists during the 1980s. Watanabe worked with the **Brecker** Brothers and **Jaco Pastorius** in addition to starting several of his own groups, which frequently toured. Watanabe is also very active as a composer and has written many jazz-inspired pieces for solo **guitar**. *See also* ELECTRIC GUITAR; JAPAN.

WATANABE, SADAO (1933–). Working as an alto saxophonist while in his twenties in Tokyo with **Toshiko Akiyoshi**'s groups, Watanabe made his first significant work in the Japanese jazz scene. Watanabe studied jazz in the United States at the **Berklee School of Music** for several years during the 1960s. After his time at Berklee, Watanabe continued to live in New York for several years working with Gary McFarland and **Chico Hamilton** before moving back to **Japan** in the 1970s. Watanabe would lead his own groups for most of the remainder of this career and frequently tour the United States and Africa.

WATERS, BENNY (1902–1998). Waters was an influential woodwind player during the 1920s and performed on all of the **saxophones** and **clarinet**. Waters was influenced by New Orleans–based groups, and the majority of his career was spent working with groups that played **Traditional Jazz**, including those led by **King Oliver** and Jimmy Archey. In the 1960s, Waters moved to **France** where he primarily led his own groups. Waters frequently switched instruments and for a while almost exclusively played **tenor saxophone** before primarily playing the **alto saxophone** in the 1990s.

WATERS, ETHEL (1896–1977). Water's career is defined by her ability to sing a variety of styles and her ability to incorporate many influences, including White vaudeville **singing** and the African-American **Blues** tradition. During the 1930s, Waters, along with **Ma Rainey** and **Bessie Smith**, led the way for African-American vocalists and frequently recorded and performed. Waters also starred in several Broadway musicals and regularly recorded popular music in addition to jazz. She continued to perform professionally as a solo act throughout the 1940s and 1950s until becoming involved with a choir organized for evangelist Billy Graham.

WATKINS, JULIUS (1921–1977). Beginning his career on **trumpet** in the late 1940s, Watkins' career changed for the better when he was hired to play **French horn** with **Kenny Clarke**. Throughout the 1950s, Watkins regularly played French horn with many of the top jazz musicians, including **Thelonious Monk**, **Sonny Rollins**, **Oscar Pettiford**, and **George Shearing**. Watkins was hired by **Gil Evans** in the late 1950s and began to branch out and do studio work and Broadway shows. For the majority of the 1960s and 1970s, Watkins worked in Classical settings and did very few jazz-related performances.

WATROUS, WILLIAM "BILL" (1939–). Watrous moved around the country during his military service in the 1950s but made his mark in New York playing **trombone** in **Kai Winding**'s different trombone groups. After spending much of the late 1960s working with **Quincy Jones, Maynard Ferguson**, and doing a variety of studio-related work, Watrous began leading his own groups in the 1970s. Watrous frequently fronted his own **big band**, the Manhattan Wildlife Refuge, and appeared as a **sideman** with **trumpet** player Billy Berry, **Albert Mangelsdorff**, and Winding, among others. Throughout the 1990s and 2000s, Watrous continued to lead groups under his own name and performed as guest artist for festivals and university-related ensembles.

WATSON, ROBERT "BOBBY" (1953–). Hailing from Kansas City, Watson learned to play **saxophone** from his father. Watson pursued a collegiate education at the University of Miami and played frequently in the area until being hired by **Art Blakey** in the late 1970s. Watson stayed with Blakey until 1981 and recorded many of his own tunes during his time as a member of the **Jazz Messengers**. "A Wheel Within a Wheel" is considered to be one of Watson's most memorable compositions from this time.

After leaving the Jazz Messengers, Watson formed his own group, **Horizon**, and started a **record label** of the same name. Watson worked extensively with several musicians during the 1980s and 1990s including Victor Lewis, Curtis Lundy, and Terrell Stafford, all of whom played in the Horizon group. Watson joined the music faculty at the University of Missouri at Kansas City and remains an active performer today.

WATTS, ERNIE (1945–). Watts grew up in Delaware and took up the **saxophone** when he was a teenager. After studying at the State Teachers College in Pennsylvania and at the **Berklee School of Music** in the 1960s, Watts gained recognition playing with the **big band** of **Buddy Rich**. After relocating to Los Angeles, Watts worked with many popular West Coast bands including ones led by **Gerald Wilson, Oliver Nelson, Doc Severinsen**, and **Cannonball Adderley**. Watts freelanced during most of the 1970s and 1980s, alternating between studio work and touring performances. He gained special recognition for his work on the soundtrack to the movie *Chariots of Fire*. Watts was actively performing in the 1990s and frequently toured both the United States and Europe. In the 2000s, he appeared as a **sideman** in groups led by **Charlie Haden** and **Doc Severinsen**.

WA-WA. One of the many sounds that can be generated on a **trumpet** or **trombone**. A wah-wah can be made by use of a **plunger**, a combination of a plunger with a Harmon **mute**, or a specialized wah-wah mute. *See also* MUTE.

WEATHERFORD, TEDDY (1903–1945). Weatherford developed his basic jazz roots while learning **piano** in New Orleans. In the 1920s, he moved to Chicago and became one of the leading **Stride** pianists in the city. Weatherford spent much of the 1930s playing abroad in Asian locales, such as Singapore, Manila, Shanghai, and eventually India.

WEBB, CHICK (1909–1939). One of the most prominent **bandleaders** and drummers of the 1930s, Webb's career was almost always fronting a band. Webb's group frequently played in New York and often featured many of the up-and-coming musicians of the 1920s and 1930s. Included in his group at different times were **Johnny Hodges, Ella Fitzgerald, Benny Carter,** and Mario Bauza. Webb considered the legendary **Savoy Ballroom** in New York to be a second home, and his band was known for playing there regularly. Webb was of substantial influence to the next wave of **big band** drummers that included **Gene Krupa** and Jo Jones. Webb died in 1939 from complications with spinal surgery. *See also* BATTLE OF BANDS; LITTLE CHICKS.

WEBB, GEORGE HORACE (1917–). An Englishman, Webb was a prominent **Traditional Jazz bandleader** and pianist in London during the 1940s. Webb founded the group the Dixielanders, who were in existence for about 10 years before the group disbanded and Webb retired from playing to pursue business ventures in the music business.

WEBSTER, BENJAMIN FRANCIS "BEN" (1909–1973). Beginning his musical career as a pianist before switching to **tenor saxophone** in the 1930s, Webster would become not only one of the most influential jazz musicians of the 1930s, but of all time. Touring first with bands led by **Bennie Moten** and **Andy Kirk** before being hired by **Fletcher Henderson** and **Duke Ellington,** Webster developed a new tenor saxophone sound that garnered him much acclaim. Webster began **recording** and touring with his own groups in the 1940s and was included in **Norman Granz**'s **Jazz at the Philharmonic** groups that toured throughout the 1950s.

Webster recorded frequently during the 1950s and worked with many popular vocalists including **Carmen McRae** and **Billie Holiday,** in addition to being featured on the **Columbia Broadcasting System (CBS)** program *The Sound of Jazz.* Webster was one of the first major jazz figures to move to **Europe** in the 1950s; he lived there until his death. While living in Europe, Webster became a regular at **jazz festivals** held in various countries and played frequently in Copenhagen. Many saxophonists who developed their styles during the 1940s and 1950s considered Ben Webster to be a significant influence along with **Coleman Hawkins** and **Lester Young.**

WEBSTER, FREDDIE (1916–1947). As a **trumpet** player, Webster first gained notoriety by playing with pianist **Earl Hines** before being hired to play in many of the popular New York **big bands**, including those led by **Benny Carter**, Eddie Durham, and **Jimmie Lunceford**. Webster always held the respect of his peers and influenced both **Dizzy Gillespie** and **Miles Davis** before his early death.

WEIN, GEORGE (1925–). Wein's career in jazz is equal parts music business and performance. In the 1940s, Wein led his own groups and played **piano** in addition to working as a **sideman** in **Traditional Jazz** groups led by **Wild Bill Davison**, among others. Wein made his mark in the 1950s when he opened a Traditional Jazz **club**, **Storyville**, and formed a **record label** of the same name. Wein was a very savvy businessman, and after a few years he opened up another club in addition to starting what is now known as the **Newport Jazz Festival** in 1954.

During Wein's career, he would continue performing with artists like **Joe Venuti**, **Sidney Bechet**, **Ruby Braff**, and **Jimmy McPartland**, while maintaining the growth and development of the Newport festival. Wein continued to expand the festival and to develop festivals in other cities and countries, and he performed well into the 1970s and 1980s. Eventually Wein sold the majority of the performance rights to his production company, Festival Production, to BET in the late 1990s, but he still remained an active participant running the Newport Festival and other endeavors that promoted and supported jazz.

WELLS, WILLIAM "DICKY" (1907–1985). After spending several years playing **trombone** with bands in his native Louisville, Kentucky, Wells moved to New York at the age of 19 and found great success early on. Playing with several lesser-known groups until he worked with **Elmer Snowden**, Wells became an important figure when he performed with bands led by **Benny Carter** and **Fletcher Henderson** in the 1930s.

In the 1940s, Wells did some work as a **bandleader** but primarily served as a trombonist for **Count Basie**'s groups. Wells followed his time with Basie by working in groups led by **Jimmy Rushing**, Paul Quinichette, and **Buck Clayton**. After spending some time working with **Ray Charles**, Wells took a semi-retirement to recover from alcohol abuse before resuming playing in the 1970s. He freelanced, primarily with **big bands**, for the remainder of his career and is considered along with **Jack Teagarden** to be one of the most influential trombone players of the 1930s.

WESS, FRANK (1922–). Inspired by **Lester Young**, Wess took up the **tenor saxophone** as a youth and performed in military bands during the

1940s. Several years after being discharged, Wess found work with **Count Basie** and would remain with the band for almost 10 years until 1964. Wess was an important and influential tenor saxophonist and was, along with **James Moody**, one of the first musicians to embrace the **flute** as a jazz solo instrument.

During the 1970s, 1980s, and 1990s, Wess freelanced as a **sideman** with many groups while also becoming more prominent as a **leader**. He led several small groups during the 1980s that featured **Kenny Barron** and Rufus Reid. Wess also worked with several **big bands** later in his career, including that of **Woody Herman** and another that he led that featured many members from the Basie band.

WEST, DOC (1915–1951). A **big band** drummer, West was a first substitute player for many of the top-working drummers, filling in for **Chick Webb** and Jo Jones when they could not perform with their respective groups. West worked with many well-known players of the 1940s including **Wardell Gray**, Tiny Grimes, and **Roy Eldridge**, with whom he was playing when he died prematurely in 1951.

WEST COAST JAZZ. A style of jazz that became popular in the early 1950s and is sometimes considered synonymous with the term "**Cool Jazz**." Some historians refer to West Coast Jazz as being "White Jazz." West Coast Jazz often featured a more relaxed style of playing, warmer tones, and a focus more on melodic development than rhythmic or harmonic development, as well as an increased emphasis on arrangements. Important West Coast Jazz musicians included **Chet Baker**, **Stan Getz**, **Gerry Mulligan**, **Shorty Rogers**, and **Shelly Manne**.

WESTERN SWING. A style of Country and Folk music that incorporated many elements considered important to jazz, most notably **improvisation**. Fiddle player Bob Wills was considered one of the top musicians to work in this style, which was popular in Texas during the first half of the 21st century.

WESTON, RANDY (1926–). Weston began playing professionally with **Rhythm and Blues (R&B)** bands in the early 1950s after serving in the military. Weston befriended fellow pianist **Thelonious Monk** and landed a record deal with the **Riverside** label. Weston primarily worked as a **leader** from that point and toured constantly for the next few decades. Playing music arranged by trombonist **Melba Liston**, Weston's groups were featured in **Europe** and Africa in addition to touring the United States.

Weston maintained residences in New York, **France**, and Tangier during the 1970s and worked with musicians including Talib Kibwe, Neil

Clarke, Ahmad Abdul-Malik, and **Cecil Payne** in his groups. Weston was well respected in several different genres of jazz and teamed up with **Bebop** musicians like **Dizzy Gillespie** and **Free Jazz** giants like **David Murray** and **Pharoah Sanders**. Much of Weston's work throughout the 1980s and 1990s was in the form of tribute to his many influences, including groups that honored **Duke Ellington** and **Thelonious Monk**. Weston also contributed several songs to the jazz canon including "Hi-Fly."

WETTLING, GEORGE (1907–1968). Wettling was an important **Traditional Jazz** drummer who worked with many of the top Early Jazz musicians during the 1930s, including **Jimmy McPartland, Red Norvo**, and **Paul Whiteman**. In the 1940s, Wettling became a staple with groups led by Eddie Condon that performed at major venues including Carnegie Hall and Town Hall. Wettling became a **leader** in the 1950s when he created the Dixielanders, and he continued his association with Condon and performing with various Traditional Jazz all-star groups. *See also* DODDS, BABY; EARLY JAZZ.

WHEELER, KENNETH "KENNY" (1930–). Born in Toronto, Canada, Wheeler moved to England in the 1950s and found work playing the **trumpet** with many **England**-based **dance bands**. Being hired by **John Dankworth** in the late 1950s inspired Wheeler to study composition throughout the 1960s when Dankworth recorded several **albums** of compositions. Wheeler worked with many of **Europe**'s top jazz musicians throughout the 1960s and 1970s, including John Surman, Alan Skidmore, and Tubby Hayes.

Wheeler also openly explored **Free Jazz** and was associated with saxophonist **Anthony Braxton** during the 1970s. At the end of the decade, Wheeler began to lead his own groups, both large and small. The group **Azimuth** was an important band formed by Wheeler, John Taylor, and Norma Winstone that remained together for several decades and recorded several albums.

Wheeler was a prominent performer during the 1980s as a member of **Dave Holland**'s groups and working with guitarist **Bill Frisell**. Throughout the 1990s, Wheeler freelanced frequently and played with Jane Ira Bloom, **John Scofield**, Paolino Dalla Porta, and **Lee Konitz**. Wheeler is also credited with being a top-notch composer and has composed music for both small group and **big band** that has been recorded by other artists.

WHETSOL, ARTIE (1905–1940). Born in Florida, Whetsol was friends with **Duke Ellington** as a youth and played **trumpet** in Ellington's band for several years during the 1920s and 1930s. Whetsol suffered from frequent health problems during his tenure with the band, which led to his retirement and eventual passing in 1940.

WHITE, LENNY (1949–). White learned to play the **drum set** as a teenager and landed **gigs** playing with **Miles Davis, Jackie McLean**, and **Freddie Hubbard** before turning 21. Being at the forefront of the **Fusion** movement, White's style often included elements of Rock and **Latin** music. For this reason, he was often used in Fusion-styled groups including **Return to Forever** and the groups of **Stanley Clarke**. Throughout the 1980s and 1990s, he worked with many important jazz figures, including **Herbie Hancock** and **Chick Corea**. White continues to lead his own groups that include **John Scofield** and Geri Allen, among others.

WHITEMAN, PAUL (1890–1967). Born in Denver, Whiteman played **violin** and worked with military bands during World War I. After being discharged, Whiteman gave up playing full time to pursue a career as a **bandleader**. He successfully led bands in San Francisco, Los Angeles, and Atlantic City before establishing himself in New York in the early part of the 1920s.

Whiteman's first major success in New York was his association with composer George Gershwin, who penned the classic "Rhapsody in Blue" for Whiteman. Throughout the 1920s and 1930s, Whiteman's popularity soared, and he was often imitated and copied. Though his music was generally commercially oriented, rather than pure jazz, he was referred to in the press as "the King of Jazz." Whiteman's orchestra featured many of the rising stars of the jazz world including saxophonist **Frankie Trumbauer, Jack Teagarden, Joe Venuti, Tommy Dorsey, Red Norvo**, and **Bix Beiderbecke**.

Whiteman's great success carried on into the 1940s, and his band was included in several motion pictures and frequent **recording** sessions. Whiteman retired from band leading when he was offered a job with the American Broadcasting Company's radio division, re-forming his orchestra from time to time. Much of his music has been preserved at Williams College in Williamstown, Massachusetts. *See also* DANCE BAND; SWING.

WILBER, ROBERT "BOB" (1928–). Wilber's career began as a saxophonist and clarinetist, and he received some lessons from **soprano saxophone** legend **Sidney Bechet** in the 1940s. Originally from New York, Wilber made a point of playing **Traditional** and **New Orleans Jazz** to help keep the spirit of that music alive on the East Coast. Much of his career would be dedicated to maintaining the spirit and style of Traditional Jazz. Wilber worked with several important musicians in the 1950s including Bechet, **Bobby Hackett**,

Benny Goodman, and Jack Teagarden. He worked with a New Orleans–inspired soprano saxophone group in the late 1970s named Soprano Summit and was also active in education. In the later decades he often paired with Kenny Davern in addition to working in groups inspired by Bechet.

WILDER, JOSEPH "JOE" (1922–). Trumpeter Wilder's career started with several appearances with Lionel Hampton, Jimmie Lunceford, and Dizzy Gillespie. In the 1950s, Wilder freelanced with many artists including Count Basie, Ernie Wilkins, and J. J. Johnson, in addition to working as a studio musician. For the next few decades, Wilder would primarily work as a studio musician. He was considered to be a standout lead trumpet player, and he continued to be involved in studio work and performances in pit orchestras for Broadway shows until the 1980s when he became more active as a leader and a sideman. Finally, after more than 62 years playing for others, he led his own quartet at the Village Vanguard in 2006.

WILKINS, ERNIE (1922–1999). After learning violin and piano as a youth, Wilkins decided to try the saxophone, an instrument that he would play for the remainder of his career. Wilkins studied music in college and served in the military before his discharge granted him the opportunity to tour and perform regularly in the late 1940s. He was hired by Count Basie in the early 1950s and would play a major figure in Basie's career, writing many arrangements for the band.

In 1955, Wilkins left the band as a performer but was hired to write for it and for other groups including bands led by Dizzy Gillespie, Tommy Dorsey, and Clifford Brown. The remainder of Wilkins' career would be hallmarked by his abilities in arranging and composing, which he did frequently for many bands, most notably that of Clark Terry. Wilkins also led his own band during the 1980s and moved to Europe.

WILLIAMS, CHARLES "BUSTER" (1942–). Williams, a bassist, got his initial professional opportunities with several tenor saxophonists including Jimmy Heath, Gene Ammons, and Sonny Stitt before working primarily with vocalists for much of the 1960s. Toward the end of the 1960s, Williams spent time in Los Angeles freelancing before moving to, and permanently residing in, New York. After relocating, Williams worked with Art Blakey, Herbie Hancock, Tony Williams, and Mary Lou Williams before becoming a member of the group Sphere along with fellow Philadelphian, pianist Kenny Barron. Williams became an active leader and frequently led trios and quartets in addition to continuing his work with Sphere. Williams also became increasingly involved as an educator, teaching at the New School in New York City during the late 1990s.

WILLIAMS, CLARENCE (1893–1965). Williams initially played **piano** in the New Orleans and Chicago areas during the 1920s before moving to New York and making a career in the business side of the music world. Involved in music printing and promoting, Williams would be influential in increasing the awareness and popularity of **Stride** pianists **James P. Johnson** and **Fats Waller**, in addition to **recording** and producing **sessions** for **Louis Armstrong** and **Sidney Bechet**.

WILLIAMS, COOTIE (1911–1985). Born in Alabama, **trumpet** player Charles "Cootie" Williams made a name for himself after being invited to tour with the Young Family Band in 1925, which included a young **Lester Young**. Williams moved to New York when he was 17 to record and play with jazz stars **Chick Webb** and **Fletcher Henderson**, later being hired by **Duke Ellington** in the early 1930s. Ellington made Williams an important member of the ensemble and often wrote pieces for him, including "Concerto for Cootie," which featured the player's outstanding plunger technique.

During the 1940s, Williams took a hiatus from playing with the Ellington Orchestra to freelance, during which time he worked with **Benny Goodman**, **Teddy Wilson**, and **Charlie Christian**. He failed at leading a **big band** due to economic concerns, but he continued to lead a small group into the 1950s. After playing in **Rhythm and Blues** groups for a few years, Williams rejoined Ellington in the 1960s and remained a member for several decades.

WILLIAMS, JAMES (1951–2004). Born in Memphis, Williams, along with **Phineas Newborn, Harold Mabern, Mulgrew Miller,** and Donald Brown, became one of the many pianists to come out of the Memphis tradition. Williams attended the **Berklee College of Music** in the 1970s before working with **Alan Dawson, Joe Henderson, Clark Terry,** and **Art Blakey**. In the 1980s, Williams began working as a **leader** with a variety of musicians including **Billy Higgins** and **Rufus Reid** in addition to serving as a **sideman** for several artists. Williams was also an active educator during this time and taught at the Hart School of Music in Connecticut.

Williams ran several groups in the early 1990s, including a tribute to Newborn, the Contemporary Piano Ensemble, and a group named ICU (or Intensive Care Unit) that played **Blues**-influenced music and included the use of a **vibraphone**. Williams started his own production company during this time and presented concerts featuring pianists in the New York area. The Jazz Studies Department of William Patterson University named Williams director of jazz studies in 1995, and several years later he gained critical acclaim for many of his records.

WILLIAMS, JOE (1918–1999). A vocalist, Williams' career began in the Chicago area working with instrumentalists including **Coleman Hawkins** and **Jimmie Noone**. In the 1950s, Williams began an on-again, off-again relationship working with the **Count Basie** Orchestra, where his rich voice and bluesy style made a perfect match. For most of the 1960s and 1970s, Williams freelanced with many leading jazz artists, including **Cannonball Adderley**, **Harry Edison**, **Junior Mance**, and **George Shearing**.

Williams began leading his own groups in the 1970s and also worked in television during the 1980s, most notably as a recurring character on *The Cosby Show*. Williams primarily performed at **festivals** and on cruise ships during the 1990s until eventually settling in Las Vegas. Notable **recordings** include *Count Basie Swings, Joe Williams Sings* (1954, **Verve**) and *The Definitive Joe Williams* (2001, Verve). An NEA Jazz Master, he garnered eight Grammy nominations, winning in 1984 in the category of Best Jazz Vocal Performance. Williams died due to complications from a respiratory disease.

WILLIAMS, MARY LOU (1910–1981). One of the most significant women in jazz, Williams was influential on many levels. She was a performing pianist, a **bandleader**, and a composer and arranger, having produced hundreds of arrangements and compositions. Williams worked almost exclusively with the **Andy Kirk** band during the 1930s, both playing in the band and acting as the band's primary arranger. In addition to writing for the Kirk band, Williams also wrote for many other groups and artists including **Tommy Dorsey**, **Earl Hines**, **Dizzy Gillespie**, and **Duke Ellington**.

Williams took a break for several years in the early 1950s to pursue other endeavors before leading groups in the late 1950s and 1960s. She was also a record producer, music publisher, and mentor to many of the great figures in jazz. Williams was honored during the last years of her career and also became involved in teaching, working at Duke University until her death.

WILLIAMS, SANDY (1906–1991). Williams worked as a trombonist with **Fletcher Henderson** and **Chick Webb** during the 1930s and continued performing with a variety of **big bands** in the 1940s, including ones led by **Coleman Hawkins**, **Benny Carter**, and **Cootie Williams**. Williams worked briefly with **Duke Ellington** before he was forced into a musical retirement due to health problems in the early 1950s.

WILLIAMS, TONY (1945–1997). A prodigious drummer as a youth, Williams studied and worked as a teenager with fellow drummers **Alan Dawson**, **Art Blakey**, and **Max Roach**. **Jackie McLean** is credited with convincing Williams to move to New York, an important move that led to his hiring by

Miles Davis. Williams would be affiliated with Davis for most of the 1960s and was one of the revolutionary members that Davis used in this late quintet. His drum style was unique, and he was very influential in helping to further develop the **drums** as a melodic and solo instrument.

Williams would be affiliated with his Davis counterparts, most notably **Herbie Hancock** and **Wayne Shorter**, for the next few decades and frequently recorded with both. Williams led his own group, Lifetime, toward the end of the 1960s and maintained the name for the next few decades, although the group frequently changed personnel. In the 1970s, Williams worked with **Stan Getz** and the supergroup **V.S.O.P.**, which used the same personnel as Davis' later quintet but with **Freddie Hubbard** assuming the role of Davis. Williams continued to work throughout the 1990s until he died due to complications from gall bladder surgery.

WILSON, GERALD (1918–). Wilson's career began as a **trumpet** player working with the band of **Jimmie Lunceford** in the late 1930s. Shortly after Wilson ended his tenure with Lunceford, he relocated to Los Angeles where he would be one of the city's primary **big band leaders** for decades. Wilson was mostly active as a composer and **bandleader**, although he also performed with some groups. His **arrangements** were played by the bands of **Count Basie, Dizzy Gillespie**, and **Duke Ellington**.

In the 1960s, Wilson wrote for many vocalists and ran a new edition of his big band that garnered much acclaim. Wilson frequently hired the best West Coast musicians, and his bands were constantly loaded with talent. Wilson became involved in education during the next few decades and taught at a variety of schools including the University of Utah, San Fernando Valley State College, and California State University at Los Angeles. Wilson's band recorded and toured often, most notably giving several important performances at the **Monterey Jazz Festival**.

WILSON, NANCY (1937–). Wilson's career as a jazz vocalist blossomed when she sat in with **Cannonball Adderley**'s quintet during a tour in the late 1950s, which led her to a record deal with **Capitol** records. Throughout the 1960s, Wilson's vocals would be heard on her own feature records in addition to dates with Adderley and **George Shearing**. Wilson took several breaks from singing jazz to record Pop **albums** until she returned to her jazz roots in the late 1970s, working with **Hank Jones, Joe Henderson**, and **Art Farmer**. Much of the 1980s was dedicated to performing worldwide at numerous **jazz festivals** while also **recording** more contemporary, Pop-related material. She is still actively performing today and received a National Endowment for the Arts (NEA) Jazz Master award in 2004.

WILSON, THEODORE "TEDDY" (1912–1986). Wilson was hired to play **piano** with **Louis Armstrong** in Chicago, an event that introduced Wilson into the 1930s jazz scene. Shortly after, Wilson moved to New York and worked with **Benny Carter** and **Benny Goodman**, the latter of whom was important because Wilson and Goodman helped break down racial boundaries by performing together. Wilson worked primarily as a **leader** for much of the 1940s until being hired to teach jazz at Juilliard in New York in 1950.

Wilson maintained a stellar reputation in terms of being a professional musician and was praised by his peers. He performed and made significant **recordings** with vocalist **Billie Holiday**. Despite recording several **albums** with **Lester Young** and **Roy Eldridge** in the late 1950s, Wilson primarily worked under his own name for the remainder of his career. Along with **Nat "King" Cole**, Wilson is considered to be one of the most important pianists to come out of the 1930s.

WINDING, KAI (1922–1983). Originally from Denmark, Winding moved to the United States when he was 12 and took up the **trombone** shortly after. In the late 1940s, Winding caught on with many of the top working bands, including those led by **Benny Goodman, Stan Kenton**, and **Gerry Mulligan**. Winding was very active in the new **Bebop** movement that was taking place and worked with **Charlie Parker** and **Miles Davis**.

During the 1950s, Winding dedicated much of his work to trombone-based ensembles. He formed a long-lasting relationship working with fellow trombonist **J. J. Johnson** and put together several groups of multiple trombones throughout the 1950s and 1960s. Winding worked with **Bill Watrous, Carl Fontana, Wayne Andre, Albert Mangelsdorff**, and Jiggs Whigham at various points. During the 1970s, Winding freelanced with many groups including those led by **Dizzy Gillespie, Curtis Fuller**, and **Lionel Hampton**. Winding retired to Spain before passing away in 1983.

WOLVERINES. An influential Early Jazz group formed in Chicago that was inspired by many of the New Orleans bands. The Wolverines recorded a few times, and included in the personnel was a rising **cornet** player, **Bix Beiderbecke**. The Wolverines were only in existence from 1923 to 1930.

WOODS, PHILIP "PHIL" (1931–). Woods received early jazz training from pianist **Lennie Tristano** before studying **clarinet** and **saxophone** at the Manhattan School of Music in the early 1950s. Shortly after graduating, Woods began working with several New York–based groups including ones led by George Wallington, **Kenny Dorham**, and **Dizzy Gillespie**. For most of the late 1950s and 1960s, Woods worked frequently as a **sideman** with artists including **Quincy Jones** and **Buddy Rich**, while also leading his own groups with fellow alto saxophonist Gene Quill. Woods moved several times during the 1970s and formed bands in both **France** and Los Angeles before settling down in Pennsylvania. During this time, Woods formed the beginnings of his band by hiring bassist **Steve Gilmore** and drummer **Bill Goodwin**, both of whom would play with Woods for the next three decades. The piano chair would alternate, as a well as the second horn chair, which was filled at times by trumpeters **Tom Harrell** or Brian Lynch. Woods would continue to record and tour well into the 2000s and is still playing today.

WOODYARD, SAM(UEL) (1925–1988). After Woodyard's drumming with various New York–based small groups was heard by **Duke Ellington** during the early 1950s, he was hired to take over the drum chair for Ellington's orchestra. After an 11-year tenure with the Ellington band, Woodyard freelanced for several years until he moved to **Europe**. Health problems and alcohol abuse led to a steep decline for Woodyard who all but retired from playing before his death in 1988.

WORKMAN, REGGIE (1937–). Born in Philadelphia, Workman's career as a bassist began working with fellow Philadelphian musicians **McCoy Tyner** and Odeon Pope in the mid-1950s. From 1955 to 1969, Workman played with many of the best groups in jazz including long stays with **Art Blakey** and the **Jazz Messengers, John Coltrane**'s famous quartet, **Jackie McLean, Cedar Walton**, and **Bobby Hutcherson**. Throughout the later decades, Workman formed a series of groups with drummer Andrew Cyrille and would play music that leaned toward the **Avant-Garde**. Workman also became interested in education and held teaching positions at the University of Massachusetts and Long Island University, and he eventually became a key member of the faculty of the New School's Jazz and Contemporary Music Program.

WORLD SAXOPHONE QUARTET (WSQ). Founded in 1976 and based on a commission received by **Anthony Braxton**, the World Saxophone Quartet remained in existence for over three decades. Braxton wrote for fellow saxophonists **Julius Hemphill, Oliver Lake** and Hamiet Bluiett, and **David Murray**, but did not play in the group himself. The group recorded several times and had several members leave or take a hiatus from the group. At various points, Arthur Blythe, John Purcell, and James Carter were all involved with the World Saxophone Quartet. The WSQ has made several records and continues to record on the Justin Time **record label**.

WORLD'S GREATEST JAZZ BAND. The culmination of several groups including the Eight, Nine, or Ten Greats of Jazz, the World's Greatest Jazz Band was formed in the late 1960s in Denver, Colorado. In existence for almost 10 years, The World's Greatest Jazz Band featured many top players and at times included **Billy Butterfield**, **Carl Fontana**, Bob Wilder, Bud Freeman, **Roger Kellaway**, **Hank Jones**, and **Urbie Green**.

WORLD WIDE. Founded by Herman Lubinsky, World Wide served as an opportunity for jazz musicians to be recorded more effectively using newer **recording** capabilities in the late 1950s. World Wide was affiliated with the Savoy **record label** and recorded **sessions** with musicians including **Frank Wess**, Pepper Adams, and **Joe Wilder**.

X

XANADU. Established in 1975, Xanadu became a highly successful jazz **record label**. Xanadu created two divisions or series of **recordings**: one for reissues of **Swing** and **Bebop** artists and the other for recording new material of artists inspired by those eras. Artists to record on Xanadu include **Sonny Criss**, **Dexter Gordon**, **Barry Harris**, and Al Cohn. Xanadu eventually stopped recording new music in the 1990s and served as a label just for distributing and reissuing.

XYLOPHONE. A percussion instrument that is made up of bars or keys of various lengths that sound various pitches when hit by a stick or mallet. The bars or keys are pitched and arranged the same way as a piano, are made out of wood or various types of synthetic alternatives, and usually have a range of two to four octaves. The instrument has roots in African, Asian, and European cultures. The xylophone is not as common in jazz as a similar instrument, the **vibraphone**. The vibraphone differs from the xylophone in that it has metal bars instead of wood, and it employs the use of a sustain pedal. The xylophone was used sparingly during the 1920s and 1930s and would make occasional appearances in modern jazz settings, but it is rarely used by performers other than vibraphonists.

Y

YANCEY, JIMMY (1894–1951). Known for his enthusiasm, Yancey began a career as an entertainer at an early age performing in vaudeville shows that toured the United States and Europe. Yancey was first a singer and tap dancer but decided to teach himself **piano** after he settled in Chicago. Yancey also attempted a career playing baseball in the African-American league but was unsuccessful. He did, however, land a job working as a groundsman for the Chicago White Sox at Comiskey Park. This steady work allowed Yancey to continue to develop as a pianist and release records under his own name while also establishing himself as a prominent **Blues** player. He was not known as being an innovator or technician as many of his peers were, but he had a strong following thanks to his enthusiastic playing style.

YERBA BUENA JAZZ BAND. A jazz group formed in the late 1930s by San Francisco–based **cornet** player Lu Watters. The band primarily played **Traditional** and **Dixieland** jazz and performed regularly at the Dawn Club in San Francisco until 1950 when the group disbanded. The group sometimes went by the name "Lu Watters & the Yerba Buena Jazz Band." Prior to disbanding, the group recorded several times, most notably *The Complete Good Time Jazz Recordings* (1947, Good Time Jazz). The Yerba Buena Jazz Band was an important group for musicians in later years who wished to emulate the Traditional or **Dixieland** jazz styles. *See also* EARLY JAZZ; JOHNSON, WILLIE GARY "BUNK."

YOUNG, EUGENE EDWARD "SNOOKY" (1919–2011). Born in Dayton, Ohio, Young took up the **trumpet** at the early age of six and toured with his family, all of whom were musicians. At the age of 20, through a referral from pianist **Gerald Wilson**, Young was hired to play **lead** in **Jimmie Lunceford**'s band. Performing with Lunceford's band was Young's big break, and he quickly became a very popular trumpet player. He subbed in many of the other popular **big bands** of that time, including the groups of **Benny Carter, Lionel Hampton,** and **Count Basie.** After his tenure with the Lunceford group ended in 1942, Young continued to freelance with many of these groups but did not stay with a single group for very long. Young did a few **recordings** under his own name during the 1940s and led his own small group back in his hometown of Dayton.

Young continued freelancing with bands until 1957 when he rejoined the Basie Band. He remained with the group for almost five years and was on many of Basie's most famous records including *April in Paris* (1956, **Verve**) and *Atomic Mr. Basie* (1957, Roulette). In 1962, he landed a job as a NBC **studio musician** where he worked until he relocated to Los Angeles in 1972. He was also an initial member to the **Thad Jones–Mel Lewis** Orchestra that was founded during the mid-1960s.

Young moved to Los Angeles in 1972 to join **Doc Severinsen**'s *Tonight Show* Band, a chair that he held until Johnny Carson left the show in 1992. In addition to performing with the band, Young also maintained steady freelancing work in Los Angeles, performing with groups like the **Gerald Wilson** Orchestra, the Capp-Pierce Juggernaut, and the Clayton-Hamilton Jazz Orchestra. He is considered one of the greatest lead trumpet players in jazz history.

YOUNG, JAMES OSBORNE "TRUMMY" (1912–1984). Young began his professional career as a trombonist at the age of 16 performing with groups in Washington, D.C. One of these groups was led by the drummer Tommy Myles and featured **arrangements** by **Jimmy Mundy**, who would soon be hired by **Earl Hines**. Young followed Mundy into Hines' band but not before receiving the nickname "Trummy" from Myles. This nickname would stick for the remainder of Young's career. Hines' band recorded and performed frequently during the 1930s, and many of Young's best work were recorded during that time. Young also sang and assisted with arrangements for the band. In 1943, Young left the band to freelance and worked with **Roy Eldridge** and the **Jazz at the Philharmonic** group before deciding to move to Hawaii where he would live on and off over the next two decades.

Louis Armstrong hired Young in 1952 to join his newly formed All Stars, and Trummy would remain with the group until the group ended in 1964. Young faced some criticism for playing music that was simple and not up to the standard that he had achieved for himself with his fairly modern and advanced playing in the 1930s. After leaving Armstrong's group, Young continued to tour the United States and **Europe** with various groups until his death in 1984.

YOUNG, LESTER WILLIS "PREZ" (1909–1959). Born close to New Orleans, Young's family relocated to Minneapolis, Minnesota, when Lester was four years old. Young was born into a family of musicians and was well versed in several instruments by the age of 13, including **violin, drum set,** and most notably, **alto saxophone**. Young's talents were constantly on display with his family's bands, but Young felt that it was important for him to break away from those groups due to disagreements they had about touring in the southern United States. In 1927, Young toured with groups not affiliated with his family. During this time, Young also switched to the **tenor saxophone**, and it became the instrument he would use primarily for the remainder of his career. From 1929 to 1933, Young bounced between various groups, including the **Blue Devils** (led by **Walter Page**), the **Count Basie** Orchestra, and short stints back with his family band.

Basie gravitated toward Young's approach and hired him to be in the band on a full-time basis in 1934. For a brief period, Young was hired by **Fletcher Henderson** to replace jazz saxophone pioneer **Coleman Hawkins**; however, Young's approach was more appreciated by Basie and the members of his band. Young stayed with Basie until the late 1930s, when Young decided to relocate first to New York and then to Los Angeles to form his own groups. Young was drafted into the military in 1944, but his stay was not a good experience for him, and he was discharged for drug abuse. In addition to some performances with Basie's band, Young resumed his jazz career performing with **Norman Granz**'s **Jazz at the Philharmonic**. Young enjoyed a popular solo career in the 1950s, **recording** many times, including numerous live dates for the Pablo recording label and with **Oscar Peterson**'s famous trio on the **Verve** release, *With the Oscar Peterson Trio* (1952, **Verve**). Mental health setbacks stemming from his time in the army and an excessive drinking problem led to his untimely and unfortunate death at the age of 50.

Young's time with Basie in the 1930s was considered his prime, and he was the ultimate musical complement to the innovations that were taking place with the saxophone and with players such as **Coleman Hawkins**. Using a much softer, whisper-like tone, Young crafted **solos** that were melodically strong and contrasted the harmonic inventiveness of Hawkins. Solos on *The Lester Young Story, Volumes 1, 2, & 3* (1938, Columbia) are great examples of this approach. In addition to influencing other saxophonists, Young also provided a musical blueprint for the **West Coast** or **Cool Jazz** movement that swept jazz in the 1950s. *See also* JONES-SMITH INC.

YOUNG TUXEDO BRASS BAND. Created in 1938 in New Orleans, the Young Tuxedo Brass Band was influential in maintaining the **brass band** tradition of New Orleans. The band fluctuated in size between 8 and 11 players and was led by clarinetist John Casimir. Casimir remained the **bandleader** until 1963, at which time saxophonist Andrew Morgan took charge of the band. Clarinetist Herman Sherman became leader of the band after Morgan died in 1972 and was responsible for one of the records put out by the band, *Jazz Continues* (1983, 504 Records). Sherman's death in 1984 led clarinetist Gregory Stafford to assume leadership of the band. The band remained very active throughout the 1990s and 2000s, performing at many jazz festivals in New Orleans.

Z

ZAWINUL, JOSEF "JOE" (1932–2007). Zawinul was originally from Austria and studied Classical **piano** during World War II at the Vienna Conservatory. After spending several years playing jazz in Austria, Zawinul applied for and was awarded a scholarship to the **Berklee School of Music** in Boston in 1959. After moving to the United States, Zawinul was at Berklee for a few weeks before he was called to perform in several local groups and was introduced to **Maynard Ferguson**. Ferguson hired him right away, and Zawinul toured with Ferguson for almost eight months before being called to tour with **Dinah Washington**. While Zawinul appreciated the work, his true passion was not to be playing with a vocalist. In 1961, when he was called to tour with **Cannonball Adderley**'s group, he excitedly accepted the position. Zawinul remained with Adderley until the late 1960s and was recorded both as a performer and composer on many of Adderley's **albums**. Zawinul's biggest jazz hit, "Mercy Mercy Mercy," was recorded while touring with Adderley.

Miles Davis hired Zawinul to record and compose for several **recording sessions** that Davis had planned. *Bitches Brew* (1969, **Columbia**); *Big Fun* (1972, Columbia); and *Live-Evil* (1970, Columbia) were the results of these recording sessions. The sessions were especially important because Zawinul had begun experimenting with electronic instruments and **synthesizers**, both of which would be an important part of his repertoire for the remainder of his career. **Wayne Shorter** was also a member of these recording sessions. Shorter left the Davis group shortly after these recordings and assembled a new supergroup, Weather Report, and asked Zawinul to be a member. Weather Report's first album was well received, and the group was quick to pioneer the **Fusion** movement. The group would remain together for 15 years and record 15 albums.

In 1988, Zawinul formed the Zawinul Syndicate, a trio that specialized in playing Jazz Fusion. Zawinul also began a career as a producer working with Malian singer Salif Keita on the album *Amen* (1991, Mango), and also as a composer, writing works including the symphony "Stories of the Danube" for the 1993 Bruckner Festival. Zawinul continued to perform with the syndicate through the mid-2000s in addition to performing Weather Report works and composing. Zawinul died due to terminal cancer in 2007.

ZENTNER, SIMON H. "SI" (1917–2000). Zentner became a trombonist at an early age and picked up the instrument rather quickly. He was awarded a college scholarship but decided to pursue performing professionally. He performed in several bands during the 1940s including the large groups of Les Brown, **Tommy Dorsey,** and Harry James before deciding to become a full-time **studio musician** in 1949. His passion for **big band** music led him to leave the studio in 1955 and resume freelancing with big bands until he formed his own band in 1959. Zenter was fortunate to maintain his band with a lot of success and even had a song penned by **Bob Florence,** "Up a Lazy River," make it onto the Top 40 *Billboard* charts. In 1965, the band was disbanded, and Zentner played as part of a house band backing up the singer **Mel Tormé.** Zentner remained in Las Vegas for the remainder of his life, serving as musical director for several shows and performing in big bands whenever he could. Zentner died due to complications of leukemia in 2000 but performed up until 1999.

ZONOPHONE. A record label established by Frank Seamon and purchased by **Victor** Records in the early 1900s. The label was rarely used in the United States before 1910 and became almost exclusively British after 1910. Zonophone was considered to be the cheaper label associated with **Gramophone** records and was used to issue **recordings** of 1920s British dance music in addition to reissuing American recordings it had acquired before 1910. Zonophone was acquired by **Electrical and Musical Industries (EMI)** and merged with the record label **Regal** to form the label Regal-Zonophone.

Bibliography

CONTENTS

INTRODUCTION

The amount of literature and other resources on the history of jazz has expanded greatly in recent years. No longer is it difficult to locate information on the life of major performers, the great big bands, the styles of jazz, or the writings of jazz critics and philosophers. The difficulty today has become selecting which resources among the vast offerings to reference. What is contained below is a sizeable sampling of books and Internet resources that provide worthwhile information and insight. Depending on the reader's area of study or interest, literature that emphasizes the sociocultural relationship of jazz to the world may be especially beneficial, while to another the specific facts surrounding the development and training of an artist's musicianship skills may be the priority. In any case, the reader will find resources that provide depth and detail among these sources beyond the basic information the dictionary can provide.

The bibliography listings begin with **Reference and General Works** and include works on certain time periods in the history, anthologies and encyclopedias, and insights into the life and world of the musician. *Thinking in Jazz*, by Paul Berliner, provides many insights into the mind of a jazz musician. Included in the text are articles, musical text examples, bibliographies, and interviews from more than 50 significant musicians. The material provides a resource for the novice *and* the professional musician. Throughout the book, a broad sense of the culture and history of jazz is provided. Stanley Crouch's *Considering Genius* is a sizeable compendium of one individual's perspective on artists and the music from throughout jazz history.

Among the works that provide an extensive overview of the history of jazz, *Jazz*, by Scott DeVeaux and Gary Giddins, stands out as a significant contribution to the field. Included in the text are listening guides to pieces provided on the accompanying CDs, lists of jazz on film, photographs, lists of musicians by instruments, and more than 500 pages of in-depth historical information on styles, musicians, recordings, and relevant societal information. Leonard Feather's works continue to be resources consulted by all jazz enthusiasts, and the substantial *New Grove Dictionary of Jazz* provides a wealth of material on all topics.

A fascinating work on the creative process of improvisation in music, art, and culture is *Free Play: Improvisation in Life and Art* by Stephen Nachmanovitch. The author has presented improvisation workshops worldwide and serves on the board of the Society for Improvised Music. His book examines the improvisational process available that all people possess and the effect and impact it has on each person.

Within this section are also found works on specific recordings or time periods of jazz that add depth to the more general discourses provided on the subject to date. Included in these are works on Miles Davis' quintet of 1965–1968 written by Keith Waters and Ashley Kahn's books on the recording sessions and background of Davis' *Kind of Blue* and the seminal John Coltrane album *A Love Supreme*. Richard Williams' *The Blue Moment: Miles Davis's Kind of Blue and the Remaking of Modern Music* is another such example of the high quality of in-depth information now available on specific topics that can enhance the reader's depth of understanding in particular areas of interest.

It is also useful to provide a listing of sources associated with particular styles and eras of jazz. Those from **Early Jazz** through contemporary styles are provided in relatively chronological order of their development. In addition to some respected and well-known jazz authors, there are also works by authors who are less known that provide a unique perspective or deeper focus on the topic.

For each subgenre of jazz, additions to the resource base are continually being produced. Karl Koenig's *Jazz in Print (1856–1929): An Anthology of Selected Early Readings in Jazz History* provides the reader with a compendium of fascinating insights into Early Jazz as it was developing. In depth and with great value to the scholar is the work by Gene Anderson, *The Original Hot Five Recordings of Louis Armstrong*, which provides valuable information on what many would consider to be the most significant early recordings in jazz. In recent years, the significant role that Chicago played in the development of jazz has been given specific notice. While William Kenney's *Chicago Jazz: A Cultural History 1904–1930* focuses on the early years of development from a cultural perspective, Gerald Majer (*The Velvet Lounge: On Late Chicago Jazz*) provides a perspective of recent decades from one who played a part in it. Placing historical anecdotes within a social and political context brings a resonance to the Chicago Jazz experience that is otherwise hard to convey, and Majer accomplishes this well.

Along with the New Orleans and Chicago developments in Early Jazz, **Kansas City Jazz** played a significant role but is often overlooked. Frank Driggs provides a current discourse on the early days of jazz from the Kansas City perspective in his book, *Kansas City Jazz: From Ragtime to Bebop—A History*. Venues, significant performers, and the political landscape that helped shape jazz in Kansas City are explored here, providing a valuable resource on an area of jazz development that deserves notice.

In **Big Bands**, readers may wish to concentrate on any number of the more recent publications that focus on particular bands (or **bandleaders**) and their history, but Scott Yanow's *Swing* (2000) should be on every scholar's reading list as a prime source for comprehensive information on Swing era bandleaders, performers, records, composers, and arrangers. Yanow then provides a follow-up to his text with *Bebop*, which is filled with essays, biographies, and reviews, and can be found in the listings under **Bebop**. His years of writing experience and personal familiarity with the music and musicians provide a valuable resource for any enthusiast. Among the listings in **Cool Jazz**, Frank Tirro has provided an insightful and thorough look at the influences and attributes of Cool Jazz, using the landmark recording *Birth of the Cool* by Miles Davis as a focal point. Information on arrangers and composers is included, as well as an accompanying CD of relevant musical examples. Within **Avant-Garde/Free Jazz**, *Music and the Creative Spirit: Innovators in Jazz, Improvisation, and the Avant Garde* is highly recommended as a source that provides a worthwhile overview with both breadth and depth on this style of jazz.

Following the extensive list of biographies, the reader will find **Jazz and Culture**. The connection jazz has had to the culture surrounding it is perhaps the greatest legacy of jazz music. Social and economic struggles and changes are reflected in the development of the music. Within this section, numerous titles on that relationship between jazz and society can be found. Although most of these texts involve social connections jazz has had within the United States, the reader may wish to delve into the impact of jazz on international cultures as well. For example, George McKay's *Circular Breathing: The Cultural Politics of Jazz in Britain* provides insight into the connection jazz had in Great Britain since 1943, while Matthew Jordon provides a French perspective in *Le Jazz: Jazz and French Cultural Identity*.

An area that deserves ongoing research and resultant publication is the role of women in jazz. Though present throughout its history, women have been overlooked to some extent until recent years, in spite of the significant impact many have had.

Some Liked It Hot: Jazz Women in Film and Television 1929–1959 is a good place for the reader to start learning about the subject, while recent additional resources on specific female musicians in the form of biography can be found under **Specific Biographical**. Recommended among these are *Ella Fitzgerald: The Tale of a Vocal Virtuosa* by Andrea Pinkney and *Billie Holiday: Wishing on the Moon* by Donald Clarke, both of which are unbiased in the presentation of biographical information. The Internet provides an additional worthwhile source, *Women in Jazz* (http://jazz women.org).

As technology and use of the Internet continue to advance, quality resources available online continue to expand. Among those included in the listings of **Internet Resources** are sites that feature articles, interviews, photographs, reviews, and video examples. Additionally, sites from countries other than the United States are provided, including Europe Jazz Network, Jazz in Japan, Jazzru: Russian Jazz Central, and the Canadian Jazz Archive Online. An excellent source on the bands and musicians prior to 1930 is the Red Hot Jazz Archive, which has become one of the primary sources for many enthusiasts. Discographies, biographical information, and information on jazz films and bands are all found within the site. PBS Jazz is based on the Ken Burns 10-part documentary video series (*Jazz: A Film by Ken Burns*) and is filled with information that would add to any reader's knowledge of the subject. In addition, PBS has developed an associated site intended for children that provides a very basic timeline as well as some biographical information on significant performers (http://pbskids.org/jazz).

REFERENCE AND GENERAL WORKS

Ake, David Andrew. *Jazz Matters: Sound, Place, and Time since Bebop*. Berkeley: University of California Press, 2010.

Arnaud, Gerald, and Jacques Chesnel. *Masters of Jazz*. Edinburgh: W & R Chambers, 1991.

Barlow, William. *Looking Up at Down: The Emergence of the Blues Culture*. Philadelphia, Pa.: Temple University Press, 1989.

Berendt, Joachim-Ernst, and Günther Huesmann. *The Jazz Book: From Ragtime to Fusion and Beyond*. Brooklyn, N.Y.: Lawrence Hill Books, 1992.

Bergerot, Frank, and Merlin Bergerot. *The Story of Jazz Bop and Beyond*. New York: Thames and Hudson, 1993.

Berk, Lee Eliot, ed. *Berklee: The First Fifty Years*. Boston, Mass.: Berklee Press, 1995.

Berliner, Paul. *Thinking in Jazz: The Infinite Art of Improvisation*. Chicago, Ill.: University of Chicago Press, 1994.

Berry, Jason, Jonathan Foose, and Tad Jones. *Up from the Cradle of Jazz: New Orleans Music since World War II*. Athens: University of Georgia Press, 1986.

Blesh, Rudi. *Shining Trumpets: A History of Jazz*. New York: Knopf, 1946.

Bushell, Garvin, and Mark Tucker. *Jazz from the Beginning*. New York: Da Capo Press, 1998.

Carr, Ian, Digby Fairweather, and Brian Priestley. *Jazz: The Essential Companion*. New York: Prentice Hall, 1988.

——. *Jazz: The Rough Guide*. London: Rough Guides, 2000.

Charters, Charles Barclay, IV. *Jazz: A History of the New York Scene*. New York: Doubleday, 1962.

——. *Jazz: New Orleans 1985–1963: An Index to the Negro Musicians of New Orleans*. New York: Oak Publications, 1963.

——. *New Orleans: Playing a Jazz Chorus*. New York: Marion Boyars, 2006.

——. *A Trumpet around the Corner: The Story of New Orleans Jazz*. Jackson: University Press of Mississippi, 2009.

Clark, Andrew, ed. *Riffs and Choruses: A New Jazz Anthology*. New York: Continuum, 2001.

Clarke, Donald. *Penguin Encyclopedia of Popular Music*. New York: Viking Adult, 1989.

Collier, James Lincoln. *The Making of Jazz: A Comprehensive History*. Boston, Mass.: Houghton Mifflin, 1978.

Cook, Richard. *Richard Cook's Jazz Encyclopedia*. New York: Penguin, 2005.

Cooke, Mervyn. *The Chronicle of Jazz*. New York: Abbeville Press, 1998.

Crouch, Stanley. *Considering Genius: Writings on Jazz*. New York: Basic Civitas Books, 2007.

Crowther, Bruce, and Mike Pinfold. *Singing Jazz: The Singers and Their Styles*. San Francisco: Miller Freeman Books, 1997.

Davis, Francis. *Bebop and Nothingness: Jazz and Pop at the End of the Century*. New York: Schirmer Books, 1996.

DeVeaux, Scott, and Gary Giddins. *Jazz*. New York: Norton, 2009.

Driggs, Frank, and Harris Lewine. *Black Beauty, White Heat: A Pictorial History of Classical Jazz 1920–1950*. New York: Da Capo Press, 1995.

Epstein, Dean J. *Sinful Tunes and Spirituals: Black Folk Music to the Civil War*. Urbana: University of Illinois Press, 1977.

Feather, Leonard. *The Encyclopedia of Jazz*. New York: Bonanza Books, 1960.

——. *The Encyclopedia of Jazz in the Sixties*. New York: Horizon Press, 1966.

Feather, Leonard, and Ira Gitler. *The Biographical Dictionary of Jazz*. New York: Oxford University Press, 1999.

——. *The Encyclopedia of Jazz in the Seventies*. New York: Horizon Press, 1976.

Fordham, John. *Jazz*. London: Dorling Kindersley, 1993.

Gennari, John. *Blowin' Hot and Cool: Jazz and Its Critics*. Chicago, Ill.: University of Chicago Press, 2006.

Giddins, Gary. *Visions of Jazz: The First Century*. New York: Oxford University Press, 1998.

Gioia, Ted. *The History of Jazz*. New York: Oxford University Press, 1997.

Goffin, Robert. *Aux frontières du jazz*. Paris: Sagittaire, 1932.

Gray, John. *Fire Music: A Bibliography of the New Jazz, 1959–1990*. Music Reference Collection, no. 31. New York: Greenwood, 1991.

Gridley, Mark C. *Concise Guide to Jazz*. Englewood Cliffs, N.J.: Prentice Hall, 1992.

——. *Jazz Styles*. 9th ed. Upper Saddle River, N.J.: Prentice Hall, 1999.

Gushee, Lawrence. *Pioneers of Jazz: The Story of the Creole Band*. New York: Oxford University Press, 2005.

Hardy, Phil, and Dave Laing. *Faber Companion to 20th Century Popular Music*. London: Faber and Faber, 1990.

Haskins, James. *Black Music in America: A History through Its People*. New York: Harper Trophy, 1987.

Hennessey, Thomas J. *From Jazz to Swing: African-American Jazz Musicians and Their Music, 1890–1935*. Detroit, Mich.: Wayne State University Press, 1994.

Hentoff, Nat, comp. *Jazz: New Perspectives on the History of Jazz by Twelve of the World's Foremost Critics and Scholars*. New York: Da Capo Press, 1974.

Hodeir, Andre. *Hommes et Problémes du Jazz*. Paris: Flammarion, 1954.

——. *Toward Jazz*. New York: Grove Press, 1962.

Jones, LeRoi. *Black Music*. New York: Morrow, 1967.

——. *Blues People: Negro Music in White America*. New York: HarperCollins, 2002.

Kahn, Ashley. *Kind of Blue: The Making of the Miles Davis Masterpiece*. New York: Da Capo Press, 2000.

——. *A Love Supreme: The Story of John Coltrane's Signature Album*. New York: Viking, 2002.

Kernfeld, Barry Dean. *The Story of Fakebooks: Bootlegging Songs to Musicians*. Lanham, Md.: Scarecrow Press, 2006.

——. *What to Listen For in Jazz*. New Haven, Conn.: Yale University Press, 1995.

——, ed. *The New Grove Dictionary of Jazz*. 2nd ed. New York: Macmillan, 2002.

King, Colin. *And All That Jazz*. London: Caxton Editions, 2003.

King, Jonny. *What Jazz Is: An Insider's Guide to Understanding and Listening to Jazz*. New York: Walter, 1997.

Kinkle, Roger D. *The Complete Encyclopedia of Popular Music and Jazz, 1900–1950*. New Rochelle, N.Y.: Arlington House, 1974.

Kirshner, Bill, ed. *Oxford Companion to Jazz*. New York: Oxford University Press, 2000.

Koenig, Karl. *Words of Mouth: Jazz Oral History Interviewing*. Covington, La.: Basin Street Press, 1989.

Kofsky, Frank. *Black Music, White Business: Illuminating the History and Political Economy of Jazz*. New York: Pathfinder Press, 1998.

Larson, Tom. *History and Tradition of Jazz*. Dubuque, Iowa: Kendall/Hunt, 2002.

Lewis, George. *A Power Stronger than Itself: The AACM and American Experimental Music*. Chicago, Ill.: University of Chicago Press, 2008.

Mandel, Howard. *Future Jazz*. New York: Oxford University Press, 1999.

Marmorstein, Gary. *The Label: The Story of Columbia Records*. New York: Thunder's Mouth, 2007.

Martin, Henry, and Keith Walters. *Jazz: The First 100 Years*. Belmont, Calif.: Thomson/Schirmer, 2006.

McCalla, James. *Jazz, a Listener's Guide*. Upper Saddle River, N.J.: Prentice Hall, 2000.

McRae, Barry. *The Jazz Handbook*. Boston, Mass.: G. K. Hall, 1989.

Meadows, Eddie S. *Jazz Scholarship and Pedagogy: A Research and Information Guide*. 3rd ed. Routledge Music Bibliographies. New York: Routledge, 2006.

Meeder, Christopher. *Jazz: The Basics*. New York: Routledge, 2008.

Megill, Donald D., and Richard S. Demory. *Introduction to Jazz History*. Upper Saddle River, N.J.: Prentice Hall, 1995.

Monson, Ingrid. *Saying Something*. Chicago, Ill.: University of Chicago Press, 1996.

Morgenstern, Dan. *Jazz People*. New York: Da Capo Press, 1993.

––––––. *Living with Jazz*. Ed. Sheldon Meyer. New York: Pantheon Books, 2000.

Nachmanovitch, Stephen. *Free Play: Improvisation in Life and Art*. New York: Tarcher/Penguin, 1991.

Nisenson, Eric. *The Making of Kind of Blue: Miles Davis and His Masterpiece*. New York: St. Martin's, 2000.

Oliphant, Dave. *Jazz Mavericks of the Lone Star State*. Austin: University of Texas Press, 2007.

O'Meally, Robert G., Brent Hayes Edwards, and Farah Jasmine Griffin. *Uptown Conversation: The New Jazz Studies*. New York: Columbia University Press, 2004.

Panassié, Hugues. *Le jazz hot*. Paris: France Empire, 1934.

Polillo, Arrigo. *Jazz*. Milan: Mandadori, 1975.

––––––. *Jazz—Geschichte und Persönlichkeiten*. Munich: Wilhelm Goldmann Verlag, 1981.

––––––. *Jazz—La vicenda e I protagonisti della musica afro-americana*. Milan: Mondadori, 1975.

Pond, Steven F. *Head Hunters: The Making of Jazz's First Platinum Album*. Ann Arbor: University of Michigan Press, 2005.

Porter, Lewis. *Jazz: A Century of Change*. New York: Schirmer Books, 1997.

Porter, Lewis, Michael Ullman, and Ed Hazell. *Jazz: From Its Origins to the Present*. Englewood Cliffs, N.J.: Prentice Hall, 1993.

Raeburn, Bruce B. *New Orleans Style and the Writing of American Jazz History*. Ann Arbor: University of Michigan Press, 2009.

Ramsey, Frederic, Jr., and Charles Edward Smith, eds. *Jazzmen*. New York: Harcourt, 1939.

Robinson, J. Bradford. *The New Grove Dictionary of Jazz*. 2nd ed. London: Macmillan, 2002.

Rosenthal, David. *Hard Bop: Jazz and Black Music 1955–1965*. New York: Oxford University Press, 1992.

Sargeant, Winthrop. *Jazz Hot & Hybrid*. New York: Arrow, 1938.

Shipton, Alyn. *New History of Jazz*. New York: Continuum, 2001.

Southern, Eileen. *The Music of Black Americans*. New York: Norton, 1971.

Stearns, Marshall W. *The Story of Jazz*. London: Oxford University Press, 1970.

Stokes, W. Royal. *The Jazz Scene: An Informal History from New Orleans to 1990*. New York: Oxford University Press, 1991.

Tanner, Paul O. W., David W. Megill, and Maurice Gerow. *Jazz*. 10th ed. Boston: McGraw-Hill, 2005.

Tesser, Neil. *The Playboy Guide to Jazz: A Selective Guide to the Most Important CD's and to the History of Jazz*. New York: Plume, 1998.

Tirro, Frank. *Jazz: A History*. New York: Norton, 1977.

Ulanov, Barry. *A Handbook of Jazz*. New York: Viking, 1960.

Vuorela, Jari-Pekka. *Finnish Jazz*. Helsinki: Foundation for the Promotion of Finnish Music Information Centre, 1986.

Walser, Robert, ed. *Keeping Time: Readings in Jazz History*. New York: Oxford University Press, 1999.

Ward, Geoffrey C., and Ken Burns. *Jazz: A History of America's Music*. New York: Knopf, 2000.

Weinstein, Norman C. *A Night in Tunisia: Imaginings of Africa in Jazz*. Milwaukee, Wis.: Hal Leonard Corporation, 1993.

Wexler, Jerry. *Rhythm & the Blues: A Life in American Music*. New York: St. Martin's, 1993.

White, Hayden. *The Content of the Form: Narrative Discourse and Historical Representation*. Baltimore, Md.: Johns Hopkins University Press, 1987.

———. *Metahistory: The Historical Imagination in Nineteenth-Century Europe*. Baltimore, Md.: Johns Hopkins University Press, 1990.

Williams, Richard. *The Blue Moment: Miles Davis's Kind of Blue and the Remaking of Modern Music*. New York: Norton, 2010.

Yanow, Scott. *Jazz: A Regional Exploration*. Westport, Conn.: Greenwood Press, 2005.

EARLY JAZZ

Anderson, Gene. *The Original Hot Five Recordings of Louis Armstrong*. Hillsdale, N.Y.: Pendragon Press, 2007.

Ballantine, Christopher John. *Marabi Nights: Early South African Jazz and Vaudeville*. Johannesburg: Raven Press, 1993.

Bradford, Perry. *Born with the Blues: Perry Bradford's Own Story: The True Story of the Pioneering Blues Singers and Musicians in the Early Days of Jazz*. New York: Oak Publications, 1965.

Brooks, Edward. *Influence and Assimilation in Louis Armstrong's Cornet and Trumpet Work (1932–1928)*. Lewiston, N.Y.: Edwin Mellen Press, 2000.

———. *The Young Louis Armstrong on Records: A Critical Survey of the Early Recordings, 1923–1928*. Lanham, Md.: Scarecrow Press, 2002.

Carney, Court. *Cuttin' Up: How Early Jazz Got America's Ear*. Lawrence: University Press of Kansas, 2009.

Case, Brian, Stan Britt, and Trisha Palmer. *The Illustrated Encyclopedia of Jazz*. New York: Harmony Books, 1978.

Dexter, Dave. *The Jazz Story: From the '90s to the '60s*. Englewood Cliffs, N.J.: Prentice Hall, 1964.

Gushee, Lawrence. *Pioneers of Jazz: The Story of the Creole Band*. New York: Oxford University Press, 2005.

Hardie, Daniel. *The Ancestry of Jazz: A Musical Family History*. New York: Universe, 2004.

——. *Exploring Early Jazz: The Origins and Evolution of the New Orleans Style.* San Jose, Calif.: Writers Club Plus, 2002.

Harwood, Robert W. *I Went Down to St. James Infirmary: Investigations in the Shadowy World of Early Jazz-Blues in the Company of Blind Willie McTell, Louis Armstrong, Don Redman, Irving Mills, Carl Moore, and a Host of Others, and Where Did This Dang Song Come from Anyway?* Kitchener, Ontario: Harland, 2008.

Hendler, Maximillian. *Syncopated Music: Frühgeschichte des Jazz.* Graz: Akademische Druck und Verlaganstalt, 2010.

Kenney, William Howland. *Jazz on the River.* Chicago, Ill.: University of Chicago Press, 2005.

Koenig, Karl, ed. *Jazz in Print (1856–1929): An Anthology of Selected Early Readings in Jazz History.* Hillsdale, N.Y.: Pendragon Press, 2002.

Schuller, Gunther. *Early Jazz: Its Roots and Musical Development.* New York: Oxford University Press, 1986.

Shafer, William John, and Johannes Riedel. *The Art of Ragtime: Form and Meaning of an Original Black American Art.* Baton Rouge: Louisiana State University Press, 1973.

Shaw, Arnold. *The Jazz Age: Popular Music in the 1920s.* New York: Oxford University Press, 1989.

CHICAGO JAZZ

Demlinger, Sandor, and John Steiner. *Destination Chicago.* Chicago, Ill.: Arcadia Publishing, 2003.

Feather, Leonard. *Jazz Chicago Style.* Los Angeles, Calif.: Hilton Credit, 1961.

Kenney, W. Howland. *Chicago Jazz: A Cultural History 1904–1930.* New York: Oxford University Press, 1994.

Longstreet, Stephen. *Jazz—The Chicago Scene: The Exhibition of the Art of Stephen Longstreet Containing Retrospective Commentary by the Artist.* Chicago, Ill.: University of Chicago Library, 1989.

Majer, Gerald. *The Velvet Lounge: On Late Chicago Jazz.* New York: Columbia University Press, 2005.

Miller, Paul Eduard, ed. *Esquire's 1946 Jazz Book.* New York: Da Capo Press, 1979.

Ramsey, Frederic. *Chicago Documentary: Portrait of a Jazz Era.* London: Jazz Sociological Society, 1944.

Sengstock, Charles A., Jr. *Jazz Music in Chicago's Early South-Side Theatres.* Northbrook, Ill.: Canterbury Press of Northbrook, 2000.

——. *That Toddlin' Town: Chicago's White Dance Bands and Orchestras, 1900–1950.* Urbana: University of Illinois Press, 2004.

Vermazen, Bruce. *That Moaning Saxophone: The Six Brown Brothers and the Dawning of a Musical Craze.* New York: Oxford University Press, 2004.

Wolf, Robert. *Story Jazz: A History of Chicago Jazz Styles.* Decorah, Iowa: Free River Press, 1995.

KANSAS CITY JAZZ

Driggs, Frank. *Kansas City Jazz: From Ragtime to Bebop—A History*. New York: Oxford University Press, 2005.
Hester, Mary Lee. *Going to Kansas City*. St. Sherman, Tex.: Early Bird Press, 1980.
Kansas City Jazz Museum. *Kansas City . . . and All That's Jazz*. Kansas City, Mo.: Andrews McMeel, 1998.
Pearson, Nathan W. *Goin' to Kansas City*. Urbana: University of Illinois Press, 1994.
Russell, Ross. *Jazz Style in Kansas City and the Southwest*. Berkeley: University of California Press, 1971.
Wilkinson, Todd R. *The Kansas City Jazz and Blues Nightlife Survival Kit*. Kansas City, Mo.: Westport, 1990.

BIG BANDS

Crowther, Bruce, and Mike Pinfold. *The Big Band Years*. New York: Facts on File Publications, 1988.
Daniels, George G. *The Swing Era, 1930–1936: Wonderful Times; Making a Lot Out of a Little*. New York: Time-Life Records, 1971.
Determeyer, Eddy. *Rhythm Is Our Business: Jimmie Lunceford and the Harlem Express*. Ann Arbor: University of Michigan Press, 2006.
Erenberg, Lewis A. *Swingin' the Dream: Big Band Jazz and the Rebirth of American Culture*. Chicago, Ill.: University of Chicago Press, 1998.
Leckrone, Michael. *Popular Music in the U.S. (1920–1950)*. Dubuque, Iowa: Eddie Bowers Publishing, 1983.
McCarthy, Albert J. *Big Band Jazz*. New York: Putnam, 1974.
McClellen, Lawrence. *The Later Swing Era, 1942–1955*. Westport, Conn.: Greenwood Press, 2004.
Morton, John Fass. *Backstory in Blue: Ellington at Newport '56*. New Brunswick, N.J.: Rutgers University Press, 2008.
Nicholson, Stuart. *Jazz: The Modern Resurgence*. New York: Simon and Schuster, 1990.
Oliphant, Dave. *The Early Swing Era, 1930–1941*. Westport, Conn.: Greenwood Press, 2002.
Payne, Philip W., ed. *The Swing Era*. New York: Time-Life Records, 1971–1973.
——. *The Swing Era, 1936–1937: The Movies; Between Vitaphone and Video*. New York: Time-Life Records, 1970.
——. *The Swing Era, 1940–1941: How It Was to Be Young Then*. New York: Time-Life Records, 1970.
Priddy, Louis H. *Jazz & Swing: In and Around Madison County before & after World War II: A Pictorial History*. Anderson, Ind.: Local 32, American Federation of Musicians, 1992.
Rollini, Arthur. *Thirty Years with the Big Bands*. Urbana: University of Illinois Press, 1987.

Scanlan, Tom. *The Joy of Jazz: Swing Era, 1935–1947*. Golden, Colo.: Fulcrum Publishing, 1996.

Schuller, Gunther, *The Swing Era: The Development of Jazz, 1930–1945*. New York: Oxford University Press, 1989.

Shaw, Arnold. *Popular Music in the 1930s*. New York: Oxford University Press, 1998.

Simon, George Thomas. *The Big Bands*. New York: Schirmer Books, 1981.

——. *Simon Says: The Sights and Sounds of the Swing Era, 1935–1955*. New Rochelle, N.Y.: Arlington House, 1971.

Stewart, Alex. *Making the Scene: Contemporary New York City Big Band Jazz*. Berkeley: University of California Press, 2007.

Stokes, W. Royal, Charles Peterson, and Don Peterson. *Swing Era New York: The Jazz Photographs of Charles Peterson*. Philadelphia, Pa.: Temple University Press, 1994.

Stowe, David W. *Swing Changes: Big-Band Jazz in New Deal America*. Cambridge, Mass.: Harvard University Press, 1994.

Studwell, William E., and Mark Baldwin. *The Big Band Reader: Songs Favoured by Swing Era Orchestras and Other Popular Ensembles*. London: Haworth, 2001.

Tumpak, John R. *When Swing Was the Thing: Personality Profiles of the Big Band Era*. Milwaukee, Wis.: Marquette University Press, 2008.

Walker, Leo. *The Big Band Almanac*. New York: Da Capo Press, 1989.

White, Mark. *The Observer's Book of Big Bands*. London: F. Warne, 1978.

Woods, Bernie. *When the Music Stopped: The Big Band Era Remembered*. New York: Barricade Books, 1994.

Yanow, Scott. *Swing*. San Francisco, Calif.: Miller Freeman Books, 2000.

BEBOP

Bergerot, Franck, and Arnaud Merlin. *The Story of Jazz: Bop and Beyond*. New York: H. N. Abrams, 1993.

Cossart, Axel von. *Vom Bebop zum Hip Hop*. Cologne: Voco-Ed., 1995.

Deveaux, Scott Knowles. *The Birth of Bebop: A Social and Musical History*. Berkeley: University of California Press, 1997.

Feather, Leonard. *Inside Be-bop*. New York: J. J. Robbins, 1949.

Gitler, Ira. *Jazz Masters of the Forties*. New York: Macmillan, 1966.

——. *The Masters of Jazz: A Listener's Guide*. New York: Da Capo Press, 2001.

Hess, Jacques B. *Bebop*. Paris: Editions de l'Instant, 1989.

Korall, Burt. *Drummin' Men: The Heartbeat of Jazz: The Bebop Years*. New York: Oxford University Press, 2002.

Mathleson, Kenny. *Giant Steps: Bebop and the Creators of Modern Jazz 1945–1965*. Edinburgh: Payback, 1999.

Meadows, Eddie S. *Bebop to Cool: Context, Ideology, and Musical Identity*. Westport, Conn.: Greenwood Press, 2003.

Oliphant, Dave. *The Bebop Revolution in Words and Music*. Austin: Harry Ransom Humanities Research Center, University of Texas at Austin, 1995.
Owens, Thomas. *Bebop: The Music and Its Players*. New York: Oxford University Press, 1995.
Tercinet, Alain. *Be-bop*. Paris: POL, 1991.
Werther, Iron. *Bebop: Geschichte einer musikalischen Revolution und ihrer Interpreten*. Frankfurt: Fischer-Taschenbuch-Verlag, 1988.
Yanow, Scott. *Bebop*. San Francisco, Calif.: Miller Freeman Books, 2000.

COOL JAZZ

Fox, Jo Brooks, and Jules L. Fox. *The Melody Lingers On: Scenes from the Golden Years of West Coast Jazz*. Santa Barbara, Calif.: Fithian Press, 1996.
Gioia, Ted. *The Birth (and Death) of the Cool*. Golden, Colo.: Speck Press, 2009.
———. *West Coast Jazz: Modern Jazz in California, 1945–1960*. New York: Oxford University Press, 1992.
Gordon, Robert. *Jazz West Coast: The Los Angeles Jazz Scene of the 1950s*. New York: Quartet Books, 1986.
Hellhund, Herbert. *Cool Jazz: Grundzüge seiner Entstehung und Entwicklung*. New York: Schott, 1985.
Marsh, Graham, and Glyn Callingham. *California Cool: West Coast Jazz of the 50s and 60s, the Album Cover Art*. San Francisco: Chronicle Books, 1992.
Tirro, Frank. *The Birth of Cool of Miles Davis and His Associates*. Hillsdale, N.Y.: Pendragon Press, 2009.

HARD BOP

Guillon, Roland. *Le Hard Bop: Un Style de Jazz*. Montreal: L'Harmattan, 1999.
Mathieson, Kenny. *Cookin': Hard Bop and Soul Jazz 1954–65*. Edinburgh: Canongate, 2002.
Rosenthal, David. *Hard Bop: Jazz and Black Music, 1955–1965*. New York: Oxford University Press, 1992.

AFRO-CUBAN

Boggs, Vernon. *Salsiology: Afro-Cuban Music and the Evolution of Salsa in New York City*. New York: Greenwood Press, 1992.
Brennen, Timothy. *Secular Devotion: Afro-Latin Music and Imperial Jazz*. New York: Verso, 2008.
Fernandez, Raul A. *From Afro-Cuban Rhythms to Latin Jazz*. Berkeley: University of California Press, 2006.
Yanow, Scott. *Afro-Cuban Jazz*. San Francisco, Calif.: Miller Freeman Books, 2000.

LATIN JAZZ

Arteaga, Jóse. *Oye Cómo Va: El Mundo del Jazz Latino.* Madrid: La Esfera de los Libros, 2003.

Chediak, Nat, Carlos Galelia, and Fernando Trueba. *Diccionario de Jazz Latino.* Madrid: Fundación Autor: 1998.

Dellanoy, Luc. *¡Caliente! Una Historia del Jazz Latino.* México: Fondo de Cultura Económica, 2001.

Fernandez, Raul A. *Latin Jazz: The Perfect Combination = La Combinación Perfecta.* San Francisco, Calif.: Chronicle Books, 2002.

Hendler, Maximillian. *Cubana de Cubana Bop: Der Jazz und die Lateinamerikanische Musik.* Graz, Austria: Akademische Druck- u. Verlagsanstalt, 2005.

Laymarie, Isabella. *Cuban Fire: The Story of Salsa and Latin Jazz.* New York: Continuum, 2002.

McGowan, Chris. *The Brazilian Sound: Samba, Bossa Nova, and the Popular Music of Brazil.* Philadelphia, Pa.: Temple University Press, 1998.

Minski, Samuel, Adlai Stevenson Samper, and Claudia Patricia Rios. *El Jazz Latino y su Trayectoria Historica.* Barranquilla, Colombia: Fundacíon Cultural Neuva Música, 2004.

Morales, Ed. *Latin Beat: The Rhythms and Roots of Latin Music from Bossa Nova to Salsa and Beyond.* Cambridge, Mass.: Da Capo Press, 2003.

Roberts, John Storm. *Latin Jazz: The First of the Fusions; 1880s to Today.* New York: Schirmer Books, 1999.

Werner, Otto. *The Latin Influence on Jazz.* Dubuque, Iowa: Kendall/Hunt Publishing, 1992.

AVANT-GARDE/FREE JAZZ

Arndt, Jürgen. *Thelonious Monk und Der Free Jazz.* Graz: Akademische Druck- und Verlagsanstalt, 2002.

Gendron, Bernhard. *Between Montmartre and the Muddclub.* Chicago, Ill.: University of Chicago Press, 2002.

Horricks, Raymond. *The Importance of Being Eric Dolphy.* Tunbridge Wells, England: Costello, 1989.

Jost, Ekkehard. *Free Jazz.* New York: Da Capo Press, 1994.

———. *Free Jazz: Stilkritische Untersuchungen zum Jazz der 60er Jahre.* Mainz: Schott, 1975.

Litweiler, John. *The Freedom Principle: Jazz after 1958.* New York: Morrow, 1990.

Peterson, Lloyd. *Music and the Creative Spirit: Innovators in Jazz, Improvisation, and the Avant Garde.* Lanham, Md.: Scarecrow Press, 2006.

Pinson, Jean-Claude. *Free Jazz.* Nantes: Éd. Joca Seria, 2004.

Sportis, Yves. *Free Jazz.* Paris: Editions de l'Instant, 1990.

Such, David Glen. *Avant-garde Jazz Musicians: Performing "Out There."* Iowa City: University of Iowa Press, 1993.

Viera, Joe. *Der Free Jazz: Formen und Modelle.* Vienna: Universal Edition, 1974.

FUSION

Coryell, Julie, and Laura Friedman. *Jazz-Rock Fusion, the People, the Music*. New York: Del Publishing, 1978.

Martorella, Vincenzo. *Storia della Fusion: Dal Jazz-Rock alla New Age; Guida Ragionata a una Musica 'Unqualificabile.'"* Rome: Castelvechi, 1998.

Nicholson, Stuart. *Jazz Rock: A History*. New York: Schirmer Books, 1998.

Reynard, Guy. *Fusion*. Paris: Editions de l'Instant, 1990.

OTHER SUBGENRES

Baumen, Dick. *The Third Stream*. Maryville: Northwest Missouri State University, 1970.

Bruyninckx, Walter. *Progressive Jazz: Free–Third Stream Fusion*. Mechelen, Belgium: 60 Years of Recorded Jazz Team, 1984–1987.

Cotgrove, Mark "Snowboy." *From Jazz Funk and Fusion to Acid Jazz: The History of the UK Jazz Dance Scene*. London: Chaser Publications, 2009.

Ertl, Franz. *Lost Grooves: The Rise and Fall: Soul-Jazz, Jazz-Funk, Jazz-Rock-Fusion*. Dessau: W. Herbst, 1994.

Fellezs, Kevin. *Birds of Fire: Jazz, Rock, Funk, and the Creation of Fusion*. Durham, N.C.: Duke University Press, 2011.

MODERN ERA

Bruyninckx, Walter. *Jazz: Modern Jazz, Modern Big Band*. Mechelen, Belgium: Copy Express, 1985.

Carr, Ian. *Music Outside: Contemporary Jazz in Britain*. London: Northway, 2008.

Godbolt, James Charles, and Jim Godbolt. *Ronnie Scott's Jazz Farrago: A Motley Assortment of Characters, Happenings, and History on the Modern British Jazz Scene*. London: Hampstead Press, 2008.

Gourse, Leslie. *Madame Jazz: Contemporary Women Instrumentalists*. New York: Oxford University Press, 1995.

Larson, Tom. *Modern Sounds: The Artistry of Contemporary Jazz*. Dubuque, Iowa: Kendall/Hunt, 2008.

Rechniewski, Peter. *The Permanent Underground: Australian Contemporary Jazz in the New Millennium*. Strawberry Hills, Australia: Currency House, 2008.

Schmidt, Uta C., Andreas Müller, and Richard Ortmann. *Jazz in Dortmund: Hot-Modern-Free-New*. Essen, Germany: Klartext, 2004.

Tomens, Robin. *Points of Departure: Essays on Modern Jazz*. Londonderry, N.H.: Stride, 2001.

RECORDING INDUSTRY

Ertegun, Ahmet M. *What'd I Say? The Atlantic Story: 50 Years of Music*. New York: Welcome Rain Publishers, 2001.

Gray, Herman. *Producing Jazz: The Experience of an Independent Record Company.* Philadelphia, Pa.: Temple University Press, 1988.

Kahn, Ashley. *The House that Trane Built: The Story of Impulse Records.* New York: Norton, 2006.

——. *Somethin' Else: The Story of Blue Note Records and the Birth of Modern Jazz.* New York: Viking, 2009.

Kennedy, Rick. *Jelly Roll, Bix, and Hoagy: Gennett Studios and the Birth of Recorded Jazz.* Bloomington: Indiana University Press: 1994.

Lake, Steve. *Horizons Touched: The Music of ECM.* London: Granta, 2007.

ANALYSIS

Baker, David. *Jazz Styles and Analysis, Trombone: A History of the Jazz Trombone via Recorded Solos, Transcribed and Annotated.* Chicago, Ill.: Maher Publications, 1973.

Gennari, John. *Blowin' Hot and Cool: Jazz and Its Critics.* Chicago, Ill.: University of Chicago Press, 2006.

Giel, Lex. *The Music of Miles Davis: A Study and Analysis of Compositions and Solo Transcriptions from the Great Jazz Composer and Improviser.* Milwaukee, Wis.: Hal Leonard, 2004.

Gridley, Mark C. *Jazz Styles: History and Analysis.* Upper Saddle River, N.J.: Prentice Hall, 2003.

Heble, Ajay. *Landing on the Wrong Note: Jazz, Dissonance, and Critical Practice.* New York: Routledge, 2000.

Jenkins, Todd S. *I Know What I Know: The Music of Charles Mingus.* Westport, Conn.: Praeger, 2006.

Knauer, Wolfram. *Zwischen Bebop und Free Jazz: Komposition und Improvisation des Modern Jazz Quartet.* Mainz: Schott, 1990.

Meadows, Eddie S. *Jazz Scholarship and Pedagogy: A Research and Information Guide.* New York: Routledge, 2006.

Miedema, Harry. *Jazz Styles and Analysis, Alto Sax: A History of the Jazz Alto Saxophone via Recorded Solos, Transcribed and Annotated.* Chicago, Ill.: Maher Publications, 1975.

Nicholson, Stuart. *Is Jazz Dead? (Or Has It Moved to a New Address).* New York: Routledge, 2005.

Ramsey, Doug. *Jazz Matters: Reflections on the Music and Some of Its Makers.* Fayetteville: University of Arkansas Press, 1989.

Tozzi, Wolfgang. *Jazz-Drumming: Studien zum Spiel Von Jack DeJohnette.* Graz, Austria: Akademische Druck- u. Verlagsanstalt, 1994.

Wright, Rayburn. *Inside the Score: A Detailed Analysis of 8 Classical Jazz Ensemble Charts by Sammy Nestico, Thad Jones, and Bob Brookmeyer.* Delevan, N.Y.: Kendor Music, 1982.

GENERAL BIOGRAPHICAL

Alexander, Charles, ed. *Masters of Jazz Guitar*. San Francisco, Calif.: Miller Freeman, 1999.

Bacon, Tony, and Dave Gelly. *Master of Jazz Saxophone: The Story of the Players and Their Music*. London: Balafon Books, 2000.

Balliett, Whitney. *American Musicians: Fifty-Six Portraits in Jazz*. New York: Oxford University Press, 1986.

——. *American Musicians II: Seventy-Two Portraits in Jazz*. New York: Oxford University Press, 1996.

——. *American Singers: Twenty-Seven Portraits in Song*. New York: Oxford University Press, 1988.

——. *Barney, Bradley, and Max: Sixteen Portraits in Jazz*. New York: Oxford University Press, 1989.

Berrett, Joshua. *Louis Armstrong & Paul Whiteman: Two Kings of Jazz*. New Haven, Conn.: Yale University Press, 2004.

Britt, Stan. *The Jazz Guitarists*. New York: Sterling Publishing, 1984.

Brocking, Christian. *Respekt!* Berlin: Verbrecher, 2004.

Chilton, John. *Who's Who of British Jazz*. New York: Continuum, 2004.

——. *Who's Who of Jazz: Storyville to Swing Street*. New York: Da Capo Press, 1985.

Crowther, Bruce. *The Jazz Singers: From Ragtime to the New Wave*. New York: Blandford Press, 1986.

Crowther, Bruce, and Mike Pinfold. *Singing Jazz: The Singers and Their Styles*. San Francisco, Calif.: Miller Freeman, 1997.

Crumpacker, Chick. *Jazz Legends*. Salt Lake City, Utah: G. Smith, 1995.

Davis, Francis. *Outcats: Jazz Composers, Instrumentalists, and Singers*. New York: Oxford University Press, 1990.

Deffaa, Chip. *In the Mainstream: 18 Portraits in Jazz*. Metuchen, N.J.: Scarecrow Press, 1992.

——. *Voices of the Jazz Age: Profiles of Eight Vintage Jazzmen*. Urbana: University of Illinois Press, 1990.

Delannoy, Luc. *Vidas en el Jazz Latino*. México: Fondo de Cultura Económica, 2005.

Dicaire, David. *Jazz Musicians, 1945 to the Present*. Jefferson, N.C.: McFarland, 2006.

——. *Jazz Musicians of the Early Years, to 1945*. Jefferson, N.C.: McFarland, 2003.

Dourschuk, Robert L. *88: The Giants of Jazz Piano*. San Francisco, Calif.: Backbeat Books, 2001.

Fell, John L., and Terkild Vinding. *Stride! Fats, Jimmy, Lion, Lamb, and All the Other Ticklers*. Lanham, Md.: Scarecrow Press, 1999.

Friedlander, Lee. *The Jazz People of New Orleans*. New York: Pantheon Books, 1992.

Gelly, Dave. *The Giants of Jazz*. New York: Schirmer Books, 1986.

Gourse, Leslie. *Blowing on the Changes: The Art of the Jazz Horn Players*. New York: Franklin Watts, 1997.

Hadlock, Richard. *Jazz Masters of the Twenties*. New York: Da Capo Press, 1986.

Holmes, Lowell Don. *Jazz Greats: Getting Better with Age*. New York: Holmes and Meier, 1986.

Horne, Chris. *Contemporary Jazz UK: Twenty One Lives in Jazz*. London: Perspectives in Jazz, 2004.

Horricks, Raymond. *Profiles in Jazz: From Sidney Bechet to John Coltrane*. New Brunswick, N.J.: Transaction Publishers, 1991.

Hunt, Joe. *52nd Street Beat: Modern Jazz Drummers, 1945–1965*. New Albany, Ind.: Jamey Aebersold Jazz, 1994.

Jasen, David A. *Black Bottom Stomp: The Masters of Ragtime and Early Jazz*. New York: Routledge, 2002.

Korall, Burt. *Drummin' Men: The Heartbeat of Jazz; the Bebop Years*. New York: Oxford University Press, 2002.

Lees, Gene. *Jazz Lives: 100 Portraits in Jazz*. Toronto: Steward House, 1993.

——. *Meet Me at Jim and Andy's: Jazz Musicians and Their World*. New York: Oxford University Press, 1988.

——. *You Can't Steal a Gift: Dizzy, Clark, Milt, and Nat*. New Haven, Conn.: Yale University Press, 2001.

Lyons, Leonard, and Don Perlo. *Jazz Portraits: The Lives and Music of the Jazz Masters*. New York: Morrow, 1989.

Mandel, Howard. *Miles, Ornette, Cecil: Jazz beyond Jazz*. New York: Routledge, 2008.

Miller, Mark. *Jazz in Canada: Fourteen Lives*. Buffalo, N.Y.: University of Toronto Press, 1982.

Monceaux, Morgan. *Jazz: My Music, My People*. New York: Knopf, 1994.

Porter, Lewis. *Contemporary Jazz Musicians: A Biographical Dictionary*. London: Routledge, 2005.

Rose, Al. *New Orleans Jazz: A Family Album*. Baton Rouge: Louisiana State University Press, 1984.

Sheed, Wilfred. *The House that George Built: With a Little Help from Irving, Cole, and a Crew of About Fifty*. New York: Random House, 2007.

Shipton, Alyn. *Handful of Keys: Conversations with Thirty Jazz Pianists*. New York: Routledge, 2004.

Unterbrink, Mary. *Jazz Women at the Keyboard*. Jefferson, N.C.: McFarland, 1983.

Vaché, Warren W. *Jazz Gentry: Aristocrats of the Musical World*. Lanham, Md.: Scarecrow Press, 1999.

Williams, Martin T. *Jazz Masters of New Orleans*. New York: Macmillan, 1967.

Wilmer, Valerie. *Jazz People*. New York: Da Capo Press, 1991.

Yanow, Scott. *The Trumpet Kings: The Players Who Shaped the Sound of Jazz Trumpet*. San Francisco, Calif.: Backbeat Books, 2001.

SPECIFIC BIOGRAPHICAL

Armstrong, Louis

Armstrong, Louis. *Louis Armstrong, in His Own Words*. New York: Oxford University Press, 1999.

——. *Satchmo: My Life in New Orleans*. New York: Prentice Hall, 1954.

Bergreen, Laurence. *Louis Armstrong: An Extravagant Life*. New York: Broadway Books, 1997.

Berrett, Joshua, ed. *The Louis Armstrong Companion: Eight Decades of Commentary*. New York: Schirmer Books, 1999.

Boujut, Michel. *Louis Armstrong*. New York: Rizzoli, 1998.

Brothers, Thomas David. *Louis Armstrong's New Orleans*. New York: Norton, 2006.

Brower, Steven. *Satchmo: The Wonderful World and Art of Louis Armstrong*. New York: Harry N. Abrams, 2009.

Collier, James Lincoln. *Louis Armstrong, an American Genius*. New York: Oxford University Press, 1983.

Giddings, Gary. *Satchmo: The Genius of Louis Armstrong*. New York: Da Capo Press, 2001.

Meckna, Michael. *The Louis Armstrong Encyclopedia*. Westport, Conn: Greenwood Press, 2004.

Nollen, Scott Allen. *Louis Armstrong: The Life, Music, and Screen Career*. Jefferson, N.C.: McFarland, 2004.

Pinfold, Mike. *Louis Armstrong, His Life and Times*. New York: Universe Books, 1987.

Storb, Ilse, *Louis Armstrong: The Definitive Biography*. New York: Peter Lang, 1999.

Strickland, David. *Louis Armstrong: The Soundtrack of the American Experience*. Chicago, Ill.: Ivan R. Dee, 2010.

Teachout, Terry. *Pops: A Life of Louis Armstrong*. Boston, Mass.: Houghton Mifflin Harcourt, 2009.

Travis, Dempsey. *The Louis Armstrong Odyssey: From Jane Alley to America's Jazz Ambassador*. Chicago, Ill.: Urban Research Press, 1997.

Baker, Chet

Baker, Chet. *As Though I Had Wings: The Lost Memoir*. New York: Buzz, 1997.

Claxton, William. *Young Chet: The Young Chet Baker*. New York: teNeues Publishing Company, 1998.

Gavin, James. *Deep in a Dream: The Long Night of Chet Baker*. New York: Knopf, 2002.

Valk, Jeroen de. *Chet Baker: His Life and Music*. Berkeley, Calif.: Berkeley Hills Books, 2000.

Barnet, Charlie

Barnet, Charlie. *Those Swinging Years: The Autobiography of Charlie Barnet*. Baton Rouge: Louisiana State University Press, 1984.

Mather, Dan. *Charlie Barnet: An Illustrated Biography and Discography of the Swing Era Big Band Leader*. Jefferson, N.C.: McFarland, 2002.

Basie, Count

Basie, Count. *Good Morning, Blues: The Autobiography of Count Basie*. London: Palladin Graften Books, 1985.

Dance, Stanley. *The World of Count Basie*. New York: Da Capo Press, 1985.
Morgan, Alun. *Count Basie*. New York: Hippocrene Books, 1984.

Bechet, Sidney

Béthune, Chrstian. *Sidney Bechet*. Marseille: Éd. Parenthèses, 1997.
Chilton, John. *Sidney Bechet: The Wizard of Jazz*. New York: Oxford University Press, 1987.
Kappler, Frank K., Bob Wilber, and Richard M. Sudhalter. *Sidney Bechet*. Alexandria, Va.: Time-Life Records, 1980.
Mouly, Raymond. *Sidney Bechet: Notre Ami*. Paris: La Table Ronde, 1959.
Zammarchi, Fabrice. *Sidney Bechet*. Paris: Filipacchi, 1989.

Beiderbecke, Bix

Collins, David R. *Bix Beiderbecke: Jazz Age Genius*. Greensboro, N.C.: Morgan Reynolds, 1998.
Deffaa, Chip. *Bix Beiderbecke: An Appreciation*. Van Nuys, Calif.: Sunbeam Records, 1988.
James, Burnett. *Bix Beiderbecke*. New York: Barnes, 1961.
Lion, Jean Pierre. *Bix: The Definitive Biography of a Jazz Legend*. New York: Continuum, 2005.
Prendergast, Curtis, and William M. Sudhalter. *Bix Beiderbecke*. Alexandria, Va.: Time-Life Records.
Scheuer, Klaus. *Bix Beiderbecke: Sein Leben, Seine Musik, Seine Schallplatten*. Waakirchen-Schaftlach, Germany: Oreos, 1995.

Blanchard, Terence

Magro, Anthony. *Contemporary Cat: Terence Blanchard with Special Guests*. Lanham, Md.: Scarecrow Press, 2002.

Bley, Paul

Bley, Paul. *Stopping Time: Paul Bley and the Transformation of Jazz*. Montreal: Véhicule Press, 1999.
Cappelletti, Arrigo. *Paul Bley: The Logic of Chance*. Montreal: Véhicule Press, 2010.

Bolden, Buddy

Marquis, Donald M. *In Search of Buddy Bolden: First Man of Jazz*. Baton Rouge: Louisiana State University Press, 2005.
Ondaatje, Michael. *Buddy Bolden: Une Lègende*. [S.I.]: Editions de l'Olivier, 1999.

Braxton, Anthony

Ford, Alun. *Anthony Braxton: Creative Music Continuums*. Exeter, Devon: Stride, 1997.

Lock, Graham. *Forces in Motion: The Music and Thoughts of Anthony Braxton*. New York: Da Capo Press, 1988.

Radano, Ronald Michael. *New Musical Figurations: Anthony Braxton's Cultural Critique*. Chicago, Ill.: University of Chicago Press, 1993.

Wilson, Peter Niklas. *Anthony Braxton: Sein Leben, Seine Musik, Seine Schallplatten*. Waakirchen, Germany: Oreos, 1993.

Brown, Clifford

Catalano, Nick. *Clifford Brown: The Life and Art of the Legendary Jazz Trumpeter*. New York: Oxford University Press, 2000.

Gerber, Alain. *Clifford Brown: Le Roman d'un Enfant Sage*. Paris: Fayard, 2001.

Stuart, Milton Lee. *Structural Development in the Jazz Improvisational Technique of Clifford Brown*. Ann Arbor, Mich.: University Microfilms, 1973.

Brubeck, Dave

Hall, Fred. *It's About Time: The Dave Brubeck Story*. Fayetteville: University of Arkansas Press, 1996.

Callender, Red

Callender, Red. *Unfinished Dream: The Musical World of Red Callender*. New York: Quartet Books, 1985.

Calloway, Cab

Calloway, Cab, and Bryant Rollins. *Of Minnie the Moocher & Me*. New York: Crowell, 1976.

Dempsey, Travis. *Cab Calloway: The King of "Hi-de-ho."* Chicago, Ill.: Urban Research Press, 1994.

Shipton, Alyn. *Hi-de-ho: The Life of Calloway*. New York: Oxford University Press, 2010.

Carter, Benny

Berger, Morroe. *Benny Carter, a Life in American Music*. Lanham, Md.: Scarecrow Press, 2002.

Cheatham, Doc

Cheatham, Doc. *I Guess I'll Get the Papers and Go Home: The Life of Doc Cheatham.* New York: Cassell, 1996.
Cheatham, Jeannie. *Meet Me with Your Black Drawers On: My Life in Music.* Austin: University of Texas Press, 2006.

Christian, Charlie

Goins, Wayne E. *A Biography of Charlie Christian, Jazz Guitar's King of Swing.* Lewiston, N.Y.: Edwin Mellon Press, 2005.

Clayton, Buck

Clayton, Buck. *Buck Clayton's Jazz World.* New York: Oxford University Press, 1987.

Coleman, Ornette

Day, Steve. *Ornette Coleman: Music Always.* Chelmsford, England: Soundworld, 2000.
Keskinen, Heikki. *Ornette Coleman.* Helsinki: Like, 1995.
Litweiler, John. *Ornette Coleman: A Harmolodic Life.* New York: Morrow, 1992.
Mannucci, Michele. *Ornette Coleman: Dal Blues al Jazz dell'Avvenire.* Viterbo, Italy: Stampa Alternativa, 2000.
McRae, Barry, and Tony Middleton. *Ornette Coleman.* London: Apollo, 1988.
Wilson, Peter Niklas. *Ornette Coleman: His Life and Music.* Berkeley, Calif.: Berkeley Hills Books, 1999.

Coltrane, John

Ansell, Derek. *It's All in the Music: The Art of John Coltrane.* Montréal: Véhicule Press, 2003.
Cole, Bill. *John Coltrane.* New York: Da Capo Press, 1993.
Fraim, John. *Spirit Catcher: The Life and Art of John Coltrane.* West Liberty, Ohio: Greathouse Co., 1996.
Kofsky, Frank. *John Coltrane and the Jazz Revolution of the 1960s.* New York: Pathfinder Press, 1998.
Nisenson, Eric. *Ascension: John Coltrane and His Quest.* Cambridge, Mass.: Da Capo Press, 1995.
Porter, Lewis. *John Coltrane: His Life and Music.* Ann Arbor: University of Michigan Press, 1998.
Ratliff, Ben. *Coltrane: The Story of a Sound.* New York: Farrar, Straus and Giroux, 2007.

Simpkins, Cuthbert. *Coltrane: A Biography*. New York: Herndon House Publishers, 1975.

Thomas, J. C. *Chasin' the Train: The Music and Mystique of John Coltrane*. New York: Doubleday, 1975.

Woideck, Carl. *The John Coltrane Companion*. New York: Schirmer Books, 1998.

Davis, Miles

Alyker, Frank, ed. *The Miles Davis Reader*. New York: Hal Leonard, 2007.

Carner, Gary, ed. *The Miles Davis Companion: Four Decades of Commentary*. New York: Schirmer Books, 1996.

Carr, Ian. *Miles Davis: The Definitive Biography*. New York: Thunder's Mouth Press, 2007.

Chambers, J. K. *Milestones: The Music and Times of Miles Davis*. New York: Da Capo Press, 1998.

Cohen, Noal. *Miles Davis: The Early Years*. New York: Da Capo Press, 1994.

Cole, George. *The Last Miles: The Music of Miles Davis, 1980–1991*. Ann Arbor: University of Michigan Press, 2005.

Davis, Gregory. *Dark Magus: The Jekyll and Hyde Life of Miles Davis*. San Francisco, Calif.: Backbeat Books, 2006.

Davis, Miles, with Quincy Troupe. *Miles, the Autobiography*. New York: Simon and Schuster, 1990.

Early, Gerald Lyn. *Miles Davis and American Culture*. St. Louis: Missouri Historical Society Press, 2001.

James, Michael. *Miles Davis*. New York: Barnes, 1961.

Murphy, Chris. *Miles to Go: Remembering Miles Davis*. New York: Thunder's Mouth Press, 2002.

Nicholson, Stuart. *'Round About Midnight: A Portrait of Miles Davis*. New York: Da Capo Press, 1996.

Szwed, John F. *So What: The Life of Miles Davis*. New York: Simon and Schuster, 2002.

Tingen, Paul. *Miles Beyond: The Electric Explorations of Miles Davis*. New York: Billboard Books, 2001.

Troupe, Quincy. *Miles and Me*. Berkeley: University of California Press, 2000.

Waters, Keith. *Miles Davis Quintet, 1965–68*. New York: Oxford University Press, 2011.

Williams, Richard. *Miles Davis: The Man in the Green Shirt*. New York: Holt, 1993.

Desmond, Paul

Ramsey, Doug. *Take Five: The Public and Private Lives of Paul Desmond*. Seattle, Wash.: Parkside Productions, 2005.

Dorsey, Tommy

Levinson, Peter J. *Tommy Dorsey: Living in a Great Big Way; a Biography*. Cambridge, Mass.: Da Capo Press, 2005.

D'Rivera, Paquito

D'Rivera, Paquito. *My Sax Life: A Memoir*. Evanston, Ill.: Northwestern University Press, 2005.

Eldridge, Roy

Chilton, John. *Roy Eldridge, Little Jazz Giant*. New York: Continuum, 2002.

Ellington, Duke

Brown, Gene. *Duke Ellington: Jazz Master*. Woodbridge, Conn.: Blackbirch Press, 2001.

Cohen, Harvey G. *Duke Ellington's America*. Chicago, Ill.: University of Chicago Press, 2010.

Dance, Stanley. *The World of Duke Ellington*. Cambridge, Mass.: Da Capo Press, 2000.

Ellington, Mercer. *Duke Ellington in Person: An Intimate Memoir*. Boston, Mass.: Houghton Mifflin, 1978.

Frankl, Ron. *Duke Ellington*. Danbury, Conn.: Grolier, 1988.

George, Don R. *Sweet Man: The Real Duke Ellington*. New York: Putnam, 1981.

Hasse, John Edward. *Beyond Category: The Life and Genius of Duke Ellington*. New York: Simon and Schuster, 1993.

Jewell, Derek. *Duke: A Portrait of Duke Ellington*. New York: Norton, 1977.

Lawrence, A. H. *Duke Ellington and His World: A Biography*. New York: Routledge, 2001.

Nicholson, Stuart. *Reminiscing in Tempo: A Portrait of Duke Ellington*. Boston, Mass.: Northwestern University Press, 1999.

Steed, Janna Tull. *Duke Ellington: A Spiritual Biography*. New York: Crossroad Publishing, 1999.

Travis, Dempsey. *The Duke Ellington Primer*. Chicago, Ill.: Urban Research Press, 1996.

Tucker, Mark. *Ellington: The Early Years*. Urbana: University of Illinois Press, 1991.

Vail, Ken. *Duke's Diary*. Lanham, Md.: Scarecrow Press, 2002.

Europe, James Reese

Badger, Reid. *A Life in Ragtime: A Biography of James Reese Europe*. New York: Oxford University Press, 1995.

Evans, Bill

Pettinger, Peter. *Bill Evans: How My Heart Sings*. New Haven, Conn.: Yale University Press, 1998.

Evans, Gil

Hincock, Larry. *Castles Made of Sound: The Story of Gil Evans*. Cambridge, Mass.: Da Capo Press, 2002.

Horricks, Raymond. *Svengali; or, The Orchestra Called Gill [sic] Evans*. New York: Hippocrene Books, 1984.

Stein Crease, Stephanie. *Gil Evans: Out of the Cool; His Life and Music*. Chicago, Ill.: A Cappella, 2002.

Fitzgerald, Ella

Colin, Sid. *Ella: The Life and Times of Ella Fitzgerald*. London: Elm Tree Books, 1986.

Fidelman, Geoffrey Mark. *First Lady of Song: Ella Fitzgerald for the Record*. Secaucus, N.J.: Carol Publishing Group, 1994.

Nicholson, Stuart. *Ella Fitzgerald: A Biography of the First Lady of Jazz*. New York: Scribner, 1993.

Pinkney, Andrea Davis. *Ella Fitzgerald: The Tale of a Vocal Virtuosa*. New York: Jump at the Sun/Hyperion Books for Children, 2002.

Garner, Errol

Doran, James M. *Errol Garner: The Most Happy Piano*. Metuchen, N.J.: Scarecrow Press and the Institute of Jazz Studies, Rutgers University, 1985.

Getz, Stan

Maggin, Donald L. *Stan Getz: A Life in Jazz*. New York: Morrow, 1996.

Gillespie, John "Dizzy"

Gentry, Tony. *Dizzy Gillespie*. New York: Chelsea House Publishers, 1991.

Gillespie, Dizzy. *To BE, or Not—to BOP: Memoirs*. Garden City, N.Y.: Doubleday, 1979.

Horricks, Raymond. *Dizzy Gillespie and the Bebop Revolution*. New York: Hippocrene, 1984.

Maggin, Donald L. *Dizzy: The Life and Times of John Birks Gillespie*. New York: Harper Entertainment, 2005.

McRae, Barry. *Dizzy Gillespie: His Life & Times*. New York: Universe Books, 1988.

Shipton, Alyn. *Groovin' High: The Life of Dizzy Gillespie*. New York: Oxford University Press, 1999.
Vail, Ken. *Dizzy Gillespie: The Bebop Years 1937–1952*. Lanham, Md.: Scarecrow Press, 2003.
Winter, Jonah. *Dizzy*. New York: Arthur A. Levine Books, 2006.

Goodman, Benny

Baron, Stanley Richard. *Benny: King of Swing; Pictorial Biography Based on Benny Goodman's Personal Archives*. New York: Morrow, 1979.
Collier, James Lincoln. *Benny Goodman and the Swing Era*. New York: Oxford University Press, 1989.
Connor, D. Russell. *Benny Goodman: Wrappin' It Up*. Lanham, Md.: Scarecrow Press, 1996.
Firestone, Ross. *Swing, Swing, Swing: The Life & Times of Benny Goodman*. New York: Norton, 1993.

Hampton, Lionel

Hampton, Lionel. *Hamp: An Autobiography*. New York: Warner Books, 1989.

Hawkins, Coleman

Chilton, John. *The Song of the Hawk: The Life and Recordings of Coleman Hawkins*. Ann Arbor: University of Michigan Press, 1990.
James, Burnett. *Coleman Hawkins*. New York: Hippocrene Books, 1984.

Heath, Jimmy

Heath, Jimmy. *I Walked with Giants: The Autobiography of Jimmy Heath*. Philadelphia, Pa.: Temple University Press, 2010.

Henderson, Fletcher

Driggs, Frank. *The Fletcher Henderson Story*. [S.l.]: Sony Music Entertainment, 1994.
Magee, Jeffrey. *The Uncrowned King of Swing: Fletcher Henderson and Big Band Jazz*. New York: Oxford University Press, 2005.

Herman, Woody

Clancy, William T. *Woody Herman: Chronicles of the Herds*. New York: Schirmer Books, 1995.

Herman, Woody. *The Woodchopper's Ball: The Autobiography of Woody Herman.* New York: E. P. Dutton, 1990.
Kriebel, Robert C. *Blue Flame: Woody Herman's Life in Music.* West Lafayette, Ind.: Purdue University Press, 1995.
Lees, Gene. *Leader of the Band: The Life of Woody Herman.* New York: Oxford University Press, 1995.

Hines, Earl

Dance, Stanley. *The World of Earl Hines.* New York: Scribner, 1977.

Hinton, Milt

Hinton, Milt. *Playing the Changes: Milt Hinton's Life in Stories and Photographs.* Nashville, Tenn.: Vanderbilt University Press, 2008.
——. *The Stories and Photographs of Milt Hinton.* Philadelphia, Pa.: Temple University Press, 1988.

Holiday, Billie

Clarke, Donald. *Billie Holiday: Wishing on the Moon.* Cambridge, Mass.: Da Capo Press, 2002.
Dufty, William, and Billie Holiday. *Lady Sings the Blues.* New York: Lancer Books, 1965.
Gourse, Leslie. *Billie Holiday: The Tragedy and Triumph of Lady Day.* New York: Franklin Watts, 1995.
James, Burnett. *Billie Holiday.* Tunbridge Wells, England: Hippocrene Books: 1984.
Nicholson, Stuart. *Billie Holiday.* London: Indigo, 1996.

James, Harry

Levinson, Peter J. *Trumpet Blues: The Life of Harry James.* New York: Oxford University Press, 1999.

Jarrett, Keith

Carr, Ian. *Keith Jarrett: The Man and His Music.* New York: Da Capo Press, 1992.

Johnson, James P.

Brown, Scott E. *James P. Johnson: A Case of Mistaken Identity.* Metuchen, N.J.: Scarecrow Press and the Institute of Jazz Studies, Rutgers University, 1986.

Johnson, J. J.

Berrett, Joshua. *The Musical World of J. J. Johnson*. Lanham, Md.: Scarecrow Press, 1999.

Jones, Quincy

Jones, Quincy. *Q: The Autobiography of Quincy Jones*. New York: Doubleday, 2001.

Kenton, Stan

Harris, Steven D., and Pete Rugolo. *The Kenton Kronicles: A Biography of Modern America's Man of Music, Stan Kenton*. Pasadena, Calif.: Dynaflow, 2000.
Lee, William F. *Stan Kenton: Artistry in Rhythm*. Los Angeles, Calif.: Creative Press of Los Angeles, 1980.
Sparke, Michael. *Stan Kenton: This Is an Orchestra!* Denton: University of North Texas Press, 2010.

Konitz, Lee

Hamilton, Andy. *Lee Konitz: Conversations on the Improvisor's Art*. Ann Arbor: University of Michigan Press, 2007.

Krupa, Gene

Crowther, Bruce. *Gene Krupa, His Life and Times*. New York: Universe Books, 1987.

LaFaro, Scott

LaFaro-Fernandez, Helene. *Jade Visions: The Life and Music of Scott LaFaro*. Denton: University of North Texas Press, 2009.

Lewis, George

Bethell, Tom. *George Lewis: A Jazzman from New Orleans*. Berkeley: University of California Press, 1977.

Marsalis, Ellis

Handy, D. Antoinette. *Jazz Man's Journey: A Biography of Ellis Louis Marsalis, Jr.* Lanham, Md.: Scarecrow Press, 1999.

Marsalis, Wynton

Gourse, Leslie. *Wynton Marsalis: Skain's Domain; a Biography*. New York: Schirmer Books, 1999.

Marsalis, Wynton. *Jazz in the Bittersweet Blues of Life*. Cambridge, Mass.: Da Capo Press, 2001.

——. *Sweet Swing Blues on the Road*. New York: Norton, 1994.

Marsh, Warne

Chamberlain, Safford. *An Unsung Cat: The Life and Music of Warne Marsh*. Lanham, Md.: Scarecrow Press, 2000.

McRae, Carmen

Gourse, Leslie. *Carmen McRae: Miss Jazz*. New York: Billboard Books, 2001.

Miller, Glenn

Simon, George Thomas. *Glenn Miller and His Orchestra*. New York: T. Y. Crowell, 1974.

Way, Chris. *Glenn Miller in Britain: Then and Now*. Old Harlow, England: After the Battle, 1996.

Wright, Wilbur. *Millergate: The Real Glenn Miller Story*. South Hampton: Wrightway, 1990.

Mingus, Charles

Coleman, Janet. *Mingus/Mingus: Two Memoirs*. Berkeley, Calif.: Creative Arts Book, 1989.

Mingus, Charles. *Underdog: His World as Composed by Mingus*. New York: Vintage, 1991.

Priestly, Brian. *Mingus, a Critical Biography*. New York: Quartet Books, 1982.

Santoro, Gene. *Myself When I Am Real: The Life and Music of Charles Mingus*. New York: Oxford University Press, 2000.

Monk, Thelonious

De Wilde, Laurent. *Monk*. New York: Marlowe, 1997.

Fitterling, Thomas. *Thelonious Monk: His Life and Music*. Berkeley, Calif.: Berkeley Hills Books, 1997.

Gourse, Leslie. *Straight, No Chaser: The Life and Genius of Thelonious Monk*. New York: Schirmer Books, 1997.

Kelley, Robin. *Thelonious Monk: The Life and Times of an American Original*. New York: Free Press, 2009.

Montgomery, Wes

Ingram, Adrian. *Wes Montgomery*. Blaydon on Tyne, England: Ashley Mark Publishing, 2008.

Morgan, Lee

McMillen, Jeffrey S. *DelightfulLee: The Life and Music of Lee Morgan*. Ann Arbor: University of Michigan Press, 2008.
Perchard, Tom. *Lee Morgan: His Life, Music, and Culture*. Oakville, Conn.: Equinox Publishing, 2006.

Morton, Jelly Roll

Charters, Charles Barclay, IV. *Jelly Role Morton's Last Night in the Jungle Inn: An Imaginary Memoir*. New York: Marion Boyars, 1984.
Lomax, Alan. *Mister Jelly Roll: The Fortunes of Jelly Roll Morton, New Orleans Creole, and "Inventor of Jazz."* New York: Pantheon Books, 1993.
Pastras, Philip. *Dead Man Blues: Jelly Roll Morton Way Out West*. Berkeley: University of California Press, 2001.
Reich, Howard. *Jelly's Blues: The Life, Music, and Redemption of Jelly Roll Morton*. Cambridge, Mass.: Da Capo Press, 2003.

Mulligan, Gerry

Klinkowitz, Jerome. *Listen—Gerry Mulligan: An Aural Narrative in Jazz*. New York: Schirmer Books, 1991.

Navarro,w Theodore "Fats"

Peterson, Leif Bo. *The Music and Life of Theodore "Fats" Navarro: Infatuation*. Lanham, Md.: Scarecrow Press, 2009.

Nichols, Red

Evans, Philip R., et al. *The Red Nichols Story: After Intermissions, 1942–1965*. Lanham, Md.: Scarecrow Press, 1997.

Parker, Charles

Giddins, Gary. *Celebrating Bird: The Triumph of Charlie Parker*. New York: Beech Tree Books, 1987.

Koch, Lawrence. *Yardbird Suite: A Compendium of the Music and Life of Charlie Parker*. Boston, Mass.: Northeastern University Press, 1999.

Priestley, Brian. *Chasin' the Bird: The Life and Legacy of Charlie Parker*. New York: Oxford University Press, 2006.

Reisner, George. *Bird: The Legend of Charlie Parker*. New York: Bonanza Books, 1962.

Russell, Ross. *Bird Lives! The High Life & Hard Times of Charlie (Yardbird) Parker*. New York: Charterhouse, 1973.

Woideck, Carl. *Charlie Parker: His Music and His Life*. Ann Arbor: University of Michigan Press, 1998.

———, ed. *The Charlie Parker Companion: Six Decades of Commentary*. New York: Schirmer Books, 1998.

Yamaguchi, Masaya, ed. *Yardbird Originals*. Reissue. New York: Charles Colin, 2005.

Pastorius, Jaco

Milkowski, Bill. *Jaco: The Extraordinary and Tragic Life of Jaco Pastorius*. San Francisco, Calif.: Backbeat Books, 2005.

Pepper, Art

Pepper, Art, and Laurie Pepper. *The Straight Life of Art Pepper*. New York: Schirmer Books, 1979.

Selbert, Todd. *The Art Pepper Companion: Writing on a Jazz Original*. New York: Cooper Square, 2003.

Peterson, Oscar

Lees, Gene. *Oscar Peterson: The Will to Swing*. New York: Cooper Square Press, 2000.

Palmer, Richard. *Oscar Peterson*. New York: Hippocrene Books, 1984.

Peterson, Oscar. *A Jazz Odyssey: The Life of Oscar Peterson*. New York: Continuum, 2002.

Powell, Bud

Groves, Alan, and Alyn Shipton. *The Glass Enclosure: The Life of Bud Powell*. Oxford: Bayou Press, 1993.

Paudras, Francis. *Danse des Infidèles: A Portrait of Bud Powell*. New York: Da Capo Press, 1998.

Reinhardt, Django

Delaunay, Charles. *Django Reinhardt*. New York: Da Capo Press, 1981.
Dregni, Michael. *Django: The Life and Music of a Gypsy Legend*. New York: Oxford University Press, 2004.
Givan, Benjamin Marx. *The Music of Django Reinhardt*. Ann Arbor: University of Michigan Press, 2010.

Rollins, Sonny

Nicholson, Stuart. *Open Sky: Sonny Rollins and His World of Improvisation*. New York: St. Martin's, 2000.
Palmer, Richard. *Sonny Rollins: The Cutting Edge*. New York: Continuum, 2004.
Wilson, Peter Niklas. *Sonny Rollins: The Definitive Musical Guide*. Berkeley, Calif.: Berkeley Hills Books, 2001.
———. *Sonny Rollins: The Man and His Music*. Berkeley, Calif.: Hi Marketing, 2001.

Royal, Marshall

Royal, Marshall. *Marshall Royal: A Jazz Survivor*. New York: Continuum, 2001.

Russell, George

Heining, Duncan. *George Russell: The Story of an American Composer*. Lanham, Md., Scarecrow Press, 2010.

Russell, Pee Wee

Hilbert, Robert. *Pee Wee Russell: The Life of a Jazzman*. New York: Oxford University Press, 1993.

Shaw, Artie

Nolan, Tom. *Three Chords for Beauty's Sake: The Life of Artie Shaw*. New York: Norton, 2010.
Simosko, Vladimir. *Artie Shaw: A Musical Biography and Discography*. Lanham, Md.: Scarecrow Press, 2000.
White, John. *Artie Shaw: His Life and Music*. New York: Continuum, 2004.

Shearing, George

Shearing, George. *Lullaby of Birdland*. New York: Continuum, 2004.

Shorter, Wayne

Carini, Stéphane. *Les Singularités Flottantes de Wayne Shorter*. Pertuis, France: Rouge Profond, 2005.
Mercer, Michelle. *Footprints: The Life and Work of Wayne Shorter*. New York: J. P. Tarcher/Penguin, 2004.

Silver, Horace

Silver, Horace. *Let's Get to the Nitty-Gritty: The Autobiography of Horace Silver*. Berkeley: University of California Press, 2006.

Smith, Bessie

Oliver, Paul. *Bessie Smith*. New York: Barnes, 1961.

Strayhorn, Billy

Hajdu, David. *Lush Life: A Biography of Billy Strayhorn*. New York: Farrar, Straus and Giroux, 1996.

Sun Ra

Szwed. *Space Is the Place: The Lives and Times of Sun Ra*. New York: Pantheon Books, 1997.

Tatum, Art

Lester, James. *Too Marvelous for Words: The Life and Genius of Art Tatum*. New York: Oxford University Press, 1994.

Tristano, Lennie

Shim, Eunmi. *Lennie Tristano: His Life in Music*. Ann Arbor: University of Michigan Press, 2009.

Trumbauer, Frankie

Evans, Philip R. *Tram: The Frank Trumbauer Story*. Metuchen, N.J.: Scarecrow Press, 1994.

Vaughan, Sarah

Gourse, Leslie. *Sassy: The Life of Sarah Vaughan*. New York: Scribner, 1993.

Waller, Fats

Shipton, Alyn. *Fats Waller: His Life & Times*. New York: Universe Books, 1988.
————. *Fats Waller: The Cheerful Little Earful*. New York: Continuum, 2002.
Vance, Joel. *Fats Waller, His Life and Times*. Chicago, Ill.: Contemporary Books, 1977.
Waller, Maurice. *Fats Waller*. Chicago, Ill.: Schirmer Books, 1977.

Webster, Ben

Büchmann-Møller, Frank. *Someone to Watch Over Me: The Life and Music of Ben Webster*. Ann Arbor: University of Michigan Press, 2006.
Valk, Jeroen de. *Ben Webster: His Life and Music*. Berkeley, Calif.: Berkeley Hills Books, 2001.

Weston, Randy

Weston, Randy. *African Rhythms: The Autobiography of Randy Weston*. Durham, N.C.: Duke University Press, 2010.

Williams, Joe

Gourse, Leslie. *Every Day: The Story of Joe Williams*. New York: Quartet Books, 1985.

Wilson, Teddy

Wilson, Teddy. *Teddy Wilson Talks Jazz*. New York: Cassell, 1996.

Young, Lester

Büchmann-Møller, Frank. *You Just Fight for Your Life: The Story of Lester Young*. New York: Praeger, 1990.
Daniels, Douglas Henry. *Lester Leaps In: The Life and Times of Lester "Pres" Young*. Boston, Mass.: Beacon Press, 2002.
Delannoy, Luc. *Pres: The Story of Lester Young*. Fayetteville: University of Arkansas Press, 1993.
Gelly, Dave. *Being Prez: The Life and Music of Lester Young*. New York: Oxford University Press, 2007.
Porter, Lewis. *Lester Young*. Ann Arbor: University of Michigan Press, 2005.

ADDITIONAL BIOGRAPHICAL

Barker, Danny. *A Life in Jazz*. New York: Oxford University Press, 1986.

Boulard, Garry. *"Just a Gigolo": The Life and Times of Louis Prima*. Lafayette: Center for Louisiana Studies, University of Southwestern Louisiana, 1989.

Chilton, John. *Red, Red, Ride: The Life of Henry "Red" Allen*. New York: Cassell, 1999.

Chilton, Karen. *Hazel Scott: The Pioneering Journey of a Jazz Pianist from Café Society to Hollywood to HUAC*. Ann Arbor: University of Michigan Press, 2008.

Coleman, Bill. *Trumpet Story*. Boston, Mass.: Northeastern University Press, 1991.

Dodds, Baby. *The Baby Dodds Story*. Baton Rouge: Louisiana State University Press, 1992.

Dupuis, Robert. *Bunny Berigan: Elusive Legend of Jazz*. Baton Rouge: Louisiana State University Press, 1993.

Erwin, Pee Wee. *Pee Wee Erwin: This Horn for Hire*. Metuchen, N.J.: Scarecrow Press and the Institute of Jazz Studies, Rutgers University, 1987.

Fairbairn, Ann. *Call Him George*. New York: Crown Publishers, 1969.

Foster, Pops. *Pops Foster: The Autobiography of a New Orleans Jazzman as Told to Tom Stoddard*. Berkeley: University of California Press, 1971.

Freeman, Bud. *Crazeology: The Autobiography of a Chicago Jazzman*. Urbana: University of Illinois Press, 1989.

Gibbs, Terry. *Good Vibes: A Life in Jazz*. Lanham, Md.: Scarecrow Press, 2003.

Green, Sharony Andrews. *Grant Green: Rediscovering the Forgotten Genius of Jazz Guitar*. San Francisco, Calif.: Miller Freeman Books, 1999.

Hill, Dick. *Sylvester Ahola: The Gloucester Gabriel*. Metuchen, N.J.: Scarecrow Press, 1993.

Hillman, Christopher. *Bunk Johnson: His Life & Times*. New York: Universe Books, 1988.

Jarvis, Malcolm. *The Other Malcolm: "Shorty" Jarvis; His Memoir*. Jefferson, N.C.: McFarland, 2001.

Kuehn, John. *Buddy DeFranco: A Biographical Portrait and Discography*. Metuchen, N.J.: Scarecrow Press, 1993.

Middlebrook, Diane Wood. *Suits Me: The Double Life of Billy Tipton*. Boston, Mass.: Houghton Mifflin, 1998.

Petkus, Ed. *Someone Out There Is Listening: The Life of Eddie Hazell, Jazz Guitar-Vocalist*. Lanham, Md.: Hamilton Books, 2010.

Porter, Roy. *There and Back: The Roy Porter Story*. Baton Rouge: Louisiana State University Press, 1991.

Price, Sammy. *What Do They Want? A Jazz Autobiography*. Urbana: University of Illinois Press, 1990.

Schuldman, Ken. *Jazz Survivor: The Story of Louis Bannet, Horn Player of Auschwitz*. Portland, Ore.: Vallentine Mitchell, 2005.

Sidran, Ben. *A Life in the Music*. New York: Taylor Trade Publishing, 2003.

Smith, William Oscar. *Sideman, the Long Gig of W. O. Smith: A Memoir*. Nashville, Tenn.: Rutledge Hill Press, 1991.

Talbot, Bruce. *Tom Talbert: His Life and Times; Voices from a Vanished World of Jazz*. Lanham, Md.: Scarecrow Press, 2004.

Tapscott, Horace. *Songs of the Unsung: The Musical and Social Journey of Horace Tapscott*. Durham, N.C.: Duke University Press, 2001.

Vaché, Warren W. *Backbeats and Rim Shots: The Johnny Blowers Story*. Lanham, Md.: Scarecrow Press, 1997.

——. *Sitting in with Chris Griffin: A Reminiscence of Radio and Recording's Golden Years*. Lanham, Md.: Scarecrow Press, 2005.

Vail, Ken. *Swingin' the Blues: 1936–1950*. Lanham, Md.: Scarecrow Press, 2003.

Wein, George. *Myself among Others*. Cambridge, Mass.: Da Capo Press, 2003.

Wells, Dicky. *The Night People: The Jazz Life of Dicky Wells*. Washington, D.C.: Smithsonian Institution Press, 1991.

Wilkinson, Christopher. *Jazz on the Road: Don Albert's Musical Life*. Berkeley: University of California Press, 2001.

Zinsser, William Knowlton. *Mitchell & Ruff: An American Profile in Jazz*. Philadelphia, Pa.: Paul Dry Books, 2000.

JAZZ AND CULTURE

Ake, David Andrew. *Jazz Cultures*. Berkeley: University of California Press, 2002.

Anderson, Iain. *This Is Our Music: Free Jazz and the Transformation of American Culture*. Philadelphia: University of Pennsylvania Press, 2007.

——. *This Is Our Music: Free Jazz, the Sixties, and American Culture*. Philadelphia: University of Pennsylvania Press, 2007.

Atkins, E. Taylor. *Blue Nippon: Authenticating Jazz in Japan*. Durham, N.C.: Duke University Press, 2001.

Austerlitz, Paul. *Jazz Consciousness: Music, Race, and Humanity*. Middletown, Conn.: Wesleyan University Press, 2005.

Baskerville, John D. *The Impact of Black Nationalist Ideology on American Jazz Music of the 1960s and 1970s*. Lewiston, N.Y.: E. Mellen Press, 2003.

Béthune, Christian. *Le Jazz et l'Occident: Culture Afro-Américaine et Philosophie*. Paris: Klincksieck, 2008.

Borshuck, Michael. *Swinging the Vernacular: Jazz and African American Modernist Literature*. New York: Routledge, 2006.

Buckner, T. Reginald, and Steven Weiland. *Jazz in Mind: Essays on the History and Meaning of Jazz*. Detroit, Mich.: Wayne State University Press, 2001.

Budds, Michael J., ed. *Jazz and the Germans: Essays on the Influence of "Hot" American Jazz Idioms on 20th-Century German Music*. Hillsdale, N.Y.: Pendragon Press, 2002.

Cassidy, Donna. *Painting the Musical City: Jazz and Cultural Identity in American Art, 1910–1940*. Washington, D.C.: Smithsonian Institution Press, 1997.

Chevigny, Paul. *Gigs: Jazz and the Cabaret Laws in New York City*. New York: Routledge, 1991.

Davidson, Robert A. *Jazz Age Barcelona*. Toronto: University of Toronto Press, 2009.

Dutton, Jacqueline, and Colin W. Nettlebeck. *Jazz Adventures in French Culture*. Nottingham, England: University of Nottingham, 2004.

Erenberg, Lewis A. *Swingin' the Dream: Big Band Jazz and the Rebirth of American Culture*. Chicago, Ill.: University of Chicago Press, 1998.

Evans, Nicholas M. *Writing Jazz: Race, Nationalism, and Modern Culture in the 1920s*. New York: Garland, 2000.

Fischlin, Daniel, and Ajay Heble. *The Other Side of Nowhere: Jazz, Improvisation, and Communities in Dialog*. Middletown, Conn.: Wesleyan University Press, 2004.

Floyd, Samuel A. *The Power of Black Music: Interpreting Its History from Africa to the United States*. New York: Oxford University Press, 1995.

Gabbard, Krin. *Hotter than That: The Trumpet, Jazz, and American Culture*. New York: Faber and Faber, 2008.

Gendron, Bernard. "After the October Revolution: The Jazz Avant-Garde in New York, 1964–1965." In *Sound Commitments: Avant-Garde Music and the Sixties*, ed. Robert Adlington, 211–231. New York: Oxford University Press, 2009.

Gerard, Charley. *Jazz in Black and White: Race, Culture, and Identity in the Jazz Community*. Westport, Conn.: Praeger, 1998.

Gioia, Ted. *The Imperfect Art: Reflections on Jazz and Modern Culture*. New York: Oxford University Press, 1988.

Hawkins, Alfonso W. *The Jazz Trope: A Theory of African American Literary and Vernacular Culture*. Lanham, Md.: Scarecrow Press, 2008.

Hurley, Andrew Wright. *The Return of Jazz: Joachim-Ernst Berendt and West German Culture Change*. New York: Berghahn Books, 2009.

Jackson, Jeffrey H. *Making Jazz French: Music and Modern Life in Interwar Paris*. Durham, N.C.: Duke University Press, 2003.

Jeffri, Joan. *Changing the Beat: A Study of the Worklife of Jazz Musicians*. Washington, D.C.: National Endowment for the Arts, 2003.

Johnson, Bruce. *The Inaudible Music: Jazz, Gender, and Australian Modernity*. Sydney: Currency Press, 2000.

Jones, Andrew F. *Yellow Music: Media Culture and Colonial Modernity in the Chinese Jazz Age*. Durham, N.C.: Duke University Press, 2001.

Jordon, Matthew F. *Le Jazz: Jazz and French Cultural Identity*. Urbana: University of Illinois Press, 2010.

Kater, Michael H. *Different Drummers: Jazz in the Culture of Nazi Germany*. New York: Oxford University Press, 1992.

———. *Gewegtes Spiel: Jazz im Nationalsozialismus*. Cologne: Kieperheuer and Witsch, 1995.

Lopes, Paul Douglas. *The Rise of a Jazz Art World*. Cambridge, England: Cambridge University Press, 2002.

McCann, Paul. *Race, Music, and National Identity: Images of Jazz in American Fiction, 1920–1960*. Madison, N.J.: Fairleigh Dickinson University Press, 2008.

McGee, Kristin A. *Some Liked It Hot: Jazz Women in Film and Television 1929–1959*. Middletown, Conn.: Wesleyan University Press, 2009.

McKay, George. *Circular Breathing: The Cultural Politics of Jazz in Britain.* Durham, N.C.: Duke University Press, 2005.

Morris, Ronald L. *Le Jazz et les Gangsters: 1880–1940.* Paris: Abbeville, 1997.

Myers, Gerald E. *Modern Dance, Jazz Music, and American Culture.* Washington, D.C.: John F. Kennedy Center for the Performing Arts. 2000.

Newton-Matza, Mitchell, ed. *Jazz Age: People and Perspectives.* Santa Barbara, Calif.: ABC-CLIO, 2009.

Ogren, Kathy J. *The Jazz Revolution: Twenties America and the Meaning of Jazz.* New York: Oxford University Press, 1989.

O'Meally, Robert G. *The Jazz Cadence of American Culture.* New York: Columbia University Press, 1998.

Ostransky, Leroy. *Jazz Cities: The Impact of Our Cities on the Development of Jazz.* Englewood Cliffs, N.J.: Prentice Hall, 1978.

Panish, Jon. *The Color of Jazz: Race and Representation in Postwar American Culture.* Jackson: University Press of Mississippi, 1997.

Peretti, Burton W. *The Creation of Jazz: Music, Race, and Culture in Urban America.* Urbana: University of Illinois Press, 1992.

——. *Jazz in American Culture.* Chicago, Ill.: Ivan R. Dee, 1997.

——. *Lift Every Voice: The History of African American Music.* Lanham, Md.: Rowman and Littlefield, 2009.

Quirino, Richie C. *Mabuhay Jazz: Jazz in Postwar Philippines.* Pasig City, Philippines: Anvil, 2008.

Ramsey, Guthrie P. *Race Music: Black Cultures from Bebop to Hip-Hop.* Berkeley: University of California Press, 2003.

Salamone, Frank A. *The Culture of Jazz: Jazz as Critical Culture.* Lanham, Md.: University Press of America, 2009.

Saul, Scott. *Freedom Is, Freedom Ain't: Jazz and the Making of the Sixties.* Cambridge, Mass.: Harvard University Press, 2003.

Townsend, Peter. *Jazz in American Culture.* Jackson: University Press of Mississippi, 2000.

Vale, V., and Marian Wallace. *Swing! The New Retro Renaissance.* San Francisco, Calif.: V/Search, 1998.

Wagnleitner, Reinhold, ed. *Satchmo Meets Amadeus.* Innsbruck: Studienverlag, 2006.

Werner, Craig Hansen. *Playing the Changes: From Afro-Modernism to the Jazz Impulse.* Urbana: University of Illinois Press, 1994.

Wiernicki, Krzysztof. *Dal Divertimento dei Nobili Alla Propaganda: Storia del Jazz in Russia.* Naples: Edizioni Scientifiche Italiane, 1991.

BIBLIOGRAPHIES

Friedwald, Will. *A Bibliographical Guide to the Great Jazz and Pop Singers.* New York: Pantheon Books, 2010.

Greenberg, Janice Leslie Hochstat. *Jazz Books in the 1990s: An Annotated Bibliography.* Lanham, Md.: Scarecrow Press, 2010.

Meadows, Eddie S. *Jazz Reference and Research Materials: A Bibliography*. New York: Garland Publishing, 1981.

INTERNET RESOURCES

All About Jazz. http://www.allaboutjazz.com.
Canadian Jazz Archive Online. http://www.canadianjazzarchive.org.
DownBeat. http://www.downbeat.com.
Ejazz News. http://ejazznews.com.
Europe Jazz Network. http://www.europejazz.net.
International Association of Schools of Jazz. http://www.iasj.com.
Jazz Clubs Worldwide. http://www.jazz-clubs-worldwide.com.
Jazz Corner. http://www.jazzcorner.com.
The Jazz Image. http://www.jazzimage.com.
Jazz in Japan (clubs and venues, artist interviews, CD reviews). http://jazzinjapan. com.
JAZZIZ. http://www.jazziz.com.
Jazz Music Tube. http://www.jazztube.com.
Jazz On Line. http://www.jazz-on-line.com.
Jazz Photos. http://www.jazzphotos.com.
Jazz Review. http://www.jazzreview.com.
JazzRu: Russian Jazz Web Central. http://www.jazz.ru/eng.
Jazz Site (British jazz history, jazz in the UK). http://www.jazzservices.org.uk.
JazzTimes. http://jazztimes.com.
Latin Jazz Club (artist interviews, CD reviews). http://www.latinjazzclub.com.
PBS Jazz. http://www.pbs.org/jazz.
PBS Kids: Jazz. http://pbskids.org/jazz.
Red Hot Jazz Archive. http://www.redhotjazz.com.
Thelonious Monk Institute of Jazz. http://www.monkinstitute.org.
Women in Jazz. http://jazzwomen.org.

About the Author

John S. Davis is associate dean and director of jazz studies in the College of Music at the University of Colorado Boulder. He holds a bachelor of arts from Metropolitan State College, a masters of arts from the University of Denver, and a doctorate of arts from the University of Northern Colorado. He joined the University of Colorado faculty in 1999, having previously served as assistant director of jazz studies at the University of Northern Colorado from 1994 to 1999 and festival coordinator for the UNC/Greeley Jazz Festival. He has appeared as guest conductor for honor and all-state jazz bands in the United States and Canada and is active internationally as a clinician and performer. From 2008 to 2010, he served as artistic director for the Jazz en Vercors festival held each summer in the Vercors Region of France, and he has performed as a trumpet player in Thailand, Canada, France, and the Philippines, in addition to most of the 48 contiguous United States. Groups under his direction have been recognized numerous times for excellence in *DownBeat* magazine's Annual Student Music Awards.